The Western Range Revisited

D0209234

Legal History of North America

Legal History of North America

General Editor
Gordon Morris Bakken, *California State University, Fullerton*

Associate Editors
David J. Langum, *Samford University*
John P. S. McLaren, *University of Victoria*
John Phillip Reid, *New York University*

The Western Range Revisited

REMOVING LIVESTOCK FROM PUBLIC LANDS
TO CONSERVE NATIVE BIODIVERSITY

By Debra L. Donahue

University of Oklahoma Press : Norman

FOR CATHY

Library of Congress Cataloging-in-Publication Data

Donahue, Debra L.
    The western range revisited : removing livestock from public lands to
conserve native biodiversity / Debra L. Donahue.
        p.   cm.
    Includes bibliographical references.
    ISBN 0–8061–3176–4 (cloth : alk. paper)
    ISBN 0–8061–3298–1 (paperback : alk. paper)
    1. Biological diversity conservation—West (U.S.)   2. Range ecology—
West (U.S.)   3. Public lands—West (U.S.)—Management   I. Title.
QH76.5.W34D66   1999
333.95'16'0978—dc21   99–34538
                                                                                    CIP

*The Western Range Revisited: Removing Livestock from Public Lands to Conserve
Native Biodiversity* is Volume 5 in the series Legal History of North America.

The paper in this book meets the guidelines for permanence and durability of
the Committee on Production Guidelines for Book Longevity of the Council on
Library Resources, Inc. ∞

Copyright © 1999 by the University of Oklahoma Press, Norman, Publishing
Division of the University. All rights reserved. Manufactured in the U.S.A.

        2   3   4   5   6   7   8   9   10

Contents

Preface

     This project began as a simple exploration of the original meaning, and possible modern interpretations, of the Taylor Grazing Act qualification for establishing "grazing districts"—that the land be "chiefly valuable for grazing." The topic, and my thinking about it, evolved continually along the way. But this book is the product of much more than a couple of years of research and writing. Was it Ralph Waldo Emerson who wrote, "I am the sum of all whom I have met"? This book is in many ways the sum of all the people whom I have met and all that I have done, particularly in the past twenty-seven years.

     The book's multidisciplinary approach reflects my own experiences—in science, resource management, and the law; in government, industry, academia, and the nonprofit, public interest sector. For the past six years I have taught public land law to law students at the University of Wyoming, but I first observed the effects that livestock grazing can have on arid western ranges twenty-five years ago as a wildlife science major, with a secondary emphasis in range science, at Utah State University (USU). I took courses from or read works by some of the range and wildlife science professors cited herein. When I was a student, range science programs were still teaching Frederic Clements's model of vegetative succession. Its application to arid rangelands has since been discredited. During the summers and in my spare time while earning my undergraduate degree, I worked for federal land management agencies, USU professors, and a range science graduate student. Only after embarking on this project did I discover that this graduate student, Mark Westoby, is the range ecologist widely credited with proposing the "state-and-transition model" of "xeric rangeland succession," discussed in chapter 5. I went on to earn an M.S. degree in wildlife biology and take more range courses at Texas A&M University. USU and Texas A&M "pioneered range studies as a serious discipline."[1]

     After graduate school I worked for the federal Bureau of Land Management (BLM) in three western states doing a wide variety of fieldwork, including riparian and stream habitat inventories, range survey, and inventories of raptors, sage grouse, and big game species and their habitats. Later I worked for the mining industry and conservation groups, acquiring a broad familiarity with environmental regulations and natural resource policy issues. Law school and a short stint in legal practice followed, preceding my academic career.

The nearly thirty years I have spent in various corners of the West have only sharpened and deepened my appreciation of the incredible diversity of western landforms and plant and animal life. Those years have also taught me some troubling things about some of my neighbors—both "natives" and newcomers who have adopted the mythical West as their own. One of these is the desire to make over nature—get rid of predators and mosquitoes, tame the wind and relocate water, replace native sod or shrubs with bluegrass, teach deer to eat handouts while expecting them to shun nursery stock.

Another tendency of some westerners, increasingly prevalent in recent years, is to blame their woes on the federal government, especially bureaucrats inside the Beltway. Livestock growers, and public land ranchers in particular, are the prototypes for this category. They blame government (federal or state, but the feds are favorite targets) for everything—predator problems, over-populations of game animals, low water years, low crop yields, plant and insect pests, escalating land prices, high taxes. If they can't blame government they will blame something or someone else, even for problems clearly of their own making. While working for the BLM in Elko, Nevada, I received a letter from a rancher who attributed the erosion along a stream running through his grazing allotment to a long list of causes, including river otters. His cattle were conspic-uously absent from the list. At the time, the only river otters in recent memory in Nevada were rare sightings near the Idaho border, at least forty air miles away and on a different stream system.

Ranchers who happen to be politicians are even more vocal in blaming their woes on others. A bill introduced in 1997 by a Shoshoni, Wyoming, rancher-legislator would have given a cause of action "for damages and any other appro-priate relief" to any "agricultural or livestock producer 'who suffers damage as a result of another person's disparagement of any such perishable food or fiber product.'" Resolutions chastising the federal government or warning it to take or forego some action are commonplace in the Wyoming State Legislature.[2]

Perhaps because they see government as the cause of their troubles, ranchers also look to Uncle Sam to bail them out of their financial difficulties—and with good cause. The availability of federal loans, the emergency feed program of the U.S. Department of Agriculture (USDA), and similar government subsidies nurture these expectations.

In the culture of the West, ranchers are "cowboys" and cowboys are "kings." This is especially true of two of the states in which I have lived. I had just gone to work for the BLM in Elko when the Sagebrush Rebellion, led by Elko rancher-legislator Dean Rhodes, broke out. More recently, I witnessed the fitful beginnings of Interior Secretary Bruce Babbitt's "rangeland reform" campaign in the "Cowboy State," Wyoming. Babbitt objected when Governor Jim Geringer insisted on a BLM Resource Advisory Council loaded with "heavy hitters from the ranching community." The state and the federal agency subsequently went their separate ways.[3]

I can see a BLM range allotment from my front door. Wet springs bring bumper crops of cheatgrass, which carpets the steep slopes above the river, turning a characteristic shade of red-purple as it cures. Later in the summer I watch the obliteration of a small perennial stream and the degradation of its steeply sloped watershed by the BLM permittee's cattle. At the same time I take twice-daily walks on nearby state and private lands, from which livestock are excluded, and marvel at the diversity of grasses, forbs, shrubs, and lichens that flourish there. Cheatgrass, unfortunately, is present too, but the native vegetation seems to be holding its own against this ubiquitous invader.

These are just a few of the perspectives and experiences that I bring to this book. They have motivated me to attempt a difficult mission—to persuade readers of the pressing need to reconsider our federal grazing policies.

The purpose of this book is to propose and defend a landscape-level strategy for conserving native biodiversity on rangelands managed by the BLM. The chief ingredient of this strategy is eliminating livestock grazing on large blocks of the most arid BLM lands in ten western states. The proposal rests on an interdisciplinary analysis. Livestock grazing policies and practices on BLM lands are examined from historical, ecological, legal, and socioeconomic perspectives. The book concludes that grazing by domestic animals on these lands is unsupportable as a matter of sound public policy. It argues that the strongest justification for removing livestock from, or at minimum reducing drastically their use of, these lands is to restore, where possible, the natural ecological functions of rangeland ecosystems in order to protect and conserve their native biodiversity.

Invariably, discussions of federal grazing policy, whether in the halls of Congress, in agency planning documents, or in meetings of advisory councils or "stakeholders," have been artificially constrained. They have been paper exercises, in which possible adjustments of numbers, seasons of use, or fees have been bandied about. Occasionally, serious consideration is given to excluding livestock from especially sensitive areas, such as riparian zones. The "no grazing" option, where it has been raised, is a straw man, a bare nod to federal regulations governing preparation of environmental impact statements (EISs). A novel suggestion was recently advanced by Carl E. Bock et al., who proposed setting aside as permanently ungrazed reserves 20 percent of every federal permittee's allotted grazing area. They opined that removing livestock from all public lands would be a "defensible" position "on purely ecological grounds," but in their view it would be "impractical, insensitive, and probably unnecessary to so completely disregard the human element." Bock and his colleagues displayed no reluctance to continue current grazing practices, which they admitted invariably impact the diversity of native species on western rangelands.[4]

A no-holds-barred reexamination of federal grazing policy is sorely needed and long overdue. All options must be on the table during that discussion. This book promotes the reexamination process by suggesting the "unthinkable": that removing livestock from many western rangelands makes economic sense, is ecologically expedient, and is legally justifiable.

Despite the proliferation of literature on biodiversity conservation, land use policy, and natural resources and environmental law, no other work that I know of takes an interdisciplinary, geographically focused approach to this subject or makes the policy argument made herein. One explanation may be the "unthink-ableness," as a matter of western policy or politics, of drastically cutting back public land grazing. Indeed, after reading the initial manuscript, one university press editor expressed uneasiness about how the book's topic would "play with our very rural state legislature (and congressional delegation)."

I am indebted to the University of Oklahoma Press for deeming this topic not only "thinkable" but publishable. Many individuals were encouraging and supportive throughout the processes of researching and writing and editing the manuscript, in particular my colleagues Rich McCormick, Brad Saxton, and Mark Squillace. Thanks as well to my hard-working and underpaid research assistants, Susan Schell and Ken Shelton, and to cartographer Linda Marston for producing a clear, informative map. Summer funding was provided by a George Hopper Faculty Research Grant.

A final note regarding style: It is a historical fact that early stockgrowers were chiefly men, that owners of large ranches are still men, that political power has been concentrated in stockmen, and that stockgrowers' representatives and political advocates have by and large been men. Indeed, part of chapter 4 is devoted to the masculine dimension of western mythology. Moreover, the statutes that regulate grazing use "man"/"men" to refer to both livestock producers and government regulators. The use of "cattlemen," "sheepmen," or "stockmen" in portions of the text reflects these circumstances, not a neglect of modern style conventions.

Acronyms and Abbreviations

ACEC	area of critical environmental concern
AUM	animal unit month
BLM	Bureau of Land Management
CAMUA	Classification and Multiple Use Act
CEQ	Council on Environmental Quality
CMA	Cooperative Management Agreement
CRM	coordinated resource management
CWA	Clean Water Act
DEIS	draft environmental impact statement
DOI	Department of the Interior
EA	environmental assessment
EIS	environmental impact statement
EMAP	Environmental Monitoring and Assessment Program
EMT	Ecosystem Management Team
EPA	Environmental Protection Agency
ESA	Endangered Species Act
FACA	Federal Advisory Committee Act
FEIS	final environmental impact statement
FLPMA	Federal Land Policy and Management Act
GAO	General Accounting Office
NABC	National Advisory Board Council
NAS	National Academy of Sciences
NCA	National Cattlemen's Association
NCOR	National Conference on Outdoor Recreation
NEPA	National Environmental Policy Act
NFMA	National Forest Management Act
NLSA	National Live Stock Association
NRC	National Research Council
NRCS	Natural Resources Conservation Service
NWF	National Wildlife Federation

PLLRC	Public Land Law Review Commission
PNV	potential natural vegetation
PRIA	Public Rangelands Improvement Act
RMP	Resource Management Plan
SCS	Soil Conservation Service
SRHA	Stock Raising Homestead Act
SRM	Society for Range Management
TGA	Taylor Grazing Act
TNC	The Nature Conservancy
USDA	U.S. Department of Agriculture
USFS	U.S. Forest Service
USFWS	U.S. Fish and Wildlife Service

The Western Range Revisited

There is perhaps no darker chapter nor greater tragedy in the history of land occupancy and use in the United States than the story of the western range.

EARL H. CLAPP,
in *The Western Range*, 1936

Introduction

In 1985 a federal judge in Oregon dismissed as "practically unthinkable" the policy choice to remove domestic livestock from public grazing lands in the Reno, Nevada, area. This book argues that evicting livestock from certain public rangelands is not unthinkable at all. On the contrary, in the face of irrefutable evidence that public land grazing is economically inefficient and inequitable and causes severe, sometimes irreversible, impacts to the land, it is unthinkable that we would continue to allow cattle and sheep to graze large portions of our public lands.

Management of public lands to produce livestock is vulnerable to challenge on several grounds. It is "out of sync" with changed public values and demands, with policies currently expressed in federal law, and with the historical legislative and popular intent regarding use of public rangelands. Moreover, it is beyond cavil that for decades neither ranchers nor land managers have understood range ecology; as a consequence, rangelands that never should have been grazed were, and continue to be, used by domestic livestock.

Demands for public land use are constantly escalating, and priorities for use of these lands have shifted significantly in recent years. The changes are most pronounced with respect to lands managed by the federal Bureau of Land Management. As Samuel Hays noted in 1984, BLM lands had, within the "past few decades," "taken on new meaning to the American people as lands which are valuable in their more natural and less developed state as natural environment lands." Professor Hays considered especially noteworthy "the evolving attitudes of the American people toward western drylands and deserts." More than half of those polled in a 1976 Gallup survey of American attitudes toward the southern California desert, he reported, "felt that they knew enough about the western desert so that they wished to respond to questions about how it should be managed." A majority "preferred natural environment management to development or vehicular use." In Hays's view, this reflected "a change in American attitudes toward many different types of natural environment lands, formerly thought of as relatively 'useless,' but now thought of as valuable in their natural condition."[1]

Respondents in the 1976 poll might have considered livestock grazing compatible with natural management, but it is now widely recognized that the "natural condition" of deserts cannot be maintained while producing cattle or sheep from the same lands. In spite of this, the BLM continues to allow grazing in many deserts and semideserts. Congress even authorized grazing to continue in one portion of the California desert recently designated for protection as the Mojave National Preserve. A similar, but more specific, poll conducted today probably would not uncover general public support for these policies. In fact, researchers in a national survey conducted in 1993 found "widespread public disapproval of current range policies, reflecting a growing disenchantment with commodity-focused management on public lands as well as a belief that range condition is deteriorating." "Generally speaking," the investigators concluded, "Americans favor greater protection for nonmarket rangeland resources and a shift away from commodity-oriented management." Respondents disagreed that range management should emphasize livestock, believing instead that fish, wildlife, and rare plants should receive greater protection. They favored protection of more rangeland as official wilderness and opposed livestock grazing in wilderness areas.[2]

Thus, the trend in public attitudes noted by Hays has not only continued but intensified in the past ten to fifteen years. The debate over the use and management of public lands is marked by a growing interest in conservation biology and ecosystem management, including management to conserve native biological diversity. Fundamental issues, such as public versus private ownership, the sustainability of resource uses, and the propriety of federal subsidies, attract attention from politicians, scientists, legal scholars, and interest groups. Management of BLM lands for livestock grazing implicates the full panoply of contemporary public land issues. While the agency has modernized its thinking on paper—taking strong positions in favor of ecosystem-based approaches to management, the importance of conserving biodiversity, and revising its range condition assessment methods, for instance—it has done little to follow through with on-the-ground action. To borrow Hays's expression, its management policies aren't "synchronized with the real world."[3]

Today millions of people use the public lands for recreation; federal grazing permit holders number about 20,000. Recreational users of BLM lands generate hundreds of millions of dollars in taxes and revenues for local businesses and equipment manufacturers and retailers. Livestock are permitted to use more than two-thirds of all public lands, yet those lands contribute but a tiny fraction of national livestock production. Revenues to the federal treasury from fees paid by stockmen fail even to cover the BLM's costs to administer grazing activities. More troubling still, livestock and grazing-related facilities and improvements have a negative impact on all other public land uses and values, particularly water quality, wildlife and fisheries habitat, watershed (including soils) characteristics, recreational values, and scenic and other aesthetic attributes. Livestock grazing has altered and diminished the presettlement diversity of native fauna and flora on many western rangelands. Some of these ecological effects appear to be irreversible, at least within ordinary management time scales.[4]

Despite these powerful reasons *not* to graze public lands, the practice has continued essentially unabated since the 1870s (earlier in some areas). As Dale Jamieson notes, "the idea that grazing . . . and other extractive uses should have priority because they are the 'senior' uses . . . often goes with a romantic view of both western history and contemporary realities. Whether justified or not, this view tends to defend traditional uses because they are traditional, even if these uses clearly lead to what everyone would regard as land degradation."[5]

In this "romantic view," ranchers are "cowboys," who are seen as synonymous with the American West. Yet ranchers have never filled the boots of the mythical cowboy—the independent, freedom-loving, self-reliant figure of the open range. The public land ranchers of today are something of a paradox. Their numbers are few, but their political power is substantial. They act like they own the range when, in fact, their toehold on it is but a revocable "privilege." They pride themselves on their self-reliance and rail against government meddling in their affairs, while availing themselves of every government benefit and fighting to maintain a grazing fee that fails to recoup even the government's administrative costs. They replace their own cowboys with newfangled balers and four-wheelers and snowmobiles and yet appeal to public sentiment and nostalgia to help preserve their traditional way of life. Arguing that the economy of their local community depends on their staying in business, they "moonlight" to make ends meet. The animals they raise on the range deplete the very capital upon which their, and the animals', living depends. They call themselves the "original conservationists," but they have a rifle slung behind the seat of their pickups for picking off coyotes and other "varmints." They poison prairie dogs and willows and sagebrush and replace native meadows with water-guzzling alfalfa.

The foregoing is not an accurate depiction of every western rancher, of course. One of the tasks of this book, in fact, is to produce a composite picture of the interest group who will be most affected by the conservation strategy proposed here. The western livestock industry is not monolithic, nor was it in the early West. As Donald Pisani has written, even the term "western livestock industry" suggests "a uniformity of interests and objectives that never really existed among stock growers." Nor have the public's or the government's perceptions of public land ranchers through the years been uniform or even clearly developed. This book explores why we have livestock—and stockmen—on federal rangelands today, examining who these stockmen were and are, how they have been perceived by others, how they came to use the public lands, and the circumstances under which they have managed to remain.[6]

The book also chronicles the early and severe degradation of western ranges and recounts government efforts to regulate grazing activities on the public domain—a somewhat imprecise term used herein to refer to unreserved federal lands managed by the Department of the Interior (DOI) and, beginning in 1946, by the BLM within that department. A principal focus is on the impact that grazing practices have had on the biodiversity and normal ecological functioning of arid and semiarid rangelands. The breadth and complexity of these impacts render an adequate treatment difficult, if not impossible, in a single book. But their significance for future land management, and indeed the national public interest, renders it imperative that they be understood as well as possible and that steps be taken immediately to mitigate or avoid them.

Politicians, the stockmen themselves, and even many environmentalists increasingly rationalize public land grazing as (1) a means of sustaining an important, traditional culture and lifestyle; (2) key to the economic stability and prosperity of small rural communities in the West; and/or (3) crucial to the preservation of open space and large blocks of wildlife habitat. As we will see, however, strong rebuttals to each of these arguments exist, and weighty countervailing considerations merit more serious attention than they have received to date. This book explores several critical issues that will bear on this analysis: to what can the image and modern political power of western ranchers be attributed, and is that power justified; is there an identifiable ranching "culture" that merits preservation; what does the law require of public rangeland managers, and what discretion does the law afford those managers; and for what uses are rangelands valuable?

Although domestic livestock grazing of all public lands could easily be challenged on economic and public policy grounds, the focus herein is on arid rangelands receiving 12 inches of precipitation or less annually. Ecologists generally agree that drier lands are most at risk of losing biological diversity to livestock grazing and other human-caused disturbances: the more arid the climate, the more likely and more severe are the ecological impacts of grazing by introduced ungulates. These lands are not all true "deserts," which ecologists sometimes relate to a precipitation threshold of less than 10 or even less than 6 inches. Nor is the amount of precipitation the only factor influencing aridity. Other factors include the timing and distribution of precipitation, evaporation rates, and the amount of solar radiation. But considerable support can be found in the current and historical literature for using the 12-inch precipitation line to identify areas where grazing poses special concerns. Significantly, the BLM and Forest Service point out in the draft environmental impact statement (DEIS) *Rangeland Reform '94* that the condition of BLM lands receiving less than 12 inches of annual moisture is unlikely to improve under current grazing management practices.[7]

As figure 1 illustrates, broad areas of the West receive 12 inches or less of rain and snow annually. These dry lands are located in the Southwest, portions of the Rocky Mountains, and the Intermountain, or Great Basin, region. Included within these broad regions are the northern extension of Mexico's deserts into the Southwest—the Mojave Desert in California and Nevada, Sonoran Desert in Arizona and California, and Chihuahuan Desert in eastern Arizona and New Mexico; portions of the Columbia Plateau in eastern Washington and Oregon and in Idaho; most of Nevada and western Utah, including the Humboldt Desert in northwestern Nevada and the Great Salt Lake Desert; and much of the Colorado Plateau in the Four Corners area. The proposal also embraces less-well-known arid lands, such as the Big Horn Basin and Red Desert of Wyoming.[8]

BLM lands are specifically targeted for two reasons. First, the bureau is the largest federal land manager and manages the greatest share of arid and semiarid rangelands. Second, its land holdings include large, contiguous tracts that lend themselves to landscape-scale management strategies.

Scale is an important feature of the conservation proposal. Conservation biologists generally agree that successful biodiversity conservation programs cannot be limited to habitat sites, communities, or even ecosystems, but must encompass whole landscapes. A frequent lament of these scientists is that parks, refuges, and other reserves are rarely large enough or connected adequately with other protected areas to function effectively as biodiversity preserves. Greater opportunities to design reserves of adequate size and configuration exist in the West, thanks to the relative abundance of federal public lands. Large blocks of BLM lands in Utah, Nevada, Oregon, Colorado, Idaho, New Mexico, Arizona, California, Wyoming, and, to a limited extent, Washington offer an opportunity for broad-scale experimentation in landscape ecology not found elsewhere. In Utah alone, tracts of BLM lands totaling 5.7 million acres meet the nominal requirements for wilderness designation, one of which is sufficient size (generally, 5,000 acres or more). A landscape approach to conserving biodiversity need not be limited to areas with wilderness qualities, but wilderness and wilderness study areas, because of their size, comprise one category of lands that may be amenable to landscape-level management.[9]

Interweaving threads from history, ecology, conservation biology, economics, and the law, this book (1) explores the premise that livestock grazing can and does cause irreversible ecological impacts on arid rangelands that did not develop in conjunction with large ungulate grazers; (2) argues that the current federal grazing policy is a largely unintended artifact of history, perpetuated by myth; (3) examines the precarious economics of public land ranching; and (4) demonstrates that the BLM, the federal agency in charge of most grazing lands, possesses the legal authority to remove livestock from at-risk lands and, indeed, has a *mandate* to prevent the kinds of damage currently being wrought by

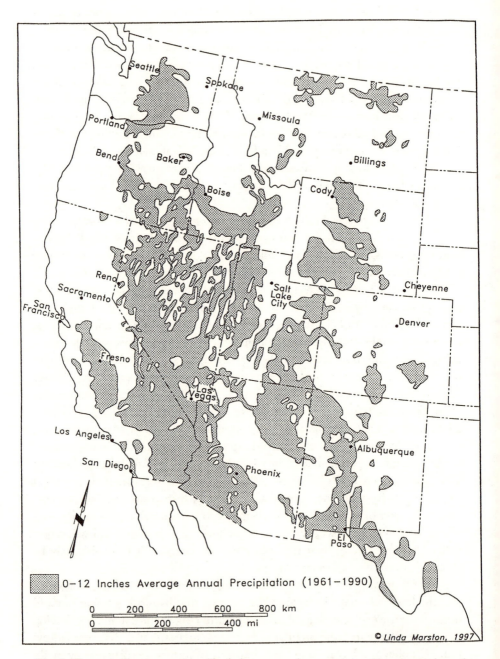

Fig. 1. The western range region. Shaded areas are those receiving 12 inches or less of annual precipitation.

livestock in many areas. The book concludes that livestock grazing on arid public lands is indefensible public policy and argues for its elimination to facilitate conservation of native plant and animal diversity.

Some working definitions are called for. The distinction between "arid" and "semiarid" is not precise, and ecologists differ as to whether and where to draw a dividing line. For purposes herein, "arid" is often used as a shorthand expression for "arid and semiarid" and refers to any area averaging 12 inches or less of annual precipitation. Similarly, various definitions of "range" or "range-lands" exist. "Rangeland" is not an ecological term, although it is occasionally defined by certain ecological characteristics. Bobbi Low and Jesse Berlin refer to "deserts and semideserts" as "typical rangelands." Mark Brunson and Brent Steel define "rangeland" as "places that have arid climates, where grasslands or desert environments are more common than heavily forested ones." In practice, "rangelands" refers to lands that are, or historically have been, used by domestic livestock. This is the meaning that "range" and "rangeland" are accorded in this volume; the terms are used interchangeably. Use of these terms suggests nothing about the land's suitability for livestock production or the appropriate uses of the land. On the contrary, it is a fundamental premise of this book that arid rangelands are *not suited* for livestock grazing.[10]

A third term that could prove troublesome is "grazing" or "grazer." "Grazing" is a subset of "herbivory," which is what all organisms that eat plants do. Likewise, "grazer" is a subset of "herbivore"; that is, all grazers are herbivores, but not all herbivores are grazers. Some, for instance, are browsers. All livestock are herbivores; most are classified as grazers. These terms are examined in more detail in chapter 5. For now, suffice it to say that when "grazing" is used without qualification, it refers (for the sake of brevity) to grazing by livestock. If a broader or narrower meaning is intended, it is spelled out in the text or should be clear from the context.

This book points out a need and an opportunity—the pressing need to conserve native biodiversity on western rangelands and the rare opportunity to pursue this objective most efficiently, at the landscape level, on BLM lands across the arid West. Endeavoring to manage these BLM lands for biodiversity may enable us to check, if not undo, the disruption and degradation wrought by more than 100 years of livestock grazing and to maximize our ability to conserve the remaining natural diversity of species and processes that arid western landscapes support. This is a worthy goal that can be pursued now by courageous land managers and concerned citizens. It is time to chart a new course for the public lands—a course that will preserve for future generations not a set of outdated and destructive myths, but an enduring legacy of healthy rangelands.

CHAPTER 1

The Historical and Cultural Landscape

Public land ranching is popularly perceived as a historical and cultural "institution." Several assumptions underlying this view have largely escaped question in lay and political circles. Among the assumptions that seem firmly entrenched are that the "livestock industry" is some monolithic entity, that ranching helped establish the West, and that cattlemen and cowboys have always been beloved by Americans. More critical appraisal by some historians and legal scholars, however, offers a startlingly different account. Our purposes are served by considering how early western stockgrowers and the livestock industry were viewed by themselves and by others, both nationally and regionally, and what place grazing had on the public lands during the early, pre–Taylor Grazing Act era. A story of paradoxes and inconsistencies, it is a relevant context for both examining livestock's current claim on the public lands and interpreting attempts to regulate public land grazing.

Stockgrowers occupied a unique place in the early West. Then as now they faced various quandaries: they sought government assistance (for instance, protection from itinerant sheepherders or predators) while simultaneously attempting to avoid government regulation and fees. They emphasized the "differences" between public and private grazing lands and between forest reserves and the public domain to justify a low grazing fee on the latter, but eschewed sharing these "public" ranges with other users. Many larger operations monopolized the range, but shunned opportunities to take title to the lands. And they emphasized the business nature of their enterprise, all the while resisting governmental efforts to price the forage commodity according to the market. These and other factors have frequently put livestock interests at cross-purposes with the government and their neighbors.[1]

Unlike miners or homesteaders or even lumber producers, stockgrowers never succeeded in convincing Congress to convey to them a property interest in the public domain. Rather, their use of the public lands was first by license or sufferance and later (and still today) by revocable permit or lease. In the nineteenth and early twentieth centuries Congress's land policies and sympathies were trained on small farmers and homesteaders. Historian Samuel Hays has observed that the stock industry's efforts to persuade Congress to pass a bill to serve its needs—whether a transfer of lands in sufficient quantities for growing stock in the sparsely vegetated West or a leasing bill—"fell on deaf ears" for fifty years. As Walter Prescott Webb put it, "It was not until 1916 that Congress recognized in its land legislation that such a class as cattlemen existed in the West." Most land disposal bills authorized homesteading for farming purposes and provided for an amount of land believed workable by a single family—160 or later 320 acres. Prior to 1904 all homestead or land entry bills were for non-grazing, agricultural purposes; most (with the exception of the Desert Lands Act of 1877, which allowed entry on 640 acres) had been limited to 160 acres, far too small an area for grazing stock in the West.[2]

Stockgrowers, though not the industry as a whole, began lobbying in 1862 for legislation that would authorize leasing the public domain for grazing and prevent or minimize any encroachment by homesteaders. But, as William Rowley has reported, "Western stockmen, the grazing interest, did not command broad based support outside their grazing region." Many conservationists believed that grazing injured tree growth and water supplies. Among stockgrowers themselves, the "nomadic sheepmen" were uniformly "'dreaded and despised.'" The first leasing bill advanced by western grazing interests was not introduced until 1899, although most entries under the Desert Lands Act, passed in 1877, were used for grazing. The act, which provided for the sale of 640 acres at $0.25 per acre, with proof that a portion of the land had been irrigated, was largely a failure. The acreage requirement was too large for one entryman to irrigate and too small to constitute a viable ranch for stockraising purposes. Ranching on sparsely vegetated western ranges required much larger tracts of land than in areas of the country already settled. Inevitably, speculation and fraud marked implementation of this ill-designed legislation.[3]

John Wesley Powell put Congress on notice of conditions in the West. In 1878 he reported that grasses were "'nutritious but scanty'" in much of the West, though in the true deserts of southern California, Nevada, Arizona, and New Mexico grasses were "'so scant as to be of no value.'" These deserts, where "'broad reaches of land are bare of vegetation,'" were believed "beyond redemption, even for grazing." Powell argued that grazing was the only safe use of the short-grass region, pointing to the Spanish-Mexican system of large land-grant ranches. Consistent with his recommendations, the first National Public Lands Commission in 1880 advised that, to be efficient, ranching units in the West should be at least 2,560 acres, or four sections. But Congress never approved land grants in tracts that large. According to Donald Worster, the "American political establishment would not tolerate such a 'feudal,' undemocratic policy that supposedly would set up great land-owning barons against the small yeoman homesteaders." Because "Congress could never swallow disposal to ranchers in such large amounts[, it] persisted for fifty more years in pursuing the vision of the small homestead, despite overwhelming evidence that 160 acres or even 640 acres was far too small."[4]

As the more productive, more eastern lands were disposed of—leaving in federal hands those lands that received less precipitation, were located in rougher terrain, and had shallower, less fertile soils—Congress began to experiment in its land disposal policies. The Kincaid Act of 1904, applicable only in northwestern Nebraska, was the first federal act expressly to contemplate disposal of the public domain for grazing purposes. Recognizing that most of the land was not suitable for cultivation, Congress authorized entry on 640 acres, an amount of land designed to allow homesteaders to farm and raise a few head of stock. Cattlemen had opposed a homesteading bill, preferring some form of leasing instead. Farmers objected to leasing. The Kincaid Act was engineered as a compromise. As a land disposal mechanism, the act was a success; it resulted in the transfer to private hands of nearly all the available land in Nebraska. Most of the ranches eventually carved out of the Nebraska prairie, however, were much larger than the 640-acre limit in the law. By 1928 the average ranch in one Nebraska county sprawled over 6,681 acres; ranches ranged from 1,300 to more than 29,000 acres in size. Cass G. Barns reported that "for some time ranches were at least twenty miles apart and each ranch kept thousands of cattle."[5]

Encouraged by the disposition success of the Kincaid Act, but perhaps concerned that it had been too generous in offering section-sized tracts, Congress passed the Enlarged Homestead Act of 1909, limiting entry to 320 acres. The 1909 act was intended to facilitate dry farming ventures. It allowed the homesteaders to live within 20 miles of the tracts if no water was available for domestic purposes, but in that case they were required to cultivate *half* instead of one-fourth of the land. As Webb noted: "The absurdity of requiring cultivation of 160 acres of land on a tract so destitute of water that none could be had for domestic purposes evidently did not occur to the legislators, who seemed determined to have the land farmed whether or no. Their farmer background was getting the better of them." Webb was not alone in this criticism. Dry farming's detractors were widespread even in 1909. The states of California, Idaho, Kansas, North Dakota, and South Dakota all tried unsuccessfully to persuade Congress not to extend the law to them. But dry farming was widely viewed by politicians as the next wave of "agricultural foundationalism." People had great faith in dry farming and irrigation as the most likely means of facilitating "home-building" in the West.[6]

During the early 1900s the West experienced a homestead rush—the result of "dryland farming promotion, increased precipitation, rising land values, and escalating agricultural commodity prices." The 1909 act, followed by the Three-Year Homestead Law of 1912, hastened the stampede. From 1870 to 1900, 430 million new acres had been cultivated in the United States—more than in the previous 250 years. But more homestead patents were issued *after* 1900 than before. According to Rowley, the Kincaid and Enlarged Homestead Acts were chiefly responsible for this land rush. Most of the land homesteaded, however, "was marginal and never should have been brought under the plow." Consequently, most homestead entries under the 1909 and 1912 statutes failed; the range was plowed up and eventually abandoned. These failed homesteads "largely became the Dust Bowl of the Great Depression." Many were repurchased by the government during the 1930s. Bust followed the boom, as it always has in the West. America's entrance into World War I ended the homestead rush, but not before much of the plains and western range had been destroyed. The bust continued after World War I; drought was widespread, and agricultural commodity and livestock prices collapsed.[7]

The Stock Raising Homestead Act of 1916 (SRHA) was Congress's next failed attempt at designing an effective disposal policy for arid western lands. It was also the first legislation (other than the geographically restricted Kincaid Act) targeted specifically at grazing. It allowed entry on 640-acre tracts that had been designated chiefly valuable for grazing. SRHA patents conveyed title only to the surface; the federal government retained all rights to coal and other minerals. In the first year of the act's operation, 60,000 entries were filed on approximately 20 million acres of public land. But the measure was too little, too late. By then the "remaining public land was generally of such low productivity that 640 acres was inadequate to support a family." Indeed, in many parts of the West 640 acres was then, as now, sorely inadequate to support a ranch operation. According to the General Accounting Office (GAO), "more than 160 acres of land [are] sometimes required to support one cow for 1 month in southern New Mexico, Arizona, southwestern Utah, southeastern California, and most of Nevada." In discussing why the SRHA was so poorly suited to its purpose, Webb mused:

> Perhaps the bungling was due to ignorance, but every consideration indicates that the lawmakers could have been informed. The Department of the Interior was in a position at any time to give information; Powell had given it long before, when there was an excuse for being ignorant. The effect of the law was to lure into the region people who were ignorant of conditions and sure to fail. There was no chance of fooling the real cowman. . . .[8]

Within a very few years the writing was on the wall. In 1923 the General Land Office contended that "few making entry under the [SRHA] could comply with the law's requirements in good faith." According to Webb, "the chief of the Bureau of Forestry declared it a crime to open land under the act of 1916." By 1927 both the secretary of the interior and the secretary of agriculture had recommended repeal of the law, and a Senate committee took official note that a 640-acre tract of grazing land would "not permit a homesteader to make a living therefrom." Modern public land law scholars George C. Coggins, Charles F. Wilkinson, and John D. Leshy have condemned the SRHA, which they claim "not only caused the usual settler heartbreak, speculation, and acreage engrossment for the rich, but also, in breaking up the great public domain grazing areas, led directly to the destruction of much of the range."[9]

As Congress experimented with land disposal schemes, it turned a blind eye to conditions on the western range—"[c]haos and anarchy" and severe over-grazing. Both resulted from competition between cattlemen and sheepmen and between homesteaders and stockmen and from the "[a]bsence of the most elementary institutions of property law." By the turn of the century, the depleted condition of the western range had long been apparent to Congress, conserva-tionists, and the stockmen themselves, who, according to Hays, "often expressed fear that continued intensive use would destroy the entire industry." The 1870s and 1880s had seen the industry boom and bust; the bust was a result of a saturated beef market, overgrazing, and the killer winters of 1886–88. President Theodore Roosevelt appointed a Public Lands Commission in 1903, whose primary objectives included investigating range conditions and developing proposals for stabilizing the range. The commission issued a questionnaire to stockmen; of the 1,400 replies received, 1,090 (78 percent) favored some govern-ment control of public land grazing. The commission subsequently recom-mended that grazing be allowed by permit, issued for up to ten years.[10]

Congress continued to ignore or misread the stockmen's needs, but their interests gained some credence with the Roosevelt administration due largely to forestry chief Gifford Pinchot's influence. Two main schools of thought con-cerning federal land policy were then extant. One held that public lands valu-able for commodity uses, particularly agriculture (*not* including grazing) and mining, should be disposed of. The other maintained that public lands should be preserved for the benefit of all Americans. Forest reserves, created under the authority of congressional acts dated 1891 and 1897, were distinguished from the public domain by their regulation and in the opinion of users and the public. The public domain remained open to grazing and unregulated, but grazing in forest reserves was regulated, at least minimally, beginning in 1901. At that time no fee was charged, and the season was not limited unless grazing interfered with economic use of the reserves. The reserves provided generally better forage, and competition for it was growing fiercer. Controversy simmered, and occa-sionally flared, between those who viewed the forests as parks and watershed areas and thought grazing should be outlawed and stockmen who wanted the forest reserves opened more extensively to grazing. Eastern sportsmen, including the Boone and Crockett Club, attempted to persuade Congress to convert forest reserves to game preserves or at least to make selected "breeding areas" off limits to commercial exploitation. Even Ethan Hitchcock, Roosevelt's interior secretary and Pinchot's boss until 1905, "looked upon the public lands either as areas to be preserved from use or distributed to settlers." Hitchcock preferred that commercial uses of the forests, including grazing, be minimized; Pinchot advocated opening the reserves more fully. Pinchot eventually won out.[11]

Questions concerning the proper uses of public lands also raised issues of ownership. According to Hays, public versus private ownership of federal lands was, in the general public's view, "the crucial conservation issue." Conservationists argued for retention. Worster characterizes these arguments as having at least three dimensions. One was moral, an "appeal to social democratic ideals of equality and commonwealth" that argued for retaining these last remnants of a great heritage of land. Another was economic, embracing the premise that public ownership could better "insure the greatest return to the greatest number of people" (the classic Pinchot criterion). A third held that the "private entrepreneur simply could not be trusted to look out for the long-term ecological health of the range resource." The view that nonagricultural federal lands could be used and managed rationally only if retained in public ownership became dominant during the Roosevelt administration and continued under William Howard Taft.[12]

Roosevelt administration land policies were premised on the Roosevelt-Pinchot brand of conservation philosophy and view of science. According to Worster, Pinchot's conservation philosophy was not new at all, but dated back to the eighteenth century and progressive agriculture notions; Pinchot's contribution was to adapt those ideas to the forest reserves. He thought nature could be improved upon and that renewable resources should be dealt with as crops. Both Pinchot and Roosevelt had "an almost unlimited faith in applied science"; both "looked upon the conservation movement as an attempt to apply this knowledge." But they faced a dilemma. Although conservationists often differed on the issue of preservation versus use, they shared the administration's view of the importance of integrated, scientific planning and centralized control or direction. Individual resource users (lumber producers, graziers, etc.), however, opposed integrated planning. Hays writes:

> Indeed, each group considered its own particular interest as far more important than any other. Resource users formed their opinions about conservation questions within the limited experience of specific problems faced in their local communities. They understood little and cared less about the needs of the nation as a whole. This approach stood in direct contrast to the over-all point of view of the conservationists. . . . While resource-use groups held a multitude of diverse aims which stemmed from many limited and local experiences . . . , conservationists held comprehensive and unified objectives. . . .

The straightforward contest between graziers and irrigators was illustrative: "Rigid grazing control might benefit the irrigator in the lower basin, but curtail the activities of the stockmen in the headwaters."[13]

In these early debates Pinchot perfected a delicate balancing act. He managed both to assuage livestock interests by encouraging grazing in the forest reserves and supporting leasing outside the forests and to impose controls on grazing, which he viewed as a serious threat to vegetative resources and watershed stability. By expanding livestock use of the forests, and reopening areas previously closed to grazing by Hitchcock, Pinchot appeared to weigh in on the side of livestock interests and their advocates in Congress. These actions went far in securing the backing of stockmen. Ranchers in Colorado actually recommended "that the reserves be turned over to 'our friend, Mr. Pinchot.'" Hays and others have argued that Pinchot cultivated the favor of the stockmen in part, if not chiefly, to facilitate a transfer of his forestry bureau from Interior to Agriculture. If so, the strategy worked. Pinchot succeeded in 1905 in convincing Congress to make the transfer; as the first chief of the Department of Agriculture's new forestry bureau, he had absolute control. Stockmen may not have been entirely fooled by Pinchot's political machinations, however. According to Rowley, livestock interests in 1905 "suspected that the government had only grudgingly admitted the importance of grazing" and that their "privileges would be short-lived."[14]

Regardless of other motives he may have had, Pinchot's efforts on behalf of stockmen reflected his conviction that forests should be used, not left in their natural state: "The object of our forest policy is not to preserve the forests because they are beautiful . . . or because they are refuges for the wild creatures of the wilderness," he wrote, "but the making of prosperous homes. . . . Every other consideration comes as secondary." Grazing soon became the "primary commercial use of the forests, far more important than lumbering."[15]

Prior to Pinchot's rise to power, graziers had not gotten preferential, or even favorable, treatment in the forest reserves. As intimated earlier, the Interior Department had initially rejected grazing as a legitimate use of the forest reserves. The first forest reserve regulation ever issued (at the behest of irrigators in 1894) forbade livestock to be grazed on or driven across the reserves. In 1897 a government botanist recommended that grazing be forbidden in public recreation areas and in watersheds with major reservoirs and that it be strictly regulated elsewhere. The General Land Office's 1899 grazing regulations stated that "stockmen used the forests only as a privilege and not as a right, and that the Secretary could exclude them entirely at his discretion." By 1902 departmental grazing policy employed the terms "privilege and allotment," which, according to Rowley, "reinforced the government's contention that stockmen did not possess unlimited rights to graze on the reserves. . . . [F]orest administrators spoke of a 'restrictive right' as opposed to what stockmen sometimes wished to consider a 'prescriptive right.'"[16]

Forest reserve grazing was limited to 1.2 million sheep and fewer than 500,000 cattle in 1902. Revised, more complex regulations issued that year favored stock owners whose home bases were in or near a reserve. An administrative "redistribution" strategy, accomplished in part by reducing large cattle and sheep operators' allowed herd sizes to provide permits for smaller herds to new settlers, served the national policy in favor of homesteaders and also resulted in steadily increasing livestock use of the forests. It was common knowledge that many of the new residents who applied for permits to run ten head of stock on the reserves actually ran more. Under Pinchot grazing use increased from 7,981 permits for 600,000 cattle, 59,000 horses, and 1.7 million sheep in 1905 to 27,000 permits for 7.7 million sheep, 1.5 million cattle, 90,000 horses, 4,500 hogs, and 140,000 goats in 1909. The administration believed that it was achieving better utilization of the range and pointed to higher animal weights as proof. By 1915 grazing use of the forest reserves had increased by more than half.[17]

At the same time, Pinchot, the scientist and conservationist, knew grazing could damage both range and forest resources. Further, like other conservation leaders during the Roosevelt era, he believed that resource policy questions "could be left to local groups, or to political pressure in Congress only at the risk of 'selling out' the national welfare to 'special interests.'" He was determined that grazing not interfere with other forest uses, especially with other uses of water—agriculture/irrigation, mining, and domestic consumption. He considered grazing and irrigated agriculture "the most important problems facing the forest reserves" in 1901. Thus, concomitantly with his dramatic expansion of permitted grazing use, Pinchot began to regulate the *conditions* of that use. Grazing levels were not to exceed the land's carrying capacity, and livestock numbers were to be reduced where "overstocking was apparent and the range deteriorated." The policy was enforced, but reductions were generally moderate. In addition, permits carried a limited term, "so that if an area later could be developed *for a more valuable use*, it could be reclassified."[18]

This latter provision is consistent with what Hays termed Pinchot and Roosevelt's "rough system of priorities" for use of the public lands. As it suggests, grazing was not especially high on the list. Despite the fact that the value of forage in most cases exceeded the value of timber harvested from the forests, other uses of forest reserves were preferred over grazing. On lands considered agricultural, homesteading enjoyed priority over grazing, and farmers with small herds of livestock had priority over the larger operators. In the granting of rights-of-way across forest reserves, domestic use of water had first priority; irrigation took precedence over stockwatering. And while commercial uses of forests, including grazing, were favored over recreational use, the homesteaders' needs trumped all other interests.[19]

The Roosevelt-Pinchot grazing policy preference for forest reserve residents and neighbors—especially small operators—coincided with the administration's policy of favoring homesteaders and its adherence to Jeffersonian doctrine. Outside the forest reserves, however, "Roosevelt stood squarely for a grazing lease program, clearly favoring the larger operators." According to Hays, the "necessity for range conservation" all but forced the Roosevelt administration to side with the big cattle operators on the leasing issue: without their support the range would have continued to deteriorate. But this decision cost the administration dearly among small farmers, who from then on identified Roosevelt and Pinchot with the "cattle barons" whom they despised. A 1901 leasing bill, which had the support of cattlemen, the Public Land Commission, and Roosevelt, was opposed by settlers, farmers, and sheepmen. In 1907 Roosevelt and the General Land Office urged enactment of comprehensive western range legislation. Leasing proposals and other reform bills were introduced through 1929 but made no headway. In 1925 a leasing bill was reported out of committee for the first time.[20]

At least two factors contributed to the failures of public domain leasing proposals during the first three decades of this century. First, the antiquated Jeffersonian ideal of the yeoman farmer was still widely held; many in Congress, as well as Roosevelt himself, held a blind, unshakable faith in the small homesteader and expressed it in their land policies. The Roosevelt administration seemed not to appreciate the inconsistency between this sentiment and its dedication to science. "Roosevelt's emphasis on applied science and his conception of the good society as the classless agrarian society were contradictory trends of thought," Hays wrote, one looking to the future and "accept[ing] wholeheartedly" the new technology, the other "essentially backward-looking, long[ing] for the simple agrarian Arcadia which, if it ever existed, could never be revived." Indeed, Roosevelt idealized both homesteaders, whom he described as "the most desirable of all possible users of, and dwellers on, the soil," and cattlemen, who exemplified for him "perhaps the pleasantest, healthiest, and most exciting phase of American existence."[21]

A second factor in the failure of leasing proposals was the widespread aversion to monopolies. Grant McConnell has suggested that "antimonopoly" was "the most characteristic appeal" of Pinchot's brand of conservation—that "'natural resources must be developed and preserved for the benefit of the many, and not merely for the few.'" Western cattle barons were a favorite target of this antipathy. Even Roosevelt, an ardent supporter of cattlemen and the ranching life, once during the controversy over the first U.S. Forest Service (USFS) grazing fee compared cattlemen to "the Eastern business community," warning against the selfish exercise of power by any single economic group. Congressman Oscar Underwood of Alabama warned his colleagues in 1901 that, if reclamation were not begun soon, "this great American desert will ultimately be acquired by individuals and great corporations for the purpose of using it for grazing vast herds of cattle. They will acquire the waterways and water rights for the purpose of watering stock and become land barons. Then it will be impossible to ever convert it into the homestead lands for our own people or to build up the population of this country." Such sentiments were not uncommon. Any proposal perceived as benefiting stock owners or impeding western settlement received a cool reception in Congress.[22]

Historian Karen Merrill's informative, often colorful account of this chapter in history helps fill some gaps in our picture of the early stockmen, both real and as perceived by politicians and the public. She describes the progress of the western livestock industry beginning in the 1870s with the Texas cattle drives, explaining how stockmen acquired and wielded their power, how that power varied over time and from state to state, and how these range users interacted with and were viewed by others. Her dissertation sheds light not only on the place of grazing interests in western history but on the underpinnings of the modern debate over preservation of rangelands versus maintenance of the ranching way of life (a topic to which we will return in chapters 4 and 8).[23]

Beginning in the early 1880s, Merrill reports, livestock owners formed "national associations which lobbied for governmental action in their industry." Hays also describes the new "pattern of making resource decisions" that grew up around nationwide pressure groups, such as the National Live Stock Association (NLSA; later the American NLSA). These groups developed relationships with the appropriate congressional committees and gave their members "a sense of participation in and control over resource development which they did not receive from the more centrally directed methods of the conservationists" in the executive branch, notably Pinchot and Roosevelt.[24]

Livestock interests also formed statewide and regional organizations. According to Merrill, "livestock owners achieved their most legendary, if not infamous, power" in Wyoming. The Wyoming Stock Growers' Association (WSGA), whose members were principally ranchers in and near Laramie County (the location of Cheyenne, the eventual state capital), was established in 1879. By 1883 it had 363 members who owned 2 million head of stock; in 1886 membership was 443. "Throughout the 1880s the WSGA wielded extraordinary power in the territory, getting legislation passed that made the Association 'almost an instrumentality of the territorial government.'" Wyoming was an "extreme example" of the large cattle owners' power, Merrill asserts, because "it had virtually no other industry." In contrast, in Montana, "where agriculture and mining had made earlier appearances, the stock growers' association met with more conflict" and enjoyed correspondingly less influence.[25]

Despite, or perhaps because of, their collective power, the big livestock operators had to contend with a negative image, particularly in national and eastern circles. Their reputation derived from numerous factors, including the "range wars" among cattlemen, sheep growers, and homesteaders and the years of overgrazing of the range. Merrill cites the well-known Johnson County War in Wyoming as an example of this competition, particularly among large and small ranchers, over the already overgrazed range. The vast majority of historians, she says,

> argu[e] that the "war" was a product of a power-hungry, declining cattle industry and long-standing economic and political tensions. . . . [Actually, the] "invasion was the culmination of another kind of conflict, economic and savagely personal, between the few who had and were determined to keep and the many who wanted their share." That none of the cattlemen were brought to trial "was accomplished by means of one of the ugliest, most unscrupulous, most shameful cases of bulldozing and oppression in the history of the late nineteenth century—which is saying something."[26]

Competition over the range, often violent, tended to increase as the range's condition deteriorated—and ranges began to deteriorate early on. As David Adams wrote:

> The range cattle business [had] boomed following the Civil War. But in [only a few years], the seemingly infinite grass resources of the West Texas ranges were consumed, their roots destroyed and trampled into the dust. Reckoning came with the severe winters of the mid-1880s. Many herds were almost wiped out by cold, hunger, and thirst; fortunes were lost; and the limitations of free and unlimited use of the public rangelands were becoming apparent.

Editorials in western newspapers as early as the 1880s pointed out the need for improving the western range. The eminent botanist P. B. Kennedy recommended near the turn of the century that the lands be revegetated and that native species be used. Unfortunately, his advice went unheeded. No rangelands were reseeded until the 1930s, and they were planted with nonnative wheatgrass. Meanwhile, other exotics—drought-resistant plants from Europe, Asia, and Africa—were imported to meet the needs of dry farming. In 1900 the president of the Arizona state cattle producers' organization warned that the western range "had suffered 'tremendous damage' and might never 'completely' recover" without government intervention. He called for a federal leasing system.[27]

The American National Live Stock Association also took a position in 1900 in favor of leasing the public domain. "From this point until the early 1930s," Merrill writes, "the western cattle association consistently supported federal control of the range." But national fears of monopoly loomed large. "Opponents— ranging from many leaders in the sheep industry, Congressional representatives, and western politicians— . . . interpreted the recommendation for leasing as the cattle industry's desire to monopolize the range. . . ." Spokesmen for the cattle industry "argued that Congress had been overly optimistic about the agricultural potential of the semi-arid range. This area, they argued, was good only for forage. Leasing . . . would also provide more and cheaper beef for Americans, thus benefitting the rest of the nation." The ANLSA split in 1906 over the leasing question. The residual ANLSA, which continued to support leasing consistently until 1920, consisted almost solely of cattle growers. Sheep producers, who by and large opposed leasing, formed the new National Wool Growers Association (NWGA). While highlighting the differences between the two groups, this schism probably only increased concerns over the big cattlemen's monopolistic intentions.[28]

Leasing proposals also led to friction between those who advocated retaining arid western lands and leasing them for grazing and would-be settlers, fired up by reports of the new dry-farming techniques, who supported additional dispositions for agricultural purposes. For the time being the settlers were winning. As already noted, the clear national policy preference in the federal land policy debates was for the homesteaders, or "home-builders," who epitomized western agrarian ideals. It was widely believed that "the region needed more people, not more cattle." As Louis Pelzer explained: "[T]he individual settler meant more than the corporation; his plow was of greater promise than a cattleman's fence. . . . The thousands of plain settler folk constituted a greater asset than the non-resident shareholders of cattle companies. . . ." A mid-1880s government report disdained proposals to make long-term leases of the public domain for grazing purposes, asserting that it would "'be much more promotive of the public interests if the lands now held by the Government shall be dedicated to the rearing of men rather than the rearing of cattle.'" Even in the land where the cattleman was king, a typical editorial (in the 28 February 1908 *Grand Encampment [Wyoming] Herald*) proclaimed: "[W]hat Wyoming wants and must have is people. Men and women who will come here to make homes and, making, enrich the state financially and socially. The home is the foundation even as it is the unit—or should be—of the commonwealth. In the fierce strife that is being waged over the range question this must be kept ever in sight."[29]

As noted earlier, Roosevelt administration land policies exhibited a tension, favoring leasing of the public domain for grazing by large cattle operators, while championing homesteaders on and near the forest reserves. Looking back later, Roosevelt noted with some regret that all national land policy eventually sided with settlers: "[T]he homesteaders, the permanent settlers, the men who took up each his own farm on which he lived and brought up his family, these represented from the national standpoint the most desirable of all possible users of, and dwellers on, the soil. Their advent meant the breaking up of the great ranches; and the change was a national gain although to some of us an individual loss."[30]

Some of the strongest opposition to grazing on public lands during the Roosevelt era and the first three decades of this century came from agriculturalists, particularly irrigators. Along with water and power supply companies, they opposed any commercial use of public lands, especially the forest reserves. They organized in California, Colorado, and Arizona, seeking to ban grazing and logging in many watersheds. Their opposition to grazing focused primarily on sheep, whose foraging habits "vastly accelerated erosion." Close relations developed during this period among hydrologists, foresters, and irrigation associations. Concomitantly, and perhaps understandably, cattlemen "vigorously opposed almost every phase of the irrigation movement in the late 1880s and early 1890s because it would divert rangeland into cropland."[31]

The early split between stockgrowers and agriculturists was enhanced by the public's perceptions of ranchers, particularly cattlemen, not as settlers, but as wealthy businessmen. At least initially, stockmen themselves considered their occupation a business, not a form of agriculture. This point was made perhaps most succinctly by the governor of Texas at the 1900 ANLSA convention, when he called the cattle industry "'next to agriculture, the greatest interest in Texas.'" The distinction was evident as early as the 1860s. Stockraising was touted not as a way of life but as an "adventure" or get-rich-quick scheme. A leading politician in Wyoming Territory, Joseph M. Carey, called cattle ranching "a sure road to fortune." The "collapse of 1885 converted ranching from an adventure into a business" and dampened the more unrealistic aspirations to wealth. But stockmen continued to be distinguished from homesteaders, who were busy settling the country and building homes for their families. In 1912 the president of the ANLSA reinforced the "big business" image of cattlemen when he publicly decried Congress's failure to impose protective tariffs on animal hides at the same time that he was "on his way to Sao Paulo, Brazil, to become involved in the South American cattle industry."[32]

Moreover, for many large ranchers stockraising was a secondary enterprise. These men lived not on the land, Merrill reports, but in cities and towns, "'in their magnificent mansions.'" They were first and foremost "bankers, real estate dealers, lawyers, lumbermen, or merchants." Historian T. A. Larson relates that in 1880 "35 percent of cattlemen who were Wyoming residents lived in cities or towns, the largest number of them in Cheyenne. They would visit their ranches in summer. . . . Other owners lived in the East or abroad, and rarely set foot in Wyoming." In other words, many cattle and sheep growers were "anything but homebuilders."[33]

In fact, according to Webb, the cattleman was long regarded as "a trespasser on the public domain, an obstacle to settlement, and at best but a crude forerunner of civilization of which the farmer was the advance guard and the hoe the symbol." Webb was a staunch supporter of cattlemen; their critics went so far as to label cattle ranching "barbaric." William E. Smythe, editor of *Irrigation Age* and a frequent contributor to *Harper's* and the *Atlantic*, "argued that irrigation was the key to opening up a new kind of society in the West. In this vision ranching would fast become a thing of the past. . . . 'The conflict is between the civilization of irrigated America and the barbarism of cattle ranching.'"[34]

In the minds of some, "barbarism" came with the territory, especially the drier regions believed suited to little but ranching. Explorer John C. Frémont's views on this point are revealing. Frémont described deserts as bringing out the worst in human character; they were "'peculiar and primitive place[s]'" and "'forced the natives into remaining peculiar and primitive themselves.'" He also wrote that "'humanity here appeared in its lowest form, and in its most elementary state.'" Frémont's view that the Indians were "savages" was widely shared, of course, but it also seems plausible that many shared the view that living "on the edge" in such a harsh land brought out similar characteristics in humans generally. And who lived in such terrain but ranchers and a few prospectors? The human successional analogues advanced by Frederic Clements and Frederick Jackson Turner seem to bear this out. Turner predicted that subsistence farmers would succeed ranchers and in turn be succeeded by farming communities and eventually cities. Historian Patricia Nelson Limerick points out, however, that his theory ignored areas of the West where water was absent or scarce. Factoring in the lack of water arguably could cut short his "Darwinian" sequence at the "primitive rancher" stage.[35]

The barbarian image was fueled by lawlessness and violence, particularly among the big ranchers and their cowboys. In fact, Larson identified distance "from the civilizing institutions—law, in particular" as a "characteristic important to the making of the cowboy." The cowboy was "a borderline character between law and outlawry"; "most people, East and West, considered them to be uncouth ruffians." Barns related his Indiana neighbors' efforts to dissuade him from moving to the Nebraska frontier in 1881. One neighbor "warned against all the ills he had ever heard of, Indians, *cowboys*, horse thieves, blizzards in winter, cyclones in summer, drouths, hot winds, grasshoppers, and rattlesnakes," contending that "it was a shame to expose [Barns's] wife to all such evils."[36]

Many big stockraising operations contrived to exclude others from the public range by fencing it illegally, employing threats and violence, and monopolizing water. In the Unlawful Inclosures Act of 1885 Congress addressed some of these problems. The statute prohibited "[a]ll inclosures of any public lands in any State or Territory" as well as "the assertion of a right to the exclusive use and occupancy of any part of the public lands." It further provided: "No person, by force, threats, intimidation, or by any fencing or inclosing, or any other unlawful means, shall prevent or obstruct any person from peaceably entering upon . . . any tract of public land . . . or shall prevent or obstruct free passage or transit over or through the public lands. . . ." While the act allowed an exception for persons with a good-faith "claim or color of title" to the enclosed lands, the exception did not apply to the general "license" to graze public domain lands, nor, later, to holders of Taylor Grazing Act permits. Enforcement of the act was difficult and spotty. In 1888 alone the Interior Department documented 531 enclosures of 7.2 million acres of public domain in 15 states and territories. Illegal fencing by big ranches killed many cattle every winter and was a significant factor in the loss of thousands of head during the blizzards of 1886–87.[37]

Webb suggested that the "blame for a great deal of western lawlessness" rested "more with the lawmaker than with the lawbreaker," explaining that Congress never recognized the ranchers' rights on the public lands and that federal laws were "wholly unsuited to any arid region." But, as William K. Wyant fairly countered, "surely there were other factors, including greed and confidence that nothing would be done about it," that gave rise to the aggression and intimidation.[38]

In addition to the big ranchers' capacity, if not propensity, for violence and/or disdain of the law, their manner of treating their herds probably contributed to the view of them as "barbaric." Merrill explains that in the winter of 1886–87:

> Before the boom years of the 1880s, cattle owners simply left their animals out on the range to forage for themselves during the winter. While there were losses, they never made enough of a dent in profits to encourage any change in method. This changed with the winter of 1886–87. . . .
>
> Loss of cattle, by most estimates, averaged around 30 percent, and the resulting descriptions of the carnage provoked widespread disgust over the industry's inhumane treatment of its animals. It was a disaster that reverberated in a number of ways for cattle operators. Thereafter, for instance, ranchers fought continually against a popular perception of them as cruel, a perception that had political consequences as the Humane Society grew in influence and lobbied Congress to increase safety standards in transporting animals.

In Wyoming alone, 300,000–400,000 of 2 million cattle died; most that survived were "hardly worth shipping to market." According to Pelzer, some operators lost all, or nearly all, of their herds. Those that died bunched up against illegal fences "perish[ed] miserably . . . from thirst and famine, and exposure to storms and cold 'northers.'" Worster writes that the 1880s "collapse of what we might call the 'laissez-faire commons' was one of the greatest, as measured in the loss of animal life, in the entire history of pastoralism." His remark that "Americans do not like to remember that they once failed abysmally in a form of husbandry where illiterate African tribesmen had succeeded" calls to mind the image of stockraisers as barbaric or primitive.[39]

Horses, the "cowboy's best friend," fared a little better. Like cattle, they had no shelter on the range. They were tools, employed to do a job. Larson describes the cowboys' attitude toward horses as ambivalent—they were often "devoted to a particular animal," but "typically hard on their animals." J. Frank Dobie relates that one "of every three mustangs captured in southwest Texas was expected to die before they were tamed [and] the process of breaking often broke the spirits of the other two."[40]

By 1889 the "'range system' of raising cattle and horses with its attendant cruelties and losses" was reportedly "'giving way to more humane and thrifty methods.'" But ranchers' altered behavior was a function of economics, not concern for their animals' welfare. "It was all right to let a longhorn steer or bull die if he were not strong enough to survive the blizzard and the drought or fight off the wolves," Webb observed sardonically, "but a blooded Hereford bull that cost from $100 to $500 was a different matter. He must be protected, sheltered, and fed if necessary, in order that the investment might be saved and the herd improved." Even so, range husbandry methods, and thus the public's perceptions of ranching, did not change markedly after the turn of the century. "Modern" livestock management methods are still perceived as cruel by some. Scientific surveys of Americans' attitudes toward animals conducted in the 1970s documented the distinctly utilitarian attitudes of farmers and ranchers toward animals and their "relative lack of objection to human exploitation of animals."[41]

Disputes about the appropriate uses and users of public lands, along with the view of ranching as commercial activity, not home-building, carried over to the debates in Congress over leasing the public domain for grazing. According to Merrill, Congress's ultimate choice in the Taylor Grazing Act to assign public domain grazing regulation to the Interior Department rather than to the Forest Service in the Department of Agriculture reflected these philosophical differences:

> [T]his placement [in part] expressed a long-standing conflict over what the public grazing lands were and over what kind of economic activity ranching encompassed. . . . [W]hile ranchers [after 1900] usually grew their feed, they still needed an enormous amount of acreage on which to graze their cows or sheep. As odd as the division may seem, ranching continued to be about *land*, farming about *crops*; and that distinction helped justify its placement in the Department of Interior, despite [Interior's] lack of experience in grazing management.[42]

The debate over whether to establish a leasing system for federal land grazing was also perceived as having social ramifications. The popular term "range barons" itself suggested the existence of a class structure in the West more akin to forms of social organization in parts of Europe than in America. Leasing was opposed by many who believed it would benefit the large operators and disadvantage all others. A speaker from Flagstaff, Arizona, at an ANLSA–Public Land Commission conference in 1904 predicted that federal leasing for grazing would "'build up a system of serfdom, of peons. . . .' While large land and cattle owners might gain from government control, . . . such control 'strikes at the root of society, at the foundation of all that is best and most sacred in our Government.'" Though perhaps exaggerated, this view seems consistent with the democracy and antimonopoly themes of the conservation movement.[43]

The "class structure" of public lands ranching has drawn the attention of some modern historians—though Merrill calls it ranching's "greatest uncharted territory." William Voigt describes the "layering or class-creating effect" brought about within western livestock users by a variety of historical factors, one of which was the ten-year grazing permit initiated by the Forest Service in 1924. Voigt labeled the permit "anathema to a deeply ingrained cultural and political resistance in America to 'special privileges.' Especially at its bargain-basement price, the ten-year permit seemed to embody a kind of class legislation, providing public resources to a very limited number of people." Stockmen countered such criticism by arguing that "the permits were just a recognition of their use and improvement of the semi-arid land."[44]

To shake their image as "barbarians" and monopolistic "cattle barons" and to establish a "more legitimate and more permanent place on the range," ranchers adopted a strategy of identifying with, or at least speaking in support of, the "home-builders." In the early 1900s, Merrill reports, both the ANLSA and the Forest Service used the language of "home-building" to support a leasing bill for the public domain: "this discursive shift worked effectively to change ranchers' position within the developing visions for the developing West. . . . [B]y using the most prominent idiom of western agrarianism, cattlemen were able to shoe-horn ranching into the category of 'agriculture.'" By taking a position "in favor of the 'bona fide settler,' [the ANLSA] helped to re-make its own image along the lines of farming; to give it a kind of cultural and political currency that it did not have nationally; and to insert cattle production as a legitimate form of homesteading."[45]

The Roosevelt administration and Forest Service Chief Pinchot invoked the home-building concept in defending forest reserve grazing by stockmen, especially the small, local graziers. Roosevelt himself proclaimed: "Our whole purpose is to protect the public lands for the genuine home-maker." The home-builder theme was repeated so often in discussions of federal land policy that it came to resemble an "administrative mantra."[46]

Not everyone in the West, however, subscribed to this attempted identification of cattle producers with "home-makers." In a 1907 speech Colorado's Senator Henry Teller described as "'absolutely insignificant'" the "issues of the cattle industry . . . when 'compared with the question' of how freely settlers could build homes on the public lands." And according to Merrill, despite Roosevelt's rhetoric and Pinchot's efforts, "ranchers and USDA officials still did not place the range livestock industry squarely within 'agriculture,' within the notion of 'productive' land use."[47]

Stockgrowers suffered another setback about this time in the form of a fee imposed on forest reserve grazing. The industry reacted violently to the new policy, adopted in 1905. Likened to taxation without representation, the grazing fee formed the basis of at least one proposal that the western states secede from the Union. As Hays put it, "To the administration it was 'perfectly obvious that the man who pastured his stock should pay something for the preservation of that pasture.' But to the stockmen it was not so obvious." Relations cooled between cattlemen and the Roosevelt administration over the grazing fee; Roosevelt "rejected the Western Insurgency" because "it expressed the aims of only one economic group in society which, if dominant, would exercise power as selfishly as did the Eastern business community." The first organized western reaction to the fee policy was the Denver Public Lands Convention of 1907. Wyoming and Colorado interests dominated the convention, with 531 of 644 delegates, and consequently "alienated many delegates from other states." Thereafter, it was principally Wyoming and Colorado political leaders who advocated cession of public domain lands to the western states. Eastern interests consistently opposed transferring the public domain to the states.[48]

Western ranchers' political legitimacy may have peaked with the passage in 1916 of the Stock Raising Homestead Act. But by virtue of the act's acreage limitation, it was only the *small* stockman who thereby acquired the status of bona fide settler or home-builder. A. A. Jones, acting secretary of the interior, testified during hearings on the SRHA in 1914: "I believe that all economists agree that the smallest unit of successful operation of an enterprise of this kind is the most profitable one. The man who has a sufficient body of land on which to make his business successful will make it much more successful and productive relatively than the man with a large area." Merrill opines that Jones's argument "said much more about societal models for the West" than it did about economics.[49]

World War I brought a national emphasis on commercial production, and federal officials began to talk less of the virtues of homesteading and more approvingly of the larger, more efficient stockgrowers. According to the Forest Service's grazing director, Will C. Barnes, the larger operators "are more interested in their stock and the use of the range, give their stock far closer supervision than do the little men, obey our regulations much more willingly, and in every way make what may be considered ideal users of National Forest range." The emphasis on stockraising as a business returned. By 1920, Merrill writes, "'home-building' [had] virtually dropped out of sight in discussions about the public domain, and in its place arose a new emphasis on the relationship between the 'business' of ranching and the administration of the public range." Chief Forester William Greeley in 1923 stated: "The efficient live-stock unit—as a business enterprise—should, I believe, become more and more the key-point in the grazing management of the national forests. . . . The government should encourage such well-established and well-equipped live-stock enterprises."[50]

This attitude went hand in hand with the view that a public resource, grass, would be wasted without cows or sheep to harvest it. Pinchot himself, through his utilitarian brand of conservation, was at least partially responsible for this notion. The author of a 1924 article in the *National Wool Grower* argued simplistically that "without livestock growers on the national forests 'there would be no market for the grass; it would simply dry and shrivel on the range.'" Forest Service grazing chief Barnes concurred: "[T]he man who uses the public domain for his winter feed is utilizing a natural product which, if not fed off by grazing animals would . . . become a dead loss and of no value to anyone." Moreover, Barnes asserted, when stockmen had access to "cheaper feed on the national forests," they would then "return those gains to their community whenever they hired extra labor, paid taxes, or made improvements to their land."[51]

Disagreement persisted, both in the West generally and among livestock groups, as to whether cession of the public domain to the states or a leasing system was the preferable federal grazing policy. When President Herbert Hoover in 1930 proposed a land transfer, but proposed to retain federal ownership of the minerals located under the lands, the western states uniformly declined the offer. They had no interest in taking title unless they could select the more desirable tracts and get them intact, minerals and all. They undoubtedly recognized the truth—that Hoover "simply wanted to unload the grazing lands from federal administration: 'They bring no revenue to the federal government. The federal government is incapable of the adequate administration of matters which require so large a matter of local understanding.'"[52]

Hoover's plan met "[o]verwhelming opposition" in the East as well as the West. Indeed, E. Louise Peffer wrote: "Perhaps no more universally unpopular public land bill had ever been introduced in Congress." Some opposed the reservation of minerals; others simply opposed cession in any form. Conservationists feared that state ownership would lead to private ownership and, in turn, to "even more serious deterioration" of the land. Easterners opposed cession because of their "equity in the lands as a national heritage." The ANLSA initially favored cession, but only if the underlying minerals were included. Ultimately, it followed the states' lead, advocating giving each state the option of choosing whether it wanted the federal lands. One widely debated concern was that disposal "would benefit only the large cattle operations." The eastern press sided with small livestock operators, labeling Hoover's proposed transfer "one of monopoly and eviction, antisocial, [and] undemocratic," and recommending that the plan be "shelved."[53]

The disinterest and antagonism in the West should have come as no surprise. The lands subject to Hoover's proposal were generally considered the least valuable remnants of the original public domain. Homesteaders had either passed up the land or tried their luck and failed. Without the minerals, the lands were perceived as having little value. Moreover, many stockgrowers feared the economic consequences of obtaining title to public domain grazing lands. They wanted the use of the lands but not the expense or liability of ownership. As early as 1878 the Wyoming Stock Growers' Association had opposed sale of federal grazing lands to ranchers, even at the modest price of five cents an acre, fearing that state land taxes would cut deeply into members' profits. Ranchers and others also feared the resultant loss of federal funds, for highways and other purposes, that hinged on the presence within their borders of federal lands. As Professor (now Interior Solicitor) John D. Leshy explains, "numerous special programs of federal financial assistance . . . constituted an umbilical cord for the western economy. A substantial restructuring of federal lands . . . would sever that cord and eliminate any useful rationale for special treatment."[54]

Hoover's aborted cession plan led to a renewed interest in leasing the public domain for grazing. The result, four years later, was the Taylor Grazing Act. A leasing system, it was believed, would address two concerns. It would ensure that the federal government retained responsibility for the condition of the lands and their management, while preserving the states' eligibility for "special treatment." But the leasing arrangement ultimately devised had another, less predictable, result: the until-then neglected, if not maligned, western livestock industry began its entrenchment, both on the public domain and on the national political scene.[55]

CHAPTER 2

The Early Legal Landscape

While livestock interests, states, Congress, and conservationists continued alternately to debate or ignore the western range, conditions on those lands deteriorated as a result of many factors, including the lack of regulation, overstocking, and drought. Stockmen and western promoters greatly inflated the stocking rates that the ranges could sustain. Stocking rates exceeded the capacity of the range, especially as it was further diminished by drought, well into the early 1900s.[1]

The fact of overstocking was, then as now, uncontested, although statistics vary as to its prevalence and even as to the numbers of animals on the range. The first domestic livestock (500 cattle, 5,000 sheep, and 1,000 horses) were introduced to what is now the American Southwest in 1540. An estimated 50,000 sheep and 20,000 cattle were brought from Mexico to missions in Texas and the Southwest in the 1700s. By 1860 California was home to an estimated 3.5 million cattle; Texas supported 4 million. Sheep herds in Utah increased from 1 million head in 1885 to 1.5 million in 1890 and 3.8 million by the turn of the century. Cattle numbers followed a similar pattern, increasing from approximately 4.6 million in the seventeen western states in 1870 to 35–40 million in 1884. Cattle herds in Arizona alone ballooned from 50,000 in the mid-1800s to 1.5 million in 1891. In 1860 Oregon was home to about 200,000 cattle, but only 65,000 people; in 1897 the state supported 2.5 million sheep.[2]

Louis Pelzer describes the overstocking of western ranges as "murderous." Symptoms included "outbreaks of pleuropneumonia," open ranges cut up by barbed wire, a drop in the cattle price, and major ranches shipping significant numbers of steers and bulls to Omaha for fattening. Even stockgrowers admitted that overstocking had occurred by the early 1880s; some were concerned that overgrazing might "*destroy* the range." Twenty cattle companies in the vicinity of the Musselshell River in the Montana Territory "declared the range already overstocked" by 1883. Ironically, just months before losing much of his herds along the Little Missouri River in the 1886–87 blizzards, Teddy Roosevelt had written:

Overstocking may cause little or no harm for two or three years. But sooner or later there comes a winter which means ruin to the ranches that have too many cattle on them; and in our country, which is even now getting crowded, it is merely a question of time as to when a winter will come that will understock the ranges by the summary process of killing off about half of all the cattle throughout the Northwest.

Roosevelt's forecast was not far off. Some operators lost nearly all of their herds; overall losses were in the vicinity of 30 percent.[3]

Albert F. Potter, head of the U.S. Forest Service grazing section and himself an Arizona grazier, described 1880–1900 on the western range as a period of "spoilation": "[P]ioneer ranchers, looking for quick profits, overstocked their ranges, an action which led to increasing speculation and incredible numbers of stock on the range." Use of the range "became a struggle in which only the fittest survived, 'and the permanent good of the industry was sacrificed to individual freedom.'" In some instances, "feed was deliberately wasted to prevent its utilization by others." These circumstances were attributed in part to the uncertainty of government regulation. Government botanist Frederick Coville explained that it was in each operator's interests to "get all the grass possible without reference to next year's crop, for he is never certain that he will be able to occupy the same range again." The West was witnessing a classic "tragedy of the commons."[4]

War also took its toll on the range. The national forests were ordered "to make available every acre of grazing lands for the greatest possible utilization," in order to "meet the [World War I] emergency." According to Rowley, the policy failed its purpose, resulting not in greater production but in "thin and poorly fed" stock. Livestock numbers on national forests increased from 1.76 million cattle and 7.84 million sheep in 1916 to 2.14 million cattle and 8.45 million sheep in 1918; numbers were almost as high in 1919. Many local rangers were alarmed at these stocking rates, which coincided with declining forage production in some areas due to weather. William Voigt paints a grim picture of wartime western rangelands:

All the liberties the livestock industry took in the boom-and-bust years of the 1870s and 1880s could not equal the havoc wrought on the ranges in that world war. It was devastating, and government was fully as responsible as industry. It insisted that ever more stock be crowded on the ranges. . . . [T]he environment being depleted . . . was subordinated to the short-term production of red meat, wool, hides, and tallow for which hungry allies and the defense establishment clamored.

Some federal officials attributed range deterioration after the war to wartime policies, but conditions undoubtedly reflected the steadily increasing use ranges had undergone since 1905.[5]

Worsening range conditions were due as much to government inaction on the public domain as to government promotion of grazing in the forests. Although Congress passed a few experimental grazing measures prior to 1934, none applied to the western range as a whole. Public domain ranges came under no federal regulation until after 1934; the principal state regulation consisted of a few inconsistent efforts to define property interests and control the peace. Open to all, the range deteriorated because every user was trying to get his share before someone else did. Sheep and sheep graziers were particularly vilified. The animals cropped plants closely, sometimes uprooting them, and their herders often set fires to burn off the understory and encourage new forage growth, thus exacerbating runoff and erosion. Conservationists, both within and outside government, urged the ouster of sheep from public ranges. Conservationist John Muir believed that fire and grazing were the chief threats to forested lands and to watersheds. In 1895 he called for military guards in forest reserves to prevent the desolation that sheep could cause. Even Pinchot subscribed to Muir's proposal for a while. A National Academy of Sciences committee, with whom Muir toured the forests in 1896, concluded that the value of the sheep industry was "'insignificant relative to the injury it inflicts on the country.'"[6]

A few outspoken nay-sayers—industry spokesmen and apologists—argued that range conditions in the West were "natural," not human-caused. For instance, in an address to the National Wool Growers Association in 1932, Dr. S. W. McClure blasted as "a damned, insidious program" the government "propaganda" campaign, led chiefly by the Forest Service, to poison the public mind about the erosion caused by sheep. This erosion, he said, "dates back to the time that the Almighty God made the first grain of sand. . . . Nothing that man has done anywhere in the world has owed much to erosion and nothing that he can do will have a perceptible effect in preventing it." "Here and there," McClure admitted, the public domain had been overgrazed, "but in the main it has not been injured." In fact, he argued, "that old public domain that they are telling us is destroyed is today carrying as many sheep as it ever did in history. . . . [I]n my country what the public domain needs is just one good rain."[7]

The fundamental reasons for overstocking were traceable to the users themselves. As stockman and American Society of Range Management president A. P. Atkins put in in 1955, "overgrazing of ranges has been the besetting sin of stockmen since Biblical times." Many early stockmen also failed to plan ahead for contingencies such as harsh winters. Whether due to lack of foresight or caution, pure greed or misguided efforts to increase profits, or overoptimism about the capacity of the land to "provide," the result on the range was the same. When range conditions—or the market—worsened during this era, pressure on forage resources only intensified. From 1931 to 1933, for example, "livestock prices fell by 50 percent, forcing cattle ranchers to produce more stock for the same return, further overstocking the public domain and compounding the degradation of the range."[8]

Congress was on notice of the escalating western range problem. According to John T. Schlebecker, Congress passed the 1916 Stock Raising Homestead Act in "an effort to retard the destruction." But "[p]rivate ownership and control [were] to no avail" in sustaining, much less restoring, range condition and productivity, George C. Coggins and Margaret Lindeberg-Johnson point out, "because the owners were largely unable to exercise self-restraint in stocking their own lands." As crop yields declined on homesteads, particularly those where dry farming had been attempted, "farmers recklessly grazed the land. They grazed not only their own, but anything at hand. . . . If farmers had no stock, they accomplished the same destruction by leasing to those who did."[9]

Most western livestock operations at the time relied on both public and private grazing lands; consequently, both classes of lands were usually over-stocked. But if stockmen could benefit at someone else's (including the public's) expense, they would. A "mentality of getting all the grass one could was part of even the most respectable outfits," Merrill reports, citing as an example a letter from Wyoming sheep rancher and senator Francis Warren to his son Fred. Warren, dubbed "the 'greatest shepherd since Abraham,'" admonished Fred as to what he should do if he were charged too much for grazing a certain section of private rental lands: "I hope you will eat every hair off that part of the range, getting it just as close as you can without injury to the sheep, and save our own range accordingly." Similarly, Schlebecker notes that stockmen kept cattle on the open (public) range as long as possible to keep down the expense of raising feed on their private lands.[10]

In 1926 a Senate committee with responsibility for the public lands stated flatly that "the range has been overgrazed. It has carried more livestock than can be fed on its forage. . . . Insufficient, if any, care has been taken to permit natural reseeding. The forage resources . . . have been seriously depleted. Erosion has been excessive. . . . There is every probability that the continuation of the present grazing policy will result in further waste and destruction." In the same year Congress considered a bill that would have established a leasing system for grazing on both national forests and the public domain. With the exception of its coverage of forests, the bill was substantially similar to the Taylor legislation passed eight years later. In authorizing the interior secretary to exclude from any grazing district "any lands which he determines are *no longer valuable for grazing purposes*," the bill left no doubt that some rangelands had already been exhausted.[11]

By 1934 Congress had been entertaining proposed grazing measures for nearly fifty years; 25 million acres of rangeland had been plowed and abandoned, an estimated 50 million acres of relatively good range had been converted to sub-marginal cropland, and the public domain was "seriously overstocked." Congressman Don M. Colton (R-Utah), who first introduced the bill that eventually passed as the Taylor Grazing Act, described "how badly irrigation reservoirs . . . were silting up because of grazing-induced erosion." Congressman Edward T. Taylor (D-Colorado) called the public domain ranges "fast deteriorating and vanishing." The prize for hyperbole—or perhaps frankness—went to Chief Forester Ferdinand A. Silcox for his description of range conditions in 1934 as a "'cancer-like growth and [the] establishment of a great interior desert.'" It was universally agreed that the federal "grazing common" was seriously depleted and deteriorating. According to Coggins and Lindeberg-Johnson, it was this "crisis [that] produced the Taylor Grazing Act, and the federal [land] disposition policy was finally interred with barely a whimper."[12]

The first federal grazing regulation to pass either house of Congress was the Colton-French bill, a leasing bill sponsored by Congressmen Colton and Burton L. French (R-Idaho); it passed the House in 1932 but died in the Senate. Congressman Taylor introduced a nearly identical bill the following year. Until the 1930s, he had been "as staunch an advocate of disposing the public domain lands as one could find." But after Congress failed to act on the Hoover Commission's report and cession proposal, the "waste, competition, overuse, and abuse of valuable range lands and watersheds eating into the very heart of the western economy" convinced Taylor of the pressing need for a federal leasing system. When hearings opened on his bill, the range situation was viewed as an emergency.[13]

The Taylor Grazing Act, passed in 1934, was the culmination of many factors too numerous and intertwined to do justice to here. One precipitating event was the dust storms that occurred in May 1934, while the Senate was considering the Taylor bill; one senator characterized them as "the most tragic, the most impressive lobbyist that has ever come to this Capitol." Ironically, William L. Graf notes, the dust was generated by drought conditions in the western Great Plains where private lands predominated, while the states farther west with the greatest acreages subject to the Taylor bill had "had only brief periods of dry conditions" that year. Those provisions of the TGA most relevant to the proposed biodiversity conservation strategy are discussed in chapter 7; grazing boards are addressed in chapter 4.[14]

Coggins has called the Taylor Grazing Act the "watershed in public land policy development"; it "clearly marked the end of free land and the start of permanent federal management" of the public domain. As a result of its passage, "the old public domain passed into history." Despite opposition from some diehard cession proponents, notably Wyoming's Congressman Vincent Carter and Senator Carey and certain stockmen's organizations (e.g., the Arizona Cattle Growers Association, California Cattlemen's Association, and the Wyoming Stock Growers), support for the bill was widespread. Several livestock associations (including the Colorado Wool Growers Association, New Mexico Cattle

Raisers Association, and Utah Wool Growers Association), the Forest Service, and Interior Secretary Harold Ickes were vigorous proponents. Ickes advocated comprehensive rather than piecemeal range reform and had threatened to exercise his executive authority to withdraw all of the public domain unless Congress enacted appropriate legislation. Speaking during debate on the Taylor bill, Representative Fuller of Arkansas asserted: "Who is in opposition [to this bill]? No one on earth except a few sheepmen and a few cattlemen who have a selfish interest, who care nothing for the present welfare of this country, and who think of nothing but getting theirs while the getting is good." Fuller was referring specifically to livestock operators who drove their herds from one state to another, making free use of public domain grazing lands.[15]

Taylor's bill passed the House 265–92. A month after the May 1934 dust storm, the Senate followed suit, after scarcely debating the bill. The secretary of agriculture and Chief Forester Silcox withdrew their support for the bill, however, largely because of amendments offered by Senator Patrick McCarran (D-Nevada). The bill, they said, was "no longer a conservation measure." According to Silcox, the Taylor Act "'abdicat[ed]' strong federal control over the range" and "would be completely ineffective in halting the spread of the 'great interior desert.'" He criticized the act's "pending final disposal" language, which he said rendered the statute a "stopgap measure"; its weak enforcement provisions; and the fact that it applied only to a small portion (80 million acres) of the land area that should have been included. Secretary Ickes's and the attorney general's views differed sharply from those of Agriculture, however, and the president ultimately disregarded Silcox's advice. Upon signing the measure, Franklin Delano Roosevelt proclaimed it "a great forward step in the interests of conservation, which will prove of benefit not only to those engaged in the livestock industry but also [to] the nation as a whole."[16]

The three chief purposes of the Taylor Grazing Act, set forth in its preamble, are to "stop injury to the public lands by preventing overgrazing and soil deterioration, to provide for their orderly use, improvement, and development, and to stabilize the livestock industry, dependent on the public range." Although the preamble was never codified, it is important evidence of Congress's intent. Interpretations of these purposes, and their respective significance, vary. According to Coggins and Lindeberg-Johnson, the need to improve range conditions is the "one explicit theme running throughout the statute." They note that, while the "Act has meant different things to different people," some believe that it is "a conservation law that was never implemented." Forty years after its passage, a federal court described the act as "an operative and effective method of protecting the environment of the public lands," while conceding that it was "not purely an environmental act."[17]

Paul Culhane argues that it was the TGA's second purpose—its "managerial function supporting the dominant user industry"—and not its first, "regulatory function"—to "preserve the land and its resources"—which "dominated the history of the legislation and was most important to its crucial supporters in the western livestock industry." Coggins and Lindeberg-Johnson counter that the "codified statute on the books does not expressly require either stabilization or subsidization of the livestock industry," although they acknowledge that the former "remains an important goal of the Act" and the latter policy has been "validated by later legislation"—referring, respectively, to the stabilization requirement in section 3 of the act and to the subsidies inherent in low grazing fees. Implementing regulations can provide some evidence of congressional intent. One BLM regulation, since amended, provided: "Approval of the transfer [of a grazing preference] shall not disrupt the stability of the livestock industry in the general area within which the public lands involved are located." One commentator construed this rule as protecting "the wealth positions of livestock operators and those that sell inputs to the industry and market and transport the output." If this interpretation is correct, and if the rule was an accurate implementation of congressional intent to "stabilize the industry," the term would seem to mean little more than protecting the economic status of those who hold grazing permits and of those who do business with permittees.[18]

Section 1 of the Taylor Act, as amended, states in relevant part:

> In order to promote the highest use of the public lands pending its [sic] final disposal, the Secretary of the Interior is authorized, in his discretion, by order to establish grazing districts . . . of vacant, unappropriated, and unreserved lands from any part of the public domain which are not in national forests, national parks and monuments, [etc.,] and which in his opinion are chiefly valuable for grazing and raising forage crops. . . .

Lands "more valuable or suitable for the production of agricultural crops than for the production of native grasses and forage plants" could be classified under section 7 as suitable for entry "under the applicable public-land laws" (e.g., for homesteading). Section 1 further specifies that "[n]othing in this chapter shall be construed as in any way altering or restricting the right to hunt or fish within a grazing district."[19]

Section 2 of the act provides:

> The Secretary of the Interior shall make provision for the protection, administration, regulation, and improvement of such grazing districts as may be created under the authority of section [1 of the act], and he shall make such rules and regulations, . . . and do any and all things necessary to accomplish the purposes of this chapter and to insure the objects of such grazing districts, namely, to regulate their occupancy and use, to preserve the land and its resources from destruction or unnecessary injury, to provide for the orderly

use, improvement and development of the range; and . . . to continue the study of erosion and flood control. . . .[20]

Section 1 implies that grazing districts were to be temporary. It authorized their establishment "[i]n order to promote the highest use of the public lands, *pending its [sic] final disposal*." Many commentators, relying on this phrase, have described the act as "transitional legislation" or "an interim measure." It was because of this language that USFS Chief Forester Silcox termed the act a "stopgap measure."[21]

The act provided for the continuation, in the meantime, of all other lawful uses of the lands that might be included in grazing districts: hunting, fishing, and use by owners of adjacent land as a stock driveway; the free grazing of domestic stock by homesteaders; and the continued use by miners, prospectors, and others. Specifically, the act provided that "nothing contained in this chapter shall prevent the use of timber, stone, gravel, clay, coal, and other deposits by miners, prospectors for mineral bona fide settlers and residents, for firewood, fencing, buildings, mining prospecting, and domestic purposes" and, further, that

> [n]othing contained in this chapter shall restrict the acquisition, granting or use of permits or rights-of-way within grazing districts under existing law; or ingress or egress over the public lands in such districts for all proper and lawful purposes; and nothing contained in this chapter shall restrict prospecting, locating, developing, mining, entering, leasing, or patenting the mineral resources of such districts under law applicable thereto.[22]

Section 7 of the Taylor Act delineates the interior secretary's authority to consider the lands' value for a variety of other purposes and to manage or dispose of them accordingly. As amended, it authorizes the secretary to

> examine and classify any lands [withdrawn or reserved per the TGA] which are . . . more valuable or suitable for any other use than for the use provided for under this chapter, or proper for acquisition in satisfaction of any outstanding lien, exchange or script rights or land grant, and to open such lands to entry, selection or location for disposal in accordance with such classification under applicable public-land laws.

Section 7 allowed some homesteading to continue within grazing districts, if the lands were classified by the secretary as "more valuable or suitable for the production of agricultural crops than for the production of native grasses and forage plants."[23]

A key provision in section 3 makes clear that a grazing authorization issued under the TGA is a revocable privilege: "So far as is consistent with the purposes and provisions of this subchapter, grazing privileges shall be safeguarded, but the creation of a grazing district or the issuance of a permit . . . shall not create any right, title, interest, or estate in or to the lands." Several courts have described the ephemeral nature of the interest in a Taylor Act grazing permit. One of the earliest and most oft-cited cases is *Red Canyon Sheep Co. v. Ickes*. The District of Columbia circuit court analogized the "the right or privilege of grazing upon the public lands" to the "right to hunt upon public waters," noting that "[n]either is an interest in the land itself, and both are subject to restriction or withdrawal . . . in the interest of the protection of the public domain." Some commentators have mischaracterized the nature of the grazing permit, and a recent federal district court decision, which referred to grazing permits as "rights," was appealed successfully by the federal government.[24]

The act gave "preference" in issuing permits to "those within or near a district who are landowners engaged in the livestock business, bona fide occupants or settlers, or owners of water or water rights, as may be necessary to permit the proper use of the lands, water or water rights." This policy resembled the nearly four-decades-old Forest Service policy of giving preference in issuing grazing permits to residents and neighbors of forest reserves. But the analogy is incomplete; the TGA preference system does not incorporate the Forest Service's redistribution policy, which provided for newcomers at the expense of the larger operators and was thus very unpopular among the big, politically powerful ranchers. In fact, McConnell described the TGA preference system as

> a capture of formal power for the benefit of established stockmen to the exclusion of would-be newcomers. Certainly it was the best of two worlds for the established stockmen: it secured the benefits of the public lands as though they were privately owned, but largely avoided the costs of private ownership. Fees were paid for the arrangement, but they were largely spent for improvements on the land for the users' benefit.

Moreover, the fees were low.[25]

The Taylor Act's characterization of the grazing privilege in section 3 and its broad recognition and continuation of existing uses in section 7 are difficult to reconcile with the view, widely held among ranchers, that the 1934 statute was Congress's way of according public land grazing some new, elevated status. Even Coggins, who once opined that the Taylor Act "is not the sort of 'Magna Carta' that miners have in the 1872 Mining Law," elsewhere asserted that the act "on its face appears to subordinate other goals to range management" and that "Congress intended the main public land use to be domestic livestock grazing." I disagree with the latter interpretations (see further discussion in chapter 7).[26]

The Taylor Act was initially limited to 80 million acres. Stockmen and others urged that its leasing provisions be extended to all public land ranges. The statute was subsequently expanded, by executive order and by congressional amendment in 1936, to encompass 142 million acres. President Roosevelt's 1934 executive order withdrew "from settlement, location, sale, or entry and reserved for classification" all unappropriated lands in the twelve western states, "pending determination of the most useful purpose to which such land may be put." As explained by BLM biographers James Muhn and Hanson R. Stuart, this order was designed to withdraw from homesteading and other nonmineral entry "all vacant, unreserved and unappropriated public lands in the West so that grazing districts could be set aside and the *remaining lands* classified as to their best use." But like Coggins and Lindeberg-Johnson's interpretation this suggests, inaccurately I think, that establishment of grazing districts took precedence somehow over classification of "remaining" lands as to their "best use."[27]

"The need [in 1934] for prompt action to protect the range was great," Paul W. Gates wrote, "and officials of the Department of the Interior did not intend to delay in putting the Taylor Act into operation." A new Division of Grazing was established, and Farrington ("Ferry") Carpenter, a rancher from Congressman Taylor's home district in Colorado and a Harvard-educated lawyer, was chosen to direct the new agency. The division's other chief officers "were not drawn from the major universities and law schools [but] selected from men who had been residents of public land states at least a year." Soon Congressman Taylor was lauding the "'amazing change' that had come to the public rangelands and the 'renewed confidence [in] the entire social and economic structure of the West' that had resulted from the adoption of the Grazing Act," and Ickes referred to the act as the "'Magna Carta' of the conservation movement." But such optimism was undoubtedly overstated. Director Carpenter reported that his division was hampered by a lack of funds and maps. Indeed, no one in authority even knew the locations of the lands for which the new agency was responsible. The all-important—and exceedingly difficult—process of determining or "adjudicating" preference rights was not completed for decades. Meanwhile, the overgrazing continued.[28]

Despite the high hopes of its sponsors and others, the Taylor Grazing Act did not fully succeed at any of its purposes. Schlebecker reports that overgrazing diminished, but he also notes that the "Division of Grazing tended to continue range rights which were attached to inferior private land" and that ranchers setting grazing policy, via the district grazing boards, "tended to perpetuate an inefficient and outmoded form of cattle husbandry." Coggins and Lindeberg-Johnson likewise charge that the new Division of Grazing "abdicated management responsibility by undue deference to the major users, a pattern that has haunted well-meaning public rangeland management ever since." They note that the act's requirement that permits be limited to "carrying capacity" "turned out to have a different meaning in practice than in science because capacity was determined (primarily by stockmen) within the first year or two of Taylor Act administration without the benefit of survey or biological opinion." In most cases, in fact, permits were "issued for many more livestock than the range could properly support." Coggins and Lindeberg-Johnson and other modern commentators have called for the act's repeal.[29]

Thus, although the Taylor Act arguably prevented range overstocking and competition from getting worse, it did not fully correct past abuses or even halt the declining trend of much of the range. Moreover, it undoubtedly allowed marginal livestock operations to stay in business longer than they otherwise would have. As a result, degradation of the public domain range continued.[30]

CHAPTER 3

The Physical Landscape

It may be an exaggeration to say that overgrazing is "in the eye of the beholder," but the term is clearly subject to divergent interpretations. This is due in part to its inherent imprecision, the various standards used to measure range conditions, the confounding effects of other environmental factors such as climate or fire, and the alternate purposes for which a given rangeland may be managed. Merrill claims there is a further complicating factor: the charge of "overgrazing" is "not a non-ideological description," but rather "mark[s] a matrix of geographical, political, and socioeconomic boundaries."[1]

Writing about the pre–Taylor Act era, Merrill describes overgrazing as involving "various sites of struggle at local levels": neighbors accusing each other of overgrazing, cattlemen accusing sheep growers, residents pointing their fingers at nomadic herders (read: "non-home-builders"), ranchers vilifying homesteaders, and so forth. Merrill's own predisposition is suggested by her reference to the "overstocking of the range and the attendant depletion of forage [which] caused tremendous concern among ranchers, politicians, and bureaucrats alike." The focus of her concern as a historian seems to be the availability of "forage," presumably for livestock, and not the effect of grazing on other species or the environment or even on soil erosion, water quality, or water yield.[2]

Ranchers, federal land managers, and range scientists have often disagreed, since passage of the Taylor Act, about the condition of the range. In those relatively infrequent instances where the BLM attempts to reduce grazing due to its concern that drought and/or overgrazing of an allotment would cause serious, possibly permanent damage to the range, ranchers almost always argue that grazing would result in no substantial injury. Similarly, ranchers "invariably" describe range conditions as better, and carrying capacities as higher, than do range scientists. Describing the tension between stockgrowers and scientists during the first half of the twentieth century, Schlebecker wrote: "Usually scientists recommended that cattlemen run only 65 per cent of the cattle which a ranch farm could support in an average year. Almost all of the cattlemen carried far more stock than this suggested maximum." Implying that the conflict over stocking rates may be irresolvable, Marion Clawson wrote:

> [The range user's] quest is not only for security of use, but for security of expectations. The Federal range administrators sympathize with this objective but are faced with other considerations. They recognize the multiple uses to which much Federal range may be put and cannot agree to an exclusive use whenever there is any real prospect of conflicting use. . . . The stockman's quest for security of expectations, though natural, is perhaps in the nature of things partly unattainable.[3]

Regardless of whether the term "overgrazed" is considered an indictment or accusation, as Merrill argues, or simply an imprecise description of the land's physical and biological conditions, few observers, including stockmen, disputed that ranges had been seriously overstocked in the late 1800s or that by the 1930s range forage and soil conditions had been severely damaged.

The process of overgrazing varies with the site, weather, class of livestock, and circumstances of use. A modern ecology text summarizes the general scenario:

> Grazing animals that are foreign to the community are used to harvest a larger share of its primary productivity than under natural conditions. Some of the plant species native to a grassland are unable to survive this increased harvest. Effects of overgrazing appear first in the decline of these species (decreasers). Meanwhile other species (increasers), that are more tolerant of grazing and are now relieved of the competition of the decreasers, expand their coverage. At the same time the biomass, height, and total coverage of the grassland decrease. Continued overgrazing can overharvest and reduce the increaser species, while still other species (invaders) that are not part of the undisturbed community appear. These may then increase in coverage, and in time the grassland may become a weed field dominated by them. With still continued overgrazing and trampling the weeds, in turn, can be reduced in coverage and the soil further exposed to erosion. The final result of overgrazing to its limit may be a virtual noncommunity—a mudfield or eroded rocky slope, depending on location.

A pioneer rancher offered an abbreviated, though perceptive, description of what had happened to overgrazed Utah ranges:

> Grazing livestock take the most flavorful forage first, and when those forms are killed out they adjust their tastes to the kinds of lesser nutrition. This process under a regime of unlimited grazing goes on until in a tragically short time the vegetation left alive on ranges of six to twelve inches of annual rainfall bears little resemblance to the original forms.[4]

Utah's overgrazing problem in the early 1900s was called one of the worst in the West; one commentator even suggested that livestock there "often lived on nothing but 'fresh air and mountain scenery.'" According to Clarence Forsling, who headed Interior's Grazing Service from 1944 to 1946 and spent several years with the Forest Service in the Intermountain Region earlier in his career, Utah had been plagued by "disastrous floods since the turn of the century because of overgrazing in the mountains."[5]

Although grazing began relatively early in Utah, range conditions were comparably bleak in many areas. Nearly all the range in southeastern Oregon, for example, was considered fully occupied by livestock by 1870. More than 182,000 sheep grazed Steens Mountain in eastern Oregon for a four- to five-month period during the 1900 growing season—this equates to an estimated density of 450 animals per square mile. By 1901 some of this flock had to be moved to lower winter pastures "due to a shortage of feed caused by over-stocking." One writer from this era reported traveling for three days over Steens Mountain and finding "no good feed except in the very steep ravines." Invasion by nonnative plants also began during this period, due chiefly to inadvertent importation with wheat seed. "The decline of palatable forage species and an increase in plant species of low palatability and bare ground took only 10 to 15 years at any given site under heavy uncontrolled grazing." Such impacts were recorded for several areas within the Intermountain sagebrush region as early as 1870.[6]

This chapter documents the progression and persistence of the "western range problem." Part A, based almost entirely on a 1936 government report, describes then-current conditions on national forest, public domain, and private rangelands. Part B, which is concerned with the aftermath of the Taylor Act, focuses on the public domain ranges to which the Taylor Act applied.[7]

A. RANGE CONDITIONS CIRCA 1936:
THE WESTERN RANGE

Shortly after the Taylor Grazing Act passed, Congress directed the Forest Service, within the Department of Agriculture, to submit to the U.S. Senate a report on the "original and present condition of the range resource, the factors which have led to the present condition, and the social and economic impor-tance of the range and its conservation to the West and to the entire United States." The agriculture secretary was further instructed to submit "recommen-dations as to constructive measures." The resulting 600-page report—known variously as Senate Document 199, *The Western Range*, or the "green book"—was the first and, until 1992, apparently the only comprehensive evaluation of western range conditions. *The Western Range* has been both praised and berated.

A National Academy of Sciences (NAS) committee in 1970 referred to it as "that epochal work." Worster lauded the survey as "the most thorough ecological accounting we have of the first half-century of western pastoralism." A symposium held in 1992 was described by one of its participants as "perhaps the first attempt to examine comprehensively the implications of livestock grazing on the western range since Senate Document No. 199 was compiled in 1936."[8]

Most criticism of the report, which painted a rather bleak picture of range conditions, has focused on its perceived political motivations. Prior to passage of the Taylor Grazing Act just two years earlier, the Forest Service and the Interior Department had vied for authority over the public domain grasslands. The Taylor Act named Interior the winner, but many suspected that Agriculture had not yet given up the contest. According to Merrill, *The Western Range* was "produced in response to a Senate Resolution [which] was clearly intended to try to have the public domain [placed] under the jurisdiction of the Forest Service and the Department of Agriculture." She claims that the report was concerned with "proving these two assertions": that "'the administration of the range resource and its use is agriculture'" and consequently that "'the grazing districts and the public domain should be transferred to the Department of Agriculture.'" Rowley referred bluntly to the survey as propagandist and "sour grapes," although he ventured that the report "may have been a necessary defensive tactic on the part of Agriculture to keep the national forest ranges under its control, free from the growing power of [Interior Secretary] Ickes." The ANLSA was less open-minded. The organization's secretary condemned *The Western Range* as a "self-serving compilation of falsehoods" by a "bigoted, conceited bureaucratic" agency.[9]

Graf labeled the report "Interior bashing" and said it was "a full-scale attempt by the Forest Service to obtain exclusive control over all the western grazing lands." Western grazing interests, keen on retaining "their hard-won local control" over the new Grazing Service, "reacted to the 'green book' with alarm," he said. They "did not want to see the well-developed controls of the forestry agency expanded."[10]

Contemporary critics could be found even within the Agriculture department. According to Rowley, Forest Service director of range management Walt L. Dutton charged that "the report was full of inaccuracies": "The evidence was manipulated, [Dutton] said, to show a greater contrast between national forest ranges and the unreserved and unregulated public domain than was actually the case. There was no question, Dutton conceded, that the public domain stood in disrepair, but he emphasized that forest ranges were certainly no shining example of successful protective administration, either." While they corroborate the political nature of the report, Dutton's remarks seem a weak indictment of *The Western Range*. They suggest that the public domain probably was in no better shape than depicted, but that the national forests' condition may actually have been worse. Forsling, a report author and chief of Forest Service research beginning in 1937, candidly acknowledged that one of the document's purposes "was to point out the inadequacies of the Taylor Grazing Act as an instrument of administration."[11]

Despite the reprobation, *The Western Range* was and is a remarkable report, especially for its time. Its "significance . . . lay in the national recognition its publication gave to problems that existed in the utilization of grazing resources on public and private rangelands." The report has been viewed both "as the most thorough appraisal of the range" and as a "highly articulate attempt to differentiate the functions of the state when it came to land-use planning." Worster defended the report's "trustworthiness," noting that "every survey of the western range made since the 1930s has tended to the same conclusion: the combination of scientifically trained, disinterested supervisors and public land tenure provides better protection for the range environment, on the whole, than simple private ownership."[12]

The green book was authored in major part by seventeen high-ranking, professional foresters in the U.S. Forest Service (including the forest and range experiment stations). According to Worster: "More than a hundred Forest Service officials examined vegetation on over 20,000 plots, some of them relict samples of the native vegetation. . . . They combed through reports by early explorers, travelers, and naturalists to supplement those measurements and push back their understanding of the land's history into the nineteenth century." Their survey covered 728 million acres, or about 40 percent of the continental United States.[13]

The Western Range provides a context for interpreting significant provisions of the Taylor Grazing Act. Its account of depleted range conditions also serves as a yardstick by which to measure future improvements, if any, attributable to management under the act. The discussion below focuses on the conditions and effects of overgrazing. Chapter 8 takes a closer look at the report's comparisons of range resource values and the 1934 understanding of the phrase "lands chiefly valuable for grazing."

The Western Range's many statistics concerning conditions on western ranges were impressive and troubling. Even if we assume that the report was biased, its comprehensive accounting of range deterioration on all categories of land— private, public domain, and national forest—should mitigate that reservation. Clearly, western ranges *were* depleted. Among the document's summary figures are the following:

> Watershed values have been seriously impaired. . . . Approximately 149 million acres, or 98 percent of the available public domain . . . is eroding more or less seriously, and 67 million acres is contributing silt to major streams. . . .

Over 80 percent of private land is eroding and 195 million acres [are] contributing silt. . . . Even on the national forests, which have a watershed objective in [their] administration, 32 million acres [are] eroding and will require additional attention.

The report chronicled significant flooding episodes, and the attendant damage and siltation of reservoirs, in several western states. One example involved Elephant Butte Reservoir in New Mexico. In just seventeen years it had lost 13 percent of its storage capacity as a result of siltation. The report's authors traced these phenomena to overgrazing, noting the ample scientific evidence that depletion of plant cover is a primary cause of erosion and floods.[14]

In transmitting the report to Congress, Secretary of Agriculture Henry A. Wallace spoke of "the astonishing degree to which the western range resource has been neglected, despite its magnitude and importance." The range was then overstocked by 43 percent. Range stocking capacity had been depleted by an average of 52 percent; the rate of depletion ranged from 30 percent in forest reserves to 67 percent on the public domain. Private lands had been depleted by 51 percent. One author described the range as "[p]ersistent, long-suffering, [and] now badly depleted and eroded"; another contributor termed the loss of topsoil from western ranges a "black picture." Depletion of the range was reported to have caused "excessive run-off and water or wind erosion almost everywhere," with attendant flooding and maintenance problems. Concerns were expressed about insect pests associated with certain "host plants, which have come in as a result of overgrazing." One author observed that it had "taken little more than half a century to reduce the productivity of the range by about half" and estimated that it probably would "take at least as long to bring it back to a grazing capacity equivalent to present stocking."[15]

Documented effects were not limited to depleted livestock forage and erosion. A chapter by Forsling et al. reported that the land's capacity for supporting wildlife and recreation also had been greatly diminished: "So far, in fact, have numbers been reduced," they wrote, "that any recital of what remains is in itself an indication of both tangible and intangible social and economic losses. A few outstanding examples will suffice":

The former millions of buffalo have declined to [a] few thousand . . . ; the thirty or forty million antelope to about 65,000; the few mountain sheep, goats, moose, and grizzly bear are barely holding their own; the scattered remnants of upland game birds and furbearers are still declining; the reduction of waterfowl has become a matter of national concern. Most of the big game animals have been crowded off their original range into much less favorable conditions.

This last sentence surely refers to "crowding" by domestic livestock, since the acreage of vacant public lands in the 1936 West was vastly greater than the area actually occupied by human settlements or crops.[16]

Forsling et al.'s interpretation of extant conditions can readily be criticized, of course, for overlooking other, possibly more influential factors in the declines of some wildlife species. The near-extirpation of bison, for instance, was a result of several phenomena, including market hunting, the government's Indian policy, and railroad expansion. Another chapter of the report attributes wildlife declines in the West to nine "chief factors and causes," including (listed in order) "deterioration of the habitat through range depletion"; lack of incentives to private landowners to protect wildlife; failed attempts to convert to crop production lands, such as "swamps," whose "highest social and economic return [would have been] in wildlife production"; "unrestricted or poorly controlled hunting and fishing"; the selection of wildlife agency personnel for political reasons rather than technical expertise; and inadequate technical knowledge. Both chapters thus recognize that livestock use and competition for habitat had contributed to the declines of large ungulates and other native species on western ranges.[17]

Senate Document 199 observed that the impacts on wildlife of overuse or misuse of the land for stock grazing in turn affect recreational values. In the introductory, overview chapter, Forest Service associate chief Earle Clapp stated: "The serious depletion of most range areas, the reduction in wildlife, the erosion and silting of streams, have all been reflected in impaired recreational values. Where originally the mind was inspired . . . it is now depressed by the sight of a terrain scored and dissected by erosion and only thinly covered by plants."[18]

The report's overall conclusion as to the "fundamental cause" of western range resource degradation is intriguing: it blamed "the typical American philosophy of prodigal destruction rather than conservation of natural resources." Clapp declared: "Other peoples have destroyed their natural resources but none have shown greater efficiency in the process." He asserted that "immediate profit" was the western stockman's "compelling motive" and that "care and restraint seemed far-fetched and visionary." Livestock producers' historical "natural tendency . . . to stock at a rate that leads gradually to some degree of rangeland deterioration" has been noted by modern range scientists, citing the stockgrowers' rationale of "[p]erceived higher monetary returns." Some commentators have simply described stockmen as greedy or selfish; Director Clawson defended them as probably "no better and no worse than" miners, loggers, and homesteaders. In theory, Clapp wrote in *The Western Range*, "the incentive of ownership should have kept large areas in good condition, but actually it has been so ineffective that the original grazing capacity has been reduced by more than half." Only 12 percent of all privately owned range was in good or fairly good condition in the mid 1930s.[19]

Consistent with Congress's directions, the green book was not limited to characterizations of range conditions. Lyle Watts, scientist and director of the Forest Service's Northern Rocky Mountain Forest and Range Experiment Station (appointed chief of the Forest Service in 1943), offered this astute explanation for the "western range problem":

> The lack of [a] constructive national land policy designed to fit the semi-arid and mountain grazing lands of the West has been a major factor in the depletion of our once great range forage resource. The belief in universal private ownership of land, the application to such a region of land laws designed to fit humid conditions, the failure to classify lands according to their highest use, and interpretation and administration of the statutes all played a definite part. The adverse effects of our past land policy on the ownership pattern of range lands and its influence on forage depletion are matters for national concern.

Watts's assessment remains uncomfortably on target today.[20]

The Western Range is both impressive for its time and instructive today in its appreciation of several points, notably: the causes of wildlife declines in the West were principally habitat-related; Americans' appetite for resources was a major factor in both wildlife population declines and the condition of rangelands generally; and watershed, wildlife, and wildlife-related recreation on rangelands were viewed in the 1930s as having significant value. The fact that livestock production was not viewed in 1936 as necessarily the highest and best use of all rangelands, or even a permanent use of the range, is an important underpinning of this book's policy argument for removing livestock from the BLM lands least suited to grazing.[21]

Sadly, Congress's receipt of *The Western Range*, with its wealth of information about the conditions of the range and the value of range resources, failed to precipitate either additional oversight of the managing agencies or further legislation to address "the western range problem." Congressman Taylor's ebullience in 1934 notwithstanding, "overgrazing," however defined, continued. Range conditions failed to improve, where they did not actually worsen.

B. RANGE CONDITIONS AND CAUSES AFTER THE TAYLOR ACT: THE NEXT SIXTY YEARS

Little if any evidence exists to suggest that passage of the Taylor Grazing Act resulted in noticeable improvement in range conditions. According to the Interior Department, "at least 115 million acres of the public rangelands [still] needed remedial attention [in 1947], and . . . 46 million acres were in critical condition because of overgrazing and erosion." The diagnosis was much the same four years later, when BLM director Marion Clawson admitted that "large areas [of the public rangelands] were still deteriorating." Clawson "even hinted that all stock might be removed from some badly abused ranges."[22]

One nonagency observer characterized the overgrazing that continued through the first half of the twentieth century as "massive." As demand for forage and other rangeland resources increased, so did range problems. According to Samuel Trask Dana, the government tried to avoid during World War II the overgrazing that it had encouraged during the first war. But the increased demand for meat, wool, and hides "emphasized the depleted condition of much of the Western range and the need for improved range management if the supply of livestock was going to be increased or even maintained." Muhn and Stuart report that the demand for range resources continued to grow after the war. During Clawson's tenure as BLM director, 1948–53, the enhanced demand for public land commodities, including forage, "had a substantial impact on the public lands."[23]

Range conditions remained poor on both national forest and unreserved public rangelands—the latter despite the creation of a new agency, the BLM, with oversight authority for public rangelands. The BLM devoted considerable attention to range management and soil and moisture conservation during its early years. Its Division of Range Management was subdivided in 1950 into two branches, Grazing Supervision and Surveys and Soil and Moisture Conservation. Noxious weed infestations on depleted western ranges had become widespread problems; a poisonous, introduced weed, halogeton (*Halogeton glomeratus*), was one of the more intractable. Starting from an initial congressional appropriation of approximately $2 million, obtained specifically to halt the spread of halogeton, the BLM launched a massive program for reseeding rangelands. Halogeton eradication efforts failed, but a "range improvement" program with significant political and ecological ramifications was born.[24]

Clawson's general assessment of deteriorating range conditions in the 1950s was confirmed by a "scientific appraisal of the public lands" authorized by Congress in 1962. Resulting reports on range conditions in Oregon, Colorado, and Montana revealed that 1.6 percent of the range was in excellent condition; 15 percent, good; 53.1 percent, fair; 25.8 percent, poor; and 4.5 percent, bad. These figures resemble closely the West-wide range condition statistics reported by the Public Land Law Review Commission's forage resource contractors in 1969 and by the BLM in 1975.[25]

A dire view of the range situation was proffered by the chief forester of the American Forestry Association. Noting that conditions had actually worsened between 1953 and 1963, he predicted that "it would take more than a century to restore the range." Even a livestock industry witness at a congressional hearing in 1963 testified that 80 percent of the range "is shot or said to be shot." Reciting a refrain that would be heard with increasing frequency in grazing policy debates, he contended, however, that "grazing people alone" were not responsible.[26]

An article published in 1963 recommended closing to all grazing "many million acres of arid and semi-arid land" in the West. The proposal, authored by Forsling (a *Western Range* contributor and head of the Grazing Service from 1944 to 1946), targeted the "steeper slopes between mesas and valleys, and between different levels of plains or mesas, the lower slopes of many desert mountains and foothills, badlands, and sandy lands subject to blowing"—lands that he described as "too poor and vulnerable to damage to sustain grazing use." Forsling estimated that about 50 million acres of "frail lands" should be withdrawn from grazing; an additional 20 to 25 million acres in the Rio Grande, Colorado, and Great Basins *should be withdrawn from livestock use strictly for watershed protection.*" Two years later, a "frail-lands study" undertaken by the BLM "identified 6.5 million acres of lands in the critical stages of erosion and over 38 million acres as being highly vulnerable." From 1963 to 1966, under Director Charles Stoddard, the agency entered into 168 agreements with the Soil Conservation Service (SCS) in an attempt to improve range soil and vegetative conditions. By the early 1970s stagnant or deteriorating BLM range conditions "were attracting criticism from environmental groups and national attention from the news media."[27]

The degraded condition of BLM ranges also came to the attention of the courts in the 1970s. Three leading public land law scholars have identified the 1974 court decision in *Natural Resources Defense Council v. Morton (NRDC v. Morton)* as "probably the true beginning point of a new, more rigorous body of federal range law." The court held for the first time that the National Environmental Policy Act (NEPA) requires the BLM to assess the site-specific impacts of its grazing program before making grazing permit decisions. The court recited evidence of overgrazing and its impacts on BLM lands, including data from a study conducted by the agency itself. According to the court, the BLM report "state[d] flatly that wildlife habitat [was] being destroyed" and streams were being damaged due to "'[u]ncontrolled, unregulated or unplanned livestock use [occurring] in approximately 85 percent of [Nevada].'" The court cited similar evidence in other BLM reports and in a 1970 Council on Environmental Quality (CEQ) report on the widespread degradation of public rangelands.[28]

While its ultimately unsuccessful appeal in *NRDC v. Morton* was pending, the BLM made public new 1975 statistics concerning the condition of its ranges. These condition ratings were based on actual forage production compared to the potential for that site. In a report to Congress the agency disclosed that 17 percent of public rangelands were in good or excellent condition; 50 percent, fair; 28 percent, poor; and 5 percent, bad. These figures are nearly identical to those produced by the congressionally mandated study in 1962. The agency predicted that conditions would continue to deteriorate. A GAO report released about the same time suggested that the actual area of deteriorated rangeland was even larger than that reported by the BLM.[29]

The Rio Puerco Basin in northern New Mexico provides a stark illustration of these rather anonymous statistics. BLM studies of this deteriorating watershed showed that, despite past reductions in livestock use, permitted numbers in 1975 still exceeded the area's forage capacity. Soil erosion was "moderate" to "severe" over 55 percent of the area grazed (an estimate that was likely understated). U.S. Geological Survey and Soil Conservation Service surveys of the area showed that annual water erosion of soils ranged from 2 to 8.7 tons per acre; wind erosion was also significant. Perennial grasses had been greatly reduced; valuable cool season perennials, once common, were absent. This phenomenon—reduction in, or loss of, perennial grasses—has been a principal effect of overgrazing in the Intermountain sagebrush region and many other areas of the West.[30]

Congress seemed to be getting the message. In the Federal Land Policy and Management Act (FLPMA) of 1976 it proclaimed that "a substantial amount of the Federal range is deteriorating in quality." The act endorsed the agency view that "installation of additional range improvements could arrest much of the continuing deterioration and could lead to substantial betterment of forage conditions with resulting benefits to wildlife, watershed protection, and livestock production." Specific range improvement needs were identified; they ranged from seeding and reseeding ranges, to controlling weeds, to enhancing fish and wildlife habitat.[31]

Two years later, in the Public Rangelands Improvement Act (PRIA), Congress registered continuing dissatisfaction with degraded range conditions, again relying heavily on range improvements to accomplish the new legislation's objectives. Not surprisingly, the statute does not expressly identify the causes of degraded range conditions. PRIA had broad support—from groups as diverse as the Sierra Club and the American Cattlemen's Association—which clearly would have been eroded by finger pointing. Nevertheless, the statute implicitly recognizes overgrazing as an important, if not the major, factor insofar as it acknowledges that grazing might have to be "discontinued (either temporarily or permanently) on certain lands" in order to achieve rangeland productivity objectives.[32]

One impetus for PRIA was a report to Congress by the comptroller general of the United States about the condition of western ranges. In his transmittal letter the comptroller had stated bluntly: "These lands have been deteriorating for years and, for the most part, are not improving." While the report did not cite FLPMA's policies (enacted the previous year) for managing the public lands, it did remind Congress that "[a]llowing the public rangelands to deteriorate conflicts with the Taylor Grazing Act's objectives," that is, "stopping damage to the public rangelands and providing for their orderly use, improvement, and development." To "comply with the intent of the Taylor Grazing

Act," the comptroller warned, the "Bureau needs to manage its lands more aggressively and effectively."[33]

In the mid-1970s, BLM officials had assured the Senate Appropriations Committee that allotment management plans providing for rest-rotation grazing would prevent range deterioration. According to the comptroller, however, such plans had been completed for only about 16 percent of BLM rangelands by 1976, and some of those plans "were obsolete because they did not protect wildlife habitat and watershed." Moreover, of the 107 million acres of range *not* covered by a plan, 49 million "were being subjected to continuous grazing throughout the forage-growing season . . . , [a practice] which the Bureau considers to be unacceptable because it destroys range vegetation." BLM estimated that continuous grazing on these lands would further deplete forage productivity by 25 percent over the next twenty-five years. The comptroller noted that even on the 58 million acres not grazed year-long BLM "had no assurance that [its] requirements were being followed and the deterioration of the land was being abated."[34]

At first blush, the agency practice of allowing year-long grazing despite a clear policy against it seems inexplicable. It was not just a matter of the bureau making an occasional exception. According to the comptroller, the BLM had "revised its grazing policies" in 1968 to reflect its position that continuous grazing was unacceptable, but five years later 1,486 of 1,760 grazing allotments in fourteen districts and six western states remained subject to continuous use. The majority of Nevada's 47 million acres of BLM rangelands were grazed year-long in 1974. BLM field managers were ignoring the policy, the comptroller explained, because they believed that enforcement "would adversely affect the financial condition of the livestock operators." Yet in failing to take steps to halt continuous grazing, the BLM was perpetuating the declining condition of the western range, contrary to two of the three stated purposes of the Taylor Grazing Act. Ironically, this resulted in undermining the act's third objective—"to stabilize the livestock industry, dependent on the public range"—as well.[35]

Overgrazing and the degradation of western rangelands also attracted the attention of academics and range professionals during this period. Frederic H. Wagner, range-wildlife specialist and professor of wildlife science at Utah State University, wrote in 1978:

> [T]he western ranges are finite and have for three-quarters of a century been stocked near or in excess of their allowable limit. Since present stocking rates are of this magnitude, it seems almost a certainty that there is no long-term potential for large increases in livestock numbers. . . . [S]ince most ranges are now overgrazed, increased grazing pressures without greatly intensified management would lead to a long-term decline in carrying capacity and productivity of western ecosystems.

A few years later Denzel and Nancy Ferguson, outspoken critics of federal range policy, asserted that "cattle alone exert more grazing pressure on western rangelands than did all the pristine populations of native ungulates." They estimated that combined grazing pressure from livestock and wild ungulates in 1984 was probably 50 percent greater than the presettlement grazing pressure on those lands.[36]

One of the most forthright indictments of grazing on arid western rangelands is the 1981 Council on Environmental Quality publication *Desertification*, written by David Sheridan. As a starting point for his discussion, Sheridan offered several scientists' definitions of "desertification," including those of Australian geographer J. A. Mabbutt and Harold Dregne, head of the International Center for Arid and Semi-Arid Land Studies at Texas Tech University. Mabbutt defined desertification as a "'change in the character of the land to a more desertic condition' involving 'the impoverishment of ecosystems as evidenced in reduced biological productivity and accelerated deterioration of soils and in an associated impoverishment of dependent human livelihood systems.'" Stated more simply, desertification is "the diminution or destruction of the biological potential of land." The process occurs "usually at times of drought stress, in areas of naturally vulnerable land subject to pressures of land use." It is a "subtle and insidious" process of "patchy destruction"; it does not progress as an advancing front.[37]

According to Dregne, desertification is "the impoverishment of arid, semi-arid, and some subhumid ecosystems by the combined impact of man's activities and drought." The term thus encompasses the impoverishment of ecosystems even within natural deserts—for example, the loss of native plants and animals and floodplain vegetation during the past 100 years in the Sonoran and Chihuahuan Deserts. Desertification "can be measured by reduced productivity of desirable plants, alterations in the biomass and diversity of the micro and macro fauna and flora, accelerated soil deterioration, and increased hazards for human occupancy. Loss of biodiversity is an inevitable accompaniment of desertification."[38]

Any form of land abuse, if it involves excessive rates of erosion, can initiate a "spiraling pattern of deterioration [that] eventually results in desertification." Beyond a certain point, the damage due to erosion is irreversible. The reason is simple: "Soil loss cannot be effectively restored through management since topsoil formation occurs at the rate of 1 in. formed every 300–1000 years."[39]

Sheridan identified overgrazing as "the most potent desertification force, in terms of total acreage affected, within the United States." Other causes are overdraft of groundwater, unsustainable cultivation, salinization of irrigated soils, and severe erosion. The predominant role of grazing comports with experiences elsewhere: excessive or abusive livestock grazing has contributed to desertification around the globe, and its effects have long been recognized.[40]

"Desertification in the arid United States is flagrant," Sheridan announced. An estimated "1.1 million square miles, or 36.8 percent of [North America's] arid lands, have undergone 'severe' desertification." Desertification of approximately 10,500 square miles has been "very severe." Within the United States alone about 225 million acres, or 350,000 square miles (an area about the size of the original thirteen states), have experienced severe or very severe desertification; the area threatened with desertification is almost twice as large. Desertified areas extend from southern Canada well into Mexico; the degree of desertification is moderate over the northern half of this region, severe or very severe in portions of southern California, southern Nevada, Arizona, New Mexico, and western Texas. More recently, conservation biologists Reed F. Noss and Allen Y. Cooperrider interpret these and similar figures as suggesting that "few arid or semiarid lands in the United States have not been degraded or desertified"; indeed, they cite "reports of at least moderate desertification on 98 percent of the arid lands of the United States."[41]

Sheridan postulated that federal subsidies, whose "net effect" is to "encourage production, not conservation," are a "major force behind desertification of the United States." He reasoned that these subsidies, combined with powerful market incentives "to exploit arid land resources beyond their carrying capacity," produce development incentives that have become increasingly attractive over the years. The "short-run economics of conserving arid land resources," on the other hand, "appear to be almost always unfavorable." Sheridan cautioned that any increase in the "agricultural output from the arid West" could come only "at the expense of the region's soil, water, and vegetational resources."[42]

The report described in detail several areas in the West where livestock grazing has been a major factor in the process of desertification. These include the Rio Puerco Basin in New Mexico; the Santa Cruz and San Pedro River Basins in southern Arizona; the Challis, Idaho, area; and the San Joaquin Valley in central California. The Rio Puerco Basin's history is illustrative. Grazing and farming began there in the late 1700s. By the 1870s 240,000 sheep and 9,000 cattle grazed in the 3.9-million-acre basin. The water table began dropping in the late 1880s, and arroyo cutting and other evidence of severe erosion appeared. "Between 1885 and 1962 an estimated 1.1–1.5 billion tons of soil washed from the Rio Puerco Basin into the Rio Grande." The number of livestock that the range could support declined steadily after 1910, with one brief increase in the 1930s. By the 1950s agricultural settlements in the basin had become "ghost towns."[43]

Paleobotanists who had studied the Rio Puerco Basin attributed the soil erosion and excessive runoff to the drying effects of overgrazing on soils and vegetation. This can result from trampling-induced soil compaction, removal of litter and topsoil, and other processes. A geologist who studied the area called the soil erosion and arroyo cutting "ongoing and incredible." Arroyos that had been 121 feet wide in the 1930s were 300 feet wide forty years later; one arroyo widened by 50 feet in one year! In his 1963 article advocating removal of livestock from certain western ranges, Forsling had cited the Rio Puerco as a "classical example of a trenched desert valley." He acknowledged that gully, sheet, and wind erosion all had occurred "under aboriginal conditions," but expressed "no doubt that erosion has been greatly accelerated and extended within the last century under the ever-increasing pressure of man's range livestock, vehicles, and implements."[44]

Sheridan warned that conditions in the Rio Puerco watershed might never stabilize. "[T]hree factors militate[d] *against* the swift return of . . . pregrazing richness," he said: the low precipitation in the basin (9 to 14 inches—typical of much of the West), the extensive loss of topsoil and the low organic content of the remaining soil, and the existence of firmly established invader species.[45]

Another instance of desertification in which grazing was implicated was the Challis area of central Idaho. Heavy grazing began there in the 1880s; in the mid-1970s soil erosion ranged from moderate to severe on 52 percent of BLM lands, shrubs had invaded the mixed sage-grasslands, and perennial grasses were sparse and of "very poor vigor." The Challis area was a focus of litigation against the BLM in the 1970s over the agency's management of its grazing program.[46]

The overall conclusion of Sheridan's report for the CEQ was pessimistic: desertification in the American West "will continue. Indeed, it will spread."[47]

Beginning a few years after publication of *Desertification*, and continuing through the mid-1990s, the General Accounting Office prepared a number of reports—some of them scathing indictments—on the grazing programs of both the BLM and Forest Service. These studies documented a variety of resource and administrative problems, including poor range conditions, especially in riparian areas and the "hot deserts"; inadequate enforcement of grazing regulations; and deficient recordkeeping, range condition monitoring, and reporting. The very titles of the reports illustrate the myriad problems identified by the government auditors: *More Emphasis Needed on Declining and Overstocked Allotments, Some Riparian Areas Restored But Widespread Improvement Will Be Slow, BLM Efforts to Prevent Unauthorized Livestock Grazing Need Strengthening, Interior's Monitoring Has Fallen Short of Agency Requirements, BLM's Range Improvement Project Data Base Is Incomplete and Inaccurate.*[48]

The GAO consistently identified overgrazing as the principal cause of deteriorating western range conditions. In one document it declared that "overgrazing, together with periodic droughts, has permanently changed the face of this rangeland"—a conclusion that the agency subsequently defended as "not a contention, but a well-established fact." In its *Hot Deserts* report, covering the Chihuahuan, Sonoran, and Mojave Deserts, the agency concluded that "[c]urrent livestock grazing activity on BLM allotments in hot desert areas [of the Southwest] risks long-term environmental damage while not generating grazing fee revenues sufficient to provide for adequate management. . . . Some damaged lands may take decades to recover if they recover at all."[49]

A contemporaneous land management plan prepared by the BLM lends credibility to certain GAO findings and reveals that the agency was continuing to flaunt its policy against year-long grazing. The BLM was proposing to expand the Afton Canyon Natural Area in the Sonoran Desert of southern California and to designate it an area of critical environmental concern (ACEC), pursuant to authority in FLPMA. A 1989 plan for management of the natural area described Afton Canyon as containing "one of the few true riparian areas in the Southern California desert. The existing ponds, marshes, and streams, with a diversity in riparian plants, provide habitat for a wide variety of wildlife." The chief provisions of the plan involved "rehabilitation of riparian and scenic values through the restriction of vehicle use in the expanded ACEC," eradication of nonnative tamarisk (*Tamarix* spp.) and revegetation with native species, and control of human and livestock disturbances. The report disclosed that year-long grazing was allowed in the adjoining grazing allotment and noted that the "majority of the allotment boundary is not fenced and unauthorized cattle grazing has been documented in Afton Canyon." The Afton Canyon plan was released a year after the GAO report documenting riparian conditions on BLM lands and twenty years after the ostensible adoption of BLM's no-year-long-grazing policy.[50]

A thorough review of the literature on the condition of western rangelands and on range ecology was neither possible nor warranted for the purposes of this book. Instead, I have drawn heavily from symposia and other compilations and from government reports, particularly the Department of Interior's 1994 draft environmental impact statement (DEIS), *Rangeland Reform '94*. Discussion of range ecology—the ecological processes and impacts of livestock grazing on arid rangelands—is reserved for chapter 5.[51]

In 1992 an important symposium was sponsored by the American Institute of Biological Sciences; the proceedings were compiled in the book *Ecological Implications of Livestock Herbivory in the West* (1994). This symposium has been described as "perhaps the first attempt to examine comprehensively the implications of livestock grazing on the western range since Senate Document No. 199 [*The Western Range*] was compiled in 1936." Another similarity between the two reports is their political overtone. The introduction notes somewhat cryptically that the symposium was "called to evaluate the credence of livestock grazing on western range lands." A paper by Wagner elaborates:

> This symposium was organized in part because of the range profession's concerns about the future of livestock grazing, particularly uncertain on public lands in the western U.S. Range professionals are somewhat caught in the middle between the stockmen's reluctance to change and demands for policy change by other interest groups, including demands for complete elimination of livestock use on public lands.[52]

The proceedings of the symposium reveal significant points of convergence in the participants' thinking. All agree that at least localized overgrazing of western ranges has occurred. Most if not all concur that grazing's impacts in some areas have been severe. The introduction summarizes the historical phenomenon this way: "The rapid expansion of the livestock industry coupled with the improper cultivation of vast acreages of nonarable land . . . resulted in drastic changes in syn- and aut-ecological relationships of plants and plant communities. The concomitant unwitting introduction of exotic plants added to the ecological disarray. . . ." One writer, addressing the sagebrush region specifically, states that changes in plant composition had occurred at "unprecedented rates" over the past 120 years and attributes those changes to various factors, notably grazing, climate changes, water diversions, and introduction of exotics. (Note that three, if not all, of these factors implicate livestock.) Another participant concludes: "Although herbivory, lack of fire, atmospheric CO_2 enrichment and climate have interacted to produce vegetation change [in the Southwest], selective grazing by large numbers and high concentrations of livestock has been the primary force in altering plant life-form interactions to favor unpalatable woody species over graminoids [grasses and grasslike plants]."[53]

More recently, a National Academy of Sciences Committee on Rangeland Classification published a report on range inventory and monitoring methods. The committee stated: "Although most observers agree that rangeland degradation was widespread on overgrazed and drought-plagued rangelands at the turn of the century, the present state of health of U.S. rangelands is a matter of sharp debate." The committee explained that the debate stems in large part from the variety of methods that have been employed. It summarized various surveys and assessments of western range conditions by land management agencies, the Soil Conservation Service, Society for Range Management (SRM), General Accounting Office, Thadis Box, and others, noting that all have been criticized and "none are based on comprehensive inventories of rangelands." Accordingly, "some ecologists now challenge the validity" of the methods used by the BLM, SCS, and Forest Service to assess condition and trend. As the committee pointed out, the fact "that it is impossible, with current methods and with current data, to determine whether federal and nonfederal rangelands are improving or degrading is itself a cause for concern."[54]

Still more recently, the BLM, in cooperation with the U.S. Forest Service, released an appraisal of public rangeland conditions, in preparation for revising its range regulations to incorporate rangeland health standards. The appraisal, published as *Rangeland Reform '94: Draft Environmental Impact Statement*, is the most comprehensive assessment available of current BLM range conditions. While claiming "improvements" in range conditions since the 1930s, the agencies warn that "there is still much progress to be made. Rangeland ecosystems are not functioning properly in many areas of the West. Riparian areas are widely depleted and some upland areas produce far below their potential. Soils are becoming less fertile." Later in the DEIS, the authors clarify that the asserted improvements have occurred only in upland areas. Public land riparian areas, they concede, "have continued to decline and are considered to be *in their worst condition in history*." Livestock grazing is identified as the chief cause of this deteriorated condition. Careful reading of the DEIS reveals that the current riparian situation is even worse than these condition figures indicate. The information reported fails to account for "extensive areas that have been degraded to the point that they are *no longer recognized as having riparian or wetland values or potential*." The authors' ultimate prognosis is hardly optimistic: "Riparian areas will not recover on a large scale without changes in policy, regulations, and management." Even if livestock were removed entirely from riparian areas, over "the long term, [only] about 65 percent of BLM riparian areas would be properly functioning (an increase of 91 percent from 1993)."[55]

Rangeland Reform '94's initial pronouncement about improvements in upland areas is also misleading. The authors subsequently explain:

> Once altered, upland vegetation communities change or improve only gradually. Native grasses revegetate slowly, annual grasses cannot be removed once established, and disturbed or eroded soils require a long time to rebuild. When management improves, upland communities that receive more than 12 inches of annual precipitation have shown improvement within 20 years. Drier areas generally have not improved.

The last sentence is especially ominous, considering that the vast majority of BLM rangelands receive less than 12 inches of precipitation annually, a fact not found in the DEIS. The more arid the rangeland, the more susceptible it is to damage by disturbances, including grazing, and the more likely that the injury may be irreversible (see chapter 5). Undermining still further its report of "improvements," the DEIS states that "monitoring studies indicate continuing resource damage and a *declining* economic feasibility of livestock grazing."[56]

Rangeland Reform '94 describes current trends in vegetative condition on BLM lands as follows: 28.4 million acres upward: "moving toward management objectives"; 91.8 million acres static: "not moving anywhere or have reached objectives"; 16.6 million acres downward: "moving away from objectives"; and 22.1 million acres undetermined. The agencies report that 90.5 million acres of uplands are properly functioning, 48 million acres are functioning but susceptible to degradation, and 20.5 million acres are nonfunctioning. Curiously, they define "proper functioning" as "the lowest condition needed to ensure ecological health and condition *while allowing livestock grazing*." This definition simply assumes that livestock grazing can be compatible with "ecological health." But as we will see, the definition is ill-suited, if not wholly inappropriate, to the more arid rangelands where grazing necessarily disrupts natural ecological processes and alters native biodiversity patterns. The definition is also at odds with the Committee on Rangeland Classification's conclusions in *Rangeland Health*: "The minimum standard for rangeland management should be to prevent human-induced loss of rangeland health" (defined as "the degree to which the integrity of the soil and the ecological processes of rangeland ecosystems are sustained"), and "[r]angeland health should be a minimum standard *independent of* the rangeland's use and how it is managed."[57]

The trend category "static" comprises the largest fraction of BLM lands, nearly 100 million acres. The term "static"—"not moving anywhere *or* hav[ing] reached objectives"—is ambiguous about the actual condition of those lands: they could all be in fair or poor condition, but not getting worse or better, or they could in theory be in very good, though unchanging, condition. The agencies provide figures in millions of acres on the "ecological status" of its lands, but these figures cannot be directly compared to the trend statistics.[58]

Rangeland Reform '94 further reports that watershed functions and water quality on federal rangelands are declining, addresses the causes and control of nonpoint source pollution due to livestock grazing practices, and predicts that water quality will worsen under current management. These conclusions comport with the results of a survey of fifteen western states a few years earlier, which identified grazing, among all nonpoint sources of pollution, as having the greatest impact on the surface water quality. The DEIS contains the remarkable admission that "[w]atershed and water quality conditions would improve to their maximum potential" if livestock were removed from western rangelands. The improvement would result from increases in vegetation and litter, which would improve soil conditions, facilitate infiltration of moisture, and reduce erosion. The glaring message is that livestock grazing is by far the chief factor affecting surface water quality on public rangelands.[59]

The DEIS predicts substantial improvements in wildlife habitat quality if livestock grazing were discontinued. "About 75 percent of degraded anadromous fish habitat would be restored. Waterfowl populations would increase. . . . Upland game and nongame species would benefit from improved riparian habitat and from increased vegetation for winter food and cover." The report also forecasts that "scenic quality, wildlife viewing, hunting, and fishing" would prosper, and "[i]mproved ecological conditions would benefit all wilderness values." Livestock affect recreational uses in several ways: by "fecal matter, foul odors, and increased insects" and by causing soil erosion and degrading water quality, thus "assaulting some users' sense of aesthetics and creating health risks." Indeed, the predicted consequences of the "No Grazing Alternative" are almost universally positive. In contrast, only much smaller improvements are predicted to occur under the agencies "Proposed Action." In particular, BLM lands receiving less than 12 inches of annual moisture would benefit little.[60]

Rangeland Reform '94's account of range conditions is especially noteworthy in view of the BLM's assertion in 1990 that its ranges were "'in better shape today than ever before in this century'"—a claim for which the agency was widely criticized. The GAO concluded that the claim "lacked supporting documentation" and was "of questionable validity." Similarly, Noss and Cooperrider found "virtually no data to back up this assertion." In fact, they wrote, BLM's own estimates indicated that at least 36 percent of BLM ranges were in fair condition and 16 percent were rated poor; "only 3 percent of its rangelands [were] in Potential Natural (Excellent) condition."[61]

Despite the lack of evidence to support it, the "better than ever before in this century" claim has enjoyed widespread popularity. It is alternatively credited to Thadis Box, who apparently first made it in 1975. The GAO describes Box, former dean of Utah State University's College of Natural Resources and SRM president, as a "recognized and frequently cited range expert." Box later conceded that this "conclusion was his professional opinion and could not be well documented" and admitted that he "was not optimistic about future rangeland trends." He also qualified the claim, noting that BLM range condition had improved substantially from 1936 to 1961, but little between 1961 and 1981. Yet twice in a paper scarcely three pages long, which he presented to lead off a 1987 conference, Box repeated the "best in this century" claim. A mere year later he called "alarming" the "revelation that the condition of more than a fourth of our rangeland is simply unknown, that another 40 percent of the data reported is [*sic*] more than 10 years old, and that more than half of grazing allotments do not have management plans."[62]

Discredited or not, the claim persists. New Mexico State University professor of range science Rex D. Pieper recited it, without explanation, in a paper published in *Ecological Implications of Livestock Herbivory*. Brunson and Steel alluded to it in reporting the results of their survey of public attitudes toward public rangeland management. They played down respondents' concerns about continued overgrazing, asserting, as if it were gospel, that these "attitudes appear to be based on misconceptions about the overall state of range resources on federal lands. Professional range conservationists *know* that environmental conditions have *steadily improved since the turn of the century*, with the probable exception of riparian areas which until recently were treated as 'sacrifice zones.'"[63]

The message is: Readers beware. Attempting to use the literature to generalize about current range conditions, or about the individual contribution of livestock, is problematic not only because vegetation, soils, and climate vary widely and because historical and current land uses and thus disturbance factors differ. Investigators' methods, objectives, and predispositions can also dramatically influence results. Results may be portrayed carelessly or even misrepresented, intentionally or otherwise, by the investigators or others.

Both academics and the land management agencies may be culpable. Several papers in the 1992 grazing ecology symposium bear this out, as does Wagner's comment that the symposium, "organized and largely contributed to by university range-management professors, ha[d] a defensive tone over the public challenges to continued livestock grazing." Noss and Cooperrider recently warned that the BLM could use its new range assessment methods to "manipulate data and misrepresent what is happening," and they justified their suspicion as based on "a cynical but largely well-deserved mistrust of the agencies by many people."[64]

The public lands grazing debate is fueled by misrepresentations or biased characterizations of range condition and other grazing-related issues. Discerning inaccuracies, misrepresentations, or bias in technical articles can be difficult for lay readers; some shortcomings, however, are readily apparent. Much of the range science and range management literature exhibits "a defensive tone" or an obvious pro–livestock production bent. A survey article cited herein only rarely specifies whether the studies being reported had involved cattle or sheep, even though the differences in diets and foraging habits—and thus the effects on the land—of the two animals are well known. Harold F. Heady's classic text, *Rangeland Management*, contains numerous photographs that depict animal effects, including overgrazing, but only one that identifies cattle as the cause of the depicted overgrazing (and none in the chapter entitled "Physical Effects of Grazing Animals").[65]

Many reporting flaws and misrepresentations are less obvious. Consider a paper prepared for the 1992 symposium *Ecological Implications of Livestock Herbivory in the West* by Pieper, who cautioned that variations among range-lands, "as well as the variety of methods used to assess rangelands," make it difficult to evaluate range conditions and their causes. The professional Society for Range Management had "attempted to summarize the existing data," Pieper said, "but the data are difficult to interpret." Apparently ignoring his own cautionary note, he proceeded to interpret the data. Using the SRM summary, he produced a table showing the "percent of rangeland in stable trend" on BLM and nonfederal rangelands by state. He then summarized the information as follows:

> [M]ore than 60% of western rangeland is *in stable trend* (i.e. there is no mea-
> surable change in range condition). Non-federal rangeland *in stable condition*
> appears to be about 10% greater than that on BLM rangeland. Data were not
> readily available for National Forest rangeland. However, only about 15% of
> western rangeland is classified as having a *declining trend*. The [BLM] in
> Oregon estimated more than 60% of the rangeland was in *satisfactory condition*
> for the intended use. These data need to be viewed with caution, but they do
> give us some idea of how ranges are *changing*.[66]

Pieper seems to use the terms "condition" and "trend" interchangeably, when in fact they describe different concepts. For example, a range site with a stable trend could be in good, fair, or poor condition. He went on to report the percentage of range in "stable condition" as varying from 56 percent of federal land in Utah to 84 percent of private land in California. He did not say whether the "condition" or trend of the remaining 25 percent of the range where the trend was not stable or declining was improving or whether data were simply unavailable. Furthermore, he did not define "range condition" for purposes of his assessment, nor explain how it is possible to discern "how ranges are changing" from these one-point-in-time statistics. Finally, his reference to the "satisfactory condition *for the intended use*" of Oregon rangelands suggests strongly that ecological health was not his concern.[67]

The "difficulty" in interpreting range condition data of which Pieper warned can be attributed in part to casual interpretations by range professionals, including Pieper himself. Some of these "assessments" or summaries add little to an informed discussion of the impacts of livestock grazing on arid lands, although they can shed light on the origins of, and tactics employed in, the public land grazing debate. The excerpt from Pieper's paper illustrates the need to examine the literature critically, especially for inconsistencies or logical flaws within individual works.

Wagner's criticism of the "defensive tone" of some of the papers in the 1992 symposium rings especially true for William A. Laycock, another presenter and an editor of the proceedings. Consider, for example, the following excerpt from Laycock's paper:

> Ehrlich (1990), Wuerthner (1990), and the *popular environmental press claim* that continued overgrazing on the public lands has resulted in serious reduction of species diversity. The pertinent questions are: 1) has overgrazing that occurred 80–100 years ago been curtailed? and 2) has [sic] past *heavy* grazing and the current level of *more moderate* grazing affected species diversity? The answer to the first question . . . is an obvious "yes." The type of abusive grazing which occurred 100 years ago on some of the land has not existed on the *majority* of public lands for at least 50 years. With regard to the second question, the *range management literature* is filled with *evidence* that prolonged *heavy* grazing can change the productivity and/or composition of most rangeland ecosystems. However, *moderate* grazing the last half century probably has not decreased species diversity of either plants or animals and may have increased diversity.[68]

Laycock's statement is objectionable both for what he says (and how he says it) and for what he does not say. Note that his second question presupposes the answer to the first by describing "current" grazing as "more moderate," a term he does not define, but merely implies is something less "abusive" than "past heavy grazing," which he also does not define. Second, he implicitly discredits the antigrazing "claim" by relegating it to the "popular press," while alluding to "evidence" from the "range management literature" to support his own assertion concerning the effects of "heavy grazing." Laycock repeatedly disparages public land grazing's critics, whom he never refers to as ecologists or conservation biologists, but only implicitly as environmentalists and explicitly as uninformed. He fails altogether to address the question whether the historical "heavy grazing" affected species diversity. Nor does he address whether "abusive grazing" continues on a "minority" of public lands or what percentage of the land area that might encompass. Finally, he cites no "evidence" for his assertion about the effects of "moderate grazing" on species diversity, nor does he explain how moderate grazing's effects can be distinguished from the effects of prior heavy grazing on the same site. He simply says moderate grazing "probably" has not decreased diversity and "may" have increased it.

Laycock continues, faulting "[d]iscussions on the effects of grazing on biodiversity" for "ignor[ing] long-accepted principles in ecology and wildlife habitat biology." The principles to which he refers, for which he cites sources dated 1947 and 1933, relate to "edge effect" and habitat "patchiness." But Laycock simply ignores the *adverse* effects on biodiversity of habitat patchiness, which conservation biologists have more recently come to understand. Specifically, he disregards evidence showing that grazing and other habitat manipulations tend to increase community-level diversity by increasing nonnative and weedy species and species typical of domesticated environments. In other words, grazing favors species that are most widespread and "rarely in danger of extinction in a human-dominated landscape." (These principles are examined in greater detail in chapter 6.)[69]

Livestock industry apologists thus dismiss or cast doubt upon evidence that does not support their position by ignoring the scientific credentials of their critics and disparaging their information and conclusions, yet offering little of substance to refute the unwelcome opinions. Behind the protestations of public land grazing's defenders can often be found facts that tell a different story. The comprehensive evaluation of range conditions contained in *Rangeland Reform '94* should have set the record straight. But debate over numbers and data interpretation persists, fueled by misconceptions and misrepresentations.[70]

The ongoing, grazing-induced deterioration of the range can be attributed to a variety of factors. First, the chronic underfunding of the Grazing Service, and then the BLM, thwarted efforts to improve the condition of the range or to enforce regulations, especially in the agencies' early years. The livestock industry itself "favored financial starvation of the Grazing Service" as a means of bringing the agency to its knees on grazing fees and other issues. When Director Forsling tried to employ range specialists and raise the grazing fee, Nevada's Senator McCarran and other congressional advocates for western livestock interests secured Forsling's dismissal and the dismantlement of the service; agency personnel were reduced by 79 percent. The BLM resulted from the merger of two weakling agencies, the General Land Office and the Grazing Service—a "shotgun wedding carried out at the insistence of triumphant cattle and sheep lobbies."[71]

The young BLM had a staff of 86 to oversee grazing on 150 million acres. From the beginning, stockmen "willfully grazed excess numbers of cattle or sheep, knowing that they were safe in so doing." The appropriations situation became so dire that the grazing district advisory boards stepped in and began paying BLM employee salaries out of TGA range improvement monies. In effect, "the regulators were being supervised by those who were to be regulated"—which undoubtedly exacerbated trespass and enforcement problems. Thirty years later the comptroller identified the BLM's lax enforcement record as a causal factor in continuing poor range condition. The BLM's own records disclosed frequent permittee infractions of grazing requirements. Yet the BLM had "rarely penalized operators who violate grazing regulations by suspending, reducing, or revoking their grazing privileges." From 1971 to 1975, for example, the BLM made "only 37 suspensions, reductions, or revocations of livestock grazing privileges," even though it processed 655 grazing violation cases in 1973 alone. An audit by the Interior Department's Office of Survey and Review determined that most grazing violations were "willful and repeated," but "most violators of livestock grazing limitations were fined merely an amount equal to the estimated amount of vegetation consumed by the unauthorized number of livestock." No penalty was levied to redress any damage done to range resources; the errant "livestock operators had to pay no more than they would have had to pay for grazing elsewhere." Even today, BLM appropriations fall far short of Forest Service funding on a per-acre basis.[72]

A second factor was the protracted process of allocating range use. The first "permanent" grazing permit under the Taylor Act was not issued until 1941; the range was not fully "adjudicated" until 1967. During this time, unpermitted use and overstocking continued in many areas. The dilatoriness reflected not only funding and staffing problems, but political manipulation at the local level. Even when finally established, permitted livestock numbers were not based on science or inventory data and thus tended to remain at unsustainably high levels.[73]

A third reason for the ongoing, grazing-induced deterioration of the range is traceable to the land users themselves. According to public land law scholars Coggins and Lindeberg-Johnson, "Excessive optimism promoted by hopes of quick profits has always characterized public land use; in many areas it still does." Coggins argues that this tendency, combined with an ability "to control local resource allocation and use," has usually led western economic interests to "'cut and run,' rather than to use self restraint in the interests of conservation and sustainability."[74]

Americans have also been unduly optimistic about the land's ability to recover from overuse. Speaking specifically of cultivated agriculture, a National Academy of Sciences committee wrote in 1970: "Our commonest miscalculation has always been to overuse the land, especially during periods of exceptionally favorable weather. Even the disastrous drought years of the thirties did not result in complete adjustment of cropping demands to soil-climate limitations." Attitudes toward grazing were no less sanguine. Many believed, erroneously, that simply removing livestock temporarily would allow deteriorated ranges to recover. Warnings over the years issued from a variety of sources—John Wesley Powell, the authors of *The Western Range*, even the Wyoming Stockgrowers—but they went unheeded.[75]

As the foregoing suggests, land abuse stemmed not just from overoptimism but from ignorance about the laws of nature—the harsh nature of the western environment. Indeed, an inadequate understanding of range ecology has been a crucial factor in the ongoing deterioration of the range. Another is the social and political influence of public land ranchers. These topics and their significance for rangeland management are explored in detail in the following two chapters.

The legacy of a century of optimism, shortsightedness, and greed in use of western ranges is—to borrow Coggins's expressions—"torn up deserts," "severely diminished grazing capacity," and "invasions of pest species." Never one to mince words, Coggins charges: "The local people did it, and the managing agencies did not do their jobs." Worster argues that ranching's "degrading effect on the environment of the American West" has come mostly "from turning pastoralism into a capitalistic enterprise, but ranching under supervision by the federal government has often not mitigated that impact and, in some ways, has made it worse." He laments: "[M]uch of the range is still, in Edward Abbey's phrase, 'a cow-burnt wasteland.'"[76]

CHAPTER 4

The Political and Cultural Landscape

A fundamental reason for the "western range problem" has to do with a characteristic of stockmen that we have not yet considered—their influence in politics and western society.

A. THE CATTLEMEN'S CLOUT

As BLM director Clawson recognized more than forty years ago, the "most important aspect of the range livestock industry is not economic but political. Range livestock producers possess political power in the nation and in their respective states far greater than their numbers alone would suggest." In fact, Clawson said, stockmen "are a minority in every western state, and only a very small minority in the nation." The range region (roughly the western half of the United States, west of the 98th parallel) supported fewer than 70,000 ranches in 1930. No more than 800,000 people were employed in the range livestock industry—about 5 percent of the total regional population and only a fraction of a percent of all Americans.[1]

Not only have stockmen always been a small fraction of the overall population, but they are "outnumbered by other interests concerned with public lands." Culhane wrote that "ranches are one of the smallest categories of firms dealing with the public lands agencies." Most stockmen's groups involved "in local public lands politics are very small organizations," with "very low annual budgets, usually less than $1,000, and memberships of thirty to sixty ranchers." A few state stockmen's associations have "several thousand members and large budgets," Culhane noted, but the total number of ranchers that hold permits to graze public lands is no more than 23,000 today.[2]

"Yet in spite of their small numbers," Clawson wrote, "range livestock producers exert a powerful influence, decisive at times, over government within their states and over their Congressional delegations." Many commentators have remarked on this phenomenon. Christopher M. Klyza described "the disproportionate political power of the less than thirty thousand ranchers holding grazing permits for BLM lands," calling them "key political actors in many sparsely populated western states." Significantly, it is *public land* ranchers who seem to wield the greatest clout. Consider the 1975 moratorium on public land grazing fee increases. Klyza wrote that the secretaries of interior and agriculture justified the moratorium on the basis of the "'difficult economic and drought conditions facing much of the livestock industry throughout the Western states.'" But, he pointed out, "the drought of 1975 was not a significant one, and . . . no aid was made available to ranchers on private lands." Phillip Foss too was speaking of public land ranchers when he wrote that there "are few groups of comparable size, if any, which are as politically powerful as are the western stockmen."[3]

Ranchers' inflated impact on national politics stems in large part from their influence in Congress, particularly the U.S. Senate. There are several reasons for this. Clawson pointed out that the relatively unpopulous range livestock region accounts for approximately one-third of the total Senate membership; thus, westerners generally wield disproportionate influence in the Senate. For many years eastern congressmen deferred to their western colleagues on so-called western issues. Public land grazing was high on that list. Calef noted that the BLM "offend[s] no one by responding to political pressure from western interests." In some cases stockgrowers had more than the ear of their representatives in Washington. Gates noted, for example, that when the Grazing Service was being investigated in 1946 by a Senate Public Lands and Surveys sub-committee, "[s]ome members of Congress who participated in the attacks . . . on the Grazing Service were themselves personally interested in the livestock industry and . . . were particularly distressed at the proposed increase in fees."[4]

Finally, ranchers' influence with the BLM is enhanced by the BLM's structure. Because the agency is organized by state offices, rather than multistate regional offices, as in the Forest Service, "[p]ower in the BLM is . . . highly concentrated in the state directors, and the state directors' power base is in turn strongly entrenched in state and local interests still heavily influenced by the grazing industry." Maintaining close contacts with governors' offices and con-gressional delegations has been the western livestock industry's formula for control. A BLM manager who sought to take some unpopular action, Sheridan explained, "found himself the center of a small political storm stirred by the affected livestock interests. His superiors at the agency received inquiries and complaints from Members of Congress from the area. Concerned about next year's budget before the Congress, they often intervened—ordering the manager to retract his decision or risk being transferred to another district." Calef called the western livestock industry "extraordinarily effective in enlisting whole-hearted and strenuous congressional support of its position in any disagreement with the BLM."[5]

While agency attempts to reduce grazing occur relatively infrequently, the backlash that Sheridan described is the rule rather than the exception when cuts *are* proposed. BLM and Forest Service managers have been transferred, threatened with transfer, or compelled to resign for proposing to reduce livestock use to protect other resources or for clamping down on trespass and other violations by grazing permittees. A manager who proceeds with the action may be reversed, reprimanded, or threatened with a transfer. Some of these employees become "whistle-blowers." If the situation becomes public, however, upper-level managers generally relent. If the employees have already been transferred, they are generally returned to their former positions. Recently, permittees have sued both BLM and Forest Service officials for enforcing agency regulations prohibiting trespass or for attempting to reduce allowable use. The experiences of BLM manager Darrel Short and Forest Service district ranger Don Oman are illustrative. Oman's story attracted widespread attention from several sources, including the *New York Times, High Country News, People, Audubon,* and at least one book.[6]

Anecdotes about the power of livestock interests in Congress are legion. They often revolve around one of the industry's many champions in Congress during the past sixty years. Men like Frank Barrett, Pete Domenici, Jim Santini, Cliff Hansen, Paul Laxalt, Malcolm Wallop, and Al Simpson have engineered field hearings to air industry concerns, introduced pro-industry resolutions and legislation, and kept up the heat on BLM and Forest Service field officials.

Nevada's Senator McCarran was one of the industry's staunchest supporters. His constituents were "the closest thing to mythical cattle barons using the public lands. Of the fifty largest grazing district operators in 1944, 30 percent (fifteen) were Nevadans, and their average of 9,185 animal units was almost twice as large as the average of the other thirty-five large operators." McCarran was responsible for the 1939 Taylor Grazing Act amendment (section 18) that required the interior secretary to consult with district advisory boards. But he may be best remembered for a four-and-a-half-year investigation of the Grazing Service's administration of the Taylor Act. McCarran introduced the resolution calling for the investigation, and his "committee staff worked closely with the livestock industry in setting up the hearings and getting its support to renew [the committee's] operating budget each year." The committee held sixty-two days of hearings in several cities in nine western states, most often in Nevada. According to Rowley, the investigation "so intimidated" many Grazing Service administrators "that they fully accepted the views and demands of the industry." Voigt tells the story of a hearing on grazing fees, which McCarran chaired, on 11 May 1945—Victory Day in Europe. The record of the hearing, Voigt marvels, "says nothing about it. . . . The livestock associations were fighting their own war [over the grazing fee] and were not to be diverted by the collapse of the Hitler regime or the accelerating advances against the Japanese in the Pacific Theater."[7]

The next committee to investigate the public land agencies (the third since the 1920s) was organized in 1947 and chaired by another industry advocate, Senator Frank Barrett of Wyoming. Like McCarran's road show, it held field hearings in seven western states. The committee's proposal to sell grazing lands was reviled in the press as an attempted land grab by the western livestock industry. But even the "overwhelming majority of ranchers" were "bitterly opposed to it," believing that it would benefit only a small group of wealthy stockmen. The committee's recommendations did lead to a one-year moratorium in livestock reductions, which "was hailed by stock organizations" but condemned by those concerned about eroding watersheds. A Grand Junction, Colorado, city council member charged that "the interests of the twenty-five thousand people of Grand Junction were being slighted for the interests of eighteen stockmen who used the ranges in question."[8]

Another ally of stockmen during this era was Barrett's Democratic colleague, Wyoming's Senator Joseph C. O'Mahoney. In 1944, during a committee hearing on the nomination of Clarence Forsling to serve as Grazing Service director, acting chairman O'Mahoney "invited a delegation of stockmen to sit with the committee and interrogate Forsling as though they were Senate members"![9]

Stockmen's advocates have held sway not only in committee rooms but on the floor of Congress, seeking and procuring aid in controlling livestock diseases; financial assistance in the forms of loans, price supports, and emergency feed payments; federal intervention in meat packer strikes; and regulation or subsidization of railroads, highways, and trucking. They have succeeded for sixty years in keeping grazing fees low and in avoiding widespread cuts in permitted numbers or seasons of use to improve range conditions. As Clawson observed, there is simply no accounting for some legislation apart from the industry's political influence. He offered the domestic wool price support approved by Congress in 1947 as an example: (1) the "gross value of wool produced in this country was [then] only about 100 million dollars . . . or less than 1/10 of 1 per cent of the gross value of all production in the United States," (2) the measure was "contrary to widely accepted national policy for the encouragement of freer international trade," and (3) the price support "seriously embarrassed this country in its trade negotiations with other nations."[10]

Fifty years later, the industry's influence seems not to have waned. In 1995 western Republicans were incensed when the Forest Service announced that it would not be renewing grazing permits for the coming season because it had been unable to complete the environmental analyses required by the National Environmental Policy Act. Ignoring NEPA's purpose, which is to ensure informed decision making by federal agencies, Republicans tacked onto a rescissions bill a provision ordering the Forest Service to renew the permits and do the environmental reports later.[11]

The next year the full Senate by a vote of 51–46 and the House Resources Committee by 23–15 passed a major grazing reform bill. The package of reforms would have effectively allowed ranchers "a dominant use of the public lands." Introduced by Senator Pete Domenici (R–New Mexico), the bill "touched off one of the great [and "most bitter"] public lands policy debates of the decade. Eventually, the administration and environmentalists convinced the House the Domenici bill would effectively allow ranchers to have a dominant use of the public lands, and the bill died."[12]

Domenici's bill, S. 1459, provides an excellent case in point for our purposes. It began by proclaiming that "the western livestock industry . . . plays an important and integral role in maintaining and preserving the social, economic, and cultural base of rural communities . . . [and] an important and integral role in the economies of the 16 western States" and that "maintaining the economic viability of the western livestock industry is essential to maintaining open space and habitat for big game, wildlife, and fish." It would have repealed Congress's findings in PRIA that relate to the "unsatisfactory condition" of the public rangelands, replacing them with the infamous and indefensible claim that "the Federal rangelands are in the best condition they have been in during this century."[13]

The measure contained numerous substantive provisions designed to further stockgrowers' interests. It increased grazing permit terms from ten to twelve years; exempted issuance of a grazing permit from assessment under NEPA or any other law; limited agency discretion by authorizing reductions in livestock use "only if . . . a change in management practices would not achieve management objectives"; changed from five to seven the number of sheep or goats equivalent to an animal unit month (AUM); expressly limited the conditions that grazing permits may contain; and required the renewal of a grazing permit "that has been pledged as security for a loan" if certain conditions are met.[14]

S. 1459 provided for both "grazing advisory councils" and "resource advisory councils." Livestock permittees would serve on both; indeed, the membership qualifications for resource advisory councils required inclusion of "permittees and lessees." The bill also specified that the "grazing advisory council *shall set* range improvement objectives."[15]

The bill prohibited the "refus[al] to issue, renew, or transfer a grazing permit" on the basis of "[i]nsufficient monitoring data." In other words, if the local grazing manager's professional judgment that resource damage may result from continued grazing is not backed up by "monitoring data"—a common occurrence due to insufficient funds—grazing must be allowed to continue. The bill even required the BLM to give prior notice to permittees of agency monitoring activities on federal lands.[16]

Domenici lay low on grazing issues in 1997. Late in the year a watered-down reform bill sponsored by Representative Bob Smith (R-Oregon), H.R.

2493—termed "Domenici Lite" by *Public Lands News*—passed the House after several provisions objectionable to the administration had been removed. It remains to be seen whether some form of range reform will pass the full Congress; President Bill Clinton has promised a veto of any Domenici-type measure. Still, the Domenici bill's significant success is further evidence of the inordinate, almost inexplicable influence that some 23,000 persons still exert in our national legislature.

Even though public land ranchers have not always succeeded in achieving the grazing policy reforms they sought, they have had tremendous success in thwarting changes that would be detrimental to their interests. Clawson opined that the ranching industry's "influence is probably greatest in a negative way, in [the] prevention of the measures it opposes," and he doubted whether "any public land policy could be adopted which was unitedly and strongly opposed by the range livestock industry." Pinchot had recognized this talent forty-five years earlier. Knowing that livestock interests could block any effort to pass legislation requiring a grazing permit or fee for the forest reserves (national forests), in 1905 he resorted to an elaborate ploy to determine whether he had administrative authority to require such permits. He had the secretary of agriculture submit three questions to the attorney general

> concerning "an application for the use of forest reserve land in Alaska for a fish saltery, oil, and fertilizer plant." Could such a permit be issued? Could the permit be for longer than one year? Could he "require reasonable compensation or rental for such permit?" When all three answers came back in the affirmative, Pinchot had his answer. If fees could be charged for fish saltery permits, they could be charged for grazing permits!

While ranchers could not avoid grazing fees, their perennial ability to keep fees below market levels is the classic example of the ability that Clawson described.[17]

Ranchers have also enjoyed considerable success in their dealings with the land management agencies even without congressional intervention. The agencies know from experience what consequences to expect if they antagonize stockgrowers or are insufficiently responsive to their concerns. During his research Calef was told repeatedly that any changes adverse to ranchers recommended by the BLM were "postponed, held in abeyance, or profoundly modified if the affected ranchers oppose them strongly enough." "On occasion," he conceded, "the BLM technicians can persuade ranchers to reduce range use or make other grazing changes; but if persuasion proves impossible, such changes are not likely to be made." A reduction in permitted livestock numbers "is seldom officially proposed unless it has the unqualified approval of the grazing district board, and it is rarely made unless there is almost universal approbation from the permittees concerned." It sometimes seems that the managing agency is the regulated community's best friend. Foss related this remarkable story. The

National Advisory Board Council (NABC) agreed in 1954 to a new grazing fee formula based on cattle/sheep prices rather than the cost of administering the grazing program, which would have increased the grazing fee from 12 cents per AUM to 18 cents. But BLM director Edward Woozley decided it was too big a jump in one increment and proposed a fee of 15 cents instead. Needless to say, neither the NABC nor permittees resisted.[18]

In Clawson's view, ranchers' political strength "differs in no essential respect from the political influence of other economic groups. It is simply more powerful, in relation to the number of people involved." He implied, however, that stockgrowers' political influence *was* different, when he theorized that it derived in part from their social stature:

Many of the oldest and best known families . . . are and always have been identified with range livestock production. The early pioneers were fre-quently ranchers. . . . Some of the families established then have remained active in the range industry, or sympathetic with it if engaged in other business. . . . These old and prominent families give the limited population engaged in the range industry more leadership, more prestige, and more political influence. . . .[19]

At least in part because of the social status associated with ranching, Clawson noted, ranchers were willing "to follow this type of life for much lower financial rewards than they might have obtained elsewhere." He described the "inheritance and family nature of some of the better known large-scale ranches" as resembling the "feudal prototype." Foss also employed the adjective "feudal" to describe public land ranching and further observed that stockmen "rank high in wealth, prestige, and influence." Sally K. Fairfax explains that the Taylor Grazing Act helped ensure that "the most prosperous property owners" would continue to benefit from federal range policy by defining "historic use," for the purpose of allocating grazing permits, in terms of range use between 1929 and 1934—the Depression years. Because many livestock operators were forced to reduce or liquidate their herds during those years, the operators remaining in business, who benefited from the 1934 legislation, were generally the most affluent.[20]

At some later date, the demographics of ranch ownership began to change. A study performed for the Public Land Law Review Commission reported that 60 percent of operating ranches in the late 1960s "were purchased from those who had no close blood relationship" with original homesteaders or permittees. But even though ranches were not staying in the hands of the original families, Clawson's theory about the social stature of ranchers remained sound. This was confirmed by a survey conducted in the early 1970s by agricultural economists Arthur F. Smith and William E. Martin. They reported that recent buyers who purchased ranches for speculative purposes also desired to "capture" the social benefits of ranch ownership. Calef made a similar observation, noting that when large ranches are inherited they often are retained by the heirs "partly as investments and partly for the prestige which in the West accrues to the owners of ranching operations." This incentive for ranch ownership holds true today.[21]

It seems to me that western livestock interests' power differs both as a matter of degree and in kind, the latter precisely because of the social aspects Clawson identified. On the other hand, McConnell describes "a fundamental reality of American politics," of which the stockmen's power could be seen as merely a peculiar manifestation: "power in the United States is primarily *local* power." Speaking specifically of the Forest Service, McConnell observed that the "elites to which the agency responded were the local elites in the areas where the Service operated, and the values it came to serve were their values." Western stockmen were the "local elites" in many areas, and they became a potent force in local public land decision making.[22]

The almost inexplicable influence of western stockgrowers, especially within the BLM, can be traced to a related factor—the grazing advisory boards established under the Taylor Grazing Act. Because the Forest Service lacked a grazing advisory board system comparable to the BLM's, McConnell's observation about local power may be even more apt in the context of the BLM. Grazing boards were one element of the "power elites" that developed from the historical "intersection" between the BLM and western livestock interests. These elites—which, as Worster puts it, "don't quite look like" power elites in other parts of the country—grew out of "struggles over power and hierarchy in the West." In 1902, long before the Taylor Act, the Interior Department had adopted a policy of allowing local woolgrower associations to recommend which operators should receive permits. Later, with no express statutory authorization, Ferry Carpenter set up state and district advisory boards to help him organize and administer the new grazing districts. Membership was limited to local stockmen. Operation of the Taylor grazing boards prompted one commentator's observation that "[p]olitical pressure from the livestock industry from 1934 to 1976 effectively hamstrung the implementation of the [Taylor Grazing Act]." According to Merrill, "nearly all historians of the public lands . . . have noted the failures of the Taylor Grazing Act—*particularly its domination by local interests.*"[23]

Foss was one of the early BLM's most vocal critics. He described stockmen's political power from 1934 to approximately 1960 as essentially a "monopolitical system" and identified grazing boards as among the "principal decision-makers of the federal grazing activity." He suggested that the advisory boards were the "formalization and legal recognition of the upper strata of a rural caste system." Foss further asserted that the grazing decision makers (advisory boards, range managers, permittees, western legislators, and committee members) constituted a "special private government," which "functions in many ways as a private, commercial organization." Similarly, Voigt described the "layering or class-creating effect" brought about within the western livestock community by a variety of historical factors, including the district grazing boards, which he claimed constituted "the basic government of grazing on 142 million acres of Taylor lands."[24]

It "is no wonder," Merrill argues, that the Taylor Grazing Act has been cited as "one of the most egregious examples of a private take-over of a public agency, for the western range users literally helped draw up the plans." BLM ranges were managed for livestock by government employees with close ties to the graziers and with heavy input from the grazing advisory boards, which were composed chiefly of permittees. McConnell reports that the advisory boards' advice was "followed in decisions on 98.3 per cent of the more than 14,000 [grazing] licenses issued during the first fourteen months of the [Taylor] Act's operation." Even Director Clawson observed candidly that, in some states, the advisory boards were "assuming some functions as land management agencies, in addition to their role as advisers to [BLM]."[25]

The grazing board system undoubtedly contributed to the aggrandizement of western stockmen. When Congress was considering in 1939 whether to give the boards legislative authorization, Interior Secretary Ickes submitted a letter relating his lack of "objection to statutory provision for the [grazing boards'] existence, so long as there can be no question that their functions are advisory only." Congress nominally heeded this advice: the Taylor Grazing Act, as amended, consistently uses the terms "advisory," "adviser," "advice," and "recommendation" to describe the boards' role. But despite these precautions, Foss relates, the "users of the range apparently came to believe that they were to administer the [grazing] program through the advisory boards, and it does not appear that [the 1939 amendment], giving the boards only advisory authority, made any particular impression on the stockmen." The boards' "recommendations" over the years were seldom "overruled by district graziers or higher authority." An NABC member testified before Congress that the Grazing Service followed the national board's "decisions" 90–95 percent of the time. As of 1972 the statutory provision authorizing the secretary to remove a board member "for the good of the [Grazing] Service" had never been exercised— even though there had been approximately 600 board members in any given year ever since the mid-1930s.[26]

It was clearly the view of ranchers that they should govern BLM range decision making. Culhane describes BLM field managers as "vassals" to the district boards. He relates the story (first recorded by Foss) of the Soldier Creek grazing district in southeastern Oregon. The local grazing board had "resisted all efforts" from 1936 into the 1950s to set range use in accordance with BLM determinations of carrying capacity. A letter from the Malheur County Court to the interior secretary and Oregon congressional delegation in 1954 left no doubt as to the prevailing local view of the role of grazing boards. The letter writers asserted: "Certainly it was never the intent of Congress that this one bureaucrat [the BLM district manager] should override the considered judgment of the cumulative experience of the members of the Advisory Board. The Manager and his paid personnel should furnish the information and the board should fix the policy. If this is not the theory, it should be." Culhane comments: "It is hard to imagine a more comprehensive assertion of the right of a self-interested clientele group to control a public agency."[27]

By 1936, Gary D. Libecap tells us, the grazing advisory boards were "estimating grazing capacity, setting stocking levels, ruling on license applications, arbitrating disputes, and helping to determine seasons of use for pastures. Their influence over almost every aspect of range management made them essential institutions for advancing the interests of ranchers and for restricting bureaucratic authority." Some western states even granted them expenditure authority over state shares of federal grazing fees.[28]

The stockmen's "organization of power" was based on an amalgam of boards and associations by which ranchers transformed their preexisting power "into a working approximation of publicly sanctioned authority." The "large-scale ranchers" were the "most influential livestock men"; they were especially well represented on grazing boards, particularly the NABC. Furthermore, NABC officials "showed a remarkable coincidence of positions in the [district] board system and positions held in stockmen's associations," and "in general the local boards reflected the existing patterns of social and economic power in their communities." As McConnell put it, "public authority was for practical purposes in the hands of the organized ranchers—more particularly of the larger and previously more influential ranchers." "[I]n probably no other public program of substantial size," he asserted, "are the elements of power and control so easily visible or so stark." And he mused: "Perhaps there is a long-term possibility, given the still remaining formal responsibility of the public bureaucracy to the constituency of the nation as a whole, that the ranchers' power to retain autonomous control of public land resources may be checked. But the long history of these lands hardly encourages optimism about such an outcome."[29]

This concentration of power over public land grazing decisions came to the attention of the Public Land Law Review Commission (PLLRC) in 1970. In the commission's view, the situation cried out for a remedy, and the remedy would necessitate diluting the influence of grazing boards. Noting the "broad roles of the public land agencies," it recommended that "members of each citizen advisory board be chosen to represent a broad range of interests." It further recommended that "representation [on such boards] should change as interest in, and uses of, the lands change. We believe that the appropriate range of representation includes not just the obvious direct interests, such as grazing, recreation, mining, fish and wildlife, and wilderness, but the professor, the laborer, the townsman, the environmentalist and the poet as well."[30]

Shortly afterward, Congress passed the Federal Advisory Committee Act of 1972 (FACA). Section 9 of FACA directs that, "[u]nless otherwise specifically provided by statute or Presidential directive, advisory committees shall be utilized *solely for advisory functions*." In response to this and other directives in FACA, the BLM terminated the district grazing boards and "realigned membership" on the NABC to reflect a wider range of interests: "livestock members were reduced from 20 to 10 and wildlife interests from 10 to 6. Representatives of other groups increased—three for outdoor recreation, and one each for forestry environmental quality, mining, county and state governments, leasable minerals, and public utilities."[31]

The 1976 Federal Land Policy and Management Act (FLPMA) provided for "advisory councils" comprised of "persons who are representative of the various major citizens' interests concerning the problems related to land use planning or the management of the BLM lands located within the area for which an advisory council is established." Muhn and Stuart claim that these field-level, multiple-use boards were intended to "supplement" district grazing boards. In many cases, however, they were essentially ornamental. I can attest to the tardy implementation and general ineffectualness of one such council. The Wells Resource Area in the Elko District of northeastern Nevada was one of the "pilot" resource areas selected by the BLM for initial implementation of FLPMA's new land use planning procedures. The Elko District did not select a multiple use advisory council until 1980 or 1981, and the council was only nominally involved in helping to prepare the Wells Resource Management Plan or in consulting with BLM staff on district management.[32]

The cattlemen's clout was not appreciably diminished by passage of FLPMA in 1976, even though FLPMA directed the BLM to manage the public lands in the national interest for a wide range of multiple uses. Stockgrowers continued to wield considerable influence in range policy and management decisions, especially decisions regarding the development of allotment management plans, range improvement projects, and adjustments of grazing fees. In the early 1980s the BLM sought to "reward" certain grazing permittees for their good stewardship records by entering into "Cooperative Management Agreements" (CMAs), which essentially abdicated authority for public range management to the private ranch operators. CMAs could not be canceled before they expired—at the end of ten years. Former BLM director Frank Gregg attacked the CMA program as "'a policy that amounts to a give-away of the public lands to private interests.'" When environmental groups challenged the program, a federal court invalidated it, holding that it violated FLPMA. The judge warned that grazing permittees "must be kept under a sufficiently real threat of [permit] cancellation or modification in order to adequately protect the public lands from overgrazing."[33]

Culhane has advanced a perspective on the phenomenon of local control of public land grazing decisions at odds with that of most observers, based in part on interviews conducted during the 1970s "with local agency officials and key interest group leaders" and "administration of questionnaires to other group leaders" in three regions of the West. His survey was nonrandom and included nine BLM resource areas in four BLM districts (primarily grazing districts). To maintain anonymity, the regions/states were not identified by name. Culhane conceded that grazing boards wielded significant power for at least two decades after Taylor Act passage, but he discounted their importance by the late 1970s. Arguing that agencies are not "captured" by their constituents, Culhane seemed particularly intent on discounting the influence of stockmen. In his view, the "primary reason for the decline of advisory board influence was that the BLM had taken on the boards over the central issue of levels of grazing leases in the 1950s and early 1960s and won." The "BLM succeeded in lowering the level of range use through the long and difficult process of adjudication," he wrote, and thus advisory board "power was undermined." By the 1970s the "license-level situation had become stable," and "the boards' functions were routine." Culhane avoided the weightier issue of whether BLM ranges were properly stocked. Had the BLM tried to reduce grazing to ecologically justifiable levels, or to remove stock from ranges that should not have been grazed at all, it is highly doubtful that the boards would have been as complacent or passive as he described them.[34]

Culhane also noted that grazing boards were terminated in 1975 after passage of FACA and replaced with administratively established multiple-use advisory boards. These boards, he asserted, were "attacked by stockmen as the symbolic final nail in the coffin of their boards' influence." He failed to point out, however, that grazing advisory boards were reestablished a mere one year later by section 403 of FLPMA. Culhane neither acknowledged what reenactment of the grazing boards suggested about the grazing lobby's power nor confronted an obvious issue—why are both grazing and multiple use boards needed, when grazing is simply one of the various multiple uses of BLM lands?[35]

Culhane reported that stockmen had "one of the lowest total influence scores" in his study. This, he said, supports their claims that, "far from being masters of the agencies, their influence was on the wane." Yet he conceded in a note that differences among participant scores were not statistically significant, and he described other "grains of salt" with which the stockmen's low influence score needs to be taken.[36]

Culhane repeatedly undermined the credibility of his assessment of the modern livestock industry's influence. For instance, he wrote:

There are a number of important alliances among the consumptive users [of the public lands], and the livestock industry is usually at their center. Stockmen constitute the largest single category of participants in local public lands politics. They have ties to the professional community (including agency professionals) through the [Society for Range Management]. Many local government officials in the three regions [of the study], including a number of town mayors and most county commissioners, were stockmen; almost all the irrigation groups, and many of the conservation and RC&D districts, were led by or primarily served stockmen. Finally, stockmen were a primary constituency or customer group for all the local government officials, local businessmen, and realtors in the sample, irrespective of formal affiliations with the livestock industry. . . .

He opined that "a large local livestock constituency (or one with very well developed access or very strong views) can stave off reductions in range use down to carrying capacity"—a view reminiscent of Clawson's assessment of stockmen's influence thirty years earlier.[37]

Culhane conceded that "large proportions of most [USFS] rangers' and [BLM] area managers' contacts are direct consumptive users" and that "the interests of many of their other local contacts (for example, local businessmen and local government officials) reinforce consumptive users' interests." While arguing rather weakly that most local constituencies "also include some conservationists or recreationists" who provide "a good degree of balance," he admitted that "the environmentalists' belief that the agencies failed to respond to their key explicit demands had some validity." BLM and Forest Service administrators, he explained, "did not respond to environmentalists by giving them what they most wanted . . . but by playing them off against users. Forest Service and BLM officials had a real commitment to accommodating economic uses of the public lands or 'economic demands' or the 'needs of the people.' They were not committed to recreation or Wilderness as primary uses of the public lands."[38]

Still, Culhane doggedly maintained that there is "mounting evidence that the capture thesis does not reflect the real world" and that the thesis is "most popular among the agencies' environmental critics." "If the bureau's rangeland is in poor condition," he contended, "the BLM is viewed by environmentalists as having been captured by the cowboys." He offered no explanation for his finding, reported on the very next page, that grazing leases in his sample regions "averaged 112 percent of carrying capacity." Moreover, he suggested implicitly that "environmentalists" are not "users" of public lands and overlooked the fact that outdoor recreation is a "principal use" of BLM lands under FLPMA and one of several co-equal multiple uses of national forests.[39]

Culhane seemed more concerned with semantics than with substance. His failure to offer alternate, plausible explanations for his findings undermines the significance and credibility of his conclusion that agencies are not "captured" by constituents. Capture by an individual interest group may be difficult to prove, but if capture is viewed more broadly as subservience to one group of interests Culhane's study offers plain evidence for such a phenomenon. He criticized oversimplified theories of capture while ignoring or at least downplaying the realities of the influence that certain groups, notably stockmen, actually exert. I think Fairfax had it closer to right: "For much of the [BLM's] history, it has looked like they were working for the livestock industry because that is all that was expected, all that was authorized, all that was funded."[40]

Evidence of BLM "capture" by the grazing industry continues to be amassed. This is so despite legislative measures such as FLPMA and PRIA and official investigations that should have had a diluting effect on graziers' influence. In comments presented to a congressional committee in 1988, an associate director of the GAO stated that the BLM "is often more concerned with meeting the immediate needs of its livestock permittees than with ensuring the longer-term, broader-based viability of the resource." These remarks reflected findings of numerous investigations into USFS and BLM grazing programs conducted by the agency in the 1980s. During one such audit, GAO officials were advised *by BLM field personnel* that "[grazing] permittees are managing BLM," rather than vice versa. During an audit of riparian conditions on western public lands, the GAO learned that BLM managers had "not taken strong action on . . . compliance problems" because they "fear[ed] the political power wielded by some permittees." A particularly graphic example was related by one BLM resource area manager who had ordered a permittee to stop unauthorized cutting of trees in a riparian area. The area manager had been directed by his supervisor, presumably the district manager, to "apologize to [the] permittee." The chagrined official was then further instructed to "deliver the wood to [the same permittee's] ranch"![41]

Noss and Cooperrider note that, "[l]ike forestry, the range conservation profession has developed close ties to industry." They offer the following anecdote, which illustrates both the fact of BLM "capture" and the enduring vitality of Foss's private, commercial organization analogy:

> Several years ago, a conference speaker asked a group of professional range conservationists in the Bureau of Land Management two questions. The speaker first asked: "How many of you consider that you are in the business of managing the vegetative resources of the public lands?" Two or three tentatively put up their hands while most of the others looked rather puzzled. The second question was, "How many of you consider that you are in the business of facilitating livestock production from the public lands?," to which everyone immediately raised their hand. "This is the problem," the speaker dryly noted.[42]

The influence of stockgrowers has not been limited to the extremes of local (BLM district-level) and national politics; it has been felt at the state level, too. In the 1910s through the 1930s livestock interests benefited from the common practice of several western states, including New Mexico, Idaho, Wyoming, Nevada, and Arizona, of making their state land selections so as to facilitate consolidation of ranch units or enable ranches to control water sources. (All western, or "public land," states were granted one, two, or four sections of federal land per township as part of their statehood compacts with the federal government.) Furthermore, ranchers have long been overrepresented in western state legislatures, at times even controlling them. Graf reported that "ranchers were disproportionately represented" in legislatures until at least the late 1960s; they held one-third of the seats in the legislatures of several states during the Sagebrush Rebellion era of 1979–81. According to Larson, a majority of members of the Wyoming Senate have often been members of the Wyoming Stock Growers Association. From 1890 to 1985 in Wyoming, twelve of twenty-one governors, half of U.S. senators, and three of fourteen congressional representatives were stockmen. The representation rates in legislatures are lower today, but, as table 1 reveals, they still exceed (significantly, in some states) the percentage of livestock interests in the general population. Wyoming is the extreme example. More than 23 percent of its state legislators are ranchers, even though "all of agriculture," livestock and crops combined, "accounts for only about 2 percent of the state's economy."[43]

Another mainstay of the industry's political and economic influence is the long, close association between university range scientists and other academics and western livestock interests. Noss and Cooperrider explain that the profession of "range management developed in response to a perception that rangelands were deteriorating—from overgrazing. The history of the profession has followed a . . . path of resourcism [similar to forestry], with livestock production becoming the primary focus." The result, according to Ed Marston, editor of the regional newspaper *High Country News*, is that the agriculture colleges of the land-grant universities in many western states, and indeed the "discipline of range science" generally, are "the obedient hand-maidens of traditional ranching." The connection between the ranching industry and state universities is reflected in the composition of the professional Society for Range Management: its 4,500–5,000 members hail from the livestock industry, academia, and federal agencies. In 1996, when the SRM board of directors endorsed the pro-industry Domenici grazing bill, its president and first and second vice-presidents were all western university faculty members. The liaison between industry and academia provides a context for interpreting Wagner's apology for the "defensive tone" of the 1992 range ecology symposium as well as for construing comments and omissions like those of professors Pieper, Laycock, and Heady, all noted in chapter 3.[44]

TABLE 1.

PERCENT OF WESTERN STATES' POPULATIONS AND

LEGISLATURES EMPLOYED IN AGRICULTURE AND AS RANCHERS

State	% of Population Employed in Agriculture[1]	% of Legislators Employed in Agriculture[2]	% of Legislators Employed as Ranchers[3]	Factor: % Agric. Legislators ÷ % Agric. in Pop.[4]
Arizona	2.5	3.3	5.6	1.3
California	3.6	7.5	2.5	2.1
Colorado	2.3	7.0	5.0	3.0
Idaho	7.8	23.8	7.6	3.0
Montana	7.1	26.7	21.3	3.8
Nevada	1.1	4.8 (6.2)	6.2	5.6
New Mexico	2.7	7.1	2.7	2.6
Oregon	3.8	6.7	2.2	1.8
Utah	3.1	11.5 (13.5)	5.8	4.4
Washington	2.8	7.5	4.8	2.7
Wyoming	7.4	22.2	23.3	3.0

[1] U.S. Department of Labor, Bureau of Labor Statistics, *Geographic Profile of Employment and Unemployment, 1995,* Bulletin 2486, February 1997.

[2] National Conference of State Legislatures, *State Legislators Occupations,* 1995. Where two figures are given, the second is a more current figure obtained from an individual state.

[3] Individual states' legislative directories, or equivalent, for current (1996–97 or 1997–98) legislatures.

[4] The figures in this column represent the factor by which agriculturists are disproportionately represented in the legislature. For instance, in Nevada agriculturists are 5.6 times more prevalent in the legislature than in the general population.

Universities' curricula frequently reflect this relationship and the influence of livestock interests. Several western universities use Allan Savory's book *Holistic Resource Management* (1988), even though range ecologists widely criticize the scientific hypotheses on which his proposed management system (known as HRM and popular among ranchers) is based. Savory's approach calls on landowners to examine their spiritual as well as material values and goals with respect to the land and to consider compatible methods for achieving those goals. Montana State University (MSU) has developed an HRM curriculum, which includes "work[ing] with sociologists to see whether ranchers believe the methods help them reach their quality-of-life goals." Significantly, while MSU considers this curricular endeavor academically worthy, it canceled the "sustainable ecosystems and economics" research proposed by a graduate student ecologist ostensibly because "multi-disciplinary studies lacked 'scientific rigor.'" Outside funding had already been obtained for the research, but the student was known for his antigrazing views.[45]

Recently, *High Country News* reported that the president of New Mexico State University (NMSU) may have been removed as "punishment for offending the state's traditional ranching interests." The saga reportedly began when media giant Ted Turner, who owns ranches in several states, including New Mexico, told a class of NMSU students that cattle ranching is "a foolish thing to do, a mistake," and that "[b]ison don't really belong [in New Mexico] either." Turner's remarks inflamed New Mexico's ranching community. Representatives of state livestock interests, including a rancher who is a member of the NMSU Board of Regents, called on the university to "repudiate Turner's remarks." Within two months after he refused to do so, the president was fired.[46]

A milder, humorous example of this "incestuous relationship" arose at the University of Wyoming. This incident is recounted in the official minutes of the first meeting of the School of Environment and Natural Resources (SENR) Citizens' Advisory Board in 1994. The minutes report that the university's Board of Trustees had "tabled a motion to change the name of the Department of Range Management to the Department of Rangeland Ecology and Watershed Management. [The dean of the College of Agriculture] thought the motion was tabled because of the negative connotations that the word 'ecology' sometimes has." Subsequently, the newly formed SENR Citizens' Advisory Board "agreed to support a name change in which a comma separates Rangeland from Ecology." Appropriately, this first meeting of the Citizens' Advisory Board was held in the Stockgrower's Room at the University of Wyoming's American Heritage Center.[47]

Western livestock interests have also enjoyed influence in the courts. Or at least that seems to be the only explanation for some surprising judicial decisions in the industry's favor. A classic example is *Hinsdale Livestock Co. v. United States*, which seems to stand for a novel principle of administrative law—that a party challenging an agency action is entitled to deference from the reviewing court. A federal district court in Montana baldly rejected a BLM decision to terminate grazing early on an allotment because of overgrazing and drought conditions—presumably matters within the agency's expertise. Yet the court did not even pay lip service to the agency's professional credentials. Instead, the court recited at length the plaintiffs' ranching experience, concluding: "they know how to judge the conditions of the range resource and have acted appropriately in managing their herds." With that, the judge expressly adopted the plaintiffs' opinion and rejected the BLM's, thus dismissing some thirty-five years of BLM range management expertise and a roughly equivalent history of federal judicial deference to agency decisions, particularly factual findings such as these.[48]

Another example of judicial deference, bordering on obeisance, to ranchers can be found in *Natural Resources Defense Council v. Hodel* (*NRDC v. Hodel*). The plaintiff environmental groups raised a broad set of challenges under several statutes, including FLPMA, to the BLM's land use plan and environmental impact statement for the Reno planning area. The complaint was filed in federal district court in Nevada, but a federal judge from Oregon, the Honorable James M. Burns, was designated to hear and decide the case, raising the question whether an impartial judge could not be found in Nevada. Judge Burns upheld the BLM's plan and EIS in all respects.[49]

The plaintiffs objected that, despite ample evidence of overgrazing in the area, only one of the BLM's several management alternatives had considered *any reduction* in livestock numbers. All alternatives would leave at least half of the rangelands in "poor" condition. Judge Burns conceded that "the enormous record in this case [demonstrated] that there has been overgrazing in the Reno area." But, he continued, "in only four allotments could it be *conclusively* determined that the overgrazing was due to livestock use." Although he approved the BLM's plan, in a footnote he queried rhetorically: "Why the agency would propose a course of action that can, with little effort, be seriously criticized as being more expensive, resulting in less long-run environmental improvement, and even less grazing in the long run can only be [a] source of speculation to the outsider" ("less grazing in the long run" presumably refers to the declining capacity of the range to support cattle). Despite this thinly veiled criticism, the judge concluded that the BLM had taken "its best cut" at the problems it faced and that principles of federal administrative law required him to defer to that administrative judgment.[50]

Judge Burns rejected out of hand the plaintiffs' argument that the agency should have considered a no-grazing alternative. Pointing to the century-long tradition of grazing in the region, he declared: "The complete abandonment of grazing in the Reno planning area is practically *unthinkable* as a policy choice. . . ." He admitted, however, that "ranching plays only a negligible role" in the "economy of the Reno area as a whole," and commented, somewhat ambiguously, that the "Bureau is legally free to change its mind, depending on how the political 'wind blows' in Nevada."[51]

Judge Burns's decision itself can be "seriously criticized" on several grounds. The BLM had no actual livestock use data, let alone information on vegetative utilization and trend for much of the planning area. The absence of use data suggests a serious dereliction of duty by the BLM. Moreover, the judge's description of the BLM's reasoning as a "source of speculation" misperceives both the agency's duty to explain its decision and the court's role in reviewing it. Why an agency chooses a particular course of action should be rationally explained or at least apparent from the record. In addition, the decision should be based on considerations specified in the agency's governing statutes and regulations. Yet Judge Burns ignored provisions in both FLPMA and the Public Rangeland Improvement Act, which govern BLM actions and which contemplate the reduction or elimination of livestock grazing under certain circumstances. In fact, the court erroneously construed PRIA as mandating that livestock grazing continue. Finally, the judge candidly admitted that the agency had considered "subjective" factors, which the BLM is neither directed nor authorized to consider, such as "the BLM's obvious desire to maintain for ranchers, what it describes (romantically perhaps) as a 'preferred lifestyle.'"[52]

The courts in *Hinsdale Livestock Co.* and *NRDC v. Hodel* adopted very different approaches to the deference owed by a federal court to an administrative agency. Yet the two opinions can be rather easily reconciled as manifesting judicial favoritism toward a segment of the local community perceived as economically, politically, socially, or culturally significant. Examples of the courts' susceptibility to western stockgrowers' influence span the century. Legal scholar Valerie Weeks Scott reported that in 1905 the Wyoming Supreme Court ignored binding precedent and "refused to apply" an 1897 U.S. Supreme Court opinion, *Camfield v. United States*, to a case with "similar facts." Both cases were brought under the federal Unlawful Inclosures Act of 1885; *Camfield* should have determined the outcome in the 1905 dispute. Scott understatedly described the Wyoming court's decision as "a good example of bias that might have existed on the court in favor of the cattle interests in Wyoming, even so far as to ignore a United States Supreme Court holding." The decision was skewed "heavily in favor of the larger ranchers." A pre-*Camfield* Wyoming case had also ruled in favor of a rancher who built a fence so as to enclose "a great number of sections of public domain," despite the clear prohibition in the 1855 act.[53]

Ninety years later, an arguably similar instance of a court ignoring or manipulating federal law occurred, again in Wyoming. Judge Clarence Brimmer's 1996 opinion in *Public Lands Council v. Secretary of the Interior* (subsequently reversed in large part by a federal appeals court) stands as yet another example of irrational deference to the livestock industry. In *Public Lands Council* the federal district court in Wyoming struck down four provisions of the Interior Department's 1995 livestock grazing regulations and only reluctantly approved others. To achieve this result the court played fast and loose with certain Taylor Grazing Act terms, attempting, it seemed, to substitute for statutory language the lexicon and understandings of public lands ranchers. For instance, after a very abbreviated account of the provisions of one section of the Taylor Act and the Interior

Department's initial adjudication process to determine grazing preferences, the judge asserted: "The term 'grazing preference' thus came to represent an adjudicated right to place livestock on public lands." As used in this context, "thus" is imbued with a tremendous amount of rationalization—historical, social, and legal. The statement quoted wholly ignores the distinction that the statute makes between the establishment of "[p]reference . . . in the issuance of grazing permits" and the "specifi[cation in permits of] numbers of stock and seasons of use," and it erroneously characterizes the nature of the grazing license.[54]

Indeed, a fundamental flaw of the opinion was Judge Brimmer's repeated use of the term "right" to graze. This contradicts Congress's choice of the term "privilege" in the Taylor Act and the act's unambiguous caveat in section 3 that the "issuance of a permit pursuant to [this Act] *shall not create any right*, title, interest, or estate in or to the lands." Congress ratified this language in FLPMA, forty years later, by specifying that the new act shall not "be construed as modifying in any way [existing law] with respect to the creation of any right, title, interest or estate in or to public lands . . . by issuance of grazing permits and leases." In a classic example of the "pot calling the kettle black," Judge Brimmer proclaimed: "With a mere stroke of his pen, the Secretary has boldly and blithely wrested away from Western ranchers the very certainty, the definitiveness of range rights, and the necessary security of preference rights that their livestock operations require." He continued: "[T]he Secretary's disregard of his congressionally imposed duty . . . must be stopped before it wreaks havoc with the ranching industry that Congress has tried to preserve."[55]

The court's pronouncement may be Judge Brimmer's view of what federal range policy ought to be, but it bore little if any resemblance to what the law is. Nor did he cite FLPMA in his discussion of preference, even though FLPMA expressly recognizes the secretary's authority to cancel, suspend, or modify grazing permits and to dispose of grazing lands or devote them to another public purpose. Both FLPMA and PRIA authorize administrative decisions to terminate grazing altogether. Even the BLM's pre-"reform" grazing regulations specify both that grazing preference can be changed, or "canceled or suspended in whole or in part," and that grazing "permits or leases may be canceled, suspended, or modified." Judge Brimmer may agree with Judge Burns in *NRDC v. Hodel* that removing livestock from public ranges is "unthinkable," but the law suggests otherwise.[56]

A panel of the Tenth Circuit Court of Appeals, with one judge dissenting, reversed the district court on three rules, thus reinstating them, but affirmed Judge Brimmer's conclusion that the TGA does not allow the issuance of conservation use permits—essentially, a grazing permit issued to someone who agrees *not* to graze livestock for the duration of the permit. While the agency has other means of curtailing grazing, "[p]ermissible ends such as conservation," the court ruled, "do not justify unauthorized means." The court approved the agency's new definitions of "preference" and "permitted use," the rule providing for federal title to all future range improvements, and the rule eliminating the requirement that a permittee be "engaged in the livestock business."[57]

In several respects, the *Public Lands Council* dissent's reasoning paralleled that of the district court. Both were concerned with the regulations' impact on the security or "certainty" of range rights, but neither explained how grazing "preferences" that can be changed at any time to reflect changes in forage or other relevant conditions provide "certainty." Indeed, the Taylor Act itself provides that the interior secretary "shall specify from time to time numbers of stock and seasons of use" and that grazing privileges "shall be safeguarded," but only "[s]o far as is consistent with the purposes and provisions of this subchapter," which include conserving and protecting rangeland. Both the dissent and the lower court accorded significantly less deference to the agency's rules than administrative law principles prescribe. The Tenth Circuit criticized the dissent and, implicitly, the district court for "substituting [its] own unattributed assertions for the plain meaning of the regulations." With respect to the range improvements rule, the court noted that "the dissent's interpretation is just that, its own interpretation." Like Judge Brimmer, the dissent placed "far too much weight" on the act's purpose of stabilizing the livestock industry. As the majority explained, the Taylor Grazing Act "clearly states that the need for stability must be balanced against the need to protect the rangeland."[58]

Livestock interests enjoy preferential treatment from yet another sector of government: conservation agencies other than the BLM and Forest Service. Grazing is allowed in many national wildlife refuges administered by the U.S. Fish and Wildlife Service and in more than twelve units of the National Park System. The California Desert Protection Act of 1994, which established the Mojave National Preserve east of Baker, also preserves cattle grazing. The 1.4-million-acre desert preserve (a unique federal designation) is home to 800 plant species and 300 animal species, including at least 2 threatened ones. One critic of the grazing compromise said, "The Park Service is giving the cowboys everything they want." Grazing is also permitted in Grand Teton National Park. Over the past twenty years the adjacent ranches to which the grazing rights attach have been the subject of (1) a bill that would have authorized federal expenditures of $200 million for the purchase of scenic easements; (2) 1997 legislation that requires the National Park Service to study how the lands can be protected from development and guarantees that grazing rights will continue during the study (expected to cost taxpayers $200,000); and (3) a controversial exchange proposal that would have traded hundreds of thousands of acres of federal lands and mineral rights of equal value in southwestern Wyoming for the Teton County ranches, while allowing the families to keep their homes and buildings in Teton County and guaranteeing them ranching privileges on the exchanged lands.[59]

Former BLM director and New Mexico lands commissioner Jim Baca, who was forced to resign his BLM position after angering western livestock interests, characterized the power of public land graziers this way: "I have never found any compromise in the livestock industry—and it always works for them." Conversely, Baca admitted with chagrin, "all we [the federal government] ever did on grazing was compromise." As a formula for maintaining the stock-growers' place on the public lands, this has been an effective strategy.[60]

B. DEMYTHOLOGIZING THE RANCHING MYSTIQUE

For many Americans the West is ranching, and the cowboy is the "ultimate symbol of western ranch agriculture." Many identify with, or at least aspire to imitate, those legendary figures of the West. Worster writes: "'Again and again, [westerners] told themselves and others that they were the earth's last free, wild, untrammeled people. Wearing no man's yoke, they were eternal cowboys on an open range.'" Thad Box, noted range scientist, academic dean, consultant, and spokesman for western ranching interests, asserts matter-of-factly: "As a nation, we will continue to be emotionally tied to the West and the cowboy and the imagined Western ethic." Even the National Academy of Sciences committee, which authored the 1994 report *Rangeland Health*, waxed poetic, describing western rangelands as "the legendary wide open spaces of American history and mythology." Never mind that "the popular song 'Home on the Range' contains not one word about livestock" or cowboys or that American history textbooks devote to cowboys and ranching "less than two pages' worth of attention out of almost a thousand pages of text." These pesky facts are starkly at odds with the popular impression of the historical and cultural importance of cowboys and cattlemen.[61]

Teddy Roosevelt was one of western ranching's earliest and biggest pro-moters. Bemoaning the passing of the cattlemen's frontier, he wrote: "We who have felt the charm of the life . . . and have exulted in its abounding vigor and its bold, restless freedom, will not only regret its passing for our own sakes, but must also feel real sorrow that those who come after us are not to see, as we have seen, what is perhaps the pleasantest, healthiest, and most exciting phase of American existence." Roosevelt romanticized and "exoticized" ranching. Merrill writes that Roosevelt described the "whole existence" of ranching as "patriarchal in character," comparing the life of a "free ranchman" to that of an "Arab sheik." But Roosevelt "undermined his own myth-making," Merrill points out, "by other depictions of western ranch owners as proper, if not superior, versions of eastern businessmen." In this way, Roosevelt exposed ranching as "an industry that was both in and out of time: run on modern business principles, it also allowed men to return to a kind of primitive social unit."[62]

The images of Roosevelt's vision of the West that have retained greatest vitality relate to the ability of ranch life to cultivate rugged masculinity and similar desirable male characteristics. "[R]anching in Roosevelt's text (and elsewhere)," Merrill writes, "was constituted by the absence of women, by the presence of a single-sex male world." As a result of living and working on the range, "men became more like their supposedly essential beings." "[H]ome was simply where a man could sleep and get his meals, and without a woman at the hearth it had no moral or sentimental qualities that informed middle-class and agrarian paeans to domesticity." Roosevelt "mentioned women only twice in his book," in the context of the "old and true border saying that 'the frontier is hard on women and cattle.'" This "single-sex male world" stood in stark contrast to farming, where the "farm wife/mother occupied a symbolic space." This, Merrill suggests, helps explain why the occupation of ranching was long considered different in kind from agriculture.[63]

Other historians have also commented on the gendered nature of the mythical West. Webb attributed the maleness of the West, particularly its dry plains and deserts, to the harshness of the environment: "The early West was strictly a man's country. It was no place for women, and women were very scarce there." "Men loved the Plains, or at least those who stayed there did. There was zest to the life, adventure in the air, freedom from restraint; men developed a hardihood which made them insensible to the hardships and lack of refinements." Webb argued that "the Plains—mysterious, desolate, barren, grief-stricken—oppressed the women, drove them to the verge of insanity in many cases." He hypothesized that women feared and distrusted the country because there "was too much of the unknown, too few of the things they loved." Much more recently, Katherine Morrissey characterized the "ideology of the West" as "celebrat[ing] a particular, and gendered, form of American identity." Morrissey points to the male-dominated "cast of characters that peoples the stereotypical West"—"[c]owboys and soldiers, gold miners and fur traders"— and to the "masculine image" of ranching (perceived as "men's work") as "conquering a virgin land."[64]

The myth of the Old West as a male-dominated world overlooks some significant physical and political realities, of course. Women were first accorded the right to vote in the West. The Territory of Wyoming enfranchised them and gave them the right to hold office in 1869; the state of Wyoming conferred the same rights in 1890. Other leaders in granting women suffrage included Utah and Colorado. The first woman to serve as judge or justice of the peace, first women appointed to juries, and first women elected to state political office were all in the West. Many women, whether by choice or necessity, oversaw ranch operations or worked alongside their menfolk. Even the legends accommodated a few women—Calamity Jane, Annie Oakley, Molly Brown.[65]

Still, the West was personified by *cowboys*. One of the greatest promoters of cowboys and the ranchers for whom they toiled was Webb, who described range life, the cowboy way of life, as "idyllic." "The land had no value, the grass was free, the water belonged to the first comer, and about all a man needed to 'set him up' in the business was a 'bunch' of cattle and enough common sense to handle them and enough courage to protect them without aid of the law." There was "something fascinating about a ranch," Webb wrote, "about riding over the green pastures on spirited horses and watching a fortune grow. . . . To be a cowboy was adventure; to be a ranchman was to be a king."[66]

On the other hand, Webb criticized, even bemoaned, the distended cowboy mystique. Describing the "haze of romance [that] has enveloped life in the West and threatens to make the Western man a legendary figure," he stated:

> Each year the haze grows, emphasized by story and picture, and there is danger that the ordinary 'bow-legged human' who had to make his living by working on horseback will disappear under the attributes of firearms, belts, cartridges, chaps, slang, and horses, all fastened to him by pulp paper and silver screen. If we could dispel this haze we could view Western life as it was in reality—logical, perfectly in accord ultimately with the laws laid down by the inscrutable Plains.

In Webb's formulation, the cowboy, as "the first permanent white occupant of the Plains," "had to adapt himself more perfectly because he was without the artificial supports of an established civilization. When he made this perfect adaptation he departed farther and farther from the conventional pattern of men, and as he diverged from the conventional pattern he became more and more unusual: he made better copy for news-writer, artist, and cartoonist." Ironically, with these and similar remarks, Webb himself did much to contribute to the romance and perpetuate the myth.[67]

Webb plainly admired cowboys' "unusual" characteristics. Near the top of his list of admirable traits was the ability to handle a horse. "No one . . . who could not ride a horse was happy in the West, for the reason that he did not fit into a society where everyone rode and had to ride." In Webb's estimation, in fact, horsemanship and association with the horse were at the root of the whole cowboy persona: "Throw fifteen or twenty men who have been selected on the basis of proved courage and skilled horsemanship into one camp, let them live all day in the open air and sunshine, ride horseback fifty or a hundred miles, and wear six-shooters as regularly as they wear hats, and you have a social complex that is a thing apart."[68]

Two distinctive components of this "social complex" were cowboys' bravery and self-reliance. While these are virtues widely admired in individuals, they are less often ascribed, as Webb and western politicians did, to whole groups or classes of persons. (In 1886 Wyoming's Congressman Carey described cowboys as "brave and generous young men.") "The Western man of the old days had little choice but to be courageous," Webb wrote. "The germ of courage had to be in him; but this germ being given, the life that he led developed it to a high degree. Where men are isolated and in constant danger or even potential danger, they will not tolerate the coward." Not everyone agreed with Webb's assessment. Cowboys were not "looked upon with favor" by most residents of Laramie and Cheyenne in the nineteenth century, and Wyoming newspaper-man Bill Nye quipped that one cowboy in twenty was brave when armed.[69]

Webb detected evolutionary principles at work on western ranges. "The great distances and sparse population of the West compelled and engendered self-reliance," he hypothesized. "A process of natural selection went on in the cattle country as it probably did nowhere else on the frontier. . . . [I]t has resulted in a rather distinct type of Western man and in a distinct Western psychology." Following Webb's lead, modern supporters of public land grazing often tout the self-reliance of ranchers in arguing that this way of life should be preserved.[70]

The stuff of legends seems inextricably bound up with Webb's own thinking. Consider his characterization of an easterner's view of a westerner, offered in the course of considering why the West is "considered spectacular and romantic":

> "Ah," said the Easterner, here is a new species of the genus *Homo*. I must observe him carefully and note all his manners and customs and peculiarities. There is something romantic about him. He lives on horseback, as do the Bedouins; he fights on horseback as did the knights of chivalry; he goes armed with a strange new weapon which he uses ambidextrously and precisely; he swears like a trooper, drinks like a fish, wears clothes like an actor, and fights like a devil. He is gracious toward ladies, reserved toward strangers, generous to his friends, and brutal to his enemies. He is a cowboy, *a typical Westerner.*

Webb may have lamented the exaggerated myth of the cowboy and sought to explain it in terms of man's interactions with a new and harsh environment. But given lapses like this, is it any wonder the myth survives?[71]

The courageous, quiet cowboy version of life on the range has been embel-lished and perpetuated by artists and writers down through the years—by western painters and photographers, songwriters and novelists, filmmakers and actors. John Wayne's roles in dozens of Westerns personify the cowboy in the minds of millions of Americans. Other notable myth-makers include Charles M. Russell, Frederic Remington, Owen Wister, Zane Grey, Louis L'Amour, and John Ford; even Ansel Adams has been included among this group. A new generation, which includes transplanted-Wyomingite Gretel Ehrlich, are doing their part to perpetuate the mythical Old West. Writer Tom Wolf notes that, while Ehrlich offers a few new characterizations of westerners as selfless, compassionate, and "androgynous," she also subscribes to all the old, clichéd ones as well—courageous, manly, laconic.[72]

The myth gets fuel from unexpected sources. One such source is "that peculiarly Western institution," the "dude" or guest ranch. Dude ranches have been part of the western scene for more than a century; their popularity was fanned initially by ranch-life aficionados like Teddy Roosevelt. The earliest examples date to the 1870s in Colorado; by 1937 Wyoming alone had 102 guest ranches. Graf pointed out that "some of the most important opponents" of Wyoming's Senator Barrett's proposed disposal of federal grazing lands in the 1940s were the dude ranchers, who saw disposal as "the end of their livelihood." Dude ranchers and conservationists eventually became "active western allies." For instance, the Wyoming Outdoor Council's membership, at least through the mid-1980s, included a significant number of Wyoming dude ranchers.[73]

Dude ranch operations got a big boost in popularity from the 1991 movie *City Slickers*. These resorts—some part working ranch, part vacation experience; others wholly recreational—give a few Americans an opportunity to experience firsthand the culture of the Old West or at least some facsimile of the myth. In many cases, it turns out, dude ranches arguably expose the myth as a fraud. Guests may want to experience a cattle drive, but they seldom yearn to return to a hard bed in a cold bunkhouse for a dinner of hardtack and beans. Accordingly, ranch owners accommodate their patrons, installing private baths and new "period" furnishings in private rooms and developing menus to rival those of the best restaurants in their guests' hometowns. The renovated Vista Verde Ranch in north-central Colorado, for instance, reportedly offers a dinner menu that includes "veal chop *brunoise*, Jamaican jerk shrimp with corn fritters and peach-mango chutney, [and] chocolate-lemon mousse torte"—hardly cowpoke fare. One reporter concludes that "it's the diversity of activities, as much as the [horseback] riding," that attracts many guests. In fact, some ranches "threaten to relegate horses to the petting zoo," favoring instead recreational pursuits and facilities that would have been unimaginable in the "good old days"—rock-climbing, rafting, heated pools, hot-tub therapy, championship golf courses, Nordic and alpine skiing, mountain biking, even hot-air ballooning. One ranch advertises an "upscale Texas experience" and an "excellent wine cellar"; another, in Oregon, boasts its own private elk herd. Lamenting "the decline of a business that is also a way of life," some ranch owners observe that "changes in dude ranching reflect changes in the West itself."[74]

For those who cannot afford to savor the Old West for a week or two at a price of $80 to $270 per day, rodeos and stock shows offer a less costly, but tantalizing, taste. A common, even weekly, summer attraction in many small western towns and an indispensable component of county fairs, rodeos reflect the continuing appeal of the Old West. The endless "rituals of rodeo combat" reflect an "attitude of human domination over nature," Worster writes, and the "cowboy trying to break the independent spirit of the wild horse" is "one of the West's favorite images of itself," showing up even on Wyoming license plates. Worster understates. The bucking bronco shows up *everywhere* in Wyoming.[75]

Many commentators have undertaken to explain—and to debunk—the cowboy myth. William Cronon explains that the real cowboy was not the idealized figure of the cattle drives of the 1860s–80s, which he says spawned the popular image, but simply a hired laborer: "Far from being a loner or rugged individualist, he was a wageworker whose task was to ship meat to the cities. . . ." Montana economics professor Thomas Michael Power describes the cowboy in similar terms, contrasting him with Jefferson's idealized yeoman farmer:

[The cowboy] was not an independent businessperson responsibly managing his land, livestock, and buildings. He was a migrant worker employed by a ranch owner, working for meager wages and engaged in backbreaking labor. It was antisocial, this life of the single male who owned nothing but his saddle, a horse, and a change of clothes, and who had a reputation for barging into western towns disrupting them with his trigger-happy carousing.[76]

Graf further rejects the collective view of western society—"still dominated by the image of the independent cowboy, the ranching family surrounded with its hard-won herds of cattle, and a rural lifestyle"—which he claims is held by easterners. The "reality," which Graf says "was invisible in the popular mind," is that western towns by the 1920s "had streetcar systems, automobile garages, department stores, and movie houses (that also showed Western films)."[77]

The cultural myth of the cowboy and the economic myths of western self-reliance and independence are closely related and replete with contradictions. Contemplating the idealized view that most people still have of the cowboy as "living a life of total freedom in an open country, living in a West beyond restraint," Worster theorized:

Pastoralism has always had that effect on people toiling in fields and cities; though they may see that the herders are often poor, primitive, and uncouth, they nonetheless admire them for their freedom to roam the high mountains, the distant savannahs, the deserts, to possess all the untrammeled freedom of space. In America we have added to that old set of pastoral idealizations some up-to-date ones: our cowboy-rancher somehow has come to stand for the ideal of free enterprise and for the institution of private property.

Given that stockmen began, and public land ranchers still operate, not predominantly with their own land but with land belonging to the American people, this is the most remarkable, most persistent facet of the myth.[78]

This view apparently took root around the turn of the century. According to Graf, it was generally believed that "[o]nly in ranching could the individual operator play a significant role, and so the rancher became the ultimate role model of the region—independent, rugged, oriented to an outdoor life-style that for other western residents was rapidly fading into a myth." In this way the "owner of a small ranch with leased federal land for grazing . . . expresses individualism as success in resource development, and he views restrictive federal regulation as a threat to individual opportunity."[79]

"Western politicians used the myth of the 'Old West' when it served their purpose," Graf observes, "especially when arguing against increased federal controls of the supposedly independent cattle operators." But the "argument seemed not to appear when these proud, independent westerners asked for federal dollars." Schlebecker also rejected the economic independence of ranchers:

> Nothing is so striking in the records of the Plains cattle industry as the divergence between the history and the legend. Cattlemen have always seen themselves as fiercely independent, neither seeking nor receiving help from anyone, and certainly not getting help from the government. They represent themselves, without guile and without deceit, as the last-surviving defenders of ancient American liberties. Oddly, most Americans do not even take offense at these airs. Yet the slightest glance at the record reveals countless efforts by cattlemen to get government help of one sort or another.

Western cattle ranchers "not only endured, they actively sought government intervention in their affairs." In the 1920s, for instance, they

> wanted federal help in controlling tick fever, and foot-and-mouth disease. When credit was hard to get, cattlemen appealed to the government for help, and when packers threatened, cattlemen once again turned to the government. . . . [T]he government brought the railroads under fair control for the cattlemen. [Then, a]s trucks became important, cattlemen insisted on federal and state subsidies for road building, that is, subsidies for truck transportation.[80]

The pattern has not changed; stockgrowers' reliance on federal and, to a lesser extent, state assistance continues to the present. The emergency feed program of the U.S. Department of Agriculture was a prime example. Until 1997 program benefits were available to private or public lands ranchers. In 1996 Congress suspended the program for the 1997 through 2002 crop years. Program expenditures had ranged from $100 to $500 million annually. Ranchers in New Mexico (more than half of whom participated) received annual cash payments averaging $4,000 each, which was "about 15 percent of their ranching income." Payments to Oregon ranchers averaged $11,000. Karl Hess, Jr., and Jerry L. Holechek reported that *every* rancher in the area of Vale, Oregon, received $30,000–$50,000 in emergency feed payments in 1994. According to the writers, those payments—which were "to make up for the grass that their overgrazed public and private ranges could not grow"—reflected the ultimate failure of a $56 million federal program to reclaim Vale district BLM lands that were overgrazed by 40 percent by 1963.[81]

To be fair, financial dependence on the federal government applies not just to ranchers but, to a significant extent, to the West as a whole. Extrapolated regionally, the myth of economic independence becomes even more strained. As Graf observed, western politicians' claims of independence never got in the way when the region sought federal funds "to build dams and roads or to fund Civilian Conservation Corps activities." Graf noted that by 1980, "for every tax dollar sent to Washington, the West received $1.20 in return." Leshy relates that,

> when the Attorney General of Nevada came calling on the Department of the Interior [in 1979] shortly after the Nevada legislature had officially claimed ownership of the federal public lands within its borders, he was concerned not with developing an orderly method for testing the constitutionality of the claim, but rather with obtaining assurance that federal payments based on federal title would continue to flow uninterrupted by Nevada's claim that it, and not the federal government, owned these lands.[82]

A prime example of westerners "on the dole" is Catron County, New Mexico—a hotbed of county supremacists, "Wise Use" proponents, and advocates of the "Cowboy Way." According to a report in *High Country News*, "Catron County is a national leader in attracting food stamps, Social Security, and other transfer payments from the federal government." Citing census records showing that county residents "took in $3,224 per person in such payments in 1994," the reporter asserted: "That's $500 per person higher than the national norm and $800 per person higher than the New Mexico average." On the whole, the federal government injects $6,500 into the local economy for each of its citizens. The county is poor; 25 percent lived below the poverty line in 1990. "The county has always lived off grass, trees, and minerals," he wrote, "and today those natural resources are in terrible shape." One consequence is that the "vast majority of Catron County ranchers [have taken] second jobs." Federal subsidies amount to about $1,000 annually to each rancher; they include payments for range improvements, such as fences and tanks; "hundreds of thousands of dollars' worth" of emergency feed payments annually to Catron and neighboring Grant County; and "flood and drought payments, sometimes in the same year."[83]

Numerous commentators have been blunt, if not bilious, in exposing the West's self-sufficiency charade. In the 1980s Edward Abbey dubbed western cattlemen "welfare parasites." George Will suggested that "a welfare mother is the soul of self-reliance compared to a westerner who receives federally subsidized range privileges, water, and various benefits." Jon Margolis was especially caustic in denouncing westerners' airs of independence and self-sufficiency:

> Western denial takes the form of claiming to be the fiercest individualists and the truest believers in free enterprise. Actually, the whole region is on the dole. Its economic system is America's only venture into state socialism, a uniquely American brand of socialism, which protects only the strong and wealthy. Half the cities of the West (it's a desert, folks), would be tiny villages were it not for federal water projects.[84]

Margolis is not the only writer to ascribe communist or socialist attributes to the western economy or to the federal system of issuing grazing permits. Robert H. Nelson called government intervention in forage production "a virtual pocket of socialism maintained in the U.S. market system." Foss, Worster, and Power have made similar observations. Stockmen themselves vehemently opposed the Forest Service "redistribution" policy of the 1930s and 1940s, by which large grazing permits were reduced to make room for new, small operators, calling it "pure socialism." Ironically, as Bernard DeVoto noted, the "western stockmen viewed themselves as the great defenders of free enterprise against the 'communism' of government interference. Yet they constantly called for government tariff protection from Argentina and government improvement of the rangelands for their benefit."[85]

Another important tenet of the myth is that ranching is an economic mainstay of the West and western communities. Like the notions of independence and self-sufficiency, this too is a delusion (explored further in chapter 8). Across the West, tourism vastly surpasses ranching in generating jobs and revenues. But this inconvenient fact does not dissuade myth proponents. Officials of four Big Horn Basin, Wyoming, counties, for instance, wrote in a letter to BLM that "Wyoming must have cowboys, cows and sheep to be of value to tourists." They could have been reading the manual prepared by the Wyoming Department of Commerce in the 1930s, which urged Wyoming residents "to wear 'real western garb during the tourist season,' and to 'give our guests what they expect.'" Even one prominent range scientist has asserted: "Tourists flock to the West because the cowboy was once king. Most people identify with this cowboy, and the past has a positive effect on the present." He did not identify the "positive effect." Plainly, the western myth appeals to tourists and helps explain the popularity of dude ranches, rodeos, and similar attractions. But tourism in the West depends much more heavily on other amenities, some of which, notably water quality and aesthetics, are seriously jeopardized by cows and cowboys.[86]

Historian Ann Fabian offers an explanation for the western chamber-of-commerce view, typified by the Big Horn officials' comments: the "popular history of the West has become an industry in its own right, an industry with an economics and history of its own." She cites clothing designer and New York native Ralph Lauren as an example. Lauren has "elaborat[ed] on the Marlboro Man" in his perfume for men, "Chaps," and in his clothing, which offers what people *perceive* to be the way one dresses in the West. Lauren started his clothing line, Fabian notes, because he couldn't find a snap-button, western shirt in Denver. According to Fabian: "Like pioneers before him and like the pioneer entrepreneurs of western images—Theodore Roosevelt, Owen Wister, and Frederic Remington—Lauren used the West to market himself." In much the same way, ranchers today market themselves and their romanticized "way of life" in an attempt to keep alive a subindustry that by rights should have foundered long ago.[87]

Power, an outspoken critic of the West's natural resource–based economic policies, has given considerable attention to the connection between economics and culture in the myth of the Old West. He describes old-line policymakers' views as an "exercise in nostalgia." In his opinion, the strongest argument for government support of these industries, which include grazing, is the cultural argument: "'It's about protecting a way of life.'" "'The question,' he says, 'is whether taxpayers will tolerate supporting the Western culture.'" A more fundamental question, however, is whether the "way of life" still exists or, indeed, whether it ever existed in the form in which it is embraced today.[88]

Columnist Ed Quillen's rejection of cowboy mythology goes beyond denigrating the economic importance of agriculture or ranching or other traditional natural resource–based industries. He asserts that the western "myth is so strong" that it actually "transcends economic self-interest" and points to former president Ronald Reagan's policies, which led to high unemployment and greatly reduced prices for many natural resource commodities. "Reaganomics" was "worse than cruel to the Mountain West," Quillen charges. But did the West rebel? "Of course not. Reagan wore a cowboy hat, rode a horse and said all the right things about gun control and rugged individualism. His share of the West's vote rose from 62 percent in 1980 to 66 percent in 1984."[89]

Like Power, Graf, and others, Quillen describes the mythical West as "a land of small family farms, skillful artisans and wholesome little towns, all populated by the descendants of courageous rugged-individualist pioneers who moved into a vast empty space without any help from that pernicious government in Washington." But Quillen's demythologization has a different twist. He claims that Republicans created the myth and exploit it by claiming that their "founding ideology somehow took root" in the Mountain West.

> That mythology persists in every Republican campaign in the West, from the good ol' boy seventh-generation rancher running for county commissioner to Jack Kemp in Grand Junction, Colo., last fall, pledging to end the Clinton administration's "War on the West."

The GOP mythology comports with the way Westerners like to think of themselves, as rural individualists taking control of their own destinies and not as urban flotsam bobbing with the ebbs and flows of global markets. Anything that stands in the way of implementing that myth, such as public control of public land, is deemed an attack on the West.

Quillen might have been thinking of the announcement by Senator Orrin Hatch (R-Utah), opposing range reforms proposed in 1993 by the Clinton administration: "The Old West is still alive. The Old West is still here. And a lot of us belong to it."[90]

Quillen's hypothesis has intuitive appeal. Stockgrowers and their advocates, by and large, are Republican. "At least 80 percent of the stockmen [in Wyoming] have been Republicans," according to Larson. Environmentalists, perhaps grazing policy critics especially, tend not to be Republicans. The expression "War on the West" was coined by Republicans intent on undoing, or at least making political hay from, the Democratic Clinton administration's economic and environmental policies in the West—most of which do not fit the myth.[91]

Despite the early "virtual extinction of the Jeffersonian farmer" and his independence (the 1880 census revealed that more than 25 percent of farms and farm acreage were operated by tenants), the myth persisted, clung to by farmers and ranchers and their promoters. A lingering "reverence" for the imagined role of small farms and ranches as feeding America and forming the foundation of small towns and rural communities continues to induce Congress both to subsidize agriculture and to exempt it from environmental regulation.[92]

This reverence reflects a religious dimension of the western myth, traceable to the view that Jefferson's yeoman farmers were "the chosen people of God." Small farmers and stockraisers were idealized, if not idolized. BLM director Clawson explained that the Jeffersonian ideal, "that of the yeoman farmer, economically and politically independent and free, tilling his own plot of land," was the "moral underpinning of the free soil free land movements of the mid-nineteenth century." Religion, of course, inspired much of western settlement; in the American mind, religion and agriculture were partners in the inevitable expansion. Land speculator Charles Dana's 1881 exhortation to settlers is illustrative: "To those who possess the divine faculty of hope—the optimists of our times—it will always be a source of pleasure to understand that the Creator never imposed a perpetual desert upon the earth, but, on the contrary, has so endowed it that man, by the plow, can transform it, in any country, into farm areas." Cattlemen, too, were convinced that they could "transform" deserts, by making them produce meat and fiber, and they claimed, though (as we saw in chapter 1) they were not always accorded, a kinship with Jefferson's yeoman farmers.[93]

Many western settlers, including ranchers, saw their mission as approved, if not directed, by the Almighty. Webb wrote that cattlemen "accepted the country as God made it, and wanted to keep it in the hands of 'God, the government, and us.'" Ronald Reagan may have had this appeal in mind when he nominated William Clark to the post of interior secretary, describing him as "'a God-fearing Westerner [and] fourth-generation rancher.'" The favored status of stockmen was caricaturized by Dr. S. W. McClure in an address to the 1932 national woolgrowers' convention. Pointing out that "Almighty God singled out men who were representing your industry, to tell the world that a new Savior was born," he proceeded to devote the first half of his address to why God had selected shepherds instead of some other group (lawyers, the Forest Service, the secretary of agriculture, etc.) to be the recipients of the "good news."[94]

Graf has suggested that religious motivations play a broad role in western resource politics generally. One explanation for this may be growing influence of the Mormon Church (Church of Jesus Christ of Latter-Day Saints, LDS). Graf recounted a League for the Advancement of States' Equal Rights conference held in Salt Lake City in 1980, at which Utah's Senator Hatch "compared the mission of the sagebrush rebels with the mission of Mormon pioneer leader Brigham Young" and "placed the [sagebrush] rebellion in the mainstream of Mormon history as a logical outgrowth of God's command to subdue the earth." The chief proponents of the Sagebrush Rebellion of 1979–81 were stockmen and their political representatives, many of them Mormon. According to Graf, both Hatch and former Utah senator Jake Garn

> in part derived their conservative values regarding public land and its management from their religion; both were Mormons. . . . In the LDS religion there is great emphasis on productivity in all respects, including economic productivity related to the land. Preservation of natural areas without economic conversion of their resources to economic benefits to humans is largely antithetical to the Mormon philosophy. The religion, which dominates Utah politics, also has a long tradition of antifederalism dating from the 1850s when federal troops were sent to Salt Lake City to enforce federal demands on the territory, which was then an LDS theocracy.[95]

Many would agree that Utah is still "basically a Mormon theocracy" and that official attitudes toward the environment have not changed. State decisions about wildlife management have been attributed to church dogma. For instance, the state wildlife agency has been criticized for pouring research funds into studying economically important species (especially brine shrimp, which support a multimillion-dollar business), while ignoring jeopardized fauna (e.g., amphibians) that have little or no market value. A disgruntled scientist complained: "[I]f these species aren't important to leaders of the theocracy—if they can't benefit from them financially—they won't be of any importance to the people down below. . . . It doesn't matter how much you wreck the environment on earth because everything will be rosy in heaven."[96]

The pervasiveness of Mormon thinking in Utah politics also surfaced in a congressional hearing in late 1997 on a Utah wilderness bill. Attacking the Southern Utah Wilderness Alliance (SUWA) for taking a position on "the extreme polar edge of this debate" and for using "extreme words" like "breathtaking wildlands," Utah's new congressman Chris Cannon (R) began to question SUWA legal director Heidi McIntosh about her qualifications: "'Can you give me a little bit of background about yourself personally? You know, you mentioned you were raised in the West. What part of the West, what your beliefs are, what your religion is possibly? An idea of where you derive your views from that you are representing here?'" He was roundly chastised in the *Deseret News*, a major Salt Lake City newspaper, for his "McCarthy-esque" grilling of McIntosh. The editorial "noted that the 'clear presumption of [Cannon's question] is that he wanted to establish that she—and by association the group she represents—is outside Utah's mainstream . . . [t]he implication: if you're not Mormon, you're not credible.'" Cannon subsequently apologized to McIntosh.[97]

Not all westerners or even all western ranchers are Mormon, but the LDS Church's membership would surprise many. It is large and growing. In fact, by 1990, the LDS Church was the largest religious organization in Utah and Idaho, the second largest in Arizona, California, Nevada, Oregon, Washington, and Wyoming, and third largest in New Mexico. Note that of the ten states containing BLM lands targeted by the conservation strategy proposed in this book this list omits only Colorado. Membership growth has exceeded even the church's own projections and has led sociologists Rodney Stark and D. Michael Quinn to predict that "non-Mormons in the West will become increasingly isolated religiously." The church's growth also has implications for western resource politics and policy making. Stephen R. Kellert pointed out nearly twenty years ago the "need for greater management recognition and understanding of the religious factor, particularly in situations where major land-use decisions affect regions of strong and traditional religious activity."[98]

Most non-Mormon westerners reportedly are "unchurched," meaning they claim no religious affiliation or do not attend any church regularly. In fact, "65 to 80 percent of the West's adult population . . . has historically shunned formal religion." They are, by and large, "believers," however. Sources suggest that their religious views come principally from reading the Bible. The biblical origins of dominionistic attitudes have been widely studied and discussed. The seminal work is Lynn White, Jr.'s essay "The Historical Roots of Our Ecologic Crisis." Drawing from White's work, Roderick Nash has argued that exploiting nature is acceptable in the Judeo-Christian tradition. "'Christianity,'" he writes, "'is the most anthropocentric religion the world has ever seen.'" According to Nash, Christians (a diverse group that includes Mormons) believe that humans are the masters of nature. As did White and others, Nash points for support to

Genesis, which reveals that man was created in God's image, that God directed man to "be fruitful and multiply, and fill the earth and subdue it; and have dominion over the fish of the sea and over the birds of the air and over every living thing that moves upon the earth." God reaffirmed this mandate, when, after the flood, He gave to Noah all living creatures. "Human dominion, in other words, was complete and unqualified."[99]

White argued that "for nearly two thousand years . . . people used Scripture to justify the exploitation of nature in the same way that defenders of slavery used it to justify ownership and exploitation of certain classes of humans." Even though he was writing as a historian, he was condemned as a "heretic," Nash observes, for assertions such as these. Nash finds support for White's view in the "original significance of the language employed in the Bible." He examines the "two operative verbs" in the early Genesis passage: the Hebrew words "'*kabash*,' translated as 'subdue,' and '*radah*,' rendered as 'have dominion over,' or 'rule.'" According to Nash, both words are used throughout the Old Testament to "signify a violent assault or crushing," to convey the image "of a conqueror placing his foot on the neck of a defeated enemy, exerting absolute dominion." Moreover, both are also used to refer to enslavement. The alternate, more modern interpretation of "dominion" in terms of exercising "stewardship" is inapt, Nash argues, in the context of Genesis.[100]

The modern construction to which Nash refers is embraced by a new religious-environmental movement, known as the "evangelical environmental movement," which arose in 1993 and is founded upon the so-called National Religious Partnership for the Environment. The movement's approach to biblical teachings and environmental issues is stewardship-oriented. According to an evangelical Christian minister, "the environment is a biblical matter" to movement members. There is little evidence that the movement is active in the West, despite a bumper sticker occasionally seen in western communities, which proclaims, "And on the 8th day God created ranchers to care for all His other creatures." Two western congressmen, Don Young (R-Alaska) and Richard Pombo (R-California), reportedly suggested that "the evangelicals were a 'front group' for President Clinton's re-election campaign." A journal article describing the movement had little or nothing to report about the movement in the West. Conservative political commentator Rush Limbaugh's assertion that "'no environmentalist can be a Christian, and vice versa,'" suggests that conservative western Republicans—his ideological colleagues—are not likely to subscribe to evangelical environmental views.[101]

White distinguished the attitudes of early American settlers, who were predominantly Christians, toward animals and the natural world from those held by Native Americans. According to White, "'by destroying pagan animism, Christianity made it possible to exploit nature in a mood of indifference to the feelings of natural objects.'" American Indians were animists; they believed that all animals and elements of nature had spirits and personalities. Nash is quick to point out that these "first Americans were not 'ecological saints'—but there is little doubt that they accepted more restraints in their relationship to their environment than did the people who displaced them." Clements's model of vegetative succession similarly distinguished between Indians and European settlers: while the Indian "belonged with the other animals in the ecological community," the white settler was "a complicating presence that overturned or disobeyed natural laws." Nash quotes Lakota Sioux Luther Standing Bear's view that it was "better to hunt wild creatures" because "herding 'enslaved the animal' and deprived it of its basic rights: 'the right to live, the right to multiply, the right to freedom.'" Standing Bear's view, and the Indian view of animals generally, contrasts particularly starkly with the views of ranchers and farmers.[102]

The familiar passage of Genesis to which White, Nash, and others have referred describes, if it is not the actual source of, the "attitude of human domination over nature" commonly included in the cowboy image. A utilitarian, mastery-over-nature attitude, along with its biblical roots, is considered fundamental to the Wise Use Movement in the West, in which livestock and other commodity interests are prominent. According to University of Colorado geography professor William Riebsame, ranchers hold the attitude "that humans have an obligation to improve on nature, a sort of 'theory of necessary human intervention.'" This is a more manipulative version of the "Jeffersonian faith" of the 1930s to 1940s that "the farmer is nature's ally, if not her benefactor." For instance, Riebsame notes, ranchers are "proud of having created water sources for cattle and wildlife where none previously existed." Ranchers further "see livestock grazing as necessary to maintain healthy rangeland," and they consider "quaint and illogical" the "notions [of environmentalists] that nature is best left . . . alone."[103]

Clayton Koppes reports similar opinions among turn-of-the-century Americans. Influenced by "a combination of economic incentives and religious constraints, [they] felt a virtual compulsion to convert unclaimed natural resources into productive goods." Even the early explorers, fascinated by vast, uncharted territories, subscribed to the notion that western landscapes were unproductive in their natural state. Limerick quotes Frémont's "musings" about the "sterile and barren" Great Basin, which, he also wrote, was nevertheless "oddly life-filled, stocked with its own adapted flora and fauna." "A 'barren spot' filled with plants?" Limerick queries rhetorically before answering her own question: "One realizes that this is a specialized version of the word: the desert was 'barren' by virtue of the absence of familiar and useful plants, especially forage for domestic animals, and by virtue of the lack of a continuous ground cover." Ranchers have always argued that ranges are worthless and wasted if not grazed.[104]

A formal survey in the late 1970s of attitudes of livestock operators and others toward nature and animals corroborated the utilitarian and dominionistic tendencies of agriculturists. In 1984 Hays called this research, conducted for the U.S. Fish and Wildlife Service (USFWS) by Stephen Kellert of the Yale School of Forestry, "one of the most extensive studies of environmental values which has yet taken place in the United States." The study consisted of an in-depth, national survey (conducted and reported in phases) of adult Americans' attitudes toward animals, wildlife, and natural habitat issues and of their activities relating to animals. In addition to the nationwide survey, mail questionnaires were sent to randomly selected members of the National Cattlemen's Association (NCA) and American Sheep Producers Council to ensure that the opinions of those "important groups" would be adequately represented.[105]

Among the findings of greatest interest here was the following description of livestock producers, including ranchers:

> A highly pragmatic orientation towards animals among Association livestock producers [i.e., members of the National Cattlemen's Association and American Sheep Producers Council] was reflected in extremely high utilitarian scores . . . , twice the next highest scoring activity group. Additionally, Association livestock producers appeared to strongly support the notion of human mastery and control over nature, as suggested by very high dominionistic scores. Perhaps relatedly, cattle and sheep producers had by far the lowest moralistic scores of any activity group, clearly indicating their relative lack of objection to human exploitation of animals.

The researchers continued: "What appeared to be a generally unsentimental and highly pragmatic orientation to animals among livestock raisers was further suggested by quite low humanistic and comparatively high negativistic scores. Moderately high naturalistic and ecologistic scores, however, indicated general interest in wildlife and some support for an ecological perspective of natural resources."[106]

Kellert and his colleagues provided a one-sentence definition of each attitude type and cited references for more detailed descriptions. "Utilitarian" describes those persons whose "primary concern [is] for the practical and material value of animals or the animal's habitat." A "dominionistic" attitude is characterized as a "primary interest in the mastery and control of animals." "Negativistic" refers to an "active avoidance of animals due to indifference, dislike or fear." The "primary concern" of people with "moralistic" attitudes is "for the right and wrong treatment of animals, with strong opposition to exploitation or cruelty towards animals."[107]

For the most part, the investigators found it difficult to evaluate occupational differences; that is, demographic factors other than occupation tended to be more significant. The "[o]ne occupational group which did stand out was farmers." Like the narrower sample group of livestock producer association members, this group had very high utilitarian, dominionistic, and negativistic scores; very low moralistic and endangered species protection scores; relatively low naturalistic and knowledge scores; and the lowest humanistic scores of any demographic group. These scores were reflected by "non-emotional pragmatism and mastery-over-nature attitudes," a "pronounced lack of sympathy for most cruelty and animal protection concerns," a "limited interest in wildlife, the outdoors, or animals in general," and an "emotionally detached view of animals."[108]

Having lived in several rural and small town areas of the West and worked on federal natural resource issues for more than twenty-five years, I found the results of the livestock group attitude survey right on target. I would add that ranchers "moderately high naturalistic and ecologistic scores" might be attributable to a selective interest in wildlife—principally game species—and a knowledge of wild animals, particularly predators, that stems from their efforts to avoid or combat predation and to lobby state and federal agencies and legislatures for increased control. Another portion of the USFWS study tends to support this assessment.[109]

The researchers observed that the attitudes of ranchers toward nature and wildlife may pose serious obstacles to promoting effective wildlife management on an important segment of this country's private lands. Their recommended solution was that "new incentives and methods [be] developed to enhance greater appreciation and a more protectionistic ethic toward wildlife among farmers." In light of their finding that education is one of the most crucial factors in Americans' attitudes toward animals, with more highly educated persons showing a greater willingness to protect endangered wildlife, I found it curious that they did not expressly advise greater attention to educational efforts.[110]

Kellert turned to White's hypotheses for insights into the possible reasons for differences among Americans' attitudes toward animals and nature. Kellert's survey found that respondents "who rarely or never attended religious services had among the highest knowledge scores" concerning wildlife; they possessed "considerably greater affective interest and cognitive understanding of animals." In contrast, respondents who participated once a week or more in formal religious activities "had very low knowledge scores." Respondents who "rarely or never attended religious services" had among the highest naturalistic and humanistic scores; they also "scored far higher on the moralistic and lower on the utilitarian [and dominionistic] scales than respondents who attended services at least once a week." Kellert suggested that that these findings were enlightened by "the importance of the anthropocentric Western religious tradition emphasizing the notion of a single God endowed with human image and characteristics, and the related belief that only man possesses the capacities for reason and immortality."[111]

Christian views of both Mormons and the "unchurched" have been influential in shaping and maintaining "homogeneous or communal social orders" in many parts of the West. Religious beliefs also affect how land has been and continues to be used. Rowley points to "the Mormon desire to hold the family together," which he says has "resulted in dividing and subdividing the family lands. The pressure to support an increasing ranch population resulted in overgrazed ranges and impaired watersheds." While the early Mormon Church apparently did not officially sanction such land abuse, the practical effect of church teachings regarding the family, combined with a rapidly growing population, was severe overuse of the land, resulting in its impoverishment in less than twenty years. Regardless of the source of utilitarian and dominionistic attitudes toward the environment, they can be fostered or extended by a declining resource base and by increasing population or demand pressures.[112]

Perhaps it is in the natural order of things that the same qualities and factors that contribute to ranchers' presence as a political force and, arguably, as a cultural group have also triggered antipathy from those outside the fold. Ranchers' political influence, and their popularity or mystique in the abstract, also seems to have spawned mistrust, animosity, and resentment. This paradox is not only a recent phenomenon.

As we saw in chapter 1, in the eyes of many homesteaders, easterners, and conservationists, the early livestock industry consisted of "cattle barons," range monopolists, and even "barbarians." As Wyoming's Senator Warren put it, "eastern people" believed that, in the chain of human evolution and development, ranchers "represent the first link, away out on the end of the chain next to the uncivilized Indian, the first link in that long line of links that connect the aborigine with those away down on the other end that are the most intelligent [and] most educated." Warren was being facetious, but the deepseatedness of such sentiments is evident in an 1887 newspaper editorial, which proclaimed: "'[A]t no period of the world's history has any nation or people who devoted themselves exclusively to stock-raising ever risen much above semi-barbarism.'" This rhetoric is even more remarkable in view of the forum—Wyoming, bastion of the range ranch industry. Even Teddy Roosevelt, who idolized ranchers and cowboys and lauded their way of life, described ranching as a "'primitive' industry, . . . 'an iron age that the old civilized world has passed by.'"[113]

Ironically, it was the widely respected "sturdy pioneer spirit of self-help and independence" of the early ranchers—which "found expression in such methods" as exclusionary fencing and violence and which resulted in social conflict and "serious destruction of the range through overgrazing"—that gave rise to much antiranching sentiment. Similarly, the ideals of private property and free enterprise, tarnished in practice in the ranching business, evoked widespread opposition to ranchers. Bernard DeVoto's excoriating criticism of stockmen, paraphrased here by Gates, illustrates these conflicts and contradictions:

They kept out the homesteader by terror or bankrupted him if he could not be otherwise eliminated, squeezed out the small stockman by grabbing the water rights and even resorting to murder. Though they owned but a minute fraction of the range they convinced themselves that it was theirs and tried to gain title through the final liquidation of the public domain. They paid in fees only a small part of the value of the forage; in effect, they received a subsidy from the Federal Treasury. Worst of all, they plundered the public lands by overgrazing, destroying the natural forage and leaving only desert areas covered with weeds unfit for forage.[114]

The early enmity between ranchers and their neighbors has been widely documented. Scott described several "devious and illegal methods" that ranchers employed to monopolize the range in the pre–Taylor Act era: land law frauds; "use of force . . . to scare farmers and settlers"; offering to "buy a farmer out, and [then] destroy[ing] his crops if he refused"; "appropriat[ing] the stray cattle of the small rancher, who had no power to retaliate, [forcing him] to leave an area if he were to keep his herd intact"; claim-jumping by falsely contesting claims of settlers; controlling scarce water supplies by various methods, crude and elaborate; and, through their control of legislatures, passing laws relieving stock-growers from liability for damage to crops unless farmers fenced their lands, which they could not afford to do. Newspapers at the turn of the century carried stories of the conflicts between cattle and sheep interests, noting the violence particularly by the former, including shootings, ambushes, and destruction of sheep herds. In one incident, cattlemen lynched two homesteaders, one of them a woman, for filing on federal land on which they ran their stock.[115]

Although western lawlessness has been exaggerated in the legend, the use or threat of violence by some westerners to defend their perceived rights and way of life is not as rare an occurrence as readers might suspect. Violence directed against the federal government actually increased throughout the West in the 1990s. BLM records document one such incident in 1991 (a confrontation with a rancher), eight in 1992, and thirty-two in 1993. Recent episodes include bombings of national forest campground facilities, a Forest Service official's vehicle parked at his home, and both BLM and Forest Service offices. Other, arguably lesser incidents included illegally developing or fencing springs on public lands and bulldozing roads into wildernesses or wilderness study areas. The perpetrator of one such escapade, a Nevada county commissioner and alleged militia member, filed a criminal complaint against the Forest Service official who had ordered him not to blade the road. He subsequently got his picture on the cover of *Time* magazine.[116]

Many of these incidents have been linked to the Wise Use and/or County Supremacy Movements, which can be seen as reincarnations of the Sagebrush Rebellion of 1979. Ranchers now as then are especially active in the movements, whose proponents openly defy federal authority over public lands and oppose most environmental regulation. The National Cattlemen's Association was a founding organization of the county movement. Others included the American Mining Congress, the National Rifle Association, and the American Motor-cyclists Association. Not long after the Sagebrush Rebellion fizzled out, Utah conservationists were dragged in effigy up and down the streets of Escalante, Utah, and then hung, for protesting nearby timber sales in an unroaded area of scenic Boulder Mountain. One of these conservation leaders also received numerous death threats, one of which was accompanied by a pistol shoved in his face. A Moab rancher told him that "if it had been me over there [in Escalante], you'd have been dead a long time ago."[117]

The Don Oman story mentioned earlier also had a violent dimension. As related by Sharman Apt Russell in *Kill the Cowboy*, Oman was the target of a variety of threats and innuendo, all originating with local ranchers. The harass-ment ranged from outright threats by grazing permit holders to "cut his throat" if they "could get him alone," to suggestions that he'd have a "wreck" or an "accident" if he did not clear out of the district or desist from enforcing agency grazing regulations. Russell reports that the Fergusons' experiences in Oregon were similar. After speaking out about the effects of livestock overgrazing on the Malheur National Wildlife Refuge and urging that stocking rates be reduced, the couple were thrown out of a community social event and advised to be "out of the county" by a certain day or they would be "dead." They received harassing and threatening phone calls from livestock owners and even ranchers' children, and the local and state cattle producers' organizations sought to get them dismissed from their refuge jobs. In the face of examples such as these, it is difficult to shrug off Margolis's accusation that westerners react with whining or violence when their lifestyle is threatened by "outsiders" or the government.[118]

More recently, the antagonism has taken on a different look. In 1997 in Elko County, Nevada, a grand jury was convened to investigate and prosecute federal land managers essentially for doing their jobs. A court later ruled the jury unconstitutional. Certain federal grazing permittees in Nevada and New Mexico have openly defied federal authority, refusing to heed Forest Service or BLM orders to remove their livestock from allotments. Both federal agencies now provide their employees wallet-sized instructions, outlining what to do if they are arrested.[119]

Westerners' antifederal sentiments and their tendencies to violence may feed on the political rhetoric that developed during the 104th Congress. Western Republican senators began using the expression "War on the West" to describe what they perceived as the insensitiveness of federal policies (particularly envi-ronmental and economic policies) to westerners' needs and autonomy, especially in the area of property rights. One is reminded of Webb's defense of stockmen's lawlessness and violence in the late 1800s as traceable, at least in part, to the government's failure to pass and enforce sensible laws that took account of the West's unique circumstances. Former BLM director Baca, less sympathetic, chastises these modern western senators for their inflammatory rhetoric. While stopping short of blaming them for the surge in militia popularity and activity in western states, he warns that the "'War on the West' battle cry" "doesn't do any good." "When elected officials use that language," "it means something." One of the senators to whom Baca referred, Larry Craig (R-Idaho), asserted that "agents" of the federal agencies "should be disarmed because they frighten the people of the West. 'There has always been a healthy suspicion of the federal agent,' the Associated Press quoted Craig. 'Now there is developing a healthy fear especially if the agent is armed.'"[120]

Predator control provides additional evidence of ranchers' violent methods; it certainly reflects their attitudes toward the environment and many of the animals with which they share the landscape. Worster noted western sheepmen's "almost metaphysical hatred" for coyotes and wolves. Predator control programs can also be viewed as a manifestation of the "state socialism" to which Margolis referred.[121]

Long and widely conducted in support of farming and grazing operations, predator control has depended on poisoning, trapping, shooting, and other measures. Government control of "undesirable" animals began in this country with bounties on wolves during colonial times. Since then animal damage control efforts have targeted myriad pest species and "varmints," from coyotes and wolves to sparrows and even seals. Throughout the early 1900s, Merrill reports, "western ranchers called on the government to help them exterminate" these nuisances from the public lands. "The government was doing nothing to 'clean up' its own lands, they argued." Ranchers accused the government of engaging "in the breeding of wolves and coyotes that destroy these useful animals," cattle and sheep.[122]

The government took heed of the industry's demands. In 1915 the federal Bureau of Biological Survey (which, not accidentally, was housed in the Department of Agriculture) was assigned responsibility for predator control. Within two years the agency had 175 to 300 hunters and trappers in the field, depending on the season, in the western states and boasted of an impressive kill record:

> 980 gray wolves, over 34,000 coyotes, about 110 bob-cats besides several stock-killing silver-tipped grizzly bears. . . . There is little question that in five years we can destroy most of the gray wolves and greatly reduce the numbers of other predatory animals. In New Mexico we have destroyed more than fifty percent of the gray wolves and expect to get the other fifty percent in the next two or three years.[123]

In 1931 Congress passed the Animal Damage Control (ADC) Act, which authorized the secretary of agriculture to "conduct campaigns for the destruction of" any "animals injurious to agriculture, horticulture, forestry, animal husbandry, wild game animals, fur-bearing animals, and birds," including "mountain lions, wolves, coyotes, bobcats, prairie dogs, gophers, ground squirrels, [and] jack rabbits." According to Merrill, the act helped establish a "close working relationship" between stockmen and federal animal damage control officials "that continues to this day."[124]

The language of the ADC Act makes it plain that neither Congress nor agricultural interests were concerned about extirpating species. All animals, even all wildlife species, clearly were not viewed as having equal value. Game animals and furbearers, for instance, were worthy of at least limited protection, while predators and certain rodents warranted "destruction." From 1937 through 1983 the federal animal damage control program was responsible for killing approximately 26,000 bears, 500,000 bobcats, 3.7 million coyotes, 50,000 red wolves, 1,600 gray wolves, and 8,000 mountain lions. Such "campaigns" were authorized on private lands as well as national forests and the public domain. Federal funding for the taking of red wolves continued until 1964; for gray wolves, until 1971. Both, of course, are listed as endangered species today. The coyote has proved much more resilient. Although it is still widely, even indiscriminately, hunted, its numbers are apparently secure and its range more extensive than ever.[125]

The federal government has not been alone in conducting "campaigns for the destruction" of animals considered "injurious to agriculture." Ranchers and farmers have participated on both public and private lands. The prairie dog may be the best example. With its historic habitat reduced by 98 percent, populations of this rodent have been decimated. Privately organized "Varmint Militias" such as that convened recently near Wray, Colorado, "for two days of shooting prairie dogs on local ranches" are not uncommon where "dogs" still exist. Privately organized coyote hunts are also popular; a prize is offered to the participant who kills the greatest number of animals. Over the years, animal damage control "campaigns" have often taken on the appearance of war games or even religious crusades.[126]

A portion of Kellert's studies for the U.S. Fish and Wildlife Service investigated and contrasted attitudes toward animal damage control held by four groups: informed and uninformed segments of the general public, sheep producers, and cattlemen. Respondents were asked to register their level of approval for each of various coyote control options. Nearly all stockgrowers—96 percent of sheep producers and 94 percent of cattlemen—approved of shooting or trapping as many coyotes as possible, while only 38 and 44 percent, respectively, of the informed and uninformed general public registered such approval. Asked whether they would approve "poisoning, because it is the least expensive solution even though other animals besides coyotes may be killed," 75 and 70 percent of sheep producers and cattle ranchers said yes. Only 8 and 10 percent of the informed and uninformed general public agreed.[127]

Questioned about the alternative of hunting whenever possible "only individual coyotes known to have killed livestock," 71 and 77 percent of the informed and uninformed public approved of this control method, but only 43 and 52 percent of the sheep and cattle producers approved. The option of using general tax revenues to pay ranchers for sheep losses, rather than to kill coyotes, was approved by only 25, 26, 11, and 7 percent, respectively, of the informed and uninformed general public, sheep producers, and cattlemen. These last results, viewed in the context of the results on other control option questions, suggest to me that the general public respondents should have been asked whether they would approve of a "do nothing" predator policy.[128]

The investigators noted that sheep and cattle producers "constituted just about the only group in the entire study to favor poisoning as a control strategy" and that "differences between the general public and livestock producers on the poisoning and shooting/trapping control options were among the greatest of any found in the study." Remarkably, 81 percent of cattle producers and 72 percent of sheep producers found "nothing wrong" with "farmers shooting golden eagles if the eagles kill their sheep." The report did not indicate whether respondents were advised that shooting eagles was prohibited by federal law, but association members surely were aware of this fact.[129]

Asked whether "cattle and sheep grazing should be limited on publicly owned lands if it destroys plants needed by wildlife, even though this may result in higher meat costs," 60 percent of the general population answered affirmatively, while only 41 and 26 percent, respectively, of sheep and cattle producers agreed. Thirty-three percent of cattlemen strongly disagreed that grazing should be limited in such circumstances. Consistent with their utilitarian attitudes, "[l]ivestock producers significantly opposed reductions in livestock grazing allotments to increase recreation or hunting [65% and 68% opposed, respectively], but nearly 70% supported this change to increase timber production."[130]

The researchers concluded that "livestock producers indicated significantly more negative views toward predators or predatory omnivores. [T]he only two animals which received relatively positive ratings from livestock producers were two exclusively herbivorous animals, the white-tailed deer and the pronghorn antelope."[131]

Kellert's study highlighted the stark contrasts between livestock producers' and the general public's views toward predatory wildlife and provided land managers important insights into appropriate means of predator control (particularly on public lands) and the tradeoffs between animal damage control and other resources. At least some livestock producers and producer associations have themselves come to recognize these differences and to appreciate the modern-day political liability of the animal damage control legacy. While the industry as a whole continues to press for animal damage control, some spokespersons endeavor to paint a very different picture of stockmen. A favorite self-appellation of modern ranchers is that they are the "original conservationists." A National Cattlemen's Association slogan hails the organization's "proud history of conservation." Several years ago NCA spokesman Ronald Micheli declared to a major meeting of scientists, managers, and various BLM observers that "[m]ost cattlemen are true conservationists and are interested in the wildlife, aesthetics, and other potential resources of the land," but he lamented that "cattlemen often do not get credit for the contributions they make to such benefits which accrue to the general public."[132]

Claims like these are easily challenged. Micheli himself provides ammunition. In the same address, he admitted tacitly (though he seemed oblivious of the admission) that ranchers' conservation-mindedness is often bought or coerced. He noted the "federal assistance guidelines [that] encourage [ranchers] to consider measures for wildlife and water quality benefits" and the "requirements and restrictions" in public range management programs "intended to enhance nonlivestock benefits." He also complained about the costs that these restrictions impose on ranchers using public lands. Economist Darwin Nielsen points out that claims like Micheli's are also suspect as a matter of economics:

> Wildlife benefits that occur as a result of range improvements on private lands are meaningless to the rancher unless he can capture them by selling hunting leases or by some other means of forcing wildlife users to pay. . . . Thus, there is very little, if any, incentive for the rancher to plan for wildlife in his improvement program. In fact, in the public land states, many private landowners see wildlife as a threat not an asset.

Nielsen's point is corroborated by Kellert's study, which found "limited interest in wildlife, the outdoors, or animals in general" among farmers.[133]

Granted, some ranchers are responsible stewards of their own lands and the public ranges that they share with other users. But most, as Kellert's study suggested, are "selective" conservationists. A classic example is South Dakota rancher Lawrence Kruse, who scoffs: "'What are prairie dogs good for? . . . They might make homes for ground owls and rattlesnakes, but I don't see any use for them.'" Any industry-wide claim that ranchers are "true conservationists" is simply refuted by the evidence—eighty years of organized government pest and predator control conducted largely for the benefit of stockmen and the billions of tons of "soil washed to the sea, bunchgrass destroyed, [and] riparian zones eradicated." Grazing critics conclude that, on public rangelands, stockmen have earned instead the undisputed title of the major nemesis of conservation.[134]

Predator control issues can be seen as a microcosm of the current debate over federal range reform in Congress and among the agencies, range users, and environmental groups. Despite popular disapproval of predator control activities on public lands (and even popular support for wolf reintroduction in several areas) and in the face of considerable evidence that market conditions, not predators, are responsible for the low profitability of livestock operations, stockmen have managed to retain the sympathy of their elected representatives on this issue. Worster offered an example from national forest lands in California in 1962: $90,000 was expended to control predators, while the value of sheep lost was only $3,500! More recently, Congresswoman Barbara Cubin (R-Wyoming) chaired a House Resources subcommittee hearing on the "predator problem" in Gillette, Wyoming. In opening the hearing, plainly staged for the livestock industry's benefit, Cubin asserted: "'I believe there's a predator control problem. . . . We have people saying it's not a problem—and that itself is a problem.'" Clearly, ranchers and their traditional use of western public lands are not generally approved of today. Yet, inexplicably, the political clout and social influence of this group have not diminished appreciably over the years.[135]

Some commentators, I should point out, may see the matter differently. Graf, notably, argues that beginning in approximately the 1940s "new forces were at work in the West that diversified the economies and public policies of the western states. Urbanization and massive industrial development began the slow process of diluting the grazing interests." By the late 1940s "it was impossible for western political representatives to depict their states as monolithic in support of antifederal positions." Changes in the "social and cultural environment of the western states" between 1960 and 1980 further "weakened the position of the sagebrush rebels," whose position was "strongest in states with strong grazing lobbies and much BLM land." "Migration to the western states from other parts of the nation brought new people into western society who did not share the ranching-mining-lumbering backgrounds of long-term residents." By 1980, Graf asserts, "cities had come to dominate the western life-style": "urbanization diluted the political base of the rebels, who could not even command solid support in their home states."[136]

There can be no question that the Sagebrush Rebellion of the late 1970s and early 1980s failed. But as we have seen, that movement has been replaced by new ones with similar ideological roots and agendas. Furthermore, the myth of the Old West and its cowboys is alive and well, thanks in part to the continuing efforts of writers, filmmakers, chambers of commerce, and even scientists and academics. Thus, while Graf is undeniably correct that western policies and economies have diversified, many western leaders continue to tout or to hide behind the cowboy culture, and many Americans—westerners and easterners alike—cling to the dream.

Moreover, as Graf himself noted, the "mythical quality of western independence does not diminish its influence": "as long as citizens of the region believe in the myth, it guides their political actions as though it were reality." Fabian reminds us of the editor's admonition to the young reporter in the movie *The Man Who Shot Liberty Valance*: "This is the West, sir. When the legend becomes fact, print the legend." Myths may be "patently false," she says, but their consequences can be "all too real." The cowboy myth is one of the "mythic constructions of the frontier," which, Richard Slotkin argues, "have been used to explain the glories of white expansion—to justify conquest, genocide, and environmental destruction."[137]

Although it may not be possible ever to "demystify" the West totally, there are good economic and ecological reasons for trying. As Worster writes:

> Historians need to take all these images and ideals [of the cowboy and ranching] seriously—more seriously than they have—but historians must also reveal what our celebration of pastoral freedom has produced on the land and in society. We need, therefore, a more honest account of cowboy ecology. It should be based not only on one hundred-plus years of ranching but also on the much longer span of pastoral activity on the planet. . . .

More specifically, "cowboy history has to be presented more forcefully than it has in terms of comparative human ecology, emphasizing the relation of people to other animals, of animals to vegetation, and of vegetation to patterns of tenure."[138]

As Worster intimates, a "more honest account of cowboy ecology" will depend on more than broader input from historians. It will require greater attention to the land and less to the legends. The public and policymakers must look to ecologists, not myth marketers, for guidance in charting a course for the West's future. Meanwhile, ranchers continue to succeed in obstructing policy changes they oppose. That power, whatever its source or ontology, remains a significant obstacle to achieving substantive "range reform" or improving range conditions.

CHAPTER 5

The Ecological Landscape

In the words of environmental historian Donald Worster, "the invasion [of the West] by millions of head of exogenous horses, cattle, sheep, and goats in the span of a few decades must have come with the explosive, shattering effect of all-out war." The "war" did not end with the invasion, of course; it has continued with varying intensity for more than 100 years. Mythic depictions of cowboys and ranch life have ignored or obscured the toll that abusive grazing practices have taken on western rangelands. "While the cowboy may have enriched our culture with movies, stories, and song," Noss and Cooperrider write, "his general lack of understanding of how to manage cows and rangelands has caused serious damage to the West." Adherence to cowboy propaganda continues to excuse land abuse.[1]

The profession of range management, Noss and Cooperrider have observed, "developed in response to a perception that rangelands were deteriorating— from overgrazing. The history of the profession has followed a . . . path of resourcism [similar to forestry], with livestock production becoming the primary focus." Similarly, Thomas Fleischner asserts that "[r]ange science has traditionally been laden with economic assumptions favoring resource use." These opinions are supported by the early and standard range management texts. L. A. Stoddart and A. D. Smith (1943) defined range management as the "science and art of planning and directing range use so as to obtain the maximum livestock production consistent with conservation of the range resources." Stoddart, Smith, and T. W. Box (1975) revised the definition to "the science and art of optimizing the returns from rangelands in those combinations most desired by and suitable to society through the manipulation of range ecosystems." Still more recently, Holechek et al. (1989) defined "range ecosystem" as the "living and nonliving elements comprising a piece of rangeland on which man has placed boundaries for management purposes." As a consequence of such views, Noss and Cooperrider assert, the emphasis in range management has been "on products and production (returns), on improvement over nature (optimizing), and on technology."[2]

Concomitantly, "the ecological merit of livestock in the West has generally gone unchallenged." In many cases, "the fundamental ecological questions have not even been posed, much less studied or answered." Even applied ecological research is rare. For instance, researchers R. E. Eckert and J. S. Spencer reported in 1986 that the "effects of grazing management systems on plant communities in the Great Basin are largely unknown." In fact, "our understanding of the long term effects of light to moderate grazing on plant communities and ecosystem processes in the Intermountain Sagebrush Region has progressed little since the turn of the century." Thomas L. Fleischner's 1994 article in *Conservation Biology* has been called "one of the first syntheses of literature on the effects of livestock management." Noss's charge that "[w]e really do not know what we are doing. . . . Everything we do in land management is an experiment" seems a fair description of applied range science.[3]

The consequences of this "experiment" are profound. Livestock grazing is "the most widespread land management practice in western North America," occurring over 70 percent of the western United States. The near ubiquity and the duration of unregulated or underregulated grazing over much of this region, coupled with grazing's "classic cumulative effect," have led to "tremendous" impacts on the landscape. In Noss and Cooperrider's estimation, livestock grazing is "the most severe and insidious of the impacts on rangelands," "the most widespread" source of disturbance, and "one of the most complex impacts ecologically." Specifically, they claim that livestock grazing is the *most insidious and pervasive threat to biodiversity on rangelands.*"[4]

This last pronouncement was not without precedent; about fifteen years earlier, R. J. Smith had described livestock grazing as "'the single most important factor limiting wildlife production in the West.'" In 1970 a National Research Council committee asserted that "grazing probably is the greatest single year-after-year agricultural influence on wildlife." And in the 1930s Aldo Leopold, a vocal critic of livestock grazing in the Southwest, wrote: "What remains of our native fauna and flora, remains only because agriculture has not got around to destroying it." Yet, according to Worster, the "least-studied impact [of ranching] has been on the native fauna of the West."[5]

The last ten to fifteen years have seen significant growth in the literature on grazing's ecological impacts, in particular its effects on biodiversity. Fleischner's 1994 survey article provides a concise, but thorough, overview. As a general matter, grazed systems and natural vegetation exhibit "important differences in species, energy and nutrient fluxes"; these differences vary widely with the site and other variables. Although ecologists and other scientists are not in complete accord on grazing's ecological impacts, Fleischner's conclusion, based on his survey of the literature, is representative: "Undoubtedly," he wrote, "grazing has led to soil erosion, destruction of those plants most palatable to livestock, changes in regional fire ecology, the spread of both native and alien plants, and changes in the age structure of evergreen woodlands and riparian forests." The negative effects of grazing on western riparian communities (not just forests) have been widely documented. In addition, there seems to be broad agreement that vegetative diversity decreases generally with grazing intensity in arid and semiarid environments, especially under a continuous grazing regime.[6]

Some scientists play down the significance of grazing as a source of environmental disturbance or attribute ecological impacts to other factors. Richard F. Miller et al., for example, have asserted that "[c]hanges in plant composition would have occurred throughout the [Intermountain Region] without livestock grazing because of the introduction of alien plant species, cultivation, increased CO_2 levels and altered fire frequencies." This observation and others like it, however, ignore the fact that livestock grazing has contributed to each of these causes of vegetative change, even atmospheric carbon levels. Most objectionable is the suggestion that changes in plant composition, specifically, the introduction of "alien plant species," would have occurred without grazing. Agriculture, including grazing, is by far the principal source of nonnative plant introductions.[7]

Similarly, the cumulative and interrelated effects of grazing and fire were recognized long ago. In a 1923 essay Leopold wrote: "All our existing knowledge in forestry indicates very strongly that overgrazing has done far more damage to the Southwest than fires or cuttings, serious as the latter have been. Even the reproduction of forests has now been found to be impossible under some conditions without the careful regulation of grazing, whereas fire was formerly considered the only enemy." Leopold pointed to the Sapello watershed, in New Mexico's Gila National Forest, which had "not been overgrazed," yet was ruined by a mere decade of grazing and no fire. "The lesson," he warned, "is that under our peculiar Southwestern conditions, any grazing at all, no matter how moderate, is liable to overgraze and ruin the watercourses." He conceded that "one example does not prove that grazing is the outstanding factor in upsetting the equilibrium of the Southwest," but he claimed that this was "rapidly becoming the opinion of conservationists." Much more recently, Laycock cited grazing as a causal factor, along with changes in fire frequency or introduction of nonnative plants, in the existence of most altered "stable state [vegetative] communities in North America."[8]

Assessments of grazing's impacts that, like Miller et al.'s, understate its ecological effects may, in addition to overlooking cumulative effects with other environmental factors, take an overly narrow view of the activities and processes encompassed by "grazing." Many authorities recognize that a broader view, which encompasses the impacts of both the grazers themselves and the attendant livestock management and land use practices, is more appropriate.[9]

A. THE IMPACTS OF GRAZING AND GRAZING-RELATED ACTIVITIES ON RANGELANDS

"[M]ost human impacts on biodiversity," Noss writes, "represent one or both of two things: (1) a change in the environmental regime, often related to disturbance; [or] (2) an increased rate of change." Livestock grazing, as well as grazing-related practices, can act as an agent of either type of change, but is usually considered a form of ecological disturbance. F. A. Bazzaz defines disturbance as "a sudden change in the resource base of a unit of the landscape that is expressed as a readily detectable change in population response." Richard Hobbs and Laura Huenneke explain that disturbance "usually acts primarily by affecting the availability of suitable microsites" (e.g., for vegetation establishment), "although some forms of disturbance may affect the availability of invasive propagules." Grazing alters microsites by trampling, depositing urine and feces, removing vegetation and litter cover, etc. Cattle and other nonnative herbivores introduce invasive propagules by "bring[ing] seed into an area either on their coats or in feces." The dramatic spread of mesquite (*Prosopis juliflora*) into former grassland areas of the Southwest, for instance, has been attributed to cattle, which eat the mesquite beans and then move out onto the grasslands, where the beans are deposited in feces, "undigested and viable, with water and fertilizer to get them established."[10]

To be sure, grazing can be considered a disturbance *or* a natural process. Grazing is a form of "herbivory," which is a natural process in all ecosystems involving a multitude of vertebrates and invertebrates. "[R]oot-feeding nematodes, leaf-chewing grasshoppers, termites, herbivorous rodents, lagomorphs, large mammals and granivores" are all herbivores, and each contributes to the effects of herbivory in an ecosystem. "Depending on the scale at which it is observed, herbivory may be considered as a continuous process of nutrient cycling or as a disturbance." Herbivores "mediate species abundance and diversity through differentially utilizing plants variously susceptible to defoliation." The emphasis here is on "differentially." Grazing may "either increase or decrease plant species diversity," but it is an "effective diversifier," Low and Berlin point out, only "if the grazer eats unequally on the variety of species available."[11]

The introduction to the West of new species of herbivores—namely, cattle, sheep, horses, goats, and swine—not only increased existing *rates* of herbivory, but "altered the *process* of herbivory at the species, community and landscape levels." The primary herbivores on any given western range site are not necessarily ungulates (hooved mammals). This is true not only for sites currently ungrazed by livestock but also, historically, for much of the West prior to the introduction of livestock. The chief herbivore historically may have been bison or elk, or it may have been hares, deer mice, or insects. Today, however, the chief grazer on rangelands is likely to be a cow or steer. This change is highly significant because, as we will see, livestock grazing is most appropriately considered a disturbance when it occurs in a vegetative community whose members have not coevolved with large grazing animals.[12]

The effects of both grazing and grazing management practices on biotic and abiotic components of rangeland ecosystems, as well as on ecosystem functions and processes, can be direct or indirect. Impacts include changes in fire frequency and hydrology, loss of soil and altered soil characteristics, loss of native vegetation and invasions by alien plants, decline or loss of aquatic organisms due to dewatering of streams for irrigation, degradation of riparian communities, alteration of predator/prey relations, and the introduction of disease. While our chief concern is with biodiversity, it must be recognized that any and all grazing-related environmental impacts hold the potential, ultimately, to affect biodiversity.[13]

Many of grazing's more direct impacts are obvious and essentially undisputed. Grazing results in trampling or removal of vegetation, trampling and compaction of soils, erosion of streambanks and hillsides, competition with big game animals for forage and water, etc. Trampling by livestock or by other large herbivores "compacts the soils, reduces soil aeration, inhibits root elongation, and reduces water infiltration," all of which reduce vegetative productivity. The full range of grazing's effects, which may never be thoroughly comprehended, is much more diverse and complex than a simple enumeration of individual impacts would suggest. Fleischner categorizes the "ecological costs of livestock grazing" into three types: (1) alteration of the species composition of communities, (2) disruption of ecosystem functioning, and (3) alteration of ecosystem structure. These "costs" can plainly overlap. For instance, the introduction and contribution to the spread of nonnative ("exotic" or alien) plant species result eventually in all three types of ecological change and thus in some of livestock grazing's most serious and pervasive impacts. Invasions of plant communities by nonnative and so-called weedy species have become "major conservation and management concerns in natural ecosystems."[14]

The "decline in native perennial grasses and their replacement with nonnative annual grasses over vast areas of the Midwest and West" are associated with the introduction of "large numbers of livestock following European settlement." This process has been chronicled by scientists and historians. Specific examples include invasion of the Intermountain West "by cheatgrass, medusahead, leafy spurge, and salt cedar" and of California by Mediterranean annual grasses and forbs (broad-leaved herbaceous plants). According to BLM botanist Roger Rosentreter, most native species "can tolerate moderate amounts of grazing. However, even one season of misuse may cause degradation and subsequently invasion by exotic annuals. . . ." Large portions of the West have suffered not just one season but more than a century of misuse.[15]

Livestock operators are not likely to refer to their animals as exotics, but domestic livestock are, of course, nonnative species. Livestock, in turn, are directly or indirectly responsible for subsequent invasions by other nonnative plants and animals, which may outcompete or otherwise adversely affect native organisms. According to Low and Berlin, it is "commonplace in evolutionary theory that non-native species frequently, when introduced to habitats similar to those of their origin, do extraordinarily well, establish strongly, increase in number and outcompete native species." This occurs, they explain, because the "transplanted species are, often for the first time in their existence, in a climatically suitable habitat in the absence of most or all of their natural predators, parasites, and competitors." William Reiners points out that the "European origin of the majority of weeds in the U.S.A. probably derives from the much longer time for evolution of disturbance-adapted species in Europe."[16]

Many nonnative plant species whose introduction and spread are related to livestock or grazing-related practices take hold and spread simply because they outcompete native species "on their own turf," but more often it is because livestock grazing has changed the environment in ways conducive to nonnatives' establishment and proliferation. Livestock grazing facilitates not only the spread of nonnative plant species, but of some animals as well. The brown-headed cowbird is commonly associated with cattle. A strong competitor, it parasitizes the nests of native birds (including, apparently, the endangered least Bell's vireo), often causing population declines. Other fauna benefited by livestock grazing range from egrets to grasshoppers.[17]

Vegetative manipulations conducted for the benefit of livestock work even more obviously to the detriment of native biodiversity. In some cases, the very purpose of these so-called range improvements is to replace native vegetation with a nonnative species, commonly crested wheatgrass (*Agropyron cristatum*). Furthermore, the area converted is often subsequently invaded by noxious weeds, defined as "exotic, undesirable, unpalatable plants." Once established intentionally or otherwise, nonnative plants displace native species and disrupt ecosystem functions.[18]

In arid areas where native vegetative communities developed in the absence of grazing by large ungulates, grazing is very likely to lead to proliferation of weedy species. Weedy species, or simply "weeds," are a large, indefinite class of native and nonnative plants, principally annuals, including but not limited to various members of the Chenopodiaceae (chenopod), Brassicaceae (mustard), and Asteraceae (composite) families, jointly termed ruderals, and certain grasses. They may be unpalatable (e.g., medusahead wildrye, *Taeniatherum asperum*) or even poisonous (e.g., halogeton and knapweed, *Centaurea* spp.) to livestock and/or native ungulates. Poisonous plants are often categorized as "noxious weeds" and may be identified as such by law or regulation. In general, weedy species "usually occupy habitats that have been only recently disturbed by humans." The disturbance can take the form of any land clearing activity—farming, gardening, road or fence construction, grazing. Plants may "become weedy because their genetic uniformity and low plasticity [the adaptability to environmental change of a species or phenotype] fortuitously favor some particular uniform, extant habitat created by human activity." Their success derives from "a fortuitous abundance of a uniform habitat to which they happened to be suitably adapted."[19]

According to plant ecologist Edith Allen, the "arid and semiarid lands of the western U.S. are experiencing an unprecedented invasion by exotic plant species that threatens native ecosystems and reduces the success of restoration." Invasion by nonnatives almost invariably leads to a reduction in the diversity of native plant communities, since many nonnative plants "form persistent near-monocultures." Examples include the Mediterranean annual grasses, cheatgrass (*Bromus tectorum*), knapweeds, and some mustards (e.g., *Brassica* spp.). Sites "converted to annuals have lost genetic, species, and structural diversity," Rosentreter explains. "They represent low-quality watersheds with increased susceptibility to soil erosion and are prone to desertification. Annual vegetation is more susceptible to drought. . . ." He points to the Intermountain steppe ecosystem (encompassing southwestern Idaho), which "is now largely dominated by initial floristics due to the introduction of exotic animals"—a function of abusive grazing and altered fire patterns.[20]

Rangelands in the Chihuahuan Desert in southern New Mexico and southwestern Texas have also been excessively grazed by livestock and consequently invaded by weeds. Anna Gillis describes studies in this region, showing that heavily overgrazed areas had nearly twice the biomass of poisonous plants as ungrazed areas. Twenty or more years' rest from grazing had fostered little or no recovery of degraded native forage species.[21]

Cheatgrass, or downy brome, is perhaps the most widespread nonnative problem plant on western ranges. W. D. Billings called it "a biotic cause of ecosystem impoverishment in the Great Basin." Originally from Europe and the trans-Caspian steppes, cheatgrass was imported to the West inadvertently with wheat and other grains in the 1890s and early 1900s. It spread so rapidly, according to Leopold, "as to escape recording. One simply woke up one fine spring to find the range dominated by [the] new weed." It became "the most abundant seed plant in the region and changed the nature of the sagebrush steppe ecosystem forever." In the Intermountain West alone, cheatgrass now "dominates more than 41 million hectares [100 million acres] . . . and is continually expanding." Wildfires "had been rare or nonexistent in the original open bunchgrass-sagebrush vegetation of the nineteenth century." Once cheatgrass became established, wildfires occurred with increasing frequency and thus ensured cheatgrass's dominance on the range. Like a few other persistent plants, cheatgrass, once established, "may not feasibly be extirpated." The "seedlings of native perennials are virtually excluded" by "this aggressive annual"; cheatgrass is even "invading undisturbed sites." In parts of Utah, Nevada, Oregon, Idaho, and Wyoming, stands of cheatgrass "form virtual monocultures."[22]

Billings cites several "long-term implications of the cheatgrass-fire problem" in the Great Basin. He believes that a "number of native plant and animal species are at risk of being eliminated, locally and even regionally"; that entire ecosystems (chiefly the sagebrush biome but also pinyon-juniper woodlands) are functionally threatened; and that cheatgrass may actually be favored by the buildup of carbon dioxide in the atmosphere. Many others have expressed similar concerns. BLM state director Delmar Vail calls the "loss of plant diversity, especially shrubs, that are continually burned because of the presence of cheatgrass" one of the BLM's "biggest concerns" in Idaho. Allen has observed that the "cheatgrass problem is probably one of the most difficult to solve for [range] restoration purposes," explaining that "restoration, if possible, would probably require numerous spring burns followed by seeding and planting with native species." Cheatgrass stands are sometimes invaded by medusahead wildrye, another introduced annual grass. Medusahead can outcompete even cheatgrass and is more undesirable because it provides less forage and is more flammable.[23]

Another widespread nonnative pest, halogeton (a member of the Chenopodiaceae Family), is also associated with livestock grazing on certain ranges. Halogeton is highly toxic to sheep but can also affect cattle under certain conditions. Once introduced, this annual forb spread quickly across degraded salt desert ranges, especially in Nevada, but in more northern ranges as well. Early BLM efforts to eradicate halogeton, including seeding 300,000 acres with crested wheat in the 1950s, failed miserably. The plant has since spread over 11 million acres in several western states. James A. Young and Raymond A. Evans have called the spread of halogeton "the most problematic product of prolonged, chronic abuse of grazing on public lands."[24]

Tamarisk, or salt cedar (*Tamarix* spp.), is a "noxious, introduced" shrub whose spread along stream courses throughout the Intermountain West and Southwest is linked to livestock grazing. A phreatophyte, salt cedar poses special problems for the water-limited West. It outcompetes other, more shallow-rooted, plants for water, thus "displacing native vegetation and making the habitat unsuitable for wildlife." It can actually lower the water table by evapotranspiration. In the Afton Canyon area on BLM lands in southern California, tamarisk invaded riparian areas, displacing more than 70 percent of the native vegetation. In 1963 Forsling reported estimates of water loss to tamarisk and other phreatophytes ranging from 500,000 to more than 850,000 acre-feet annually in New Mexico alone. (One acre-foot is equivalent to approximately 330,000 gallons.) Eradication of tamarisk is difficult and expensive.[25]

Other direct impacts of livestock grazing include destruction of bird nests and loss of hiding cover for newborn animals; competition with native animals for water and space; transmission of disease to native animals; surface water pollution and impacts on aquatic organisms; prevention of sprouting in certain shrubs; and destruction of cryptogamic soil crusts. Livestock probably also negatively affect production of most waterfowl species, although reports in the literature are mixed. Donald D. Dwyer et al. reported that waterfowl "may be adversely affected by grazing during breeding, nesting, and brood-rearing periods," but they further noted that certain species, "notably the blue-winged teal (*Anas discors*), are benefited by moderate grazing over no grazing." Keith E. Severson and Philip J. Urness analyzed two literature reviews concerning livestock and waterfowl: one reported fifty-five studies showing that grazing was detrimental and one study that detected higher nesting success; the other review reported more mixed results. Grazing is also known to have adverse impacts on neotropical migratory birds in various habitats, including "grasslands of the Great Plains and the Southwest, riparian woodlands, intermountain shrubsteppe, and open coniferous forests."[26]

The effects of competition between livestock and native species can be direct or indirect. Competition takes many forms; effects vary depending on the species involved, location, and other circumstances and are often not easily detected. Some native species simply avoid areas where domestic animals are grazing. Cooperrider reports that he "has often observed elk departing sites in spring within hours of cattle arriving," a phenomenon also "observed through radio-telemetry studies in other areas." But competition for resources, and the manifestations thereof, is often much more subtle.[27]

Dwyer et al. caution that negative effects should be expected any time livestock displace wildlife into "habitats less suited to their well-being." This "displacement" can be geographic (e.g., the avoidance response observed by Cooperrider) or temporal. For instance, several researchers have documented the "high-grading" of available forage by livestock when they are turned onto the range during periods of peak plant growth. The immediate result is less nutritious feed available for wild animals that use the range later in the season. According to Dwyer et al., even when use by livestock and native ungulates is simultaneous, "vegetation composition is altered" through livestock grazing, and "nutrition of competing wild animals declines in comparison with that of the more flexible domestic animals." Nutritional impacts can have long-term consequences, including effects on reproduction, and may be compounded by other stresses, such as severe weather. Ultimately, it appears that the survival and populations of other herbivores are generally reduced. The mechanisms, and effects, can be complex. For example, heavy use by cattle of bighorn winter range in the Salmon River region of Idaho has been blamed not only for "high level of disease and parasitism" among bighorns, but also for the low reproduction in native sheep.[28]

Little is known about the long-term effects of livestock on animals other than ungulates. The rare desert tortoise is of particular concern. Livestock eat or trample the same plants that tortoises feed on; one tortoise eats less vegetation in a year (about twenty pounds) than a cow does in one day. In addition, cattle trample the tortoises themselves and crush burrows containing tortoise eggs. Being more mobile, livestock possess an obvious competitive advantage in the harsh environments that these species share. The tortoise is listed as threatened throughout most of its range in the Southwest, except in the Sonoran Desert. Their numbers have declined by about 70 percent since 1970 on BLM's 16,000-acre Desert Tortoise Natural Area in California. The natural area is open to both cattle and sheep grazing. One study showed that just two days of sheep grazing reduced available annual forage by 90 percent. Land managers and scientists disagree, however, about the chief cause(s) of the tortoise's decline. Some blame principally land development and recreational activities, particularly off-road vehicle use. Range scientist Neil West suggests that removing cattle from tortoise habitat "is an action that is more politically than scientifically supportable."[29]

The masked bobwhite quail may also be a casualty of livestock grazing. Its decline has been "correlated with the expansion of tall shrubs into formerly desert grasslands along the Arizona-Sonora border," a phenomenon attributable primarily to livestock. Other game birds, such as sage grouse and sharptail grouse, have also been impacted by grazing and grazing management practices. Cattle and sheep compete directly with native mammals and birds for desert water sources. Cattle are known to impact birds by trampling or eating important food plants. When livestock deprive other herbivores of forage, those animals may decline in abundance, and the carnivores that feed upon them may in turn decrease. Very little is known about the effects of livestock grazing on insects, although there is evidence that livestock effects on interspecific competition can contribute to *increases* in the populations of certain species, such as grasshoppers and other small herbivores, and in turn the animals that feed upon them.[30]

Domestic livestock also serve as reservoirs of foreign microorganisms. Certain pathogens and parasites pose well-known dangers to populations of humans or animals. In general, whenever "exotic animals are brought into an area, there is a risk of disease transmission to the detriment of the native species." Native species that have not been exposed to a disease may "lack genetic or acquired resistance to the new pathogens or parasites." This is especially well documented where domestic sheep have been introduced to native bighorn sheep ranges. In some cases, "[e]ntire populations of bighorns have died off within a year or two of coming in contact with domestic sheep." Diseases introduced by domestic sheep, in combination with overhunting, have been blamed for "the extinction of the Audubon's subspecies [of bighorn] and loss of the Rocky Mountain bighorn from much of its prior range."[31]

The ramifications for native wildlife of brucellosis, which originated in cattle rather than sheep, are less direct. This disease is at the center of an ongoing controversy involving management of Yellowstone National Park. Scientists generally agree that brucellosis is not native to bison and elk, but rather that these mammals were initially infected with the *Brucella* bacterium by exposure to cattle. Nor does the disease pose a serious hazard to the health of bison or elk. Instead, the presence of the organism in these native ungulates is perceived by the livestock industry and regulatory agencies as threatening reinfection of cattle, in which it causes abortions—even though there is no evidence of disease transmission from bison or elk to cattle in the wild. Stockgrowers, concerned about the impact on their pocketbooks if cattle herds lose their certification as "brucellosis free," are lobbying and litigating to require testing and vaccination of Yellowstone area bison and elk and removal of infected animals. The fear of brucellosis transmission was directly responsible for the slaughter of at least 1,100 bison crossing the northern boundary of Yellowstone National Park during the winter of 1996–97.[32]

The impacts of livestock (particularly cattle) grazing on riparian areas have been widely studied. Direct effects include elevated levels of fecal coliform bacteria and sediment in streams, degradation of stream banks and bottoms, reduced shrub reproduction, and increased shrub mortality. Cattle foraging can eliminate a willow stand in thirty years and prevent regeneration of cottonwood. Capitol Reef National Park in southern Utah, which underwent early, and hard, livestock grazing, suffered drastic changes in the vegetative composition, including loss of willows and other riparian trees and shrubs. Researchers who compared then-current conditions in and around the park with available historical data concluded simply that "riparian zones are probably not well adapted to support large concentrations of herbivores." Livestock grazing can also have an impact on rare plant species; grazing is a contributing factor in the status of many western plants on the federal lists of threatened or endangered species. In 1997, for instance, the U.S. Fish and Wildlife Service added three southwestern wetland plants to the endangered list. "All depend on cienegas, perennial streams, and wetlands, which are extremely rare in the desert southwest" and which are used disproportionately by livestock.[33]

The destruction of cryptogamic soil crusts by livestock has only recently been recognized as significant. Cryptogamic crusts—also referred to as crytobiotic, microbiotic, or microphytic crusts—exist on the surface of soils in certain areas. Consisting of cyanobacteria, mosses, and lichens, the crusts "are an important component of ecosystems in semiarid areas. These crusts may represent up to 70 percent of the living [ground] cover in some of these systems." "[I]ncreasing evidence indicates that microbiotic crusts play several vital roles in arid and semiarid rangeland ecosystems." Their ecosystem functions include "enhanc[ing] soil stability, reduc[ing] water runoff . . . , improv[ing] nutrient (nitrogen and some essential mineral elements) relations for at least some vascular plants, and enhanc[ing] germination and establishment for some vascular plants." Fleischner reports that the "availability of nitrogen in the soil is a primary limiting factor on biomass production in deserts. In the Great Basin Desert, at least, it is second in importance only to the lack of moisture." The contribution of these crusts "to the nitrogen economy of these arid ecosystems is substantive." Removal of or damage to cryptogamic crusts can have significant adverse impacts on desert soils and nutrient cycling.[34]

Cryptogamic crusts are vulnerable to disturbance—cattle or sheep trampling, off-road vehicles, and other recreational use. According to St. Clair and Johansen, "domestic grazing animals seriously damage the integrity of the microbiotic crust through trampling of the crust, particularly during dry periods of the year." Impacts can be especially severe in arid and semiarid regions in and west of the Rockies, which "developed without the pressure of large herds of grazing ungulates." Vehicular use can have similar effects. On many arid lands even "a single pass of an off-road vehicle will reduce nitrogen fixation by cyanobacteria and increase wind and water erosion of surface soils." Furthermore, cryptogamic crusts are "slow to recover from severe disturbance, requiring 40 years or longer to recolonize even small areas." Full recovery reportedly can require up to 50 years in the Great Basin and 100 years on the Colorado Plateau.[35]

The consequences for nutrient cycling of damaging cryptogamic crusts are an example of an indirect effect of grazing. Indirect consequences are less readily discernible and thus more difficult to document than many of the more direct effects discussed above. The dividing line between direct and indirect effects is, to be sure, not always clear; for instance, the spread of exotics, discussed above as a "direct" effect, is labeled an "indirect grazing-induced process" by the federal land management agencies. Dwyer et al. describe "direct" effects as occurring "when livestock modify or become part of a species's ecological requirements" and "indirect" effects as occurring "when livestock-induced modifications in the ecosystem cause pertinent environmental pressures." The federal land management agencies assign the following impacts to the "indirect" category:

- changes in stream channel characteristics and water quality . . . ;
- wholesale changes in plant communities . . . ;
- altered precipitation infiltration and evapotranspiration regimes due to soil compaction exposure; and
- accelerated soil erosion as a result of hillside trailing.

Other indirect consequences include modification of microenvironments, alteration of fire return intervals, and influences on ecosystem processes, including nutrient cycling (noted above), energy flow, and hydrology. F. Stuart Chapin points out that agriculture and grazing "generally cause a short-term increase in nutrient availability above that of undisturbed ecosystems through reduced uptake by plants, increased organic matter mineralization rates, and fertilization." The long-term effects often differ, however, depending on several factors. He suggests that long-term nutrient availability is reduced by grazing. This seems inevitable since cattle remove nutrients from the system when they are taken off the range. Overgrazing, especially heavy grazing, has been implicated in reductions in the diversity, abundance, and density of macroinvertebrates, including aquatic invertebrates, but the mechanisms are subject to speculation.[36]

Numerous studies of the effects of livestock grazing on small mammals have shown that species diversity is generally reduced. Other studies indicate that diversity of small mammals may increase with grazing intensity up to a point, but that "[a]bundance and biomass often diminish." Leopold observed that overgrazing on Southwest ranges was "probably the basic cause of some or most outbreaks of range rodents, the rodents thriving on the weeds which replace the weakened grasses." But available data today indicate that "fewer species are benefitted by heavy grazing than by no grazing."[37]

Changes in species composition of the vegetation may be just as difficult to discern and explain. Such changes can result from one or more of a variety of causes. The most obvious have been mentioned—trampling, selective foraging, and introduction of nonnatives. Other factors include a "change in nutrient cycles caused by reduced diversity in rooting depth or changes in energy flow because of a reduced period during which the remaining plants photosynthesize." Livestock contribute to all of these processes. In general, "vegetation diversity decreases with grazing intensity, especially under continuous grazing." Dwyer et al. warn that recognition of this relationship "is basic to understanding and predicting impacts of domestic livestock management on wildlife populations." Taken to its extreme, this principle suggests that few species can persist in the face of disturbances that are sufficiently frequent or severe.[38]

Perhaps the best example of an indirect consequence of grazing is its potential to impact climate by contributing carbon to the atmosphere. According to David A. Perry and Jeffrey G. Borchers, "[h]istorically, soils disturbed by intensive agriculture, forestry, and grazing have been significant sources" of atmospheric carbon. Livestock themselves contribute carbon in the form of carbon dioxide (CO_2) and methane (CH_4). Even if livestock's individual contribution to atmospheric carbon levels is minor, its cumulative effects should not be overlooked.[39]

Another category of indirect, but highly significant, ecological impact is traceable not to grazing per se, but to the accoutrements of grazing, including those referred to collectively as "range improvements": facilities and activities such as fencing, roads, water developments (including irrigation), predator control, grazing systems, and vegetation manipulation (seeding, chaining, plowing, application of herbicides, etc.). The effects of livestock-related range improvements on native species, both plant and animal, and ecosystems can be substantial, if not devastating.[40]

"Range improvements," or "range rehabilitation" measures, are undertaken to enhance livestock production. While they are often touted as having non-wildlife benefits—for instance, benefits to vegetative condition, soil, or water quality—their actual and potential impacts on wildlife are chiefly adverse and have long been of concern to wildlife managers. Wagner advised twenty years ago that the "entire ecology of reseeding [rangeland] ecosystems needs to be studied," noting that the effects on wildlife were poorly understood. More recently, Dwyer et al. cautioned that grazing systems should not be counted on to benefit both livestock and native herbivores:

> Livestock management programs using specialized rotational grazing systems are usually not designed to accommodate significant increases of potentially competing wild herbivores. Presumed "benefits" to wildlife from selected grazing systems are regrowth of vegetation on the areas recently vacated by livestock. If these benefits are realized, resulting in an increase in wild herbivores during the growing season, the benefits accrued from pasture deferment could be negated and the intent of the grazing system thwarted.

They concluded that the survival of native species depends largely "on their ability to survive more and more complicated situations resulting from man's preoccupation with increasing livestock production."[41]

Every so-called range improvement is an environmental disturbance; it can have both direct and indirect effects on the ecosystem. Fencing, supplemental feeding, and maintaining artificially high concentrations of grazing animals all exacerbate livestock's impact on natural systems. Fencing can prevent livestock from moving to better forage areas, "resulting in higher frequencies and intensities of defoliation [on grazed areas] than would occur otherwise." Fences also can obstruct wildlife (particularly pronghorn antelope) movements, even to the point of fragmenting habitat and causing reduced vigor and mortality. Barbed wire fences cause injuries or mortalities when animals such as deer attempting to jump or pass through the fence get entangled in the strands. The cleared rights-of-way along fences and roads facilitate the invasion of weedy species (see the discussion of edge effect and species diversity in chapter 6). Fencelines also inhibit travel by recreationists and can affect the scenic qualities of an area.[42]

Water developments are among the most common range improvements. The ramifications for biodiversity of both livestock-related water developments and water use in the arid and semiarid West are of special concern. Developing a spring by excavation or impoundment may deprive wildlife of access to it or to its downstream flow or may destroy the associated riparian habitat. Drilling wells to provide stockwater can deplete aquifers or disrupt hydrologically connected surface flows. Areas surrounding livestock watering sites often become "sacrifice areas"—trampled down, with compacted soils, supporting only trampling-resistant species or no vegetation at all, attractive to flies, and a source of pollution of adjacent watercourse. As Low and Berlin remark: "No one who has seen a sacrifice area around a watering point can doubt the effects of trampling by grazers."[43]

Use of water to irrigate livestock feed crops, principally alfalfa, is especially damaging. In very few areas of the West can livestock be pastured year-long; this necessitates the growing of a forage crop, hay, for feeding during the rest of the year. The most common forage crop, alfalfa, is notoriously water consumptive. In the arid West, alfalfa must be irrigated. Making matters worse, it requires late season irrigation when western stream flows are at their lowest. Diverting water for irrigation can actually dewater natural stream courses, stressing or killing riparian vegetation and aquatic organisms. Irrigated agriculture consumes 8–90 percent or more of all water used in western states; in several states a substantial fraction of this water is lavished on alfalfa. In California, for instance, cattle and alfalfa are the two largest water users. Alfalfa fields can also be an "attractive nuisance" to wildlife. Deer, which find alfalfa highly palatable, are often struck by automobiles as they cross highways traveling between cultivated fields and upland areas.[44]

Animal damage control efforts, conducted chiefly for the livestock industry's benefit, have had massive and far-reaching impacts on populations of target predator and pest species, on nontarget organisms, and undoubtedly on western ecosystems. As we saw in chapter 4, both livestock producers and the government in the early 1900s were bent on exterminating predators. By the 1920s gray wolves were extinct in nearly all western states outside of Alaska, though federal funding for their "control" continued until 1971. As Leopold pointed out, the "scourge of deer and elk" that resulted from eliminating cougars and wolves from many ranges "simply transferred the role of pest from carnivore to herbivore." Coyote numbers also increased at least in part due to reduced numbers of, and hence competition from, less resilient predators, such as wolves, foxes, and mountain lions. The coyote is now the most numerous and widely distributed predator on western rangelands. Although it is still hunted and trapped indiscriminately, especially on sheep ranges, its status is nevertheless apparently secure. If anything, local reductions in coyote populations seem to increase reproductive rates.[45]

The direct and indirect impacts of animal damage control measures on ecosystems are complex and substantial. Not only the intended victims, predators and pest species, are at risk. Many nontarget species, including carrion-eaters and other "[w]ide-ranging vertebrates," are also in jeopardy; indeed, whole ecosystems may be significantly altered. Animal Damage Control kill statistics for one year (1991) revealed that more than *150,000 nontarget animals of 23 species* had been destroyed. The endangered black-footed ferret, the rarest mammal in the world, is the most famous nontarget casualty. Disease and drastic reduction of its prey species, the prairie dog, pushed it nearly to extinction. A variety of "control" measures, but particularly the widespread use of poisons until the 1970s, reduced prairie dogs to only 2 percent of their historic range from Mexico to Canada. In Wyoming alone poisoning reduced prairie dog numbers by 75 percent from 1915 to 1981. Of five species in North America, the Mexican prairie dog is listed as endangered and the Utah prairie dog is threatened.[46]

Not only prairie dogs and ferrets have been affected by the tireless campaign to eradicate these rodents. Ecologists and conservation biologists refer to the black-tailed prairie dog (the most widely distributed of the five species) as a "keystone" or "umbrella" species; they believe that it "plays an important role in maintaining the biotic integrity of the western grasslands." The BLM recognized a "prairie dog ecosystem" at least as early 1979. Many ecological processes, including nutrient cycling, depend on this rodent's presence, and scores of species find habitat—food, shelter, even breeding grounds—in prairie dog colonies or "towns." Scientists believe that the vegetation in prairie dog towns is more nutritious and more digestible, noting that bison and pronghorn prefer it to forage in other areas. Tim Clark et al. studied colonies of three species of prairie dogs from Hobbs, New Mexico, to the Utah-Wyoming line in 1982. They observed 107 vertebrate species and subspecies (1 amphibian, 25 reptiles, 51 birds, and 30 mammals) on prairie dog colonies; a review of the literature revealed 140 vertebrate species associated with colonies. Associated invertebrate species are also numerous. The disappearance of black-tailed prairie dogs, it is believed, "can cause the collapse of an entire natural community."[47]

The term "range improvements"—whether used to refer to animal damage control or some other livestock support activity or facility—is a misnomer, of course; what it means is enhancement of the range's livestock-producing capacity. The term plainly reflects range management's livestock-production bias. Conversely, both ranchers and range scientists occasionally use the term "range deterioration" to refer to the effects of natural ecological processes, such as fire or herbivory by native organisms, which are not conducive to livestock grazing. Black-tailed prairie dogs again serve as an example. Ranchers call these rodents "'prairie rats,'" complaining about the vegetation they consume and the hazard that their burrow entrances pose to livestock, especially horses. Several states have branded them pests or "varmints," and even some range scientists charge that these animals "can contribute to further range deterioration by their own feeding and digging activities." These perspectives contrast starkly with the prevailing scientific view, described above, that the black-tailed prairie dog is an ecological linchpin. Ironically, scientists suggest that vegetation on prairie dog colonies is probably more nutritious for cattle, as it is for native ungulates. C. Knowles suggested several reasons for preferential use of prairie dog colonies by cattle in northeastern Montana, including higher production, higher nutrient content, and higher nitrogen content of vegetation and increased abundance of forbs on prairie dog towns.[48]

Given the livestock-production orientation of the term, it is not surprising that range improvement projects are seldom if ever designed to restore or enhance natural/native biodiversity. They usually have the opposite effect, whether intentional or inadvertent. "Rehabilitation" of degraded or overgrazed (usually shrub-dominated) ranges often consists of converting the existing vegetation to a monoculture of a nonnative grass that is palatable to cattle. The conversion typically involves application of herbicide and/or some mechanical brush control measures, both of which are ecologically disruptive.

Perhaps the commonest precept of range improvement dogma is that many shrub species—usually lumped under the pejorative term "brush"—are "undesirable." Those who hold this view may not even distinguish between native and introduced species. The native big sagebrush (*Artemisia tridentata*) is a chief target. Darwin Nielsen writes that in much of the West the sagebrush-grassland "range type has high potential for improvement," that is, the replacement of sage with "more desirable forage plants." Nielsen concedes that sagebrush does have forage value for "game animals" as well as livestock, but he argues that, except on some critical deer or elk winter ranges and in critical sage grouse habitat, "the opportunity cost of leaving [i.e., not replacing] the sagebrush [is] very high."[49]

Other "undesirable" shrub species include mesquite, which has spread from Mexico into large areas of the Southwest, creosotebush (*Larrea tridenta*), and tarbush (*Flourensia cernua*) in the Southwest and saltbushes, such as shadscale (*Atriplex* spp.) and greasewood (*Sarcobatus* spp.), in cool deserts where alkaline soils predominate. According to Carlton H. Herbel, mesquite is "considered detrimental throughout the semidesert range area," creosotebush "has no grazing value," and the presence of tarbush "results in a dramatic decrease in the production of herbaceous [read "forage"] plants." Herbel asserts that "present [livestock] stocking rates could increase dramatically" in the Southwest "[i]f the potential of these ecosystems could be realized." He describes seeding and herbicidal treatments that can improve many vegetation types, but laments that "[p]ractically no range improvement techniques exist for salt desert [shrub] ranges."[50]

The species of choice for "improving" most ranges is crested wheatgrass, imported originally from Asia. Extensive areas of the West that once supported sagebrush-bunchgrass communities have been seeded with crested wheatgrass. This introduced species has several advantages: it is drought- and grazing-resistant as well as palatable to livestock, and it proved adaptable to degraded ranges throughout the northern Great Plains and Intermountain West. Once established, it "suppressed the growth of cheatgrass and brought stability to the eroded, abandoned croplands."[51]

While some wildlife species make use of crested wheat, particularly in the spring (because it greens up before native grasses do), crested wheat seedings are necessarily adverse to animals that depend on the replaced native vegetation. Sagebrush, the principal species reduced or replaced by crested wheat seeding efforts, is important or essential in the diets of pronghorn, sage grouse, and mule deer, and elk make extensive use of sagebrush communities in the winter.[52]

Sage grouse, a sagebrush obligate, are especially hard hit by crested wheat seedings. Historically, sage grouse were found wherever big sagebrush occurred. The bird is apparently still present in thirteen western states and parts of southern Canada, but its distribution and numbers have been greatly reduced. At least one subspecies found in west-central Colorado, in the vicinity of Gunnison, has been proposed for listing as endangered. Sage grouse are susceptible to habitat disturbances, especially vegetative conversions in the vicinity of their breeding areas (strutting grounds, or leks). Young grouse depend heavily on riparian areas, which have been seriously degraded and reduced in area by overgrazing. Research scientists with Battelle Memorial Institute's Pacific Northwest Laboratory have identified "loss of quality sagebrush habitat" as the most likely cause of the decline of sage grouse in the sagebrush steppe regions of eastern Oregon and Washington. The apparent causes were fire and grazing.[53]

Little evidence supports the claims of wildlife benefits from range improvement projects. These claims invariably accompany attempts by industry apologists or project proponents to justify proposed improvements or to rationalize completed projects that have come under fire by conservationists or fiscal conservatives. Most often touted are water developments, which are said to "open up new areas for wildlife." Seldom do the actual effects of water developments on wildlife species receive any scientific scrutiny before or after construction. Apologists also overlook the possible negative effects of competition for the "new" water, the potential impacts on hydrologically connected water supplies, and the ability of the rest of the habitat to support additional wildlife use.[54]

The twentieth-century increases in mule deer and elk populations have been attributed in part to water developments and predator control. But such increases, if they occurred, may be better explained as reflecting "longer term, region-wide trends traceable to better regulation of harvest by state agencies" or as long-term comebacks from population lows earlier in the century. Wagner cautioned in 1978 that "we have few conclusive data on which to form judgments" about the impacts of predator control on wildlife populations. He observed, reasonably, that the "answers undoubtedly differ for various ungulate and predator species, their relative numbers, and other aspects of the ecological context." More recently, Noss and Cooperrider also found "limited" evidence "supporting arguments that 20th century populations of big game animals are greater or smaller than 19th century populations."[55]

The tendency to exaggerate, if not actually fabricate, the benefits to wildlife of range improvements, along with the failure to consider their negative impacts, skews grazing policy and range management decisions. Because livestock grazing imposes costs on natural systems and on other rangeland resources and users—costs that are nearly always discounted or overlooked—managers and politicians make economically inefficient and inequitable choices about public land use (see chapter 8 for a discussion of the significance of these costs in the grazing debate).

No scientist disputes that livestock will contribute to changes in the floral and faunal diversity of the area grazed, if grazing occurs at sufficient intensities or over a sufficiently broad area or for a sufficiently long time. Biodiversity may be altered even on ungrazed areas adjoining or near grazed areas, as in the case of the spread of nonnative plants. Not all scientists agree with the conclusion that grazing is the "most insidious and pervasive threat to biodiversity on rangelands," however. Many scientists avoid such generalizations, preferring site-specific depictions of impacts. But even these scientists recognize the need for concern about grazing's potential impacts on biodiversity. Pieper, for instance, agreed that livestock "grazing does alter vegetational patterns and changes habitats for many animals," but he advised that each situation "should be evaluated on the basis of the animals involved and the degree of vegetational change. If livestock grazing leads to reduction in general diversity, then the situation may become critical."[56]

A variety of factors in addition to grazing—both natural and human-induced—can also impact biodiversity; this can make it difficult to attribute ecological change to a particular cause. Indeed, ecological effects are generally the product of multiple, and dynamic, factors. Still, the fact that off-road vehicles, climate, or some other source of disturbance may interact with grazing to produce cumulative, or even counteracting, impacts does not mean that grazing's impacts are insignificant or irrelevant or that it is pointless to address problems of abusive grazing.

Herbel summarized the factors responsible for vegetation changes as including "(1) climate, (2) grazing by wild or domestic herbivores, (3) fire, (4) plant adaptations, and (5) governmental policies." Climate is a particularly important variable in ecological change. It may be the "most important factor affecting the evolution of vegetation" in areas where native herbivory played a lesser role in the development of vegetation such as arid portions of the Southwest and the Great Basin. Beyond this generalization, however, scientists frequently disagree as to the relative significance of grazing and other environmental factors. According to Dwyer et al., the "effect of grazing on total vegetal production is much less significant than the effect of climate." But grazing is as important as, if not more significant than, "weather variation" in determining species composition. Fleischner acknowledges older research, which suggested that "a shift toward greater aridity [in the West] is the primary factor for regional vegetation changes" and that "climatic oscillations since 1870 have resulted in short-term fluctuations in vegetation." But in his view, more recent work indicates that "long-term directional changes, including degradation of riparian habitats and spread of exotic species, have resulted from *human* disturbances, including overgrazing by cattle."[57]

Clements, whose vegetative succession theories have pervaded range science and range management throughout most of the professions' history, believed that climate (temperature, moisture, and wind) was the most important variable in determining the plant community and vegetative condition of a site, at least after the early stages of succession, when soil was most crucial. In Worster's estimation, "the simple, stark correlation between climate and the climax [vegetative] community remains the essence of Clements's system." Given the influence of Clements's thinking, his focus on climate may explain in part why so many ranchers and range scientists believe that climate outweighs all other factors in determining range condition.[58]

In any event, climate must be recognized as a confounding factor in research on the effects of grazing. Because long-term ecological changes caused by climate "may mask or confound impacts due to grazing," range scientists and managers must bear in mind that research "based on short-duration studies may not effectively detect such changes or determine their causes." Climate change, or "global warming," may further complicate matters.[59]

Aridity is a potent climatic factor. Only relatively recently have ecologists come to understand how important aridity and the developmental history of a vegetative community are in determining the severity of livestock grazing impacts. Both factors have important ramifications for the proposed biodiversity conservation strategy.

B. THE RELATION OF COEVOLUTION AND ARIDITY TO CHANGES IN RANGELAND BIODIVERSITY

1. COEVOLUTION

In 1931 Webb declared confidently that "cattle-herding, as practiced in the West, was conditioned by environment. It was a natural occupation which used the land in its natural state and altered it hardly at all." Ranchers have long subscribed to this view. Even today, livestock graziers and certain range specialists often claim that "livestock grazing is merely substituting a nonnative animal for native ones that have been removed from the system." The assertion heard most frequently is that cattle simply "replace" bison: they occupy the niche vacated by bison in the 1870s. (The reference is to the Holocene *Bison bison* that roamed the plains of North America for about 5,000 years.) Even the land management agencies have subscribed, at least in part, to this theory, referring to the "function" performed by bison in "keeping parts of the plains grassland open and more suitable for burrowing rodents" as having "been replaced by livestock grazing."[60]

The "niche" theory fails, however, for at least two reasons. First, it misuses the term. A niche is not a *site* occupied by a species. "Niche" describes "the way a species population is specialized within a community." It encompasses all habitat requirements of, or resources required by, a particular species, as well as the species' place, both geographically and temporally, within the community. "Niche" reflects evolutionary and co-evolutionary specializations. In other words, there is no such thing as an "empty niche"; "niche" has no meaning when divorced from the species under consideration. The bison's "niche" disappeared with the bison. It strains the meaning of "niche" to apply it to domestic animals like cattle that did not evolve in, and thus are not specialized members of, the communities in which they are now found.[61]

Even apart from this arguably semantic point, the "replacement" view is just too simplistic. In fact, Noss and Cooperrider urge, if the land management objective is to conserve biodiversity, "replacement," or "substitution," arguments are simply "untenable, untrue, or irrelevant." Cattle and bison are ecologically distinguishable, as they explain:

> Cattle do have similar (not identical) forage preferences to bison, but their foraging habits differ. . . . Modern-day cattle, in spite of thousands of years of domestication [from their ancestor, the wild ox], still retain a tendency to stay in the riparian zones—those remnants of their ancestral Pleistocene habitat. . . . [Thus,] their natural tendency on North American rangelands is to concentrate in small scattered groups near water, where they can do considerable damage. . . .
>
> Bison, on the other hand, moved in large herds across vast areas, and did not concentrate in riparian areas for long periods of time. Furthermore the bison has many adaptations to more northern climates such as the ability to get moisture from eating snow. . . . The impacts of these two disparate foraging patterns on the vegetation and landscape are predictably quite distinct.[62]

Noss and Cooperrider go on to explain that there are also geographic limits to the replacement hypothesis. Bison "were found in only token numbers in both the Great Basin and the southwestern deserts, the two areas where livestock grazing is most contentious and, in the opinion of many ecologists, most damaging." Furthermore, no other large herding herbivores were found in these regions, at least since the Pleistocene.[63]

Opinions vary somewhat as to the exact historical distribution and numbers of *Bison bison* beyond the Great Plains. According to Miller et al., the species was "widely distributed throughout the sagebrush steppe, but most abundant [within that region] in southwestern Wyoming and southeastern Idaho." They depict the sagebrush steppe as lying to the north and east of the Great Basin sagebrush region, encompassing large parts of western Wyoming, southern Idaho, and eastern Oregon, and smaller portions of northern Nevada, southeastern Washington, and southwestern Montana. "Throughout most of the sagebrush steppe, however, bison herds were probably small and isolated," and by the 1830s the animal had disappeared west of the Rocky Mountains. Dirk Van Vuren proposes that low bison numbers west of the Rockies resulted from "low overall forage production, and from discontinuous habitat which isolated bison populations and slowed recolonization following periodic local extinctions." He reports that skeletal evidence from eastern Washington and Oregon and southwestern Idaho comes primarily from areas of steppe vegetation that contain graminoid vegetation preferred by bison, but that those habitats were mosaics, many parts of which were unsuitable for bison. The evidence further indicates that some inbreeding occurred in these area. Van Vuren and Frank C. Deitz suggest that a breeding population of bison *may* have inhabited the Humboldt River drainage in northeastern Nevada, citing the discovery of remains of one female bison. Fleischner concludes from his review of the literature that, west of the Rocky Mountains, "bison were rare or absent during Holocene times. The species was present in the northern Rockies region, marginally present along the northern and western perimeter of the Great Basin, and absent altogether from Arizona, western New Mexico, [and] most of Nevada and California."[64]

Pieper elaborates on the distinct food habits of bison and cattle, a difference to which Noss and Cooperrider allude in their reference to "forage preferences." "Bison were primarily grazers," he states, noting results from two studies showing that grass comprised as much as 90 percent of bison diets. "Cattle, in contrast, consume more browse and forbs." According to these two studies, "[b]ison diets were more digestible than cattle diets suggesting that bison were more adapted to native forage than cattle." Other research, in Colorado, shows an even stronger preference for grass. In nearly every sample, Pieper reports, bison diet consisted of more than 90 percent grass. W. K. Lauenroth et al. surmise that "replacement of bison by cattle [in shortgrass steppe] may have had an influence on plant and wildlife communities due to differences between bison and cattle in diet selection and grazing behavior" and conclude that "replacing" bison with cattle resulted in "greater competition with pronghorn and a greater negative effect on winter-stressed wildlife obtaining spring forage," as well as differential effects on vegetative diversity.[65]

To borrow Fleischner's succinct recapitulation of the relevant literature, "the ecological analogy between cattle and bison is incomplete."[66]

An ecological analogy between cattle and other native ungulates is even more strained. Again, Noss and Cooperrider explain:

Native North American ungulates have different forage preferences from livestock. More importantly, native ungulates move about (especially away from riparian zones) much more freely than livestock. Most wild ungulates on western ranges are migratory and thus only graze an area for one season. Moreover, because wild ungulate populations are generally limited by something other than total year-round forage supply, most North American species (with the possible exception of bison) existed in much lower densities than livestock currently do.[67]

This assessment is not subject to serious dispute. Lauenroth et al. apparently subscribe to the replacement theory as applied to cattle and bison in shortgrass steppe regions, but otherwise seem to agree with Noss and Cooperrider: "Plant communities with a short evolutionary history of grazing are more likely to change when grazed by domestic animals than are those with a long evolutionary history of grazing . . . and the change is more likely to be away from background conditions." Similarly, the federal land management agencies report that impacts of livestock have been "particularly destructive to ecosystems where native grazing ungulates were scarce or absent." The heavier the livestock use, the more severe the impacts. Southeastern Arizona, where native ungulate populations have always been low but livestock grazing has been nearly continuous in some areas since stock were first introduced, illustrates this principle. C. J. Bahre asserted that "'probably no single land use has had a greater effect on the vegetation . . . or has led to more changes in the landscape than livestock grazing'" in this area.[68]

Steven Archer and Fred E. Smeins concur that heavier grazing in "grasslands with a short evolutionary history of grazing" eventually causes diversity to decline, and they note that the "Intermountain grasslands [that] evolved with light grazing . . . have changed markedly since the introduction of livestock." As for the sagebrush type, they observe:

Selective grazing by the native herbivores as a group in the sagebrush steppe may have been minimal, reducing their affect [sic] on interspecific competition. As a group, the native herbivores in this region readily grazed forbs, grasses and shrubs. . . . Spring forbs are grazed by many classes of animals including large ungulates, lagomorphs [rabbits and hares], small rodents, birds and insects. Grasses were consumed by elk, bison, and to a lesser degree pronghorn and deer. Lagomorphs and insects . . . also readily consumed many grass species. If preferential grazing was minimal, the physiognomy of the sagebrush steppe may have evolved primarily to be adapted to cold wet springs and hot dry summers rather than [to] herbivory.

They conclude that, "while grazing has been an important selection process in many ecosystems, man has substantially changed its frequency, intensity, extent, and magnitude with the introduction of livestock. The result has been rapid and widespread changes in species composition and productivity of plant communities."[69]

Some investigators may suggest inadvertently that they subscribe to the substitution argument, at least with respect to bison. Pieper, for instance, reports that livestock grazing "probably has had much larger impacts on vegetation of the Intermountain Region, Great Basin, and the Southwest, than the Great Plains *where livestock replaced bison* as the dominant herbivore." Yet as we have seen, Pieper has described the differential food habits of cattle and bison and conceded that even on the Great Plains "replacing bison with cattle was not without some impacts." Livestock impacts have been greatest, he concludes, in the Great Basin/ Intermountain Region, where native large herbivores were scarce after the widespread extinctions of the Pleistocene and where native pronghorn, bison, deer, and elk "probably had minimal impact on other ecosystem components."[70]

It bears noting that the terms "evolution" and "coevolution" are often used imprecisely by these scientists and others writing on this topic. Strictly speaking, only species, subspecies, and populations "evolve." "Coevolution" refers to the joint or paired evolution of two species or populations of organisms, each of which influences the other. Vegetative communities, ecosystems, or sites develop or form over time, but do not themselves "evolve." I think readers may fairly infer, however, that the point is the same regardless of the terminology. Where large grazers were historically absent or uncommon, the potential ecological impacts of livestock grazing are greatest.[71]

Readers also should understand that large herbivores are classified tradi- tionally as grazers if they feed primarily on grasses and forbs or as browsers if they feed primarily on woody vegetation. The key is "primarily," because the feeding habits of most ungulates are complex, varying with myriad factors, including season, location, condition of the forage, and characteristics of the animal, such as condition, sex, and age. Mule deer in the Intermountain and Rocky Mountain West subsist principally on browse in the winter, but eat sub- stantial amounts of forbs (broad-leaved herbaceous plants) during the summer and some grass in the spring. Cattle are considered grazers, but also browse, especially in riparian areas and when other forage is scarce. The differences among the diets and foraging habits of livestock and wild ungulates have been the subject of considerable research. Significantly, as Wagner has explained, herbivores that "would not compete materially in a system with healthy, diverse vegetation might converge in their feeding patterns where vegetation is degraded and would be driven to competition." The likely result of such conver- gence is further degradation of the habitat with potential negative impacts to the native herbivores.[72]

The differential effect of livestock on western ranges, as compared to that of native ungulates, is not due solely to their selective use of certain plant species and their preference for riparian areas and other moist habitats. It is also a product of their management by humans. Livestock husbandry on western ranges enhances the ecological differences between livestock and native ungulates. Livestock management results in levels of herbivory greater in both intensity and duration than natural (native) levels, historic or current, of herbivory in the same areas. Whereas native ungulate herbivory tends to be seasonal and to fluctuate in intensity and duration from year to year and place to place, livestock populations are maintained at "unnaturally" high levels and might graze an area for multiple seasons or even year-long.[73]

This difference is crucial to understanding why western ranges are so susceptible to damage from grazing by livestock. Noss and Cooperrider explain:

[O]n most North American rangelands, evolutionary pressure to develop resistance to grazing has not been strong for the last 10,000 years because populations of large herbivores were limited by factors other than year-round availability of forage. . . . In fact, most wild ungulates of North American rangelands concentrate seasonally on either (1) open, low-elevation winter ranges . . . , or (2) near sources of free water . . . during the dry season. . . . These concentration areas are usually a small percentage of the year-round range of the species, but [are] most limiting to the population in terms of forage. Thus on large portions of rangelands, plant species evolved with minimal grazing pressure from large herbivores.[74]

Livestock populations, in contrast, are limited by none of these environmental factors, but by human management constraints. Many writers have reported the adverse effects of season- or year-long livestock grazing on arid rangelands. Laycock observed that "heavy grazing during the wrong season can cause severely reduced yields or cause death of many shrubs on salt desert shrub rangelands." The adverse impacts of concentrated livestock use of riparian areas have been widely documented. The BLM long ago recognized the hazards of year-long grazing but, as discussed in chapter 3, has failed to halt the practice in all areas. Year-long grazing continues to be allowed on many BLM ranges in the Southwest, with disastrous consequences.[75]

Even if use is not year-long, livestock behavior, such as cattle's tendencies to congregate near water and to avoid steep slopes, can lead to animal distribution problems with consequent environmental impacts. This is particularly true where cattle are grazed in large pastures in rugged topography and where riparian zones or other watering areas are limited—as in the Intermountain sagebrush steppe region. The effect on the landscape is compounded by the management, or mismanagement, of livestock by ranch operators. Leaving cattle to fend for themselves in these areas ensures that they will spend a disproportionate amount of time feeding and resting in valley bottoms, along streams, and near other sources of water. Dwyer et al. report that "even under moderate grazing of adjacent upland" riparian zones "are usually abusively grazed." The use and placement of feed supplements, like salt, also have implications for the environment. Before the federal land management agencies adopted regulations, those stockgrowers who used salt "generally dumped it only along the creeks and near the springs," further assuring that livestock would congregate there. Requiring salt and mineral supplements to be placed on ridges, in saddles, or outside riparian zones would help prevent such concentrations. But there are no generally applicable regulations. The net result of livestock behavior and management has been a disproportionate impact on valley and canyon bottoms and riparian and wetland habitats on arid and semiarid ranges across the West.[76]

2. ARIDITY AND GRAZING OPTIMIZATION

In addition to claiming that cattle have simply replaced bison on many western ranges, stockgrowers and some range specialists frequently assert that livestock grazing can actually *enhance* the growth and productivity of grasses. Accordingly, so the theory goes, grazing can be beneficial for both domestic grazers and native wildlife. "Central to the grazing optimization theory," Pieper writes, "is the idea of coevolution of grasses, plants and herbivores that feed upon them. . . . Many believe grasses have been shaped by grazers, but recently several workers have suggested that grasses depend on, or could not exist in the absence of, grazers." This "grazing optimization" or "compensatory growth" theory, Pieper further observes, has "important implications for livestock grazing in the western United States." For this reason, and because of conflicting research results, the theory is highly controversial.[77]

The theory is actually quite tentative, as A. J. Belsky concluded in 1986 after reviewing the evidence. She recounted Lincoln Ellison's (1949) "review of the effects of grazing on rangeland species and communities" and his conclusion that "there was no evidence to support the claims that grazing benefits plants." Since then, she noted, "there have been more reports claiming the benefits of grazing to plants. However, other than for plants grown under artificial conditions, no new evidence has been reported that renders Ellison's conclusion any less accurate today." In other words, Belsky asserted, "no convincing evidence supports the theory that herbivory benefits grazed plants."[78]

The artificial conditions to which Belsky referred include so-called clipping studies. Researchers grow forage species (grasses and/or forbs) in containers in the greenhouse or laboratory and clip them at various stages of their development. Total growth, or herbage production, is compared between clipped and unclipped plants, and the results are extrapolated to the foraging by grazing livestock that occurs under field conditions. Heady warns that the "grazing optimization hypothesis" is based solely on container studies and thus "lacks vegetational or ecosystem testing." Dwyer et al. assert that "there is no published evidence that shows any grazing system to increase long-term plant and litter cover on watersheds." Few if any scientists argue that the effect of cattle on range vegetation could be directly analogized to mechanical clipping in a laboratory setting. As Low and Berlin explain, "standard clipping techniques for estimating plant response to grazing will not give an accurate reflection when the herbivore(s) generating the grazing pressure are highly selective, nomadic, or seasonal." Furthermore, cattle "produce other effects besides defoliation. They walk, sit, lie, urinate, and defecate, all usually in very localized and nonrandom patterns."[79]

In spite of these criticisms, the literature contains ample examples of purported "grazing optimization." Gillis offers one illustration. Citing work by New Mexico State University range scientist Jerry Holechek, she reports that, in "areas thought to be representative of the Chihuahuan Desert before European settlement, forage production is approximately 20% lower than on moderately grazed pastures." According to Gillis, Holechek used this research finding to suggest that "grazing can be sustainable and even beneficial" even in arid areas. But Holechek's conclusion contains two flaws (or a premise and a flaw) that should be acknowledged. First, labeling an increase in forage production "beneficial" indicates that Holechek's goal, or the goal of land management in this area, is to enhance livestock production. The objective might, arguably, have been to enhance forage for wildlife. But increasing forage production on a seasonal range could lead to a population increase that might not be supportable year-long. Second, because every ecosystem has finite, albeit variable, supplies of nutrients and water, an increase in production of forage species is obtainable only at the expense of some other element(s) of the system, probably the more sensitive and/or less competitive plant species. Enhancing "forage production" is *not* desirable if the management goal is to conserve natural processes and native biological diversity.[80]

Furthermore, Holechek's conclusion cannot be squared with what range ecologists today widely recognize—the more arid the landscape, the less likely the grazing optimization theory will apply. More mesic (moist) communities are generally more resistant to grazing pressure and, if degraded, able to recover more quickly after grazing is reduced or stops.[81]

Pieper explains that "stimulation by grazing" is most likely "related to [the] regrowth potential of the plants and the amount and timing of precipitation. Consequently *if* grazing optimization does occur, it is more plausible in mesic rangelands and less likely to occur in arid and semi-arid ecosystems." Severson and Urness have reported that livestock grazing may decrease plant structural diversity on xeric (dry) sites while increasing it on more mesic sites. They claim that most benefits to wildlife habitat credited to livestock grazing "have been fortuitous rather than planned" and conclude that the application of "livestock grazing as a tool to improve habitat . . . may indeed be very limited." Using grazing to attempt to stimulate plant growth would seem to be risky business, particularly in the arid and semiarid ecosystems typical of the West.[82]

Even if (or where) grazing stimulates plant growth, it seems reasonable to assume that no single, simple "grazing optimization" mechanism exists. According to M. Lamotte: "All that is certain is that there are different responses according to climate, soil, and intensity and timing of grazing." Variations also derive from differences in the plants themselves. Pieper explains: "Plants vary in their response to herbivory. Some plants are detrimentally impacted by even low levels of grazing. . . . Other plants may not be detrimentally impacted until defoliation reaches a certain point. . . . Still other plants can be stimulated until a certain level of defoliation is reached and then detrimentally impacted. . . ." Furthermore, as discussed above, the foraging habits of grazers and browsers vary. Some are selective; some are generalists. Some crop leaves and other plant tissue relatively indiscriminately; others preferentially take young, green leaves and shoots. Such differences are to be expected, given natural variability and principles of coevolution. Thus, one would expect, as Noss and Cooperider point out, that populations of some plant species, which have evolved in the presence of herbivores, "have a competitive advantage under conditions of grazing." This clearly is *not* the case where vegetation has not developed in conjunction with heavy or sustained grazing pressure.[83]

Noss and Cooperrider conclude that much of the controversy over the grazing optimization theory is "traceable to confusion over temporal and spatial scales, and to attempts to generalize across vastly different rangeland systems and to equate naturally evolved herbivore grazing [patterns] with current livestock management practices." Furthermore, they note, the "'question of compensatory growth is of relevance to management of Western rangelands for livestock production, but of relatively little relevance to conservation goals. No region-wide answers can be expected.'"[84]

A similar debate simmers over the effects of livestock trampling or "hoof action"—"the damage or alleged benefits caused by soil compaction and other direct effects of livestock"—especially in arid areas. This debate usually implicates the livestock management methods of Zimbabwean Allan Savory. Some of Savory's adherents are almost fanatical in their zeal, while others dismiss his views as irrelevant to much of the western United States. Noss and Cooperrider describe, and debunk, Savory's hypotheses:

Savory (1988), however, claims that animal impact, which he describes as "all things animals do besides eat" is necessary in arid lands ("brittle environments" as he terms them) to advance succession. Little evidence supports this contention. Animal impact, as Savory defines it, is hard to separate from [the] impact of livestock eating. On the Appleton-Whittell Research Ranch Sanctuary (a relatively brittle environment) grazing was eliminated in 1968. Savory's theory predicted an initial improvement (following the elimination of the stress of grazing), followed by deterioration as the residual beneficial effect of animal impact wears off. The deterioration he predicts would eventually lead to a loss of diversity and relative instability of the ecosystem. Sixteen years later, with neither grazing nor animal impact, both plant species diversity and diversity of several animal groups studied (birds, small mammals, grasshoppers) had all increased. Brady et al. (1989) concluded that the data on vegetation and wildlife changes after 16 years did not support the hypothesis that continued animal impact is needed to prevent ecosystem deterioration. Rather, cessation of grazing allowed recovery.[85]

Savory's theories have been criticized by many range ecologists. According to Miller et al., there is scant empirical support for the hypothesis that hoof action by large herbivores enhances seed establishment. Dwyer et al. concur, contending that the "literature does not support" the belief that "seeds trampled by livestock . . . enhance production of new seedlings and thus improve the range." Belsky asserts that she has "never read one experimental paper that concluded that trampling was beneficial to a community." Pieper has been quoted as stating simply, "Savory's biology is shaky." Savory's beliefs, which were formulated in Africa over a twenty-year period, are premised significantly on the ecological importance of large, herding ungulates, many of whom are migratory, in "brittle" environments. He contends that "domestic animals, like cattle, have to be managed in a way that mimics the grazing patterns of wild herbivores." This advice seems highly dubious when imported to a different continent and applied to areas where historical wild ungulates were *not* large herding animals. Evolutionary principles suggest that Savory's methods would be least effective or appropriate on ranges that have not developed with large herding, migratory ungulates.[86]

We will return to both principles—the significance of aridity and evolution. But for now the critical point to understand is that plants on North American rangelands, particularly the drier of those lands, are not adapted to withstand the artificial pressures of grazing by domestic livestock. Vegetation will be affected by livestock grazing; the effects will depend "upon grazing intensity, the evolutionary history of the site and climatic regimes." The most severe impacts can be expected on arid sites where plants did not coevolve with large ungulates (herding or otherwise). Moreover, livestock grazing should be considered a disturbance not only "where the evolutionary history of grazing is short" but in any situation involving a significant change in grazing regime. As Hobbs and Huenneke put it, "imposition of grazing animals (or different herbivores) on a system not previously subject to that type or level of grazing will constitute a disturbance. So, too, will the removal of grazing from a system with a long grazing history." In either case, they warn, "[s]pecies diversity *will* be affected."[87]

C. RANGELAND VEGETATION DYNAMICS

It is now necessary to delve into another, crucial issue of range ecology. Because of certain hoary misunderstandings about vegetative succession on arid rangelands, a preliminary discussion of the succession theory, and the range condition and range assessment methods based thereon, is in order. Traditional methods for describing and measuring rangeland management goals have some inherent flaws, due largely to their foundation on now largely discredited notions of how (or whether) vegetative succession operates on arid rangeland sites. Range measurement systems have been based on a linear view of succession, usually referred to as the Clementsian model, named after its originator, turn-of-the-century Nebraska ecologist Frederic E. Clements. This view of vegetative succession holds that, absent significant disturbance, vegetation on a given site under given climatic, soil, and other environmental conditions will pass through defined, predictable stages, termed seral communities, until some "vaguely final climax" vegetative community is achieved. Two themes pervade Clements's work: that ecological succession in plant communities is dynamic and that the "character of the plant formation" is "organismic," that is, development of the site plant community is analogous to development of individual plants. According to Worster, the plant succession model "owed much to the example of human settlement on the prairie frontiers of America, of pioneering in a new land": "first trapper, then hunter, pioneer, homesteader, and finally urbanite."[88]

Clements developed his model for grasslands, specifically, the grasslands/bison/Plains Indian community of the prairies and semiarid high plains—a biome that, ironically, would soon disappear. As noted earlier, he believed that temperature, moisture, and wind were the crucial variables during the middle and later stages of succession. Soil was more important in the early stages because as each sere develops it "transforms the very soil itself and thus creates a more benign medium in which the future climax can grow." Just as Clements's emphasis on climate may have predisposed modern range scientists to credit (or blame) climate chiefly for range condition, his conviction that the grassland prairie plant/animal mixture "must be the climax stage in any region where there is limited rainfall and much exposure to drying winds, [and] where moisture is seasonal and confined to the upper soil layers," may be responsible for modern range scientists' prejudice in favor of grasses and against shrubs.[89]

Although Clements recognized, and other scientists surmised, that humans might disrupt the normal pattern of vegetative succession and even cause permanent changes in the vegetation of a particular site, Clements's model predicted that changes were generally reversible. As Worster puts it, "Upset or deflect this [successional] process and eventually nature will find a way to get back on track." Disturbances, such as fire or grazing, were viewed as causing "retrogression"—movement in a linear direction away from the site's climax condition. "Forward" succession would begin again, it was believed, following removal of the disturbance.[90]

Notions of retrogression as applied to overgrazing originated with an early student of Clements, Arthur W. Sampson; they were revised by E. J. Dyksterhuis in a landmark article in 1949. Relying on the succession/retrogression model, farmers, scientists, and bureaucrats all came to believe that if the "disturbance" ceased, succession would soon get back on track and the land would recover. According to Wagner, the presumed ability of an ecosystem to "rehabilitate itself through natural processes if freed of disturbances" led to extensive reductions in livestock numbers by land management agencies. This reversibility is also a premise behind rest-rotation grazing, which BLM adopted wholeheartedly in the early 1970s. Rest-rotation grazing—along with the belief that grazing impacts are reversible—still has its adherents, including the federal Natural Resources Conservation Service (NRCS, formerly the Soil Conservation Service).[91]

Clements's model attracted criticism essentially from the beginning, as early as the 1920s. Recently, Worster has labeled the "issue of the climax" an "enduring conundrum," noting that it is "inextricably wrapped up in those muddled, subjective things called human values" and ultimately unanswerable by science alone.[92]

Many ecologists now believe that "[o]nly the more mesic rangeland vegetation types" follow the Clementsian model. Laycock and others conclude that the Clementsian model "ceases to be effective in explaining changes" when applied to the "shrub-dominated and semi-arid vegetation types west of the Great Plains." The "traditional concept of single equilibrium communities" is simply inapplicable to many arid and semiarid systems. In 1992 the professional Society for Range Management announced that "the Clementsian theory of succession has been largely abandoned by ecologists," particularly in its application to "arid and semiarid shrub-grass range."[93]

An alternative model, described by Westoby et al. in 1989, is attracting growing support. Westoby and his colleagues explain that their model was prompted by the identification of "[w]eaknesses of the range succession model [that] are most apparent in arid and semiarid rangelands, where episodic events are important and influences of grazing and intrinsic vegetation change act intermittently." They had made several observations in shrubland and grassland that were inconsistent with the model: removing livestock from desert shrubland and grassland often does not change the vegetation at all, does not change it in the direction predicted, or may result in increased production but no change in species composition. They also determined that "plant abundance may vary discontinuously and *irreversibly* in response to changes in stocking rate." These and similar findings prompted them to propose a new model, "the state-and-transition formulation," which they describe as "a practicable way to organize information for management, not [a hypothesis that] follows from theoretical models about dynamics."[94]

Westoby et al.'s model was not entirely novel. Twenty years ago wildlife biologist Ray Dasmann offered the following simple, though partial, description of a threshold model, which recognized evolutionary principles:

> Ecosystems can be damaged or destroyed even without species extinction if exploitation exceeds past thresholds of irreversibility. Such thresholds are affected not only by the amount of disturbance but by its nature. Disturbances that are in the evolutionary experience of a biotic community are more easily assimilated. . . .
>
> Overgrazing of rangelands on mountain slopes, for example, which exceeds the capacity of the grasses and other forage to reproduce and grow, creates bare ground subject to accelerated erosion by water or wind. If overgrazing is stopped in time, vegetation and soil can recover. If it is pushed to the point where too much soil is lost and bedrock is exposed, recovery may not take place in thousands of years. . . .

Dasmann's explanation is only "partial" because it does not describe what range ecologists now believe also to be true—that alternative stable vegetative communities, such as cheatgrass or medusahead, may exist for a given site, particularly in more arid areas. If disturbances cause site conditions to exceed some threshold, not only will plant community development not proceed toward the presumed climax community, but some alternative "steady state" adapted to the disturbed conditions may become established instead.[95]

According to Laycock, the concept of "relatively stable states of vegetation," which the state-and-transition model incorporates, seems to have been raised initially in 1955. A "multiple climaxes" or multiple steady states model, including the notion of "[p]ermanent alterations in rangeland ecosystems" resulting from disturbances such as grazing, was presented by Heady in 1973, though it failed to gain wide acceptance at the time. The concept has only recently (since about 1988) "received much attention in the range management literature." Noss and Cooperrider also report that the model apparently began to gain acceptance about 1989 or 1990. Fleischner cites Westoby et al. (1989) as pioneering the state-and-transition model, which Fleischner termed still "in its infancy" in 1996.[96]

The notion of permanent, disturbance-induced vegetative change—a feature of the Westoby model—is reminiscent of Ellison's "destructive change" concept, formulated in 1949. Ellison distinguished between "secondary succession," which occurs on sites where original vegetation has been disturbed (e.g., by fire or drought), and "destructive change," which he considered "beyond the limits of normal change and to be induced by accelerated erosion." According to a National Academy of Sciences committee, Ellison considered changes in plant composition resulting from grazing "normal adjustments." But destructive change, in his view, "could not easily be reversed, even with the discontinuation of grazing"; it "results in the permanent loss of productive capacity." In its 1994 report, *Rangeland Health*, the committee observed that Ellison's hypothesized "destructive change" process could "be thought of as leading to a threshold shift between two ecological states." This threshold concept is another feature of Westoby's and other modern models.[97]

Rangeland Health was prepared by the National Academy of Sciences National Research Council (NRC) Committee on Rangeland Classification. The committee was convened in 1989 to "examine the scientific basis of methods used by" the BLM, Soil Conservation Service, and Forest Service "to inventory, classify, and monitor rangelands." It also was charged with recommending better methods for evaluating rangeland health. *Rangeland Health* cites numerous studies, including the work by Westoby and his colleagues, that support theories embracing multiple equilibria, thresholds, and transitions between alternative vegetational states. These theories and models are known by various names, including Westoby et al.'s "state-and-transition" model; threshold, or site conservation threshold, model; "multiple climaxes" model; and "alternative steady states" concept. A crucial feature of each is the recognition that various "combinations of climatic and grazing conditions" can lead to a "change in plant species composition that is not readily reversible." In such instances, "the system has crossed a threshold." The NRC committee defined "threshold" as "a boundary in space and time between two ecological states" and observed that, although the ecological threshold concept has long been recognized, "the concept has not been explicitly included in assessments of rangelands."[98]

Despite its tardy incorporation in range condition assessment techniques, the threshold concept has great significance for our purposes and for range management generally. Models incorporating a threshold principle predict that, when disturbances in a community cause site changes in vegetation or soils or both that exceed some threshold condition, the vegetation will continue to change until it reaches a new, or alternate, steady state, even if the disturbance ceases. "[A] plant community may be rather resilient up to a certain threshold, after which it can no longer return to its previous stable state." As explained by Allen, "Arid lands are especially subject to changes in trajectory of succession when the interval of disturbance becomes too short for recovery, as with increased anthropogenic disturbance." Grazing is included in this class. "Retrogression" is seen as "step-wise rather than continuous," or linear, as in the Clementsian model. The transitions contemplated by the models are "different from other changes from one state to another because they are not reversible on a practical time scale without human intervention." In some cases, such as "severe soil erosion," the committee pointed out, even "human intervention may not be sufficient to reverse these changes."[99]

The state-and-transition model and its variants are believed to be broadly applicable. BLM biologists Michael M. Borman and David A. Pyke venture that it is "appropriate for semiarid communities of North America, Australia, and South Africa." The models are also continually gaining converts. In addition to the SRM, proponents now include the NRC committee that authored *Rangeland Health*, numerous ecologists and conservation biologists, including Noss and Cooperrider, and (at least tentatively) the federal land management agencies. After reviewing the available research, the NRC committee concurred with the models' premise that not all rangelands have a "single, definable, and predictable climax plant community." Instead, it concluded, "succession may follow multiple pathways," and the particular pathway may depend on "the kind of disturbance and the environmental conditions during secondary succession." There are "practical difficulties," it warned, in determining what the climax vegetation for any site "should be." The BLM and Forest Service now recognize the occurrence of alternate steady states, each of which they refer to as a "disclimax community" and define as "a relatively stable ecological community that has displaced the climax community as a result of repeated or continuous disturbance by humans, domestic animals, or natural events." Because it is "based on a more complex and realistic view of plant dynamics" (a "more accurate term than succession," Noss and Cooperrider point out), the state-and-transition model is better able to explain such phenomena.[100]

Note that the state-and-transition model retains a reversibility principle: vegetative impacts should be reversible where disturbance has *not* caused a site conservation threshold to be exceeded. This helps explain studies such as those surveyed by Miller et al., which report increases in native plants, including perennials, in the sagebrush steppe following the cessation of grazing or implementation of intensive management under certain circumstances. Similarly, Laycock cites a Nevada study in which "30 years of protection from grazing . . . resulted in increased vegetal cover of all life forms" and an Idaho study in which plant abundance increased, although species composition did not change, following twenty-five years of "rest" from grazing. Another example, cited by Noss and Cooperrider, is the Appleton-Whittell Research Ranch Sanctuary, where sixteen years of no grazing led to increased plant and animal species diversity. Several writers have described how the overgrazing-induced invasion of Camp

Creek in eastern Oregon by sagebrush and juniper was corrected essentially by excluding cattle from the riparian zone. Presumably, in none of these situations had a site conservation threshold been exceeded.[101]

Four "examples of apparent regional shifts of North American vegetation to alternative steady states" have been identified. Several researchers have reported these shifts, summarized here by Noss and Cooperrider:

1. The Great Basin—from perennial bunchgrasses and open stands of sage-brush to dense sagebrush and annuals such as cheatgrass and medusahead.
2. Southwestern Desert Grasslands and Savannas—from tobosa and black grama grasslands to creosotebush, tarbush, or mesquite shrublands.
3. Southern Grasslands and Savannas—from tallgrass prairies and savannas to oak, juniper, mesquite, or thorn scrub woodlands.
4. California Mediterranean Grasslands—from perennial bunchgrasses to annual grasses.

All of these shifts have occurred since European settlement; each, according to the model, reflects the passing of some threshold. Similar shifts can occur at a local, rather than regional, level.[102]

Livestock grazing has been a major factor in each of these vegetation transitions. According to Laycock: "Most of the stable state communities in North America appear to involve either a change in fire frequency or introduction of an alien species in addition to other factors such as grazing." The suppression of fire in communities that have developed with it can result in drastic vegetative changes. Conversely, as we saw earlier, the introduction of frequent fires to an ecosystem or landscape that developed largely in its absence (e.g., by invasion of cheatgrass in the sagebrush steppe) can have equally dramatic, and devastating, effects. While fire, rather than grazing, is sometimes blamed for the vegetative condition of rangelands, both factors have usually been present and are jointly responsible for the condition of the range.[103]

A caveat is in order with respect to the fourth transition listed above. The view that portions of California now dominated by Mediterranean annuals were, in presettlement times, perennial bunchgrass communities has been widely repeated. Clements apparently originated the view, which may help explain its tenacity. At least one researcher, however, believes that the native herbaceous vegetation of low elevation areas of California consisted primarily of annuals, not perennial grasses. The North Coast ranges, Mark Blumler says, are an exception.[104]

Each of the four "shifts" reflects one or both of two "transition thresholds," which range ecologists characterize as "readily identifiable" in arid and semiarid rangelands. One threshold separates grassland from shrubland or woodland; the other, stable from degraded soil. In the Intermountain sagebrush steppe the applicable thresholds are crossed when:

> (1) the abundance of woody plants reaches a level that reduces fine fuels so fires are unlikely to occur . . . (2) the occurrence of fire is unlikely to return the plant community to its previous state due to the depletion of deep rooted native perennial[s;] or (3) the herbaceous understory [has been] replaced by introduced annuals and short lived perennials, thereby increasing fire frequency to greater frequencies than during presettlement times.[105]

The conversion of native vegetation to cheatgrass is a prime example of the first shift. Robin J. Tausch et al. describe cheatgrass as both a threshold and "an additional stable state community" in many areas where "thresholds were crossed during the late 19th and early 20th centuries as a result of heavy livestock use." But they caution: "While different stable states in community composition are common, and potentially important, the reasons for their existence and for the threshold between them can be subtle and difficult to identify. Several possibilities may be involved." The causal factors include "[f]ire, in combination with the presence of large juniper," the "intensity and timing of fire," "nutrient islands . . . beneath juniper canopies," soil nitrogen, effects of fire on soil mycorrhizae, grazing regimes, and the availability of seed sources for nonmycorrhizal dependent species such as cheatgrass. University of Idaho range science professor Kenneth Sanders reports further that cheatgrass-dominated ranges, which he describes as existing "in a stable lower successional state," "normally will *not* respond to a change in grazing or even to no grazing." Allen and Miller et al. cite similar processes and results in the sagebrush steppe region generally. According to Miller et al.: "Heavy grazing, altered fire frequencies, variable climate, introduction of exotic plant species and other perturbations have changed the composition and structure of vegetation on many parts of the landscape to new steady states." Rest from grazing "did not result in reduced shrub density with improved grass productivity in the under-story as classic succession theory would predict"; thus, removal of livestock "may not return these communities to the pre-grazed state."[106]

According to Hobbs and Huenneke, the third vegetative shift, "from peren-nial grassland to shrub-dominated desert scrub," has occurred in many areas of the Southwest. The transformation in the "physiognomy" of these semiarid grasslands is accompanied by a decline in species diversity. *Rangeland Health* describes a specific example from the Jornada experimental range in south-western New Mexico. This portion of the Chihuahuan Desert, which averages 8 inches of precipitation annually, was originally black grama (*Bouteloua eriopida*) grassland. Today the site is shrubland, characterized by patchy mesquite and creosotebush. Heavy grazing and moderate drought are believed to have caused the crossing of a threshold. According to the NRC committee, the range will not return to black grama without human intervention; and even human intervention may not succeed, given the changes that have occurred in concentrations and locations of moisture and nutrients.[107]

The advancement of pinyon-juniper (*Pinus* spp. and *Juniperus* spp., often abbreviated P-J) woodlands in the West also illustrates the third regional shift. Herbel reports:

> Six species each of pinyon pine and juniper trees dominate woodlands occupying approximately [125,482 square miles] in semiarid portions of the western United States. The extent of these ecosystems is much greater now than when settlers first came . . . because livestock grazing has reduced competition from herbaceous plants, and fires have not occurred frequently enough to kill the young trees.

Up to a point, the grasses may return with reduced grazing pressure and reintroduced fire. But beyond some threshold, as in cheatgrass-dominated areas, reducing livestock numbers "will not reverse or stop these successional changes." At this point, the trees "outcompete grasses for soil moisture and sunlight, and grasses can no longer become [re]established."[108]

Site conservation thresholds likely have been exceeded in the Four Corners area, near the conjunction of Utah, Colorado, Arizona, and New Mexico. P-J woodlands in this region have been "subjected to heavy livestock grazing for more than 100 years." That would explain why "50 years of protection [from grazing] of the Chaco Canyon Culture National Historical Park in northwestern New Mexico resulted in little difference in . . . grasses between the grazed area outside the park and the protected area within the park." Even one palatable grass, sensitive to livestock grazing, was not more dense on all of the protected sites—as the Clementsian model would predict.[109]

A partial explanation for transitions like these is that overgrazing, which reduces grass cover, can change soil moisture regimes, usually resulting in less surface moisture and more moisture reaching the subsoil. This favors shrubs and longer-rooted species (e.g., P-J and sagebrush) and disfavors grasses and shallow-rooted species; potential secondary consequences are changes in the frequency and kinds of fire and, ultimately, soil erosion. The conditions extant at Camp Creek in Oregon, prior to the removal of livestock grazing, were attributed to this basic sequence of events. There, however, no threshold had apparently yet been crossed, and the availability of water no doubt facilitated recovery.[110]

Laycock offered an example involving aspen (*Populus tremuloides*), which differs from the foregoing patterns in that it involves the loss, rather than the encroachment, of a woody species. He reported that stands of aspen had degenerated and disappeared as a result of "heavy, prolonged browsing" and, further, that the aspen failed to return even after grazing and browsing were eliminated. The decay and gradual disappearance of aspen are of concern in many areas of the mountain West.[111]

There is a further dimension to disturbance-induced vegetative change patterns on arid sites not yet considered. After a threshold has been exceeded, site deterioration may actually worsen, leading to yet another alternate steady state and, eventually, to desertification. The reinvasion of a cheatgrass community by medusahead may be the clearest example of a *subsequent*, alternate steady state. Establishment of medusahead represents deterioration of a vegetative community; it is a step toward desertification. New Mexico's Rio Puerco Basin also exemplifies the process of desertification. Recall Sheridan's account of the BLM's repeated, unsuccessful attempts there to halt arroyo-cutting and other symptoms of advancing erosion by means of cutting back livestock grazing. He and many contemporary observers of the Rio Puerco questioned whether the agency's measures would be strong enough to halt the downward slide in range conditions. One geologist familiar with the area doubted that elimination of grazing would allow vegetation to recover in areas with the most fragile soils. Finally, Laycock offers a compelling, though somewhat ambiguous, illustration involving continuous declines in plant cover (he does not identify the species) on a New Mexico site twenty-two years after exclusion of livestock. The continuing decline suggests that an alternative steady state had not yet been achieved.[112]

The crossing of a threshold has immense significance for land management. As Kenneth D. Sanders puts it, "once a threshold is crossed to a more degraded state, improvement cannot be obtained on a practical time scale without a much greater intervention or management effort than simple grazing control." But this should not be taken by land managers as an invitation to simply "give up" on a site where a threshold has been exceeded. Some sites may warrant more expensive and management-intensive "intervention" because of the value of certain remaining or preexisting, recoverable resources or uses. Removal of livestock will be a component of the management or restoration plan in such areas. Similarly, it may be possible to halt or slow the downward slide in vegetative conditions on those sites where a new steady state has not yet been established. This might be achievable solely with the removal of livestock, but will more likely require additional intervention. In all cases restoration success will be affected by the aridity of the site.[113]

The connection between aridity and disturbance-induced alternative steady states is garnering increasing recognition. "Examples of alternative steady states, abrupt thresholds, [etc.,] are becoming increasingly abundant for both succession and retrogression," Archer and Smeins report, and most of this evidence comes from arid and semiarid rangelands. This is not surprising since the state-and-transition model was developed for, and is particularly applicable to, such areas.[114]

Not only are arid areas more vulnerable to disturbance (specifically, to the exceedance of thresholds as a result of disturbance), but, once degraded, arid and semiarid sites improve extremely slowly if at all after the disturbance ceases. The drier the site, the less likely it is that it will recover from disturbances such as overgrazing if a threshold has been approached or exceeded. According to Laycock, "Almost all of the arid and semi-arid rangeland types remain stable at one or more of the lower successional states for long periods of time, even when grazing is removed." Bruce Munda and Steven Smith's report of "numerous, largely unsuccessful attempts to revegetate degraded desert rangelands in the southwestern U.S." and Allen's similar research bear out the connection between disturbance-induced steady states and aridity. Sanders's work in cheatgrass communities reveals that cheatgrass ranges may be reclaimed by native perennials where annual precipitation is 14 inches or more. But where precipitation is less than 12 inches, there is "little evidence that annual rangelands . . . can be successfully converted to perennial grasslands through grazing management alone."[115]

Conversely, water availability is the "key to rapid recovery" in more mesic communities. Practical experience supports the hypothesis that more mesic conditions make sites more resilient. Evidence includes the general, if slow, success achieved in restoring riparian areas by removing livestock. The hypothesis also gains support from the belief, especially common earlier in the century, that one or two years of good moisture conditions would promote recovery of abused rangelands. Studies in southern Utah reflect this principle. Researchers there reported that "the more favorable the growing conditions, the faster the recovery process following disturbance." But they also noted that "resiliency to perturbation is highly site and species specific," citing examples of slow recovery of willow (*Salix* spp.) following overgrazing. Willow is typically found only in moist sites, where conditions are presumably conducive to regrowth.[116]

Interestingly, the connection between precipitation and grazing impacts was recognized a century ago. The interior secretary issued an order in 1897 prohibiting sheep grazing in forest reserves "in regions where rainfall is limited." Sheep were permitted only in the wet Cascade Mountains of Oregon. Forsling's 1963 recommendation to close millions of acres of "arid and semi-arid land" in the West to all grazing reflected his appreciation of the link between xeric conditions and vulnerability to grazing. And in a departure from the then-prevalent view that grazing effects were reversible, Wagner observed in 1978 that "natural recovery" from overgrazing in arid and semiarid lands was likely to be especially slow, perhaps "a century or more."[117]

Despite the extensive empirical evidence in support of the state-and-transition-type vegetative models and their growing acceptance among range ecologists as well as the ample theoretical criticism of the Clementsian model—from Ellison's

(1949) destructive change ideas to Margaret H. Friedel's (1991) threshold concepts—a blind faith in the reversibility of grazing-induced vegetative changes has persisted. At least until very recently, no attempt was made to incorporate the "new community ecology ideas" into the methods used to inventory, classify, or monitor rangelands. Traditional range measurement systems, based on linear-succession principles proposed in the first half of this century, are still in use. The NRC committee points out that the debate over the validity of the climax concept was missing from early range management texts "and is still missing from the later textbooks of Stoddart and colleagues (1975) and Heady (1975) and the most recent range research methods book edited by Cook and Stubbendieck (1986)." Worster also found that the climax idea had been modified little or not at all "in many science texts of recent years." Likewise, the books and technical papers leading to development of the Soil Conservation Service method, now basically used by all agencies, "make no mention of papers . . . that questioned the successional model."[118]

Thus, while the SRM can accurately claim that *ecologists* have "largely abandoned" Clementsian successional theory, Laycock can reasonably counter that *"range science* has not kept pace with ecology."[119]

The BLM illustrates Clements's enduring legacy. Under long-standing BLM methods, determinations of range site condition classes are based on the similarity of a site's species composition to the "purported potential natural (climax) vegetation" at that site. The closer to climax, the higher the condition; lower seral stages are deemed "poor" or "fair." The agency equates "climax vegetation" with a site's "potential natural plant community" and defines it as the "final vegetation community and highest ecological development of a plant community that emerges after a series of successive vegetational stages. The climax community perpetuates itself indefinitely unless disturbed by outside forces." BLM methods for rating vegetative condition reflect these principles. Technicians assess the percentage of vegetation that is

> similar to what is believed to be a site's potential natural or climax plant community. The potential natural community is the one that would develop on a site if successional sequences were completed without human disturbances.
>
> Poor land is in an early seral stage—less than 25% of the plants that are expected to be in the climax system are present. Land rated as fair is in mid-seral stage—25 to 50% of the site's potential community is present. Good corresponds to late seral [50 to 75% potential], and excellent equals climax conditions [75 to 100%].[120]

Other agencies' techniques for assessing condition and trend resemble the BLM's, though each differs in some respects. All incorporate some version of the SCS "range condition classes." SCS techniques were based on Dyksterhuis's range site and condition method (described in his landmark 1949 paper noted earlier), which in turn was founded on Clements's, Sampson's, and Ellison's successional theories. Dyksterhuis proposed that range condition be evaluated in terms of the "departure from climax vegetation for a specific range site." He believed that range condition improved as succession advanced; hence, condition is directly related to the climax community for the site. In his view, "[f]oliage on rangeland in top condition will be almost all forage." According to the NRC committee, this became the "fundamental basis" of range inventory methods: "All major inventory and classification methods in use today are modifications of that basic concept." Per Dyksterhuis's model, grazing drives "plant composition toward the early stages of succession," thus reversing the pattern of natural succession. Grazing, ironically, lessens forage quality. Grazing could be manipulated, however, to maintain rangeland at any stage of succession.[121]

In recent years, range survey methods based on these principles have come under increasing scrutiny. Scientists and the General Accounting Office, among others, have questioned not only the BLM's definitions, methods, and inventory data, but the alternate proposals of Laycock and other members of the Society for Range Management. These questions led to the NRC Committee on Rangeland Classification's charge to review existing methods used by the BLM, SCS, and Forest Service "to inventory, classify, and monitor rangelands" and to recommend better methods for evaluating rangeland health.[122]

From 1989 until its report was published in 1994, the NRC committee reviewed the findings of numerous inventories and assessments of western range conditions, conducted by the land management agencies, SCS, SRM, GAO, and individual scientists, including Box. All of these surveys have been criticized, the committee reported, and "none are based on comprehensive inventories of rangelands." For instance, no trend data were available for more than one-quarter of the BLM ranges included in Box's survey. The committee noted that the land management agencies do not conduct nationwide inventories, but rather gather data to manage individual grazing allotments. Even though these "data are not collected by a statistically designed sampling method that would allow confident aggregation of results on a national basis," the committee reported, the data have been so used, for example, in certain planning documents. The committee reported the challenges being raised by ecologists to the validity of range assessment methods now in use and noted that range science experts disagree as to whether the SCS range condition classes are useful for measuring rangeland health. The mere fact "that it is impossible, with current methods and with current data, to determine whether federal and non-federal rangelands are improving or degrading," the committee noted pointedly, "is itself a cause for concern."[123]

While the committee's work was in progress, the Society for Range Management sponsored a new approach for evaluating rangeland condition. The SRM measurement system, adopted in 1992, incorporates principles of nonlinear succession and "site conservation thresholds," employs a "desired plant communities" concept, and assigns a "site conservation rating" of either sustainable or unsustainable. Portions of the new system have been adopted by the BLM, which recognized the criticisms of its existing range assessment methods. In particular, the BLM embraced the "desired plant communities" concept for evaluating range condition. "Desired plant community" is defined as

> [t]he plant community that has been determined through a land use or management plan to best meet the plan's objectives for a site. A real, documented plant community that embodies the resource attributes needed for the present or potential use of an area, the desired plant community is consistent with the site's capability to produce the required resource attributes through natural succession, management intervention, or a combination of both.[124]

According to the BLM, its new system is "based on whether rangeland conditions on a site can sustain natural plant communities and basic ecological functions. The system describes three categories of rangelands: Proper Functioning . . . Functioning but Susceptible to Degradation . . . [and] Nonfunctioning." "Functioning but susceptible to degradation" means that "the capabilities of proper functioning areas are threatened by livestock grazing activities." Using this system, the BLM has estimated that 57 percent of its uplands are in proper functioning condition, 30 percent are "at risk" (susceptible to degradation), and 13 percent are not functioning properly. The respective figures for riparian areas are 34, 46, and 20 percent. Curiously, these latter figures bear little resemblance to riparian condition statistics reported by the agency four years earlier.[125]

Noss and Cooperrider have already expressed reservations about the new BLM approach to measuring range condition, warning that it could be used to "manipulate data and misrepresent what is happening" and pointing to the BLM's unsupported 1990 claim that "ranges were 'in better shape today than ever before in this century.'" They express support for "the intent of" the SRM guidelines (from which the BLM methods borrow) and their belief that the SRM preference for sustainable communities would help alleviate though not eliminate some of their concerns about the potential for abuse of the "desired community" concept. But they "don't believe the guidelines go far enough in recognizing the limitations of using individual sites as a basis for management and evaluation."[126]

The most recent pronouncement on the matter was the NRC's long-awaited report, *Rangeland Health*. The committee concluded that the "current system of rangeland assessment will not serve as an adequate evaluation of rangeland health, as defined by the committee," and it described the approach it had developed "for evaluating the ecological health of rangeland ecosystems."[127]

"Rangeland health," the committee announced, "should be defined as the degree to which the integrity of the soil and the ecological processes of rangeland ecosystems are sustained." Ecological "integrity" has "recently been defined as 'maintenance of the structure and functional attributes characteristic of a particular locale, including normal variability.'" Accordingly, the "determination of whether a rangeland is healthy, at risk, or unhealthy should be based on the evaluation of three criteria: degree of soil stability and watershed function, integrity of nutrient cycles and energy flows, and presence of functioning recovery mechanisms." The committee identified the "threshold of rangeland health" as a "boundary between ecological states of a rangeland ecosystem that, once crossed, is not easily reversible and results in the loss of capacity to produce commodities and satisfy values." "Commodities" include resources such as forage and water. "Values" are defined broadly as "intangible products," including "natural beauty, open spaces, and the opportunity for the ecological study of natural ecosystems." Rangeland health is not synonymous with capacity to produce commodities or satisfy values, the committee cautioned; two healthy rangelands may have very different capacities.[128]

The varying (and variable) "capacity of rangelands to produce commodities and satisfy values," the committee explained, "depends on the integrity of internal nutrient cycles; energy flows; plant community dynamics; an intact soil profile; and stores of nutrients and water." "Serious degradation can result in the irreversible loss" of this capacity, along with "the loss of some or all options for using and managing rangelands in the future." Conversely, conserving rangeland health "preserves the option to change the use and management of a site as the desired resources and values change." The committee's fundamental conclusion is straightforward and deceptively simple: the "minimum standard for rangeland management should be to prevent human-induced loss of rangeland health."[129]

Although the committee defined "rangeland health" in terms of *sustaining* the "integrity of the soil and the ecological processes of rangeland ecosystems," "healthy" is obviously a mutable concept. This is evidenced by the ambiguity and anthropocentrism in the committee's application of the definition: "Given soil reclamation or reseeding efforts or other external inputs, transition across the threshold of rangeland health from unhealthy to healthy is possible. Even though *health is restored*, the rangeland may not produce the same mix of resources and satisfy the same values as it did in the *original healthy* state." In other words, the committee allows for more than one "healthy" state on a given range site, including a "restored" healthy condition that plainly reflects human-induced changes. The committee confirmed this when it stated: "A change from an at-risk to a healthy state, however, does not necessarily entail a return to the original plant community composition of the site." Clearly, in the committee's view, sustaining ecological integrity does not necessarily entail pre-serving native, or "original," site conditions.[130]

The committee's anthropocentrism was also evident in its remarks about "extreme environments," like the South Dakota badlands and Mancos shale sites in Utah, where soils are poorly formed and/or erosion is severe. Such sites would be considered "unhealthy" by its definitions, even though the "unhealthy" conditions are "natural," not human induced. The committee observed that "even the best management of these landscapes may not be sufficient to achieve healthy conditions." It admitted, however, that such areas "often satisfy impor-tant aesthetic and recreational values, and recreational use of these areas is often an important source of economic activity in the local area." The committee's approach here seems contrived and would seem to subsume too many arid western rangelands. Ultimately, the committee conceded that "the evaluation of rangeland health is a judgment, not a measurement."[131]

The NRC committee concluded that current methods for assessing range-land condition are deficient because they do "not adequately assess soil stability or the integrity of ecological processes such as nutrient cycles and energy flow." The committee repeatedly emphasized soil stability, warning: "[I]t is important to recognize that rangelands are often located in arid or other extreme environ-ments where the processes of soil formation are slow or impeded. Destructive processes such as wind and water erosion can easily exceed constructive processes such as the accumulation of soil organic matter. Naturally destructive processes are thus highly probable on many rangelands."[132]

The deficiencies of current systems for assessing rangeland conditions have significant management implications. One of the biggest "practical difficulties," to use the NRC committee's term, is that the climax theory, which underpins cur-rent range condition assessment techniques, justifies the assumption that "a site that has retrogressed can recover if the process [of disturbance] is reversed." But recovery is not possible, the committee points out, if "severe soil erosion, invasion of a new and very dominant species, or change from a fire-dependent to a fire-safe plant community has resulted in near-permanent changes in the abiotic or biotic community." The climax concept may also be irrelevant where ranchers or range managers have legitimate reasons for desiring to maintain the range condi-tion at a stage other than the presumed climax—for instance, to optimize winter deer habitat or summer sheep range.[133]

Current methods are also inadequate to serve biodiversity conservation goals. This shortcoming stems from what Gillis describes as treating all plants "as equal." As described above, the methods equate condition with the percent of climax species present. A site could lack up to 25 percent of the presumed climax species and still be classified in "excellent" condition. The range manager or technician might not detect the loss of "minor species," including rare plants or plants listed as threatened or endangered. Even functionally more important species, such as perennial grasses, might be absent. Alternatively, managers might predict that natural succession will resume, notwithstanding the presence of a fierce competitor, such as medusahead.[134]

Some scientists might dispute that range condition methods are defective for treating all plants as "equals." West, for instance, claims that the

> functional consequences of species-level diversity at the ecosystem level is [sic] still being debated. . . . Functional groupings have been proposed as a means of aggregating species having similar effects on ecosystem processes. Because we can never determine how each species affects all ecosystem functions, such groupings may be a practical necessity. Where there is more than 1 species per functional group, it implies that species within a functional group may be equivalent or redundant . . . and that [the] ecosystem could function equally well with fewer species.[135]

West's reasoning has some practical appeal, but it suffers from at least two shortcomings. It discounts the genetic, aesthetic, and intrinsic value of species, and it suggests implicitly that we can understand the functions of species sufficiently well to identify those that are truly "redundant." Noss concedes that some species "may be redundant or nonessential to ecosystem function," but asserts that "they nonetheless constitute unique genetic material and would be worthy of equivalent ethical consideration." Some conservationists might reject even Noss's limited concession regarding functional redundancy. It is difficult to imagine a species that could substitute completely for all functions (e.g., predator/prey or parasite/host relations, nutrient cycling, energy consumption,) performed by some other species. Perhaps Norm Peck had this in mind when he wrote: "That biodiversity is integral to the health of an ecosystem should be self-evident. Nature does not often waste energy producing meaninglessly iso-lated parts." Until we know enough to make such fine judgments regarding species' functionality or the value of their genetic material, the safer course is the more conservative one—attempt to conserve all species.[136]

The foregoing disagreement suggests one reason why land managers and scientists have failed to reach accord on improved range survey techniques, despite the wide recognition that the old methods and the results they produce are flawed. Another reason, no doubt, is simple inertia. The NRC Committee on Range Classification identified two additional factors. First, the current successional model "apparently adequately explains vegetation dynamics on a significant portion of rangelands"; and second, there exists no "single coherent theory that can explain all of the current anomalies or that has been sufficiently tested." New models of rangeland change have been proposed, but none has gained general acceptance. Westoby et al.'s model "seems well adapted to rangelands where episodic events may well be the primary factors responsible for determining vegetation composition." But, the committee concluded, it probably is not generally applicable. The committee noted that the Environmental Protection Agency is conducting research to "develop ecological indicators and rangeland classification systems."[137]

Inventory and monitoring procedures will no doubt undergo continued fine-tuning and perhaps even major overhaul. But even in the absence of scientifically acceptable range assessment techniques, public range management can, in the meantime, be improved by adapting or correcting current land use practices to incorporate the threshold concept. It is not surprising that conservation biologists—practitioners of an applied science—would be leading the way in urging both new range survey techniques and enlightened land management. Conservation biologists Noss and Cooperrider, for instance, have proposed that the SRM guidelines be "expanded to incorporate landscape-level thinking." In other words, the model should embrace not only desired plant communities, but also desired landscape-scale conditions and processes.[138]

Range condition assessment and rangeland management should, of course, go hand in hand. Just as it is true, to borrow riparian researchers Wayne Elmore and Boone Kauffman's aphorism, that the "closer an ecosystem is managed to allow for natural ecological processes to function, the more successful that management strategy will be," so too will range condition models and assessment techniques that recognize those processes be more reliable. Because both aridity and evolutionary principles play crucial roles in the ecology and current condition of a site, it follows that both factors should be incorporated in any model of plant community dynamics. All three—models, measurement methods, and management—must be informed by contemporary ecological understanding. On western ranges that will include, in many cases, an appreciation of the threshold and alternative steady state principles of plant community dynamics.[139]

This understanding, in turn, suggests two broad management objectives: "First, management should avoid altering plant communities beyond thresholds. Second, areas that have moved beyond thresholds [and "are continuing to degrade"] but not yet into another steady state . . . should receive a high priority for restoration to a steady state." Granted, the ability to identify site thresholds may be of little utility to range managers or ecologists attempting to discern a trend in order to enable corrective action to be taken before a threshold is reached. Indeed, the Committee on Rangeland Classification urged an "accelerated effort by ecologists" to "develop and test models of rangeland change that will assist in identifying rangelands that are *approaching* thresholds of change." In the interim, however, land managers need not be paralyzed by what they do not yet know. As Dasmann advised twenty years ago, "It is far better, if we are concerned for the future, to keep exploitation rates within obviously safe limits. . . . Since we do not yet know where the thresholds may lie, caution is imperative." The landscape-level biodiversity conservation strategy proposed in the next chapter would allow managers to accommodate much of the uncertainty in our current understanding of arid and semiarid land ecology.[140]

CHAPTER 6

Preserving Biological Diversity on Arid Western Landscapes

The strategy I propose for beginning the essential task of conserving the remaining native biodiversity of arid western rangelands has several elements. It targets large contiguous blocks of BLM lands, which contain whole landscapes, located principally in the Intermountain, Great Basin, and Southwest Regions of the West. It encourages managers to determine the vegetative condition and trend of these lands with respect to any threshold between vegetative stable states. And it calls on the agency to modify management of these areas as necessary to prevent exceedance of thresholds or to stabilize the sites in desirable alternate steady states, so as to conserve naturally functioning ecosystem processes and native biodiversity profiles. The chief component of the revised management will be the elimination or drastic reduction of domestic livestock grazing.

A. BIODIVERSITY

Popular writers, philosophers, and scientists, along with politicians and courts, have found many ways of expressing the importance of biodiversity. As a general matter, "species can have value as commodities and amenities, and they can have moral value." This book is concerned with biodiversity's ecological value; hence, its approach might be called biocentric or ecocentric. But a more accurate description would be holistic. In my view arid land biodiversity is worth preserving because it has all these values. Only where its amenity values, such as serving ecosystem functions, would be jeopardized to produce a product, such as livestock forage, need its commodity values be foregone.[1]

Biodiversity is integral to ecosystem health. As the "shock absorber for any catastrophe in the ecosystem," diversity may be the element most crucial to sustaining ecosystem functions and processes. An ecologically healthy ecosystem, characterized by a full complement of its native biota, provides commodities such as water, forage, and wood supplies and amenities such as *clean* water, clear vistas, and rare flowers. Ecosystem health embraces not only organismic diversity, but abiotic elements as well. The NAS Committee on Developing Strategies for Rangeland Management defined "rangeland health" as "the degree to which the integrity of the soil and the ecological processes of rangeland ecosystems are sustained."[2]

West has opined that "many means of measuring community diversity [exist], but all of them are value laden. That is, choice of variables to measure and how they are indexed betrays what we consider are important." This is an anthropocentric perspective and can take as many forms as there are human priorities for uses of nature. Congress has taken an anthropocentric view of biodiversity, indicating, for instance, that the "diversity of life forms" in the country "enrich[es] the lives of the American people." Similarly, John V. Krutilla linked future human welfare with avoiding the "conversion of natural environments." The U.S. Supreme Court, quoting a congressional committee, described as "incalculable" the value of genetic resources, which is only one aspect of biodiversity.[3]

Biological diversity also has moral value, just as the individual components of biodiversity do. That value may be deemed intrinsic or derivative from one's religious or theological views. The "fundamental value assumption that biodiversity is good and ought to be preserved" is an essential underpinning of conservation biology—and of this book.[4]

"Biodiversity" has nearly as many definitions as characterizations of its significance. Considered broadly, biodiversity encompasses the variety of life at various levels, ranging from genetic, through individual species, to communities of organisms existing in particular habitats. Simple species diversity, or "richness," is literally "the number of species (or habitats) within a defined area."[5]

Three "scales" of species diversity are recognized by conservation biologists: alpha, beta, and gamma diversity. There are some discrepancies among scientists in the use of these terms; for instance, Noss and others refer to diversity at the landscape scale as gamma diversity, while Hobbs and Huenneke label it beta diversity. "Regional diversity" is another expression for landscape-level, or gamma, diversity. Discrepancies in terminology can cause confusion. In this discussion, I use Noss's characterizations:

> *Alpha diversity* is the number of species within a single habitat or community. In most cases [this is] a few hectares or less . . . of uniform vegetation structure. *Beta diversity* reflects the change in species composition along an environmental gradient or series of habitats. . . . [A]lpha and beta diversities [are] roughly equivalent to . . . within- and between-habitat diversities. . . . Finally, the total species diversity of a large geographic region (e.g., a landscape or larger) has been called *gamma diversity*.

Noss explains that he follows the "within-patch" and "between-patch" distinctions for alpha and beta diversity, respectively, even though the latter is "counter to a strict definition of beta diversity," because it "is more useful for land managers." "Gamma diversity" is employed here to refer to landscape or "landscape plus" diversity.[6]

Noss sets out methods for, and the advantages and disadvantages of, managing for diversity at each of these scales. Gamma diversity is best managed by "[p]reserv[ing] sufficiently large areas of unaltered indigenous ecosystems on a regional scale; interconnect[ing] habitat patches; [and] limit[ing] human intrusion in sensitive areas." Noss's view, adopted here, is that managing for gamma diversity should be the goal of a biodiversity conservation strategy. The advantages of managing at this scale are that "[a]dequate population levels and genetic variation of indigenous species [are] maintained; critical ecosystem processes [are] perpetuated; [and] long-term human welfare [is] promoted." Disadvantages include "[s]ome loss of local species richness with declines in edge species; more land taken out of 'productive' human use; [and] short-term economic losses."[7]

Noss reports the advantages of managing for alpha and beta diversity: for alpha—increased number of species within the particular and/or larger populations of certain species and desired community structure; for beta—greater species richness at the local level and larger populations of edge-adapted species, such as game animals, with a concomitant increase in recreational potential. The disadvantages: for alpha—difficult and expensive implemention and uncertain effects of management efforts on various individual species; for beta—reduced numbers or possible extirpation of "interior specialists," increases in weedy or pest species, "community destabilization," and possibly decreased regional diversity.[8]

The proposal herein for conserving arid lands biodiversity proceeds on the premise that preserving gamma diversity should be the objective of rangeland conservation efforts. The choice of gamma diversity over one of the other scales is best explained in terms of a wildlife ecology principle known as "edge effect."

B. EDGE EFFECT

As we have seen, the ecological effects of livestock grazing, particularly prolonged or heavy grazing, including impacts on biological diversity, are generally adverse. Grazing can, however, *increase* species diversity. Indeed, Laycock and other range scientists who advocate grazing on western rangelands have recently adopted as an additional basis for their position grazing's contribution to habitat "patchiness," or "edge effect," and hence to species diversity. Assessing this argument requires an understanding of the scale at which biodiversity may be affected by grazing or other disturbances and the implications of those effects.[9]

Leopold may have been the first to recognize the ecological concept known as "edge effect"—that boundaries between habitat types or successional stages within a habitat type are often rich in wildlife species because of the coincidence and diversity of cover and food. Examples of such boundaries include the transition zone between a meadow and the adjacent forest or shrub community, the conjunction of a greasewood flat and a pinyon-juniper woodland, the riparian-upland community boundary, and the forest-alpine boundary, to name just a few. Wildlife managers have long believed in the importance of edge effect. A text long considered the bible of wildlife managers advises managers to "'[d]evelop as much "edge" as possible because wildlife is a product of the places where two habitats meet.'" The emphasis on creating edge has been due in large part, one suspects, to the fact that many game animals (such as deer and grouse) are "edge-adapted." But not only game animals are edge-adapted; many other birds and small mammals found in urban and agricultural areas also benefit from habitat "patchiness" (which Noss describes as the "horizontal complexity of vegetation profiles"). Plants too are benefited by the convergence of habitat features; thus, edges also exhibit greater plant species diversity. Faunal diversity is, in turn, largely a function of the vegetative diversity.[10]

When considering alternative biodiversity conservation strategies or the effects on biodiversity of various land uses or disturbances, it is essential to consider scale. Maintaining a variety of patches of different successional age increases edge effect and is the primary way to increase beta (between-patch) diversity. But seeking to maximize local (alpha or beta) diversity can have "complications." "Emphasis on sheer numbers of species and habitats can . . . be dangerous," Noss warns, "when applied simplistically and irrespective of regional ecology." "Particularly in manipulated areas, beta diversity may include nonnative species and species typical of domesticated environments." These "[e]dge species . . . are mostly widespread and 'weedy,' [and] are rarely in danger of extinction in a human-dominated landscape."[11]

Similar caveats have been offered by others. Texas A&M University professor of range science Fred Smeins observes that "species diversity increases as environmental heterogeneity—or the patchiness of the habitat—does," and he cautions that management "intervention[s]" to "increas[e] the diversity of habitats within an ecosystem . . . can be a double-edge[d] sword." Writer-ecologist George Wuerthner criticizes the "tendency among range managers to ignore native species that may have narrow niches and [instead] look at big-game species as a barometer of wildlife health. . . . '[D]eer and elk are like pigeons and rats; they're more adaptable to change than other species. . . .'"[12]

Edge-adapted species are benefited by habitat fragmentation; breaking up blocks of habitat into smaller patches literally creates additional edge habitat. Much has been written about the adverse effects on species diversity of habitat fragmentation and reductions in the sizes of "habitat islands." Noss points out that "in many cases of habitat insularization, species *richness* does not seem to change or may even increase; species *composition*, however, often shifts toward taxa with low area requirements or high edge affinities." Habitats are fragmented by a variety of causes, natural and anthropogenic. Humans fragment habitats intentionally or inadvertently, by periodic burning or mowing, grazing, cutting small stands of trees, clearing land, and otherwise "interrupting" uniform habitats. Habitat fragmentation, and the concomitant creation of new edge habitat, can also result from clearing land for linear facilities, such as "roads, electric transmission lines, sewer lines, and even wide trails."[13]

Although these land uses and practices "enhance habitat patchiness and edge effect," and may consequently increase beta diversity, "this local increment is obtained at the expense of those species most in need of protection. The increment generally comprises species that are common in the urban-agricultural matrix"; the species lost are those "interior specialists" that require greater solitude or space or some other attribute of larger blocks of habitat. The disruptive mechanisms are diverse. Facilities and activities that fragment habitat "not only stress the mesic (moist) habitat of certain species, but can destabilize entire faunal communities." Linear developments such as road and powerline corridors may "serve as at least partial barriers to the movements of small mammals and could potentially disrupt normal dispersal patterns and population dynamics." Furthermore, "[c]orridor edges are frequently colonized by avian brood parasites (e.g., cowbirds), nest predators, and nonnative nest-hole competitors (e.g., starlings). These opportunists are usually abundant in the urban-agricultural matrix. . . ." For conservation purposes, it is crucial to know "which species are being favored by edge effects. A higher total species richness could be primarily due to an increased number of ruderal or weedy species of low conservation value . . . or to a higher number of legitimate community members."[14]

Managers thus must be wary of trying to *maximize* diversity, especially over a limited geographic area. An "uncritical acceptance of the maximum habitat diversity philosophy," Noss explains, "may be inimical to the preservation of regional diversity if applied routinely in a number of management units across a landscape." "Sensitive species that inhabit forest interiors or that are easily disturbed by humans suffer from this kind of management and may disappear from landscapes where no large, unmanipulated natural areas remain." Similar concerns exist for other biomes. Researchers in grassland ecosystems contend that the result of "replacing" bison with cattle has been "greater community heterogeneity at the square meter scale but greater homogeneity at the catena [i.e., soil type] and landscape scales." An emphasis on enhancing diversity at the local scale can actually "lead to regional impoverishment."[15]

Consider a large, contiguous block of habitat, area *A*, that is fragmented by some significant disturbance. Interior-adapted and reclusive species, as well as large, territorial predators or other animals with large home ranges, may be lost from area *A*. However, the edge effect created by conjoining disturbed and undisturbed sites may actually create new habitat for other species. The result within the perimeter of the former area *A* may actually be a larger number of species than before, but the new, edge-adapted species are likely to be species that already existed along *A*'s shared boundary with adjoining communities. The net result: more species within *A* but fewer species over the larger landscape of which *A* is a part. The greater the perimeter to area ratio, the greater the edge effect. A sufficiently small habitat may be effectively *all* edge habitat. Noss reports "increasing evidence that birds characteristic of forest interior habitats are unable to maintain their populations where edge is abundant." The same principle surely operates with respect to other interior specialists.[16]

Despite conservation biologists' warnings concerning the risks of ignoring scale, management and policy guidelines for diversity (where such guidance exists) generally do not acknowledge the issue. As Noss explains:

> The area of land over which maximum diversity is attained is usually not specified, but the general emphasis on edge development and measurement suggests that [the scale] is the individual management unit rather than the regional landscape. Hence maximum beta diversity is the goal and gamma diversity (except in the case of very large units) is ignored. Alpha diversity is also generally ignored. . . .

To illustrate his point, Noss cites the diversity provision of the National Forest Management Act (NFMA), which mandates guidelines for management plans that "provide for diversity of plant and animal communities based on the suitability and capability of the specific land area." While Noss fails to point out that the NFMA provision also calls for "preserv[ing] the diversity of tree species similar to that existing in the region," his concern is well founded. Given the statute's general language and the unexplained references to community diversity as well as diversity within the region, it is likely that neither Congress nor the drafters of this language considered issues of scale. The statute also gives forest managers no guidance regarding what components of biodiversity to conserve or how to achieve diversity goals.[17]

Congress is in good company. Most commentators on the effects of grazing or other land uses on biodiversity simply overlook the issue of scale; when they claim that grazing enhances biodiversity, they are referring (whether cognizantly or not) to edge-effect–induced increases in local (beta) biodiversity. Issues of scale may also be skirted intentionally. Laycock, for instance, clearly recognizes the implications of scale, but in one recent paper he overtly disregards or manipulates what conservation biologists have written about it, asserting: "Heavy livestock grazing, unless extremely widespread, increases the variety of habitats on a landscape level, improving both habitat diversity *and* edge. Thus, even if plant and animal species diversity is [*sic*] reduced, this grazing could *increase* habitat diversity on a larger total landscape level, theoretically increasing overall bird and animal diversity."[18]

Laycock cites no authority for this assertion or the effects of disturbances on landscape-level diversity. He also does not explain what he means by "heavy" grazing, "extremely widespread," "improving . . . edge," or *could* increase" (emphasis added). His assertions seem directly contrary to the conclusions of Noss, Cooperrider, and other conservation biologists and ecologists that grazing "homogenizes" habitats at the landscape level. Alternatively, Laycock's statement could be viewed as reflecting his own definitions of the various scales at which biodiversity can be measured; he does not explain what he means by "landscape" versus "larger total landscape." His use of "extremely widespread" might refer to a regional scale; if so, he implicitly admits that grazing may not increase diversity at the regional scale and, indeed, may reduce it. I prefer the more critical view of Laycock's statement, especially since he does not acknowledge that livestock grazing does not have to be "heavy" to affect species diversity, nor that grazing has been more widespread than any other land use in the West.

Another rather remarkable example of an unqualified claim that grazing can increase diversity also appears in the same compendium of range ecology papers. Discussing "patch dynamics," Pieper writes: "Not all consequences of grazing are detrimental, however. Domestic cattle, for example, produce seemingly endless quantities of dung, which is generally deposited in small heaps. These create local concentrations of nutrients returned to the system, and these enriched patches often exhibit clearly greater productivity or altered composition from the surrounding sward." He offers absolutely no explanation for why these changes should not be considered detrimental. He also introduces ambiguity with the phrase "greater productivity or altered composition." It is not clear whether he is attempting to equate the two or if he means them as alternate possibilities. In the latter case there is no reason to think that an "altered composition" resulting from nutrient input is necessarily desirable (as he clearly intimates).[19]

More importantly, the process that Pieper describes, at least if sufficiently widespread or intensive, poses potential negative consequences for natural ecosystem functioning and for species distribution and possibly composition. Hobbs and Huenneke report that increases "in baseline nutrient status," such as those resulting from "input from livestock feces," can "exacerbate the likelihood of invasions by weedy pest species." Deposition of feces and urine by livestock can alter the "baseline nutrient status" of ecosystems, causing "nutrient enrichment"; for most arid western rangelands, which have "a naturally low nutrient status," this "gradual enrichment" is an "important problem" with "important implications for the whole ecosystem." Those "endless quantities of dung" can have other detrimental impacts as well, such as water pollution and possible disease vectoring.[20]

Pieper also exaggerates the purported beneficial effects of the deposition of livestock feces. As Low and Berlin explain: "A 350 kg cow covers 0.75 [square meters] of ground each day with approximately 34 kg of feces . . . , smothering the plants beneath, changing the local nutrient balance, and providing a small 'island' for every nitrogen-tolerant plant or coprophagous animal species. In very dry habitats, degradation of feces may take years if suitable coprophages are absent." While seeds "eaten with herbage may pass through [a cow's] digestive tract unharmed," these "seeds, of course, are concentrated in the dung deposits. Few seeds will germinate until the dung has decomposed"—which, again, "may take years." This suggests that the species composition-altering effects of livestock feces—desirable or not—may continue long after livestock are removed from a range.[21]

Apart from the issue of scale, the extent to which enhancing edge effect will enhance species diversity surely has a limit. Two factors that influence that limit—aridity and coevolution—are discussed in chapter 5. Grazing may increase local diversity by increasing habitat patchiness and, hence, edge effect, but even local species diversity begins to decline as grazing intensity increases above some limit in arid and semiarid environments. In areas where plant species have evolved in the absence of grazing by large ungulates, livestock grazing is not likely to benefit native species. "Only on subhumid grasslands with long history of grazing does diversity reach a maximum at intermediate levels of grazing." In drier areas, weedy species, unpalatable species, and non-natives are most likely to thrive. An arid or semiarid rangeland community that is more diverse because it contains more weedy species that are widely distributed or more nonnative invaders such as cheatgrass is not a management goal to be strived for.[22]

The goals of management are, of course, key. As West remarks, whether creation of a "patchwork" of habitats to "optimize the mix of cattle and wild ungulates" is "desirable or not depends on who is paying the bills and benefiting from the consequences." He is referring to manipulations of biodiversity for reasons other than restoring or maintaining native diversity. Even where an objective of management is to use grazing to alter the natural vegetative community, it still must be determined whether the desired change can be achieved in this way. The side effects of achieving that change should also be considered. For instance, a management plan targeted at improving big game habitat and livestock forage may have a negative impact on other animals. The effect of any land use management plan other than one designed to conserve native biodiversity will have unintended consequences for diversity. Indeed, given the state of our knowledge, even a plan targeted at conserving diversity is likely to fall short of its goal.[23]

Unqualified claims by a land manager, range scientist, or stockgrower that some habitat manipulation will increase diversity should not be taken at face value. When range managers or industry apologists attempt to justify public land grazing on the ground that it enhances biological diversity, the assertion must be examined more closely. Is the prediction based on relevant information for the specific site conditions? How will species composition be affected? What species will be benefited, or increased, by grazing, and at what geographic or ecological scales? What species may be harmed or even eliminated? Are the benefited species native to the area? Are they rare or common or even weedy? What will be the eventual species composition of the site, and how will it compare to what might be expected in the absence of human-caused disturbances? How will species abundance compare to natural conditions? Can livestock be used to help return the community to a composition, or seral stage, from which it has "retrogressed" as a result of human disturbances, or will grazing simply bring about another artificially induced condition? These are among the questions that managers should address before implementing any biodiversity conservation strategy that allows livestock grazing to continue or uses grazing as a tool.

C. RESERVE CONSIDERATIONS: SIZE, CONFIGURATION, HABITAT TYPE AND QUALITY

Biologists disagree over the optimum features, such as size and configuration, of biodiversity preserves. Many argue "the bigger, the better"; most would at least agree that "the *more*, the better": "redundancy . . . is a very desirable character-istic of an ecosystem conservation system." Two decades ago Dasmann opined: "It is probably true to say that we can't have too many ecological reserves. . . . With the increasing rate of human modification of all lands and waters on earth, the time for establishing such reserves grows distressingly short."[24]

The first three steps in a biodiversity conservation strategy, according to Donald M. Waller, are to identify areas with the highest levels of biodiversity and then to "protect as many as possible in the largest blocks possible." The reserve size criterion has attracted considerable attention in recent years. Eco-systems "seem to have a minimum critical size." Reserves can be too small to be effective, but they probably can't be too big. Large preserves are undoubtedly essential for some species (e.g., species with large home range requirements or highly diverse habitat needs); they are also more likely than smaller preserves to contain a greater proportion of any given species' habitat requirements and at least some higher-quality habitat. In addition, larger preserves, especially those with relatively small perimeter to area ratios, have a greater capacity to insulate or buffer against disturbances. Small, isolated preserves are not "well suited to maintaining viable populations in the long term, due to problems of demo-graphic and genetic stochasticity, and to natural catastrophes . . . even if we assume a stable climate."[25]

Larger preserves may effectively be created by connecting smaller preserves. But the connecting corridors must themselves meet certain requirements; for example, they must be wide enough to be usable by animals moving between habitat areas and not so long that movement would be discouraged, and they must contain appropriate habitat (at a minimum, sufficient cover). Noss distinguishes between strip corridors, which are "wide enough to maintain interior conditions in their centers," and line corridors such as fence rows and treelines, which are "essentially all edge habitat." Ideally, preserves would protect complete ecosystems and would be larger rather than smaller, unfragmented, and several.[26]

The bigger the area preserved, the more likely it will contain complete ecosystems or, more accurately, connected ecosystems and regions, and the greater the potential for preserving "indigenous ecosystem structure, function, and integrity." Preserving "whole ecosystems with [their] full complement of indigenous genetic diversity is the ideal," Noss states. As a practical matter, regional landscape planning "demands a complex of both large and small preserves and as many as possible, taking advantage of auspicious protection opportunities when they arise," and "recognizing the importance of broad corridors connecting habitat islands." It is also important to preserve as many kinds of ecosystems as possible. Indeed, "preservation of multiple examples of all natural communities occurring in the U.S. should be a national goal."[27]

Reserve size is important for another practical reason—it is inversely proportional to the level of management and affirmative protection efforts required to restore or maintain an area's "natural" conditions. Noss illustrates, using an old-growth forest example:

> In natural landscapes *unmodified by man*, disturbances are patchy in time and space and range from the removal of individual trees to devastation of many square kilometers. . . . But in fragmented systems, both disturbance and lack of disturbance can be threats to regional diversity. . . . This dilemma arises because of the small sizes and artificial boundaries and spacing of most surviving habitat islands. . . . The smaller the preserve, the more necessary is [*sic*] vigorous protection *and* management to retain or restore the conditions for which the preserve is set aside.

This advice suggests, conversely, yet another advantage of preserving large contiguous areas: active management may not be required to achieve diversity restoration and protection goals. As we saw in chapter 5, however, simply terminating the unnatural disturbances on deteriorated, semiarid ranges may not lead to the restoration of predisturbance conditions—and certainly will not accomplish that objective if the overgrazing and/or other disturbances have caused site conservation thresholds to be exceeded.[28]

This potential for "passive restoration" in large reserves is important, nevertheless, for several practical reasons. First, and most fundamentally, given the current limits of science we may not know what management prescriptions will achieve the desired conditions on a given site. Second, for the foreseeable future funds for such management will be in short supply. And finally, larger areas will allow a greater margin for error for management efforts that, being largely experimental, are bound to fail occasionally, perhaps more often than not.

The idea of setting aside land to preserve it for its natural values dates to at least 1872 in the United States when Yellowstone Park was reserved from the public domain. A few regional biodiversity initiatives are now being implemented, for example, in the Greater Yellowstone Ecosystem, Pacific Northwest forests, and coastal sage scrub in California. But few areas have actually been set aside for biological diversity conservation purposes, based on modern scientific knowledge concerning the importance of, and most effective strategies for, preserving that diversity. As a result, most reserves are too small or are improperly configured: their boundaries are nearly always politically determined, rather than based on biological, geological, or other relevant considerations.[29]

In addition, many community types and landscapes are under- or unrepresented in preserve systems. David W. Crumpacker et al. concluded that at least 33 of 135 Kuchler potential natural vegetation (PNV) types are inadequately or not represented on federal and Indian lands. Waller reported that "22 percent of the various kinds of ecosystems recognized in this country are not represented" on federal lands in blocks of 10,000 hectares or larger. Research natural areas, which are relatively small (generally 15 to 400 hectares), "represent only a small fraction of the diversity of plant communities" in national forests. Crumpacker et al., however, observed that some PNV types were well represented and, at least in 1967, were still in "natural or seminatural condition." Of 27 million hectares of sagebrush steppe type on federal and Indian lands, 85 percent were "estimated to be in natural or seminatural condition in 1967."[30]

Cooperrider correctly points out that current preserve systems in the United States "were not established to preserve biological diversity," and he offers western rangelands as evidence. Both grasslands and deserts "are poorly represented in United States reserves, particularly where they do not exist in landscapes with scenic geological features," which make it more likely that the area might be protected as a park or wilderness. Even though it is a "fundamental purpose" of national parks and monuments "to conserve the scenery and the natural . . . objects and the wild life therein," and every wilderness area is to be managed "to preserve its natural conditions," traditionally neither kind of preserve has been established for its biological values. As Graf observes, scientists were "[n]otable by their absence during the move to establish the Wilderness Act."[31]

Furthermore, many under- or unrepresented communities and landscapes are deteriorating; the need to preserve them is thus even more pressing. West notes that, while most western rangeland is "less fragmented than ecosystems in wetter parts of the country, even low levels of fragmentation may result in ill-functioning communities. [Thus, we] must expect greater efforts to protect declining and under represented ecosystem types [and] to restore missing species and community types. . . ." The lion's share of this fragmentation has been caused by grazing. Less than 1 percent of the sagebrush steppe vegetation type, a major vegetation type in the Intermountain West, has never been grazed; 30 percent has been grazed heavily. Grazing continues to be allowed in more than one-third of designated wilderness areas and will likely be even more prevalent in BLM wildernesses (final designations for which are pending in several states). Miller et al. cite the need for "designated research sites throughout the sagebrush region to conduct long term research." But Noss and Cooperrider warn that *grazed* areas, even within designated wildernesses, "cannot possibly serve as reserves or as benchmark areas for evaluating effects of grazing."[32]

Appropriately selected reserves may serve one or both of two specific purposes: "(1) [as] core areas for protecting sensitive elements of biodiversity, and (2) [as] benchmark or control areas with minimal human manipulation so that the effects of multiple-use management can be compared." Currently, "[m]ost rangeland landscapes suffer from a lack of reserves large enough to serve either purpose adequately." The proposal set out here would go a long way toward addressing these deficiencies. First, it would establish large preserves, which would protect not only "sensitive elements of biodiversity," but the full complement of native biota. Second, although reserve areas would remain available for a wide range of multiple uses, they could still serve as "benchmark or control areas with minimal human manipulation" because the most significant disturbance, livestock grazing, would be eliminated.[33]

Designating large blocks of BLM lands as biodiversity preserves is an example of "taking advantage" of one of the "auspicious protection opportunities" to which Noss refers. Law professor Robert Keiter observes that the "[b]iologically rich yet still relatively undeveloped western public lands offer an ideal setting for" establishing a "large system of interconnected nature reserves." While Keiter opines that national parks, wilderness areas, and wildlife refuges "come closest to meeting these prescriptions," others point to the huge, untapped potential of the BLM lands. Crumpacker et al. report that a "surprisingly large number of major terrestrial and wetland ecosystems"—53 percent of all PNV types—are represented on BLM lands. They conclude: "This emphasizes the importance of [BLM] in developing a national strategy for conservation of ecosystem diversity." Cooperrider also recognizes BLM lands' significance, pointing out that in 1991 "BLM wilderness study areas represent 111 of 138 Bailey-Kuchler [habitat] types in the West, many of which are not now in any wilderness system."[34]

It will not be sufficient, however, to preserve only the available large tracts of relatively intact habitat on BLM lands. As many scientists and managers and even the public are coming to recognize, the success of diversity preservation efforts will depend on employing a multifaceted strategy that targets private, state, and federal lands. An essential facet of any biodiversity protection effort in the West will be protection of riparian zones.[35]

Healthy desert streams and associated riparian communities are uniquely productive. Riparian vegetation shelters streams, providing sustenance and shade for the lotic community. Riparian communities "may provide habitat for the majority of the Rocky Mountain region's amphibians and reptiles." They are crucial not only to the animals that reside there but to a large fraction of all animal species found on arid and semiarid lands. "Studies of riparian areas in southeast Oregon, Wyoming, Arizona, and New Mexico have shown that 75% to 80% of wildlife species depend on these green patches for some or all of their life cycles." Intensive inventories of the San Pedro River in southern Arizona, a stream that has been the subject of intensive restoration efforts, reveal that it is home to 382 species of birds, 82 mammals, 45 amphibians and reptiles, and 12 fish. Its avifauna represents "almost one-half of the bird species found in the continental United States." The diversity of the San Pedro is presumed to be typical of the diversity of the few remaining riparian habitats in southern Arizona. While some species once found along the river, including the "grizzly bear, jaguar, Mexican wolf, two native desert pupfish subspecies, . . . squawfish, razorback sucker, [and] humpback sucker," are now missing, the "area still holds surprises." A new vascular plant species, never before described, was recently discovered here.[36]

Western riparian habitats, which two U.S. Fish and Wildlife Service biologists have described as "important and endangered," are extremely vulnerable to damage by livestock grazing. Riparian zones produce a disproportionate amount of the forage on a given area, but, because of cattle's fondness for low, moist, shady spots, the disproportion of riparian vegetation in cattle diets is even more lopsided. In one Oregon allotment riparian areas comprise only 2 percent of the allotment area, but produce 20 percent of the total available forage and *80 percent* of the forage actually consumed by cows. Similar heavy use by cattle is endangering riparian zones across the West.[37]

Despite these reasons for concern, the condition of public land riparian areas, at least until recently, was largely unknown. Barely 10 percent of the BLM's 7.3 million acres of riparian lands are in the eleven western states; the rest are in Alaska. Yet in 1992 the agency professed not to know the status of more than 85 percent of these lands, because it either had not inventoried them or had not set condition objectives. Two years earlier the agency had reported that only 7 percent of BLM riparian areas outside Alaska were "meeting objectives," and 10 percent "were not meeting objectives"; the status of 83 percent was "unknown."[38]

In 1994 the BLM reported riparian area conditions based on its new range condition methods, which assess "whether rangeland conditions on a site can sustain natural plant communities and basic ecological functions." Using this system, the BLM estimated that 34 percent of riparian areas are in proper functioning condition; 46 percent are "at risk" or susceptible to degradation (which means that "the capabilities of proper functioning areas are threatened by livestock grazing activities"); and 20 percent are not functioning properly. In other words, two-thirds of BLM riparian lands are not, or may not be, healthy, functioning ecosystems. This is a far cry from the agency's goal of not less than 75 percent of riparian areas in proper functioning condition by 1997. Furthermore, the 1994 condition figures do not account for the riparian habitats already lost on BLM lands. As we saw in chapter 3, federal land managers consider public land riparian areas "to be in their worst condition in history."[39]

Very little public land riparian habitat has been protected. Most streamside habitats remain available for stock grazing, the human activity known to have had the most deleterious impacts. The severest losses, not surprisingly, have been in the most arid regions. According to the director of research at the Rincon Institute, in Phoenix, many riparian ecosystems in the Southwest "have disappeared completely." In Arizona and New Mexico, where "riparian zones comprise only 1 or 2 percent of the total land area," "90 percent of these habitats have been lost or degraded over the last century." In California, less than 1 percent of all riparian habitat types are protected.[40]

Protecting riparian zones on western pubic lands is crucial in meeting the habitat needs of hundreds of plant and animal species. It also would provide important linkage areas and travel corridors between habitat islands—a significant step toward preventing the insularization of populations and ensuring genetic diversity. The health of riparian habitats is a reflection of watershed health, and protecting riparian zones goes a long way toward ensuring the quality of the water in the stream. Everything we know about these crucial habitats compels the conclusion that *all* riparian areas on western federal lands should be restored where necessary and preserved.[41]

D. THE BASICS: LANDSCAPE-LEVEL CONSERVATION BIOLOGY

What does it mean to manage land in order to preserve biodiversity and properly functioning ecosystem processes at the landscape level? To begin, we need some working definitions. According to M. Godron, R. T. T. Forman, Noss, and others, a landscape is "a kilometers-wide area where a cluster of interacting stands or ecosystems is repeated in similar form." An "ecological unit with a distinguishable structure," a landscape is "defined by a common geomorphologic process and a common disturbance regime." In contrast with ecosystems, landscapes are "almost always highly heterogeneous." Landscape ecology, in turn, has been defined as "the study of the interactions and fluxes of energy, mineral nutrients, and species among clustered stands or ecosystems." The science of landscape ecology "deals with an ecological mosaic of patches with continuously varying degrees of connectedness and recognizes the importance of matrix and corridors to terrestrial habitat island dynamics." Landscapes are dynamic; paleoecological research shows that the composition of communities, or patches, changes continually as species' geographic ranges shift in response to climate.[42]

Ecology in its early years focused on individual ecosystems, but ecosystems are not, and should not be viewed as, discrete entities. Noss proposes the "landscape mosaic [as] a more appropriate unit of study and management than single sites or ecosystems." Looking at landscapes rather than at the components of landscapes also offers some advantages for management. "Through an integration of concepts, the landscape paradigm identifies patterns that might otherwise go unnoticed. These patterns include regional trends in extinction and colonization, relative abundances of species and habitat types, and spatiotemporal dynamics of the structural components of a landscape." When the concern is preserving landscapes or regions, "species composition and abundances, not simple number of species, assume primary importance."[43]

As we have seen, efforts to maintain overall native diversity will be most likely to succeed if conducted at the landscape or regional scale. A "reasonable goal" for maintaining biodiversity at the landscape scale would be "to maintain a shifting mosaic of seral stages that resembles that which would occur over large areas in the absence of human interference." This would facilitate not only the preservation of plant and animal communities, but also the continuation of natural landscape conditions and processes. Admittedly, the approach is fraught with complications and uncertainties. The lack of detailed information concerning presettlement vegetative conditions is one example. Still, an advantage of "measuring the landscape against some defined mix of vegetation communities" is that the approach would "apply over a planning period of decades." A planning horizon of "decades" or longer allows for natural variability and adjustments in management to accommodate unforeseen developments; it is also compatible with a goal of sustainability.[44]

What does "sustaining" a certain mix of plant communities mean, on the ground? At least a couple interpretations seem possible. First, range managers could endeavor to maintain indefinitely a specific plant community on each range site. In this way, the prescribed mix of communities across broad areas also would be maintained. Alternatively, once the desired mix of communities (and range of condition or seral stage within communities) was determined, community boundaries could shift as long as the relative proportions of types and conditions were maintained. Either approach would require management based on an understanding of plant community dynamics, including an ability to predict and thus facilitate or manipulate macroscale fluctuations.

Applied landscape ecology might be analogized to ecosystem management, but it is actually an extrapolation thereof. It focuses not on single ecosystems, but on a "mosaic" of interrelating ecosystems or communities. "[F]ield naturalists have known for a long time that many organisms habitually move among 'different' communities." This counsels in favor of managing to conserve habitats on a landscape, or regional, basis. Birds, for instance, often move among two or more distinct habitat types (communities) to meet their needs for food, space, and shelter. It would be just as absurd to expect these birds to subsist in only one community or the other as to attempt to manage for theoretical "average" habitat requirements.[45]

I can offer a striking example from my own BLM field experience. Bald eagles wintering in the cold deserts of Nevada and Utah make use of certain common features of the Great Basin landscape. They spend the day in open, relatively flat areas, feeding on rodents or lagomorphs, often road-killed jackrabbits. They may perch on powerlines, fence posts, or elevated topographic features (even gravel piles) to get a better view of the hunting terrain, but they often simply rest on level ground. Each afternoon or evening they fly to a nearby mountain range to a communal roosting area, usually in mature conifer trees, where they presumably remain until the next morning. These two very different habitat requirements do not lend themselves to "averaging." It seems certain that bald eagles wintering in these areas require *both* kinds of habitat within reasonable proximity. As this example reveals, landscape structure and habitat type are important and interrelated. The eagles apparently require both elevational, topographic, and structural variation and distinct vegetative communities.

The goal of preserving a landscape, Noss writes, is to preserve its "indigenous ecosystem structure, function, and integrity."

> For any landscape, the model natural ecosystem complex is the *presettlement* vegetation and associated biotic and abiotic elements. Preservation activities would ideally maintain high-quality examples of presettlement-type ecosystems in approximate proportion to their former abundance in the region. This does not mean trying to hold nature static. Rather, *preservation* should imply perpetuating the dynamic processes of presettlement landscapes.

As this prescription reveals, one of the first steps in planning for the conservation of a landscape's biological resources should be to sort out natural and human-caused disturbances and identify the influences of each.[46]

Natural, presettlement disturbance factors, which influence the constantly changing appearance and composition of a landscape, include climate and meteorology, the evolution and natural extinction of species, and geological processes. An objective of conservation biology is a landscape shaped by these forces, rather than by human activities. Why attempt to exclude or minimize human-caused disturbances from certain landscapes? After all, we hear so often in this era of growing interest in managing ecosystems that human beings are a part of, not separate from, the environment. The reason is simple: "Total diversity of species at the landscape level [is predicted to] be greatest when disturbance occurs at its historical frequency and in its historical pattern." This seems reasonable, given that ecologists generally agree that greater diversity promotes greater environmental resilience (the "shock absorber" concept) and, hence, stability.[47]

The greater diversity in unmodified habitats reflects the fact that humans, for the most part, modify rather than adjust to their environment. As Sheridan explains, "in their struggle for survival against aridity, certain plants and animals have evolved 'fantastic—sometimes unbelievable—adaptations.' Humans, on the other hand, have evolved no significant physiological adaptations, such as water-storing organs." A landscape approach to conserving biodiversity is predicated on the realization that humans have altered their environment in ways and to degrees that exceed landscapes' natural capacities to absorb such change. We affect the environment in ways that no other species can or ever has—by drastically hastening extinction rates, altering the global climate, consuming and translocating resources, etc. In some instances we may simply be accelerating changes that would have occurred eventually, though over a much longer time scale. Or we may be causing disturbances that deflect succession or evolution in radically different directions. For instance, would cheatgrass have migrated to North America and established itself so resolutely on this continent if humans had not migrated from Eurasia? We often do not know even whether we are altering the environment, much less what the ramifications of changes may be and whether they are reversible.[48]

Knowing what the "model natural ecosystem complex" is or should be suggests what the objective of biodiversity conservation at the landscape level should be, but it does not tell us how to get there. Noss advises that we "can attempt only to approximate the pristine, presettlement condition, and this new landscape will not 'manage itself.'" He and Cooperrider have outlined several recommendations for managing reserves, with special emphasis on rangelands:

1. "Make management and [the] legal/administrative designation congruent,"
2. "Remove or control incompatible uses,"
3. "Control exotics,"
4. "Distinguish internal and external problems and implement appropriate programs,"
5. "Establish connectivity between reserves,"
6. "Determine key ecological processes and manage to maintain or restore them,"
7. "Identify opportunities or needs for expansion of reserves and take appropriate action," and
8. "Identify needs for buffering and take appropriate action."[49]

Note that Noss and Cooperrider do not propose large, new reserves; instead, they emphasize managing and possibly expanding extant reserves. They also suggest that "hot spots" of biodiversity on BLM lands be protected via designation as "areas of critical environmental concern" (ACECs), wilderness areas, research natural areas, "or whatever designation is feasible." None of these designations is tailored to achieve landscape-level biodiversity conservation. Still, each can promote biodiversity conservation goals if utilized to good advantage by managers, and all will be useful components of any broad-scale conservation program, including the proposal advanced herein.[50]

E. THE SPECIFICS: MANAGING ARID WESTERN RANGELANDS AS BIODIVERSITY PRESERVES

Two scientists writing in 1985 characterized ranching in the Great Basin as the "'Grand Experiment.'" I propose an even grander experiment: removing livestock from these and other arid western public lands so ill-suited to that use as the key mechanism of a program to reestablish and maintain the native species composition and ecosystem processes in these areas.[51]

A necessary preliminary step in implementing or even considering such a proposal will be to identify BLM rangelands of a suitable size and shape with respect to the landscape in which they occur. So-called checkerboard areas probably should be excluded from the program unless significant exchange opportunities are feasible, except along the boundaries of the checkerboard where public sections adjoin larger blocks of BLM lands. ("Checkerboard" land ownership patterns exist along railroad rights-of-way in the West, a result of the mid-1800s federal policy of granting alternate sections of land to railroad companies to encourage new construction. The legacy is a 20- to 40-mile swath of country in which alternating sections, or square miles of land, are federal and private, with scattered state-owned sections.) Larger, "kilometers-wide" tracts managed by BLM are widely dispersed:

Utah: southeastern, central, and western portions of the state;
Nevada: throughout the state, excluding only military reservations, the Union Pacific Railroad (checkerboard) corridor, and two national forests;
California: relatively limited areas in northeastern and southeastern portions of the state;
Colorado: chiefly northwestern and west-central parts of the state, and scattered areas in the southwest and central region;
Idaho: southwestern, south-central (Snake River Plain), and east-central (Challis area) portions of the state;

Wyoming: southwestern, south-central, central (Great Divide Basin), and
    north-central (Big Horn Basin) portions of the state;
Arizona: scattered areas in the northwest, along the western border, and in
    the southwest, and a limited area in the southeast;
New Mexico scattered areas across the state, except the northeast;
Oregon: south-central and southeastern portions of the state;
Washington: very few scattered parcels in the central portion of the state.[52]

The next step will be to determine the condition of these rangelands. In
particular, this will entail attempting to ascertain whether deterioration has
exceeded some site conservation threshold(s). Range managers will not lack
technical guidance for this task. As noted in chapter 5, the EPA is conducting
research, as part of the arid lands portion of its Environmental Monitoring and
Assessment Program (EMAP), to "develop ecological indicators and rangeland
classification systems." In addition, the technical literature contains useful information. Miller et al. have summarized field ecology studies that shed light on
how site condition and threshold determinations might be made and on
assessing restoration potential. One study determined that the "potential for
increased cover of perennial native herbaceous species generally occurs when
sagebrush species cover is below the maximum potential level, a residual of
perennial herbaceous species is present and competition from Eurasian weeds is
absent or minimal." These and similar determinations will be at least partly
subjective. Where expertise beyond that currently possessed by BLM range
conservationists is required, professionals from the range science and ecology
departments of western universities and others will be available for consulta-
tion. Training, if it is not already underway, should be provided in the near
future in conjunction with the BLM's adoption of a new system for evaluating
range condition.[53]

If natural, or relatively natural, conditions exist in the area, elimination or
continued exclusion of livestock should help facilitate the maintenance or
restoration of native biodiversity and natural ecological processes. As we saw in
chapter 5, increases in plant species diversity have been documented in several
areas after termination of grazing. Miller et al. predict that, where "plant communities have not crossed a threshold into another steady state," protection
from grazing can produce "a return to good ecological condition." Thus, if no
site conservation threshold has been exceeded, a plausible conservation strategy
would be simply to allow natural plant community dynamics to operate. This
would entail removing "unnatural" disturbances, including domestic livestock,
and monitoring ecological conditions. This is not to suggest that "pristine conditions" can be reestablished merely by removing livestock or that any recovery to
more natural conditions will be rapid. Such expectations would, as Pieper has

observed, be "too simplistic in light of other changes that have occurred . . . and many extrinsic factors," such as weather variations. Severson and Urness further caution that the results will depend on the specific characteristics of the site; implementation of grazing management changes will require "an intimate knowledge of the ecological processes controlling rangeland biota."[54]

If the range site is dominated by weedy species and nonnative annuals and soils are severely eroded, however, a threshold may have been crossed. Such sites "have lost genetic, species, and structural diversity"; they have lost their "shock absorber." Presumed climax conditions (the potential natural community that would exist in the absence of human-caused disturbances) probably could not be reachieved in these areas. Maintenance of the existing steady state or rehabilitation to some improved condition will require removal of livestock *and* active management intervention.[55]

If the site is currently in an alternate steady state, or in transition between seral stages, it may be impossible to achieve potential natural conditions, at least given our current knowledge and expertise. In either case, however, management should be able to influence the direction and character of changes in the vegetative condition and "improve the habitat value for many declining species." Measures may include "rehabilitat[ing] damaged soils, streams, and watersheds" as well as "reintroduc[ing] extirpated species wherever possible." The argument advanced by some range scientists that it "does not necessarily follow that management for climax is necessary, desirable, or achievable" usually reflects a land use agenda having livestock production as a fundamental component. Archer and Smeins plainly demonstrate this bias when they cite management considerations based on producing livestock to support the assertion.[56]

The literature contains considerable evidence that rehabilitation of degraded arid rangelands is difficult at best. According to Allen, "Of the many restoration projects in the western U.S. and elsewhere, none have achieved the goal of bringing back the diversity of species that once existed at a particular site." Even "the best examples of restoration have been able to reintroduce only a fraction of the plant species richness, and natural recolonization is slow." Similarly, Munda and Smith report "numerous, largely unsuccessful attempts to revegetate degraded desert rangelands in the southwestern U.S." These studies may simply reflect the limits of the knowledge and technological skills employed at the site, or they may indicate that vegetative thresholds had been crossed at the study sites and that "restoration," indeed, was not feasible.[57]

An option in the latter circumstance would be to attempt to achieve and maintain a desirable alternate steady state—which might be the site's current condition or some other desired plant community achievable by management measures, perhaps even grazing. Well-managed goats, for instance, have shown promise as a tool for reducing or eliminating certain intractable introduced plant pests, such as leafy spurge. No livestock grazing should be allowed in biodiversity reserves, however, "unless it can be clearly established that grazing is *necessary* to substitute for a natural process (e.g., native ungulate grazing) that for some compelling reason cannot be reestablished." This is likely to be the case in few if any areas.[58]

By intimating that grazing might be used to achieve desired vegetative conditions I do not intend to open up the subject of available management tools and methods for managing degraded rangelands to restore natural biodiversity. The focus herein is on the utility of removing livestock as a biodiversity conservation tool. It is worth noting, however, that most available guidance for rehabilitating degraded ranges is tainted with the livestock production bias noted in chapter 5; consequently, it may be of little use to managers whose aim is to conserve native biodiversity.

Heady, for example, counseled that, because "the land manager has little or no control over climate, large and small native herbivores, pathogens, alien species, fire, and carbon dioxide in the atmosphere," control over vegetation "lies mostly with domestic herbivores, pest control chemicals, and prescribed fire." As "wild space decreases, the need for more knowledgeable *and intensive use* of herbivores, chemicals, and fire as tools for vegetational management will increase." Heady's premises are overstated and his advice is inconsistent and reactionary. Missing is any mention of integrated (or biological) pest manage-ment methods other than "intensive use of [domestic] herbivores." He ignores *removal* of livestock as a management tool. He also disregards any need or ability to conserve "wild space"; he simply presumes the inevitability of its continued loss. If biodiversity is to be conserved, range managers must become more crea-tive and less hidebound in their efforts to repair ranges damaged by a century of livestock use.[59]

Once a site is identified as appropriate for inclusion in a biodiversity reserve, the next step will be to decide what land uses are compatible with the goal of conserving rangeland biodiversity and how those uses must be managed. According to Noss and Cooperrider, the relevant inquiry "is not 'Is the system going to be altered?' but rather 'How much is it going to be altered' and 'For how long will it be affected?' and 'What is the probability that it can be returned to its natural state?'" "Management," they note, "should be designed to avoid moving plant communities beyond those irreversible thresholds that lead to unstable or impoverished ecosystems. Practices are not justifiable if they result in loss of species or in soil erosion in excess of soil formation." The old adage "An ounce of prevention is worth a pound of cure" will be a useful guiding principle. "The philosophy underlying conservation biology and other applied sciences," Noss explains, "is one of prudence: in the face of uncertainty, applied scientists have an ethical obligation to risk erring on the side of preservation."[60]

In the case of livestock grazing, prudence is especially warranted but has long been in short supply. There have been warnings down through the years—

from seers as well as the land itself—about the impacts of grazing in the arid West. None has been heeded. Powell instinctively knew that if livestock grazing were to be sustainable in the West it must be very carefully managed and at low stocking levels. Even Clements recommended "that millions of the most fragile areas in the Southwest and Great Basin be set aside wholly for recreation or as wilderness" because grazing could cause permanent damage there.[61]

G. A. Pearson, a Forest Service scientist in the Southwest in the 1930s, doubted that "any system of commercial grazing could have avoided the decline" in western range carrying capacity, given the region's aridity. He concluded that about half of the range was at best marginal, "[i]f not distinctly submarginal," for livestock production. Twenty years later grazing practices had changed little, and another Forest Service scientist argued bluntly that millions of acres of arid and semiarid western lands should be closed to all grazing. This land, Forsling wrote, "is too poor and vulnerable to damage to sustain grazing use."[62]

Today we know that grazing can irreversibly alter natural vegetative communities. There is no longer any excuse for what scientists term a "Type II error," that is, "claiming no effect when one actually exists." Type II errors are dangerous because "they can result in irreversible damage." Livestock grazing is incompatible with preserving landscape-scale native biodiversity on western ranges averaging 12 inches or less of annual precipitation. Leaving livestock on these ranges poses the risk of irreversible damage, where it has not already occurred, and continued decline of already-converted communities.[63]

Grazing advocates may argue that livestock grazing should be allowed to continue, since "removing livestock may not suffice to improve range condition." While this may be true, it "does not mean that unrestricted grazing should prevail." Scientists cannot deny, Coggins argues, that "lowering grazing intensity will be a necessary element in any overall scheme for improvement." But merely "lowering grazing intensity" will be inadequate or inefficient to achieve biodiversity conservation goals in many areas. *Any* grazing poses a risk of loss of native species, and the cost of lowering grazing levels would in many cases only make grazing even less profitable and thus even more objectionable as a use of public lands.[64]

The choice of land use should depend on application of a sustainability criterion. "If livestock can be grazed in such a way as to preserve the biological diversity and ecological integrity of the landscape," Cooperrider writes, "there are few reasons to oppose such grazing." But he and Noss conclude:

> In light of the detrimental effects of livestock and the difficult challenge of grazing an area sustainably, livestock will need to be removed from many areas where they are now grazed, particularly those areas of the West that receive less than, say 10 to 15 inches of annual precipitation. A policy such as this may require removal of livestock from over 50 percent of the West. . . .

[I]t is difficult to see how grazing in these areas, which supported few large herbivores in pre-Columbian times, can be made sustainable.[65]

Noss and Cooperrider have suggested certain guidelines designed to help ensure that, where livestock grazing is allowed to continue, grazing is compatible with the goal of conserving biodiversity. Readers should keep in mind that these guidelines are not tailored to the more arid lands that are our focus. I pass on these recommendations as general guidelines only. If public land managers choose to allow livestock grazing to continue on arid lands unsuited to livestock production, these guidelines might help mitigate the adverse ecological effects. My comments respecting the guidelines are noted parenthetically.

First, Noss and Cooperrider advise, grazing should be planned at the landscape level because planning at a smaller scale can fragment the habitat and lead to a loss of gamma diversity. (Landscape-level planning will necessitate landscape- and regional-scale evaluations of environmental consequences in agency NEPA analyses.) Second, predator control, *if necessary*, should be accomplished by removing only occasional problem animals, not by a wholesale eradication program. Third, timing, intensity, and frequency of grazing should be managed so as to prevent livestock from high-grading the forage. (Implementing this guideline will require careful monitoring and timing of use.) Fourth, degradation of sensitive areas, such as riparian zones, must be avoided. (Degradation of BLM riparian lands, if judged "unnecessary or undue" by agency managers, would be prohibited by FLPMA.) Fifth, "grazing should try to mimic the natural [grazing] pattern, for instance by bison. Ideally, . . . the native herbivore should be reintroduced." (Recall that in most of the areas that are the focus of this book, bison were not historically present or were present only sporadically or in very small numbers.)[66]

Noss and Cooperrider's sixth recommendation is that grazing should be compatible with natural disturbance regimes, such as fire. (This would seem to preclude grazing in all areas already invaded, or prone to invasion, by cheatgrass.) A seventh, key guideline is to minimize the risk of exceeding irreversible thresholds. Eighth, management must recognize the averages and extremes in site environmental conditions. (Grazing practices cannot be designed for average conditions when precipitation will be less than average half the time; stocking a range on the basis of its average carrying capacity results in overstocking almost half the time.) Ninth, grazing management must be much more flexible than it currently is in order to take advantage of, or withstand, rare events. (But stockgrowers may lack the fiscal and logistical flexibility necessary to adjust their business practices accordingly.) And finally, the "bottom line": "Grazing should not result in the loss of any native plant or animal species from the regional landscape, or impoverishment of any other measure of native biodiversity (genetic integrity, natural relative abundance patterns, etc.)." (This reinforces the conclusion that grazing will be an unacceptable land use on the more arid sites because, as we have seen, species loss will be likely there.)[67]

Probably the strongest biodiversity-based argument against allowing grazing to continue on arid public lands is the unavoidable link between livestock grazing and the introduction and spread of nonnative species. According to one scholar, "exotics are the most overlooked threat to biodiversity." Exotics are a factor in the decline of 46 percent of species listed as federally threatened or endangered, second only to habitat loss and degradation.[68]

Hobbs and Huenneke have observed that, "when the choice is between natives and non-native pest species," the decision should be "easy." Preferring native species over nonindigenous biota is not mere parochial "purism." The goal of preserving a landscape is to preserve its "*indigenous* ecosystem structure, function, and integrity." Species diversity at the landscape level is predicted to be "greatest when disturbance occurs at its historical frequency and in its historical pattern." By definition, nonnative species constitute an unnatural disturbance; their presence diminishes the integrity of the natural ecosystem.[69]

Nonindigenous plants or animals do not function in their new ecosystem as did the species they replaced or as do the species with which they compete for available resources. While their role and function in the "adopted" ecosystem will likely overlap with those of existing, native species—even to the point, possibly, of outcompeting a native for space or nutrients—the simple fact that the introduced species did not evolve at that location, under those conditions, ensures that it cannot substitute perfectly for a native. For instance, an introduced species of grass might thrive at least temporarily on the new site's soil and climatic conditions, but its root system might not hold the soil as well as the native it replaced, or its seeds might be unpalatable to the granivorous bird that had depended on the native grass.

A nonnative species, which possesses a competitive advantage over a native species that it replaces, may not only cause a loss of native species, it may actually destabilize the ecosystem. A graphic example, though a nonrangeland one, is the threat posed by the introduction of lake trout to Yellowstone Lake. It is feared that these fish will prey on and eventually eliminate native cutthroat trout—a key food source for at least forty-two species of birds and mammals. Because the lake trout's habits differ from the cutthroat's (for instance, they spawn during a different season of the year and in deep water, rather than in shallow tributary streams), these fish will be unavailable to many of the species, such as grizzly bears, otters, and birds, that now feed on cutthroat. Cheatgrass might be considered the "lake trout" of rangelands.[70]

A final reason to avoid introducing nonnative species is that they threaten genetic diversity by posing a risk of interbreeding with native species or by crowding out native organisms. Yan B. Linhart has pointed out that plant genomes show such "precise adaptations to local conditions" that vegetative rehabilitation projects may fail where "non-local materials" are introduced, and "the long-term biological health of nearby populations" may also be endangered.[71]

Still, not all scientists see the nonnative issue so starkly. West cautions that "not all introduced, alien, or exotic species are equal threats; it depends on how they fit into ecosystems."

> Most communities do not consist of highly co-evolved species pairs, but exhibit some substitutability by species within groups. This is not to deny mutualism and the existence of keystone or critical link species, but rather to acknowledge that not all species play those roles. We need to differentiate between the exotics to worry about and those that are of less worry, based on what they do.

This is a corollary to West's view (noted in chapter 5) that it is neither necessary nor feasible to preserve all species, given the existence of ecologically functional equivalents. The argument here has the same practical appeal and the same shortcomings. Scientists do not know enough in most cases to make the fine distinctions that would be required to avoid Type II errors in these matters. In general, "[e]cosystem-level diversity declines and distinct communities are lost" as a result of invasions by introduced organisms.[72]

If politics or misguided notions of tradition continue to preclude removal of livestock from arid public lands, management of grazing in these areas will need to be more active than it has been in the past. Noss advises:

> [I]n general, species that have evolved in an area have evolved ways of avoiding, tolerating, or exploiting a particular disturbance regime. Management practices that mimic the natural disturbance regime, in terms of spatial scale, frequency, intensity, seasonality, effects on habitat structure, and other attributes, are more likely to maintain [native] biodiversity than are management practices that create conditions that are unlike those occurring in the natural landscape.[73]

Even taking such care, the risks of livestock grazing on arid lands will continue to be high. Hobbs and Huenneke point out that, in communities displaying "a nonequilibrial series of alternate states"—the presumed situation on many arid western rangelands—grazing will require "much more active management to 'seize opportunities and to evade hazards.'" It is not at all clear that we know enough to manage a disturbed rangeland either to maintain the extant vegetation in a particular "steady state" or to achieve and maintain some other vegetative condition. An even more basic hurdle is the cost of attempting such intensive management. The range livestock business is, at best, only marginally profitable. When federal administrative costs and subsidies are factored in, the enterprise is flatly uneconomic. There can be no justification for continuing grazing in the face of increased costs.[74]

Even if managers are willing to assume the risk that livestock can be safely grazed in some areas, or used effectively to manipulate vegetation to achieve biodiversity goals, domestic grazing animals should be excluded from all riparian areas and wetlands. While season-long and spring-summer grazing of riparian areas are most objectionable, any livestock use of these invaluable habitats can contribute to declines in vegetative condition, water quality, and watershed condition. The appropriate and efficient solution is to ban all livestock use. If exclusion cannot be accomplished without fencing, livestock should be removed from the surrounding upland areas as well. Any additional fencing of public lands should be avoided in view of fencing's cost, its adverse effects on native ungulates and recreational use, and its potential for fragmenting habitat.[75]

Although "the damage being done by livestock to waters, riparian areas, and forest patches far exceeds any done by humans," grazing is not the only land use that hinders the conservation of arid land biodiversity. Many other human activities also have the potential to impact rangeland biodiversity, depending on their timing, frequency, distribution, and intensity. Noss and Cooperrider suggest that in "Class I reserves," where biological resources are accorded the greatest protection, the following uses should be "removed or controlled to the greatest extent possible": "livestock grazing, mining, higher-impact (more intensive or developed) forms of recreation, most motorized activity, water diversions or depletions, and human settlement." Their approach to "multiple-use" lands is considerably less well defined: the "challenge is to learn how to use these lands while preventing long-term deterioration."[76]

The strategy proposed here is essentially an approach for conserving biodiversity on "multiple-use" lands; it advocates eliminating incompatible uses, principally livestock grazing, and regulating other, compatible uses appropriately. Small-scale mining, for instance, might be an acceptable use *if* it does not significantly fragment the habitat or disrupt critical ecosystem functions, such as hydrology. But additional road construction and improvements, construction of other linear facilities, and new water developments or diversions should be avoided in reserves.

Two other activities, camping and off-road vehicle (ORV), or all-terrain vehicle (ATV), use, merit additional consideration.

Camping should not be allowed in particularly sensitive areas like riparian zones or where rare plants occur. Dispersed, backcountry camping is probably compatible with biodiversity protection. Reasonable regulations, such as restricting use of woody vegetation for firewood and requiring minimum setbacks from water sources, may be expedient. It also may be necessary to enforce use thresholds in popular areas. Camping may be a problem in high-use areas like Utah's red-rock desert, for instance, but will not cause immediate concern in most landscapes subject to this proposal. Established campgrounds are not likely to be significant threats to biodiversity unless they provide habitat for rare species, disrupt wildlife movements or other behavior, or generate undue impacts due to campers migrating into surrounding areas. According to Hobbs and Huenneke, "mechanical disturbance" of soil "in the absence of nutrient addition may not necessarily lead to enhanced invasion" of a site by exotics or weedy species, thus suggesting that the impacts of recreation on rangeland may be less severe than those of grazing. Managers will need to exercise a case-by-case approach in deciding whether and how to regulate camping to protect biodiversity.[77]

ORV use is another story. To borrow one critic's expression: "First and foremost, ORVs eat land." Dirt bikes, "dune buggies," three- and four-wheelers, and the like are popular forms of entertainment on public rangelands near western population centers and on certain other BLM desert lands. In fact, over half of all ORV use occurs on lands managed by BLM. ORVs impact the environment by removing or damaging vegetation and soil, enhancing wind and water erosion, and harassing wildlife. Desert soils are "exceptionally vulnerable to ORV attack"; ORV-caused damage to desert soils and plant life heals slowly if at all. ORVs are objectionable on other grounds as well: they contribute to noise and air pollution, consume fossil fuels, and annoy or displace non-motorized recreationists. ORV use is plainly incompatible with the conservation of biodiversity and maintenance of ecosystem functions. Accordingly, a management plan for conserving biodiversity on arid BLM rangelands should disallow or strictly regulate ORVs, along with livestock.[78]

Finally, wild horses and burros may pose local problems. Horses are found chiefly in Nevada and Wyoming; burros, in New Mexico and Arizona. Non-native herbivores, these animals are objectionable biologically for the same reasons livestock are. But wild horses and burros enjoy special legal distinction. Congress and the Supreme Court have accorded them the status of protected wildlife. Under the Wild, Free-Ranging Horses and Burros Act, these animals are considered "an integral part of the natural system of the public lands." If populations are properly managed and kept in check so as to meet the act's objectives—that is, to "achieve and maintain a thriving ecological balance" and "protect the range from the deterioration associated with overpopulation"— these animals should not pose undue threats to native biodiversity. Whether such management is possible or likely is beyond the scope of this book. In general, though, wild horses and burros are fewer and more dispersed than are cattle or sheep; this mitigates their impacts in most situations. They also pose less risk of introducing new nonnative plant species. While I would prefer to see these animals removed from public lands, such an undertaking would require amending, if not repealing, the federal statute. Livestock are clearly a greater threat to biodiversity, and they can be dealt with under current law.[79]

F. JUSTIFYING THE PROPOSED BIODIVERSITY CONSERVATION STRATEGY: SOME CONCLUDING THOUGHTS

The costs or disadvantages of managing extensive tracts of BLM rangelands as biodiversity reserves would be minor and vastly outweighed by the benefits. The only arguably "'productive' human use" (Noss's term) that would be eliminated or significantly curtailed would be grazing. But public land grazing, especially on more arid lands, is a marginally productive activity at best and an unsustainable one on the native landscapes in question. As Forsling explained in 1963, when he proposed closing millions of acres of public rangelands to grazing: "The proposed solution may sound drastic, but it is needed to avoid more drastic action in the more distant future. As a matter of fact, the land involved has so little grazing capacity at best, that its removal from use would have little effect on the over-all range capacity." The "short-term economic losses" attributable to evicting livestock would be commensurably small, limited principally to the relative handful of permittees whose grazing privileges are canceled or reduced. These and other purported economic impacts of terminating public land grazing are examined more closely in chapter 8.[80]

Off-road-vehicle usage of biodiversity preserves also would be disallowed or strictly limited under the proposed program, but this activity cannot qualify as one of Noss's "productive uses." Its energy, environmental, and aesthetic costs, if fully accounted for, surely outweigh its benefits. Moreover, as Culhane's survey demonstrated, "ORV clubs have few friends among other users of the public lands." The reason is simple: ORVs are "simply not compatible with the quality of outdoor experience being sought by a majority of Americans." Interest in areas closed to ORV use would probably rise among other recreationists. The resulting increase in use of BLM lands for nonmotorized forms of recreation would help offset, if not replace or overcompensate for, income losses to the community from prohibiting ORV use. These new uses might in turn have to be limited, however, if the demand exceeds the absorptive capacity of the resource. But even limits on use, if accompanied by fee requirements and/or managed commercial recreational services, can generate revenues.[81]

The benefits of the proposed biodiversity conservation program are potentially great. Many scientists and other writers have recounted myriad reasons for conserving biodiversity. Realization of biodiversity's economic, scientific, medical, moral, and aesthetic values would be the potential reward of a successful conservation strategy. Preserved species are untapped sources of scientific information and biological wealth, including new "medicines, crops, pharmaceuticals, timber, fibers, pulp, soil-restoring vegetation, petroleum substitutes, and other products and amenities." Species, their genetic material, and their interconnections in communities and ecosystems are literally irreplaceable.[82]

What uses of arid public rangelands could continue if the proposed conservation strategy were implemented? The most fundamental "use" of biodiversity preserves, though not immediately apparent as such, is the maintenance of the protected area's ability to provide ecological services. Another "use" is the preservation of the area's historic and prehistoric resources. Other, more obvious land uses that could be accommodated, and perhaps enhanced or expanded, include low-impact recreational activities, such as hiking, hunting, catch-and-release fishing, dispersed camping, water sports, spelunking, amateur archeology, and photography. These activities would bring dollars into the local area. In addition, reserves would provide field laboratories in which scientists could do much-needed research. Scientific study is not only compatible with reserve protection, but, as noted above, itself serves as a justification for designating biodiversity preserves.[83]

In 1970 a National Academy of Sciences Committee on Agricultural Land Use and Wildlife Resources cited the lower Rio Grande Valley—a riparian landscape in a semiarid setting in Texas—to highlight the diverse reasons for preserving functioning native habitats. Its comments are especially germane here:

> It may be said of most such remnant ecosystems that relatively few people see them and they will contribute little in the way of mass public benefits. This usually is true also of alternative uses for the lands they occupy—in this case more fields of vegetables and citrus groves. It probably is public business if a sample of primitive biota anywhere is to be preserved for long-term casual use. Such historic and biological landmarks help to maintain the character of a locality. More broadly, their service to science and intellectually curious minorities probably helps to assure the integrity of our heterogeneous society. In a degree these are abstract and sophisticated viewpoints, but such terms of reference must be considered admissible if our resource management context is not to be completely utilitarian.[84]

The educational and scientific value of reserves cannot be exaggerated. Dasmann recognized that reserves serve important purposes in both "public education and the training of specialists." Reserves provide new fora for conservation education, thus helping to meet a need recognized by many writers, past and present. Leopold believed that conservation would "follow" only after conservation education succeeded in building "an ethical underpinning for land economics and a universal curiosity to understand the land mechanism." Recently, law professor Eric Freyfogle has argued: "Today's paramount need, without question, is ecological education. . . . Once Americans understand the ecological roles of particular lands, they can support new land-use limits. . . . Without that education, without that knowledge, ownership norms will remain in a pre-ecological age." Freyfogle's comment about outdated ownership norms is reminiscent of Laycock's, Noss's, and others' observation that range management is still in a preecological age.[85]

I readily concede that there is much we don't know about biodiversity conservation. This is so partly because there is much we haven't tried. Biodiversity losses have resulted largely from our ignorance, but they needn't continue for the same reason. Pieper wrote: "Restoration may be centuries away, but not having a scientific answer does not alleviate the need for some working goals" or at least a set of basic management prescriptions to begin pursuing those goals. Despite our continuing needs for information (which are unlikely ever to be fully met), we know enough now to take action. The apology that "[e]verything we do in land management is an experiment" is not a reason not to conduct informed experiments. Ongoing research efforts should be continued, expanded, and refined. We need "[t]rue ecological research" that looks "holistically at the entire ecosystem—at soils, soil microbes, plants, insects, and all vertebrates, and the myriad ecological processes such as nutrient and hydrologic processes." In the meantime, much will be lost if we fail to manage public rangelands on the basis of what we do know.[86]

The current thinking regarding rangeland community dynamics and landscape ecology justifies certain fairly simple conclusions. First, management to conserve biodiversity would be simpler and more feasible on large tracts of land under single ownership or management, if land managers were able—and willing—to create preserves in those areas and to implement the knowledge available to them. Second, given what we know about the potentially irreversible effects of grazing on arid and semiarid sites, public rangeland management strategies should incorporate a precautionary principle. We should seek to avoid impacts that we do not yet know how to, and may never be able to, repair once they occur. We should seek to preserve options. In the familiar words of Aldo Leopold: "To keep every cog and wheel is the first precaution of intelligent tinkering." Removing livestock from public lands forecloses only one narrow land-use option, while helping to maintain and protect nearly all other public uses and values of the land.[87]

In sum, we should think bigger and more long term and be less willing to exploit resources than we have in the past. Harvard entomologist Edward O. Wilson's advice is unequivocal: "The ethical imperative should therefore be, first of all, prudence. We should judge every scrap of biodiversity as priceless while we learn to use it and come to understand what it means to humanity." But we cannot afford to wait until we think we have all the answers. By then the questions may be moot, and our opportunity to preserve a full measure of native biodiversity may be lost forever. Our task now is to act cautiously, but *to act*—or *not* to act in ways that we have come to realize are unwise. Noss agrees on the need for prudence, the need to "err on the side of preservation when science is unable to provide clear answers." But he also urges managers to avoid complacency or delay. "Because the threats to biodiversity are so immediate," he writes, "our imperative is action." The "battle may be won or lost in the 1990s."[88]

We must not be too timid. The livestock industry and the BLM will certainly resist this proposal, and even some conservationists are likely to protest that it seeks to change too much, too fast. But if Noss and others are right about the immediacy of the crisis, such caution is not only misplaced but counterproductive.

Consider the following advice from Phillip Hoose, former director of preserve selection and design for the widely respected conservation organization The Nature Conservancy (TNC). In chapter 7 of his book *Building an Ark: Tools for the Preservation of Natural Diversity through Land Protection*, Hoose discusses existing systems for preserving federal lands and why more areas haven't been designated despite existing authority. Then he sets forth the circumstances under which he believes a "public resource manager is most likely to agree to designate property":

1. The area is really important.
2. Its importance—relative to any other parts of his domain—can be demonstrated clearly.
3. [The manager] has relatively little to lose in setting aside the area as opposed to using it in some other way.
4. Designation will not disrupt an existing program, particularly one regarded as important.
5. Designation helps the manager meet a legal obligation or a policy requirement.
6. Designation has popular support.[89]

Initially, it may seem hard to quibble with any of this practical, "real world"–informed advice. But most of Hoose's recommendations share an important common premise—and weakness: they assume that candidate biodiversity reserves will be only, or at least primarily, relatively small, discrete areas. While this concession is likely to facilitate designation of reserves, it will not promote the goal of conserving biodiversity at the landscape level. Proposals like Hoose's, and even the recommendations of Noss and Cooperrider, which emphasize use of existing designations, such as wilderness or ACEC, can be viewed as encouraging a form of triage. Landscapes, and the full range of biodiversity they support, will be in continual jeopardy as long as federal biodiversity conservation strategies are limited to such piecemeal efforts.

It is not just the geographic scale, of course, but the substance of the proposal—to *eliminate*, not just reduce, livestock grazing—that is likely to elicit faintheartedness. The view that public land grazing is somehow inviolate is behind many compromises on public land range management, including the recent "sustainable ranching" demonstration projects, usually involving the rancher, the land management agency, and a conservation group or land trust. These projects may be popular, but they cannot be justified in arid environments. Livestock grazing is simply not ecologically sustainable, at least on a scale that is economic, on arid western rangelands. TNC is preeminent among nongovernmental organizations involved in biodiversity conservation efforts; it also advocates "sustainable ranching." But its endorsement of livestock production on public lands, where grazing is not compatible with conserving native biodiversity, will do considerable harm to any group or agency's effort to end this ecologically damaging practice. Sanctioning livestock grazing anywhere on desert or semidesert ranges will frustrate, if not doom, BLM attempts to eliminate grazing on unsuitable ranges generally.[90]

Conservationists must "keep their eye on the prize." Merely curtailing livestock use will not achieve the goal of preserving and restoring arid land biodiversity. Evicting livestock will be essential.

CHAPTER 7

The Current Legal Landscape

The principal statutes that bear significantly on the conservation measures proposed here are the Taylor Grazing Act, Federal Land Policy and Management Act, Public Rangelands Improvement Act, National Environmental Policy Act, Endangered Species Act (ESA), and Clean Water Act (CWA). The Taylor Act has legal and historical significance for any examination of public domain grazing policy. Defending a conservation program that entails eliminating livestock requires understanding the circumstances that spawned this first grazing law, Congress's legislative goals, and the flexibility of the act's grazing policy. Also crucial is an appreciation of the scope of, and limitations on, agency authority. That's where FLPMA, the BLM's organic act, comes in. FLPMA is the single most important statute governing management of BLM lands, including administration of the public land grazing program.[1]

A. TAYLOR GRAZING ACT

The Taylor Grazing Act was the first federal legislation concerning grazing on the public domain. It applied only to unreserved federal lands administered by the Department of the Interior. The act's principal provisions are described in chapter 2, and its history has been thoroughly examined by others.[2]

The Taylor Act's preamble states three chief purposes: "To stop injury to the public lands by preventing overgrazing and soil deterioration, to provide for their orderly use, improvement, and development, and to stabilize the livestock industry, dependent on the public range, and for other purposes." The act authorizes the secretary of the interior, "in his discretion," to establish grazing districts from lands "which in his opinion are *chiefly valuable for grazing* and raising forage crops." This discretion is to be exercised "[i]n order to promote the highest use of the public lands pending its [*sic*] final disposal." Section 2 empowers the secretary to do any and all things necessary to accomplish the purposes of this chapter and to insure the objects of such grazing districts, namely, to regulate their occupancy and use, to preserve the land and its resources from destruction or unnecessary injury, to provide for the orderly use, improvement and development of the range; and . . . to continue the study of erosion and flood control.

The act neither mandates the creation of grazing districts nor prescribes the specifics of a grazing program.[3]

Establishment of a grazing district had no effect on existing rights in, or to the use of, the public lands under any other law, and authorization to run stock on a grazing district is a revocable privilege, which conveys no "right, title, interest, or estate in or to the lands." Section 7 of the act authorizes the interior secretary to

examine and classify any lands [withdrawn or reserved per the TGA] which are . . . *more valuable or suitable for any other use than for the use provided for under this chapter*, or proper for acquisition in satisfaction of any outstanding lieu, exchange or script rights or land grant, and to open such lands to entry, selection or location for disposal in accordance with such classification under applicable public-land laws.

Section 7 also allowed homesteading on tracts not to exceed 320 acres to continue on lands within grazing districts, if classified by the secretary as "more valuable or suitable for the production of agricultural crops than for the production of native grasses and forage plants."[4]

The meanings of the section 1 terms "chiefly valuable for grazing" and "highest use of the public lands" merit scrutiny because they relate to the continuing discretionary authority of the BLM to allocate grazing lands to other uses, including biodiversity conservation. Because these two terms occur in the same section of the law, they should draw meaning from each other and, absent some compelling reason to the contrary, should be applied together. Insights to their construction can be gleaned from the act itself, prior use of the terms by Congress, interpretations by the administering agency, and other sources.[5]

The expression "chiefly valuable" apparently was first used by Congress in this context in the Stock Raising Homestead Act of 1916. The act authorized the interior secretary to "designate as stock-raising lands" those lands "the surface of which is, in his opinion, chiefly valuable for grazing and raising forage crops, do not contain merchantable timber, are not susceptible of irrigation . . . , and are of such character that [640] acres are reasonably required for the support of a family." The SRHA reserved to the United States "all the coal and other minerals" beneath the surface of lands patented under the act and subordinated surface rights to rights in the mineral estate. That is, the statute authorized miners to go upon the surface of a homestead to develop the underlying minerals and provided for payment of damages to the surface owner for any resulting harm to crops or improvements. Taken together, these provisions imply that lands "chiefly valuable for grazing" meant lands *not more valuable* for other uses or resources. Timber, minerals, and irrigable land were all deemed of higher value.[6]

This interpretation seems borne out by a grazing bill introduced in Congress subsequent to the SRHA but prior to Congressman Taylor's bill. This 1926 measure, a precursor to the Taylor Act, would have established a leasing system for grazing on both national forests and the public domain. Its drafters were meticulous in pointing out where grazing ranked among the panoply of federal land uses:

> [T]he use of these lands for grazing *shall be subordinated* (a) to the development of their mineral resources, (b) to the protection, development, and utilization of their forests, (c) to the protection, development, and utilization of their water resources, (d) to their use for agriculture . . . , and (e) to the protection, development, and utilization *of such other resources as may be of greater benefit to the public*.

Apart from its application to the national forests, the 1926 bill was substantially similar to the Taylor Act passed eight years later. Like Congressman Taylor's measure, this bill authorized the secretary to "establish grazing districts upon any lands [designated in the bill] which, in his opinion, are valuable for grazing" and to "exclude from such district any lands which he determines are no longer valuable for grazing purposes or are more valuable for other purposes." The term "no longer valuable for grazing" apparently alluded to lands already exhausted by overgrazing.[7]

This comparative value theme ran throughout the Senate committee's report on the 1926 bill. The report stated that "development of these lands for more beneficial uses than grazing will be encouraged." It also explained that the "policy of this bill is in large part economically necessary because large areas of public grazing land would be of no benefit to persons other than those who own or control near-by lands." The Senate report concluded by admonishing: "Grazing on the public lands and national forests should be encouraged and stabilized but should be subordinated to more beneficial uses of the land." Note the similarity between the terms of this bill (e.g., "Grazing on the public lands . . . should be . . . stabilized") and those of the TGA (e.g., the preamble purpose "to stabilize the livestock industry, dependent on the public range"). Industry stability, however, was plainly not a principal goal of the 1926 proposed legislation. The secretary of agriculture opined that the 1926 measure would "promote stability" in the western livestock industry, but he cautioned: "Such stability should be afforded to the extent that it will not impair the primary resources of the national forests."

Very recently a federal court made an intriguingly similar remark about BLM grazing lands. The Tenth Circuit Court of Appeals in *Public Lands Council v. Babbitt* observed that under the Taylor Grazing Act the interior secretary "is free to consider" BLM lands' minor contribution to livestock production when "balancing the need for industry stability against the need to protect the federal lands from deterioration."[8]

The 1926 legislative language reflected the view, widespread during the 1920s and early 1930s, that public domain grazing lands were not especially valuable. Range depletion was "nearly universal," and the lands were desperately in need of rehabilitation. Many believed that the cost to manage the lands would exceed their worth unless they also contained minerals or other resources. The report by President Herbert Hoover's public lands commission and the public reaction thereto illustrate these opinions.[9]

Released in 1931, the Hoover Commission Report recommended that additional public lands be reserved for "oil, coal, forests, parks, wildlife, and national defense, and that the remaining public domain (grazing lands) be ceded to the states," reserving their minerals to the United States. According to Gates, the cession plan was motivated by Hoover's "realization of the need for action to prevent further deterioration of the unappropriated rangelands" and his "belief that [the states] would give them the kind of management their condition called for." National and regional reactions to his proposal, however, caught Hoover off guard. He had not "foreseen that the West would look upon the lands as a liability without the minerals which constituted by far the greater part of their actual value. Furthermore, he did not sense the strength of the conservation movement. The great resources of the West were regarded by conservationists as belonging to the Nation and all its people, to be retained for them and not conveyed to the western states."[10]

Western governors and congressional delegations disapproved especially of Hoover's proposal that they take title to the "grazing lands with their low potential for revenue, but not the more lucrative mineral, oil, and forest lands." The lands to be ceded were referred to variously and colorfully as "skimmed milk," the "lid without the bucket," a "shell," and unable to support a jack-rabbit. Utah's Governor George H. Dern declared disdainfully: "The states already own, in their school-land grants, millions of acres of this same kind of land, which they can neither sell nor lease, and which is yielding no income. Why should they want more of this precious heritage of desert?" These politicians were, in part, echoing the sentiments of their stockgrower constituents. The National Wool Growers Association secretary scoffed: "A public lands commission, consisting partly of inexperienced visionaries, has recommended that the Federal Government after withdrawing everything of value from the remaining public lands, shall turn the worthless residue over to the states, under conditions that would bring heavy expenditures to the unhappy residents." The lands to be divested, he added, were that "part of the public domain that never was worth anything and never will be."[11]

Merrill reports that it was not unusual for livestock industry spokesmen to refer to "grazing lands as not having much value, even though they were the mainstay of the industry's production." Ferry Carpenter, first director of the Grazing Service, reminisced about issuing the first permits under the Taylor Act: "One funny thing I found was that the drier the land is and the more worthless it is, the harder stockmen fight for it. Just why that is, I don't know, but they do. I have had them fight over land on which 640 acres wouldn't support a nightcrawler."[12]

There were two main dimensions to the states' and stockgrowers' opposition. First, they believed that large portions of the remaining public domain had but limited value—and then only, or at least principally, for grazing. Second, the public domain grazing lands were thought valuable chiefly to those persons who resided nearby and owned the necessary, complementary base lands (e.g., for stock handling facilities and growing hay) and water. Each notion became an important impetus for a leasing plan for public land grazing; both are incorporated in the Taylor Grazing Act. The act gives "preference" in the issuance of grazing permits to "those within or near a district who are landowners engaged in the livestock business, bona fide occupants or settlers, or owners of water or water rights, as may be necessary to permit the proper use of the lands [or] water." And the act directs the secretary to identify lands "more valuable or suitable for any other use than [grazing]"—a proviso that surely reflects the general opinion that grazing was not an especially valuable use of public lands.[13]

Elucidated by this historical evidence, the Taylor Grazing Act, especially its section 7, is strikingly reminiscent of the 1926 grazing bill's prioritization of public land uses. It can be fairly surmised that Congress's opinion of grazing's value, given expression in the Taylor Act, had not changed much from the more explicit perspective in the 1926 bill.

The legislative history of the Taylor Grazing Act supports the conclusion that the public domain consisted of grazing lands and lands supporting other (or multiple) uses and that the two categories of lands were perceived as having very disparate values. Congressman Taylor referred to the public domain as "this great national asset of ours," but he also stated that a "very large part of the remaining public domain is utterly worthless for anything else than for grazing." Public records indicate that most of the then-remaining public domain lands, often referred to as "waste land," were believed to be of little value other than for grazing. Texas's Congressman Richard M. Kleberg's view was typical: "[T]he only way by which [the] surface production [of these lands] can be converted into wealth is through the grazing of livestock." In a 1933 letter to the House Committee on Public Lands, Interior Secretary Ickes stated: "With the exception of their mineral content and of limited areas suitable for cultivation . . . , most of the remaining public domain is valuable chiefly for grazing."[14]

This view was one of two recurring themes that marked the 1934 congressional land policy debates. The other was that the public domain's value even for grazing was diminishing as a result of overuse and abuse. The *Congressional Record* and the House and Senate reports on the Taylor bill are replete with observations on the serious erosion and forage depletion over much of the public domain. Taylor admitted that much of the western range was "a very poor quality of grazing land." The House of Representatives reportedly responded with applause to the observation of Congressman Martin (D-Oregon) that "much of [the public domain] is not worth a damn, even for grazing." Note the unmistakable suggestion that grazing was considered the *lowest* use of public lands. Taylor warned the House: "Today we are, by overgrazing, creating sand dunes in every one of these [western] states," and without "some system of controlled and orderly use . . . a very large part of every Western State will soon be a barren desert." Martin and Utah's Congressman Robinson agreed, asserting that unless the ongoing "land destruction" could be arrested, "entire sections of the country would eventually be worthless" and the grazing lands "absolutely unproductive" in twenty-five to forty years. Reviving a statement from the earlier debates on the Colton grazing bill, Wyoming's Representative Carter characterized the western public domain as "an economic problem and responsibility rather than an economic opportunity."[15]

Comments such as these are significant not only because they reflect Congress's awareness of grazing's contribution to desertification (although no one used that term). They also reveal some understanding that deserts, natural or human-caused, *cannot support livestock grazing*. The logical inference is that some western lands, including arguably the "true" deserts and perhaps other arid regions that are the subject of this book, were never meant to be included in Taylor grazing districts.

Such was the mood of Congress and the livestock industry when the Taylor bill passed in 1934. Thirty years later, the Taylor Grazing Act was still the only federal grazing law, and the view of grazing as a low-value, if not last-resort, use of the public lands persisted. In testimony before the House Subcommittee on Public Lands in 1963, the assistant interior secretary in charge of BLM lands, John A. Carver, Jr., described grazing as the lowest-ranking public land use. This, he believed, was the unavoidable interpretation of section 7 of the Taylor Grazing Act. Carver recited to the committee section 7's key language authorizing the interior secretary to "classify any lands . . . within a grazing district, which are . . . more valuable or suitable for any other use than for the use provided for under this act . . . and to open such lands to entry, selection, or location for disposal." To Carver, the message in this language was clear. Candidly, he told the legislators: "If there is any value judgment as to which is the low man on the totem pole, that is the way I read it. I know the way that it works is that a homestead entryman, if the land is suitable for homesteading, takes the grazing permittee out without a sou, so to speak, and so do any of the other entry statutes." Carver's translation of the grazing law was corroborated by BLM associate director Harold R. Hochmuth. Testifying before the same committee, he described section 7 as "put[ting] grazing low and everything else above it." These views, espoused by officials of the very agencies charged with administering the public domain under the Taylor Grazing Act, supply yet more evidence that the act was intended to promote livestock grazing on lands not more valuable for some other use.[16]

My assessment of the Taylor Act varies somewhat from that of Coggins and Lindeberg-Johnson. They label the statute "a grazing law." Plainly, it is. But as readers can now see, it is not so plain that "Congress intended the main public land use to be domestic livestock grazing," as they further assert. It is not apparent whether Coggins and Lindeberg-Jonson considered the import of section 7 in this context. This is a crucial difference. My interpretation varies with theirs largely because of section 7, viewed through the prism of legislative and western history. They opine that the Taylor Act "on its face appears to subordinate other goals to range improvement," although they concede that "no court has squarely faced or resolved the question," and they describe the need for "range improvement" as the "one explicit theme recurring throughout the statute." But to the extent that they equate "range improvement" with improvement of rangelands solely for livestock, they overstate their case. As we saw in chapters 2 and 3, the need for rehabilitating western ranges, which the Taylor Act was intended to address, was perceived not solely as an exigency of the livestock industry but as necessitated by watershed, wildlife, and recreation concerns, as well.[17]

Furthermore, there is no doubt that the concept of multiple use of federal lands was familiar to Congress in 1934 when it passed the TGA. Multiple use had been practiced on the forest preserves, many would argue, since their beginning near the turn of the century. The Taylor Act itself preserved other lawful uses of public lands, including mining, hunting, and use of native materials by settlers, on lands formed into grazing districts. Just three years after the Taylor Act was passed, Congress conferred on one of BLM's predecessors, the General Land Office, authority to manage the revested Oregon and California Railroad grant lands for multiple uses. The Oregon and California Revested Lands Sustained Yield Management Act of 1937 (O & C Act) required sustained-yield production of timber from the lands, authorized use for grazing and recreation, and called for protection of wildlife, watershed, and other resources. This multiple-use mandate is even broader than the legislation applicable to the national forests until passage of the Multiple-Use, Sustained-Yield Act of 1960.[18]

It seems likely that Congress would have provided similar, explicit multiple-use authority in the TGA—or perhaps enacted entirely different legislation—had it more fully appreciated the values of the much more extensive public domain lands. But, as we have seen, like much of the nation Congress believed that the public domain grazing lands had value for little but grazing and that the more valuable public lands would not be included within Taylor grazing districts.

The O & C Act also yields further evidence that Congress did not consider grazing an especially valuable land use. The act provided for sustained-yield harvesting of timber "for the *purpose[s]* of providing a permanent source of timber supply, protecting watersheds, regulating stream flow, and contributing to the economic stability of local communities and industries, and providing recreational facilties [*sic*]." Grazing was allowed on O & C lands but plainly was not a "purpose" for which the O & C lands were to be managed. This is revealed by section 4, which authorizes the interior secretary to lease for grazing any lands "which may be so used *without interfering with the production of timber or other purposes* of this Act as stated in section 1." This provision calls to mind the 1926 grazing bill's subordination of grazing to all other land uses.[19]

The federal government continued to distinguish between grazing lands and more valuable, multiple-use lands. Discussing the various proposals over the years to transfer federal grazing lands to the rancher-operators, BLM director Marion Clawson observed in 1950: "Practically none of these suggestions included all Federal lands in the West, but only those 'chiefly valuable' for the purpose in question." Even livestock interests considered those lands having uses other than, or in addition to, grazing more valuable and hence not suitable for disposition. Voigt notes that few stockmen protested in 1943 when 3 million acres of grazing lands in southern Utah, which "supported little vegetation," were withdrawn for the benefit of mining interests. A public lands disposal plan advanced in 1946 by the NWGA advocated, in essence, disposal of only those lands chiefly or solely valuable for grazing. It proposed that "all lands in the grazing districts and in the national forests that were not multiple use, [or] important for timber growing or water conservation, should be sold at a reasonable price, on long terms, and at low interest." The stockmen's organization further conceded that the minerals underlying any lands sold should remain in federal ownership.[20]

According to Gates, the "distinguished agricultural economist" Marshall M. Kelso in 1947 examined the advantages and disadvantages of private ownership of the western ranges and identified three factors that counseled against conversion of federal lands to private hands: "(1) the multiple use of much of the land for wildlife, for recreation, and for watershed protection . . . ; (2) the economic impossibility of much of the land paying its own way in private ownership; and (3) the fact that much of it was 'not amenable to division into areas for single enterpriser control.'" In the same year Congress passed a grazing fee statute, which required that the interior secretary "take into account the extent to which [BLM grazing] districts yield public benefits over and above those accruing to the users of the forage resources for livestock purposes." Dana interpreted this "ambiguous language" as "apparently legaliz[ing] the stockmen's claim that grazing fees should be based on the cost of administration and not on the value of the forage." But it also reflects an expanding legislative recognition that grazing lands were productive of benefits other than forage.[21]

Around 1960 the secretary of the interior took the position that the Taylor Grazing Act was "a multiple purpose act." In *LaRue v. Udall* the federal District of Columbia Circuit Court of Appeals approved this interpretation. Quoting at length from a secretarial opinion concerning the land exchange provision in section 8 of the act (43 U.S.C. § 315g), the court wrote: "It seems to us that the Secretary correctly construed [the statute] when he said . . . ":

> [T]he benefit to the public interests, which is the criterion of the statute, need not be related exclusively to conservation of Federal grazing resources nor need it be shown that a proposed exchange will promote range management. . . . The Taylor Grazing Act is a *multiple purpose act*. . . . [S]ection 1 of the Act authorizes the Secretary of the Interior to establish grazing districts in order to promote the highest use of the public domain. . . .
>
> Thus, nothing in the other sections of the act suggest [sic] that private interests may not acquire public land being used for grazing purposes to the detriment of those licensed to use the land [for grazing].[22]

Few legal scholars or land managers today would describe the Taylor Act as a "multiple purpose act," at least in the same sense as is FLPMA or the Forest Service's Multiple-Use, Sustained-Yield Act. Still, TGA sections 7 and 8 (the latter of which was repealed by FLPMA in 1976) plainly reflect the interior secretary's authority to consider the lands' value for a variety of purposes and to manage or dispose of them accordingly.

The interior secretary's 1960 pronouncement also was consistent with the BLM's long-held view that it possessed a "multiple-purpose" orientation. In a sense, a "multiple-use" perspective predated the BLM itself, created in 1946 to administer the public domain. A 1939 amendment to the TGA had required each district grazing board to have a representative of wildlife interests. Even earlier, the 1936 USDA report, *The Western Range*, left no doubt that the Department of Agriculture viewed the public domain as possessing multiple values and supporting a variety of uses, specifically, watershed services, the production of timber, providing for the "rapidly growing need for recreation," and the "sustained production of wildlife," in addition to livestock production. At least some Agriculture officials believed that the "broad authority conferred upon the Secretary of the Interior" by the Taylor Act might be sufficient to enable the "correlated use . . . and development of resources," which they deemed necessary to "obtain the maximum use or service consistent with the conservation of the resource, and hence the highest current public benefits."[23]

The BLM's first director also recognized that "Federal lands in the West are capable of multiple use and have *value for many purposes*." "Although range livestock use 76 per cent of the land in the range region," Clawson wrote in 1950, "grazing is the sole use of but little of it. Most western land is capable of multiple use." Clawson noted that "[m]ost range land is also watershed land of some importance," that the range includes forests and supports game and other wildlife, and that "[m]uch of the range area has recreational values in addition to those associated with wild life." He candidly admitted, however, that "policy with respect to [the range's] management has been formulated largely in consideration of its effect upon grazing use."[24]

BLM biographers Muhn and Stuart and political science professor and prominent BLM observer Sally Fairfax cite additional evidence of the agency's multiple-use perspective. Fairfax opines that the BLM "appears to have begun to view itself as a land-management agency" sometime during the 1950s. "Emulating Forest Service approaches, the Bureau designed a number of legislative proposals drawing heavily on Multiple Use Sustained Yield Act concepts. . . ." The early BLM had a "wildlife habitat management" program, built recreational facilities, such as campgrounds and picnic areas, and classified many potential sites for acquisition under the Recreation Act of 1926—all despite the lack of any express delegation from Congress of wildlife or recreation management authority.[25]

Later the bureau tried to "parlay temporary classification and management authority," which it was delegated in the Classification and Multiple Use Act (CAMUA) of 1964, "into a multiple-use mandate." It "undertook many activities on public domain lands for which express statutory authority was uncertain or nonexistent." These activities included establishing research natural areas, primitive areas, and areas dedicated to wildlife conservation. Even so, the BLM had no actual *management* authority over recreation or wildlife prior to the CAMUA or following that statute's expiration in 1970 until passage of FLPMA in 1976.[26]

While the Taylor Act does not explicitly authorize, much less mandate, "multiple-use" management, the act does contain numerous references to the secretary's discretion. Courts, including the court in *LaRue v. Udall*, have consistently affirmed secretarial actions taken under the TGA, noting the ample discretion conferred on the secretary for carrying out his overriding duty under the act—that of "promot[ing] the highest use of the public domain." According to the Tenth Circuit Court of Appeals, which most recently considered the matter, "the means the Secretary may employ to accomplish the purposes of the Act are nearly completely in his discretion." In view of two of the act's purposes—

stopping injury to the public lands by overgrazing and soil deterioration and providing for their orderly use and improvement—the secretary's discretion should promote, not hinder, implementation of the proposed biodiversity conservation strategy.[27]

The foregoing analysis leads me to conclude that grazing was not intended to be the predominant use of public lands under the Taylor Act; in fact, grazing was at best a co-equal use of the public domain, where it was not actually subordinated to other uses. Consistent with this interpretation, the act has never been interpreted to limit the other uses to which "grazing" lands might be put in the public interest. The interior secretary's broad discretion under the act to establish grazing districts (or not) and otherwise to provide for use and management of the public domain is limited essentially only by the requirement to "promote the highest use of the public lands." The Interior Department and the courts have recognized that uses of the lands, and the public purposes they serve, will change. Accordingly, the statute's provisions for establishing grazing districts on "lands chiefly valuable for grazing" and for promoting "the highest use" of the lands must be construed to allow for review and reappraisal of the appropriateness of grazing in any particular location and over time. Public lands that become "more valuable or suitable for any other use"—including biodiversity conservation—should be reclassified for that use. Furthermore, where lands may be irreparably damaged by continued grazing, the agency is obliged to terminate such abuse. If this analysis is correct, the Taylor Grazing Act presents no impediment to the biodiversity conservation strategy proposed herein.

B. FEDERAL LAND POLICY AND MANAGEMENT ACT

Congress finally enacted organic legislation for the Bureau of Land Management on 21 October 1976. The Federal Land Policy and Management Act established national policy with respect to the public lands and conferred on the secretary of the interior, acting through the BLM, overall authority to administer those lands. The act amended certain provisions of the Taylor Grazing Act and repealed the homesteading laws, with an exception for Alaska; in all respects relevant here, however, the Taylor Act remained intact. Section 402 of FLPMA sets forth conditions for the grazing permits issued pursuant to the TGA and expressly reaffirms TGA section 3's proviso concerning the nature of the interest in a grazing permit. Consequently, livestock grazing on BLM public lands today is subject to both FLPMA and the Taylor Grazing Act, and grazing permits on both BLM lands and national forests are privileges, not compensable property interests.[28]

1. CONGRESSIONAL FINDINGS AND POLICY

FLPMA provides the nuts-and-bolts authority for regulating livestock grazing on the public land, but it is the statute's more general tenets that are fundamental to our inquiry.[29]

FLPMA begins with Congress's unequivocal policy declaration that "(1) the public lands be retained in Federal ownership, unless as a result of the land use planning procedure provided in this Act, it is determined that disposal of a particular parcel will serve the national interest." This is significant for our purposes for at least two reasons: it reveals Congress's belief that, with certain relatively narrow exceptions, retaining the federal lands will serve the national interest; and concomitantly, it laid to rest any lingering notion that the public lands were merely being held "pending [their] final disposal," as suggested in the opening lines of the Taylor Grazing Act.[30]

History discloses that Congressman Taylor inserted the "pending final disposal" language in his bill to ensure the support of the western legislators who still favored transfer of these lands to the states, but who realized that transfer in 1934 was politically infeasible. The language remained on the books for forty years, and its meaning was subject to recurring debate. "Was ['disposal'] intended to arrange merely for 'orderly management,' or actually to 'get rid of'?" Voigt queried rhetorically. "A desk dictionary gives both definitions and puts the latter in a subsidiary position." It is presumably a reflection of this uncertainty that some commentators (even prominent public land scholars Coggins, Wilkinson, Leshy, and Fairfax) have referred to the TGA's "pending final *disposition*" provision. "Disposition" seems even more equivocal than "disposal" regarding the ultimate fate of the lands. Prior to FLPMA's passage, states' righters and livestock interests had frequently invoked the "pending final disposal" provision in support of their claims to the federal lands. While such claims did not cease in 1976 (witness the Sagebrush Rebellion), proponents were basically forced to turn from Congress to the courts in their search for a forum. Congress had spoken: the public domain had value to the nation and should, therefore, remain public.[31]

Several other elements of FLPMA's policy statement bear on any biodiversity conservation proposal. The section pronounces Congress's determination that "the national interest will be best realized if the public lands and their resources are periodically and systematically inventoried and their present and future use is [*sic*] projected through a land use planning process coordinated with other Federal and State planning efforts." It directs that management of the public lands be "on the basis of multiple use and sustained yield unless otherwise specified by law"; that "the public lands be managed in a manner that will protect the quality of scientific, scenic, historical, ecological, environmental, air and atmospheric, water resource, and archeological values; [and] that, where

appropriate, will preserve and protect certain lands in their natural condition";
and that "plans for the protection of public land areas of critical environmental
concern be promptly developed." The statute also admonishes that the public
lands "be managed in a manner which recognizes the Nation's needs for
domestic sources of ... food ... and fiber from the public lands."[32]

2. Implementing FLPMA's Multiple-Use Policy

The statute's multiple-use and sustained-yield policies are given force in the
mandate: "The Secretary shall manage the public lands under principles of
multiple use and sustained yield, in accordance with land use plans developed
by him under section 1712 of this title. . . ." Congress supplemented this
command in the next paragraph: "In managing the public lands the Secretary
shall, by regulation or otherwise, take any action necessary to prevent unnecessary or undue degradation of the lands." Read together, these directives surely
mean that public land uses may not be authorized in combinations or at levels
that would result in "unnecessary or undue degradation." The degradation
standard in turn must, at a minimum, mean that resource condition may not be
allowed to decline to a point that would interfere with the sustained yield of
that, or any other, resource or with realizing the land's values.[33]

This reasoning is informed by FLPMA's definitions of the key terms.
"Sustained yield" is "the achievement and maintenance in perpetuity of a high-
level annual or regular output of the various renewable resources of the public
lands consistent with multiple use." The definition of "multiple use" is a bit
more complex:

> The term "multiple use" means the management of the public lands and their
> various resource values so that they are utilized in the combination that will
> best meet the present and future needs of the American people; making the
> most judicious use of the land for some or all of these resources or related
> services over areas large enough to provide sufficient latitude for periodic
> adjustments in use to conform to changing needs and conditions; the use of
> some land for less than all of the resources; a combination of balanced and
> diverse resource uses that takes into account the long-term needs of future
> generations for renewable and nonrenewable resources, including, but not
> limited to, recreation, range, timber, minerals, watershed, wildlife and fish,
> and natural scenic, scientific and historical values; and harmonious and coor-
> dinated management of the various resources without permanent impairment
> of the productivity of the land and the quality of the environment with
> consideration being given to the relative values of the resources and not neces-

sarily to the combination of uses that will give the greatest economic return or the greatest unit output.[34]

The meaning of this convoluted language, and of the substantially similar guidance applicable to the national forests, has been debated by scholars and in the popular press. Section 202 of FLPMA confirms that Congress intended this definition to be consistent with the term's traditional meaning. It calls for land use plans to be developed "us[ing] and observ[ing] the principles of multiple use and sustained yield set forth in this and other applicable law." But few courts have construed the language, and those that have done so found little "law to apply." In recent years, Wise Use proponents have adopted the term for their own purposes to connote chiefly commodity resources and uses. No consensus on the term's meaning exists among legal scholars, although the bulk of opinion seems to hold that the definition is ambiguous and "fuzzy." In the minority, Coggins has argued that the definition does contain law to apply, including some fairly strong guidance, such as "without permanent impairment," the emphasis on supplying future needs, and the rather detailed specification of resources and values. He concludes that the "series of 'shalls' and 'shall nots' [in the multiple use laws] ought to be binding on public land managers." Similarly, Coggins asserts that FLPMA's definitions of multiple use and sustained yield "require fairly definite management emphases and practices."[35]

Several particulars of FLPMA's "sustained yield" definition have significance for us: its admonition to consider the "relative values" of resources; its focus on the "present and future needs of the American people," and the absence of any mention of local needs; its inclusion of "natural scenic, scientific and historical values" as resources; and its recognition of the appropriateness of managing land for the "related services" of these "uses" rather than any particular "use" per se; and, finally, the direction to manage all resources without impairing the land's productivity or environmental quality. All of these management guidelines are compatible with a policy decision to preserve biodiversity across landscapes.

The BLM's organic act also identifies six "principal or major uses," which overlap with, but are not identical to, the uses identified in the definition of multiple use. These "principal or major uses" are "domestic livestock grazing, fish and wildlife development and utilization, mineral exploration and production, rights-of-way, outdoor recreation, and timber production." The legislative history concerning the provision is spare, but straightforward. The House Report stated simply: "'[P]rincipal or major uses' is defined for the purposes of section 202 of the bill. They represent the uses for which Congressional oversight is particularly needed. The definition does not mean to imply that other uses such as 'watershed' are not of great public significance."[36]

The act's only substantive reference to "principal or major uses" is in one paragraph of section 202, which deals with preparation and implementation of land use plans. Specifically, paragraph 202(e)(2) provides:

> Any management decision or action pursuant to a management decision that excludes (that is, totally eliminates) one or more of the principal or major uses for two or more years with respect to a tract of land of one hundred thousand acres or more shall be reported by the Secretary to the House of Representatives and the Senate. If within ninety days . . . Congress adopts a concurrent resolution of nonapproval . . . then the management decision or action shall be promptly terminated by the Secretary.[37]

Thus FLPMA reflects Congress's intent to authorize decisions to terminate grazing on tracts of 100,000 acres (approximately 156 square miles) or less made in the course of the normal BLM planning process. This is consistent with section 402 of FLPMA, which expressly recognizes the secretary's authority to cancel, suspend, or modify grazing permits and to dispose of grazing lands or devote them to other public purposes. BLM's grazing regulations specify both that grazing *preference* can be changed, or even "canceled or suspended in whole or in part," and that grazing "*permits* or leases may be canceled, suspended, or modified." FLPMA, as amended, provides that grazing cuts that exceed 10 percent in one year will not take effect until the completion of any administrative appeal. In 1978 Congress again acknowledged, in the Public Rangelands Improvement Act, the administrative authority to terminate grazing altogether.[38]

FLPMA section 202(e)(2) raises an interesting, though not immediately pertinent, issue: does it authorize an unconstitutional "legislative veto"—that is, does it violate the constitutional requirement that legislation be presented to the president for signature before it becomes law? A court directly confronted with the question would, if it answered the question in the affirmative, next have to determine whether the objectionable provisions of 202(e)(2) are "severable"; that is, whether they could simply be excised from FLPMA, leaving related provisions intact. FLPMA itself provides: "If any provision of this Act . . . or the application thereof is held invalid, the remainder of the Act and the application thereof shall not be affected thereby." It is not clear how a court would resolve this issue. Conceivably, the court could conclude, drawing from section 202(e)(1) and (2), that Congress intended to limit the interior secretary's authority to eliminate principal uses to areas less than 100,000 acres in size or to larger areas if for less than two years. On the other hand, a court might simply sever section 202(e)(2), which contains the objectionable provision, leaving the secretary with arguably blanket authority to eliminate principal uses.[39]

3. AREAS OF CRITICAL ENVIRONMENTAL CONCERN

Section 201, which implements FLPMA's inventory requirements, directs the
secretary to "prepare and maintain on a continuing basis an inventory of all
public lands and their resource and other values (including, but not limited to,
outdoor recreation and scenic values), giving priority to areas of critical environmental concern." The prominent placement of this directive in the act and its
explicit emphasis on identifying ACECs are not fortuitous. The next section of
FLPMA, containing the statute's planning provisions, instructs: "In the development and revision of land use plans, the Secretary shall— . . . give priority to
the designation and protection of areas of critical environmental concern." Congress defined ACECs as "areas within the public lands where special management attention is required (when such areas are developed or used or where no
development is required) to protect and prevent irreparable damage to important historic, cultural, or scenic values, fish and wildlife resources or other natural
systems or processes, or to protect life and safety from natural hazards."[40]

The preeminence that Congress accorded the designation and protection of
areas of critical environmental concern may come as a surprise, but it would be
difficult to deny in the face of such clear language. Still, some observers have
noted that ACECs have been "greatly misunderstood." Some, even within BLM,
view ACECs "as an impediment to the bureau's emphasis on production of
energy and minerals, timber, and livestock forage. They argue that ACECs are
'anti-multiple use.'" In other circles, BLM's performance in designating ACECs
has been criticized as "highly uneven."[41]

In any event, the ACEC designation is one tool expressly authorized by
FLPMA that could be used in implementing a landscape-level biodiversity
conservation program. Arid and semiarid landscapes whose native biological
diversity is vulnerable to traditional grazing practices or to other human-caused
disturbances easily meet the ACEC designation criteria. To date, however, most
ACEC designations have been smaller than the size recommended for protecting
whole landscapes. Only a few, principally in Alaska, have been sufficiently extensive. Nothing in FLPMA would limit use of the ACEC designation to conserve
biodiversity at the landscape level; neither the statute nor agency regulations
impose a maximum limit on the size of ACECs. But the agency's erratic record
in making designations and its tendency to keep their size small suggest that
ACECs alone will be inadequate to the task of preserving regional biodiversity.
An alternate approach might be to give ACEC designation to certain core areas or
especially vulnerable sites (such as riparian corridors or wetlands, areas of fragile
soils, areas containing listed or candidate threatened or endangered species, communities approaching a threshold in vegetative condition, etc.) and use less
stringent designations or limited multiple-use management for the balance of the
landscape.[42]

The "prevent irreparable damage" standard in the ACEC definition seems incongruously lax for an area where "special management attention is required" to protect "important" values, especially in view of FLPMA's directive that *all* public lands and resources are to be managed so as to prevent "unnecessary or undue degradation." According to standard rules of statutory construction, "irreparable damage" and "unnecessary or undue degradation" must be accorded distinct meanings. Accordingly, the terms might refer to different kinds or degrees of impacts. Clearly, the no "unnecessary or undue degradation" standard applies to ACECs, which are "public lands." It seems sensible to infer that the no "irreparable damage" standard, applicable specifically to ACECs and not to public lands generally, is more rigorous. This reasoning suggests that, elsewhere on the public lands, outside ACECs, irreparable damage may be permissible if it is not "unnecessary" or "undue." In ACECs, on the other hand, *no* irreparable damage, however slight, is permissible.[43]

A useful hypothetical illustration can be constructed using mining activities outside ACECs. The impacts of surface mines can be quite significant; indeed, mining can irreparably damage other resources or values. On arid or high-elevation mined sites, for instance, it might not be possible to reestablish the premining vegetative composition. Similarly, the hydrology of a site could be irreparably damaged, either by drilling and blasting activities or by the actual excavation of the mine pit (or the tunnels, shafts, adits, etc., of an underground mine). These impacts might be "irreparable," but if they are necessary in order to develop the mine (one of the multiple uses recognized by FLPMA), and if they are kept within prescribed limits, they probably would not constitute "unnecessary or undue degradation" and thus would be permissible on most BLM lands, excluding ACECs, wilderness, and other special status areas.

Cattle grazing, as we have seen, can irreversibly alter vegetative conditions on arid or semiarid rangelands. If such a landscape received ACEC designation, grazing would have to be eliminated because it would violate the no "irreparable damage" standard. Outside ACECs, however, the applicable standard is no "unnecessary or undue degradation." The "degradation," or vegetative impact, that would occur if livestock grazing continues might be "unnecessary" if it could have been avoided (e.g., by grazing fewer head, or at a different season, or for a shorter time). It might also be "unnecessary" in the sense of being ill-advised: that is, if, given the relative scarcity of the resources, the long- and short-term benefits, and/or FLPMA's requirement to manage the lands sustainably, livestock should never have been permitted to graze on these lands. This is an argument to be made during agency planning activities, before grazing is authorized. Because of the deference generally accorded agency decisions, the claim would not likely prevail as the basis for an after-the-fact judicial challenge to a decision to allow grazing or to renew a grazing permit.

Alternatively, or perhaps additionally, the impacts of grazing might constitute *"undue* degradation." On certain sites, some impact on vegetation due to
grazing could be viewed as "necessary" or unavoidable. This presumes the
irrelevance or failure of the "unnecessary because ill-advised" argument, above.
"Necessary" impacts are nevertheless limited to those that are not "undue."
"Undue" can take meaning from several other provisions of the statute, perhaps
principally the requirement to manage according to multiple-use and sustained-
yield principles. In other words, grazing may not interfere with the "achievement and maintenance in perpetuity of a high level annual or regular periodic
output" of any other resources or values for which the grazed area is also being
managed. Nor may grazing result in "permanent impairment of the productivity of the land and the quality of the environment." More difficult arguments
concerning the likelihood of an "undue" impact might be premised on language
in the "multiple use" definition concerning the "relative values of the resources"
or the "long-term needs . . . for renewable and nonrenewable resources."[44]

Prevailing on any of these arguments, in or outside of ACECs, however,
may ultimately entail convincing a court that the BLM's decision to permit
grazing in the first instance, or its conditions on that permission, was arbitrary or
capricious—a decidedly difficult proposition, as noted in chapter 4. Winning
such a contest will require good inventory data or proving that the agency
inexcusably lacked the inventory data called for by FLPMA, sound science,
useful statistics concerning the values of the various resources, and, lamentably,
time and a change in the philosophies and attitudes of many of our land managers
and judges. Principled adherence to and enforcement of FLPMA's inventory and
planning provisions should ensure that most information needs are met. Courts
have overturned agency decisions when they determined that the agency failed
to consider an important aspect of the problem or ignored available information
about the likely impacts of its proposed action. Thus, the BLM's failure to
consider available scientific information concerning irreversible, grazing-induced
changes to arid rangeland ecosystems should be an adequate ground for holding
invalid an agency decision to continue grazing on many western ranges.[45]

4. OTHER PLANNING CRITERIA

The ACEC and inventory requirements in section 202, discussed above, are the
third and fourth of nine criteria listed in FLPMA for developing and revising
BLM land use plans. They are preceded by directives to "use and observe the
principles of multiple use and sustained yield" and to "use a systematic interdisciplinary approach to achieve integrated consideration of physical, biological,
economic, and other sciences."[46]

Of the remaining five planning criteria, three merit particular attention. In relevant part, they require the secretary to "(5) consider present and potential uses of the public lands; (6) consider the relative scarcity of the values involved and the availability of alternative means . . . and sites for realization of these values; [and] (7) weigh long-term benefits to the public against short-term benefits." The final two criteria require the secretary to (8) provide for compliance with applicable pollution control laws, including state and federal water standards, and (9) coordinate federal land use planning and management activities, to the extent practical and consistent with law, with similar activities of other federal agencies, state and local governments, and Indian tribes. These latter criteria may be especially relevant to a landscape biodiversity protection strategy where livestock grazing activities in the area threaten surface water quality or where an interagency or interjurisdictional approach to conserving biodiversity will be necessary or expedient because the landscape is under multiple ownership or management.[47]

It is significant to the grazing debate that criterion 9 does *not* require the BLM to consider local communities' needs for resources, but only to (1) "coordinate" planning and management with any "land use planning and management programs" of local governments; (2) "to the extent practical . . . assure that consideration is given to . . . local . . . plans that are germane in the development of land use plans for public lands"; and (3) provide for "meaningful public involvement." Recall that the O & C Act of 1937, which provides for management of certain BLM lands in the Pacific Northwest, calls for sustained-yield harvesting of timber to serve the *"purpose* of . . . contributing to the economic stability of local communities and industries." FLPMA contains no counterpart. The lack of a comparable provision, applicable to BLM lands generally, seriously undermines the oft-heard argument that BLM grazing policies should promote local community stability. Elevating local economic concerns to the level of a "purpose" for which the public lands are managed is neither mandated by nor defensible under FLPMA.[48]

FLPMA's planning criteria are procedural, rather than substantive, requirements. They do not dictate outcomes; rather, they guide agency discretion by prescribing a rational approach to planning for the future use and conservation of public lands. But as the Supreme Court has observed (albeit in the NEPA context), such "procedures are almost certain to affect the agency's substantive decision." Moreover, as discussed above, the planning criteria draw meaning from and lend meaning to other, *substantive* provisions of FLPMA, such as the no "unnecessary or undue degradation" standard. When considered in conjunction with FLPMA's substantive provisions, the planning criteria plainly suggest that a weighting, or balancing, of factors in favor of environmental considerations will be appropriate in making public land management decisions. Joseph

L. Sax has argued that FLPMA possesses the "potential to *mandate* ecologically-based decision making."[49]

Taken in the aggregate, FLPMA's "present and potential uses" language, sustained-yield mandate, and directives for protecting ecological and environmental values and meeting the needs of future generations convincingly demonstrate that present uses are not to be satisfied at the expense of future needs or land productivity. This conclusion is reinforced by the seventh planning criterion, which directs the BLM to "weigh long-term benefits to the public against short-term benefits." Clearly, a balancing process is indicated, with a thumb on the scale for the management alternative that offers long-term benefits. The issue facing the land manager when "consider[ing] the present and potential uses of the public lands" might be the sustainability of a particular use, i.e., whether present uses of a site are impairing the site's productivity for future uses (either the same or other uses) or simply whether the present use is the best, or most valuable, or most desirable use.[50]

The juxtaposition in criterion 7 of "long-term benefits *to the public*" (emphasis added) and the unembellished "short-term benefits" invites the conclusion that Congress had in mind short-term private benefits or perhaps benefits to some subset of "the public," such as a local community. Assuming this to be so, several potential "balancing" situations come immediately to mind: (1) the choice between "production of beefsteaks and spiritual stimulation" suggested by Forest Service assistant chief Leon F. Kneip in 1936; (2) the short-term benefits to permittees or the local community of some level of beef/mutton/wool production from local public lands versus the long-term benefits to the public of greater forage and cover for native biota and less pollution of area streams; or (3) the short-term benefits to local ORV interests of allowing dirt bikes in a particular canyon versus the long-term benefits to the wider public interest in avoiding damage to vegetation, soils, watershed, and aesthetics and disturbance of wildlife populations. Choices like these are the stuff of land management. Land use planning continually requires managers to balance various, often conflicting, uses and demands on the land and its resources.[51]

Coggins has called FLPMA's sixth planning criterion, the "relative scarcity" proviso, "the heart of planning." "The whole point of [FLPMA]," he writes, "is the need to deal with resource scarcity. . . . Resource allocation by pricing alone is inappropriate for the nation's natural heritage." The proper construction of this criterion seems readily apparent. Calling on planners to "consider the *relative scarcity* of the values involved and the availability of *alternative* means . . . and sites for realiz[ing] those values" surely indicates that scarcer values should receive some preference, at least where competing, more common, values can be realized by other means. And, again, when construed in light of other statutory guidelines—e.g., those calling for protecting ACECs, ensuring sustainability of resources, and considering the "relative values" of resources, "not necessarily . . .

the greatest economic return" that they are capable of achieving—this interpretation seems not merely fair but inescapable.[52]

The "relative scarcity" proviso also informs FLPMA's policy that "the public lands be managed in a manner which recognizes the Nation's need for . . . food . . . and fiber from the public lands." Livestock production lands and facilities are not scarce in this country. More importantly, as we will see in chapter 8, the contributions of public lands to the nation's red meat and fiber supplies are negligible. The nation has no "need" for food or fiber "from the public lands." This policy thus poses no obstacle to removing livestock from arid public rangelands.[53]

5. FLPMA's Planning Criteria and Biodiversity Conservation

Multiple use and sustained yield: While some land uses and activities will need to be curtailed on a landscape designated for biodiversity preservation, the area would continue to be productive of many "resources" and "resource values" to which FLPMA refers, namely, dispersed, low-impact forms of "recreation," "watershed, wildlife and fish, and natural scenic, scientific and historical values." The "output" of these resources and their related values could be sustained "in perpetuity" if the ecosystems on which they depend are allowed to continue to function naturally. Protecting native biodiversity is inseparable from sustaining properly functioning ecosystems. The public must be educated, however, that ecosystems are not static; levels of use and resource "outputs" will vary from year to year, for instance, because of drought, wildfire, or normal cycles in wildlife populations.[54]

Systematic, interdisciplinary approach: By definition a landscape approach is interdisciplinary; it requires that managers take a holistic, ecological view of the interrelating elements and processes that define and govern a landscape. A management strategy formulated around the interrelationships of ecosystems, as is applied landscape ecology, would comply with FLPMA's directive to use a "systematic approach to achieve integrated consideration of physical, biological, economic, and other sciences." It would also further compliance with NEPA's requirement that all federal agencies "utilize a systematic, interdisciplinary approach . . . in planning and in decisionmaking."[55]

Priority to ACECs: Landscape-level management could be the preferred method for protecting an area that meets ACEC criteria. It would protect interrelating ecosystems, not just single communities, and would require less active management and afford greater buffering, or "insurance," against unforeseen disturbances. It also would promote the intent of "multiple use" as defined by FLPMA: "making the most judicious use of the land . . . over areas large enough to provide sufficient latitude for periodic adjustments to conform to changing needs and conditions." Given what we now know about grazing's potential impacts, arid and semiarid rangelands easily meet Congress's criteria for ACEC designation—areas "where special management attention is required . . . to protect and prevent irreparable damage to important . . . resources or other natural systems or processes." Cooperrider and others have recommended ACECs as tools for conserving biodiversity, though not expressly at the landscape scale.[56]

Relying on inventory data: Inventories, particularly of vegetation and soils, will be critical to identifying landscapes in need of protection and capable of being managed to conserve native biodiversity. Performing thorough inventories and employing the findings thereof in land-management decisions will help ensure that at-risk ecosystems and landscapes receive necessary recognition and protection.[57]

Relative scarcity of values: Most in need of protection are (1) landscapes that contain uncommon and/or especially valuable communities; (2) communities that reflect presettlement conditions, particularly if the communities are elsewhere widely degraded; and (3) perhaps landscapes that contain unusual aggregations of communities and landforms. The attribute of scarcity should be a factor in prioritizing landscapes for protection. Managers will need to explain to the public, however, that a landscape that appears to be common in the region— for instance, an area where sagebrush or greasewood is dominant—may indeed be "scarce" and thus worthy of protection insofar as its condition, including its species diversity, is relatively natural or restorable.[58]

Consideration of present and potential uses of the public lands: No evaluation of this sort could be thorough or complete without consideration of local and regional biodiversity, both of which are essential to maintaining a full complement of future management options and to sustaining the productivity of any land area. Approaching land management at the landscape level would preserve a greater variety of options for future land use—which is synonymous with ensuring that present uses are sustainable.[59]

Weighing long-term public benefits against short-term benefits: It is this consideration that most clearly supports a decision to protect biodiversity at the landscape level. Long-term benefits may be difficult to quantify; indeed, some may not even be known. But many such benefits will be identifiable, and their valuation will be possible, if imprecise. Resource economist Krutilla's comments on this policy choice are particularly useful:

> [F]irst . . . unlike resource allocation questions dealt with in conventional economic problems, there is a family of problems associated with the natural environment which involves the irreproducibility of unique phenomena of nature—or the irreversibility of some consequence inimical to human welfare. Second, it appears that the utility to individuals of direct association with

natural environments may be increasing while the supply is not readily subject to enlargement by man. Third, the real cost of refraining from converting our remaining rare natural environments may not be very great. Moreover, with the continued advance in technology, more substitutes for conventional natural resources will be found for the industrial and agricultural sectors. . . . For all of these reasons we are confronted with a problem not conventionally met in resource economics. The problem is of the following nature.

At any point in time characterized by a level of technology which is less advanced than at some future date, the conversion of the natural environment into industrially produced private goods has proceeded further than it would have with the more advanced future technology. Moreover, with the apparent increasing appreciation of direct contact with natural environments, the conversion will have proceeded further, for this reason as well, than it would have were the future composition of tastes to have prevailed. Given the irreversibility of converted natural environments, however, it will not be possible to achieve a level of well-being in the future that would have been possible had the conversion of natural environments been retarded. That this should be of concern to members of the present generation may be attributable to the bequest motivation . . . as much as to a sense of public responsibility.[60]

Krutilla's advice has heightened urgency today. Americans increasingly value and enjoy unspoiled nature and comprehend the irreversibility of some environmental damage. Yet the damage continues. But the law now provides an additional stimulus for, and means of addressing, the "concern" to which Krutilla referred—FLPMA *requires* consideration of "the future needs of the American people," and the "long-term benefits" and "potential uses of the public lands."[61]

FLPMA policy, like Krutilla's reasoning, plainly supports a preference for the "long-term public benefits" derivable from conserving natural environments over the short-term advantages of "industrially produced private goods." Humans will inevitably develop means of producing more beef or other livestock products more cheaply from less land. Private land is already capable of compensating handily for the 2 percent of the nation's beef supply produced from public lands. Improvements in breeding, nutrition, or other aspects of livestock production would only further minimize the significance of public lands. But our species is not apt to learn how to replicate natural environments. The object of a landscape-level biodiversity protection strategy would be to conserve those "irreproducible" attributes of landscapes that have long-term value, while limiting land uses to those that are, along with landscape processes, sustainable.[62]

FLPMA's term "short-term benefits," in contrast, connotes benefits that are not sustainable over the long term and/or presupposes that achieving them will require tradeoffs with long-term uses and values. Such tradeoffs are permissible

under FLPMA only if they do not contribute to "unnecessary or undue degradation" of the land. Regardless of how this degradation is defined, irreparable,
human-induced alteration of biodiversity and ecosystem processes on arid and
semiarid rangelands should qualify. Activities that do not pose such hazards
should be sustainable and, if so, would provide long-term benefits; they should
be preferred in managing rangelands. Tradeoffs will be inevitable, of course—
meaning that *some* potential short-term benefits will be foregone in order to
conserve biodiversity (see chapter 6). But the kinds of "benefits" foregone are
likely to be obtainable elsewhere or through advancements in technology,
whereas, to put it bluntly, "they're not making any more land."[63]

Short-term benefits, in addition to their potential to be unsustainable and to
pose a risk of undesirable, even unlawful, impacts, may benefit only local or
other narrow interests. FLPMA calls for managing the public lands so as to
"best meet the present and future needs of *the American people*" and refers
repeatedly to serving or considering the "national interest." It does not direct the
agency to promote local interests or to meet local or individual needs. The
statute does call for attention to state and local land use plans, but it requires
"consider[ation]" and "coordinat[ion]" only "to the extent consistent with the
[public land] laws" and "to the extent . . . practical." Any management action
designed to achieve some short-term benefit that would impair or jeopardize
long-term, or more widespread, uses or values is clearly not the "most judicious
use of the land." Such a choice reflects poor judgment and is poor policy; it also
probably violates FLPMA. Arguably, too, it is inconsistent with the Taylor
Grazing Act's purpose "to promote the highest use of the public land."[64]

Both grazing and ORVs are examples of uses with largely local, short-term
benefits. Likewise, "range improvements," as traditionally undertaken, can be
viewed as seeking short-term benefits at the expense of long-term uses and
values otherwise obtainable from the land. FLPMA describes range improvements as "including, but not limited to, seeding and reseeding [rangelands],
fence construction, weed control, water development, and fish and wildlife
habitat enhancement." The statute's separate enumeration of "fish and wildlife
habitat enhancement" strongly implies that the other listed improvements may
not "enhance" fish or wildlife habitat. In fact, in a joint report concerning
grazing fees, mandated by section 401(a) of FLPMA and submitted to Congress
just one year later, the Departments of Agriculture and Interior recited the ways
in which livestock may impact wildlife, including the "negative impact on
wildlife habitat" of "fences, canals, and roads." They concluded: "In effect range
developments are a trade-off with wildlife." BLM officials customarily tout the
wildlife benefits of range improvement projects, but many wildlife and range
experts have offered views more in line with those expressed in the 1977 report.
Finally, many range "improvements" have limited useful lives or are of limited
effectiveness in achieving their intended result. Thus, as Voigt reported for the

national forests, "annual injections of rehabilitative money . . . , no matter where or in what volume spent, seem unable to check the inexorable decrease in forage production."[65]

BLM policies and biodiversity: Certain recent developments within the BLM hold out some hope for the eventual adoption of a landscape-level bio-diversity conservation strategy by the agency. First, BLM has embarked (at least on paper) upon an agency-wide mission to implement ecosystem management on its lands. In a recent annual report, the agency acknowledged that "[b]iodi-versity issues cut across virtually all BLM land management programs," and it promised to "keep this focus in the forefront." The agency's operating manual and a recent fish and wildlife planning document call for ecosystem manage-ment "to ensure self-sustaining populations and a natural abundance and diversity of wildlife" and to "manage habitat to maintain populations at a level that will avoid the need to list species and to conserve rare, vulnerable, and representative habitats, plant communities, and ecosystems."[66]

A "concept paper" prepared by the BLM Ecosystem Management Team (EMT) expressly states that ecosystem management "is consistent with BLM's mission and direction under [FLPMA] and is supported by other laws guiding the Bureau's mission." The BLM director forwarded this paper to all state dir-ectors, explicitly affirming the agency's "strong commitment for [*sic*] ecosystem management."[67]

The EMT identified "maintaining landscape functions" and "reconnecting portions of the landscape that have been managed separately in the past" as important components of managing ecosystems. "Determining how future land-scapes should function," the team wrote, "is an integrated process involving coor-dination across ecosystems. Descriptions of these desired landscape functions should integrate ecological, economic, and social considerations."[68]

Moreover, the EMT advised, successful ecosystem management will require integrating science "with operational management at all geographic levels," and research and technology "should be directed at solving problems and answering questions at the landscape and regional levels." The EMT reported that the "BLM is increasingly moving to manage local environments in relation to more regional, landscape levels." The concept paper placed special emphasis on the need for the agency to "think big"—to "[e]xpand [its] thinking to higher, larger levels and longer term (temporal and spatial)." These are themes typically sounded by conservation biologists (see chapter 6). Indeed, the EMT's advice seems entirely consistent with a biodiversity conservation strategy like the one proposed here.[69]

Informal policy statements, such as the EMT concept paper or even BLM manual provisions, may not be enforceable, but they nevertheless reflect the BLM's view that FLPMA authorizes, if not requires, agency efforts to conserve biological diversity. Because grazing is the most widespread and damaging land use on BLM lands, grazing management is the major tool available to the BLM for managing ecosystems and landscapes and conserving native biodiversity.[70]

Second, the BLM is involved in several interagency initiatives designed to conserve biodiversity at the regional or landscape levels. The agency was responsible for securing a memorandum of understanding among several county, state, and federal entities to develop the California Bioregions Initiative, a planning effort with "the long-term goal of sustaining the rich natural heritage of each major bioregion in California." Broad-perspective management plans are in place for Oregon forests, riparian areas, neotropical birds, and watersheds that are managed jointly by the BLM and Forest Service. The "Bring Back the Natives" watershed and fisheries restoration program is one example. The BLM is reportedly collaborating with The Nature Conservancy on ways to conserve biodiversity on BLM lands. It and TNC have teamed up in ill-advised demonstration projects designed to show that working ranches and fragile desert environments can be simultaneously sustainable. Summaries of the BLM's biodiversity policies and initiatives, including publications and training programs, can be found in the agency's 1992 annual report and in the Keystone Center report, *Biological Diversity on Federal Lands*.[71]

A third internal development that may foreshadow landscape-level biodiversity conservation efforts by the BLM is its training course "Applied Biodiversity Conservation." The BLM developed and teaches this course in conjunction with other federal agencies, scientists, and conservation organizations. Training has been offered in several locations, and many key BLM employees have participated.[72]

In summary, FLPMA's policies and principles and the agency's self-proclaimed management direction are consistent with a landscape-level approach to biodiversity conservation on large, arid rangelands managed by BLM. FLPMA empowers the BLM to take the single action most crucial to achieving this goal—removing livestock from lands unsuited to grazing. In particular, the statutory requirement to weigh long-term benefits to the public (benefits attributable to conserving native biodiversity) against short-term benefits (the private advantage to a few livestock permittees and, perhaps, economic benefits to a few local economies) counsels in favor of the proposed conservation program.[73]

C. PUBLIC RANGELANDS IMPROVEMENT ACT

PRIA belongs in this discussion chiefly because it evinces Congress's continuing awareness of both the ongoing degradation of western rangelands and the value of range ecosystems. It also recognizes that livestock might have to be removed from some ranges to accomplish the legislative goal of range rehabilitation.

In PRIA Congress declared that "vast segments of the public rangelands are producing less than their potential for livestock, wildlife habitat, recreation, forage, and water and soil conservation benefits, and for that reason are in an unsatisfactory condition," and that "such rangelands will remain in an unsatisfactory condition and some areas may decline further under present levels of, and funding for, management." The statute's recitation of the myriad costs and problems posed by 1978 range conditions reads like a range management text:

> [U]nsatisfactory conditions on public rangelands present a high risk of soil loss, desertification, and a resultant underproductivity for large acreages of the public lands; contribute significantly to unacceptable levels of siltation and salinity in major western watersheds . . . ; negatively impact the quality and availability of scarce western water supplies; threaten important and frequently critical fish and wildlife habitat; prevent expansion of the forage resource and resulting benefits to livestock and wildlife production; increase surface runoff and flood danger; reduce the value of such lands for recreation and esthetic purposes; and may ultimately lead to unpredictable and undesirable long-term local and regional climatic and economic changes.

FLPMA had contained a legislative finding that "a substantial amount of the Federal range lands is deteriorating in quality." PRIA reflected Congress's growing concern over these conditions.[74]

The statute's definitions section would also seem more at home in a scientific tome. The term "range condition" is defined broadly:

> the quality of the land reflected in its ability in specific vegetative areas to support various levels of productivity in accordance with range management objectives and the land use planning process, and relates to soil quality, forage values . . . , wildlife habitat, watershed and plant communities, the present state of vegetation of a range site in relation to the potential plant community for that site, and the relative degree to which the kinds, proportions, and amounts of vegetation in a plant community resemble that of the desired community for that site.

"Native vegetation," in turn, is defined as "those plant species, communities, or vegetative associations which are endemic to a given area and which would normally be identified with a healthy and productive range condition occurring as a result of the natural vegetative process of the area."[75]

In PRIA Congress reaffirmed "a national policy and commitment to . . . manage, maintain, and improve the condition of the public rangelands so that they become as productive as feasible for all rangeland values in accordance with management objectives and the land use planning process established by [FLPMA]." The act relies heavily on range improvements, particularly structural improvements, to accomplish this objective and authorizes funding for this purpose. Congressional confidence in range improvements was also evident in FLPMA, which expresses the legislative belief "that installation of additional range improvements could arrest much of the continuing range deterioration."[76]

Reliance on range improvements to compensate for lost productivity of grazing lands has long characterized public rangeland management. It dates to the early 1930s, when BLM's predecessor, the Grazing Service, engaged Civilian Conservation Corps workers to develop water sources, build fences, reseed ranges, control weeds, and perform other rehabilitative functions. The Forest Service too depended on range improvements, long before passage of FLPMA, which governs BLM and Forest Service grazing programs alike. BLM acting director (now Forest Service chief) Mike Dombeck, speaking in Cheyenne, Wyoming, in July 1996, intimated that this is still the BLM's preferred approach— despite the agency's much publicized efforts to achieve "range reform." Dombeck reportedly assured his stockgrower audience that the "BLM does not intend to reduce ranching on public lands despite fears to the contrary." Similarly, a common refrain heard during the early stages of the Clinton administration's rangeland reform campaign was that range condition problems "are mainly problems of the past that can be corrected by modern range management techniques." As we have seen, however, range "improvement" really means enhancing the range's livestock production capacity. Modern thinking concerning rangeland ecology and the practical irreversibility of disturbance-induced stable vegetative states exposes the pitfalls of overreliance on "range improvements" to restore or improve degraded grazing lands.[77]

As the definition of "range condition" reveals, PRIA recognizes several range values other than livestock forage. Even so, range improvement funding has been extremely lopsided in favor of livestock production. According to one investigator, 96.5 percent of the money spent in the field since 1980 for specific range improvement projects has been used to benefit livestock. (She qualified this accounting, however, noting that the BLM was "able to account for only half the [range improvement] money spent" during the period.) It should come as no surprise that grazing permittees support range improvement projects. Improvements hold out the hope of increased forage and, consequently, increased AUMs. According to Fairfax, PRIA's provision for range improvement funding was a "classic agency-approved buy-off. The Bureau was attempting to sweeten deep cuts in grazing allotments with the thought that productivity improvements resulting from increased investment would make the cuts only temporary." In addition to PRIA appropriations, a portion of all grazing fees paid by permittees is plowed back into the ground into "rehabilitation, protection, and improvements" of the lands grazed. Advising land managers how to use these "range betterment" funds was a longstanding function of BLM district grazing advisory boards.[78]

Contrasting with the pro-livestock bias in implementing federal range improvement policy is PRIA section 4(b): "Except where the [FLPMA] land use planning process . . . or the Secretary determines . . . that grazing uses should be discontinued (either temporarily or permanently) on certain lands, the goal of such management shall be to improve the range conditions of the public range-lands so that they become as productive as feasible [for all rangeland values]." According to Coggins, this language is "the most important provision in all the range management statutes." The paragraph directs that range "improvement is *the* goal under the statutes, not just a goal," Coggins asserts; as such, it consti-tutes "the first nonambiguous policy statement in rangeland legislation." Keep in mind that PRIA did not *confer* the authority to remove livestock from public lands; both the Forest Service and the BLM already had power under FLPMA and prior legislation to take such a step.[79]

Fairfax disagrees with Coggins's interpretation. She describes PRIA's provi-sions as "an odd bag of rancher concerns," all of which "undercut the ostensibly multiple-use emphasis of FLPMA. Certainly, they attest to the continuing political strength of the range-livestock industry in Congress." I would side with Coggins. Far from securing or entrenching stockgrowers' interest in public grazing lands, PRIA ratifies the administrative power to reduce or eliminate livestock use to promote values such as watershed, wildlife, and soil quality. It also equates "native vegetation" with healthy range condition. The legislation was more of a consolation prize than a victory for ranchers.[80]

How would a biodiversity conservation strategy that precludes, or greatly limits, livestock grazing fare under PRIA? First of all, PRIA is not organic legis-lation; it does not impose new duties on BLM, nor grant it additional authority. Instead, by specifying that its policies are to be "construed as supplemental to and not in derogation of the purposes for which rangelands are administered under other provisions of law," PRIA reaffirms that BLM rangelands shall continue to be managed in accordance with the Taylor Grazing Act and FLPMA.[81]

Plainly, Congress sought in PRIA to promote domestic livestock grazing as a use of western rangelands. But this objective is constrained by section 4(b). Where grazing interferes with the range's capacity to produce other resources, grazing will be curtailed or eliminated. Thus, PRIA can be seen as elevating the goal of healthy range condition over the objective of livestock production.[82]

PRIA does nothing to weaken my assessment of the legality or propriety, under FLPMA or the Taylor Grazing Act, of the proposed biodiversity conser-vation strategy. In fact, by clarifying that "improving range conditions" is *"the* goal" of range management, even where livestock grazing continues, and by expressly recognizing that grazing may have to be discontinued in certain circumstances, PRIA probably strengthens the case for a biodiversity conser-vation plan on arid lands unsuited to livestock grazing. Section 4(b) could even be viewed as reflecting Congress's understanding that manipulation of grazing will be the key ecosystem management tool on BLM and Forest Service rangelands.[83]

PRIA further confirms the interior secretary's broad discretion to determine the condition of and to manage public rangelands. The secretary's discretion is arguably limited, however, by PRIA's attention to "potential plant communit[ies]" and "natural vegetative process[es]," and its recognition of issues such as the feasibility of increasing rangeland productivity and rangelands "potential for [producing] livestock." These latter provisions help bolster an argument that the secretary is required to assess whether livestock production is feasible and appropriate on a particular site or whether grazing would impact native vegetation or functioning ecological processes. In these respects, PRIA complements FLPMA's requirement that livestock production, one of the multiple uses, be sustainable. It would be illogical at best to infer that Congress intended, via PRIA, to perpetuate the "unsatisfactory conditions" extant on "vast segments of the public rangelands" by sanctioning continued, unsustainable grazing on lands unsuited to that purpose. PRIA thus confirms that conservation of biodiversity and/or prevention of irreversible, grazing-induced vegetative changes would be legitimate bases for a decision to terminate grazing on arid and semi-arid rangelands.[84]

D. OTHER STATUTORY AUTHORITY

The statutes examined thus far are those that most directly govern or guide the BLM's grazing-management authority—the Taylor Act, FLPMA, and PRIA. Many other statutes bear upon the BLM's grazing-related decision-making authorities and responsibilities. The most significant of these are the National Environmental Policy Act, Clean Water Act, and Endangered Species Act.

1. NATIONAL ENVIRONMENTAL POLICY ACT

NEPA dictates no substantive outcome in agency decision making, but it does require federal agencies to fully consider the impacts of "major Federal actions significantly affecting the quality of the human environment." NEPA review takes the form of an environmental impact statement. Agencies may do a preliminary "environmental assessment" (EA) to determine whether an EIS is required. All BLM resource management plans are accompanied by an EIS; agency actions that are more limited in scope, such as granting a right-of-way to construct a pipeline, approving a mining plan of operation, or renewing a grazing permit, are addressed in an EIS or EA.[85]

Impacts on biodiversity are clearly within Congress's contemplation in NEPA. Section 101 of the statute proclaims that "it is the continuing responsibility of [all federal agencies] to use all practicable means . . . to improve and coordinate Federal plans, functions, programs, and resources to the end that the Nation may . . . preserve important . . . natural aspects of our national heritage, and maintain, wherever possible, an environment which supports diversity." The section containing the EIS requirement speaks of "environmental impact," "adverse environmental effects," "relationship between local short-term uses of man's environment and the maintenance and enhancement of long-term productivity," and "irreversible and irretrievable commitments of resources." Each of these is relevant to a consideration of impacts on biodiversity and consistent with BLM's land planning and management responsibilities under FLPMA. Numerous commentators have discussed NEPA's application to the potential biodiversity impacts of proposed agency actions. Such impacts are clearly within the scope of effects that an EIS must consider.[86]

This last conclusion is fortified by NEPA-implementing regulations issued by the Council on Environmental Quality. These rules specify that all reasonably foreseeable impacts, including cumulative impacts, flowing from agency actions be considered in NEPA documents. The CEQ has admonished: "To the extent that federal actions affect biodiversity, and that it is possible to both anticipate and evaluate those effects, NEPA *requires* federal agencies to do so." The CEQ has issued informal guidance specifically addressing the treatment of biodiversity in the NEPA process. In the council's view, "conceptual frameworks, analytical tools, and information are currently available to support [biodiversity impact] analysis."[87]

The CEQ has formulated several "recommendations for improving consideration of biodiversity in NEPA analyses." There are signs that the BLM is taking to heart at least part of this advice—the CEQ's suggestions (1) that agencies "[a]cknowledge the conservation of biodiversity as national policy and incorporate its consideration in the NEPA process" and (2) that they develop "[a]gency-sponsored environmental training courses [that] discuss biodiversity." I cannot say whether the BLM consistently considers biodiversity in its NEPA or planning documents or how its implementation record squares with its written plans. But the agency has addressed biodiversity in a number of significant planning efforts in recent years. A quick, one-time review of the agency's public notices in the Federal Register revealed: (1) a proposed land exchange, one of whose purposes was to "enhance regional biodiversity objectives"; (2) a draft Resource Management Plan (RMP) and EIS, which included a proposal for an ACEC whose purposes included "enhanc[ing] the biodiversity of the ecosystem"; and (3) a "basin-wide, ecosystem-based [planning] effort" (part of a proposed RMP amendment), which cited "declining biodiversity" among the issues to be addressed therein.[88]

Two of the CEQ's recommendations concerning biodiversity are especially noteworthy: It exhorts agencies to "seek out opportunities to participate in efforts to develop regional ecosystem plans" and to "consider establishing specific goals and objectives for the conservation of biodiversity" within any existing ecosystem management frameworks. The council further encourages agencies to "consider initiating" such regional efforts when they "are lacking entirely." As discussed in chapter 6, BLM has done this on at least one occasion. The CEQ also urges federal agencies to "actively seek relevant information ["on the status and distribution of biota"] from sources both within and outside government agencies" and to "[e]xpand the information base on which biodiversity analyses and management decisions are based," by "cooperating with academic institutions, private industry, and others on research to advance ecological understanding." These recommendations dovetail with FLPMA's requirements regarding inventories and interdisciplinary planning. Indeed, all of the CEQ recommendations have relevance for BLM's land planning and management—including its grazing program—and merit the agency's serious attention.[89]

In sum, NEPA does not require the BLM to conserve biodiversity, nor indeed to take or avoid any substantive action in managing federal lands. But NEPA and its implementing regulations flesh out the BLM's obligation to consider the impacts of its grazing program on biodiversity. And the statute's broad national goals supply an additional incentive—and justification—for considering and implementing a biodiversity conservation program.

2. ENDANGERED SPECIES ACT

The ESA has been the subject of extensive commentary, both generally and respecting biodiversity conservation specifically.[90]

The ESA imposes on the BLM, as on all federal agencies, an affirmative duty to conserve threatened and endangered ("T&E") species and their habitats. Specifically, section 7 requires agencies to "utilize their authorities in furtherance of the purposes of [the ESA] by carrying out programs for the conservation of [T&E species]." This section directs agencies to "insure that any action authorized, funded, or carried out by such agency is not likely to jeopardize the continued existence of any [T or E] species or result in the destruction or adverse modification of [critical] habitat." The act declares that it is the "policy of Congress that all Federal departments and agencies shall seek to conserve [T&E species] and shall utilize their authorities in furtherance of the purposes of [the act]." "Conserve" and "conservation" are defined as "to use and the use of all methods and procedures which are necessary to bring any [T or E] species to the point at which the measures provided by [the ESA] are no longer necessary. Such measures include, but are not limited to, . . . habitat acquisition and maintenance."[91]

While the species entitled to ESA protections and subject to its prohibitions are only those species that are officially listed or are candidates for listing as threatened or endangered, the act has profound implications for the conservation of biodiversity generally by virtue of its mandate to preserve listed species' habitats. Congress's understanding of ecology is reflected in ESA section 2(b), which states that the "purposes of this chapter are to provide a means whereby the ecosystems upon which endangered species and threatened species depend may be conserved."[92]

The agency charged with administering the ESA, the U.S. Fish and Wildlife Service (USFWS), has recognized the management limitations of focusing too narrowly on only those species on the brink of extinction. As former USFWS director Mollie Beattie wrote not long ago: "Regardless of how the ESA has been used in the past, we intend to use it to support and conserve biodiversity and ecosystems." "Prelisting conservation will be crucial," she said, in avoiding what Interior Secretary Babbitt has called "train wrecks"—crisis situations such as the imbroglio over old-growth logging and the northern spotted owl in the Pacific Northwest. It is "precisely in those places where economic activity is unsustainable," Beattie observed, "that ecosystems are in trouble." One ESA scholar has described the "new ESA" as envisaged by Beattie, Babbitt, Sax, and others in the Clinton administration as "more conscious of ecosystem-wide conservation strategies, rather than single-species preservation efforts."[93]

Given that the BLM is one of the major federal land management agencies— it manages the greatest land area and a huge fraction of this country's wildlife habitat—it would seem to bear an especially heavy species conservation burden or, depending on one's perspective, enjoy an unparalleled opportunity under the ESA. The ESA's mandates serve to reinforce, and sharpen the focus of, the bureau's wildlife and habitat-related responsibilities and authorities under FLPMA (reiterated in PRIA). The biodiversity conservation strategy advanced herein epitomizes the "[p]relisting conservation" approach advocated by the USFWS, and it would significantly further the purposes of the ESA and the BLM's affirmative obligation to promote those purposes. Finally, the ESA and implementing regulations will help ensure detection and protection of any species that "slip through the pores" of the coarse-filter approach embodied in a landscape-scale conservation effort.[94]

3. CLEAN WATER ACT

The Clean Water Act applies potentially to all BLM land use activities, pursuant to the terms of the CWA itself and to FLPMA's requirement that all land use plans "provide for compliance with applicable pollution control laws." The CWA directs that all federal agencies "engaged in any activity resulting, or which may result, in the discharge or runoff of pollutants . . . [are] subject to, and [shall] comply with, all Federal, State, interstate, and local requirements . . . respecting the control and abatement of water pollution." In addition, the act specifies that any "applicant for a federal license or permit to conduct any activity . . . which may result in any discharge" into surface waters is subject to "certification" by the appropriate state agency. Licenses and permits potentially subject to certification include grazing permits, rights-of-way grants, special use permits, etc. The state may approve the proposed activity, approve it subject to specified modifications or conditions, or deny certification, thus precluding issuance of the federal permit. The U.S. Supreme Court approved the inclusion of wetlands within the category of waters subject to CWA regulation, based in part on the ecological relationship between water and adjacent wetland vegetation. Activities conducted in wetlands are subject to certification and to the act's dredge-and-fill permitting and mitigation requirements. Taken together, these provisions require the BLM and its permittees to comply with all applicable state water quality standards when planning and implementing any land use activities.[95]

How do any of these requirements relate to biodiversity? The "objective" of the Clean Water Act is "to restore and maintain the chemical, physical, and *biological integrity* of the Nation's waters"; a "national goal" of the legislation is to attain wherever possible "water quality which provides for the propagation of fish, shellfish, and wildlife." All water quality standards must "serve the purposes [of the act]"; these standards must, therefore, take into account the biota of the surface waters to which they apply. Water quality standards consist of two parts—a designated use (such as coldwater fishery or shellfish bed) and target criteria (for chemical or biological parameters such as dissolved oxygen and fecal coliform bacteria) designed to meet and sustain the designated use(s). The water quality criteria most likely to be violated on BLM lands as a result of grazing activities are those pertaining to turbidity (sediment load), nutrients, temperature, and pathogens. Water quality standards also encompass the respective state's antidegradation policy, a set of rules according to which each state categorizes its waters and provides increasing levels of protection for higher-quality waters. Antidegradation regulations augment the protection afforded streams by designated uses and water quality criteria.[96]

The upshot of these requirements is that the BLM must insure that its land use activities do not (1) interfere with achieving or sustaining a designated use of any surface water, (2) cause or contribute to a violation of any water quality criteria applicable to surface waters on BLM or downstream lands, or (3) violate applicable antidegradation standards. EPA guidance for wetlands specifies, in addition, that wetland water quality criteria should include "a standard that wetlands must be 'free from' activities that 'would substantially impair the biological community as it naturally occurs.'"[97]

Western states' identification of grazing as their number-one cause of non-point source pollution reflects the incomplete coverage of water pollution laws and/or the inadequacy of their enforcement against grazing activities on public and private lands. The 1996 federal district court decision in *Oregon Natural Desert Association v. Thomas* (*ONDA*) was the first to hold expressly that CWA section 401 certification requirements apply to activities that may result in nonpoint pollution and to rule that federal livestock grazing permits are subject to state certification. The court's decision is a sound, defensible interpretation of the Clean Water Act. Although it was reversed by the Ninth Circuit Court of Appeals, that court subsequently withdrew its opinion from publication in the Federal Reporter. Under the appellate court's rules, the opinion thus has no precedential value and may not even be cited, except in very narrow circumstances. The result: while the district court's decision was overturned in this particular matter, the court could adopt and apply the same reasoning in future cases. *ONDA* has attracted considerable attention from the livestock industry, state and federal agencies, and environmentalists, and it will undoubtedly spawn litigation in other states.[98]

Certification of grazing permits has not traditionally been sought or required by states or by public land management agencies. Implementing the *ONDA* court's interpretation of CWA section 401 across the West would undoubtedly meet with substantial resistance, not only from grazing permittees, but also from many state environmental departments, which will consider the certification review process an unwanted addition to their workloads and a political hot potato. Nevertheless, the fact of livestock's impact on water quality is incontrovertible, and the legal requirements, while controversial, have now been recognized by one court and should be addressed by all public land grazing states. Many western environmental groups are taking an increasingly active interest in water pollution issues. One thing seems sure: public land grazing will receive more, not less, scrutiny in the future.[99]

In summary, the Clean Water Act, in conjunction with FLPMA's mandate that the BLM comply with federal and state water quality requirements, effectively charges the BLM with conserving biodiversity in surface waters, including riparian zones and other wetlands, on all BLM lands. More rigorous implementation and enforcement of federal and state water quality requirements would further biodiversity conservation objectives by helping to restore and maintain the "biological integrity" of aquatic, wetland, and riparian habitats.

The BLM's statutory authorities are fully consistent with implementing a landscape-scale biodiversity conservation program. None of these laws poses an obstacle to taking the necessary implementing steps, including, where necessary, removing livestock from the area to be protected. On the contrary, affirmative steps to conserve biodiversity would facilitate BLM compliance with several legislative mandates, including managing the public lands for sustainable uses (FLPMA), avoiding unnecessary or undue degradation of public lands (FLPMA), conserving threatened and endangered species (ESA), and restoring the biological integrity of surface waters (CWA). A biodiversity conservation strategy calling for the reduction or elimination of livestock grazing on arid BLM lands would enhance BLM's ability to comply with the letter and the spirit of the Clean Water Act, state water quality law, NEPA, the Endangered Species Act, and FLPMA.

CHAPTER 8

The Socioeconomic Landscape

Livestock remain on public lands, despite grazing's devastating ecological impacts, its historically inferior position on the "totem pole" of multiple uses, and a set of legal policies that it subverts. The status quo continues chiefly because of ranchers' political clout and the existence of a political system that they are uniquely equipped to exploit. The apologia consists of two principal arguments: public land grazing is important to the economic base of local communities, if not the region, and the ranching way of life merits preservation, both for its own sake and as a means of preserving the West's open spaces. If these socioeconomic rationalizations can be overcome, as the historical and legal arguments have been, no warrant should remain for leaving domestic livestock on arid public lands.[1]

The economics discussion here is more historical and qualitative than quantitative or scientific. Evidence is examined for the value of the public forage resource, the contribution of public lands ranching to local and regional economies, and the values of public rangelands for other uses. The chapter picks up several unfinished threads from previous chapters, including chapter 2's brief foray into the economics of public land grazing at the time of the Taylor Grazing Act, chapter 7's construction of the Taylor Act term "chiefly valuable for grazing," and chapter 4's look at the ranching culture.[2]

Consideration of economics is warranted for two basic reasons. First, Congress contemplated, in the Taylor Grazing Act, that only lands *"chiefly valuable for grazing* and raising forage crops" would be included in grazing districts and that the interior secretary would exercise his discretion under the act "to promote the highest use of the public land." Because the law still contains this language, its meaning, both circa 1934 and today, demands consideration. Second, public policy choices demand attention to economic efficiency and equity. As public priorities concerning federal public lands change, and as demands with respect to these lands escalate, it is imperative that we reconsider the fiscal soundness and sustainability of traditional land uses and how we value uses of the public lands. As Hays so cogently put it, "Uses are not inherent in resources, but are only what people want them to be." Our vastly enhanced appreciation of the importance of sustaining ecological health, which includes maintaining biodiversity, is perhaps the most compelling reason for reexamining our views concerning what public land uses are in fact "valuable."[3]

Undertaking a discussion of economics necessitates attributing some value to the benefits of conserving biodiversity. Monetary values can easily be assigned to a pound of beef or wool, and with relative ease to an entire ranching operation, but valuing a species saved is much more problematic. Putting a value on conserving the biodiversity of landscapes is not just more difficult still but, many would argue, impossible. Nevertheless, the "need for more rigorous economic and social analysis within BLM" demands that policy analysts be able to assign value to both market and nonmarket goods. Accordingly, economists have developed methods for valuing "goods" for which there is no traditional market (e.g., species and ecosystems).[4]

The analytical methods, and the results produced thereby, however, are often controversial. The methodology has been widely criticized—as "hypothetical," imprecise, useless, or confusing. According to Workman and his colleagues, there is a "near consensus in the literature that the willingness-to-pay procedure is the most appropriate conceptual framework available for valuation of nonmarket outputs." But, they warn, "values for some nonmarket products (e.g., aesthetics, endangered species, and Indian burial grounds) cannot now or perhaps ever can be expressed in monetary terms." The problem—and this is the problem for biodiversity as well—"is how to include them in a decision analysis." As assistant Forest Service chief Leon Kneip put it, more than sixty years ago: "All too frequently large intangible social values have been sacrificed to small material gains because no means existed for relative evaluation or to compel the action most in the public interest."[5]

If a solution to this problem is to be found, surely it will include some form of surveying human attitudes and values. Hays wrote that "amenity values are not held willy-nilly. There is a pattern and order to them which can be described and dealt with systematically." He praised, as "one of the most extensive studies of environmental values which has yet taken place in the United States," the 1970s research by Stephen Kellert of the Yale School of Forestry (examined in chapters 1 and 4). Hays observed that BLM lands—even "western drylands and deserts"— had, within the "past few decades," "taken on new meaning to the American people as lands which are valuable in their more natural and less developed state as natural environment lands." He encouraged all resource agencies, particularly the BLM, to make some similar effort to be sensitive to and to understand the "larger social context" of changing environmental values in their planning efforts.[6]

While understanding human environmental values should affect how agencies think about the resources that they manage, it still will not enable them to place a dollar amount on certain resources or amenities. Some conservation biologists, philosophers, and environmental ethicists argue that even the most sophisticated economic measures are inappropriate for valuing biological "resources," which have inherent value far beyond their monetary worth, assuming it could be determined. They hold that conventional economic tools are unsuited to making decisions about the conservation of biological diversity. The 1970 NAS Committee on Land Use and Wildlife Resources wrote simply: "We believe that to preserve the quality and variety of the American out-of-doors is justified by assumption and principle, rather than by economics." David Ehrenfeld much more recently opined that the "very existence of diversity is its own warrant for survival." I would add that it is a warrant for *our* survival as well.[7]

Some may criticize this tack as a "cop-out." But it seems to me indisputable that life and the world as we know it depend on sustaining natural functions and processes. We lack the knowledge or ability to recreate species or other "component parts," let alone whole, functioning systems. The conservation of natural systems must not be made to depend on our ability to assign some monetary value to their component parts. This is so even if we were able to develop "better" techniques for assigning value to such things as beetles, or fungi, or soil microorganisms—and even if economists were to agree on those improved techniques. I share Ehrenfeld's fear that "when we finish assigning values to biological diversity, we will find that we don't have very much biological diversity left." This book thus reflects the belief that people need to come to understand the "inherent wrongness" of destroying species and natural environments.[8]

A. THE VALUE OF PUBLIC GRAZING LANDS

Grazing has been conducted on the public domain for two hundred years in some places, but the history of the western livestock industry began a little over a century ago. Over that time the face of the industry has changed significantly. The 1870s to 1880s are generally considered the "high period of the reign of the cattle barons." After the initial bust—the result of a saturated beef market, a depleted range, and the killer winters of 1886–88—a "shift to smaller operations, with a permanent home base, more restricted range and a means of supplying winter forage, began to characterize the industry." Grazing according to this pattern has continued over much of the public domain (now BLM lands) and national forests to this day.[9]

For the first sixty years or so, livestock producers' use of federal western rangelands was "chiefly by default" because the land was considered "not economically useful for other purposes." Livestock grazing was the most lucrative private use of much of the public domain, over the short term, in the late nineteenth and early twentieth centuries, although even then many lands were already severely depleted and not achieving their potential productivity. For a few years, prior to the development of refrigeration and the increasing use of feedlots, the range livestock industry could claim some national significance. But at no time was its economic contribution as significant as many apologists would have the public believe.

Chapter 7 concludes that the Taylor Act's criterion for establishing grazing districts—that the lands be "chiefly valuable for grazing"—can be fairly translated as "not more valuable for some use other than grazing." The discussion that follows recounts additional, post-1934 evidence and commentary in support of this interpretation.

1. THE EARLY POST–TAYLOR ACT YEARS

Borrowing heavily from the 1936 report to Congress, *The Western Range*, this section attempts to paint a picture of the western range livestock enterprise in the mid-1930s and to delineate the contours of the TGA's term "chiefly valuable."[10]

Speaking of all agricultural products and agriculture-related investments in 1936, of which the range livestock industry was one component, Paul H. Roberts, a contributor to *The Western Range*, wrote: "It hardly need be said that the agriculture of the West affects local, national, and world trade and penetrates into the whole social and economic fabric." Roberts then presented various statistics concerning the extent and value of public land livestock production in order to give "[s]ome idea of the extent to which range livestock contributes to the possible prosperity of western agriculture."[11]

Public rangelands were said to occupy "about two-fifths of the total land area of the United States and about three-fourths of that of the range country." The West at this time "produce[d] about 75 percent of the national output of wool and mohair, and in pounds about 55 percent of the sheep and lambs, and nearly one-third of the cattle and calves"; these products came "primarily [from] the range territory." The "direct value" of livestock products from the range states amounted to $476 million. Roberts also attributed the range's importance to the "[h]uge expenditures by the Federal Government, the States, and private enterprise" in activities ranging from "irrigation, roads [and] range improvements" to developing new strains of fruits, grains, forage, and livestock "adapted to western conditions."[12]

The number of livestock in the West was reported at more than 63 million, valued at $1.4 billion. Production of wool and mohair, primarily from rangelands, amounted to more than 276 million pounds, valued at over $82 million.

The number of cattle (excluding dairy cows) in the seventeen range states was 13.7 million. Roberts did not distinguish between cattle grazed on public range-lands and those raised solely on private lands. Stock operations varied from as few as 5 to 10 head of cattle or sheep to "60,000 cattle, and 80,000 sheep, or more. Acreages of land controlled [varied] from as few as 10 acres of farm land to 400,000 or 500,000 acres of range land with some farm land. There [were] some limited instances of probably 1,000,000 acres in a single ranching operation."[13]

Roberts's report gave some attention to what constituted an economic ranch unit in the West. Far from being an easy road to fortune, successful ranching entailed several prerequisites: "In literally thousands of cases throughout the West it has been demonstrated that with an adequate number of stock, an owned ranch producing supplemental feeds commensurate with the operation, and a permit on a nearby national forest with assurance of enough reasonably cheap forage, a high plane of living is possible." This list presupposes that a ranch oper-ation without public land grazing privileges would be less profitable, or perhaps even uneconomical. The writer confirmed this elsewhere, reporting that "forage from leased land or from permits to use public land costs the livestock operator less than does ownership in fee simple." It is not apparent whether Roberts intended to specify a requirement for a national forest permit as opposed to a permit to graze any public land. His phrasing may simply reflect an inadvertent institutional bias. But because forests generally produced more, and higher-quality, forage than did public domain (now BLM) ranges, ranches holding rights only to the latter may have been less profitable.[14]

What constituted an "adequate number of stock" or an adequate ranch acreage in 1936 varied depending on the location. In the Nebraska Sand Hills, 640-acre Kincaid Act homesteads had failed, and ranchers had subsequently consolidated their holdings. According to Roberts, successful western Nebraska ranches covered 1,300 to more than 29,000 acres and produced approximately 100 head to 1,800 head of cattle, respectively. In neighboring Wyoming, ranches with fewer than 200 head "were losing on the average 3.79 percent, while the large outfits were making 2.53 percent profits above all costs." Clearly, the days of the "cattle barons" were over. Economies of scale operated on the western range, but profit margins in all ranch size categories were small.[15]

Despite its "badly depleted and eroded" condition, the range, Roberts asserted, was "still the essential ingredient of a balanced way of living in the West." He recognized that continued overgrazing and the resulting degradation of western ranges would undermine the continuing viability of public lands ranching and expressed concern about the sustainability of ranch life's benefits: "Surely, it is not too much to ask that the management of ranges and ranches be so coordinated that greater social and economic security may be enjoyed by future generations." The hard realities of the western range posed a dilemma: although ranges were already widely overgrazed, there were disadvantages to grazing too few livestock. As Roberts explained it, "where the numbers of stock grazed per permittee [were] too low," not only were ranches uneconomic, but "the sound social values which should flow from the range [also were] not realized."[16]

Other chapters of *The Western Range* concentrated on range resources other than livestock; several reported that in some areas the actual or potential value of nonforage resources exceeded that of the grazing resource. Indeed, the document as a whole evidences a widely shared conviction that many, if not most, rangelands were *not* "chiefly valuable for grazing" but could more profitably serve other uses. Forsling et al. set the stage for these analyses: "If the task [of improving the range] involved no more than the meager grazing resources, it might be argued that the land had better be abandoned without attempting conservation. But this land cannot be written off the books like a worn-out piece of machinery." The grazing lands, they explained,

> afford other important possibilities of use. They constitute the natural feeding place or breeding grounds, or both, for various species of game animals and birds. Some areas support woodlands or forests. . . . Still other parts have high potential value for outdoor recreation and the human enjoyment of desert flora, geologic forms, and scenery.
>
> In order to realize the maximum contribution to local communities and the general public welfare, there should be correlated use, protection, and development of all the resources on the grazing districts so as to obtain the highest net benefit from all combined, in accordance with actual present and probable future needs. . . .

The observations of S. B. Show were similar.[17]

Show warned that unless the TGA were "amended specifically to provide for multiple use this feature of administration may be neglected" on the public domain. Forsling et al. noted that there would be "strong and persistent contention that the act is designed wholly for the welfare of the livestock growers," but they believed that the secretary of the interior had "broad discretionary power to do whatever . . . is necessary to stop injury from overgrazing and to conserve all the resources on the public lands set aside as grazing districts."[18]

The foregoing comments reflect what the Agriculture Department considered a crucial management issue: "How, through the correlation of the various uses for which range lands are suited, [to] obtain the maximum use or service consistent with the conservation of the resource, and hence the highest current public benefits." One recommendation in *The Western Range* was that Congress pass legislation "authoriz[ing] administration of all range resources, forage, watershed, wildlife, in accordance with the multiple-use principle and for the highest public benefits." "One of the essentials in achieving highest use of the land," Forsling et al. ventured, "is to maintain sufficient flexibility to meet justifiable new demands as they arise."[19]

Several individual reports in *The Western Range* reflected considerable thought about the relative values of range resources. Reed W. Bailey and Charles A. Connaughton, director and silviculturalist, respectively, of the Forest Service's Intermountain Forest and Range Experiment Station, wrote: "Although grazing is often considered the outstanding value of range lands, watershed protection may be of even greater importance on over half of the total range area." These scientists estimated that the lands' watershed value was probably at least four times their value for livestock production. The overview chapter concluded, based on Bailey and Connaughton's economic assessment, that the "grazing value of range watershed lands may not often exceed $3 per acre" and was often actually less in the lands' "present denuded condition." The "watershed value" of the lands, while "much more difficult to determine," was calculated to be at least $12.27 for every acre of range watershed lands (a total of 475 million). This estimate was derived from water-related "dependent investments" such as "irrigation works, land, and facilities." Bailey and Connaughton noted "[i]nvestments of over 5.8 billion dollars in irrigated land and improvements compare[d] with about 4.1 billion invested in range livestock and [lands and facilities]." The estimated value of the *forage* on the public range in 1933 was, according to Gates's later report, only $10 million.[20]

Wildlife was another of the valuable "natural products of the range." In his introductory chapter Associate Chief Clapp asserted: "The reappearance of wildlife has undoubtedly been one of the factors responsible for over 38 million visitors in the national forests in 1934 as compared with 3 million in 1917." Wildlife on the western ranges was assigned a "present annual economic value" of $90 million, although this figure was said to tell only part of the story. To this figure, Clapp stated, "expenditures exceeding $40,000,000 by hunters and fishermen should be added, and, in part also, those by recreationists of over $15,000,000, because one of the intangible but chief values of wildlife is the increased recreational attraction and enjoyment which it affords."[21]

Conceding that recreation was seldom the dominant use of rangelands, Clapp argued that such lands do "have an important recreational function." Furthermore, those rangelands "possessing the qualities sought by outdoor recreationists have thus acquired economic values which often exceed those for other services. They are capital assets of their communities. They draw large sums of money that otherwise would not be received; money which contributes as fully to economic security as that from any other source." Clapp recognized that visitors paid indirectly "for the privilege of enjoying scenic charm or other recreational values" by purchasing commodities and services in the area. He warned that the "serious depletion of most range areas, the reduction in wildlife, the erosion and silting of streams, have all been reflected in impaired recreational values. Where originally the mind was inspired . . . it is now depressed by the sight of a terrain scored and dissected by erosion and only thinly covered by plants." He concluded that administration of rangelands having recreational value had to take recreational uses, along with other values, into account if the ranges were "to serve the highest public interest."[22]

The Western Range revealed not only that the value of other range resources in 1936 exceeded that of grazing, but also that grazing was not accorded any special status among range uses. Clapp advised that livestock should be removed from certain lands, "such as seriously eroding areas on the watersheds of important streams." Temporary closure to all grazing of perhaps 50 million acres would "be necessary in the public interest." In addition, Clapp warned, "[l]imited areas, such as municipal watersheds, and those of irrigation reservoirs where the plant cover is on a hair-trigger balance because of adverse conditions, will need to be *closed permanently to grazing.*" This recommendation encompassed approximately 11.5 million acres. Clapp even ventured that "local adjustments in grazing use . . . may be necessary" to accommodate recreation. Apparently seeking to mitigate the emotional and practical impact of this pronouncement, he added: "The cash value of recreation in which livestock producers share is an important factor in offsetting possible losses. The western 'dude ranch' is an example of direct returns, but community returns benefit livestock producers indirectly." The Agriculture Department's belief that rangelands had greater value if retained by the government and managed for public, rather than private, purposes was also evident in its concern over preventing "the establishment of prescriptive rights on grazing districts."[23]

One contributor to the report had an especially clear view of the potential of the western range and of the tradeoffs that producing livestock entailed. Forest Service assistant chief Kneip wrote:

> If it is impossible simultaneously to use a given area for the production of beefsteaks and spiritual stimulation, steps should be initiated promptly to determine which of the two products is more important to the economic future of the region. Frequently it will be found that continued use for the production of beefsteaks not only threatens the ultimate destruction of the resource but currently attracts to the region from other sections a far smaller amount of money than would be attracted were the resource dedicated to recreational and inspirational forms of use of a practically perpetual character.

Kneip expressed regret that decisions regarding the appropriate uses of public rangelands had been "so little characterized by analytical determinations of the degree to which any given area will contribute to taxable wealth under one form of use as compared to another, or under a logical correlation of two or more forms of use in proper balance as compared to a single use which to justify itself must be carried beyond safe limits of biological laws." These observations were echoed in part by Show, who observed that range management "has to do with . . . all related activities necessary to attain the highest use consistent with the protection and sustained yield of all the resources. In short, it is a job of applied biology."[24]

Recognizing the desirability and economic value of uses that could be considered nonconsumptive, Kneip promoted the rangelands' great potential for supporting recreation and tourism:

> The dollar brought to and left in the region by the tourist seeking only the beauty and the interest of nature has just as great a purchasing power and will contribute as fully to the economic existence of the community as will a dollar brought in through the production and sale of beef, mutton, hides, or wool. Furthermore, the tourist dollar need subtract nothing whatever from the sum total of available natural resources, while the livestock dollar inevitably means the subtraction from the soil of at least a minute part of [nutrients and] elements essential to its continued productivity.[25]

The Western Range's discussions of watershed, recreation, and wildlife values leave no doubt that in 1936 livestock production was not considered (at least by the Department of Agriculture) the highest and best use of all rangelands or even a permanent use of the range. The contributors were agreed that, if the range were "to serve its greatest usefulness, plans for stopping deterioration, and for restoration and maintenance, must be formulated around the highest form or forms of use, whether for the grazing of domestic livestock, for the services which watersheds should render, for timber production, for the production of wildlife, or for recreation."[26]

The views presented in *The Western Range*, and the statistics on which they were based, are not determinative, of course, of congressional intent behind national grazing policy. Still, they seriously undermine the apparent presumption in favor of grazing that inexplicably persists. A common argument in favor of continuing our present policy is that grazing has always been an important, and unquestioned, use of the western range and a significant component of the economies of certain western communities. Therefore, the argument goes, it should continue. But if the appropriateness or desirability of grazing in all circumstances was not a foregone conclusion at the time of the Taylor Act's passage, a fact as to which *The Western Range* leaves no doubt, then the argument's premise is faulty and its force is seriously weakened.[27]

Kneip's reference to the choice between "beefsteaks and spiritual stimulation" reveals a recognition, even in 1936, that natural resources and amenities had value transcending their market worth. Kneip referred to these values as "social":

> [C]ertain little canyons and groves which are the natural and nearby recreation areas of small farming communities have a higher social significance than the Grand Canyon or the Giant Forest. The tragedy of past land use in the

Western States lies partly in the frequency with which that fact has been overlooked or disregarded. The logging that removed the grove of trees . . . or the grazing that destroyed the ground cover and polluted and caved the banks of the stream that gave beauty and value to [an] area . . . have not always returned benefits in any measure commensurate with those destroyed. All too frequently large intangible social values have been sacrificed to small material gains because no means existed for relative evaluation or to compel the action most in the public interest.

Kneip recognized that the recreational, or spiritual, potential of public lands derived largely from nature—from the "beauty and interest" of the environment, healthy forests, "grass-covered and flower-studded flats and slopes," teeming wildlife, and "the wide diversity of forest, land and geological types." His appreciation of the factors that should be weighed in making land policy choices embraced landscape-scale biodiversity; he just had a different name for it.[28]

Kneip perceived spiritual, social, and economic values even in deserts:

But if the desert is dotted with windmills and stock-watering tanks, if its unique flora is unbalanced and its peculiar animal life is forced to change its natural habits by the grazing of domestic livestock, if its brooding silence is shattered by the engines and horns of passing motorcars, and its emptiness is filled with gaudy gasoline stations and billboards, its unusual power to serve human needs is impaired, with no real assurance that society actually has benefitted by the change, or that the new order permanently will contribute as much to the economic security of the local population as would the old order if it were wisely perpetuated.

The National Conference on Outdoor Recreation (NCOR) in 1928 had also identified the connection between recreation and the protection of natural areas. It recommended "coordinating the common functions of . . . Government which relate to outdoor recreation and administration of natural plant and animal life resources" and specifically encouraged the "[c]lassification of lands of the public domain chiefly valuable for recreation."[29]

Today the means "to compel the action most in the public interest," and avoid the tradeoffs of which Kneip warned, are available in FLPMA's provisions prohibiting unnecessary or undue degradation, requiring consideration of long-term versus short-term benefits and relative scarcity of values, and demanding that uses be sustainable.

This brief glimpse of The Western Range reveals a variety of perspectives on, and indices to, range and ranch values, even in the early Taylor Act years. Ranchers may have been the only group who considered the range "chiefly valuable" for grazing. BLM director and economist Marion Clawson conceded as much, a few years later: "Controversy can readily arise as to the interpretation of the term 'chiefly valuable.' To the range user, or to any other user of a single use of multiple-use land, most land used by him is chiefly valuable for that purpose. To other users, relatively little Federally owned land is chiefly valuable for only one use."[30]

"The *very nature* of the range livestock industry," Clawson added provocatively, "means that the land it uses has little alternative use." The unmistakable inference is that had there been conflicting demands for the use of western rangelands in the early years, their use would not have defaulted to graziers. That there were perceived to be no or few alternative uses for much of the land, and relatively few conflicts initially, was chiefly a function of the extant population—both its low numbers and distribution—and the seemingly infinite western land supply.[31]

Clawson, like the writers of *The Western Range*, understood that most western rangeland was "capable of multiple use" and, in fact, had important watershed, forest, wildlife, and recreational values, including values "in addition to those associated with wild life." Management policy had not reflected these values, however, but had been "formulated largely in consideration of its effect upon grazing use." This fact says nothing about the relative value of grazing; it merely reveals that grazing's constituency was the most powerful or otherwise best situated to secure its own interests. Indeed, Clawson cited the "effective organization and political strength of range livestock producers" as significant factors in the setting of range policy. Another factor was the difficulty land managers experienced in trying to "balance one use against another," especially when some "have no definable monetary value."[32]

Clawson appreciated that "public sentiment in this country has changed toward future use of all types of resources. There will be far greater emphasis upon conservation and upon the public interest in private uses of lands." "Closely allied" to this growing interest in conservation was the enthusiasm for recreation: "People want to use land to hunt and to fish over, to hike or camp upon, or merely to see. They feel that they have a right to use all land, but particularly public land, for this purpose." Even though recreationists lacked political clout at this time, they enjoyed "numerical superiority." Peffer reports that sportsmen were estimated in 1951 at "25 million 'hunters and anglers plus an infinity of sightseers,'" compared to "350,000 cattlemen and sheepmen in the Western range states." The ranks of *public land* ranchers were smaller by an order of magnitude.[33]

By the 1960s, if not before, it was widely believed that public rangelands supported a variety of uses and that the Taylor Grazing Act was outmoded as a vehicle for administering the public domain. A prominent Taylor Act critic was the Public Land Law Review Commission (PLLRC). Its monumental 1970 report, *One Third of the Nation's Lands*, covered all federal lands, but the report's greatest significance was for the BLM. "'Other agencies had clear statutory mandates. BLM was the primary target of the Report and everyone knew it.'"[34]

A common refrain of the PLLRC report was the recommendation that "public lands *chiefly valuable* for specified purposes," including grazing domestic livestock, "be made available for disposition on certain conditions and to a limited extent." The commission conceded there was "no good information available to define and identify that portion of the 273 million acres under grazing permit that are chiefly valuable for domestic livestock," thereby confirming that the fact of grazing says nothing about the land's suitability for grazing, much less its value for other uses. The commission pointed out that many public lands should never have been grazed. Yet, historically, "*all* public lands which could be physically negotiated by livestock" were so used. It recommended that "[f]rail and deteriorated lands"—that is, overgrazed lands with steep slopes or "in delicate ecological balance"—should be "classified not suitable for grazing" and that "grazing in such areas should be prohibited."[35]

Where public lands *could* be identified as "chiefly valuable for the grazing of domestic livestock," the commission advised, they should "be offered for sale at market value with grazing permittees given a preference to buy them." The commission qualified this recommendation, however. It advocated disposal only "when important public values will not be lost," explaining: "Consideration must be given to the fact that the public forage lands are often productive of other values." Lands retained in federal ownership should "be managed for the broadest range of values they can produce, consistent with the goals and objectives outlined . . . elsewhere in this report." "We believe," the commission announced, "that it is in the public interest to encourage the highest and best use of the public lands to the end that they contribute the most in social and economic values. . . . The end result, of course, is to achieve the maximum benefit for the general public. . . ."[36]

The commission defined "public benefits" as pertaining to "all segments of the public and their interests"—"the direct user, whether a consumptive or nonconsumptive one," as well as "those whose only interest might be an intellectual or emotional one." All were "justifiable interests" in the public lands. At the same time, the commission recognized the importance, as well as the difficulty, of weighing all the "various justifiable interests" in order to "assure maximum benefit for the general public."[37]

The PLLRC cautioned that "laws and policies should be avoided which permit public lands and resources to be used in unfair competition with resources from other sources. . . . This principle precludes tax or pricing policies which unduly favor the users of public land." As the commission recognized, the system of grazing "preference" and underpriced fees for grazing on BLM lands plainly violated this precept. Similarly, the commission advised against issuing permits for the construction of private cabins, asserting that public recreation use "should not be preempted by vacation homesites by the few who could be accommodated."[38]

The commission developed specific criteria for disposing of federal grazing lands. It advised that "the lands be chiefly valuable for grazing livestock, that they have few or no other valuable uses which would not be equally, or as well, realized under private ownership, and that their disposition not be likely to complicate unduly the management of retained public lands." The commission acknowledged that priorities and values concerning uses of public lands could change, referring specifically to abandoning grazing in favor of some other dominant use when "there is a clear, technically supportable determination that the lands are no longer chiefly valuable for grazing." This one recommendation is highly suggestive that the commission, like Congress in the 1920s and early 1930s, viewed nongrazing uses as more valuable.[39]

The commission formulated "three possible general standards" for weighing the relative values of various land uses and then allocating lands to those uses: first, giving preference to "uses that contribute most to regional economic growth"; second, favoring "nonmarket values," recognizing that federal owner-ship is "a necessary substitution for the imperfection in the market"; and third, favoring "uses that appear likely to generate the lowest degree of environmental degradation, or contribute the most to environmental enhancement." Although the commission did not speculate about the ramifications of implementing any of these standards, livestock production likely would fare poorly under any of the three. Public land grazing's contribution today to regional economies is negligible; livestock constitute a commodity, producible on private land without government intervention; and the environmental impacts of grazing are significant and widely recognized. In contrast, biodiversity conservation and the sustaining of ecosystem functions would be preferred uses under any of the standards. The commission expressly pointed out that outdoor recreation on public lands may "generate greater benefits to the particular locality in some circumstances than any market-oriented resource use."[40]

Background information on the value of rangelands for grazing was obtained under a separate contract and relayed to the PLLRC in the report *The Forage Resource*. Information included statistics on AUMs, relative contributions of public lands to regional and national livestock production, sizes of ranch opera-tions, etc.[41]

According to the report, the public lands contributed about 3 percent of the total AUMs of forage required for all cattle and sheep in the United States in 1966; in the West the contributions were 11 percent for cattle and 20 percent for sheep, or 12 percent overall. The PLLRC termed the 12 percent regional contri-bution "an important source of forage requirements in the West." Even with "intensive [range] improvement practices," it was believed that the national contribution could be expanded to only 4.6 percent. Western public lands today contribute only about 2 percent. The report stated that 10 percent of public lands supported one AUM of grazing on 5 acres or less; 26 percent required

5.1–10 acres; 21 percent, 10.1–15 acres; 19 percent, 15.1–25 acres; and 24 percent of the lands required more than 25 acres.[42]

The Forage Resource identified capital investment as the western livestock industry's "most significant influence . . . on the local and state economies." The western livestock industry as a whole (including both private and public land operations) ranked among the top three employers in eight of the eleven western states, but the number of ranches in the West had declined by 16 percent since 1940. Total grazing use of the public lands had been decreasing; declines of 9 percent in animal numbers and in forage consumption had occurred between 1947 and 1966 in the eleven western states. Cattle numbers on public lands, however, actually increased during this period, by 40 percent.[43]

A survey of permittees revealed that the larger operations derived more than 75 percent of their income from livestock production; operations with less than 151 animal units, however, averaged only 39.3 percent of income from livestock. Twenty-one percent of respondents reported using private grazing lands (other than their own) in addition to federal lands, at fees exceeding those paid for federal forage.[44]

The Forage Resource investigators noted that federal grazing policy "avoided the adoption of an economic efficiency criterion," instead "let[ting] social factors related to the range, small family ranches and local communities replace price (economic efficiency) as a means for resource allocation." As a result, "permitted ranchers obtained forage at a lower cost than those with no federal permits"; the "differential in cost was the source of the permits acquiring a capitalized value." Another consequence of federally subsidized grazing was smaller ranches. If permits were made available on the basis of competitive bidding, the study authors predicted, ranch sizes would more than double. The average, "break even"–sized cattle ranch was just over 200 head; ranches needed to be considerably larger—300 head or more—to break even in the Intermountain Region and Southwest. Furthermore, the "adjusted average cost of beef [Westwide was] just over the average selling price." These two facts meant that some "average-sized" ranches lost money. A large fraction of smaller ranches reportedly did "not cover their costs through ranching alone."[45]

Direct contributions of the livestock industry to income in eight western counties selected for study ranged from 12 to 24 percent. The researchers concluded that, "[l]ike farming generally, the livestock industry has contributed to the growth and the stability of the local community." Referring to the Taylor Act purpose of stabilizing the livestock industry, the investigators concluded, however, that any "reallocation policy that tends to increase the number of small ranchers will neither be doing the rancher, the industry nor the community a favor." The authors of *The Western Range* had recognized a comparable dilemma in the 1930s. They pointed out that the Forest Service's redistribution policy was, in some cases, actually destabilizing local communities by reducing permitted numbers below minimum ranch sizes in order to issue grazing permits to new applicants. *The Forage Resource* authors characterized the basic policy issue in 1970 as: "can we stabilize the livestock economy and at the same time secure the maximum returns to the Government in the form of fees or rentals for the public grazing lands?"[46]

The final PLLRC report acknowledged that, "[w]ithout the privilege of grazing public lands, many ranches would cease to exist as economic units, or would be forced out of business due to the high cost of substituting other sources of feed." It nevertheless recommended that the federal government "receive full value for the use of the public lands and their resources," including the forage resource, without regard to the impact on permittees or, consequentially, on local communities. Just six years later Congress made this recommendation federal policy in FLPMA.[47]

The PLLRC's advice concerning other public lands resources sheds light on the relative values of public land uses. Its modern perspective on fish and wildlife resources and habitat foreshadows some of the current interest in biodiversity conservation. Expressing concern that fish and wildlife "be properly considered in the growing competition for public land resources," the commission stated:

> The Federal Government has a responsibility to make provision for protecting, maintaining, and enhancing fish and wildlife values on its lands generally *because of the importance of those values as part of the natural environment, over and above their value for hunting, fishing, and other recreational purposes.*
>
> Protection and propagation of rare and endangered species of wildlife should be given a preference over other uses of public lands. . . .

"Following preference to rare and endangered species," the commission continued, "preference should be given to the support of those species for which the public lands provide a critical or significant portion of the habitat." The PLLRC criticized the historical federal favoritism for game, over nongame, species, warning that the "resulting imbalance in resource management policy must be redressed." It further advised that "[f]ish and wildlife populations should be maintained at levels in consonance with the ability of the habitat to support them. . . . Public land vegetation should be managed so as to sustain wildlife populations. . . ."[48]

The PLLRC recommended that forage be allocated by statute to wildlife, both game and nongame species, and it implied that, where livestock grazing needs and wildlife management concerns collided, the wildlife objectives should take precedence. It was "convinced that predator control programs should be eliminated or reduced on Federal public lands." "While these programs may have been of some benefit to livestock operators," the commission stated, "they have upset important natural mechanisms for the population control of other species." It also urged that "key fish and wildlife habitat zones" be identified and "formally designated for such dominant use." In those areas it would be essential that wildlife values "consistently receive dominant treatment in all resource decisions." Designated areas might include crucial big game habitat areas, "choice bird nesting or feeding areas, or important resting and cover zones for migratory songbirds."[49]

The PLLRC did not go as far, however, as most of today's conservation biologists would advocate. It did not contemplate that "wildlife habitat zones" would be as large as grazing districts, and while it recommended "a natural area system for scientific and educational purposes," it believed that "these requirements can be met with a relatively small amount of land." Nor did the commission envisage the preservation of biodiversity for the purpose of maintaining functioning ecosystems. Rather, it advocated preserving "examples of all significant types of ecosystems" purely for scientific study purposes. Nevertheless, the PLLRC report taken as a whole reflects the view that *all* fauna and flora have value and that public land managers have a responsibility to provide adequately for them.[50]

As noted earlier, the commission acknowledged the potentially significant contribution of public land recreation activities to local and regional economies. It recognized the "widespread public benefits" available from outdoor recreation and expressed concern that government provide efficiently for them. The commission understood that the "Federal multiple-use lands offer one of our best opportunities to supply large, extensive, and relatively undeveloped areas to accommodate these activities," and it advised accordingly that federal management should emphasize *dispersed types of recreation requiring only minimum land development and supervision, and few facilities*. Noting that the "enjoyment of scenery accounts for a significant amount of current recreation use [of] the public lands," the commission advocated *restricted use zoning of multiple use public lands to protect scenic values*."[51]

One of its bolder proposals was a suggestion that the Forest Service and the Interior Department be merged into a new department of natural resources. "Although there are still program differences between the two bureaus, caused in large part by their historical development," the commission wrote, "the *actual uses of these lands are almost identical*." The commission explained that the "increasing emphasis being placed on outdoor recreation and environmental quality" "justif[ied] separating the administration of the national forests from the *farm enterprise* orientation of the Department of Agriculture and placing it in a closer relationship to the *public land functions* of the Department of the Interior." A reasonable inference is that the PLLRC viewed the agriculture/ grazing orientation of both agencies as subordinate to their (other) natural resource functions.[52]

These excerpts from the PLLRC report do not directly answer the questions "What is the value of public land grazing?" and "What does it mean to say that lands are 'chiefly valuable' for grazing?" But because they reflect the thinking and study of a highly diverse and well-informed body assigned the specific task of determining how the public lands could best be managed or disposed of in order "to achieve the maximum benefit for the general public," they can inform our analysis.

2. FLPMA and Other Modern Evidence of the Value of Rangelands

Two years after the PLLRC's report was issued, and four years before Congress passed FLPMA, the U.S. Forest Service conducted a "comprehensive" scientific study of western range problems. According to Robert Nelson, an economist with the Interior Department's Office of Policy Analysis, the study examined forage availability from all sources, public and private, and considered the "efficient allocation of forage production from the perspective of the nation as a whole." The report was quashed almost immediately for political reasons—it concluded that "livestock grazing in the western United States was economically unjustified in many areas."[53]

The Forest Service report identified a preferred alternative for public range management, based on "minimization of the total cost to the nation of achieving the desired level of forage production." Maximizing the industry's efficiency would entail reducing the area grazed in every region, but mostly in the West. Specifically, the area grazed should decline from "86 percent of western rangelands grazed in 1970 to only 23 percent in 2000." These were "radical conclusions apparently based on a scientific approach," Nelson observed, but they "were also clearly unacceptable politically and institutionally." A proposal to eliminate even "half the grazing on western rangelands would be totally unacceptable to ranchers."[54]

Politics won out. As Nelson put it, "In deciding to be more practical and to constrain the least cost calculation to stay within reasonable bounds," Forest Service economists redid the analysis, manipulating the constraints, including "the degree of change that might be politically tolerable." "[W]hat had been a scientific management question," he charged, was "transformed into a political one."[55]

By 1974 the federal government was advocating *increasing* red meat production from U.S. ranges. In an interagency report issued by the USDA, Nelson relates, the "discussion had been turned around to the point that it now justified grazing on federal lands." In imprecise and unscientific language, which highlighted its political motivations and purposes, the document cautioned that

elimination of grazing from federal lands would require a shift of a considerable proportion of total range livestock numbers and their production to other lands and, in essence, would remove a sizeable proportion of this resource from the Nation's productive resource base. More animals on non-Federal lands would require more intensive use of private range, increases in pastures, harvested forages and feed grains, more acres in cultivation, and greater dependence on feedlot feeding for meat production. Although proportionately small in relation to non-Federal range livestock production, loss of Federal grazing would upset the supply-demand situation for beef and materially affect the sheep industry.[56]

Shortly thereafter, FLPMA was enacted. The statute ignored the findings and advice of the 1972 Forest Service study and many of the Public Land Law Review Commission's recommendations, which Congress had specifically solicited to inform its review of public land policies. FLPMA did incorporate (at least nominally) some PLLRC concepts, however, including the multiple-use and sustained-yield principles, a fair-market-value policy for public resources, and a retention policy for all public lands except where the public interest dictated disposal. FLPMA left intact the Taylor Grazing Act's substantive grazing provisions; it also left undefined the TGA term "chiefly valuable for grazing." But section 401(a) of the act called for a joint BLM–U.S. Forest Service "study to determine the *value of grazing* on the lands under their jurisdiction in the eleven Western States with a view to establishing the fee to be charged for domestic livestock grazing on such lands."[57]

Inexplicably, the report (*Study of Grazing Fees for Grazing Livestock on Federal Lands*) that resulted from the FLPMA-mandated study failed to address directly the issue of the "value of grazing." Its response to the legislative charge was, ostensibly, a single recommendation: "The fee system should collect fair market value for the forage resource." But this advice merely rephrased FLPMA's national policy directive that "the United States receive fair market value of the use of the public lands and their resources unless otherwise provided for by statute."[58]

Study of Grazing Fees gave only passing attention to the issue of the relative values of the various uses of rangelands. Pointing to the "many other users of the Federal lands in addition to grazing permittees," the report's authors observed: "These segments of the general public are also concerned about grazing fee levels. They are aware of the economic problems faced by the permittees, but generally favor a grazing fee based on fair market value for use of Federal lands. This viewpoint concludes that if grazing is low in economic value, then other uses may be more appropriate." "This viewpoint," upon which the report did not elaborate, is vaguely reminiscent of opinions expressed in the PLLRC report and *The Western Range*, namely, that economic and social values obtainable from the public lands should be maximized and that no private uses or users of public lands should be given an unfair advantage.[59]

The "many other users" of the public lands to whom the *Study of Grazing Fees* authors referred were and are, by far, recreationists. Some of the most outspoken critics of the Sagebrush Rebellion, Reagan-era privatization schemes, and more recent proposals to transfer BLM lands to states or private interests have been recreation interests, both sports enthusiasts and conservation groups. Most of the opposition has centered around the view that the lands are too valuable to dispose of and/or that their values will be more fully realized if they remain in federal hands.

The expansion of interest in public land outdoor recreation opportunities has been phenomenal. National parks visitation rose from 3 to 30 million between 1930 and 1945; today, visits to Yellowstone National Park alone number more than 3 million. Visits to national forests grew from 3 million in 1917 to over 38 million in 1934 and 52.2 million in 1955. Recreational use of forests has continued to rise; most of the increase has been on undeveloped sites. Of the 188 million visitor-days in the national forests in 1973, fewer than 40 percent were on developed sites; most were dispersed in undeveloped areas. By 1980 forests recorded 223 million recreation visitor-days—compared to 87 million in the national parks.[60]

The BLM was established in 1946; by 1963 recorded recreation use reached 30 million visitors. BLM lands were "used more for recreation than for any other purpose." By 1992 BLM recreation topped the 74-million mark. BLM lands remain largely undeveloped; according to the agency, recreation "management is focused on 5,000 developed and 24,000 undeveloped recreation areas and sites." "Most of these recreation sites are accessible to livestock" as well as to people—a reflection of their undeveloped status. The BLM "administers 1.7 million acres of designated wilderness and has recommended that 9.7 million more acres be designated by Congress." The numbers (which represent tiny fractions of the 270 million-acre BLM system) would be much larger but for the opposition of commodity interests, particularly the livestock and minerals industries.[61]

As public land recreational use increased, so did memberships of conservation organizations, particularly those listing wilderness preservation on their agendas. The Wilderness Society's membership, for example, increased from 7,600 in 1956 to 27,000 in 1964, 87,000 by 1970, 100,000 by 1983, 160,000 by 1986, and 200,000 by 1988. The Sierra Club ballooned from 7,000 members in 1952 to nearly 500,000 in 1988.[62]

In 1984 Interior economist Nelson concluded that "for many westerners the real reason for maintaining public land ownership is to ensure continued open access for recreational use." Nelson's assertion seemed validated in 1995 when a bill introduced by Senator Craig Thomas (R-Wyoming), providing for transfer of BLM lands to western states, met immediate and fierce opposition from hunters and other recreational users of federal public lands and from conservation groups.

A chief criticism, voiced repeatedly, was that the bill made no provision for continued public access to these lands.[63]

Nelson's 1984 article addressed indirectly the relative values of public lands for grazing and for recreation or other public values and examined the reasons for retaining lands in order to manage the public goods they supply. In explaining why certain BLM lands should be retained (because of the values they possess), Nelson suggested that the next logical step would be to manage them to protect and promote those values.

Private tenure arrangements, Nelson explained, are appropriate for lands that are primarily valuable for commodity production; "where dispersed recreation is the most important use," the "case is strongest for public ownership." He points out that "some recreation policies such as the creation of wilderness may create benefits that are realized by people who never directly enter on the land. Such 'existence values' involve a true public good and cannot be captured privately." This does not mean, of course, that public land management policies do not create benefits that *can* be captured privately. Many ranchers capitalize on the wildlife benefits of neighboring public lands by guiding and outfitting hunters and taking "dudes" on pack trips. And when Aldo Leopold was advocating wilderness designation of roadless portions of the Gila National Forest in the 1920s, he was serving as secretary of the Albuquerque Chamber of Commerce.[64]

In Nelson's view, the case seemed "weakest for keeping the government in the business of managing production of public timber, coal, forage, and other commodity outputs." He called government intervention in these industries "a virtual pocket of socialism maintained in the U.S. market system." In these areas there are "few public values at stake and probably greater prospects of efficient management in the private sector." Instead of outright sale, Nelson and Clawson contemporaneously recommended long-term leasing of grazing lands where grazing fees did not cover administrative costs. Lessees would pay "all costs of management, including roads, fencing, water development, and fire control," and leases would include "performance standards for the achievement of nongrazing outputs on the lands." Nelson added that it would "be important to provide a readily available mechanism for abandoning grazing and conversion to *higher values uses* [sic] *that might emerge*." In Clawson's view long-term leasing would be profitable only on lands providing one AUM of forage per four acres or less. According to *The Forage Resource*, no more than 10 percent of all public grazing lands were so productive. Clawson opined that "no rancher could afford to lease public lands without careful and relatively intensive conservation management. Short term exploitation would be too costly, as would low-producing rangelands." Nelson calculated that, even at the highest estimated purchase price of $100 an AUM on the open market, "permanent grazing rights [on public lands] probably would be worth no more than $7 per acre."[65]

Plainly, Nelson and Clawson considered grazing a nonpublic and a low-value use of the "public grazing lands." Nelson also reported that "[a]lmost all economic studies of the returns and costs to ranching have concluded that ranch values far exceed any reasonable estimate of the capitalized value of the net income that can be earned from ranching." He pointed out that "recreational 'ranchettes' are creating rangeland values far higher than livestock grazing can justify" in some areas. Proximity to public lands has a significant, positive effect on private land prices, an effect that has been growing in recent years. Ironically, Nelson's "ranchette" argument is employed by grazing advocates to resist efforts to curtail grazing on public ranges and to oppose grazing fee increases that might force some ranchers out of business.[66]

By definition, public goods are best provided by public ownership. As economist J. R. Conner explains, "[p]ublic ownership is necessary to achieve" the goals of "conservation of natural resources, preservation of environmentally unique and/or fragile areas, and creation of opportunities for present and future citizens . . . to observe and enjoy unique wildlife and 'natural' areas." If such areas were privately owned, "the resources (rangeland) would be subject to ecological deterioration through use in the production of readily marketable goods and/or services" because "a private owner uses the land to produce a product or service for which current markets exist, even if the process results in irreversible degradation of the resource."[67]

Biological diversity, like the wilderness character of a tract of land, is a classic public good, which can be realized only or at least most fully through public ownership and management of the land. Also like wilderness, areas retaining their native biodiversity possess "scarcity," an attribute that FLPMA values and BLM land-use planning is meant to promote. Landscape-level biodiversity preserves would have existence, option, and bequest values to those individuals who derive satisfaction simply from knowing that such areas exist, that they retain the option of visiting the area(s) in the future, and that they will be preserved for future generations.[68]

These nonmarket values are in addition to the direct benefits, both present and potential, of biodiversity preserves as species reserves, gene banks, high-quality watersheds, recreational or scientific study areas, etc. The potential overall value is mind-boggling. Recently, a group of scientists devised a way of quantifying just the direct benefits of ecosystems. They calculated a monetary value for seventeen of nature's "ecosystem services," such as water purification, food production, and carbon dioxide regulation, of $33 *trillion* annually, nearly double the world's gross economic product. The value of biodiversity and other nonmarket uses of rangelands will only increase as rangelands are diverted to other uses and as population pressures and urbanization increase.[69]

Research suggests that the value placed on biodiversity conservation would be further enhanced by public information and education efforts, much like those that led Americans to value wilderness more highly. In Harvard ento-mologist Edward O. Wilson's words, there is an "implicit principle of human behavior important to conservation: *the better an ecosystem is known, the less likely it will be destroyed*." As Americans become more cognizant of the need for and value of naturally functioning ecosystems—an educational challenge for conser-vation biologists, land managers, and agency specialists—the existence values of such preserves will grow. Conversely, the value of so-called grazing lands for the purpose of producing forage will continue to decline. A better under-standing of the unavoidable tradeoffs involved in grazing public lands, and of the philosophical distinction drawn by Krutilla and Kneip between the value of natural areas and the commodities that humans are capable of producing with their technology, should hasten the demise of public land grazing.[70]

B. THE ECONOMICS OF PUBLIC LANDS RANCHING TODAY

While I have disclaimed any intent to attempt a traditional economic analysis here, customary ways of looking at public natural resources and resource allo-cation questions dictate that I offer at least a rundown of some relevant statistics. This section also provides a glimpse of who public land ranchers are and what motivates them. Where possible, the federal government's own data are used in the following discussion; many current statistics have been gleaned from 1994 documents prepared jointly by the U.S. Departments of Agriculture and Interior in connection with Interior's rangeland reform efforts. The nature of the agen-cies' recordkeeping and the kinds of comparisons that I and other commentators seek to make, however, necessitate reference to grazing-related statistics and demographic information drawn from other available sources as well.

1. PUBLIC LAND GRAZING: THE NUMBERS

Public lands livestock production *seems* more important than it is in part because it has been going on since the West was first settled and in part because it occupies so much of the public domain. Wilkinson notes that "more acres of the eleven western states are dedicated to cattle ranching than to any other use." Domestic livestock are grazed on 258 million acres of BLM lands and national forests—a chunk of country equivalent to the combined areas of California, Oregon, Washington, and most of Nevada. But initial impressions can be deceiving.[71]

The size and significance of the western livestock industry have often been exaggerated, indeed, "vastly inflated," by industry representatives, administrators, and politicians. Rowley related the Barrett committee's outlandish assertion in 1947 that the Forest Service's "reduction program threatened the nation's and the world's beef supplies with higher prices." The secretary of agriculture rejected this claim outright, asserting that, "if all the ranges on the national forest were closed to grazing, less than 1 percent of the nation's total animal-months' feed requirements would be involved." BLM ranges, though more extensive, were and are even less productive.[72]

Even Webb, the cattleman's champion, cautioned that "we must not ignore the fact that, after all, the West, even including Texas, did not produce many cattle." He noted that in 1880 there were about 39.7 million head of cattle in the entire United States; the sixteen western states and territories had 12.6 million, or just 34 percent. That number was halved when the Pacific states and Texas were excluded. Donald J. Pisani reported that the number of cattle in the West "declined from as many as 1,500,000 in 1885, to 900,000 in 1886, to 300,000 a decade later." He further noted that "the assessed value of Wyoming's cattle [in 1886] was $14,651,125," an amount that had "shrunk to $3,732,558 a decade later."[73]

By 1900, Rowley reported, the "cattle industry was in major retreat," and "sheep outnumbered cattle in most western states." The rise of the sheep industry had begun in the 1840s and escalated in the 1890s. By 1900 there were 4 million sheep in Utah Territory alone, four times the number just fifteen years earlier. Sheep numbers peaked in Wyoming in 1910 at 5.5 million; the population low was in 1880 (517,000), very close to the figure today (538,000). According to Worster, the total number of sheep being raised in the United States declined after World War II due to falling markets to about half the 1910 level. The relative abundance of cattle and sheep then began to shift. Between 1947 and 1966, according to *The Forage Resource*, "cattle numbers permitted on the public lands increased by 1.5 million (40 percent), while sheep numbers decreased by 2.7 million or 23 percent." The net result in authorized AUMs, however, was almost a wash—25.9 million in 1947 and 25.3 million in 1966. In 1976–77, 3.5 million cattle and horses and 4.6 million sheep and goats were authorized to use BLM lands.[74]

Clawson reported that from the 1930s to about 1950 BLM lands provided forage for 1.5 to 2 million cattle and 8 to 10 million sheep, run by approximately 20,000 permittees. Very few of these animals spent twelve months of the year on federal land; nearly all required other pasture or were sent to feedlots when not grazing public lands. Today the number of AUMs of authorized BLM use is approximately 8.35 million for cattle and 1.2 million for sheep, for a total of 9.55 million, down from 10.8 million AUMs in 1977. These figures represent amounts of forage, not head counts, and thus are not directly comparable to most of the figures in the preceding paragraph. For example, 8.35 million AUMs of cattle use could mean 8.35 million cattle on the range for one month or, more realistically, about 2.8 million head for three months. The total number of domestic livestock using BLM lands is said to have declined continuously since 1935, when records were first kept following passage of the Taylor Grazing Act, but the reported numbers can be hard to interpret. The BLM's own annual statistical compilation does not include the actual number of animals that graze BLM lands; however, a 1994 agency EIS reported that BLM lands provide forage for about 4 million domestic livestock annually.[75]

Production of beef cattle in the United States, however, has long been concentrated in eastern Texas, eastern Oklahoma, the Gulf Coast states, and the Southeast—states having no federal rangelands. The "total number of beef cows in the 11 western states is not as great as those that exist in just Texas and Oklahoma." In January 1976 there were more than 1.4 million beef cattle in Florida, about the same number as found in Nevada, Utah, Arizona, and Washington combined. At the same time, Nevada, Utah, and Arizona each had only half as many beef cattle as did Virginia. The FLPMA-mandated *Study of Grazing Fees* reported that on January 1, 1977, the eleven western states contained about 18 percent of the beef cattle in the United States. Wilkinson notes that 81 percent of all livestock in the United States today are produced on private lands in the East; western private lands account for another 17 percent. The federal public lands produce only 2 percent of all U.S. livestock. This tiny fraction of national livestock production requires 170 of 270 million BLM acres and 100 of 200 million national forest acres.[76]

Study of Grazing Fees reported that about half of the livestock in the western states, or 9 percent of all U.S. livestock, spent some portion of the year on public lands. Seven years later D. Michael Harvey reported that 4 percent of beef cattle and 38 percent of sheep "graze on public lands at some point during their lives." The national forests and BLM lands provided only 3 to 5 percent of the feed consumed by U.S. beef cattle and sheep in the 1970s, and, according to the PLLRC, the proportion had been decreasing.[77]

As noted, about 4 million livestock graze BLM lands today. The Department of the Interior reported 1994 *authorized* use on BLM lands of approximately 8.35 million AUMs for cattle and 1.2 million for sheep. Actual use is usually less. BLM lands provide about 5 percent "of the overall annual feed requirements for sheep operations" in the country, while all federal lands provide "about 7 percent of beef cattle *forage* and about 2 percent of the *total feed* consumed by beef cattle in the 48 contiguous states."[78]

Of the more than 1 million sheep/lamb and beef cattle operators (this includes about 650,000 cattle ranches) nationwide, only an estimated 22,350, or about 2 percent, hold federal grazing permits, from the BLM, Forest Service, or both; 4,600 of these are sheep producers. Reports of the current number of BLM permittees range from 18,000 to about 19,500; these permittees operate on 22,000 allotments. Beef cattle producers with federal permits make up about 3 percent of the 907,000 producers in the forty-eight contiguous states.[79]

Even in the eleven western states, where public grazing lands are located, federal permittees and lessees make up only 22 percent of all beef producers and about 19 percent of total sheep/lamb producers. About 70 percent of cattle producers in the West "own all the land they operate." The percentage of livestock operators with federal permits ranges from 49 percent in Nevada to 3 percent in Washington; the figures in Utah, Arizona, and New Mexico are about 35 percent; in Colorado, Idaho, and Wyoming, 20–25 percent. The percent of forage provided by federal lands is comparably low. In Montana, for instance, where cattle are reportedly "more important to [the state's] economy than wheat is to Kansas or oranges are to Florida," federal lands provide only 10 percent of the total forage requirements of sheep and cattle. Arizona is an exception to these statistics: among all federal permittees in 1982, "only cattle operators in Arizona obtained more than half of their forage from public lands." This is a function of both the percentage of federal land grazed—"more than 87 percent of the 14.2 million acres managed by the BLM" in Arizona—and, presumably, the fact that many ranges are grazed year-long. Overall, only about 3 percent of the forage required by all U.S. livestock comes from public lands, and the level of dependency has declined in every state but New Mexico since 1968.[80]

The numbers of permittees also have declined somewhat since grazing first came under some regulation on the public lands. In 1963 approximately 30,000 operators in the West held federal permits, according to an official of the Nevada Wool Growers Association. A spokesman for the Public Lands Coordinating Committee and Nevada Central Committee of Grazing Boards broke this figure down into 20,000 Taylor Grazing Act permittees and 12,000 to 15,000 national forest permittees. There were only 1,500 livestock operators in all of Nevada at this time. In 1976–77 the BLM estimated that about 22,000 operators were authorized to graze livestock in 52 grazing districts or on so-called section 15 leases, outside district boundaries. Today the number of BLM permittees may be as few as 18,000.[81]

The foregoing figures help set the stage for the recent prognostications by the federal Departments of Agriculture and Interior. In 1994 these agencies predicted that *eliminating grazing altogether* on federal lands—the option termed "No Grazing"—would have minor economic impacts. According to their draft environmental impact statement, *Rangeland Reform '94*:

> No Grazing would affect about 8 percent of the beef cattle inventory in the 11 western states, and 2.4 percent of the beef cattle inventory in the 17 (including Texas) western states, and 0.8 percent of the sheep inventory in the 11 western states.

Employment and income impacts would be minor relative to the total westwide economy. In agriculture, impacts would be relatively greater. But, in the long term, continued growth of employment and income in other industries would tend to offset [these impacts].

The effect on beef prices of eliminating grazing on public lands would be slight. In the near term, liquidating sheep and cattle herds, would lower prices as more livestock are slaughtered. In the long term, a 1 percent decrease in national cattle inventory could result in about a 1 percent increase in retail beef prices. But this price could be negated by an increase in the national cattle inventory.[82]

The agencies further predicted that the "No Grazing" alternative would result in a loss of 18,300 jobs in agriculture and related industries, or about "1 percent of the total 1990 agricultural employment of 1.5 million" and "less than 0.1 percent of total westwide employment." But they also pointed out that some of these losses would be offset: "Greatly improved wildlife and fisheries habitat and recreation site improvements could increase employment and income as hunting, fishing, and wildlife viewing opportunities increase."[83]

Despite the minuscule economic impacts of eliminating public land grazing altogether, the federal agencies opined that "[p]ermittees using Federal lands in the Western States are an important part of the livestock industry in the United States." Considered in the most generous light, this assessment is simply illogical. At worst, it may be intentionally misleading. The influence of public lands on the national livestock industry is plainly negligible. Witness the increase in U.S. livestock production between 1960 and 1980, despite a reduction in authorized grazing use on all BLM and Forest Service lands of about 4 million AUMs over the same period. The continuing decline in per capita red meat consumption in the United States and the liquidation of beef cattle herds over the past three years provide still further evidence of the ever-declining need for public land grazing capacity.[84]

The numbers notwithstanding, numerous commentators over the years have argued that public land ranching makes significant contributions to local, regional, and national economies. As the industry feels more threatened, the claims multiply. In 1990 industry apologists John B. Lacey and James B. Johnson calculated "the total economic activity attributable to livestock grazing on federal lands and to associated agency expenditures" at $124.5 million annually in Montana. They argued that the BLM's and U.S. Forest Service's administrative costs and investments in range improvements should be "considered *additional benefits* to the Montana economy." "Obviously, grazing on public lands provides benefits that go way beyond the holders of grazing permits." Remarkably, these writers failed to acknowledge that the federal costs of administering the grazing program far exceed permit revenues. Nielsen has pointed out that "many range improvements are not economically feasible when evaluated only on the benefits from increased AUMs to livestock." This explains why grazing and range improvement advocates often tout the nonlivestock benefits of public land grazing and range improvements to help make their case.[85]

Few apologists today attempt to justify public land grazing on the basis of the lands' contribution to food production. The current director of the Wyoming Department of Agriculture, Ronald A. Micheli, however, is one of those few. Micheli, who was representing the National Cattlemen's Association in 1984 when he offered these comments, wrote that "beef provides 16 to 18 percent of available protein for human consumption" and then leaped to the conclusion that "rangelands have an important place in our human food supply." He predicted future "pressures to manage the ranges for highest possible animal production to meet the world food challenge."[86]

A USDA–Agricultural Research Service range scientist took an even more indefensible position. Addressing the question whether "range animal husbandry is obsolete," Young stated:

> The production of red meat from rangelands will persist because of; [sic] a) dietary demand for quality protein, b) the inherent dispersal of animal waste and nutrient cycling with range operations, c) lack of direct or more efficient means of humans utilizing range forage, and d) the unrelenting growth in demand for food. It has been projected that we must double the world's food supply not too far into the 21st century. This will have to be accomplished with less cropland and greatly restricted irrigation water.

Young's remarks display a blatant bias in favor of rangeland grazing. "Protein" can be produced more cheaply and efficiently by raising other animals in other regions; the demand for "red meat" is at or near its lowest level in history; "dispersal of animal waste" leads to pollution of surface waters, which would be prohibited if public land grazing were regulated as feedlots are; nutrients "cycled" on rangelands long before livestock were introduced there, and livestock alter natural nutrient cycles; and grazing cannot be conducted on western rangelands without concomitantly raising hay or supplemental feed, which in turn cannot be accomplished without irrigation (as Young himself concedes).[87]

Meeting any increased world demand for food will have to be done in the most efficient way—which clearly does not include raising livestock on arid and semiarid rangelands. According to Young, "the bottom line remains the eight essential amino acids that man must receive from dietary sources"; these, he says, are "most easily obtained from consumption of meat and dairy products." Young concludes that "[u]nless this basic problem is addressed on a global scale apparently rational approaches to conservation biology are doomed to failure. Perhaps the logical conclusion to this scenario is that Americans must become self sufficient in quality protein and the western range must play a role in supplying this need." Yet this "conclusion" seems not at all "logical," given the information Young himself provides or fails to provide. First, Americans *are* self-sufficient in producing protein. Second, the western range produces no dairy products. Third, Young does not explain why the meat humans require must be beef or mutton, much less range beef or mutton, when poultry and other meats can be produced more economically. And finally, the minimal contribution of public lands to the forage requirements for national beef and mutton production renders his assertions even more untenable.[88]

The comments of Young and Micheli notwithstanding, most observers would limit the economic "importance," if any, of the western range livestock industry to its contribution to local or regional economies. Diehard grazing advocate Pete Domenici's 1996 grazing bill, S. 852, asserted that "the western livestock industry . . . plays an important and integral role in maintaining and preserving the social, economic, and cultural base of rural *communities* . . . [and] an important and integral role in the economies of the *16 western States*." Holechek and Hess claim that eliminating public land livestock grazing "would severely harm some local economies."[89]

The federal agencies themselves retreated from their assessment in *Rangeland Reform '94* that federal lands are a nationally important component of the U.S. livestock industry by stating elsewhere in the report: "Federal rangelands are essential to the economic vitality of many *family* farms and ranches. . . . In *some* western communities, ranching is the main economic activity." This characterization probably exaggerates even the local importance of public lands ranching, however, given the large number of western ranches (at least 70 percent) that do not enjoy federal grazing privileges. *Rangeland Reform '94* also reported that "some local businesses [do] depend on ranchers," pointing to the $19,000 that permittee survey respondents estimated that they spend annually in local communities. This reasoning too seems a bit of a stretch, considering that all persons and businesses, not just the 23,000 public-land ranchers, spend money in the community in which they reside and that substantial permittee income comes from nonranching sources. The agencies cited no evidence to support a conclusion that this money would not be "replaced" by some other source if, for some reason, it stopped flowing from federal grazing permittees. Nor did they assert that expenditures by ranchers are subject to a different "multiplier" than comparable spending by others.[90]

This federal assessment of the impacts of eliminating grazing calls to mind economist B. Delworth Gardner's criticism ten years earlier of the kinds of social and economic analyses the BLM customarily conducted. "Left undone," Gardner concluded, "is the really solid economic and social analysis of the Bureau's policies in terms of their impact on the community." Agency claims regarding the dependence of local communities on grazing policies should thus be taken with the proverbial grain of salt.[91]

Ranchers themselves profess their belief that public land ranching is "vital," but apparently only to the "economic stability of rural communities." They claim that eliminating public land grazing would have various economic consequences, including "decreased patronage and possible closings of small businesses, less funding for . . . schools and health care, and increased pressure on social services to assist the unemployed and to train rural residents for new careers."[92]

The General Accounting Office encountered many such claims when it was researching its 1992 *Hot Deserts* report. Livestock representatives and cattlemen's associations told the auditors that "grazing provides a large portion of the tax base to many local communities," but they "did not supply any quantitative data to GAO to support this view." The GAO reported that eleven of twelve BLM EISs, which it analyzed in preparing its report, predicted that eliminating livestock grazing on BLM allotments would result in "little economic disadvantage" to the respective study areas. The GAO concluded that in the Southwest even "local economies are not dependent on public lands ranching."[93]

The GAO findings coincide with those of agricultural economists Smith and Martin, who studied ranches in Arizona in the early 1970s. Smith and Martin's interpretations of their study results gave a new twist to the debate over ranching's economic impact. "It may be said," they suggested, that

> the impact of ranching on the local economy is to be found more in terms of such dimensions as social stability and community leadership, rather than in terms of significant economic benefits, since resources employed in cattle ranching are on the average underemployed. The implication is that the *town keeps the present rancher going*; one might be so extravagant as to suggest that *ranching has no economic impact on the town.* . . .

Nearly twenty-five years later Power drew a similar conclusion for the agriculture industry as a whole: "[A]griculture increasingly depends on the vitality of urban and nonagricultural rural economies to provide the nonfarm income that keeps farm operations alive." Agriculture is "a subsidiary activity."[94]

Undoubtedly, the presence of public lands and federal policies with respect thereto have the potential to affect local economies. About three-fourths of counties in the eleven western states contain significant amounts of public lands and thus have direct interests in federal grazing, logging, mining, and recreation policies. The point here is simply that ranching's individual impact is small and growing smaller—as, indeed, are the economic impacts of other extractive, public lands-based industries. The Forest Service recently identified only two "economic impact areas" (comprising parts of four counties) within its Rocky Mountain Region that could be considered dependent on public land resources.[95]

Power is an outspoken critic of public-land natural-resource extraction policies, including grazing policies, which he includes within agriculture. As he writes in *Lost Landscapes and Failed Economies*, "[M]anipulating nature often has negative environmental consequences. Such agricultural policies are doubly irrational: they damage the environment while harming the economic activity they seek to help."[96]

Power asserts that mining, timber, and agriculture "make a much more modest contribution to local economies than is usually assumed. The ongoing transformation of local economies, including technological and market changes, has drastically reduced the relative importance of such industries. As a result, rather than being a source of economic vitality they are likely to play a *declining and destabilizing* role in local economies in the future." A later chapter of the book reveals that "more modest contribution" is a drastic overstatement of the actual individual impact of public land grazing.[97]

Power suggests that claims about the "importance of federal grazing to the economies of western states can be analyzed by asking three questions: What is the direct contribution agriculture makes to the state economy? What portion of this total agricultural activity is associated with cattle and sheep operations? What portion of the feed for livestock operations is provided by grazing on federal land?"[98]

Power's own analysis begins with the third question. Federal lands, he reports, provide only 2 percent of the feed consumed by beef cattle nationally; the percentages for the eleven western states range from 2 percent in Washington to 43 percent in Nevada and average just 12 percent. These figures are very similar to those reported by the federal land management agencies in 1994. He describes how livestock interests often exaggerate the economic impact of public land grazing. One ploy is the arbitrary classification of ranches "dependent on federal land." A recent New Mexico State University College of Agriculture study, for instance, defined ranches "dependent on federal land" as those that obtain more than *5 percent* of their forage needs from federal land. By this contrivance, Power observes, 45 percent of ranches in Washington—a state that gets only 2 percent of its total forage requirements from public lands—would be classified "federal-land dependent." Not only does this strain the meaning of "dependent," Power points out, but the approach vastly overcounts the relative numbers of livestock that actually depend on federal land. For example, if a ranch gets 5 percent of its livestock feed from public lands, the entire ranch, not just 5 percent of its cattle herd, is considered "dependent." According to Power's calculations, the degree of exaggeration resulting from this method ranges from more than 200 percent to over 2,300 percent and averages 575 percent for the eleven western states. He argues that figuring the percentage of feed actually obtained from public lands, which he calls the "direct-calculation" method, yields a more representative statistic.[99]

Power estimated the economic contribution of public land grazing using a two-step formula. First, he multiplied the "percent of reliance on federal forage" by the "percent of agricultural economic activity represented by cattle and sheep operations." He then multiplied this product "by the direct contribution agriculture makes to the economy in terms of both income and employment." The results are eye-opening. The actual number of jobs "directly tied to federal land grazing" in all eleven western states is just under 18,000; this is a mere 0.06 percent of all western jobs, or 1 of every 2,000 jobs. The percent of total agricultural income attributable to federal grazing averages 0.04 percent, or $1 of each $2,500 of income; it is highest in Wyoming, at 0.25 percent. Power estimated that it would take only eleven days of normal job growth and six days of normal income growth to replace all federal grazing jobs. He also pointed out that, of "the major occupational groups, only domestic servants earn less by the week than hired farm workers"—a useful statistic to keep in mind when considering the oft-repeated argument that converting a resource-extraction-based local economy to a tourism-based, service-oriented economy results in lower wages.[100]

The federal land management agencies did not break out the income/employment impacts of eliminating grazing with such specificity in their *Rangeland Reform '94* documents. However, their prediction of 18,300 job losses in agriculture and related industries due to discontinuing public land grazing compares favorably with Power's estimate. The agencies did offer the following statistics, which provide a broader context for evaluating Power's predictions:

> The economy of the western states is highly diversified. Between 1982 and 1990, employment in all industries grew by 11 million workers. The percentage of total employment has increased in the service, finance, insurance, real estate, construction and retail sectors. Industries that have decreased as a percentage of total employment include: government, manufacturing, agriculture, transportation, communications, utilities and mining.
>
> As with employment, income in the agriculture sector has declined relative to the rest of the economy. . . . [B]y 1990 [agricultural] income had fallen back to its 1982 level. All industries except agriculture grew during this period.

Income from agriculture declined to just 2.4 percent of total income in 1990.[101]

Some commentators reject out of hand any economic significance for public land grazing. Wyoming writer Paul Krza scoffs: "The biggest myth is contained in [Wyoming's] official nickname, 'The Cowboy State.' The reality is that all of agriculture—cows, sheep, wheat, sugar beets, and other crops—accounts for only about 2 percent of the state's economy." According to reporter Tom Bishop, the annual gross product of Wyoming's ranching industry, $200 million, is "the least of any industry in the state." As for the public land livestock industry in the West, "If [it] dried up tomorrow there would not be a consumer in the United States who would be aware of it." Bishop's assertion is consistent with the federal government's estimate that eliminating public land cattle grazing might raise retail beef prices by 1 percent, but that the increase "could be negated by an increase in the national cattle inventory." Moreover, because of the inelasticity of the demand for beef, reduced production would actually result in "*greater* total revenue for U.S. beef producers as a whole."[102]

It is important to the grazing debate and essential to a rational choice of land policy to recognize that most public land ranches are only marginally profitable. Box wrote that the "American rancher will continue his struggle to exist, not because of the 'huge' profits involved but because ranching is the way of life that he prefers." In reality, ranching profits, if any, are far from "huge." Three-fourths of BLM permittees run fewer than 100 head of cattle, an operational scale that "does not provide enough cash flow or profit to support a family." Data for cow/calf operations in various Forest Service regions indicate that operators' net returns are generally negative, and in some cases returns are even less than cash costs.[103]

Holechek et al. report that since 1900 "western cattle ranches have returned about 1–3% on capital investment, compared to 10% for stocks and 4–6% for bonds." They "strongly recommend diversification," suggesting that ranchers take up "guest ranching, nature tours, pack trips, and marketing of plants for landscaping." In fact, many public land ranchers already supplement their live-stock income by offering recreational or tourist facilities, such as "bed and breakfasts, trail rides, livestock drives, and working dude ranches." Some ranchers lease their lands to outfitters or provide guiding or outfitting services themselves. "Others can stay on their land because family members work in jobs outside the family ranching business. . . ." According to the federal Departments of Interior and Agriculture, the "economic survival" not only of ranching families but of some western communities "may depend on how well they diversify to compete in the 1990s and beyond."[104]

The GAO took a detailed look at the profitability of ranching operations in a region of special interest to us—the West's hot deserts. Its findings corroborated the economies of scale reported by other researchers and first noted in *The Western Range*. They also give long overdue credence to Powell's warning of more than a century earlier that the "'true deserts'" of this country—the same "hot deserts" about which the GAO reported—support grasses "'so scant as to be of no value'" for livestock grazing or forage production. The GAO found that 94 percent of "the typical large operations" with more than 300 head of livestock were "able to realize a positive net income," but "only 58 percent . . . of the medium operations [100–300 head] and 45 percent . . . of the small operations [100 head or fewer] realize a positive net income. Furthermore, . . . the net income of many of the operations that make a profit is small." The GAO reported "net incomes" of small to medium ranches ranging from "a loss of $207" to a gain of as much as $4,347 for operations running up to 200 head of livestock. "Many livestock operators are able to continue ranching because they supplement their income with money from outside sources." The GAO concluded that BLM grazing facilitates permittees' "ability to maintain a traditional ranching lifestyle," but that it contributes only minimally to the preservation of local economies.[105]

Smith and Martin's survey of Arizona ranchers in the early 1970s yielded similar results. They reported that 80 percent of survey respondents "had outside jobs or income to help support the ranch." Based on the "market prices of bona fide commercial ranches" in Arizona, "computed net returns to capital and management range[d] from *negative to 1 or 2 percent*"; "[s]imilar results have been obtained in other western states." Smith and Martin concluded that "purchases of Arizona ranches apparently are not made for the purpose of maximizing returns on the investment. . . . [R]anches are selling at such high prices that an extremely low return on the opportunity cost of investment is implied on all retained ranches." Foreshadowing the GAO's conclusion related above, they proposed that "cattle ranching in Arizona, and possibly by extension in the whole arid Southwest, is no longer a subject for discussion under the category of 'commercial agriculture,' but has, in fact, become a legitimate field of inquiry in 'community development and human resources.'"[106]

Smith and Martin's study results comport with those of more recent research conducted in New Mexico. At the outset of their report, investigators John M. Fowler and James R. Gray noted that the general public's "popular conception" that ranchers are "making a pretty good return on their investment" is "not necessarily the case." They tabulated historical ranch budget data for three size classes of New Mexico ranches over a 43-year period. The "most evident" feature of these data was "the presence of *negative numbers* in all three size classes"; that is, all size classes of ranches experienced years in which they did not cover expenses, including depreciation. In good years, though, "net returns were substantial especially to the extra-large [1,000 animal-unit] operations." A follow-up study revealed that in 1982 "the net return on small ranches was adequate to cover cash expenses but not enough to pay for depreciation, operator labor and management, and total capital."[107]

Fowler and Gray also reported, based on a study limited to southeastern New Mexico ranches, that "the return on owned investment of ranchers in 1978, [for] both small and medium-sized cattle ranches was zero; the return of large cattle enterprises was less than one percent; even with favorable prices in 1978, returns were less than three percent on the very large investment values in ranches." Only sheep ranches "made enough to yield a 1.5 percent return on owned investment." Extrapolating from New Mexico ranching data, Holechek and Hess speculated that more than half of all federal ranches may be economically unsustainable.[108]

A Wyoming study indicates that low rates of return are not limited to the hottest and driest rangelands. Delwin M. Stevens studied mountain valley ranches in Wyoming in the 1970s. Even though he chose to study ranches that were "considerably larger and somewhat better managed than typical Wyoming cattle ranches," average returns to capital ranged from just 4.04 to 4.48 percent, depending on the size of the ranch. These returns were posted in 1973, "a peak year in cattle prices in the United States." By the next year costs had increased by 17 percent, and the price of livestock sold in the United States was down by half. As a result of this "difficult cost-price squeeze," incomes in all ranch size categories were negative. An award-winning rancher was recently quoted in a Wyoming newspaper as saying: "The rate of return on a Rocky Mountain cow-calf operation is often so low that 'if it was a business decision, you'd sell to a developer and go on' and do something else. . . . 'You live like a coyote on these outfits.'"[109]

Fowler and Gray attributed their findings in New Mexico to a variety of factors, which they referred to as the dual "heterogeneity" of ranch economies. The first set of factors relates to environmental and physical differences among ranches (e.g., in soils, vegetation, climate, etc.); the second, to the "institutional and social aspects of ranching families." "Managerial ability, skill, and knowledge vary drastically from rancher to rancher," they said. "In addition, planning horizons differ; profit motivation is not necessarily the same; capital positions range from complete ownerships to servicing 80 percent debt; and the size and type of operation are not only different, but also dynamic in nature." Despite this variability, it is the one feature common to all cattle operations—the "cattle cycle"—that is "probably the single most important long-term aspect of the ranching business if a profit is to be made." The causes of the frequent, periodic peaks and troughs in cattle prices are complex; contributing factors include "the general level of business activity, per capita income, consumer preferences, and a host of other variables."[110]

What keeps western ranches, so many of them marginally or not profitable, afloat? Fowler and Gray pointed to the equity attributable to rising land prices. But they admitted that this phenomenon also leads to larger debt, which in turn leaves ranchers "vulnerable to the impacts of high interest rates," as it did in the 1970s and 1980s. Add to this a recurring "cost-price squeeze," and the result is a threat to the very survival of ranches, especially the smaller ones, "which are readily characterized as marginal operations and do not have a large enough base to be viewed as an economic unit." Fowler and Gray noted that the number of ranches in New Mexico had actually increased since 1978—a trend they described as "inconsistent with economic theory." They attributed the increase in part to a "shift to more 'gentleman ranching'" and to a rise in the number of "subsistence places," an artifact, apparently, of a change in New Mexico's definition of farm or ranch.[111]

Most research shows that farmers in general, and perhaps western ranchers in particular, depend increasingly on nonfarm income to make ends meet, including nonfarm jobs, self-employment, retirement plans, and interest and dividends. *U.S. News and World Report* reported in 1995 that, of America's 2.1 million farms, "1.9 million farm households derive a majority of their income from off-farm employment." The article continued:

> Two-thirds of all farms—the 1.4 million smallest, with sales of less than $40,000 a year—actually derived 101 percent of their income from off-farm sources: Their owners used their paying jobs to help cover an average $400-a-year *loss* from farming. Each of these farms nonetheless received an average of $800 in direct government payments in 1992—a subsidy of $1.1 billion for what are in truth hobbies. . . .

"Nationally," Power reported, "almost 80 percent of the income received by beef-raising operations comes from nonfarm sources." In heavily urban western states, such as Utah, Oregon, and Nevada, "off-farm income supplies 67 to 80 percent of farm family income." These figures do not distinguish between livestock-only operations and other farms, nor do they identify public land grazing operations as such.[112]

2. PUBLIC LAND GRAZING: THE ACTORS

Who are these people whose precarious lifestyle is a subject of political concern? Chapter 4 provides some description, though largely historical. More recent information is available from several sources, notably a "national study of attitudes toward rangeland management" conducted by Brunson and Steel in 1993. Results of the survey of 4,336 ranchers in the eleven western states were reported in *Rangelands*, and some of its findings are summarized in the *Rangeland Reform '94* DEIS. The sample consisted of 11 percent of all federal permittees. Each survey respondent was the ranch owner/manager or equivalent. The DEIS offers this snapshot view of respondents and their families:

> The average respondent was 55 years-old [*sic*] and [had] worked on the same ranch for 31 years. . . . [T]he average ranching family had been in the business for 78 years and in the same state for 68 years. . . . An average of two of the [average] seven people [on each ranch] were unpaid family members, and another family member worked off the ranch, contributing an average of 23 percent of the household income.

In Arizona, the DEIS reports, an average of two people work off the ranch, and they contribute 53 percent of the household's income. The survey determined that "85 percent of beef cattle ranches had less than $25,000 annual sales, [and] most operators worked full-time off the ranch."[113]

Similar statistics have been reported by others. According to a *High Country News* story, the "vast majority" of ranchers in Catron County, New Mexico, hold "second jobs." In Smith and Martin's Arizona study the median age of ranchers was "nearly 60 years." A *High Country News* writer, reporting the average age of Montana ranchers as fifty-one, called "young rancher" a "contradiction in terms." A study conducted for the Public Land Law Review Commission suggested that most ranches had not been held continuously by the same family. Only 2.5 percent of "original homesteaders were still on their ranches," and about 60 percent of operating ranches had been "purchased from those who had no close blood relationship." By 1984, 80 to 85 percent of federal grazing permittees reportedly had "purchased permits from other ranchers."[114]

In the 1993 federal survey, respondents were asked "what they would do if livestock grazing were prohibited on federal land." The response: "57 percent said they would operate on a smaller scale, 18 percent said they would retire, 9 percent said they would move out of state, and 21 percent said they would convert their land into real estate development." More than one-third of respondents from Arizona, California, and Colorado said that they would "convert their land into real estate," perhaps reflecting the relatively higher land values in those areas.[115]

Other studies over the years have yielded similar findings. The GAO's *Hot Deserts* study of the previous year reported that many ranchers, if they lost or were restricted in their public land grazing privileges, would either cut back on their operation or seek to supplement their ranch income through outside employment. J. Stephen Peryam and Carl E. Olson studied the effects of hypothesized changes in BLM grazing policies on ranches in west-central Wyoming in the mid 1970s and concluded: "It is unlikely that a ranch operator will accept the reductions in returns that are described in [this report]. Rather he will attempt to change his present operation and management practices in an effort to compensate for the loss of income caused by the changes in BLM policy." Smith and Martin found that Arizona ranchers would either cut back on their operation or seek to supplement their ranch income through outside employment.[116]

Smith and Martin's study had an additional dimension not found in later surveys. They identified and defined several "factors" that they believed "indicat[ed] the significant goals and attitudes surrounding ranch ownership commonly held by Arizona ranchers." This phase of their study not only gives us a more detailed picture of who ranchers are, but also suggests explanations for some of the findings of the later government surveys (e.g., what motivates ranchers to stay in the business). The researchers placed these factors in four categories: "ranch fundamentalism, conspicuous consumption/speculative attitudes, economic satisficing, and ties to the local area and community."[117]

"Ranch fundamentalism" characterized both "old-time ranchers" and recent purchasers and was "comprised of [1] family, [2] land, and [3] rural fundamentalism attitudes, plus [4] a resource protection goal." The first three of these attitudes are limited neither to the West nor to ranchers; the fourth, however, requires explanation. As defined by Smith and Martin, "resource protection goal" refers not to environmental values or to preserving the range, but rather to the desire of these ranchers to maintain their land holdings for their exclusive use, to fight the "reclassification of rangeland into wilderness areas," and to support "antisportsman legislation in an effort to keep other people off 'their' range." Smith and Martin suggested that this attitude was limited to "ranchers who have large holdings, do not live on the ranch, and are members of one or more cattle associations."[118]

In my experience, the attitude Smith and Martin describe is quite common, especially among long-time ranchers and operators of large operations, but is *not* limited to absentee ranch owners. It does, however, seem especially prevalent among recent purchasers or lessees of large ranches. Hunters and other recreationists are familiar with this phenomenon—losing their access to hunt or fish or hike on private ranch land after it changes hands or losing their access route across private to public lands. The 1996 Domenici grazing bill contained a rather remarkable provision prohibiting the local BLM manager, when making grazing-related decisions, from considering a permittee's or permit applicant's "past practice or present willingness" to allow public access across private to federal land. This provision represented a step backward from the PLLRC's enlightened thinking of twenty-five years ago: the federal land management "agencies should have statutory authority to *require* that public land lessees and permittees grant reciprocal public right-of-way across private land under certain circumstances."[119]

Smith and Martin's second category, "conspicuous consumption/speculative attitudes," related principally to recent purchasers of ranches who resided permanently in urban areas of the state or out of state, who purchased the ranch for speculative purposes, but who desired to "'capture'" the social benefits of ranch ownership in the meantime. The researchers hypothesized that, for this group, the "original motive for investing [in ranch property] . . . was social and psychological and the *rationalization* of this desire was economic." "Economic satisficing," the third category of attitudes, describes the view of some ranchers that a low or negative return from ranching is sufficient, presumably as long as they can supplement their income if necessary in the local community and as long as their land is appreciating in value.[120]

The fourth category, ties to the local area and community, requires little elaboration. As Smith and Martin noted, "Arizona ranchers act no differently in this regard than coal miners in Appalachia." The researchers "definitely fe[lt] that the strength of ranchers' attitudes toward land itself is the key to understanding why ranchers do not act as 'economic men'"—that is, why ranchers hold on to their lands and marginal operations even though selling (e.g., to a developer) or engaging in another business would be more lucrative.[121]

The researchers discovered that ranchers who displayed strong "rural fundamentalism" or a "conspicuous consumption/speculative attitude" were much more inclined to sell their property. That "rural fundamentalism" could contribute to a willingness to sell may seem counterintuitive. The explanation, according to Smith and Martin, is that selling a ranch at a profit might enable a rancher to stay in the local rural area, by buying a smaller ranch or a home in the local community.[122]

Other studies have examined the likely effects of various changes in federal grazing policies and the means available to ranchers to compensate for those changes. Olson and John W. Jackson, for example, interviewed operators of twenty-seven ranches, ranging in size from 150 to 400 head of breeding cows, in the vicinity of the Medicine Bow Mountains in south-central Wyoming. Ranches were divided into three size categories and a "model" ranch was chosen for each. The researchers reported that, while increased grazing fees would reduce net income, the reductions "would not force any of the three [model] ranches to a negative net ranch income" under the assumptions used. They observed that "the greater the dependency on Federal lands for feed base, the greater the impact on resource use and net ranch income as the fee increases." However, "even the high dependency ranch was able to maintain a positive net ranch income with the highest level of fees under the price assumptions used" in their study. The researchers conceded that the "loss of Federal range is difficult to cope with." But they concluded that if "ranches are able to increase productions [sic] on their hay meadows and are willing to feed the increased hay production as grazing replacement it appears the ranches can survive at their initial size in terms of livestock numbers and systems." They also noted that the "conversion of native hay to pasture was a workable alternative" for maintaining net ranch income in some instances. Significantly, Olson and Jackson concluded that complete loss of federal grazing would reduce net income "and possibly force reduced enterprise sizes," but they did not find that it would put operators out of business.[123]

Peryam and Olson's study also analyzed the ability of Wyoming ranches to compensate for increased BLM grazing fees and/or reduced AUMs. They encouraged operators to "become more efficient in [their] production." They pointed out that there are "many potential means for increasing the calving percentage," while conceding that some methods "may not be feasible for some ranch operations." Other obvious options include obtaining alternate sources of feed by buying or leasing additional rangeland or increasing the ranch's own hay production.[124]

Agricultural economists Dillon M. Feuz and W. Gordon Kearl were not concerned explicitly with federal land policies; their study's objectives were to examine "livestock management, marketing, and the effect of cropping practices on ranch profitability." Their research suggests the wide range of husbandry and ranch management techniques that could help increase ranch profitability, such as increasing weaning weights; wintering steers on alfalfa and grain and selling them as "short yearlings"; wintering heifers on improved meadow hay, retaining them through the summer and selling them as yearlings; converting to a stocker operation by allowing calves to be purchased in the fall and/or the spring; and "becom[ing] better farmers." Their work suggests that ranchers may have several operational options for dealing with lost or reduced federal grazing privileges.[125]

Yet another "remedy" for federal grazing permit reductions was addressed in a 1980 congressional report, entitled "Mitigating Reductions in Grazing Use on Public Rangelands." This report addressed the issue whether ranchers whose permits were reduced would require additional public assistance. The report's authors concluded that "'new legislation, or changes in program appropriations are not needed if ranches make use of the programs already available.'" They identified seven federal programs, including the emergency feed and several loan programs.[126]

Finally, the authors of *The Forage Resource* reported in 1969 that, absent subsidized federal grazing permits, ranches would consolidate, leading to a doubling in ranch size. This suggests yet another recourse open to ranchers faced with the loss of federal grazing privileges.[127]

The foregoing studies all have ramifications for both the lifestyle and community support rationales for preserving public land grazing. They suggest that eliminating public land grazing in certain areas would *not* mean an end to ranching, if local employment/income opportunities are available, if ranchers are creative in adjusting their ranch plans, and/or if other government subsidies remain available. When one considers that 70 percent of ranches in the West operate entirely on private lands, the overall effects on ranching of reducing or eliminating federal privileges become even more attenuated.

Smith and Martin turned the community support debate around, suggesting that the "availability of jobs in the local area may well have stronger impact on the survival of current ranchers in the area than the ranchers have on the viability of the local community." Power largely agreed. Martin later referred to this as the "Smith-Martin question of who are the chickens and who are the eggs—the ranchers or the members of the local community." He asserted that local communities "could afford to subsidize the rancher, but in fact are looking for subsidies themselves."[128]

Smith and Martin claimed that the results of their research had implications for the survival and development of small towns in the West. They proffered what they termed (perhaps facetiously) an "extravagant" suggestion: that "an alternative use of the local rangelands, such as for recreation, might enhance the town's viability and growth." Similar suggestions, of course, have been advanced by the PLLRC, Power, environmentalists, and the federal land management agencies. But Smith and Martin were quick to point out a practical obstacle to such proposals: "Economic satisficing attitudes on the part of surrounding ranchers are likely to produce the phenomenon that few, if any, economic development alternatives are seriously considered by community leaders, of whom ranchers are a part." Similar concerns have been voiced over more than four decades, beginning with Director Clawson in 1950.[129]

Smith and Martin's own study, Fowler and Gray's work, and widely available anecdotal information indicate that leadership solidarity should be expected from ranchers on few issues, given that the ranching community is not monolithic. Predator and pest control may be the principal exception. Apart from size differences, there are at least two general categories of ranchers—those whose goal is "to maintain the ranch as a business, home, and way of life" and those, usually more recent purchasers, who are likely to be "gentlemen ranchers" and/or absentee owners and who are interested in ranch land appreciation. Ranchers are no more likely to put community interests above their own than any other group. Ranchers who are in precarious economic circumstances see economic and social changes in the community as a threat to their continued way of life and thus generally resist change. Anyone who has lived in a relatively small community in the West is bound to be familiar with this phenomenon, simply from reading the local newspaper, following local politics (especially the affairs of county commissions, whose members are often disproportionately ranchers), or participating in school boards, weed and pest control planning, or other community affairs. Even if western livestock interests are not always successful in achieving the policy changes they seek, they have an aptitude, as Clawson observed nearly fifty years ago, for *resisting* change.

3. EXAMINING THE ASSERTED MERITS AND BENEFITS OF PUBLIC LAND GRAZING

The reasons cited most often for continuing federal grazing policies are (1) to stabilize the livestock industry and/or the economies of local communities, (2) to preserve the family ranch and its associated way of life, and (3) to maintain open space. The first two arguments are often employed jointly. Even if public grazing lands don't contribute significantly to the livestock industry, the argument goes, they are crucial to maintaining an important western lifestyle and the rural West's social and cultural fabric. They do this, proponents reason, by supporting family ranches and the economies of small western communities. The foregoing section has already exposed several economic weaknesses of the first two arguments: public land livestock operations yield only tiny fractions of the nation's livestock products, public land ranching is marginally profitable, ranching families depend heavily on nonranch sources of income, and a high percentage of western ranches own all the land they work.

Both arguments appeal as much to sentiment as to economics, and they rest on shaky premises concerning the ranching "culture" (explored in chapter 4). Just what version of ranch life and culture is historically and/or socially significant and thus worth preserving? "Ranchers" have been "cattle barons," range monopolists, small homesteaders and sodbusters, itinerant sheep herders, cattle rustlers, eastern or foreign capitalists, and businessmen who "oversaw" the ranch operation from their offices in Billings or Denver or Chicago and who left the day-to-day work of running the ranch to a foreman and crew. Even if we could select one of these versions to enshrine in public land policy, how would we defend the choice, and which of its accoutrements would we preserve? Illegal fencing? Range wars? Mistreatment of animals? Predator and rodent extermination? Local usurpation of the law? Parochialism and the shunning of outsiders?

The "way of life" argument is suspect not only on historical grounds, but as a matter of present reality. As E. Bruce Godfrey and C. Arden Pope, Fowler and Gray, and others have pointed out, an increasing number of ranchers are simply "hobby type operators." It could be argued quite persuasively, in fact, that most public land ranches are "hobby" ranches, given that most are too small to support a farm/ranch family. "[T]o the degree that these small operators are essentially in production for the enjoyment of the lifestyle," Godfrey and Pope write, "one could easily contend that they should not be given preferential treatment over *other recreational users* of the public land." Some ranch owners are millionaires who made their fortune in another business and now imagine themselves modern-day cattle barons. Consider Texas oilman Oscar Wyatt, former chairman of Coastal Corp., who, for $3 million, purchased the 5,600-acre S&H Ranch in the Utah Book Cliffs, concomitantly obtaining grazing privileges to 150,000 acres of public lands. The S&H Ranch was the only missing link in the Book Cliffs Conservation Initiative, a plan to reduce cattle numbers and more than triple the elk population in the area, which had gained the support of the BLM, Utah Division of Wildlife Resources, three of the four plateau ranchers, and several sports and conservation groups. Within months of purchasing the ranch, Wyatt sued fifteen defendants, "nearly everyone involved with the Book Cliffs proposal, charging that an increased elk herd would compete with his cattle for forage and make his ranch unworkable."[130]

There is no single ranching "culture" or way of life. Nor should all of the trappings of any one, much less all, of the styles of ranching be dignified by arranging federal policy for their benefit. What is likely to be commendable about small ranching communities is something that ranchers have no monopoly on—neighborliness, hard work, "clean living," and family values.

Despite their obvious flaws, economic and cultural rationales have enjoyed significant success. Culhane noted that respondents in his survey of interest group leaders, politicians, and agency officials "seemed to view policies that benefited the local economy as 'motherhood' types of policies." Consequently, respondents usually responded affirmatively, "although often with reservations," when asked whether they supported "giving preference to local economic considerations in policymaking." Responses in the 1993 national survey of attitudes toward rangeland management may have been prompted by similar sympathies, although apparently no attempt was made to ascertain the reasons for the opinions given. "About 40 percent of respondents said that the economic vitality of local communities should be given the highest priority when making decisions about federal rangelands; a similar proportion disagreed." It seems likely that this "motherhood" bias, or sympathy, is widely shared and that it is responsible in part for the success of both the cultural and the local-community economic arguments for preserving public land grazing.[131]

Even the land management agencies themselves are not immune. Recall that Judge Burns attributed the BLM's Reno area grazing plan in part to the agency's "obvious desire to maintain for ranchers, what it describes (romantically perhaps) as a 'preferred lifestyle.'" Similarly, it was the anticipated socioeconomic impacts on permittees of eliminating grazing that apparently caused the Forest Service and BLM, in the *Rangeland Reform '94* DEIS, to reject the "No Grazing" option. The alternative was clearly preferable in every other respect.[132]

The agencies' sympathy for permittees is manifest in the following discussion of impacts expected from eliminating grazing:

[L]osses in ranch income would result in declines in the economic well-being of many permittees and their families. Lifestyle changes would include families decreasing their spending, diversifying operations . . . , sending family members to work off the ranch to bring in more income, and selling ranches, either to other ranchers or to developers. Most permittees would try to absorb the income losses rather than sell their ranches because maintaining the ranching lifestyle is important to them. But, under No Grazing some operations would go out of business.

. . . Many ranchers in their 50s and older would be seriously affected (the average age of ranch managers is 55). Generally as people get older, they have a harder time finding other suitable employment.

The agencies wrote that "the social well-being of recreationists and environmentalists would improve under No Grazing" as a result of "improved riparian and wildlife habitat and improved recreation opportunities," making it patently clear that the well-being of a small number of ranchers took precedence over the interests of other, significantly larger groups.[133]

The agencies, the ranchers themselves, politicians, and other industry apologists increasingly cite maintenance of small rural communities, the ranching lifestyle, and cultural traditions, rather than supply-and-demand principles or other traditional economic arguments, to justify continuing grazing programs. "Grazing is part of our heritage," according to assistant interior secretary Bob Armstrong. Public land grazing ensures the survival of western communities, asserted range scientist Thomas M. Quigley and range science professor E. T. Bartlett. They proclaimed in their tellingly titled paper "Livestock on Public Lands: Yes!" that the "contribution of livestock grazing on Federal land to local economies is obvious. It may be the case that many of the communities that thrive in the sparsely populated portions of the west would be uninhabited if it were not for a viable livestock industry." They offered no examples to illustrate this statement, nor any other authority. As we have seen, the numbers show that even at the local level the economic impacts of public-land ranch operations are exceedingly attenuated.[134]

At least one Interior official has opined that an appropriate scale for judging the merits of ranching might even be *below* the community level. Nelson once suggested that our public range policy should incorporate a site-specific, ranch-by-ranch, analysis. He advised that we ask: "Is a public subsidy necessary to sustain grazing in an area? If not, and if private ranchers bear the cost and want to continue livestock grazing, it would make little sense to tell ranchers that their decision is economically unjustifiable." The key, however, is whether the ranchers truly "bear the cost." It makes considerable "sense" to tell ranchers that their operations are uneconomic if they are using public rangeland that is more valuable for other purposes and if (as is probable) their livestock are imposing costs on other resources and land users. All public land ranch operations are subsidized, directly and indirectly, by the public.[135]

Another fundamental objection is that sustaining a single elite group's preferred lifestyle is an inappropriate goal for public policy respecting public lands. Fur trappers helped open the West, yet they enjoy no federal protections or subsidies. Indeed, their business has been banned or drastically curtailed in nearly every state, and the federal government has not intervened in their behalf. Why should a public land use policy defend one private individual or group's choice of lifestyle over another's? The inequity exists even within the livestock industry. Producers in other parts of the country "do not have the peculiar Federal support enjoyed by the users of the public lands in the West." Even in the West a mere 22,000 individual ranch operations, perhaps 30 percent, enjoy federal grazing privileges. These operators wield disproportionate control over lands belonging to all Americans and used for many other purposes.[136]

Despite western stockgrowers' claims to the contrary, federal permittees do have an advantage over livestock operators who lack federal permits. According to the land management agencies, permittees' "costs [a]re $10 per hundred weight lower than nonpermittee costs, and receipts per hundred weight [a]re slightly higher for permittees." Moreover, "[a]s a general rule, a ranching opera- tion which possesses a [federal] grazing permit is worth more than a similarly situated ranching operation that does not possess a grazing permit." Godfrey and Pope disagree with this latter assessment. In their view, the "proportion of a [ranch's] feed coming from federal lands generally has no effect on the value of the base property." They concede, however, that the unprivileged majority of ranchers could reasonably "object to the competition as unfair." They also acknowledge that the location of the ranch in proximity to public land recreational opportunities "has a significant positive impact on the value of ranches sold."[137]

Stabilizing the livestock industry is within the purposes of the Taylor Grazing Act. But preserving western cultural traditions and the ranching "way of life" are objectives nowhere to be found in the statutes governing federal grazing policies. The contrived "custom and culture" arguments lodged by certain Wise Use pro- ponents and county supremacists have been debunked by several commentators. Those who argue that "elimination of livestock grazing from public lands would be harmful to some operators and communities" agree that it "would not elimi- nate the *industry* in any of these states." Even grazing defenders Quigley and Bartlett concede that "[t]radition may be a very poor reason to perpetuate a given management practice or use"—though they announce in the very next sentence that "traditional aspects of public land grazing use cannot be ignored."[138]

A more appropriate policy for public lands would be to recognize and protect where possible the more widely shared western "lifestyle" values that depend on the availability of open public lands. Westerners have a long history of using nearby vacant federal lands for various forms of recreation and inspira- tion, including hiking, riding, fishing, picnicking, hunting, camping, collecting natural products and artifacts, and sightseeing. Hays cited a 1978 poll conducted locally by the *Casper Star Tribune* in Casper, Wyoming, which revealed that 75 percent of those polled used wilderness areas for recreation. Casper, for those readers unfamiliar with it, is no Boulder or Bozeman or even Bend, but a small city with strong ties to the oil and gas industry. Kellert's studies also revealed strong and widespread interest in wilderness and wildlife in the West. Wilder- ness, wildlife, and opportunities for dispersed recreation are public goods, for which it is appropriate to formulate public policy. The production of livestock on public lands or the production of forage to feed those animals is a private good, as is the coveted lifestyle that accompanies this pursuit. It can be seriously questioned whether the government should be in the business of promoting, at taxpayer expense, either the resource use or its "cultural" trappings.[139]

Even if our grazing policy's asserted objective of maintaining communities and a traditional lifestyle could be justified, the means are flawed. As we have seen, it is actually off-ranch and nonranch sources of income, not federal grazing policies, that enable many ranchers to stay on their land. Moreover, assuming that a purpose of current federal grazing policy is to ensure the continued existence of family ranching, consistent with national land policy, which historically has favored the small operator, grazing policies have had an ironic and unintended consequence. "Livestock operations with federal permits ... are on average larger than operations without federal permits. . . . [P]ermittees on the average have more than twice as many cows as nonpermittees [and] average almost nine times as many sheep as nonpermittees. . . ." Most ranch operators, at least those who are members of national stockgrowers' organizations, are also "substantially more wealthy than the average Federal taxpayer."[140]

These phenomena have attracted attention from several quarters. According to a National Wildlife Federation (NWF) survey, "10 percent of the BLM's permittees control almost 50 percent of the AUMs permitted"; "the top 20 BLM permittees (or 0.1 percent of the total number) control 9.3 percent of the available forage" and "14 percent, or 20.7 million acres of the BLM's rangelands." The "top 20" permittees include corporations such as Nevada First Corp., Agri-Beef Co., and Metropolitan Life Co. (some are companies with $1 billion in assets) and such wealthy individuals as J. R. Simplot, one of the 400 richest people in the country. In 1990 the "smallest of the top 20 permittees reported ... livestock sales of over $1 million." The GAO determined that "the 500 largest permits, which represent only 2.7 percent of all permits, control about 37 percent of the BLM's total AUMs." A recent article in the *New York Times* reported that "free-market economics is driving all but some of the wealthiest public-land ranchers [such as computer billionaires William Hewlett and David Packard] out of business." Like Texas oilman Oscar Wyatt, in nearly all cases, these wealthy "ranchers" did not *acquire* their wealth from ranching.[141]

What is it costing U.S. taxpayers to keep these modern-day cattle barons on the range? According to the NWF study, the BLM's largest permittee, Dan Russell, with 220,000 AUMs, represented a loss of $948,854 to the U.S. Treasury in just one year, circa 1990 (NWF didn't explain how this figure was derived). Large operators also wreak havoc on the land. According to the *New York Times*, "Federal officials have been working for years to force Mr. Hewlett and Mr. Packard to keep their cattle out of streams and fragile meadows." The agencies blame the livestock for violations of water quality standards in the headwaters of salmon streams. NWF reports that "17.2 million acres, or 83 percent, of the 20.7 million acres where the top 20 permittees run livestock are considered to be in unsatisfactory ecological condition." This rate greatly exceeds the 58 percent of all BLM allotments that are classified in unsatisfactory condition. Furthermore, "only 33 allotments, covering 6.1 million acres (24 percent of the total acreage used by the top 20 permittees), have allotment management plans in place to address the grazing problems."[142]

A third rationale offered in support of continuing public land grazing is to maintain open space, by forestalling subdivision and other development of private ranch lands. This defense is pleaded not only by the usual roster of industry apologists (indeed, it seems to be the industry's new mantra), but by environmental groups and conservation advocates as well. A prominent example is found in the *Rangeland Reform '94* DEIS. The Departments of Agriculture and the Interior defended their rejection of the "No Grazing" option by hypothesizing that an "unintended consequence" of eliminating grazing might be "more subdivisions and real estate development," which "could result in a reduction in environmental values." This concern about development was plainly speculation. No authority was offered.[143]

Likewise, Senator Domenici's recent grazing bills proclaimed that "maintaining the economic viability of the western livestock industry is essential to maintaining open space and habitat for big game, wildlife, and fish," and they noted the current "pressures to sell the base property of the federal land ranches for subdivision or other development." Assistant Interior Secretary Armstrong stated simply that grazing "helps preserve the wide open spaces of the West." Senator Thomas suggested that if livestock grazing were disallowed in Grand Teton National Park "we'd have subdivisions right up to the park line"—as if there were no other way to control such development. Extolling the merits of "coordinated resource management," Scott E. and Ann C. Cotton claimed: "Agriculture benefits the environment by ensuring wide open spaces."[144]

At least two national environmental organizations subscribe to the open space argument. A Nature Conservancy official reportedly stated that "the key to long-term conservation . . . in Wyoming is tied to the long-term viability of ranching as an industry." The Nature Conservancy spent $4.6 million recently to "save a working ranch from developers" near Canyonlands National Park, Utah, explaining: "We didn't really want to see condos and golf courses at the gateway of Canyonlands." TNC had "already protected 525,000 acres on 77 different projects" in Utah. A Wilderness Society spokesman was quoted as saying: "If a [grazing] fee increase has the effect of driving ranching families off the land on a wholesale basis, we will lose a critical and irreplaceable piece of the western land mosaic." The reporter himself added: "Whatever the problems associated with grazing they pale beside the destruction caused by subdivisions. Public land ranching is a hedge against overdeveloping the West."[145]

"The message is clear," says range ecologist and grazing antagonist George Wuerthner: "No matter how bad you think cows are, condos are worse." Wuerthner, though, doesn't buy the argument. He scoffs: "This skeleton rattles every time anyone criticizes agriculture." The prediction of more real estate subdivisions is seldom supported by facts or even by persuasive argument. It seems to be largely an assumption—or a red herring. Such statements overlook the fact that 70 percent of western ranches operate wholly on private land. The outspoken Fergusons are critical of the notion that we have to keep public land ranchers in business to prevent land from being subdivided and developed.

They conclude that the threats are mostly hollow and that the best solution is better use of state zoning laws, supervision of building and new septic system permits, etc.[146]

Market forces, not federal grazing policies, lead to development. As Wuerthner puts it: "People are not knocking down the doors of realtors in places like North Dakota, despite inexpensive and abundant private land for sale." Perhaps these weaknesses in the argument explain why two range professionals, recently assigned the task of defending livestock grazing as a "legitimate use of the public land," omitted any mention of its utility in preserving open space.[147]

The federal agencies' own data and reasoning undermine the purported connection between maintaining grazing policies and preserving open space. As we have seen, most public land ranchers cannot support their families with their ranch income exclusively, and the market value of most western ranch land far exceeds its value as "working ranches." Still, most ranchers keep ranching anyway. To cite an extreme example, 5,000 acres of ranch lands bordering Grand Teton National Park are worth an estimated $40 to 100 million for development, yet their owners raise cattle and pay agricultural-land property taxes of only about $2 per acre. Even if faced with cuts in AUMs, increases in grazing fees, or deprivation of their federal grazing privileges, the majority of ranchers would attempt to hold onto their ranches and their lifestyle, compensating financially by obtaining other employment or taking other measures. Conversely, only a minority of ranchers would choose to sell their lands, for subdivision or other development, if faced with such circumstances. It seems reasonable to assume that these ranchers are more likely to sell their lands whether they lose their public land grazing permits or not. Those stockmen motivated more by financial gain than by the desire to maintain a ranching lifestyle and those whose financial situation is especially constrained are the groups most likely to sell, regardless of federal land policies.[148]

The preservation of open space is a valid public policy concern and a crucial conservation biology objective. But perpetuating public land grazing is an extremely inefficient and inequitable mechanism for preventing the subdivision of large blocks of private land. Nothing now prevents the owners of large ranches from selling their deeded lands to developers or others willing and able to pay a high price—nothing, that is, other than the desire to stay in ranching, to maintain their accustomed lifestyle.

"Even if . . . subdivisions were a greater threat to biodiversity than agriculture [is]," Wuerthner argues, "it is doubtful that agriculture, at least in most of the arid West, could provide a viable alternative land use that would be economically sustainable." He points to the declining numbers of farms and ranches in the West since the turn of the century and the "significant" agricultural subsidies that have prolonged agriculture's demise. Grazing clearly is not ecologically sustainable in many areas of the West; it follows that it is not economically sustainable. If public policymakers deem it desirable to prevent the possible breakup of large ranches that enjoy public grazing privileges, they should explore strategies that do not involve subsidizing a damaging, unsustainable use of public lands. An incentive system incorporating tax breaks or other financial or technical assistance designed to protect and conserve the land and its resources would certainly be preferable. Other tools are available as well. Conservation easements, land trusts, transferable development rights, and planned development zoning requirements, such as "cluster" development, all can mitigate the threat of land development and the impacts when it occurs and negate the need to perpetuate environmentally unsound grazing policies.[149]

An even weaker justification proffered for public land grazing is that ranching adds value to the range or produces benefits that would not otherwise exist. In its most extreme form this view posits that many rangelands would be worthless but for their use for livestock production. Livestock industry spokespersons throughout the century have maintained that the lands "aren't good for anything except grazing" and have scoffed at the notion of letting rangelands sit "idle." The chief use of rangelands in terms of number of users and revenues generated has long been recreation, but stockgrowers sometimes disparage recreation as a "nonproductive" use. They see themselves as both producing a product and "improving" the land. Nelson was expressing the industry view when he wrote: "By pouring greater resources and investments into the range, we could increase its productive capacity enormously. For example, much of the range could produce at much higher levels if only water could be supplied."[150]

Nelson's view is typical of the industry attitude toward "range improvements." It is the familiar boast of agriculture: "creating something out of nothing" or "[m]aking the desert bloom." Unimproved ranges are often described by land managers and stockgrowers as unproductive. Investments in range improvements have nearly always been viewed as adding value to the range; their attendant costs, particularly impacts on other resources, have seldom been figured into the equation. As noted earlier, Lacey and Johnson even argued that the federal agencies' expenditures in administering the grazing program and making range improvements should be considered "additional benefits" to the local economy. A photo in Stevens's technical paper on ranch profitability shows an ag plane spraying sagebrush; the caption reads: "Developing stock water reservoirs and spraying for sagebrush control on foothill grazing lands are two range improvement practices which usually pay good dividends." The writer found it unnecessary to specify how these practices "improve" the range or who reaps the "dividends."[151]

Rowley has pointed out that "no [range] improvements would be made without the government's willingness to pay for them." He reports that the Forest Service had spent nearly $1.2 million "on structural improvement and revegetation on the 298 livestock allotments in Nevada" as of 1960, with an additional

$133,000 budgeted for 1961. At the same time, the agency was advising stock-growers that grazing would still have to be curtailed in order to restore range and watershed conditions. Holechek recounts a similar episode on BLM lands near Vale, Oregon. The public funding enjoyed by ranchers comes not just from federal taxpayers via the land management and agricultural service agencies, but from state taxpayers through state-funded universities. Holechek offered the ludicrous example of research at New Mexico State University to "genetically engineer rumen microorganisms so that cattle can safely graze locoweed, a [poisonous] by-product of overgrazing."[152]

While Nelson agreed that range improvements may benefit wildlife—a benefit for which the public arguably should pay—he also pointed out that "there would be no need to make such investments to benefit wildlife, if the lands were not grazed by ranchers' cattle." Other writers either do not appreciate that livestock have induced the need for range "improvement" or fail to recognize that it may not benefit wildlife to create new or maintain artificial habitats. Holechek and Hess, for instance, point to the "many watering points," "crucial in supporting many wildlife populations," which would no longer be maintained if public land grazing were discontinued.[153]

Proponents of the "added value" view routinely present a skewed picture of the costs and benefits of both grazing and range improvements. Either they consider the local benefits and ignore the national costs or they ignore the costs to other resources and resource users of devoting such large expanses to grazing and altering habitats.

Herbel offered this summary list of the costs and benefits of range improvements—costs: "(1) land treatment costs; (2) structural developments (e.g., fences, water developments); (3) nonuse of grazing animals; and (4) administrative costs"; benefits: "(1) increased livestock numbers; (2) increased livestock performance; and (3) improved multiple-use options." Later in his paper he recommends: "All planning for range improvements and subsequent management should be integrated, and total benefits and costs—to wildlife, livestock, watersheds, ecological integrity, and recreation—should be assessed." But his capsule description of costs and benefits is typically misleading, in that it discounts or ignores costs such as water quality degradation, loss of native biodiversity, impaired recreational experiences, and lost wildlife forage or habitat.[154]

Program administration costs alone should be a sufficient ground on which to challenge public land grazing policies. The disparity between the costs of administering grazing programs and the revenues produced in the form of permit fees has been widely documented. Clawson observed that "total costs incurred" by the government in administering grazing on BLM and national forest lands "are substantially in excess of the revenues produced." To a large extent, he wrote, "the general taxpayer foots the bill," while a small group "gets the benefits." Schlebecker reported that BLM grazing fees "had never covered costs." Lynn Jacobs claimed that federal expenditures on ranching programs today exceed fee revenues to the U.S. Treasury by ten times. Holechek and Hess describe the federal grazing program as "running deeply in the red." According to Klyza, BLM's annual costs for managing its grazing program typically exceed revenues by $30–$50 million; Nelson reported shortfalls for BLM and Forest Service grazing programs of more than $52 million in 1990 and $78 million in 1978 and 1981. In 1980 "BLM expenditures on *rangeland inventories alone* equalled $26.1 million, more than the total revenues collected from grazing fees."[155]

Relying on government statistics, Godfrey and Pope and Neil R. Rimbey also concluded that the direct costs of public land grazing exceed permit revenues. Rimbey inferred that "BLM is spending $2.41 per AUM for each $1 received from grazing, while the [Forest Service] is spending $3.38 for each $1 received." The GAO reported a "$1.3 million shortfall" to the U.S. Treasury attributable to the grazing programs in only eight "hot desert" BLM districts. This amount does not reflect the cost of grazing-induced range deterioration. The GAO warned that "many tasks needed to adequately protect the public lands used for grazing throughout the country are not being accomplished" at the agencies' current funding levels. Thus, agency operating deficits fall short of reflecting the true net costs of livestock grazing on public lands.[156]

Many economists, fiscal conservatives, and conservationists rail at this situation. "An outright gift" to permittees would be "more sensible," the Fergusons observe with disgust. Holechek and Hess apparently agree; they have argued that "millions of dollars in annual savings could accrue to taxpayers if the federal government paid ranchers not to graze federal lands." Nelson once mused that if the BLM had used the money it had spent on preparing grazing EISs "to buy out grazing rights to public lands [instead], it might well have been able to buy out a significant part of the grazing rights in the EIS areas for no more than the costs to prepare the EIS." His suggestion aptly illustrates the low value and high costs of public land grazing, but it also implies erroneously that public land ranchers have a "right" to graze public lands. The Taylor Act and FLPMA are utterly clear on this score: the grazing privilege is not a compensable property interest. The cost of preparing grazing EISs is thus an additional, not an alternate, burden on taxpayers.[157]

Monetary outlays by the federal agencies to benefit individual graziers sometimes look very much like gifts, occasionally bordering on the fantastic. In Arizona, the Bureau of Reclamation reportedly plans to spend $191,000 per ranch to enable ranchers to continue to graze eleven allotments in the vicinity of a Tonto Basin reservoir. A national forest in the same area has committed to spend $261,000 on fencing and water troughs on one unit of one allotment so that one permittee can continue to graze 450 cattle in the Sonoran Desert; it will spend nearly $100,000 on another allotment for the benefit of one operator who runs 250 cattle year-long. The reporter of this logic-defying largesse noted that the Sonoran Desert permittee had been implicated by the Arizona Game and Fish Department as a co-conspirator in the illegal killing of mountain lions; the other permittee had not grazed the allotment or paid grazing fees for more than two years.[158]

These are not isolated incidents. Holechek and Hess have related the incredible story of the BLM's Vale Range Rehabilitation Program. From 1963 through the early 1990s the BLM spent the equivalent of $304,000 in 1992 dollars per rancher to try to reclaim the heavily overgrazed range in this area of south-central Oregon. Local participation in the federal Emergency Feed Program indicates that the rehab program has been a failure: Vale area ranchers raked in cash payments averaging $11,000 annually from 1989 to 1995; several received more than $25,000; some, as much as $50,000. Other "outright gifts" to ranchers include predator control program subsidies, one of the most blatant examples of cost-ineffective government munificence.[159]

The Emergency Feed Program was suspended by Congress in 1996 for the 1997 through 2002 crop years. The program was administered by the USDA's Agricultural Stabilization and Conservation Service. It reimbursed ranchers on private and public lands for 50 percent of the cost of additional feed needed for their stock "during drought and other disasters," when forage production on grazing lands is reduced by 40 percent. Payments to participants varied widely. Since 1988 an average of 43,000 producers per year received $3,900 in cash payments; during the drought of 1988–89, however, 152,446 producers received payments averaging slightly less. According to Holechek and Hess, with the exceptions of Arizona and South Dakota, "[r]anchers in the western states have generally received higher emergency feed payments than those in the Great Plains." Between 1988 and 1992 annual average payments to western ranchers ranged from $1,470 in Arizona to $18,581 in Nevada. Only about 10 percent of applicants were checked to verify that they met program requirements.[160]

Holechek and Hess, along with many others, criticized the emergency feed program as contributing to overgrazing and to overproduction of cattle. Program benefits were available not only in drought years, but in all years except those of above-average precipitation! "Emergency" seems as much a misnomer as "range improvement." Ranchers had no incentive to stock ranges conservatively because they could rely on the government to help them get their animals to market regardless of range conditions. As Holechek and Hess put it, the program gave ranchers "a financial incentive to stock their ranges for high precipitation years instead of average or below average years." It remained to be seen whether drought and extreme heat conditions in much of the country in 1998 would lead to pressure to reestablish the program or enact some new feed assistance program for stockgrowers.[161]

The emergency feed program clearly did not "add value" to the range, but like grazing generally and so-called range improvements it ignores the costs/

impacts imposed by livestock management on other uses and users as well as on the land itself. An even more fundamental flaw of the "added-value" argument is that it disregards what scientists, managers, and conservationists have known or suspected for years—that most of those other uses of the public lands, such as hunting, recreation, and watershed, have vastly greater value, even in traditional economic terms, than livestock grazing. Although few studies have been reported in the literature, those that have been conducted "generally show that livestock grazing does not have as great a benefit as some other alternative uses."[162]

As we have seen, several authors of *The Western Range* calculated that many rangelands were substantially more valuable for their watershed functions than for the livestock forage they produced. More recently, the GAO reported that "some studies estimate the value of public lands for the enhancement of big game animals as higher than the value of the land for livestock grazing." It cited Challis, Idaho, where the value of an AUM for enhancing elk and deer populations was estimated at $5–$20, compared to less than $2 for livestock. Range scientists John Workman et al. estimate that consumer surpluses to hunters due to grazing permit reductions are six times the lost income to ranchers; "[r]eductions in permitted livestock grazing constitute a wealth transfer from the grazing permittee . . . to groups . . . who place a high value on amenities." Bishop expressed this idea in lay terms when he wrote that "15 buffalo in the Wapiti valley [near Cody, Wyoming] are worth more to more people than every range cow in Park County," the county that includes Cody and Yellowstone National Park. Indeed, ranchers who undertake hunting- and recreation-related businesses to supplement their incomes themselves help to prove the point that rangelands possess amenities more valuable than their livestock production potential.[163]

When they fail to prevail in the argument that livestock production lends value to worthless or unproductive rangelands, grazing advocates often resort to urging that livestock grazing is a "complementary" use of these lands. Grazing advocates Quigley and Bartlett have argued that such "complementary relationships provide justification for continued livestock grazing on the public lands." But, again, this argument overlooks or minimizes costs. Livestock "benefits" almost surely come at the expense of higher-value uses; thus, livestock production is unlikely to optimize or maximize rangeland benefits. Fowler and Gray were more cautious, observing that "[a]lternative production possibilities" for rangelands, such as "[r]ecreation, wildlife viewing and hunting, water development, and timber production," are "not necessarily competitive with livestock production." Martin pointed out that, even if the tradeoffs were considered, we may have no sound mechanisms for quantifying them. He was skeptical that "we really know the production function for rangeland forage and range improvement," much less "the marginal rates of substitution between the multiple products that may be produced on the range in addition to domestic livestock." Even if we can't measure the tradeoffs, however, we can see them in eroded slopes, degraded streams, and rampant nonnative plants. Chapter 5 demonstrates that the complementarity argument is inapplicable to arid and semiarid rangelands that evolved in the absence of large-ungulate grazing.[164]

Some apologies are simply irrational or ignorant. The authors of a recent publication promoting coordinated resource management (CRM) in Wyoming claimed that the agriculture industry, within which they include ranching, "positively impacts [Wyoming's] economy . . . with programs that: improve water quality through management of riparian habitat and reduction of non-point source pollution; . . . enhance wildlife habitat; and reduce fire hazards." These claims are ridiculous. First, grazing does not reduce nonpoint source pollution; it is the chief cause of nonpoint source pollution in western states, including Wyoming. Second, the principal agent responsible for impacts on western riparian ecosystems is agriculture—principally, losses of water to irrigation and the myriad effects of livestock grazing. Thus, any "beneficial impacts" of agriculture on water-related resources could result only from reducing its historically negative impacts. Third, the net impact of agriculture on native wildlife habitat over the past 125 years has undeniably been negative. It is ludicrous to fabricate a defense for the industry by using its more recent efforts to offset some historic habitat losses by such measures as enhancing habitat for pheasants (a nonnative species), improving waterfowl habitat in specific locations, or reintroducing beaver, which ranchers were largely responsible for eliminating in the first place. Finally, grazing, along with fire suppression, is implicated in the loss of native biodiversity across many western landscapes. "Reducing fire hazards" is no benefit if an ecosystem evolved with fire and needs periodic fires to sustain itself. If fires occur too frequently, it is probably because the community is dominated by cheatgrass, an invasive species for which agriculture is to blame.[165]

This form of sophistry is not uncommon among livestock industry proponents. A National Cattlemen's Association spokesman claimed credit for "benefits accruing to the general public" from "public range management programs," apparently referring to range "improvements" that alleviate past livestock-related damage to watercourses and wildlife habitats. Nielsen made a similar assertion, couched in economic terms. Hypothesizing a "serious conflict on a critical deer or elk winter range," he asserted that if a "range improvement program is undertaken in another area that will produce enough forage to replace the livestock use on the problem range, the wildlife benefits occurring on the critical winter range should be counted as part of the range improvement project." This ploy of adding the elimination of the ecological harm initially caused by livestock grazing to the benefits of range improvement projects is a common strategy. It may seem reasonable to economists trying to tally all costs and benefits, but it makes little sense if the objective of the analysis is to ascertain whether wildlife—or the public lands generally—are indeed better off as a result of livestock grazing or so-called range improvement practices.[166]

4. ATTEMPTING TO EXPLAIN THE UNEXPLAINABLE

The foregoing discussion seems, inevitably, to have brought us right back to the original question: Why do we continue to graze public lands? It seems fair to say that we're no closer to a reasoned answer. Power intimates that the special treatment enjoyed by agriculture in general, despite what economic statistics reveal about its role in the economy, is at bottom a social/cultural phenomenon. "People view agriculture not just as another type of commercial activity, but rather as an honorable way of life, one that strengthens the social and political fabric of the nation and therefore deserves protection." Jefferson's vision of a nation of yeoman farmers is "one of the most enduring articulations of this view." By integrating work and home life, he explains, "[f]arming and ranching are seen as attractive ways of life rather than just commercial ventures seeking profit."[167]

Power queries, however, whether it is "agriculture itself, or the autonomy, self-direction, and individual responsibility associated with it" that make it "attractive." Neither the life of a migrant farm worker nor that of a plantation slave was viewed as "ennobling," he points out. And "almost any family-run business requires the same independence and responsibility" as does agriculture. He concludes:

> [O]nly some of those employed in agriculture fit the image of the indepen-
> dent, self-employed businessman. Just as important, there are independent,
> self-employed businesspeople in almost every field, not just agriculture. . . .
> Given the declining percentage of population employed in agriculture, this
> would seem an unlikely industry to protect in the name of self-employed and
> family-operated business. . . . In any event, it is not clear what the current
> justification is for supporting small businesses more generously in agriculture
> than in other fields of economic activity. It may be time to convert the
> historical accident of our agricultural support institutions to broader-based
> small-business extension services.[168]

As Power points out, explaining how agriculture has come to enjoy its place in American policy does not provide a clear, comprehensible justification for perpetuating our agricultural policies. This is especially true for public land grazing. Traditional economic criteria expose continued grazing on public lands as folly. But the ecological harm posed by livestock grazing on arid and semiarid lands threatens to undermine the entire economic base of portions of the West.

Power warns that the "long-run economic health of the community may, at times, require that the *natural landscape, part of the community's permanent economic base*, not be sacrificed to stopgap measures to maintain extractive employment at past levels."[169]

As Krutilla recognized more than thirty years ago, the "cost of refraining from converting our remaining rare natural environments may not be very great," but the level of our future well-being will depend significantly on enjoining such conversions. Eliminating grazing in arid regions of the West would offer tremendous potential benefits while imposing very few costs. The economic impacts would be minor, even at the local level; and cultural concerns—whose authenticity as a matter of both history and federal land policy is suspect, anyway—are overblown. While additional evidence could be amassed, the case as it stands should be sufficient to justify the measures proposed for conserving native arid-land biodiversity. No legitimate apology for continued domestic livestock grazing on these lands should remain. What remains is the ineluctable conclusion that public-land grazing in the arid West is unsound public policy—ecologically destructive, contrary to the intent of the applicable laws, economically inefficient, and inequitable.[170]

Conclusion

There undoubtedly would be howls of protest, indignant claims of interference with property rights, and predictions of doom for small western communities if the BLM were to propose to remove livestock from arid western rangelands. The differences in political and economic views that characterize the grazing debate are perhaps irreconcilable. While recognizing this philosophical divergence, however, two things must be kept in mind. First, the lands in question are public lands, subject to management in the public interest. There are no private property interests at stake, but there are public interests and public goods of enormous value in the balance. This public versus private rights issue is not just economic or philosophical, but ethical. Martin queries whether ranchers as private "investors have a right to get themselves into a position where short-run exploitation of the range resource is the answer to their long-run wealth-creating venture." Livestock interests, congressional delegations, and indeed the BLM itself need to be reminded, frequently, of the public interest in rangeland resources. Second, most of the opposition to the proposal would come from certain vocal but very narrow segments of society—the permit holders themselves and their allies in stockgrowers' associations, certain western legislators (principally Republicans), and leaders of some western communities. The latter two groups will need to hear from the vast majority of their constituents who do not favor turning the range over to a narrow economic interest group.[1]

Many readers may be inclined to dismiss the conservation proposal as too radical or naive to stand a chance in the political arena. I refer them to the 1993 survey of attitudes toward rangeland management conducted by Brunson and Steel. The researchers conducted random telephone surveys of 2,000 households, completing interviews with 1,360 adults. (The remainder, for the most part, declined to participate because they had no opinion on the subject.) The average respondent was in his or her early fifties, had some college education, and lived in a town with a population greater than 25,000. The interviewers defined "rangelands" for respondents as "places that have arid climates, where grasslands or desert environments are more common than heavily forested ones."[2]

According to Brunson and Steel, 34 percent of respondents favored a total ban on livestock grazing on public lands; only 21 percent opposed such a ban, while 45 percent were neutral toward the concept. The respondents showed sympathy for local communities, but they opposed by a 3:1 margin abandoning endangered species protections to protect ranching jobs. Half of the sample had "'hardly any' confidence in the livestock industry." In contrast, 40 percent expressed "a great deal of confidence in environmental groups." Only 13 percent of those responding belonged to an environmental organization; 11 percent said they depended on farming or livestock for their livelihood. The researchers construed the attitude toward the stock industry as a reflection of the public's general lack of confidence in big business.[3]

The federal agencies, in their summary of the Brunson and Steel survey results, acknowledged that more than one-third of respondents supported eliminating all livestock from public lands. They also noted that only one-fourth of the respondents thought that federal rangeland management "should emphasize livestock grazing; 43 percent disagreed" with that proposition.[4]

Brunson and Steel reported that 86 percent of respondents in their survey believed that water quality from federal rangelands had "decreased markedly" over the past fifty years—63 percent agreed strongly with this statement—and 83 percent considered the loss of streamside (riparian) vegetation a "serious problem." Sizeable majorities thought that plant and animal species "should be better protected . . . on rangelands." Specifically, 86 percent thought that wildlife should be better protected; 76 percent held the same view about fish; and 75 percent believed that rare plants needed greater protection. The researchers also determined that more than 80 percent of respondents agreed that "humans have an ethical obligation to protect plant and animal species."[5]

As noted in the last chapter, approximately 40 percent of respondents in the 1993 survey thought that "the economic vitality of local communities should be given the highest priority when making decisions about federal rangelands; a similar proportion disagreed." Responses on this topic were similar between easterners and westerners: 46 percent of westerners believed that local community vitality should be accorded the highest priority; 29 percent thought that livestock grazing should be emphasized on federal rangelands, compared to 25 percent of all respondents who thought that grazing should be emphasized.[6]

Apparently, survey respondents were provided little or no background information other than the definition of "rangeland." My guess is that most of the public equate "rangeland" with "grazing land." Even those persons who live in the vicinity of public rangelands and persons who visit public lands for recreational purposes may be so accustomed to seeing cattle or sheep on public lands that they make the same assumption. Thus, it seems likely that the general public would presuppose that communities located near public rangelands are ranching communities. Likewise, it seems reasonable that many, perhaps most, respondents would assume that lands identified as "rangeland" are suitable for grazing. As we have seen, that is not true of arid and semiarid lands.

The potential sources of bias that I am suggesting may have colored the results of the 1993 survey are analogous to those discovered by Arthur W. Magill, principal resource analyst for the Forest Service's Pacific Southwest Research Station, in an earlier survey of public attitudes toward deserts. He showed color slides to people to determine their perceptions of managed and unmanaged landscapes. Respondents completed a questionnaire while viewing slides; answers were open-ended. Magill discovered that more than twice as many people liked "arid lands that were reported as 'deserts,' 'sand dunes,' 'prairies,' and 'open range,'" than those simply reported as "having an 'arid look.'" He speculated that people "liked arid landscapes, despite not liking arid-looking lands, because landscapes such as deserts and prairies project an image of 'openness,' which was liked by most respondents." He received 37 responses about overgrazing; 95 percent said they "disliked" what they saw, and no one liked it. "The percentage of people who disliked 'overgrazing,'" Magill reported, "was greater than those who disliked 'roads' . . . or 'clearcuts.' . . ." On the other hand, of the 49 respondents who commented about grazing generally, 51 percent liked it, 16 percent disliked it, and 27 percent were indifferent. In closing, he pointed out that "managers should be aware that many lay people will perceive some arid lands as overgrazed, whether they are or not."[7]

Brunson and Steel's survey results show that, despite any preconceived notions respondents may have had about the suitability of "rangeland" for live-stock grazing or the likelihood of local community dependence on ranching, there is fertile ground in the public's mind in which to sow new, even "radical," ideas for reforming federal grazing policies. Their survey and Magill's remind us of the need to better inform the public about land management choices and consequences. Given the power of education to influence attitudes about the natural world, public support for grazing should slide even lower if the agencies and/or conservation organizations were to undertake to provide more accurate information about livestock's impacts on other rangeland values, including biodiversity.[8]

Quigley and Bartlett summarized the results of yet another survey, this one of a presumably better-informed group—U.S. Forest Service employees. Respondents were asked to rate the relative values of multiple uses of national forests. "Grazing," the authors reported, "was found to contribute about 10 percent of the value associated with the multiple uses, timber 15 percent, and water, recreation, and wildlife about 25 percent each." The authors (unabashed proponents of public land grazing, as we've seen) posited a rather strained characterization of these results, stating that the Forest Service employees' "perception of the public values associated with grazing on Federal land were [sic] not nearly zero compared to the other multiple-use values." "This would indicate," they asserted, "that grazing represents a substantial value as compared to the other uses and elimination would be inappropriate." The most obvious alternative interpretation, of course, is that Forest Service employees considered grazing the least valuable of national forest uses, outweighed by every other multiple use by a factor of 50 to 150 percent. It seems to me that the results merely reflect Forest Service employees' recognition that livestock grazing is an extant use of public lands, and their opinion that grazing's value is significantly outweighed by that of all other national forest uses. Furthermore, the resources perceived by Forest Service employees as most valuable were the "amenity" resources, those most clearly public goods—water, recreation, and wildlife.[9]

These surveys contain lessons for land managers. First, each plainly refutes the notion that eliminating grazing on public lands is "unthinkable." This reflects a more general development noted by conservation leader M. Brock Evans: it "has become more thinkable to move farther away from the notion that the public lands are primarily there to produce exploitable commodities for the personal profit of private corporations." Second, the 1993 public attitudes survey seems to corroborate the suggestion that community stability may be the toughest issue in the livestock grazing debate—although the survey also reveals that a majority do not believe that local economic concerns should be determinative of public land policy choices. The nearly equally split vote on this issue, with 40 percent in favor of giving "the economic vitality of local communities" highest priority and 40 percent opposed, further suggests that, if the public were better informed concerning the small actual impact of grazing on most local economies, their concern—and the controversy—would be significantly alleviated. Finally, the BLM and certain segments of the public, particularly Wise Use groups and proponents of the so-called county movement, need to be reminded that neither of the principal BLM grazing statutes, FLPMA and the Taylor Act, requires the level of consideration currently accorded local community concerns. On the contrary, FLPMA repeatedly emphasizes the national interest in the public lands. As for the stability of the livestock industry itself, recall that a federal court recently observed that the interior secretary "is free to consider" BLM lands' minor contribution to livestock production when "balancing the need for industry stability against the need to protect the federal lands from deterioration."[10]

Grazing by domestic livestock has had, and continues to have, significant adverse environmental consequences on arid western rangelands. These consequences include a reduction of native biological diversity, especially at the landscape scale. Grazing's ecological impacts are more widespread than those of any other human activity in the West, and elimination of grazing holds greater potential for benefiting biodiversity than any other single land use measure. Public land grazing has been occurring for 100 years or more on most public lands and, as a general matter, is authorized by law. But grazing on certain public lands was probably never contemplated by Congress, and continued grazing of these and other areas arguably violates the intent of the authorizing legislation and interferes with the achievement of other statutory goals. Public land grazing is condoned, even promoted, ostensibly because it helps sustain local western economies, preserve a traditional culture and lifestyle, and maintain desirable open space. But in fact, public land grazing, by any measure, is costly and wasteful; it is supported by, rather than supports, local communities; it survives, not because of federal land policies, but because of ranchers' desire to maintain their accustomed lifestyle and their ability to find other means of economic support; and its utility in preserving open space depends on the profit-seeking whims of private ranchland owners.

If this book has succeeded in convincing the reader that the proposal to conserve biological diversity on large tracts of arid and semiarid BLM range-lands by removing unnatural agents of disturbance, chiefly domestic livestock and grazing-related practices, is not so radical as it initially may have appeared, then it has succeeded in a significant respect. The only essential ingredient yet lacking is the political will to oppose a narrow, but powerful, interest group—the deeply entrenched western livestock industry. As preeminent range law scholar George Cameron Coggins has written: "In the end range productivity is a political problem that can be overcome only by political courage, the range resource in the shortest supply." But courage is not lacking entirely, as numerous quotations in this book from conservation biologists, political and range scientists, and environmental leaders demonstrate. Granted, the public will need to be persuaded of the proposal's merit before the agency can be induced to buck the inevitable opposition from livestock interests, certain local officials, and many western legislators. But the public—most of whom don't have an axe to grind or a political agenda—are not only educable but ready to learn the truth. What is needed now is leaders with courage.[11]

The time has come to force the issue. As conservation biologists Noss and Cooperrider put it,

> [It is] a fact that livestock grazing on rangelands has been in existence for several thousand years globally and several hundred on this continent, and is likely to continue. *This is not to say that it will or should continue in all places where it has been in the past.* We need to take a hard look at the desirability of producing beef on arid or semiarid public lands. . . . Sustainability, including maintenance of native biodiversity, should be the fundamental criterion for determining if livestock grazing should [continue to] be allowed. . . .

Comparable advice, albeit more livestock-oriented, is coming from the range science community. Dwyer and colleagues admonish range managers to "require that the entire ecosystem be healthy," rather than aiming at "improving ecological condition for livestock production," and they caution:

The immediate demand on rangeland managers is to halt practices that will contribute to any further irreversible ecological changes associated with livestock grazing. Management for human benefits, including livestock products, should fit into the total ecosystem instead of restructuring it around a single purpose.[12]

But for the traditional, nearly inexplicable, deference enjoyed by western livestock interests, the case for removing livestock from the driest public ranges should not be difficult to make. American interests and values have changed dramatically since the 1880s. As a people we are considerably better informed and more appreciative of the natural world. It makes no sense—economic, ecological, social, or otherwise—to perpetuate a use of public lands (let alone the environmental degradation that ensues) that has always been subordinate to other recognized uses and that has even less importance in today's socioeconomic and cultural milieu than it did when its place on the range was first formally recognized. Today people place higher values on preservation of the native biota, water quality, cultural and historical resources, scenic vistas, and aesthetics. Public lands are highly valued by the hundreds of millions of people who use them for recreation each year, as well as by those who never visit them but place a value on simply knowing that they exist. The interest in species diversity is burgeoning—witness the more than 100 million visits made annually to the nation's major zoos and aquariums. People are concerned about bequeathing to their children and to subsequent generations an environment that is in no worse condition—and preferably in healthier condition—than theirs and that is as richly populated with life as the world in which we now live.[13]

Where is the wisdom in borrowing from our future—in terms of land and water productivity, species diversity, and overall environmental health—in order to maintain a marginally economic lifestyle enjoyed at public expense by such a tiny minority of our population and to produce, on lands unsuited to the purpose, commodities that would scarcely be missed if their production ceased? It is beyond cavil that public land grazing affords "considerable" private benefits to a limited class of beneficiaries, while imposing immense costs on present and future generations of Americans.[14]

Wuerthner has argued that the "only secure way of preserving biodiversity and the evolutionary processes that maintain it is to restore large wildlands complexes across the landscape. In many parts of the western United States, the most logical place for restoration efforts are [sic] lands currently used for marginal resource production." I have not here proposed that grazing be halted immediately on all public lands, but I am convinced that the first step—removing livestock from those areas most unsuited to the use—is long overdue. Since the West was first settled, the destruction of our nation's biological heritage has continued nearly unabated, tacitly sanctioned and abetted by federal politicians, land managers, and agriculture service agencies. We can no longer afford to sit back and wait for them to act or for agriculture to reform itself.[15]

It is time to make hard decisions about traditional, time-honored uses of land. I invite readers to judge livestock grazing on arid public lands by Leopold's straightforward standard: "Examine each question in terms of what is ethically right as well as what is economically expedient. A thing is right when it tends to preserve the integrity, stability, and beauty of the biotic community. It is wrong when it tends otherwise."[16]

Notes

PREFACE

1. See Rowley, *Forest Service Grazing*, 219.
2. "Bill Would Allow Civil Lawsuits," 8, quoting H.B. 127.
3. Krza, "Cow Coup," 4.
4. Bock, Bock, and Smith, "Proposal for a System," 732–33.

INTRODUCTION

1. Hays, "Public Values," 1813–14.
2. Brunson and Steel, "National Public Attitudes," 77–80.
3. Hays, "Public Values," 1823.
4. See Wilkinson, *Crossing the Next Meridian*, 81. Coggins, Wilkinson, and Leshy, *Federal Public Land*, 20, 888.
5. Jamieson, "Sustainability and Beyond," 7.
6. Pisani, *To Reclaim a Divided West*, 295. See also McConnell, *Private Power and American Democracy*, 207–9.
7. Regarding precipitation thresholds, see, e.g., Noss and Cooperrider, *Saving Nature's Legacy*, 258; Forsling, "Grazing Lands," 12–13, 61–62; Sheridan, *Desertification*, 20; Sowell et al., "Cattle Nutrition," 1; Dwyer, Buckhouse, and Huey, "Impacts of Grazing Intensity," 871; Pearson, "Multiple Use in Forestry," 247–48; Barth and McCullough, *Livestock Grazing Impacts*, 19, quoting Bennion, "A Pioneer Cattle Venture." See also chapter 5. U.S. Department of the Interior, BLM, *Rangeland Reform Summary*, 28. See also Sanders, "Can Annual Rangelands Be Converted," 412; NRC, Committee on Rangeland Classification, *Rangeland Health*, 32–33.
8. See Whittaker, *Communities and Ecosystems*, 154–57; Bender, *Reference Handbook on the Deserts*; Limerick, *Desert Passages*, 4. See also Calef, *Private Grazing and Public Lands*, 240–43.
9. See, e.g., "Utahans Don't Take Kindly," 6.
10. Low and Berlin, "Natural Selection," 1169. Brunson and Steel, "National Public Attitudes," 77.

CHAPTER 1. THE HISTORICAL AND CULTURAL LANDSCAPE

1. See generally Coggins, Wilkinson, and Leshy, *Federal Public Land*, 2–3. See, e.g., Merrill, "Private Spaces."

2. See generally Coggins and Lindeberg-Johnson, "Public Rangeland Management II," 19–20, 28–30, 40–60. See also chapter 2 regarding the nature of the grazing privilege. See, e.g., *Buford v. Houtz*, 133 U.S. 320 (1890). Taylor Grazing Act, ch. 865, 48 Stat. 1269 (1934), codified as amended at 43 U.S.C. §§ 315–315p (1994). Hays, *Conservation*, 51–52. Webb, *The Great Plains*, 423. To illustrate the agriculture objective of federal land policy: from 1870 to 1900, 430 million new acres were cultivated, more than in the previous 250 years. NRC, *Rangeland Health*, 21, citing Athearn, *The Mythic West*.

3. Foss, *Politics and Grass*, 41. Rowley, *Forest Service Grazing*, 24, 28, quoting 1896 National Academy of Sciences committee report. See Nelson, "Ideology and Public Land Policy," 278. Desert Lands Act of 1877, 43 U.S.C. §§ 321–39.

4. Adams, *Renewable Resource Policy*, 101, quoting Powell, *Report on the Lands*. Limerick, *Desert Passages*, quoting Powell, *Report*, 7, 8, 30. Worster, *Nature's Economy*, 228. See Coggins, Wilkinson, and Leshy, *Federal Public Land*, 85.

5. 43 U.S.C. § 224 (repealed 1976). Foss, *Politics and Grass*, 20. See Hays, *Conservation*, 61, 65. See Coggins, Wilkinson, and Leshy, *Federal Public Land*, 86. Roberts, "Integrated Part of Western Agriculture," 417. Barns, *Sod House*, 98–99.

6. Enlarged Homestead Act, 43 U.S.C. §§ 218–21 (repealed 1976). Webb, *The Great Plains*, 423. Merrill, "Private Spaces," 82.

7. Muhn and Stuart, *Story of BLM*, 35 (quotation). Enlarged Homestead Act, 43 U.S.C. §§ 218–21 (repealed 1976). Three-Year Homestead Act, 37 Stat. 123–25 (1912; repealed 1976). Muhn and Stuart, *Story of BLM*, 35–36. Foss, *Politics and Grass*, 22. NRC, *Rangeland Health*, 21, citing Athearn, *The Mythic West*. Culhane, *Public Lands Politics*, 79. Rowley, *Forest Service Grazing*, 225. See generally Gates, *History of Public Land Law*, 495–529. Coggins, Wilkinson, and Leshy, *Federal Public Land*, 86.

8. 43 U.S.C. §§ 291–301 (repealed 1976). Muhn and Stuart, *Story of BLM*, 35. Foss, *Politics and Grass*, 27 (quotation). GAO, *BLM's Hot Desert Grazing Program*, 18. Webb, *Great Plains*, 424–25.

9. Muhn and Stuart, *Story of BLM*, 36, citing General Land Office. Webb, *The Great Plains*, 424. Senate Comm. on Public Lands and Surveys, Grazing on Public Lands and National Forests, S. Rep. No. 517, 69th Cong., 1st Sess., 17 (1926). Coggins, Wilkinson, and Leshy, *Federal Public Land*, 86.

10. Hays, *Conservation*, 50–51, 61–62, 69, 267, 272, 189–91. Foss, *Politics and Grass*, 41, citing commission's 1905 report.

11. See Hays, *Conservation*, 39–40, 57, 69, 72, 258. Rowley, *Forest Service Grazing*, 46.

12. Hays, *Conservation*, 69. Worster, *Under Western Skies*, 43. Hays, *Conservation*, 258.

13. Worster, *Nature's Economy*, 267–68. Hays, *Conservation*, 69, 189–91, 267, 272–73 (quotations).

14. Hays, *Conservation*, 39–41 (quotation), 43–44, 274. Rowley, *Forest Service Grazing*, 57.

15. Hays, *Conservation*, 41–42 (quoting Pinchot speech in 1903), 49.

16. See Hays, *Conservation*, 55, 57. Rowley, *Forest Service Grazing*, 24, 54.

17. Hays, *Conservation*, 58–59. Rowley, *Forest Service Grazing*, 46–47, 59, 83, 93.

18. Rowley, *Forest Service Grazing*, 59–60. Hays, *Conservation*, 273 (emphasis added).

19. Hays, *Conservation*, 71. Rowley, *Forest Service Grazing*, 45–46, 130. Hays, *Conservation*, 71, 273.

20. Rowley, *Forest Service Grazing*, 47, 61–62 (quotation). Hays, *Conservation*, 53–55 (quotation on 54). Klyza, *Who Controls Public Lands?* 110–11. Foss, *Politics and Grass*, 27, 43, 46.

21. Hays, *Conservation*, 267–69. Compare ibid., 268–69, noting Roosevelt's ideal "classless agrarian society," with Foss, *Politics and Grass*, 200, describing the upper level of a "rural caste system" represented by the Taylor Grazing Act's grazing advisory boards. Pelzer, *Cattlemen's Frontier*, 191, 248, quoting Roosevelt, *Ranch-Life and the Hunting Trail*.

22. See Foss, *Politics and Grass*, 27. McConnell, *Private Power and American Democracy*, 45, quoting Pinchot, *Fight for Conservation*, 46. Hays, *Conservation*, 267, citing Roosevelt. Pisani, *To Reclaim a Divided West*, 294–95, quoting Underwood.

23. Merrill, "Private Spaces."

24. Ibid., 30. Hays, *Conservation*, 274.

25. Merrill, "Private Spaces," 28, 30, 75, quoting Dale, *Range Cattle Industry*, 86. Larson, *Wyoming*, 128.

26. Merrill, "Private Spaces," 31, 35, quoting Smith, *War on Powder River*, xii, 246. Peffer, *Closing of the Public Domain*, 251. Calef, *Private Grazing and Public Lands*, 68.

27. Adams, *Renewable Resource Policy*, 91. Young and Evans, "Plant Manipulation," 59–60. Webb, *The Great Plains*, 511–12. Hays, *Conservation*, 55. Voigt, *Public Grazing Lands*, 248, citing Stanfield hearings. See also chapter 5, discussing the potentially irreversible impacts of overgrazing.

28. Merrill, "Private Spaces," 45–47, 240–41. See also chapter 2 concerning President Hoover's cession proposal.

29. See Hays, *Conservation*, 251–52. Joseph Nimmo, Jr., Report to Congress, 1885, quoted by Rowley, *Forest Service Grazing*, 12. Pelzer, *Cattlemen's Frontier*, 191. Merrill, "Private Spaces," 75–76, quoting *Grand Encampment Herald*. See also Barns, *Sod House*, 249.

30. Pelzer, *Cattlemen's Frontier*, 191, quoting Roosevelt, *Ranch-Life and the Hunting Trail*, 104.

31. Hays, *Conservation*, 23–26. See Merrill, "Private Spaces," 105–6.

32. Rowley, *Forest Service Grazing*, 5. Merrill, "Private Spaces," 91–92, citing the governor of Texas (emphasis deleted). Webb, *The Great Plains*, 240 (quotation). Pisani, *To Reclaim a Divided West*, 226, citing Carey. Merrill, "Private Spaces," 95–108 (quotation on 98–99, n. 55).

33. Merrill, "Private Spaces," 91 (quotation), 95–108. Larson, *Wyoming*, 121. Merrill, "Private Spaces," 83 (quotation).

34. Webb, *The Great Plains*, 424. Merrill, "Private Spaces," 81–83, quoting a "1982 [*sic*; presumably 1892]" editorial by Smythe.

35. Limerick, *Desert Passages*, 43, quoting Frémont's 1843–44 Report, 702. Regarding Indians as "savages," see Cronon, *Nature's Metropolis*, 31, quoting Turner.

36. Larson, *Wyoming*, 110, 122. Barns, *Sod House*, 38 (emphasis added).

37. See Pelzer, *Cattlemen's Frontier*, 114, 182, 187–89, citing a Colorado settler for the report of losses due to illegal fences. Unlawful Inclosures Act of 1885, 43 U.S.C. 1061–66 (as amended). See, e.g., *Camfield v. United States* and *United States ex rel. Bergen v. Lawrence*.

38. Wyant, *Westward in Eden*, 456, quoting Webb, *The Great Plains*, 498, 50. The subject of ranchers' image and the notion of "barbarism" is taken up in more detail in chapter 4.

39. Merrill, "Private Spaces," 31–32 (footnotes and citations omitted). Larson, *Wyoming*, 127 (quotation). Pelzer, *Cattlemen's Frontier*, 182, quoting a Colorado settler. Worster, *Under Western Skies*, 41–42.

40. Larson, *Wyoming*, 126. Dobie, *I'll Tell You a Tale*, 52.

41. Rowley, *Forest Service Grazing*, 3, quoting Ensign, *Report on the Forest Conditions*. Webb, *The Great Plains*, 239–40. Kellert, *Activities—II*, 21.

42. Merrill, "Private Spaces," 267 (emphasis in original).

43. Ibid., 97, quoting conference proceedings at 324–26.

44. Ibid., 168 n. 73, 205. Voigt, *Public Grazing Lands*, 244–45.

45. Merrill, "Private Spaces," 102–4.

46. Ibid., 104, quoting Roosevelt, in Proceedings of the 1907 Public Land Convention, 136.

47. Ibid., 105, quoting Teller, in Proceedings of the 1907 Public Land Convention, 54, 171.

48. Hays, *Conservation*, 253–54, 257, 259, 267, citing an editorial in the *Centennial [Wyoming] Post*, quoting Roosevelt. Merrill, "Private Spaces," 239.

49. Merrill, "Private Spaces," 106–7, quoting 1914 Hearings on H.R. 9582 and 10539, part I, 462 (emphasis deleted).

50. See Rowley, *Forest Service Grazing*, 112–16. Merrill, "Private Spaces," 122–23, 171 (quoting Will C. Barnes, "Sheepmen on the National Forests"), 193. Greeley, "Stabilizing the Use of Public Ranges," 35, quoted in Merrill, "Private Spaces," 124 n. 11.

51. Merrill, "Private Spaces," 141–42 (quoting *National Wool Grower* [March 1924]: 14), 171 (quoting Barnes, in *National Wool Grower* [February 1921]: 34).

52. See Merrill, "Private Spaces," 239–41. Foss, *Politics and Grass*, 48. Merrill, "Private Spaces," 223, quoting Hoover as quoted in Winter, *Four Hundred Million Acres*, 400. See the discussion in chapters 2 and 7 of the "chiefly valuable for grazing" language in the Taylor Grazing Act.

53. Muhn and Stuart, *Story of BLM*, 37. Foss, *Politics and Grass*, 48. Peffer, *Closing of the Public Domain*, 212. Merrill, "Private Spaces," 240–41. Dana, *Forest and Range Policy*, 233. Rowley, *Forest Service Grazing*, 159. Graf, *Wilderness Preservation*, 148 (citations omitted).

54. See Merrill, "Private Spaces," 240–41. Dana, *Forest and Range Policy*, 233. Pisani, *To Reclaim a Divided West*, 295. Leshy, "Sharing Federal Multiple-Use Lands," 270. See also Schlebecker, *Cattle Raising*, 102–3.

55. Dana, *Forest and Range Policy*, 259. See also chapter 4.

CHAPTER 2. THE EARLY LEGAL LANDSCAPE

1. Pieper, "Ecological Implications," 185.

2. NRC, *Rangeland Health*, 20. Pieper, "Ecological Implications," 185 (citations omitted). Coggins and Lindeberg-Johnson, "Public Rangeland Management II," 31–32, 39–40.

3. Pelzer, *Cattlemen's Frontier*, 139, 143, 149, 177, 212, quoting Roosevelt, *Hunting Trips of a Ranchman*, 290. See Pisani, *To Reclaim a Divided West*, 295 (emphasis added). See Merrill, "Private Spaces," 31–32.

4. Rowley, *Forest Service Grazing*, 15–16, 21, 33 (citing USFS grazing chief Potter), 34 (quoting Coville).

5. Rowley, *Forest Service Grazing*, 112–16; see also 95. Voigt, *Public Grazing Lands*, 311.

6. See, e.g., Gates, *History of Public Land Law*, 608–10; 78 *Cong. Rec.* 6344, 6358–59 (10 April 1934). See, e.g., Coggins and Lindeberg-Johnson, "Public Rangeland Management II," 31–32, citing Garrett Hardin's "Tragedy of the Commons" thesis. Rowley, *Forest Service Grazing*, 25–28, citing the committee.

7. McClure, "Address," 40, 57.

8. Atkins, "Report of the President," 63. See also Pelzer, *Cattlemen's Frontier*, 149–50; Schlebecker, *Cattle Raising*, 149, 194–95. Adams, *Renewable Resource Policy*, 105, citing Gates, *History of Public Land Law*, 607.

9. Schlebecker, *Cattle Raising*, 70. Coggins and Lindeberg-Johnson, "Public Rangeland Management II," 32. Schlebecker, *Cattle Raising*, 149.

10. Merrill, "Private Spaces," 58, quoting a letter of Francis E. Warren, 22 May 1914, Francis Warren Papers, American Heritage Center, University of Wyoming. The description of Warren as "the greatest shepherd" is found in Rowley, *Forest Service Grazing*, 82. See Schlebecker, *Cattle Raising*, 194–95.

11. Senate Committee, *Grazing on Public Lands*, 7–8, 18–19, quoting § 204(2) (emphasis added).

12. Foss, *Politics and Grass*, 35. Clawson, *Federal Lands Revisited*, 67. See S. Rep. No. 517, 3; Voigt, *Public Grazing Lands*, 248, citing Colton and Taylor, in 1930 *Congressional Record*, 249–50. Merrill, "Private Spaces," 251, quoting Silcox, in Gates, *History of Public Land Law*, 612. See discussion of desertification in chapter 5; Coggins and Lindeberg-Johnson, "Public Rangeland Management II," 41.

13. Graf, *Wilderness Preservation*, 150; see also Foss, *Politics and Grass*, 50–51. Merrill, "Private Spaces," 245 (citing Edward Taylor, as quoted in Peffer, *Closing of the Public Domain*, 217), 247 (citing Hearings on H.R. 2835 and 6462, 9). Dana, *Forest and Range Policy*, 259; see 78 *Cong. Rec.* 6344, 6344–46 (10 April 1934); 78 *Cong. Rec.* 11,139 (12 June 1934); Merrill, "Private Spaces," 247, citing Hearings on H.R. 2835 and 6462, 9.

14. More detailed historical accounts of the Taylor Act can be found in the works by Foss, Gates, Peffer, Coggins, and others. Graf, *Wilderness Preservation*, 152 (citation omitted). See, e.g., Foss, *Politics and Grass*; Gates, *History of Public Land Law*; Peffer, *Closing of the Public Domain*. Graf, *Wilderness Preservation*, 187. Taylor Grazing Act, ch. 865, 48 Stat. 1269 (1934) (codified as amended at 43 U.S.C. §§ 315–315p [1994]).

15. Coggins, "Some Disjointed Observations," 473. Coggins and Lindeberg-Johnson, "Public Rangeland Management II," 55. See Klyza, *Who Controls Public Lands?* 112; 78 *Cong. Rec.* 6344, 6348–49 (10 April 1934); 78 *Cong. Rec.* 11,139, 11,144 (12 June 1934); Foss, *Politics and Grass*, 49, 58; Voigt, *Public Grazing Lands*, 311. See Coggins and Lindeberg-Johnson, "Public Rangeland Management II," 32. See Graf, *Wilderness Preservation*, 151–52. 78 *Cong. Rec.* 6363 (10 April 1934).

16. Merrill, "Private Spaces," 251. See Graf, *Wilderness Preservation*, 152; Gates, *History of Public Land Law*. Merrill, "Private Spaces," 251–52, citing Silcox, as quoted in Gates, *History of Public Land Law*, 612. Dana, *Forest and Range Policy*, 259–60 (quotation). Muhn and Stuart, *Story of BLM*, 37, citing Roosevelt.

17. Taylor Grazing Act, ch. 865, sec. 1, 48 Stat. 1269 (1934). Coggins and Lindeberg-Johnson, "Public Rangeland Management II," 47. *Natural Resources Defense Council v. Morton*, 388 F. Supp. 829, 833 (D.D.C. 1974).

18. Culhane, *Public Lands Politics*, 93. Coggins and Lindeberg-Johnson, "Public Rangeland Management II," 50–51. 43 C.F.R. § 4110.2–3 (since amended). Gardner, "Role of Economic Analysis," 1450.

19. TGA § 1, 43 U.S.C. § 315. TGA § 7, 43 U.S.C. § 315f.

20. TGA § 2, 43 U.S.C. § 315a.

21. TGA § 1, 43 U.S.C. § 315 (emphasis added). See, e.g., Coggins and Lindeberg-Johnson, "Public Rangeland Management II," 40, 49. Dana, *Forest and Range Policy*, 260, citing Silcox.

22. TGA § 1, 43 U.S.C. § 315. TGA § 5, 43 U.S.C. § 315d; TGA § 6, 43 U.S.C. § 315e.

23. TGA § 7, 43 U.S.C. § 315f.

24. TGA § 3, 43 U.S.C. § 315a. *Red Canyon Sheep Co. v. Ickes*, 98 F. 2d 308, 314–16 (D.C. Cir. 1938). See, e.g., Libecap, *Locking Up the Range*, 100, describing the privilege as "[r]elatively broad and secure at first," but "eroded" by the BLM; Hage, *Storm over Rangelands*. *Public Lands Council v. Babbitt*, 929 F. Supp. 1436 (D. Wyo. 1996), *reversed in part and affirmed in part sub nom. Public Lands Council v. Babbitt*, 154 F. 3d 1160. *Public Lands Council* is discussed in more detail in chapters 4 and 7.

25. See TGA § 3, 43 U.S.C. § 315a. McConnell, *Private Power and American Democracy*, 209.

26. Coggins, Wilkinson, and Leshy, *Federal Public Land*, 694. Coggins and Lindeberg-Johnson, "Public Rangeland Management II," 50–51.

27. Gates, *History of Public Land Law*, 612, 614, and n. 16 (citing 49 Stat. 1976). *Hall v. Hickel*, 305 F. Supp. 723, 725 and n. 1 (D. Nev. 1969). See also Coggins and Lindeberg-Johnson, "Public Rangeland Management II," 54–56. Executive Order 6910 (26 November 1934), quoted in *Hall*, 305 F. Supp. at 725 n. 1. Muhn and Stuart, *Story of BLM*, 37 (emphasis added). See the discussion in chapter 7 of the Taylor Act's term "chiefly valuable for grazing."

28. Gates, *History of Public Land Law*, 613–16 (quotation on 613). Merrill, "Private Spaces," 311, quoting Carpenter, "Range Stockmen Meet the Government," 333. Culhane, *Public Lands Politics*, 89, 91. See also Carpenter, "Establishing Management"; Coggins and Lindeberg-Johnson, "Public Rangeland Management II," 58.

29. Schlebecker, *Cattle Raising*, 176–77. Coggins and Lindeberg-Johnson, "Public Rangeland Management II," 55, 59, 101.

30. See generally Coggins, Wilkinson, and Leshy, *Federal Public Land*. Ibid., 693, citing *Public Lands Statistics: 1990*, table 18.

CHAPTER 3. THE PHYSICAL LANDSCAPE

1. See generally NRC, *Developing Strategies*. Merrill, "Private Spaces," 188.

2. See Merrill, "Private Spaces," 187–88 (emphasis added). See also chapter 1.

3. Sheridan, *Desertification*, 23. See, e.g., *Barton v. United States*, 609 F. 2d 977, 978–79 (10th Cir. 1979); *Hinsdale Livestock Co. v. United States*, 501 F. Supp. 773 (D. Mont. 1980). Schlebecker, *Cattle Raising*, 194–95. Clawson, *Western Range Livestock Industry*, 117.

4. NRC, *Land Use and Wildlife Resources*, 107, citing A. P. Atkins, "Report of the President, 1955," 63–64. Whittaker, *Communities and Ecosystems*, 339. Barth and McCullough, *Livestock Grazing Impacts*, 19, quoting Bennion, "A Pioneer Cattle Venture," 315. Range ecology is examined more thoroughly in chapter 5.

5. Barth and McCullough, *Livestock Grazing Impacts*, 20, quoting Peterson, "Grazing in Utah." Rowley, *Forest Service Grazing*, 178–81 (citing Forsling), 200–201.

6. Miller, Svejcar, and West, "Livestock Grazing," 118–19, 124, citing Griffiths, *Forage Conditions*.

7. USDA, *The Western Range*, 1.

8. Ibid., iii. NRC, *Land Use and Wildlife Resources*, 81. Worster, *Under Western Skies*, 47. Young, "Historical and Evolutionary Perspectives," 1, citing *The Western Range*. Symposium papers were published in the Society for Range Management publication *Ecological Implications of Livestock Herbivory in the West* (1994), edited by Vavra, Laycock, and Pieper. See also Merrill, "Private Spaces," 257.

9. Merrill, "Private Spaces," 257; see also Graf, *Wilderness Preservation*, 162. Merrill, "Private Spaces," 257, quoting *The Western Range*, v. Rowley, *Forest Service Grazing*, 156–58. Graf, *Wilderness Preservation*, 162, citing the ANLSA secretary.

10. Graf, *Wilderness Preservation*, 162.

11. Rowley, *Forest Service Grazing*, 157, citing Forsling.

12. Young, "Historical and Evolutionary Perspectives," 1 (first two quotations). Merrill, "Private Spaces," 257–58 (quotation). Worster, *Under Western Skies*, 48–49.

13. Young, "Historical and Evolutionary Perspectives," 2, noting, however, that "[o]nly three authors were recognized as range managers (examiners)." Worster, *Under Western Skies*, 47.

14. Clapp, "Major Range Problems," 23–24 (quotation). See also Forsling et al., "Administration of Public Range Lands," 455. Bailey and Connaughton, "In Watershed Protection," 337. See Clapp, "Major Range Problems," 23–25.

15. *The Western Range*, iii. See Clapp, "Major Range Problems," 3–5, 7, 25. See also Roberts, "Integrated Part of Western Agriculture," 418. Forsling et al. "Range Conservation the Exception," 287. Clapp, "Major Range Problems," 67; see also ibid., 55.

16. Forsling et al. "Range Conservation the Exception," 286.

17. Clapp, "Major Range Problems," 26.

18. Ibid., 27–28.

19. Ibid., 26, 9. Clawson, *Western Range Livestock Industry*, 385. Pieper, "Ecological Implications," 180 (citation omitted); Coggins and Lindeberg-Johnson, "Public Rangeland Management II," 32. Cf. Graf, *Wilderness Preservation*, 261.

20. Watts, "Unsuitable Land Policy," 213. Rowley, *Forest Service Grazing*, 184. Cf. Young and Evans, "Plant Manipulation," 61.

21. See Clapp, "Major Range Problems," 9, 41. See also chapter 8.

22. Gates, *History of Public Land Law*, 622, citing Secretary of Interior Julius Krug's Annual Reports for 1947 and 1948. Voigt, *Public Grazing Lands*, 300–301, citing Clawson, *Western Range Livestock Industry*.

23. Sheridan, *Desertification*, 13. See also Noss and Cooperrider, *Saving Nature's Legacy*, 64, citing a series of reports since 1936 describing the deteriorated condition of U.S. rangelands. Dana, *Forest and Range Policy*, 281. Muhn and Stuart, *Story of BLM*, 58–59, quoting Clawson, *From Sagebrush to Sage*.

24. Muhn and Stuart, *Story of BLM*, 58–59, 61. Whitson, ed., *Weeds and Poisonous Plants*, 21. See also Libecap, *Locking Up the Range*, 100.

25. Gates, *History of Public Land Law*, 631, citing Secretary of the Interior, Annual Report (1963), 60–62. University of Idaho, *The Forage Resource*, S-26, reporting 2.5 percent of western public land was in excellent condition; 17 percent, good; 50 percent, fair; and 31 percent, poor.

26. Gates, *History of Public Land Law*, 631, citing congressional hearing testimony. House Commitee, *Public Lands Review, Hearings on H.R. 106, 255, 5498, and 5159*, at 253 (Serial No. 11, Part I, Use and Disposal of Public Lands), statement by George W. Abbott, special counsel for Public Lands Coordinating Committee and Nevada Central Committee of Grazing Boards.

27. Forsling, "Grazing Lands Must Be Restored," 12–13, 61–63 (emphasis in original). Muhn and Stuart, *Story of BLM*, 151, 205, citing a 1971 *Reader's Digest* article on overgrazing, "Nibbling Away at the West," and a 1973 *National Geographic* story on the plight of the bighorn sheep in Challis, Idaho.

28. National Environmental Policy Act, 42 U.S.C. §§ 4321–70d (1994). Coggins, Wilkinson, and Leshy, *Federal Public Land*, 711. *Natural Resources Defense Council v. Morton*, 388 F. Supp. 829, 841 (D.D.C. 1974), *affirmed per curiam*, 527 F.2d 1386 (D.C. Cir.), *cert. denied*, 427 U.S. 913 (1976). 388 F. Supp. at 834, citing BLM, *Effects of Livestock Grazing on Wildlife*. 388 F. Supp. at 834, 840. Ibid., 836.

29. See Sheridan, *Desertification*, 12, citing a 1977 GAO report.

30. Sheridan, *Desertification*, 17, 19. See, e.g., Miller, Svejcar, and West, "Livestock Grazing," 119–20.

31. FLPMA § 401(b)(1), 43 U.S.C. § 1751(b)(1).

32. 43 U.S.C. §§ 1901–8. See, e.g., 43 U.S.C. §§ 1901(a)(4), 1904. See also Coggins, "Public Rangeland Management IV," 122–27, 110 (citing Arizona's Representative Morris Udall concerning the bill's support), 116. 43 U.S.C. § 1903(b). See also chapter 7.

33. Comptroller General, *Rangelands Continue to Deteriorate*, i, 21.

34. Ibid., iii–iv, 13.

35. Ibid., 15. Taylor Grazing Act, 48 Stat. 1269.

36. Wagner, "Livestock Grazing," 141. Ferguson and Ferguson, *Sacred Cows*, 115–16.

37. Sheridan, *Desertification*, iii, quoting Mabbutt; cf. Thurow, "Hydrology and Erosion," 158. United Nations, *Conference on Desertification*, 5, quoted in Sheridan, *Desertification*, 2. Sheridan, *Desertification*, 2–3.

38. Dregne, "Desertification of Arid Lands," quoted in Noss and Cooperrider, *Saving Nature's Legacy*, 221. Sheridan, *Desertification*, 2–3; Noss and Cooperrider, *Saving Nature's Legacy*, 221.

39. See Thurow, "Hydrology and Erosion," 156, 158. See also NRC, *Rangeland Health*, 104.

40. Sheridan, *Desertification*, 121.

41. Ibid., 121, 3–4, quoting and citing Harold Dregne, and map in figure 2. Noss and Cooperrider, *Saving Nature's Legacy*, 221, quoting and citing Dregne, "Desertification of Arid Lands," 322.

42. Sheridan, *Desertification*, 121–22.

43. Ibid., 13–17 (quotations on 14 and 15), 20, 29–31, 43–47, 60–65.

44. Ibid., 15–16. Forsling, "Grazing Lands Must Be Restored," 60.

45. Sheridan, *Desertification*, 20 (emphasis in original). See also chapter 5. In 1997 the Santa Fe, New Mexico, environmental organization Forest Guardians called the Rio Puerco "the most grossly overgrazed watershed in the West." "New Lease on Life," 21.

46. Sheridan, *Desertification*, 13. See the discussion in chapter 5. See also Graf, *Wilderness Preservation*, 187, which describes the expansion of gullies and arroyos in New Mexico through the 1930s and the "similar conditions [e.g., erosion of slopes and stream channels, which] extended from Arizona to Montana and Colorado to California."

47. Sheridan, *Desertification*, 122.

48. E.g., GAO, *Comparison of Rangeland Condition Reports*; GAO, *BLM's Hot Desert Grazing Program*; GAO, *BLM's Range Improvement Project Data*. See also GAO, *Profile*.

49. See, e.g., GAO, *Declining and Overstocked Allotments*, 2–3; GAO, *Some Riparian Areas Restored*, 2–3; GAO, *BLM's Hot Desert Grazing Program*, 2–3. GAO, *Nevada Consulting Firm's Critique*, 14 (quotations). GAO, *BLM's Hot Desert Grazing Program*, 2–3.

50. BLM, *Management Plan for Afton Canyon*, 24, 33, 37.

51. See, e.g., NRC, *Developing Strategies*; Buchanan, *Rangelands*; Heitschmidt and Stuth, eds., *Grazing Management*; Vavra, Laycock, and Pieper, eds., *Ecological Implications*. Department of the Interior, BLM, *Rangeland Reform '94*.

52. Young, "Historical and Evolutionary Perspectives," 1, citing *The Western Range*. Wagner, "Changing Institutional Arrangements," 281. See also chapter 5.

53. Vavra, Laycock, and Pieper, "Introduction," in *Ecological Implications*, v. Cf. Pieper, "Ecological Implications," 192. Miller, Svejcar, and West, "Livestock Grazing," 131. Archer, "Woody Plant Encroachment," 13.

54. NRC, *Rangeland Health*, 1, 24–28.

55. Department of the Interior, *Rangeland Reform*; Department of the Interior, BLM, *Rangeland Reform '94: Executive Summary* (hereafter *Rangeland Reform Summary*). The draft reports were finalized later in 1994. The abstract of the Final Environmental Impact Statement (FEIS) indicates that it incorporates the DEIS except where otherwise noted. Differences between the two documents are summarized on page 2 of the FEIS. The data cited herein do not differ between draft and final. *Rangeland Reform Summary*, 1, 21 (emphasis added). See also Rangeland Reform, 3-29 to 3-32, discussing the myriad benefits of healthy riparian areas and wetlands, their current condition and trend, and the causes of this degradation; ibid., 3-42 to 3-47, describing wetland, riparian, and aquatic communities on federal lands and the effects of grazing thereon. *Rangeland Reform Summary*, 21. *Rangeland Reform*, 3–32 (emphasis added; citation omitted). *Rangeland Reform Summary*, 40.

56. Department of the Interior, *Rangeland Reform Summary*, 20. See also Miller, Svejcar, and West, "Livestock Grazing," 103. Department of the Interior, *Rangeland Reform Summary*, 27 (emphasis added).

57. Department of the Interior, *Rangeland Reform*, 3-26 to 3-28 (emphasis added). NRC, *Rangeland Health*, 5, 47 (emphasis added), 4. The committee's recommendations are examined in chapter 5.

58. Department of the Interior, *Rangeland Reform*, 3-27 (emphasis in original).

59. Department of the Interior, *Rangeland Reform*, 3-26 to 3-27. Department of the Interior, *Rangeland Reform Summary*, 29, 41 (quotation). "Preliminary Summary of Findings," I-B-2. See also Department of the Interior, *Rangeland Reform*, 3-36 to 3-38.

60. Department of the Interior, *Rangeland Reform Summary*, 29. Anadromous fish are those that are born in fresh water, spend a portion of their adult life in salt water, and then return to fresh water, usually their natal stream, to spawn. Ibid. See also Department of the Interior, *Rangeland Reform*, 4-29; Department of the Interior, *Rangeland Reform Summary*, 28, 31, 40; Department of the Interior, *Rangeland Reform*, 4-108 to 4-117. Under the Proposed Action, over the long term, 15 million acres of BLM uplands would remain in nonfunctioning condition, while an additional 6 million would be "functioning but susceptible to degradation." Ibid., 2-46 (table 2-9). Of the precious BLM riparian lands, 16 percent would remain nonfunctioning, and 41 percent would be "functioning but susceptible to degradation." Ibid., 2-47 (table 2-9).

61. Noss and Cooperrider, *Saving Nature's Legacy*, 250, quoting Keystone Center, *Final Consensus Report*. GAO, *Comparison of Rangeland Condition Reports*, 2. Noss and Cooperrider, *Saving Nature's Legacy*, 64.

62. See Pieper, "Ecological Implications," 202, citing Box and Sisson, "Public Ranges." Pieper, "Grazing Systems and Management," 21, citing later statement by Box. GAO, *Comparison of Rangeland Condition Reports*, 6, citing Box, "Rangelands," 113–18. Box, "American Rangeland," 1, 3. GAO, *Nevada Consulting Firm's Critique*, 13.

63. Pieper, "Ecological Implications," 202, citing Box and Sisson, "Public Ranges." Brunson and Steel, "National Public Attitudes," 77–78, citing Holechek, Pieper, and Herbel, *Range Management* (emphasis added).

64. Wagner, "Changing Institutional Arrangements," 284. Noss and Cooperrider, *Saving Nature's Legacy*, 250.

65. See Miller, Svejcar, and West, "Livestock Grazing," 101. See Heady, *Rangeland Management*, 55, 61, 114, 165, 181, 182, 241, showing a cow grazing in a southwestern desert.

66. Pieper, "Ecological Implications," 201 (emphasis added).

67. Ibid. (emphasis added).

68. Wagner, "Changing Institutional Arrangements," 284. Laycock, "Implications of Grazing," 263–64 (emphasis added). See the discussion in chapter 5 of Laycock's treatment of grazing's effects on biodiversity.

69. Laycock, "Implications of Grazing," 264. Noss, "Regional Landscape Approach," 701.

70. Jacobs, *Waste of the West*, is perhaps the most comprehensive source of information about public land grazing, compiled for the purpose of revealing its adverse environmental effects and its questionable economics. It contains hundreds of revealing photographs.

71. McConnell, *Private Power and American Democracy*, 205; Wyant, *Westward in Eden*, 137; Dana, *Forest and Range Policy*, 287. See also Libecap, *Locking Up the Range*, 60–61; Wyant, *Westward in Eden*, 137l; Klyza, *Who Controls Public Lands?* 145.

72. Gates, *History of Public Land Law*, 622. Muhn and Stuart, *Story of BLM*, 57 (quoting Foss), 226–27. Peffer, *Closing of the Public Domain*, 268. Comptroller General, *Rangelands Continue to Deteriorate*, v, 17–19.

73. Culhane describes the process of "adjudication." It began with "interim one year permits issued immediately after passage of the Taylor Act, often at pre-1934 use levels, transformed into permanent (though nominally ten-year) licenses." The process was not completed until 1967. Culhane, *Public Lands Politics*, 89–91; Carpenter, "Establishing Management." See also *Brooks v. Dewar*, 313 U.S. 354, 360 (1941), upholding the secretary's authority to issue temporary permits until "permanent permit" decisions could be made; *Public Lands Council v. Secretary of the Interior*, 929 F. Supp. 1436 (D. Wyo. 1996), *reversed in part and affirmed in part*, *Public Lands Council v. Babbitt*, 154F. 3d 1160 (10th Cir., 1998), noting the "lengthy adjudication process [that] took nearly 20 years to complete"; Comptroller General, *Rangelands Continue to Deteriorate*, i; Sheridan, *Desertification*, 17. See also Coggins and Lindeberg-Johnson, "Public Rangeland Management II," 58–59.

74. Coggins and Lindeberg-Johnson, "Public Rangeland Management II," 32. Clapp, "Major Range Problems," 9. Coggins, "'Devolution,'" 218. Vavra, Laycock, and Pieper, "Introduction," v. See also chapters 1 and 8.

75. NRC, *Land Use and Wildlife Resources*, 21. Roberts, "Integrated Part of Western Agriculture," 409–10. Pisani, *To Reclaim a Divided West*, 295.

76. Coggins and Lindeberg-Johnson, "Public Rangeland Management II," 32. Worster, *Under Western Skies*, 45, 49.

CHAPTER 4. THE POLITICAL AND CULTURAL LANDSCAPE

1. Clawson, *Western Range Livestock Industry*, 11, 4–6.

2. Ibid., 382. Culhane, *Public Lands Politics*, 160–61. See also chapter 8.

3. Clawson, *Western Range Livestock Industry*, 11. Klyza, *Who Controls Public Lands?* 126, 131. Foss, *Politics and Grass*, 198.

4. Clawson, *Western Range Livestock Industry*, 11. Gates, *History of Public Land Law*, 621. See Calef, *Private Grazing and Public Lands*, 212, 259–61.

5. West, "Power, Dependency, and Conflict Management," 1780. Calef, *Private Grazing and Public Lands*, 212, 259–61 (quotation on 260–61). Sheridan, *Desertification*, 117.

6. See, e.g., Voigt, *Public Grazing Lands*, 257; Rowley, *Forest Service Grazing*, 131; Klyza, *Who Controls Public Lands?* 135; Russell, *Kill the Cowboy*, 45–52, recounting Oman's story; "BLM Whistleblower"; Duerk, "BLM Manager in Wyoming," 3; Nokkentved, "Idaho Ranchers," 5.

7. Rowley, *Forest Service Grazing*, 174. Culhane, *Public Lands Politics*, 87. Gates, *History of Public Land Law*, 619. Rowley, *Forest Service Grazing*, 174, citing committee work files. Voigt, *Public Grazing Lands*, 276–77, 286–87 (quotation).

8. See Voigt, *Public Grazing Lands*, 83, 93–97. Robbins, *Our Landed Heritage*, 433–34, quoting *Denver Post*. Rowley, *Forest Service Grazing*, 204–9 (quotation on 209).

9. Voigt, *Public Grazing Lands*, 279–81 (quotation on 279), 286.

10. See Schlebecker, *Cattle Raising*, 102–3. Clawson, *Western Range Livestock Industry*, 11.

11. See *Public Lands News*, 26 October 1995, 4. The rescissions bill was passed as Public Law 104-19, on 27 July 1995.

12. S. 1459, 104th Cong. 2d Sess. (1996). *Public Lands News*, 2 October 1997; see also *Public Lands News*, 4 April 1996, 2 May 1996, 19 September 1996, 12 December 1996, 9 January 1997, and 13 November 1997.

13. S. 1459, § 101.

14. See S. 1459, §§ 104, 106, 111, 121–24, 131–32, 134–35.

15. S. 1459, §§ 161–64 (emphasis added).

16. S. 1459, § 106(c).

17. Clawson, *Western Range Livestock Industry*, 381–82. Adams, *Renewable Resource Policy*, 93. The Supreme Court ultimately upheld this authority under the Forest Service Organic Act of 1897, 16 U.S.C. § 551 (1994). See *Grimaud v. United States*, 220 U.S. 506 (1911); *United States v. Light*, 220 U.S. 523 (1911).

18. Calef, *Private Grazing and Public Lands*, 135, 140, 212, 259–61. Foss, *Politics and Grass*, 192.

19. Clawson, *Western Range Livestock Industry*, 12–13.

20. Ibid., 223. Foss, *Politics and Grass*, 198. Fairfax, "Coming of Age," 1721.

21. University of Idaho, *The Forage Resource*, S-35 to S-36. Smith and Martin, "Socioeconomic Behavior of Cattle Ranchers," 219. Calef, *Private Grazing and Public Lands*, 130.

22. McConnell, *Private Power and American Democracy*, 199–200 (emphasis in original).

23. Worster, *Under Western Skies*, 15. Coggins and Lindeberg-Johnson, "Public Rangeland Management II," 57. Five years later the administrative practice of establishing advisory boards was ratified by Congress. Act of 14 July 1939, 53 Stat. 1002. See Coggins and Lindeberg-Johnson, "Public Rangeland Management II," 57 n. 377, citing

Foss, *Politics and Grass*, 117; Peffer, *Closing of the Public Domain*, 230. A National Advisory Board Council was formed in 1940. Peffer, *Closing of the Public Domain*, 231. Sheridan, *Desertification*, 23. Merrill, "Private Spaces," 266 (emphasis added).

24. Foss, *Politics and Grass*, 137, 199–201, and chapter 6. Voigt, *Public Grazing Lands*, 244–45, 255. See also Peffer, *Closing of the Public Domain*, 229–31.

25. Merrill, "Private Spaces," 310, citing McConnell, *Private Power and American Democracy*; see also 266. Foss, *Politics and Grass*, 192. McConnell, *Private Power and American Democracy*, 204–5, citing Foss, *Politics and Grass*, 119. Clawson, *Western Range Livestock Industry*, 119.

26. Senate Committee, *Amending the Taylor Grazing Act*, 1–2 (letter from Interior Secretary Ickes). 43 U.S.C. § 315o-1. See also *Chournos v. United States*, 193 F. 2d 321, 323 (10th Cir. 1951), explaining that federal "officials, with the advice of an advisory board composed of permit holders within the district, shall exercise their judgment and discretion in granting permits, and determining the extent to which lands within the district shall be grazed." Foss, *Politics and Grass*, 198–200. See also Ferguson and Ferguson, *Sacred Cows*; Jacobs, *Waste of the West*; Merrill, "Private Spaces," 266; GAO, *Some Riparian Areas Restored*; GAO, *Management of Public Rangelands*, Testimony of James Duffus III; Calef, *Private Grazing and Public Lands*. Voigt, *Public Grazing Lands*, 255. See also Foss, *Politics and Grass*, chapter 8; ibid., 129–30. The NABC was not provided for by the 1939 amendment to the Taylor Act, but was organized by the district boards themselves in 1940 and was comprised of members elected by and from the district grazing boards. See Foss, *Politics and Grass*, 120–22. 43 U.S.C. § 315o-1(a).

27. Culhane, *Public Lands Politics*, 89–91.

28. Libecap, *Locking Up the Range*, 53–54.

29. Calef, *Private Grazing and Public Lands*, 77. McConnell, *Private Power and American Democracy*, 209–10, citing Calef, *Private Grazing and Public Lands*, 63.

30. Public Land Law Review Commission, *One Third of the Nation's Land* (hereafter PLLRC Report), 289.

31. Pub. L. 92-463, 86 Stat. 770, as amended, 5 U.S.C. app. 2 §§ 1–15 (1994). 5 U.S.C. app. 2 sec. 9 (emphasis added). Muhn and Stuart, *Story of BLM*, 205.

32. FLPMA § 309, 43 U.S.C. § 1739. Muhn and Stuart, *Story of BLM*, 205.

33. Klyza, *Who Controls Public Lands?* 134, quoting Gregg. *Natural Resources Defense Council v. Hodel*, 618 F. Supp. 848, 871 (E.D. Cal. 1985).

34. Culhane, *Public Lands Politics*, 30, 137, 138–41, 247–50.

35. Ibid., 257.

36. Ibid., 334, 344.

37. Ibid., 180, 333–34. Ample anecdotal and experiential evidence support a coincidence of interests between western county commissioners and the livestock business. Speaking to a reporter on condition of anonymity, a Catron County, New Mexico, businessperson recently asserted: "Our [county] commissioners don't give a shit about the local economy. The only thing they're interested in is making sure the cattle industry continues." Davis, "Catron County's Politics," 10. Stiles, "Utah County Sweeps Away."

38. Culhane, *Public Lands Politics*, 333–34, 229.

39. Ibid., 338–39.

40. Fairfax, "Coming of Age," 1727.

41. See, e.g., Foss, *Politics and Grass*, 198–200; Ferguson and Ferguson, *Sacred Cows*; Jacobs, *Waste of the West*; Merrill, "Private Spaces," 266; GAO, *Some Riparian Areas Restored*, 46–47; Calef, *Private Grazing and Public Lands*. GAO, *Management of Public Rangelands*, 5–6, testimony of James Duffus III. GAO, *Some Riparian Areas Restored*, 46–47.

42. Noss and Cooperrider, *Saving Nature's Legacy*, 77.

43. See Graf, *Wilderness Preservation*, 184. Where the designated sections were no longer available, states were allowed "in-lieu" selections. These are the selections to which Graf refers. Graf, *Wilderness Preservation*, 184, 230 (quotations), 249. Larson, *Wyoming*, 140. See also Scott, "Range Cattle Industry," 173. Krza, "While the New West Booms," 10.

44. Noss and Cooperrider, *Saving Nature's Legacy*, 74. Vileisis and Marston, "What Did the Land Look Like?" 14. Klyza, *Who Controls Public Lands?* 135. See *Public Lands News*, 12 December 1996, 12 December 1996, 9 January 1997, and 13 November 1997.

45. See Gillis, "Should Cows Chew Cheatgrass," 673; Sindelar, Montagne, and Kroos, "Holistic Resource Management," 45–46. Wuerthner, "Montana State University," 21. Savory's HRM methods are examined in chapter 5.

46. Chilson, "Did Ranchers Fire a University President?" 5; Ness, "You're Picking on Ranchers" (letter to editors), 9; Chilson, "Peter Chilson Responds," 9. Erik Ness, a spokesman for the New Mexico Livestock Board, criticized Chilson's article for inaccuracies. Chilson acknowledged errors concerning the respective positions and occupations of two persons mentioned in the article, but maintained that the gist of his story was accurate. He pointed to an article in the 19–25 June edition of the *Bulletin*, a Las Cruces, New Mexico, weekly newspaper, corroborating his account.

47. Minutes of the 28 October 1994 Meeting of the School of Environment and Natural Resources Citizens' Advisory Board, no pagination.

48. 501 F. Supp. 773, 777 (D. Mont. 1980). Deference to a party challenging agency action is directly contrary to the usual principle governing judicial review of administrative agency decisions. See generally Administrative Procedure Act, 5 U.S.C. § 706 (1994); Schwartz, *Administrative Law*, § 10.1.

49. *Natural Resources Defense Council v. Hodel*, 624 F. Supp. 1045 (D. Nev. 1985), *affirmed*, 819 F. 2d 927 (9th Cir. 1987).

50. 624 F. Supp. at 1052–53, 1056 n. 6, 1057 (emphasis in original). In contrast, *Seidman v. Gunzel*, No. CIV 94-2266 (D. Ariz., 16 January 1996), held that the Forest Service violated the National Environmental Policy Act by "failing to analyze a range of grazing rates" and that the agency "must consider alternate stocking rates as well as other uses of the habitat." See Zukoski, "Multiple Uses Must Be Considered," 14.

51. 624 F. Supp. at 1054–55 and n. 4, citing *Dahl v. Clark*, 600 F. Supp. 585, 590 (D. Nev. 1984) (emphasis added).

52. 624 F. Supp. at 1056–57. 43 U.S.C. § 1712(e). 43 U.S.C. § 1903(b). 624 F. Supp. at 1054, 1056.

53. Scott, "Range Cattle Industry," 170–71, citing constructions of the Unlawful Inclosures Act of 1885, 23 Stat. 321, by *Camfield v. United States*, 167 U.S. 518 (1897), and *Anthony Wilkinson Livestock Co. v. McIlquam*, 14 Wyo. 209, 83 Pac. 364 (1905). *United States v. Douglas-Willan Sartoris Co.*, 3 Wyo. 287, 22 Pac. 92 (1889).

54. *Public Lands Council v. Secretary of the Interior*, 929 F. Supp. 1436 (D. Wyo. 1996), *reversed in part and affirmed in part*, 154 F. 3d 1160 (10th Cir. 1998). The court's reluctant approval of some of the challenged rules is reflected in this comment: "Although the Court agrees that [the regulation's time limit on temporary nonuse] might be bad judgment, it cannot say that the Secretary's judgment was arbitrary and capricious." 929 F. Supp. at 1444. The court's comment about "preference" can be found at 929 F. Supp. at 1440. See Taylor Grazing Act § 3, 43 U.S.C. 315b.

55. 43 U.S.C. 315b (last sentence; emphasis added). FLPMA § 402(h), 43 U.S.C. § 1752(h). *Public Lands Council*, 929 F. Supp. at 1441.

56. FLPMA, 43 U.S.C. 1701–84. See FLPMA § 402(a), (g), 43 U.S.C. § 1752(a), (g); PRIA § 4(b), 43 U.S.C. § 1903(b). See 43 C.F.R. § 4110.4–2(a)(1) (1994). The court acknowledged 43 U.S.C. § 1712(e)(2) in the context of discussing the new regulations' provision for "conservation use permits," but wrongly suggested that it is the only mechanism by which the secretary can reduce grazing levels. See 929 F. Supp. at 1443–44. The relevant BLM regulations can be found at 43 C.F.R. §§ 4110.3, 4110.4–2(a)(2), 4110.4–2(a)(1) (1994).

57. *Public Lands Council v. Babbitt,* 154 F. 3d 1160, 1163, 1182.

58. Ibid., 1182–87. 43 U.S.C. § 315b. *Public Lands Council,* 154 F. 3d at 1171, 1178, 1171–72.

59. Ligorner, "Congressman Miller's Report," 30. Manning, "Mojave National Preserve," 13 (quotation). "Irony," 4. "Bill to Conduct Grazing Study," 12.

60. Comments by former BLM director Jim Baca at the Western Wyoming Congress, held in Rock Springs, Wyoming, 25 April 1996.

61. Power, *Lost Landscapes and Failed Economies*, 189–90. McGerr, "Is There a Twentieth-Century West?" 255, quoting Donald Worster. Box, "American Range-land," 3. NRC, *Rangeland Health*, 18. Noss and Cooperrider, *Saving Nature's Legacy*, 231, 220, citing Andy Kerr, of the Oregon Natural Resources Council. Worster, *Under Western Skies*, 34.

62. Pelzer, *Cattlemen's Frontier*, 248, quoting Roosevelt, *Ranch-Life and the Hunting Trail*, 104. Merrill, "Private Spaces," 86–89, quoting Roosevelt, *Ranch-Life and the Hunting Trail*.

63. Merrill, "Private Spaces," 89–91, quoting Roosevelt, *Ranch-Life and the Hunting Trail*, 97. Compare Power, *Lost Landscapes*, 190. See chapter 1's discussion of the view of ranching as separate from agriculture.

64. Webb, *The Great Plains*, 248, 505–6. Morrissey, "Engendering the West," 133.

65. See generally Larson, *Wyoming*, 76–107 (chapter 3, "The Equality State").

66. Webb, *The Great Plains*, 230, 233.

67. Ibid., 244–45.

68. Ibid., 244–47.

69. Larson, *Wyoming*, 122. Webb, *The Great Plains*, 245–46. Larson, *Wyoming*, 121.

70. Webb, *The Great Plains*, 245–46.

71. Ibid., 491, 495–96 (emphasis added).

72. See Graf, *Wilderness Preservation*, 191–93. Cronon, *Nature's Metropolis*, 219. See Wolf, "'Wyoming' Is Dead," 114–18.

73. Graf, *Wilderness Preservation*, 193.

74. Jones, "Roundup," 48–53.

75. See ibid., 50, 52; Graf, *Wilderness Preservation*, 78. Worster, *Under Western Skies*, 235.

76. Cronon, *Nature's Metropolis*, 219–20. Power, *Lost Landscapes*, 190.

77. Graf, *Wilderness Preservation*, 190, 120.

78. Worster, *Under Western Skies*, 51.

79. Graf, *Wilderness Preservation*, 120.

80. Ibid., 120, 262–63, 190. Schlebecker, *Cattle Raising*, 102–3, 240–41.

81. Hess and Holechek, "If Rain Doesn't Fall," 20. Public Law 127, § 171(b), 104th Cong., 2d session, 4 April 1996. Hess and Holechek, "Ranchers Forced," 20.

82. Graf, *Wilderness Preservation*, 190. Leshy, "Sharing Federal Multiple-Use Lands," 270.

83. Davis, "Catron County's Politics," 8, 9.

84. Abbey, "Even the Bad Guys," 51. Leshy, "Sharing Federal Multiple-Use Lands," 270, citing Will. Margolis, "Waaaaaaaaaaaaaah!" 16.

85. Nelson, "Ideology and Public Land Policy," 287. Rowley, *Forest Service Grazing*, 131, 205 (citing DeVoto).

86. "County Officials Formally Protest," B1. Ironically, the Big Horn Basin is the most arid part of Wyoming and thus the portion least suited to livestock grazing. Box, "American Rangeland," 2. Larson, *Wyoming*, 140.

87. Fabian, "History for the Masses," 227, 235–36.

88. Miller, "Economics of 'Old West' Fading," 8A, quoting Power, *Lost Landscapes*.

89. Krza, "While the New West Booms," 10. Quillen, "The Mountain West," 8–9.

90. Quillen, "The Mountain West," 9. See Williams and Lyon, "Open Letter," quoting Hatch. Quillen defines the Mountain West as Arizona, Colorado, Idaho, Montana, Nevada, New Mexico, Utah, and Wyoming. Ibid., 8. How significant politically is this Republican Mountain West? Jimmy Carter demonstrated that a "Democrat can take the White House without carrying a single state in the Mountain West. . . . California alone has 54 electoral votes, while the entire Mountain West has only 40." Ibid.

91. Larson, *Wyoming*, 140.

92. Malone, "Jeffersonian Ideal," 46. Clawson, *Federal Lands Revisited*, 132. See Donahue, "Untapped Power," 290 n. 474, citing laws containing exemptions for agriculture.

93. Malone, "Jeffersonian Ideal," 46. See discussion in chapter 1 on the agriculture/ranching, home-building/business dichotomy. Clawson, *Federal Lands Revisited*, 132. Charles Dana, quoted in Worster, *Nature's Economy*, 227; Dana coined the phrase "rain follows the plow."

94. Webb, *The Great Plains*, 502. McClure, "Address," 39. Adams, *Renewable Resource Policy*, 499, quoting Reagan.

95. Graf, *Wilderness Preservation*, 230; see also ibid., 238–39.

96. Wilkinson, "Utah Ushers Its Frogs," 13, quoting Peter Hovingh, Salt Lake City chemist and naturalist.

97. "Hansen and Cannon," 11, quoting, first, Cannon and, second, *Deseret News* editorial; Margolis, "Utah's Bumbling," 5.

98. Quinn, "Religion in the American West," 160–61, citing Stark's remarks at the annual meeting of the Society for the Scientific Study of Religion, Salt Lake City, 27 October 1989. Kellert, *Attitudes—III*, 107.

99. See Quinn, "Religion in the American West," 159. Nash, *Rights of Nature*, 88, describing White, "Historical Roots." Ibid., 88–89, quoting Genesis 1:27–28; 89, citing Genesis 9:2–3, 8.

100. Nash, *Rights of Nature*, 89–91, quoting White, "Historical Roots," 1205.

101. Smith, "Evangelical Christians" (quotations). Baker, "Reverent Approach to the Natural World," 475–78. Smith, "Evangelical Christians," quoting Limbaugh.

102. Nash, *Rights of Nature*, 91, quoting White, "Historical Roots," 1205. See Worster, *Nature's Economy*, 217–18, discussing Clements's theories. Nash, *Rights of Nature*, 117–18, quoting Standing Bear, *Land of the Spotted Eagle*, 193.

103. See Gen. 1:26, 28 (New American Bible, 1971). Worster, *Under Western Skies*, 235. A recent exposé of the Wise Use Movement included a photograph of a handmade sign, containing the subtitle "Our Community Depends on Timber," below its principal message: "Look! At the *spotted owl* of the air, they neither sow or reap or gather into barns. Our heavenly father feed's [*sic*] them. Are we his people not much better than they? Matthew 6:26." Brick, "Determined Opposition," 16–17 (emphasis in original). Riebsame, "Ending the Range Wars?" 9. See also Hage, *Storm over Rangelands*, 231–32. Worster, *Nature's Economy*, 238. Riebsame, "Ending the Range Wars?" 9.

104. Koppes, "Efficiency, Equity, Esthetics," 231. Limerick, *Deserts*, 41.

105. Hays, "Public Values," 1831. See Kellert, *Attitudes—I, Activities—II, Attitudes—III*. The survey was scientifically designed and conducted and consisted of more than 3,000 randomly selected respondents who were interviewed by telephone and asked dozens of standardized questions. Analysis of the sample showed that it reflected well the demographics of the American population. Kellert, *Attitudes—I*, 9, 12.

106. Kellert, *Activities—II*, 21.

107. Respondents' attitudes toward wildlife were identified on the basis of 65 survey questions. "Attitude scales were based on a typology of nine basic attitudes toward wildlife and the natural world." These attitudes were labeled naturalistic, ecologistic, humanistic, moralistic, scientistic, aesthetic, utilitarian, dominionistic, and negativistic. Kellert, *Activities—II*, 4–5. See also Kellert, *Attitudes—III*, 44, summarizing the common behavioral expressions and most related values/benefits associated with each attitude, as well as the estimated percent of the population strongly oriented toward each.

108. Kellert, *Attitudes—I*, 36–37. See also Kellert, *Attitudes—III*, 108.

109. Kellert, *Attitudes—I*, 63.

110. Ibid., 36–37.

111. Kellert, *Attitudes—III*, 102, 107.

112. See Quinn, "Religion in the American West," 165–66 (quotation). Rowley, *Forest Service Grazing*, 205. See Williams and Lyon, "Open Letter," citing a presentation

by "Apostle Orson Hyde, one of the 13 leaders of the Mormon Church," to the General Conference on 7 October 1865. As noted in chapter 3, Utah's overgrazing problem in the early 1900s was among the worst in the West. See Rowley, *Forest Service Grazing*, 180–81.

113. Merrill, "Private Spaces," 85 (quoting an 1887 Laramie, Wyoming, newspaper editorial), 94 n. 46 (quoting Warren, in 1905 ANLSA proceedings, 340), 86 (quoting Roosevelt, *Ranch-Life and the Hunting Trail*, 2).

114. McConnell, *Private Power and American Democracy*, 202. Gates, *History of Public Land Law*, 628, citing articles by DeVoto.

115. Scott, "Range Cattle Industry," 166, 171–74. Larson, *Wyoming*, 132–34, 129. See also Pelzer, *Cattlemen's Frontier*, 188–89.

116. See Seigel, "A Lone Ranger"; Richardson, "No-Nonsense Idaho Sheriff"; Larsen, "The Revolt of the West." *Public Lands News*, 11 May 1995, 3.

117. See generally Echeverria and Eby, eds., *Let the People Judge*; Hungerford, "'Custom and Culture' Ordinances"; Lavelle, "'Wise Use' Movement Grows"; Reed, "The County Supremacy Movement." Marston, "Coming into a New Land," 170, reporting an interview with Clive Kincaid, active in the Utah conservation movement in the early 1980s. Marston also reports that actor/director/Utah resident Robert Redford was burned in effigy in Kanab, Utah, for publicly opposing development of the proposed Kaiparowits coal mine and power plant near Canyonlands and Capitol Reef National Parks. Ibid., 172.

118. Russell, *Kill the Cowboy*, 16–20, 45–52. Margolis, "Waaaaaaaaaaaaah!" 16.

119. Coppelman, "Federal Government Response," 33, 79. *Public Lands News*, 14 September 1995, 8, citing an internal BLM memo.

120. *Public Lands News* 11, May 1995, 1–2, quoting the Associated Press, quoting Craig and Baca.

121. Worster, *Nature's Economy*, 264. Margolis, "Waaaaaaaaaaaaah!" 16.

122. Adams, *Renewable Resource Policy*, 243. Merrill, "Private Spaces," 174, quoting Warner, "Elk and Game Wardens," 31.

123. See Adams, *Renewable Resource Policy*.

124. Ibid., 244, quoting 46 Stat. 1468. Merrill, "Private Spaces," 174–75.

125. Adams, *Renewable Resource Policy*, 243–44, 247, citing Council on Environmental Quality. See also Malone, "Reflections on the Jeffersonian Ideal," 46.

126. Long, "Vanishing Prairie Dog," 118.

127. See Kellert, *Attitudes—I*, 46–48.

128. Ibid., 49–51.

129. Ibid., 52, 61.

130. Ibid., 63. Kellert, *Activities—II*, 121–22. Mixed results were obtained on a question concerning competition for forage among cattle, bighorn sheep, wild horses, and other wildlife. More than half of association members favored reducing native wildlife and wild horses but not livestock. But 42 percent favored reducing wild horses and cattle to protect native wildlife. "Only 3% favored limiting wildlife and livestock to assist wild horses." Kellert, *Activities—II*, 121.

131. Kellert, *Attitudes—I*, 63.

132. See, e.g., Ferguson and Ferguson, *Sacred Cows*, 223. The National Cattlemen's slogan was heard on National Public Radio in 1996. Micheli, "Response to 'Role

of Land Treatments,'" 1422, 1424. Micheli also stated that "the nation's cattlemen desire to be better understood." Ibid., 1424.

133. Micheli, "Response to 'Role of Land Treatments,' " 1422, 1424. Nielsen, "Economic Factors," 1379. Kellert, *Attitudes III*, 108.

134. Long, "Vanishing Prairie Dog," 124, quoting rancher Kruse. Ferguson and Ferguson, *Sacred Cows*, 223.

135. Worster, *Nature's Economy*, 264–65. Rea, "Predator 'Problem,'" B1, quoting Cubin.

136. Graf, *Wilderness Preservation*, 185–86, 230, 248–49, noting that 80 to 90 percent of Arizonans were urban residents by 1980.

137. Ibid., 120, 262. Fabian, "History for the Masses," 227, 234, citing Slotkin.

138. Fabian, "History for the Masses," 234. Worster, *Under Western Skies*, 52, 37.

CHAPTER 5. THE ECOLOGICAL LANDSCAPE

1. Worster, *Under Western Skies*, 45. Noss and Cooperrider, *Saving Nature's Legacy*, 231.

2. Noss and Cooperrider, *Saving Nature's Legacy*, 74. Fleischner, "Ecological Costs," 629, 638. Stoddart and Smith, *Range Management*, 2, quoted in Nelson, "Economic Analysis," 49. Stoddart, Smith, and Box, *Range Management*, 90, quoted in Noss and Cooperrider, *Saving Nature's Legacy*, 74. Holechek, Pieper, and Herbel, *Range Management*, 134.

3. Noss and Cooperrider, *Saving Nature's Legacy*, 252. Miller, Svejcar, and West, "Livestock Grazing," 128. Eckert and Spencer, "Vegetation Response on Allotments," quoted in Miller, Svejcar, and West, "Livestock Grazing," 128, 132 (quotation). Noss, "Cows and Conservation Biology," 614 (quotation). Noss, "Guidelines for Biodiversity Management."

4. Fleischner, "Ecological Costs," 629. Noss and Cooperrider, *Saving Nature's Legacy*, 221, 258. See also generally Lauenroth et al., "Effects of Grazing on Ecosystems," 69. Noss and Cooperrider, *Saving Nature's Legacy*, 230 (citations omitted; emphasis added).

5. Fleischner, "Ecological Costs," 638, quoting Smith, "Conclusions," 117–18. NRC, *Land Use and Wildlife Resources*, 108. Leopold, *Sand County Almanac*, 199, from the essay "The Round River." Worster, *Under Western Skies*, 45.

6. Godron and Forman, "Landscape Modification," 20 (quotation). Fleischner, "Ecological Costs," 637. See also Horning, *Grazing to Extinction*; Tausch et al., "Differential Establishment," 252–53; Wuerthner, "Living behind the Bovine Curtain," 16; Jacobs, *Waste of the West*. Dwyer, Buckhouse, and Huey, "Impacts of Grazing Intensity," 874. Smeins, "Concepts for Solving Biodiversity Problems."

7. Miller, Svejcar, and West, "Livestock Grazing," 101 (quotation), 129–33. See, e.g., Archer, "Woody Plant Encroachment," 13, Pieper, "Ecological Implications," 193; Perry and Borchers, "Climate Change," 308.

8. See Flader and Callicott, *River of the Mother of God*, 91–92, 183, 309 (compiling essays by Leopold). Laycock, "Stable States," 432.

9. Noss and Cooperrider, *Saving Nature's Legacy*, 237–40 (table 7.1), 243–46 (including table 7.2). See also generally *The Western Range*.

10. Noss, "Issues of Scale," 244. Bazzaz, "Characteristics of Populations," 272. Hobbs and Huenneke, "Disturbance, Diversity, and Invasion," 326, 328. Noss and Cooperrider, *Saving Nature's Legacy*, 237.

11. Noss and Cooperrider, *Saving Nature's Legacy*, 224. Archer and Smeins, "Ecosystem-Level Processes," 115, 121. Low and Berlin, "Natural Selection," 1203.

12. Miller, Svejcar, and West, "Livestock Grazing," 127 (emphasis added). See Wagner, "Livestock Grazing," 141; Ferguson and Ferguson, *Sacred Cows*, 115–16.

13. See Noss, "Cows and Conservation Biology," 613; Fleischner, "Ecological Costs," 630–31; "Impacts of Grazing Intensity," 867–1166 (part 3 of *Developing Strategies*).

14. The first quotation is from Belsky, Letter, 31. See also Dwyer, Buckhouse, and Huey, "Impacts of Grazing Intensity," 871–72, 880; GAO, *Some Riparian Areas Restored*; Barth and McCullough, *Grazing Impacts on Riparian Areas*; Elmore and Kauffman, "Riparian and Watershed Systems," 212; Fleischner, "Ecological Costs," 635–36; Low and Berlin, "Natural Selection," 1204. Fleischner, "Ecological Costs," 631.

15. Hobbs and Huenneke, "Disturbance, Diversity, and Invasion," 325 (citation omitted), 329. Noss and Cooperrider, *Saving Nature's Legacy*, 246. Laycock, "Grazing vs. No Grazing," 260. Rosentreter, "Displacement of Rare Plants," 174. See also Harvey, "Aliens among Us," 4–5.

16. Low and Berlin, "Natural Selection," 1217. See Hewlett, "No Easy Answer," 20.

17. Noss and Cooperrider, *Saving Nature's Legacy*, 237, 261, 246–47. Young and Evans, "Plant Manipulation," 63.

18. Noss and Cooperrider, *Saving Nature's Legacy*, 247. We have actively perpetuated some of these altered ecosystems by introducing other exotics to make use of the initial invader, such as chukar partridge (*Alectoris chukar*) in cheatgrass-dominated areas or ring-necked pheasants (*Phasianus colchicus*) in agricultural areas. See also Monsen and Kitchen, *Proceedings—Ecology and Management*, preface inside front cover.

19. Stutz, "Evolution of Weedy Annuals," 9–10. See also Whitson, *Weeds and Poisonous Plants*. Whitson adopts J. M. Torell's decidedly nonecological definition of a weed: "A plant that interferes with management objectives for a given area of land at a given point in time." Ibid., v. See also Antognini, "Implementing Effective Noxious Weed Control," noting that the USDA's Animal and Plant Health Inspection Service (APHIS) maintains a list of noxious weeds and that states have their own lists.

20. Allen, "Restoration Ecology," 7–8. Rosentreter, "Displacement of Rare Plants," 170–74 (citations omitted).

21. Noss and Cooperrider, *Saving Nature's Legacy*, 255, 261. U.S. Department of the Interior, *Rangeland Reform*, 3–51. Gillis, "Should Cows Chew Cheatgrass," 674.

22. Billings, *"Bromus tectorum,"* 301, 307 (citing studies by Mack), 307–8 (quoting Leopold). Billings cited historical data from two surveys by P. B. Kennedy. The first, in 1902, discovered no cheatgrass and no evidence of burns along a 55-mile transect in northeastern Nevada; the second, conducted fifty years later along the same transect, found cheatgrass everywhere and evidence of seventeen burned areas. Ibid., 308. Allen, "Restoration Ecology," 10. Noss and Cooperrider, *Saving Nature's Legacy*, 255. Davidson et al., "Selecting Wilderness Areas," 95, 111–12. See also Tausch et al., "Differential Establishment," 252 (citations omitted); Vail, "Symposium Introduction," 3.

23. Billings, *"Bromus tectorum,"* 320. Vail, "Symposium Introduction," 3, citing statistics showing a cheatgrass monoculture on 1.1 million acres, a cheatgrass under-story on 1.8 million acres, and an additional 1.3 million acres with "strong cheatgrass potential." Allen, "Restoration Ecology," 10. Sanders, "Can Annual Rangelands Be Converted," 412; Rosentreter, "Displacement of Rare Plants," 170. Young and Evans, "Plant Manipulation," 60. Davidson et al., "Selecting Wilderness Areas," 111–12, noting that cheatgrass can easily jeopardize threatened or endangered native plant species. See Hironaka, "Medusahead," 89. Vail, "Symposium Introduction," 4.

24. Young and Evans, "Plant Manipulation," 63. Vail, "Symposium Introduc-tion," 3. See Calef, *Private Grazing,* 240–47. See Young and Evans, "Grand Experi-ment," 63.

25. BLM, *Management Plan for Afton Canyon,* 33. Forsling, "Grazing Lands Must Be Restored," 59.

26. Fleischner, "Ecological Costs." Dwyer, Buckhouse, and Huey, "Impacts of Grazing Intensity," 872. Severson and Urness, "Livestock Grazing: A Tool," 243; see also Lauenroth et al., "Effects of Grazing," 91. U.S. Department of the Interior, *Range-land Reform,* 3-47.

27. See Dwyer, Buckhouse, and Huey, "Impacts of Grazing Intensity," 874. Noss and Cooperrider, *Saving Nature's Legacy,* 236.

28. Dwyer, Buckhouse, and Huey, "Impacts of Grazing Intensity," 873–74, 881. See Noss and Cooperrider, *Saving Nature's Legacy,* 236; Fleischner, "Ecological Costs," 636.

29. See Noss and Cooperrider, *Saving Nature's Legacy,* 236. Russell, *Kill the Cow-boy,* 85, citing biologist and professional environmentalist Steve Johnson. Manning, "Mojave National Preserve," 13. Doyle, "Ranchers Agree to Limit Grazing," A13. West, "Biodiversity of Rangelands," 8.

30. Dwyer, Buckhouse, and Huey, "Impacts of Grazing Intensity," 873, 881. Noss and Cooperrider, *Saving Nature's Legacy,* 236; Fleischner, "Ecological Costs," 636. Wagner, "Livestock Grazing," 123. See West, "Biodiversity of Rangelands," 8; Wyoming Conservation Congress, April 1996, presentation by Colorado upland game bird researcher Dr. Clait Braun; Noss, "Cows and Conservation Biology," 613–14; Wagner, "Livestock Grazing," 123, 125. Noss and Cooperrider, *Saving Nature's Legacy,* 236. Severson and Urness, "Livestock Grazing: A Tool," 243.

31. Noss and Cooperrider, *Saving Nature's Legacy,* 237 (quotations), 256–57. USDA, Forest Service, *Biological Diversity Assessment,* 13 (quotation).

32. See generally Keiter and Froelicher, "Bison, Brucellosis, and Law." Much of the scientific research has been done by Yellowstone park biologist Mary Meagher. See, e.g., Meagher and Meyer, "On the Origin of Brucellosis." See also Aguirre and Starkey, "Wildlife Disease in U.S. National Parks" (regarding bovine brucellosis and lungworm-pneumonia in bighorn).

33. See generally Donahue, "Untapped Power," 278–82, summarizing impacts, particularly on water quality, and citing sources; Dwyer, Buckhouse, and Huey, "Impacts of Grazing Intensity," 881, citing "increasing evidence . . . that herded sheep are much less detrimental to riparian zones than are traditionally managed cattle." See Barth and McCullough, *Grazing Impacts on Riparian Areas,* 115–16; Fleischner, "Ecological Costs,"

633–34; Elmore and Kauffman, "Riparian and Watershed Systems." Barth and McCullough, *Grazing Impacts on Riparian Areas*, 127 (citations omitted). "Listing Actions," 24 (*ciénega* is a Spanish word for a "distinctive type of marshy, mid-elevation community that is often surrounded by an arid environment").

34. St. Clair and Johansen, "Introduction," 1–2. See generally "Symposium on Soil Crust Communities." Davidson et al., "Selecting Wilderness Areas," 110–11; Belnap, "Potential Role of Cryptobiotic Soil Crusts," 184. See also Miller, Svejcar, and West, "Livestock Grazing," 116–17; Fleischner, "Ecological Costs," 633.

35. St. Clair and Johansen, "Introduction," 2, also noting that range scientist "[Neil] West has questioned the ecological value of microbiotic crusts and has called for more rigorous studies." Davidson et al., "Selecting Wilderness Areas," 111. Belnap, "Potential Role of Cryptobiotic Soil Crusts," 179.

36. U.S. Department of the Interior, *Rangeland Reform*, 3-51 to 3-52. Dwyer, Buckhouse, and Huey, "Impacts of Grazing Intensity," 874. Miller, Svejcar, and West, "Livestock Grazing," 101–33. Dwyer, Buckhouse, and Huey, "Impacts of Grazing Intensity," 867, 870–71, enumerating impacts of grazing on hydrologic properties of watersheds. Chapin, "Patterns of Nutrient Absorption," 175. Barth and McCullough, *Grazing Impacts on Riparian Areas*, 122, 125, 129. Dwyer, Buckhouse, and Huey, "Impacts of Grazing Intensity," 872–73.

37. Severson and Urness, "Livestock Grazing: A Tool," 242–43. Flader and Callicott, *River of the Mother of God*, 309 (Leopold essay). Dwyer, Buckhouse, and Huey, "Impacts of Grazing Intensity," 872–73.

38. See NRC, *Rangeland Health*, 92–93. Hobbs and Huenneke, "Disturbance, Diversity, and Invasion," 326. Dwyer, Buckhouse, and Huey, "Impacts of Grazing Intensity," 874.

39. Perry and Borchers, "Climate Change," 308. See also NRC, *Rangeland Health*, 101, noting studies showing that "wild and domestic grazing animals can influence soil processes"; Odum, *Fundamentals of Ecology*, 33, 96–98, 371–72.

40. See, e.g., Noss and Cooperrider, *Saving Nature's Legacy*, 24; Herbel, "Manipulative Range Improvements," 1172–73.

41. Wagner, "Livestock Grazing," 129. Dwyer, Buckhouse, and Huey, "Impacts of Grazing Intensity," 875.

42. Archer and Smeins, "Ecosystem-Level Processes," 115. See *United States ex rel. Bergen v. Lawrence*, 620 F. Supp. 1414 (D. Wyo. 1985), *affirmed*, 848 F.2d 1502 (10th Cir. 1988). See Noss and Cooperrider, *Saving Nature's Legacy*, 241. U.S. Department of the Interior, *Rangeland Reform*, 4–30.

43. Noss and Cooperrider, *Saving Nature's Legacy*, 241, 246. Braun, "Emerging Limits," 71 n. 88. Low and Berlin, "Natural Selection," 1204.

44. Wilkinson, *Crossing the Next Meridian*, 261. According to the U.S. Geological Survey, irrigation accounts for 93.3 percent of consumptive water use in Colorado. Internet source: www.cnr.colostate.edu/CWK/use_colo.htm. Pisani, *To Reclaim a Divided West*, 230. Reisner, "Next Water War," 98.

45. Leopold, *Game Management*, quoted in Adams, *Renewable Resource Policy*, 244. Flader and Callicott, *River of the Mother of God*, 309 (Leopold essay). See Adams, *Renewable Resource Policy*, 243–44, 247.

46. West, "Biodiversity of Rangelands," 8. See, e.g., "These Guns for Hire," 18, reporting ADC statistics. Long, "Vanishing Prairie Dog," 120. Campbell and Clark, "Colony Characteristics," 274–75.

47. See, e.g., Long, "Vanishing Prairie Dog," 118, 124. See also Knowles, "Some Relationships of Black-Tailed Prairie Dogs," 198, 201–2. Severson and Urness, "Livestock Grazing: A Tool," 241. Long, "Vanishing Prairie Dog," 124, noting that South Dakota has labeled the prairie dog a "noxious pest." Miller, Ceballos, and Reading, "Prairie Dog and Biotic Diversity," 677, 678. Campbell and Clark, "Colony Characteristics," 275, citing unpublished BLM documents. Clark et al., "Prairie Dog Colony Attributes," 580–81 (citations omitted). Clark et al. noted that sharp-tailed and sage grouse may strut on colonies (ibid.). Madson, "Dog Days," 8, 10.

48. Long, "Vanishing Prairie Dog," 118, 124. Long reported that "prairie dogs eat as much as 7 percent of a ranch's forage." Ibid., 124. Severson and Urness, "Livestock Grazing: A Tool," 241. Knowles, "Some Relationships of Black-Tailed Prairie Dogs," 198, 201–2.

49. Nielsen, "Economic Factors," 1373, 1380.

50. Herbel, "Manipulative Range Improvements," 1168–71.

51. Noss and Cooperrider, *Saving Nature's Legacy*, 260. See Wagner, "Livestock Grazing," 128–29. Pieper, "Grazing Systems and Management," 14. Young and Evans, "Plant Manipulation," 61.

52. Noss and Cooperrider, *Saving Nature's Legacy*, 260. Nielsen, for instance, writes: "Vegetative manipulations as extreme as converting sagebrush to crested wheatgrass have some positive wildlife benefits." Nielsen, "Economic Factors," 1378. But he offers no specific example or authority. Flinders, "Essential Habitat for Wildlife," 51. NRC, *Land Use and Wildlife Resources*, 117 (citations omitted).

53. Wyoming Conservation Congress, 26 April 1996, presentation of Dr. Clait E. Braun. Noss, "Cows and Conservation Biology," 613–14. See also Wagner, "Livestock Grazing," 125. Downs, Rickard, and Cadwell, "Restoration of Big Sagebrush," 74 (quotation). See also Rosentreter, "Displacement of Rare Plants," 174.

54. Nielsen, "Economic Factors," 1378.

55. Miller, Svejcar, and West, "Livestock Grazing," 112. Wagner, "Livestock Grazing," 131. Noss and Cooperrider, *Saving Nature's Legacy*, 260.

56. See, e.g., Fleischner, "Ecological Costs," 637; Miller, Svejcar, and West, "Livestock Grazing," 101; Archer, "Woody Plant Encroachment," 13. See Brandt and Rickard, "Alien Taxa," 104; Vail, "Symposium Introduction," 3. Noss and Cooperrider, *Saving Nature's Legacy*, 230. Pieper, "Grazing Systems," 11 (citation omitted).

57. Herbel, "Manipulative Range Improvements," 1169. Dwyer, Buckhouse, and Huey, "Impacts of Grazing Intensity," 868. Fleischner, "Ecological Costs," 637, citing Bahre, *A Legacy of Change* (emphasis added). See also Donart, "History and Evolution," 1250, regarding increasing aridity of western ranges since the Paleocene.

58. Worster, *Nature's Economy*, 214, 211.

59. Noss and Cooperrider, *Saving Nature's Legacy*, 221 (quotations). See also Gillis, "Should Cows Chew Cheatgrass," 672; Pieper, "Ecological Implications," 192; Dwyer, Buckhouse, and Huey, "Impacts of Grazing Intensity," 867. Perry and Borchers, "Climate Change," 308.

60. Webb, *The Great Plains*, 245. Noss and Cooperrider, *Saving Nature's Legacy*, 240. See also Fleischner, "Ecological Costs," 637. U.S. Department of the Interior, *Rangeland Reform*, 3–41.

61. See Whittaker, *Communities and Ecosystems*, 77–87.

62. Noss and Cooperrider, *Saving Nature's Legacy*, 240 (citations omitted). See also Cronon, *Nature's Metropolis*, 221.

63. Noss and Cooperrider, *Saving Nature's Legacy*, 240–41 (citations omitted). Pelzer's simple observation that bison and other plains animals "escaped the wholesale tragedies" of cattle herds during the 1880s winters is testament to the divergent habits and adaptations of cattle and native species. Pelzer, *Cattlemen's Frontier*, 148.

64. Miller, Svejcar, and West, "Livestock Grazing," 111, 102, citing skeletal evidence that an isolated herd of bison in eastern Oregon were inbred. Van Vuren, "Bison West of the Rocky Mountains," 65, 67. Van Vuren and Deitz, "Evidence of *Bison bison*," 319, citing the discovery of one female bison skull and explaining that females were gregarious and did not wander widely as males do. Fleischner, "Ecological Costs," 637.

65. Pieper, "Ecological Implications," 185–86 (citations omitted). Pieper, "Grazing Systems and Management," 9–11, noting also that bison diets differ from those of the pronghorn antelope, which has "occupied diverse habitats and exhibited broad selectivity of food items" throughout its historical range in central and western North America. Lauenroth et al., "Effects of Grazing," 88.

66. Fleischner, "Ecological Costs," 637.

67. Noss and Cooperrider, *Saving Nature's Legacy*, 241 (citations omitted).

68. Fleischner, "Ecological Costs," 637. U.S. Department of the Interior, *Rangeland Reform*, 3–47 (citation omitted). See also generally Dwyer, Buckhouse, and Huey, "Impacts of Grazing Intensity," 874. Lauenroth et al., "Effects of Grazing," 82, 88. Fleischner, "Ecological Costs," 637, quoting Bahre, *Legacy of Change*.

69. Archer and Smeins, "Ecosystem-Level Processes," 113–15, 121.

70. Pieper, "Ecological Implications," 177 (emphasis added), 185–86 (citations omitted). Pieper used the Chihuahuan Desert as an example.

71. See, e.g., Fowler and MacMahon, "Selective Extinction."

72. Wagner, "Livestock Grazing," 121–24. See also Murie, *Elk of North America*, 296–300. Wagner, "Livestock Grazing," 123.

73. Wagner, "Livestock Grazing," 128.

74. Noss and Cooperrider, *Saving Nature's Legacy*, 226.

75. Laycock, "Grazing vs. No Grazing," 260. University of Idaho, *The Forage Resource*.

76. Miller, Svejcar, and West, "Livestock Grazing," 128. Dwyer, Buckhouse, and Huey, "Impacts of Grazing Intensity," 880. Rowley, *Forest Service Grazing*, 77. See also Heady, *Rangeland Management*, 183. The state of Wyoming either does not regulate salt placement or, if it has such a rule, does not enforce it. On state land leased for grazing in southeastern Wyoming, I have seen salt placed in the middle of a much-overused riparian meadow, about thirty feet from the edge of the stream.

77. Pieper, "Ecological Implications," 184 (citations omitted). See Noss and Cooperrider, *Saving Nature's Legacy*, 225.

78. Belsky, "Does Herbivory Benefit Plants?" 886–87. See also Pieper, "Ecological Implications," 184, quoting Belsky; Verkaar, "When Does Grazing Benefit Plants?" (concurring with Belsky's conclusions).

79. Heady, "Summary: Ecological Implications," 291. Dwyer, Buckhouse, and Huey, "Impacts of Grazing Intensity," 871. Low and Berlin, "Natural Selection," 1213–14, 1204.

80. Gillis, "Should Cows Chew Cheatgrass," 674.

81. See, e.g., Laycock, "Grazing vs. No Grazing," 50; U.S. Department of the Interior, *Rangeland Reform Summary*, 21; GAO, *Some Riparian Areas Restored*.

82. Pieper, "Ecological Implications," 184 (emphasis added). Severson and Urness, "Livestock Grazing: A Tool," 233, 242, 245.

83. Lamotte, "Characteristics of Energy Flows," 57. Lamotte noted the difficulty of drawing "clear conclusions on how grazing affects [primary] production." Ibid. Pieper, "Ecological Implications," 183, 184 (citations omitted). See generally Low and Berlin, "Natural Selection." Crawley summarized some of the various opinions on the subject, noting the semantical difficulties with the term "good for plants." Crawley, "Benevolent Herbivores?" 167. He concluded that "herbivores could increase plant fitness," but that "the weight of the evidence suggest[s] that they almost never do." Ibid., 168 (emphasis added). It would be hard to deny that one plant "benefits" from grazing when it escapes being eaten because a neighboring plant is consumed instead. Noss and Cooperrider, *Saving Nature's Legacy*, 225.

84. Noss and Cooperrider, *Saving Nature's Legacy*, 225–26, quoting Noy-Meir, "Compensating Growth of Grazed Plants" (citations omitted).

85. Noss and Cooperrider, *Saving Nature's Legacy*, 235, citing Savory, *Holistic Resource Management*, and Brady et al., "Response of a Semidesert Grassland," 284 (other citations omitted).

86. Miller, Svejcar, and West, "Livestock Grazing," 130. Dwyer, Buckhouse, and Huey, "Impacts of Grazing Intensity," 867. Dwyer et al. note, however, that although plants "respond favorably to rest from grazing," researchers "have not discovered why this occurs." Ibid. Belsky, Letter, 31. Gillis, "Should Cows Chew Cheatgrass," 673. Regarding trampling effects, see also Laycock, "Grazing vs. No Grazing," 271; Bryant et al., "Does Short-Duration Grazing Work?" 296. See Sindelar, Montagne, and Kroos, "Holistic Resource Management," 45. Gillis, "Should Cows Chew Cheatgrass," 673 (sidebar).

87. Archer and Smeins, "Ecosystem-Level Processes," 121. Hobbs and Huenneke, "Disturbance, Diversity, and Invasion," 328 (emphasis added).

88. Noss and Cooperrider, *Saving Nature's Legacy*, 249, 227. See Clements, "Plant Succession"; Clements, *Dynamics of Vegetation*; Noss and Cooperrider, *Saving Nature's Legacy*, 227; Dasmann, "Wildlife and Ecosystems"; Archer and Smeins, "Ecosystem-Level Processes," 132–33; Gillis, "Should Cows Chew Cheatgrass," 670–72. Worster, *Nature's Economy*, 209 (quotation), 210 (quotation), 211–12, 190 (quotation), 218.

89. Worster, *Nature's Economy*, 217, 215, 210. Today Clements's theory is sometimes described as based on a "monoclimax," although he did recognize possible "subclimaxes" that were attributed by him to unusual soil conditions and thus were essentially "monoclimaxes" themselves, just much more localized. Ibid., 210.

90. Worster, *Nature's Economy*, 210.

91. Rowley, *Forest Service Grazing*, 102–6. Arthur W. Sampson, who authored *Range and Pasture Management* in 1923, is known as the "father of range science." He also co-founded the first U.S. Forest Service forest and range experiment station, in Utah. Ibid. See generally Low and Berlin, "Natural Selection." Wagner, "Livestock Grazing," 128. Archer and Smeins, "Ecosystem-Level Processes," 137–38. Laycock, "Grazing vs. No Grazing," 256, 271. See also Heady, "Summary: Ecological Implications," 293; Fleischner, "Ecological Costs," 634. Archer and Smeins, "Ecosystem-Level Processes," 137–38; Barth and McCullough, *Grazing Impacts on Riparian Areas*, 6; GAO, *Some Riparian Areas Restored*; U.S. Department of the Interior, *Rangeland Reform Summary*, 21. Dyksterhuis, "Condition and Management of Range Land," revising Sampson's application of Clements's model to rangeland management. See Gillis, "Should Cows Chew Cheatgrass," 672. Wagner, "Livestock Grazing," 128. Pieper, "Grazing Systems and Management," 16–17, describing the rest-rotation principle and noting inconsistent results. See, e.g., Gillis, "Should Cows Chew Cheatgrass," 41; Sheridan, *Desertification*, 13, discussing the "drastic action" needed to halt BLM range deterioration, stabilize the soil, and "*allow perennial grasses to return*" (emphasis added), thus implying reversibility.

92. For a wide-ranging examination of Clements's critics' views, readers are directed to Worster's *Nature's Economy*, at 239–50 (quotation on 249–50). An example of an early critic is Oxford's A. G. Tansley, who disagreed with the model's exclusion of humans. He believed instead that "heavy grazing by animals" may give rise to a "biotic climax" or an "anthropogenic climax," that is, some climax stage other than that predicted for the site by the model. Ibid. See also Joyce, "Life Cycle of the Range Condition Concept," for a review of criticisms of Clements's model applied to rangelands.

93. Laycock, "Grazing vs. No Grazing," 271, 256. See also Archer and Smeins, "Ecosystem-Level Processes," 137–38; Heady, "Summary: Ecological Implications," 293; Fleischner, "Ecological Costs," 634; Low and Berlin, "Natural Selection." Barth and McCullough, *Grazing Impacts on Riparian Areas*, 6; GAO, *Some Riparian Areas Restored;* U.S. Department of the Interior, *Rangeland Reform Summary*, 21. Society for Range Management, "Range Management Guidelines," no pagination.

94. Dwyer, Buckhouse, and Huey, "Impacts of Grazing Intensity," 868–69, citing Norton, "Impacts of Grazing Intensity." Westoby, Walker, and Noy-Meir, "Opportunistic Management," 268–71 (emphasis added).

95. Dasmann, "Wildlife and Ecosystems," 25–26.

96. Laycock, "Grazing vs. No Grazing," 254, 267–68 (citations omitted). See also Laycock, "Stable States"; ibid., 432, citing Tueller, "Secondary Succession," 57–65. Tueller reportedly observed "disturbance factors for shrub-dominated ecosystems" that can "force a stable community across a threshold into a transitional phase moving toward another stable state." Ibid.; see also NRC, *Rangeland Health*, 38–39. Noss and Cooperrider, *Saving Nature's Legacy*, 227. Laycock, "Stable States," 431–32. Fleischner, "Ecological Costs," 634. See also May, "Thresholds and Breakpoints," 477, compiling and summarizing mathematical models, which described the dynamic behavior of ecological systems, including grazing systems, where "continuous variation in a control variable can produce discontinuous effects."

97. Ellison, "Ecological Basis," as reported by NRC, *Rangeland Health*, 38–39. NRC, *Rangeland Health*, 62–63.

98. See NRC, *Rangeland Health*, 90–92, citing studies by Friedel and Sharp et al., among others. See also Laycock, "Grazing vs. No Grazing," 253–54 (citations omitted); Fleischner, "Ecological Costs," 634. NRC, *Rangeland Health*, 37–38.

99. See NRC, *Rangeland Health*, 37, 47. Noss and Cooperrider, *Saving Nature's Legacy*, 228 (citations omitted). Allen, "Restoration Ecology," 8. The threshold concept is credited to various persons, including Australian range scientist Margaret Friedel and Wyoming range ecologist William Laycock. See Gillis, "Should Cows Chew Cheatgrass," 672, citing Friedel; Fleischner, "Ecological Costs," 634, citing Friedel, "Range Condition Assessment," and Laycock, "Stable States." NRC, *Rangeland Health*, 37–38, citing Friedel et al., "Where the Creeks Run Dry."

100. Borman and Pyke, "Successional Theory," 83 (citations omitted). NRC, *Rangeland Health*, 83, 91. U.S. Department of the Interior, *Rangeland Reform*, GL-6. Noss and Cooperrider, *Saving Nature's Legacy*, 227, 249–51.

101. Miller, Svejcar, and West, "Livestock Grazing," 126. Laycock, "Grazing vs. No Grazing," 258–59. Noss and Cooperrider, *Saving Nature's Legacy*, 235, citing Brady et al., "Response of a Semidesert Grassland," 284. Wilkinson, *Crossing the Next Meridian*, 75–80, 101–3; Russell, *Kill the Cowboy*, 22.

102. Noss and Cooperrider, *Saving Nature's Legacy*, 230, citing Archer and Smeins, "Non-linear Dynamics." It should be noted, however, that P-J woodlands are more widely distributed than Noss and Cooperrider's reference to "southern grasslands and savannas" would suggest. See also Archer and Smeins, "Ecosystem-Level Processes," 135; Miller, Svejcar, and West, "Livestock Grazing," 125–26, 132, summarizing research in the western United States as well as elsewhere, demonstrating the establishment of new steady states following disturbances; Pieper, "Ecological Implications," 192–93; Laycock, "Grazing vs. No Grazing," 254–60; Laycock, "Stable States," 432, noting that "lower successional stable states" are found in the shrub-dominated vegetation types of the Great Basin, in short-grass steppe, in southwestern grasslands, and in California and Idaho annual grasslands, citing Westoby et al., "Opportunistic Management."

103. Laycock, "Stable States," 432. See, e.g., Pieper, "Grazing Systems and Management," 14–15.

104. See Blumler, "Some Myths," 23–24, noting historical accounts and his own research.

105. See NRC, *Rangeland Health*, 90–92, citing, e.g., studies by Friedel, "Range Condition Assessment," and Sharp et al. Friedel, working in Australia, attributed the grassland to woodland shift to grazing and the second shift to severe soil erosion. Miller, Svejcar, and West, "Livestock Grazing," 126–27.

106. Tausch et al., "Differential Establishment," 252, 256. Sanders, "Can Annual Rangelands Be Converted," 412, citing Friedel, "Range Condition Assessment," 422–26 (emphasis in original). Ibid., citing Laycock, "Stable States," and Heady, "Valley Grassland." Allen, "Restoration Ecology," 8; Miller, Svejcar, and West, "Livestock Grazing," 126.

107. Hobbs and Huenneke, "Disturbance, Diversity, and Invasion," 328. NRC, *Rangeland Health*, 32–33, 45.

108. Herbel, "Manipulative Range Improvements," 1170, citing West, "Successional Patterns." Noss and Cooperrider, *Saving Nature's Legacy*, 228; see also Hobbs and Huenneke, "Disturbance, Diversity, and Invasion," 331–32.

109. Pieper, "Ecological Implications," 197 (citation omitted). Hobbs and Huenneke, "Disturbance, Diversity, and Invasion," 326. It may be, as Hobbs and Huenneke observed, that few species can persist in the face of disturbances that are sufficiently frequent or severe. Ibid.

110. See Wilkinson, *Crossing the Next Meridian*, 75–80, 101–3.

111. Laycock, "Grazing vs. No Grazing," 262.

112. Noss and Cooperrider, *Saving Nature's Legacy*, 228–29, citing an example of overgrazing-induced desertification in southern New Mexico. Hironaka, "Medusahead," 89. Sheridan, *Desertification*, 20. Laycock, "Grazing vs. No Grazing," 259, 262.

113. Sanders, "Can Annual Rangelands Be Converted," 412, citing Laycock, "Stable States," and Heady, "Valley Grassland."

114. Archer and Smeins, "Ecosystem-Level Processes," 137–38. Westoby et al., "Opportunistic Management," 271.

115. Laycock, "Grazing vs. No Grazing," 261, 271 (quotation). Munda and Smith, "Genetic Variation," 288, citing Cox et al., "Vegetation Restoration." Allen, "Restoration Ecology." Sanders, "Can Annual Rangelands Be Converted," 412.

116. Laycock, "Grazing vs. No Grazing," 261. Barth and McCullough, *Grazing Impacts on Riparian Areas*, 6–7.

117. See Rowley, *Forest Service Grazing*, 31–32, concerning *Forest Service Grazing* regulations. Forsling, "Grazing Lands," 12–13, 61–62. See also Low and Berlin, "Natural Selection." Wagner, "Livestock Grazing," 128.

118. NRC, *Rangeland Health*, 62–63. Worster, *Nature's Economy*, 249–50.

119. SRM, "Range Management Guidelines." Gillis, "Should Cows Chew Cheatgrass," 672, quoting Laycock (emphasis added).

120. Gillis, "Should Cows Chew Cheatgrass," 671. Gillis's article recounts some of the discourse at the 1992 conference noted in chapter 3, papers from which were published in *Ecological Implications of Livestock Herbivory*, edited by Vavra, Laycock, and Pieper. See BLM, *Riparian-Wetland Initiative*, 14–15. See Bosselman and Tarlock, "Influence of Ecological Science," 854–56. See also Pieper, "Ecological Implications," 201. Gillis, "Should Cows Chew Cheatgrass," 670. See also Noss and Cooperrider, *Saving Nature's Legacy*, 249. U.S. Department of the Interior, *Rangeland Reform*, GL-4.

121. NRC, *Rangeland Health*, 76, 26, 54, 60–61, 76 (quoting 1958 paper, 151). The grazing hypothesis behind Dyksterhuis's and the SCS method is described, ibid., 76. See also ibid., 58–65, discussing range survey methods; 64–65 (summary table); 81–82 (trend measurement methods).

122. See Gillis, "Should Cows Chew Cheatgrass," 671. NRC, *Rangeland Health*, viii.

123. NRC, *Rangeland Health*, 24–29, 149, 31.

124. SRM, "Range Management Guidelines." See Noss and Cooperrider, *Saving Nature's Legacy*, 250; U.S. Department of the Interior, *Rangeland Reform*, 1-17, citing

NRC, *Rangeland Health*; U.S. Department of the Interior, BLM, *Riparian Area Management*, 1–4. U.S. Department of the Interior, *Rangeland Reform*, GL-6.

125. U.S. Department of the Interior, *Rangeland Reform Summary*, 21, 22 (figs. S-3 and S-4). In 1990 the BLM reported the following figures. Describing BLM riparian areas outside Alaska, the agency stated that 7 percent were "meeting objectives," 10 percent "were not meeting objectives," and 83 percent were "unknown," meaning that "inventory and monitoring data are unavailable or that specific objectives . . . have not been established." BLM, *Riparian-Wetland Initiative*, 11. The agency did not define "meeting objectives," but illustrated the classification with the example of a riparian area that lacked "the desired amount of willows." Ibid.

126. Noss and Cooperrider, *Saving Nature's Legacy*, 250–52.

127. NRC, *Rangeland Health*, viii, 82.

128. Ibid., 4, 35 (quoting an unnamed 1992 NRC report, 520), 8, 42, 19, 48–49. The committee does not define "rangeland," although it describes U.S. rangelands as extending "from wet grasslands of Florida to the desert shrub ecosystems of Wyoming and from the high mountain meadows of Utah to the desert floor of California," ibid., 1, and as including "deserts, grasslands, canyons, tundra, mountains, and riparian areas," ibid., 18. The committee also points out that rangelands "are ecosystems, not individual organisms." Ibid., 2.

129. Ibid., 5, 28, 96, 47.

130. Ibid., 42–43 (emphasis added), 48–49.

131. Ibid., 49–50, 97.

132. Ibid., 82, 100 (citations omitted). The committee notes: "Little research has been done to determine whether grazing causes loss of soil organic matter, but some studies have shown that wild and domestic grazing animals can influence soil processes." Ibid., 101. It cautions that "any factor that severely reduces soil cover opens the way for removal of organic matter via erosional events." Ibid.

133. NRC, *Rangeland Health*, 91. See Noss and Cooperrider, *Saving Nature's Legacy*, 250.

134. Gillis, "Should Cows Chew Cheatgrass," 671; Noss and Cooperrider, *Saving Nature's Legacy*, 249.

135. West, "Biodiversity of Rangelands," 9–10.

136. Noss, "Regional Landscape Approach," 703. Peck, "Ecosystem Management," 23. West does admit that "[b]y definition, there is no redundancy in the critical function of a *keystone* species." West, "Biodiversity of Rangelands," 10 (emphasis added). He offers kangaroo rats as an example, observing that in their absence "a shrub steppe quickly changed to grassland" at the Chihuahuan-Sonoran Desert ecotone in Arizona. Ibid.

137. NRC, *Rangeland Health*, 92, 127–28, 42, citing the arid lands portion of EPA's Environmental Monitoring and Assessment Program.

138. Noss and Cooperrider, *Saving Nature's Legacy*, 250–52 (quotation on 252).

139. Elmore and Kauffman, "Riparian and Watershed Systems," 217. Laycock, "Stable States," 432.

140. Noss and Cooperrider, *Saving Nature's Legacy*, 230. NRC, *Rangeland Health*, 127–28 (emphasis added). Dasmann, "Wildlife and Ecosystems," 26.

CHAPTER 6. PRESERVING BIOLOGICAL DIVERSITY
ON ARID WESTERN LANDSCAPES

1. Norton, "Commodity, Amenity, and Morality," 201. The same concepts apply to genetic and community diversity, considered later in the text. Ibid., 203. For explorations of the value of biodiversity, readers are directed to the prolific writings of Harvard entomologist Edward O. Wilson, the rich and relevant work of Reed Noss and Allen Cooperrider, Aldo Leopold's *Sand County Almanac*, and the periodical *Conservation Biology*.

2. See Peck, "Ecosystem Management," 23. The "shock absorber" description is from Dwyer, Buckhouse, and Huey, "Impacts of Grazing Intensity," 881. NRC, *Rangeland Health*, 4.

3. West, "Biodiversity of Rangelands," 2. *Wild, Free-Ranging Horses and Burros Act*, 16 U.S.C. § 1331: wild horses "contribute to the diversity of life forms within the Nation and enrich the lives of the American people." Krutilla, "Conservation Reconsidered," 784–85 (footnote omitted). *Tennessee Valley Authority v. Hill*, 437 U.S. 153 (1978). The court cited the Report of the House Committee on Merchant Marine and Fisheries on H.R. 37, "a bill which contained the essential features of the subsequently enacted [Endangered Species Act of 1973]," for the statement: "*The value of this genetic heritage [of all species] is, quite literally, incalculable.*" Ibid., 177–78 (emphasis in original).

4. See Norton, "Commodity, Amenity, and Morality," 201. Noss, "Some Principles of Conservation Biology," 895.

5. Wilson, *Diversity of Life*, 393 (glossary); see also U.S. Department of the Interior, *Rangeland Reform*, GL-3.

6. Noss, "Regional Landscape Approach," 700–701 (citations omitted, emphasis in original). Hobbs and Huenneke, "Disturbance, Diversity, and Invasion," 324 (citation omitted).

7. Noss, "Regional Landscape Approach," 703.

8. Ibid. (table).

9. Pieper, "Ecological Implications," 195–96, noting that "moderate grazing may contribute to higher species diversity than either light or destructive grazing"; 202, removing all livestock from a range "in the long run might even be negative in terms of biodiversity." Severson and Urness, "Livestock Grazing: A Tool," 242–43; Laycock, "Grazing vs. No Grazing," 263–64. Noss, "Regional Landscape Approach," 701, 703.

10. Noss, "Regional Landscape Approach," 701 (citing Leopold, *Game Management*, and Yoakum and Dasmann, "Habitat Manipulation Practices," 231).

11. Ibid.

12. Smeins, "Concepts for Solving Biodiversity Problems" (citation omitted). Gillis, "Should Cows Chew Cheatgrass," 672, quoting Wuerthner.

13. Hobbs and Huenneke, "Disturbance, Diversity, and Invasion," 331. See generally Harris, *The Fragmented Forest*. Noss, "Regional Landscape Approach," 701–2 (emphasis added).

14. Noss, "Regional Landscape Approach," 702 (citations omitted). Hobbs and Huenneke, "Disturbance, Diversity, and Invasion," 331 (citation omitted).

15. Noss, "Regional Landscape Approach," 702. Lauenroth et al., "Effects of Grazing on Ecosystems," 88. Noss, "Issues of Scale," 241–42.

16. Noss, "Regional Landscape Approach," 702.

17. Ibid., 701, referring to, though not citing, 16 U.S.C. § 1604(g)(3)(b). 16 U.S.C. § 1604(g)(3)(b) (emphasis added). Concerning the NFMA provision generally, see Siemans, "A 'Hard Look' at Biodiversity."

18. Laycock, "Grazing vs. No Grazing," 264 (emphasis in original).

19. Pieper, "Ecological Implications," 195 (citation omitted).

20. Hobbs and Huenneke, "Disturbance, Diversity, and Invasion," 332. See also Heitschmidt and Stuth, eds., *Grazing Management*; Great Plains Agricultural Council, Water Quality Task Force, *Agriculture and Water Quality*.

21. Low and Berlin, "Natural Selection," 1204–5.

22. See, e.g., Smeins, "Concepts for Solving Biodiversity Problems," no pagination; Noss, "Regional Landscape Approach," 702. Pieper, "Ecological Implications," 194–96, discussing mechanisms by which livestock contributes to patchiness, or "patch dynamics" (citation omitted). Young and Evans, "Plant Manipulation," 63.

23. West, "Biodiversity of Rangelands," 9. West's assertion is a bit too facile. Livestock interests don't "foot the bill" for most range improvements or other land management measures taken to benefit livestock. As chapter 8 points out, grazing fees cover only a small portion of the costs of administering public rangelands.

24. See generally Noss, "Some Principles of Conservation Biology," 898–99, 900–907. Regarding reserve design principles generally, see Hoose, *Building an Ark*; Reid and Miller, *Keeping Options Alive*, chapter 6. Crumpacker et al., "Preliminary Assessment," 111, regarding redundancy. Dasmann, "Wildlife and Ecosystems," 26.

25. Waller, "Introduction," xxi. Noss, "Regional Landscape Approach," 703 (citations omitted). Noss, "Some Principles of Conservation Biology." Noss, "Issues of Scale," 244.

26. Noss, "Regional Landscape Approach," 704. Shafer, "Land Conservation Strategy," no pagination. Shafer warned that large reserves must not be "dismember[ed]" in order to achieve the objective of "several" reserves. Ibid.

27. Noss, "Regional Landscape Approach," 700, 703–4. See also Salwasser et al., "Role of Interagency Cooperation," 297. West, "Biodiversity of Rangelands," 10 (citation omitted).

28. Noss, "Regional Landscape Approach," 704 (citations omitted; emphasis in original).

29. See 17 Stat. 32 (1872) (codified at 30 U.S.C. §§ 21–22 [1994]). See also Donaldson, *The Public Domain*, 1294. Vickerman, "Integrating Biodiversity Strategies"; see also Sax, "Nature and Habitat Conservation," 51–52.

30. Crumpacker et al., "Preliminary Assessment," 106. Waller, "Introduction," xv, xx. See Ryan et al., *Research Natural Areas*, 1, 3. Crumpacker et al., "Preliminary Assessment," 111.

31. Cooperrider, "Conservation of Biodiversity," 46 (citation omitted). Noss and Cooperrider, *Saving Nature's Legacy*, 252. 16 U.S.C. § 1 (1994). 16 U.S.C. § 1131(c) (1994). Graf, *Wilderness Preservation*, 244.

32. West, "Biodiversity of Rangelands," 10 (citations omitted). Noss and Cooperrider, *Saving Nature's Legacy*, 64 (citation omitted). Noss and Cooperrider, *Saving Nature's Legacy*, 252 (citing the report of a 1988 survey). McClaran, "Livestock in Wilderness," 886–87. Miller, Svejcar, and West, "Livestock Grazing," 132. Noss and Cooperrider, *Saving Nature's Legacy*, 253. See Davidson et al., "Selecting Wilderness Areas."

33. Noss and Cooperrider, *Saving Nature's Legacy*, 252.

34. Keiter, "Conservation Biology and the Law," 921. Crumpacker et al., "Preliminary Assessment," 114. Cooperrider, "Conservation of Biodiversity," 46–47, 50 (citation omitted). See also Davidson et al., "Selecting Wilderness Areas."

35. E.g., West, "Biodiversity of Rangelands," 10.

36. USDA, Forest Service, *Biological Diversity Assessment*, 14. Gillis, "Should Cows Chew Cheatgrass," 669. See also Barth and McCullough, *Grazing Impacts on Riparian Areas*, 5, 11; Wuerthner, "Grazing *The Western Range*," 28. McClure, "Meeting the Biodiversity Challenge," 5.

37. Boylan and MacLean, "Linking Species Loss," 13. Gillis, "Should Cows Chew Cheatgrass," 669.

38. U.S. Department of the Interior, BLM, *Managing the Nation's Public Lands*, 17, 19. BLM, *Riparian-Wetland Initiative*, 11. The agency did not define "meeting objectives," but illustrated "not meeting objectives" with the example of a riparian area lacking "the desired amount of willows." Ibid.

39. U.S. Department of the Interior, *Rangeland Reform Summary*, 21, 22 (figs. S-3 and S-4). See also chapters 3 and 5.

40. McClure, "Meeting the Biodiversity Challenge," 5. Gillis, "Should Cows Chew Cheatgrass," 668–69. Boylan and MacLean, "Linking Species Loss," 13. Briggs, "Evaluating Degraded Riparian Ecosystems," 63 (quotation). Waller, "Introduction," xx (quotations).

41. See generally Noss, "Regional Landscape Approach," 703–4.

42. Godron and Forman, "Landscape Modification," 13, 19 (citations omitted); Noss, "Regional Landscape Approach," 700 (quoting and citing Forman and Godron, "Patches and Structural Components," 733), 702. Hunter, "Coping with Ignorance," 272.

43. Noss, "Regional Landscape Approach," 700, 704.

44. Noss and Cooperrider, *Saving Nature's Legacy*, 251–52. Elmore and Kauffman, "Riparian and Watershed Systems," 217. See also SRM, "Society for Range Management Guidelines"; Noss and Cooperrider, *Saving Nature's Legacy*, 250–52.

45. See Godron and Forman, "Landscape Modification," 12, 19. Noss, "Regional Landscape Approach," 702.

46. See Noss, "Regional Landscape Approach," 700, 703 (emphasis in original).

47. See, e.g., Raup, "Diversity Crises," 51. See also generally Wilson, *Diversity of Life*. See, e.g., McVicker, "Ecosystem Management," 4: "Humans must be considered as members of the ecosystem . . . [and] a major change element." An extreme example of this viewpoint: "The human race has been produced by the evolutionary process and so have its artifacts. The automobile is just as 'natural' as the horse. It is just as much a species, just as much a part of the total ecological system, and the idea that there is something called 'ecology' in the absence of the human race and its artifacts at this

stage of the development of the planet is romantic illusion." Boulding, *Ecodynamics*, 19, 31, quoted in Bjork, "Ownership and Outcome," 191. Hobbs and Huenneke, "Disturbance, Diversity, and Invasion," 332. Dwyer, Buckhouse, and Huey, "Impacts of Grazing Intensity," 881.

48. Sheridan, *Desertification*, 105 (quoting George, *In the Deserts of This Earth*, 116–17). See Gillis, "Should Cows Chew Cheatgrass," 672.

49. Noss, "Regional Landscape Approach," 704 (citation omitted). Noss and Cooperrider, *Saving Nature's Legacy*, 254–57.

50. Noss and Cooperrider, *Saving Nature's Legacy*, 248; see also Cooperrider, "Conservation of Biodiversity," 50, referring to ACECs as protection "at the smallest scale." See also Ryan et al., *Research Natural Areas*, 6.

51. Pieper, "Ecological Implications," 186, quoting Young and Evans, "The Grand Experiment," 1.

52. See *Leo Sheep Co. v. United States*, 440 U.S. 668 (1979), describing the history of and rationale behind the land grants. BLM, State of New Mexico Land Status Map (1990) (scale 1:531,915): BLM, State of Colorado Wilderness Status Map (1992) (scale 1:1,000,000); BLM, State of Nevada (1990) (scale 1:1,000,000); BLM, State of California Wilderness Status Map (November 1991) (scale 1:1,000,000); BLM, State of Oregon Wilderness Status Map (May 1992) (scale 1:1,000,000); BLM, State of Arizona Wilderness Status Map (1984) (scale 1:500,000); BLM, State of Wyoming Land Status (1984) (scale 1:500,000); BLM, Surface Management Responsibility, State of Idaho (1991) (scale 1:500,000). See also BLM, Central Oregon Public Lands (1988) (scale 1:100,000). Washington holds less potential because of the smaller and more scattered BLM holdings. See, e.g., BLM Surface Management/Mineral Management Status maps (scale 1:100,000) for Walla Walla, Washington-Oregon; Omak, Washington; and Moses Lake, Washington. Surface management information apparently is not available for all of Washington.

53. See NRC, *Rangeland Health*, 42, concerning EMAP. Miller, Svejcar, and West, "Livestock Grazing" 126–27.

54. See Miller, Svejcar, and West, "Livestock Grazing," 126; Laycock, "Grazing vs. No Grazing," 258–59; Noss and Cooperrider, *Saving Nature's Legacy*, 235, citing Brady et al., "Response of a Semidesert Grassland," 284; Wilkinson, *Crossing the Next Meridian*, 75–80, 101–3. Miller, Svejcar, and West, "Livestock Grazing," 132. Pieper, "Ecological Implications," 192. Severson and Urness, "Livestock Grazing: A Tool," 241–42.

55. See Tausch et al., "Differential Establishment," 252. Rosentreter, "Displacement of Rare Plants," 170. See also chapter 5.

56. Allen, "Restoration Ecology," 7, 12. Noss, "Guidelines for Biodiversity." Archer and Smeins, "Ecosystem-Level Processes," 132.

57. Allen, "Restoration Ecology," 7, 12. Munda and Smith, "Genetic Variation," 288, citing Cox et al., "Vegetation Restoration."

58. Noss and Cooperrider, *Saving Nature's Legacy*, 254 (emphasis added). See also Noss, "Issues of Scale"; Low and Berlin, "Natural Selection," 1218.

59. Heady, "Summary: Ecological Implications," 292 (emphasis added). See Cooperrider, "Conservation of Biodiversity," 49.

60. Noss and Cooperrider, *Saving Nature's Legacy*, 257–58. Archer and Smeins, "Ecosystem-Level Processes," 138. Noss, "Some Principles of Conservation Biology," 897 (citation omitted).

61. See Foss, *Politics and Grass*, 40–41; Udall, *The Quiet Crisis*, 105–6. Worster, *Nature's Economy*, 236, citing Clements, "Ecology in the Public Service," 49.

62. Pearson, "Multiple Use in Forestry," 247–48. Forsling, "Grazing Lands Must Be Restored," 12–13, 61–62. Gillis, "Should Cows Chew Cheatgrass," 671.

63. Noss and Cooperrider, *Saving Nature's Legacy*, 258.

64. Stebbins, Letter, 31. Coggins, "Public Rangeland Management V," 538.

65. Cooperrider, "Conservation of Biodiversity," 50 (emphasis added). Noss and Cooperrider, *Saving Nature's Legacy*, 259.

66. Noss and Cooperrider, *Saving Nature's Legacy*, 258. See generally *Kleppe v. Sierra Club*, 427 U.S. 390 (1976), concerning when a regional-scale EIS may be appropriate; 40 C.F.R. pt. 1502 (1995), CEQ regulations for preparing EISs. See also the discussion of NEPA in chapter 7. FLPMA, 43 U.S.C. § 1732(b). See Hodgson, "Buffalo—Back Home," 84–85, describing Frank and Deborah Popper's proposal for a "Buffalo Commons" on the Great Plains and the smaller-scale "Big Open" proposal for a herd of 75,000 bison on the eastern plains of Montana.

67. Noss and Cooperrider, *Saving Nature's Legacy*, 259. See Low and Berlin, "Natural Selection," 1218–19. See also Sheridan, *Desertification*, 65; Hagenstein, "Federal Lands Today," 87–88.

68. Jenkins, "Harmful Exotics," 106. Wilcox et al., *Rebuilding the Ark*, 2 (fig. 1).

69. Hobbs and Huenneke, "Disturbance, Diversity, and Invasion," 332–33. Noss, "Regional Landscape Approach," 700 (emphasis added); see also 704.

70. See, e.g., "Hook, Line, and Sunk?" 23–24.

71. See, e.g., Reid and Miller, *Keeping Options Alive*; Harris, McGlothlen, and Manlove, "Genetic Resources and Biotic Diversity," 93. Linhart, "Restoration, Revegetation," 272.

72. West, "Biodiversity of Rangelands," 11. Noss, "Landscape Connectivity," 35 (citation omitted). See also Godron and Forman, "Landscape Modification," 16.

73. Noss, "Issues of Scale," 243.

74. Hobbs and Huenneke, "Disturbance, Diversity, and Invasion," 328–29 (citation omitted). See also Miller, Svejcar, and West, "Livestock Grazing," 132. Economic issues are treated in chapter 8.

75. See Elmore and Kauffman, "Riparian and Watershed Systems," 224–27, 217. See also Noss and Cooperrider, *Saving Nature's Legacy*, 256–57.

76. Noss and Cooperrider, *Saving Nature's Legacy*, 247, 254–55, 257.

77. Ibid., 247. Hobbs and Huenneke, "Disturbance, Diversity, and Invasion," 332. See also Jacobs, *Waste of the West*.

78. Sheridan, *Off-Road Vehicles*, 9. See Coggins, Wilkinson, and Leshy, *Federal Public Land*, 888–89. Noss and Cooperrider, *Saving Nature's Legacy*, 248. Sheridan *Off-Road Vehicles*, 7–12, 19–35. Noss and Cooperrider, *Saving Nature's Legacy*, 248. Sheridan, *Off-Road Vehicles*, 12, 19–35 (quotation on 19). *Sierra Club v. Clark*, 756 F.2d 686, 688 (9th Cir. 1985).

79. *Wild, Free-Ranging Horses and Burros Act*, 16 U.S.C. §§ 1331, 1333. *Kleppe v. New Mexico*, 426 U.S. 529 (1976).

80. Noss, "Regional Landscape Approach," 703. Forsling, "Grazing Lands Must Be Restored," 61–62. See also Krutilla, "Conservation Reconsidered," 784.

81. See generally Culhane, *Public Lands Politics*, 174. Sheridan, *Off-Road Vehicles*, 30–31.

82. See, e.g., Wilson, "The Environmental Ethic," 329; Wilson, ed., *Biodiversity*, 79–116, 193–223; Noss, "Regional Landscape Approach," 703; Norton, "Commodity, Amenity, and Morality"; Ehrenfeld, "Why Put a Value on Biodiversity?" 212. Cf. Dasmann, "Wildlife and Ecosystems," 26.

83. The Comb Wash litigation is illustrative. See *National Wildlife Federation v. Bureau of Land Management*, UT-06-91-1 (Department of the Interior Office of Hearings and Appeals, 20 December 1993; decision by District Chief Administrative Law Judge John Rampton). Judge Rampton's decision was affirmed and given immediate effect by *National Wildlife Federation v. Bureau of Land Management*, IBLA 94-264 (Interior Board of Land Appeals, 1 March 1994).

84. NRC, *Land Use and Wildlife Resources*, 83.

85. Dasmann, "Wildlife and Ecosystems," 26. See also Krutilla, "Conservation Reconsidered," 786. Leopold, *Sand County Almanac*, 202. Freyfogle, "Owning and Belonging," 19, 21.

86. Pieper, "Ecological Implications," 192 (citations omitted). Miller, Svejcar, and West, "Livestock Grazing," 129, 132. See also chapter 5.

87. Leopold, *Sand County Almanac*, 190.

88. See Noss, "Issues of Scale," 248, noting that in conservation practice, "the defensibility of thinking small has vanished with increasing ecological understanding"; Noss, "From Endangered Species to Biodiversity," 231. Noss and Cooperrider, *Saving Nature's Legacy*, 93–97. Noss, "Issues of Scale," 244–45. Noss and Cooperrider, *Saving Nature's Legacy*, 254. Wilson, "Environmental Ethic," 331. Noss, "From Endangered Species to Biodiversity," 239. See also generally Reid and Miller, *Keeping Options Alive*.

89. Noss, "Issues of Scale," 239. Hoose, *Building an Ark*, 77.

90. See, e.g., Lenderman, "A Ranch Rescued," 7, reporting on a TNC deal to preserve the Dugout Ranch near Canyonlands National Park in Utah, the goals of which are "to preserve the 5,167-acre ranch, plus 250,000 acres of federal grazing allotments, as a working model of sustainable ranching, as well as to save the ranch's fragile desert environment." Lenderman reports that TNC had "already protected 525,000 acres on 77 different projects" in Utah. Ibid. TNC's purchase of the huge Gray Ranch in New Mexico (on the border with Mexico), and subsequent transfer to the Animas Foundation for the purpose of continuing livestock ranching, is another example of a transaction engineered apparently for political and fundraising purposes whose ecological underpinnings are extremely shaky.

CHAPTER 7. THE CURRENT LEGAL LANDSCAPE

1. Readers interested in more thorough treatment of the Taylor Act, FLPMA, or PRIA are encouraged to consult any of several authoritative works. See especially Coggins and Lindeberg-Johnson, "Public Rangeland Management II"; Coggins, "Public Rangeland Management III"; Coggins, "Rangeland Management IV"; Coggins and Glicksman, *Public Natural Resources Law* §§ 19.02, 19.03. Regarding biodiversity

conservation and NEPA, the Endangered Species Act, and Clean Water Act, see, e.g., Cheever, "Road to Recovery"; Glicksman, "Pollution on the Federal Lands"; Braun, "Emerging Limits"; CEQ, *Incorporating Biodiversity Considerations*. See also generally Snape, ed., *Biodiversity and the Law*.

2. Taylor Grazing Act, ch. 865, 48 Stat. 1269 (1934), (codified as amended at 43 U.S.C. §§ 315–315r [1994]) (hereafter TGA). See, e.g., Gates, *History of Public Land Law*; Foss, *Politics and Grass*; Peffer, *Closing of the Public Domain*; Coggins and Lindeberg-Johnson, "Public Rangeland Management II"; Merrill, "Private Spaces."

3. TGA § 1, 43 U.S.C. § 315 (emphasis added). TGA § 2, 43 U.S.C. § 315a.

4. TGA § 2, 43 U.S.C. § 315a. TGA § 7, 43 U.S.C. § 315f (emphasis added).

5. TGA § 1, 43 U.S.C. § 315.

6. 39 Stat. 862, ch. 9, §§ 2, 9 (1916).

7. See S. Rep. No. 517 (1926), concerning the TGA predecessor bill, S. 2584. Ibid., 6–7, quoting § 1 of S. 2584 (emphasis added); ibid., 18–19, provisions of §§ 203[a] and 204[2], respectively. See also Rowley, *Forest Service Grazing*, 12, reporting that "[p]roposals to declare the [public domain] lands a permanent grazing area met with scorn" and were opposed vigorously by the railroads.

8. S. Rep. No. 517 (1926), 10, 2, 12, 17, 2. *Public Lands Council v. Babbitt*, 154 F. 3d 1160, 1172 (10th Cir. 1998).

9. Clapp, "Major Range Problems," 3.

10. Graf, *Wilderness Preservation*, 147. Gates, *History of Public Land Law*, 528, 525. See also Muhn and Stuart, *Story of BLM*, 37. Gates's book was prepared for the Public Land Law Review Commission and submitted to Congress as part of the commission's report in 1968. Prior to this assignment, Gates had spent thirty years studying history, with an emphasis on the history of the western public lands, and he chaired the history department at Cornell University from 1946 to 1956. See Gates, *History of Public Land Law*, v–vi, letter of transmittal to Congressman Wayne Aspinall from Milton A. Pearl, Director, PLLRC.

11. Graf, *Wilderness Preservation*, 147 (citation omitted). Peffer, *Closing of the Public Domain*, 208, quoting 1931–32. U.S. Senate Hearings on various public lands bills. See also Foss, *Politics and Grass*, 47–48. 78 *Cong. Rec.* 11,142 (1934). McClure, "Address," 57. See also Foss, *Politics and Grass*, 48; Peffer, *Closing of the Public Domain*, 208–9.

12. Merrill, "Private Spaces," 230. Carpenter, "Establishing Management," 108–9.

13. TGA § 7, 43 U.S.C. § 315f.

14. 78 *Cong. Rec.* at 6364, 6368, 6366. 78 *Cong. Rec.* 11,139–40 (1934). House Committee, *To Provide for the Orderly Use*, 7 (Ickes letter); see also Senate Committee, *To Provide for the Orderly Use*, 5.

15. House Committee, *To Provide for the Orderly Use*; Senate Committee, *To Provide for the Orderly Use*. 78 *Cong. Rec.* 6364 (1934). 78 *Cong. Rec.* 6366–67, 6356 (1934). 78 *Cong. Rec.* 6350–52 (quotation on 652), 6355 (1934), quoting Major Stuart.

16. House Committee, *Hearings on H.R. 106*, 253–67, 264, quoting 43 U.S.C. § 315f, 265–66.

17. Coggins and Lindeberg-Johnson, "Public Rangeland Management II," 51–52. See the discussion in chapter 3 of *The Western Range*.

18. Muhn and Stuart, *Story of BLM*, 43. See also Richardson, *BLM's Billion-Dollar Checkerboard*. Multiple-Use, Sustained-Yield Act of 1960, 16 U.S.C. §§ 528–31 (1994). See 16 U.S.C. § 475; *United States v. New Mexico*, 438 U.S. 696 (1978). 50 Stat. 874, § 1.

19. 50 Stat. 874, § 1 (1937) (emphasis added). See Richardson, *BLM's Billion-Dollar Checkerboard*, 52, 66.

20. Clawson, *Western Range Livestock Industry*, 14. Voigt, *Public Grazing Lands*, 276. Gates, *History of Public Land Law*, 623.

21. Gates, *History of Public Land Law*, 624, citing Kelso, "Current Issues." Dana, *Forest and Range Policy*, 288.

22. See TGA § 1, 43 U.S.C. § 315, preserving existing rights under federal or state law to hunt and fish within grazing districts; TGA § 5, 43 U.S.C. § 315d, concerning the "use of timber, stone, gravel, clay, coal, and other deposits by miners, prospectors for mineral bona fide settlers and residents, for firewood, fencing, buildings, mining prospecting, and domestic purposes"; TGA § 6, 43 U.S.C. § 315e, concerning "the acquisition, granting or use of permits or rights-of-way," "ingress or egress over the public lands . . . for all proper and lawful purposes," and application of mining laws. TGA § 3, 43 U.S.C. § 315a. *LaRue v. Udall*, 324 F. 2d 428, 430 (D.C. Cir. 1963), quoting interior secretary opinion (citations to §§ 3, 7, and 14 of the act omitted; emphasis added). Classification and Multiple Use Act, Pub. L. No. 88-607, 78 Stat. 986 (1964) (expired 1970).

23. See 43 U.S.C. § 315o-1. Forsling et al., "Range Conservation the Exception," 287–88; Show, "Probable Future Use," 454; Clapp, "Major Range Problems," 38. This issue is explored in chapter 8.

24. Clawson, *Western Range Livestock Industry*, 14–16 (emphasis added), noting competition from agricultural interests, recreationists, and "hobby ranchers," and 104–6, discussing multiple uses of range land and the manager's difficulty in "balanc[ing] one use against another," especially when some "have no definable monetary value."

25. According to Muhn and Stuart, BLM's predecessor, the Grazing Service, "took wildlife habitat into consideration and permitted wildlife interests to play an active role in administering the grazing districts in New Mexico and Oregon." Muhn and Stuart, *Story of BLM*, 69, 39, 41, 72, 150. Fairfax, "Coming of Age," 1727–28. See also ibid., 1728–32.

26. Fairfax, "Coming of Age," 1728–32 (quotations on 731). Fairfax describes the CAMUA as conferring on the BLM "*general* authority and an affirmative duty to analyze and assess land for a broad range of multiple uses at its own initiative and in the context of a comprehensive classification program." Ibid., 1730 (emphasis in original). *Classification and Multiple Use Act of 1964*, Pub. L. No. 88-607, 78 Stat. 986 (1964). FLPMA, Pub. L. No. 94-579, 43 U.S.C. §§ 1701–84 (1994). The BLM hired its first wildlife biologist in 1961; district offices had no biologists until 1965. Muhn and Stuart, *Story of BLM*, 150.

27. See, e.g., 43 U.S.C. §§ 315, 315b, 315f, 315m, 315m-1, each referring to the secretary's "discretion." See, e.g., *Red Canyon Sheep Co. v. Ickes*, 98 F. 2d 308, 314, 318–19 (D.C. Cir. 1938), holding that a decision to exchange grazing lands is wholly within the secretary's discretion, subject only to the TGA's public interest criterion, and

suggesting in dictum that the secretary also has discretion to devote lands previously grazed to some other public purpose; *Carl v. Udall*, 309 F. 2d 653, 657–58 (D.C. Cir. 1962), upholding the secretary's discretion, if not duty, to withhold from disposal under the public land laws any BLM lands deemed more valuable for retention for public purposes; *Chournos v. United States*, 193 F. 2d 321, 323 (10th Cir. 1951), holding that BLM officials had discretion to determine extent to which lands would be grazed; *Bleamaster v. Morton*, 448 F. 2d 1289, 1292 (9th Cir. 1971), upholding, as an exercise of his authority under 43 U.S.C. § 315f to "dispose of land," the secretary's decision to lease a tract for a desert museum under the Recreation and Other Public Purposes Act of 1926; *Hall v. Hickel*, 305 F. Supp. 723, 728 (D. Nev. 1969), following *Carl v. Udall*; *Richardson v. Udall*, 253 F. Supp. 72, 78–79 (D. Idaho 1966), noting one limit on the secretary's otherwise "complete" discretion to classify lands under 43 U.S.C. § 315f. Cf. Mary A. Van Alen, 8 IBLA 77 (27 October 1972), upholding the BLM manager's decision to cancel range improvement permit for road construction because the area had since been designated a roadless "wildlife development" area; explaining that decision was consistent with the TGA's goal of "promot[ing] the highest use of the public lands." *Public Lands Council v. Babbitt,* 154 F. 3d 1160, 1176 (10th Cir. 1998).

28. Pub. L. No. 94-579, 43 U.S.C. §§ 1701–84 (1994). See Fairfax, "Coming of Age." 43 U.S.C. § 1702(e). 43 U.S.C. § 1701 note. 43 U.S.C. § 1903(b), stating that the secretary of the interior "shall manage the public rangelands in accordance with the Taylor Grazing Act . . . , [FLPMA], and other applicable law consistent with the public rangelands improvement program pursuant to [43 U.S.C. §§ 1901–8]." See Coggins, "Rangeland Management IV," 5. 43 U.S.C. § 1752(a). "Nothing in this Act shall be construed as modifying in any way law existing on October 21, 1976, with respect to the creation of right, title, interest or estate in or to public lands or lands in the National Forests by issuance of grazing permits and leases." 43 U.S.C. § 1752(h).

29. For the most part, FLPMA's "nuts-and-bolts" grazing provisions (see, e.g., 43 U.S.C. §§ 1751–53) are only peripherally relevant to the subject of this book. With the exception of FLPMA's provision for terminating permits, they are not discussed further. For an exhaustive examination of the Taylor Grazing Act and FLPMA, see Coggins and Glicksman, *Public Natural Resources Law*, §§ 19.02, 19.03; Coggins and Lindeberg-Johnson, "Public Rangeland Management II"; Coggins, "Public Rangeland Management IV."

30. FLPMA § 102(a)(1), 43 U.S.C. § 1701(a)(1).

31. See Graf, *Wilderness Preservation*, 153. Emphasis added: Coggins and Lindeberg-Johnson, "Public Rangeland Management II," 55; Coggins, Wilkinson, and Leshy, *Federal Public Land*, 136; Fairfax, "Coming of Age," 1726, 1730. Voigt, *Public Grazing Lands*, 250. Graf, *Wilderness Preservation*, 153.

32. FLPMA § 102, 43 U.S.C. § 1701. Inventory and planning requirements are established by §§ 201 and 202, 43 U.S.C. §§ 1711 and 1712, respectively. FLPMA § 102(a)(7), 43 U.S.C. § 1701(a)(7). FLPMA § 102(a)(8), 43 U.S.C. § 1701(a)(8). FLPMA § 102(a)(11), 43 U.S.C. § 1701(a)(11) (emphasis added). FLPMA § 102(a)(12), 43 U.S.C. § 1701(a)(12).

33. FLPMA § 302(a), 43 U.S.C. § 1732(a). FLPMA § 302(b), 43 U.S.C. § 1732(b).

34. FLPMA § 103(h), 43 U.S.C. § 1702(h). FLPMA § 103(c), 43 U.S.C. § 1702(c).

35. See Multiple-Use, Sustained-Yield Act § 4, 16 U.S.C. § 531(a) (1994). FLPMA § 202(c)(1), 43 U.S.C. § 1712(c)(1). See Hardt, "Federal Land Management"; Coggins, "Public Rangeland Management IV"; Bates, *Changing Management Philosophies*. See generally Coggins, Wilkinson, and Leshy, *Federal Public Land*, 622–29. See, e.g., Brick, "Determined Opposition," 16; Power, *Lost Landscapes*, 2–3. See Coggins, Wilkinson, and Leshy, *Federal Public Land*, 628. Coggins, "Of Succotash Syndromes," 279–80. Coggins, "Public Rangeland Management IV," 50.

36. FLPMA § 103(l), 43 U.S.C. § 1702(l). See FLPMA § 202(e), 43 U.S.C. § 1712(e). H.R. Rep. No. 1163, 94th Cong., 2d Sess., reprinted in 1976 *U.S. Code Congressional and Administrative News* (hereafter *USCCAN*) 6175, 6179. See also 1976 *USCCAN* 6175, 6219.

37. FLPMA § 202(e), 43 U.S.C. § 1712(e). FLPMA § 202(e)(1), 43 U.S.C. § 1712(e)(1). FLPMA § 202(e)(2), 43 U.S.C. § 1712(e)(2).

38. See 43 U.S.C. § 1752(a), (g). See 43 C.F.R. § 4110.3 (1994). 43 C.F.R. § 4110.4–2(a)(2) (1994), 43 C.F.R. § 4110.4–2(a)(1) (1994) (emphasis added). McClure Amendment to 1979 appropriations bill, codified at 43 U.S.C. § 1752 note. PRIA, 43 U.S.C. § 1903(b).

39. See *Chadha*, 462 U.S. at 931–35. FLPMA, Pub. L. No. 94-579, § 707.

40. FLPMA contains several provisions that are thought to authorize an unconstitutional "legislative veto," such as that struck down by the U.S. Supreme Court in *Immigration and Naturalization Service v. Chadha*, 462 U.S. 919 (1983). At least two courts have addressed FLPMA § 204, 43 U.S.C. § 1714, which specifies procedures for withdrawals, including disapproval of an executive withdrawal or termination of a withdrawal by a concurrent resolution of Congress, and emergency withdrawals at the instance of the chair of either the House or Senate Interior Committee. These provisions may violate the constitutional requirements for both presentment (presentation of a bill to the president for signature) and bicameralism (approval of a bill by both houses of Congress). U.S. Const. art. I, § 7, cl. 2. *Pacific Legal Foundation v. Watt*, 529 F. Supp. 982 (D. Mont. 1981), upheld § 204 against such a charge. The *National Wildlife Federation v. Watt* court, on the other hand, opined, without deciding, that the committee action authorized by § 204(e) "will probably be held to be impermissible legislative activity." 571 F. Supp. 1145, 1155 (D.D.C. 1983). Most, though not all, commentators, conclude that these provisions *are* unconstitutional per *Chadha*. See Coggins, Wilkinson, and Leshy, *Federal Public Land*, 305; Glicksman, "Severability"; Lee, "FLPMA's Legislative Veto." Section 202(e) also may violate the requirement that a legislative act be presented to the president for signature before becoming law, although no court has considered § 202(e) in light of the ruling in *Chadha*. Section 202(e) triggers the legislative veto concern *only* if Congress exercises its disapproval authority. FLPMA § 201(a), 43 U.S.C. § 1711(a). FLPMA § 102(a)(11), 43 U.S.C. § 1701(a)(11). See also Sax, "Claim for Retention," 126. FLPMA § 202(c)(3), 43 U.S.C. § 1712(c)(3). FLPMA § 103(a), 43 U.S.C. § 1702(a). See also 43 C.F.R. § 1610.7–2 (1995); *BLM Manual* 1613 (1988); Williams and Campbell, "How the BLM Designates ACECs," 232.

41. Williams and Campbell, "How the BLM Designates ACECs," 232 (citations omitted).

42. See Cooperrider, "Conservation of Biodiversity," 50; Williams and Campbell, "How the BLM Designates ACECs," 235–36. The Natural Resources Defense Council

"question[ed] how ACEC's that small can protect the indicated values." Ibid., 236. It was not clear from the context whether "that small" referred to areas less than 40 hectares or less than 400 hectares. See ibid. The report noted that "range resources" were protected in only 9 of 357 ACECs, but that grazing was a threat to "resources and values" in 32 ACECs. Ibid., 235. See 43 C.F.R. § 1610.7–2 (1995).

43. FLPMA § 302(b), 43 U.S.C. § 1732(b). See *Babbitt v. Sweet Home Chapter of Communities for a Great Oregon*, 515 U.S. 687, 697–98 (1995).

44. See 43 U.S.C. § 1732(b): no "unnecessary *or* undue degradation" (emphasis added). 43 U.S.C. § 1732(a). See 43 U.S.C. § 1702(h). 43 U.S.C. § 1702(c).

45. See, e.g., *Natural Resources Defense Council v. Hodel*, 624 F. Supp. 1045 (D. Nev. 1985), *affirmed*, 819 F. 2d 927 (9th Cir. 1987). See 43 U.S.C. § 1711, requiring a continuing, current inventory of public lands and resources; see also 43 U.S.C. § 1701(a)(2). But see *Natural Resources Defense Council v. Hodel*, 624 F. Supp. 1045, 1057, 1061 (D. Nev. 1985), declining to overturn BLM grazing-related decisions despite lack of even most basic data. See 43 U.S.C. §§ 1711–12. See, e.g., 5 U.S.C. § 706 (1994); *Motor Vehicle Manufacturers Association v. State Farm Mutual Auto Insurance Co.*, 462 U.S. 29, 43 (1983), noting that an agency decision would be arbitrary if the agency had "entirely failed to consider an important aspect of the problem"; *Foundation for North American Wild Sheep v. U.S. Department of Agriculture*, 681 F.2d 1172 (9th Cir. 1982), overturning a Forest Service decision not to prepare an EIS largely because the agency had ignored relevant available information concerning impacts of the proposed action.

46. FLPMA § 202(c)(1)–(4), 43 U.S.C. § 1712(c)(1)–(4).

47. FLPMA § 202(c)(5)–(9), 43 U.S.C. § 1712(c)(5)–(9) (emphasis added). See generally Holst, "Unforeseeability Factor"; Williams and Rinne, "Biodiversity Management," 5.

48. FLPMA § 202(c)(9), 43 U.S.C. § 1712(c)(9). 43 U.S.C. § 1181(a) (emphasis added). On the other hand, FLPMA does require consideration of local economic needs when land exchanges are contemplated. See 43 U.S.C. § 1716(a). The economics of federal land grazing are taken up in chapter 8.

49. *Robertson v. Methow Valley Citizens Council*, 490 U.S. 332, 350. Sax, "Nature and Habitat Conservation," 53 (emphasis added).

50. FLPMA § 202(c)(7), 43 U.S.C. § 1712(c)(7).

51. Compare 43 U.S.C. § 1716(a), specifying, with respect to land exchanges, that "when considering public interest the Secretary concerned shall give full consideration to . . . the needs of State and local people, including the needs for lands for the economy, community expansion, [etc.]." Kneip, "In Supplying Areas for Recreation," 366–67.

52. Coggins, "Public Rangeland Management IV," 95, 97–98. 43 U.S.C. § 1712(c)(6) (emphasis added).

53. FLPMA § 102(a)(12), 43 U.S.C. § 1701(a)(12).

54. 43 U.S.C. § 1712(c)(1). See 43 U.S.C. § 1702(c), (h). See also chapter 6.

55. 43 U.S.C. § 1712(c)(2). NEPA, 42 U.S.C. § 4332(2)(A). See the discussion of NEPA later in this chapter.

56. 43 U.S.C. § 1712(c)(2), (3). 43 U.S.C. § 1701(a)(8). See chapter 6. 43 U.S.C. § 1702(c). Cf. Krutilla, "Conservation Reconsidered," 785, discussing the "need to consider

what we need as a minimum reserve [of natural environments] to avoid potentially grossly adverse consequences for human welfare." 43 U.S.C. § 103(a), 43 U.S.C. § 1702(a) (emphasis added). See, e.g., Cooperrider, "Conservation of Biodiversity," 50. See also chapter 5.

57. 43 U.S.C. § 1712(c)(4). 43 U.S.C. §§ 1701(a)(2), 1711(a).

58. 43 U.S.C. § 1712(c)(6). See, e.g., CEQ, *Incorporating Biodiversity Considerations*, 7; Noss and Cooperrider, *Saving Nature's Legacy* (chapter 4). Winner, "Sagebrush Steppe," E1, E4.

59. See 43 U.S.C. § 1712(c)(5).

60. See 43 U.S.C. § 1712(c)(7). See generally Godfrey, "Measuring the Economic Impact," 1517; Gardner, "Role of Economic Analysis," 1441; Noss and Cooperrider, *Saving Nature's Legacy*; Krutilla, "Conservation Reconsidered," 784–85 (footnote omitted).

61. See, e.g., 43 U.S.C. §§ 1702(c), 1712(c)(5), (7).

62. See chapter 8 for a discussion of the economics of public land livestock production.

63. 43 U.S.C. § 1732(b). See also the discussion of NEPA later in this chapter.

64. 43 U.S.C. § 1712(c)(9). 43 U.S.C. § 1702(c), defining "multiple use" (emphasis added). See, e.g., 43 U.S.C. § 1701(a)(1)–(2); 43 U.S.C. § 1701(a)(12), referring to the "Nation's need" for certain resources; 43 U.S.C. § 1702(c), referring to the "needs of the American people." 43 U.S.C. § 1702(c), defining "multiple use." Taylor Grazing Act, 43 U.S.C. § 315.

65. FLPMA § 401(b)(1), 43 U.S.C. § 1751(b)(1). FLPMA § 401(a), 43 U.S.C. § 1751(a). *Study of Grazing Fees*. Muhn and Stuart, *Story of BLM*, 69. See Wagner, "Livestock Grazing and the Livestock Industry," 140; Archer and Smeins, "Ecosystem-Level Processes," 126. Voigt, *Public Grazing Lands*, 239.

66. BLM, *1992 Annual Report*, 5. Fischman, "Endangered Species Conservation," 19–20, quoting BLM Manual § 6500.06 and citing U.S. Department of the Interior, BLM, *Fish and Wildlife 2000*.

67. See U.S. Department of the Interior, BLM, "Ecosystem Management in the BLM," Att. 1-1 to 1-2. Ibid., 5, Att. 1-1, Att. 1-6.

68. Ibid., Att. 1-6.

69. Ibid., Att. 1-7, Att. 1-9.

70. See Fischman, "Endangered Species Conservation," 20 n. 102, summarizing case law. See also *Western Radio Services v. Espy*, 79 F. 3d 896 (9th Cir. 1996), holding Forest Service Manual provisions not enforceable. See Fairfax, "Coming of Age," 1750.

71. U.S. Department of the Interior, BLM, "Ecosystem Management in the BLM," 4. Waller, "Introduction," xiv. Williams and Rinne, "Biodiversity Management," 5. BLM, *1992 Annual Report*, 6. Keystone Center, *Biological Diversity on Federal Lands*, 49–54.

72. See generally *Applied Biodiversity Conservation*.

73. See also Keystone Center, *Biological Diversity on Federal Lands*, 51, noting that the BLM "has a mandate to inventory and monitor elements of biological diversity and authority to conduct research." See FLPMA § 102(a)(8), 43 U.S.C. § 1701(a)(8).

74. Pub. L. No. 95-514 (codified at 43 U.S.C. §§ 1901–8 [1994]). See also Comptroller General's Report. 43 U.S.C. § 1901(a)(1)–(2). 43 U.S.C. § 1751(b)(1). PRIA's description of range conditions is codified at 43 U.S.C. § 1901(a)(3).

75. 43 U.S.C. § 1902(d), 1902(e).

76. 43 U.S.C. § 1901(b)(2). See, e.g., 43 U.S.C. §§ 1901(a)(4), 1904. See FLPMA, 43 U.S.C. § 1751(b)(1).

77. Voigt, *Public Grazing Lands*, 315. "Dombeck Says," 7. St. Clair, "Talkin' about Cows," 7, 8. St. Clair was reporting on the town hall–style meetings chaired by Interior Secretary Babbitt and held around the West in 1993 to discuss federal grazing reforms.

78. Gillis, "Should Cows Chew Cheatgrass," 675, citing Johanna Wald, Natural Resources Defense Council. Fairfax, "Coming of Age," 1737. See 43 U.S.C. § 1751(b)(1). 43 U.S.C. § 1904.

79. 43 U.S.C. § 1903(b). Coggins, "Public Rangeland Management IV," 115–16 (emphasis in original).

80. Fairfax, "Coming of Age," 1736.

81. 43 U.S.C. § 1901(c).

82. See 43 U.S.C. § 1702(l). Fairfax, "Coming of Age," 1736.

83. 43 U.S.C. § 1903(b) (emphasis added).

84. 43 U.S.C. §§ 1902(d), 1901(b)(2), 1903(b), 1901(a)(1). The decision could be made by the interior secretary in the exercise of his discretion or in the ordinary course of the BLM land planning process. See 43 U.S.C. § 1903(b); 43 U.S.C. § 1712(c), (e).

85. Pub. L. 91-190 (codified as amended at 42 U.S.C. §§ 4321–70d [1994]). See, e.g., *Robertson v. Methow Valley Citizens Council*, 490 U.S. 332, 349–51 (1989). 42 U.S.C. § 4332(C). See also *Methow Valley*, 490 U.S. at 349–50. The EIS is the "detailed statement" required by 42 U.S.C. § 4332(C). See also 40 C.F.R. pt. 1502 (Council on Environmental Quality's EIS regulations). See 40 C.F.R. §§ 1501.3 to 1501.4.

86. 42 U.S.C. §§ 4331(b)(4), 4332(2)(C)(i)–(v). See, e.g., Holst, "Unforeseeability Factor"; Bear, "Promise of NEPA," 178; CEQ, *Incorporating Biodiversity Considerations*; Noss and Cooperrider, *Saving Nature's Legacy*, 335. See also Keystone Center, *Biological Diversity on Federal Lands*, 48.

87. 40 C.F.R. §§ 1502.16, 1502.22. See also 40 C.F.R. §§ 1508.7, defining "cumulative impact," and 1508.8, defining "effects." *Robertson v. Methow Valley Citizens Council*, 490 U.S. 332, 354–56 (1989). CEQ, *Incorporating Biodiversity Considerations*, 23 (emphasis added), citing 40 C.F.R. § 1502.22, which "provide[s] a framework for agencies to proceed when faced with incomplete or unavailable information."

88. CEQ, *Incorporating Biodiversity Considerations*, 23. 58 Fed. Reg. 60,050 (12 November 1993); 59 *Fed. Reg.* 54,625, 54,626–27 (1 November 1994); 60 *Fed. Reg.* 37,666, 37,667 (21 July 1995).

89. CEQ, *Incorporating Biodiversity Considerations*, 23–24. See chapter 6.

90. Pub. L. 93-205 (codified as amended at 16 U.S.C. §§ 1531–44 [1994]). See, e.g., Cheever, "Road to Recovery"; Holst, "Unforeseeability Factor"; Patlis, "Biodiversity, Ecosystems, and Endangered Species," 43; Ruhl, "Section 7." See also Keystone Center, *Biological Diversity on Federal Lands*, 48–49.

91. ESA § 7(a)(1), (2) 16 U.S.C. §§ 1536(a)(1), (2). 16 U.S.C. § 1531(c)(1). See also generally Ruhl, "Section 7." 16 U.S.C. § 1532(3).

92. 16 U.S.C. § 1533. 50 C.F.R. pt. 402. 16 U.S.C. § 1531(b).

93. Beattie, "Biodiversity Policy," 13–14. Ruhl, "Section 7," 1112.

94. Beattie, "Biodiversity Policy," 13. See Noss and Cooperrider, *Saving Nature's Legacy*, 105–7; Hunter, "Coping with Ignorance."

95. Pub. L. 92-500 (codified as amended at 33 U.S.C. §§ 1251–1387 [1994]). See 33 U.S.C. §§ 1323(a), 1341. 43 U.S.C. 1712(c)(8). 33 U.S.C. § 1323(a). See also Glicksman, "Pollution on the Federal Lands." 33 U.S.C. § 1341(a), (d). See *PUD No. 1 v. Washington Department of Ecology*, 511 U.S. 700 (1994). But see *Oregon Natural Desert Association v. Dombeck*, 46 ERC 1993 (9th Cir. 1998), *reversing Oregon Natural Desert Association v. Thomas*, 940 F. Supp. 1534, 1541 (D. Ore. 1996). See also Donahue, "Untapped Power," 226–28, 286–87. The section 401 requirement places the burden on states, not the federal agency (BLM or Forest Service), however, to determine whether the permitted activity would fully comply with water quality requirements. See 33 U.S.C. § 1344; 33 C.F.R. pt. 328 (1995); 40 C.F.R. pt. 230 (1995). See also *United States v. Riverside Bayview Homes, Inc.*, 474 U.S. 121, 132–35 (1985). See, e.g., Donahue, "Untapped Power"; Glicksman, "Pollution on the Federal Lands"; *Northwest Indian Cemetery Protective Association v. Peterson*, 764 F. 2d 581 (9th Cir. 1985), *reversed in part on other grounds sub nom. Lyng v. Northwest Indian Cemetery Protective Association*, 485 U.S. 439 (1988).

96. 33 U.S.C. § 1251(a) (emphasis added). 33 U.S.C. § 1313(c)(2)(A). See, e.g., *Riverside Bayview Homes*, 474 U.S. at 134–35. See *PUD No. 1 v. Washington Department of Ecology*, 511 U.S. 700 (1994); Donahue, "Untapped Power," 215–16.

97. Pendergrass, "Rediscovering Old Tools," 165–66, 168–70, quoting U.S. EPA, *Water Quality Standards*, 18, 6.

98. "Preliminary Summary," 25–26. See also chapter 5. *Oregon Natural Desert Association v. Thomas*, 940 F. Supp. 1534, 1541 (D. Ore. 1996), *reversed, Oregon Natural Desert Association v. Dombeck*, 46 ERC 1993 (9th Cir. 1998). See 151 F. 3d 945, noting that the Ninth Circuit opinion was withdrawn from publication. Federal Rules of Appellate Procedure, Ninth Circuit, rule 36-3. See also ibid., rules 36-1 and 36-2. For a thorough discussion of the reasoning that supports the *ONDA* district court's opinion, see Donahue, "Untapped Power," 226–28, 286–87. See also *PUD No. 1 v. Washington Department of Ecology*, 511 U.S. 700 (1994).

99. See Donahue, "Untapped Power," 286–87.

CHAPTER 8. THE SOCIOECONOMIC LANDSCAPE

1. See, e.g., Behan, "Multiple Use Management," 2002; Fairfax, "Legal and Political Aspects," 1703; and the works of George Wuerthner, Denzel and Nancy Ferguson, Lynn Jacobs, George Coggins, and Johanna Wald.

2. See Power, *Lost Landscapes*, 246–47 (contrasting quantitative and qualitative indices of, and goals for, economic health and well-being), 177–83.

3. 43 U.S.C. § 315 (emphasis added). See generally "Applying Socioeconomic Techniques," part 5, in *Developing Strategies*, 1427–1681. See also Nielsen, "Economic Factors," 1373; Gray, "Response to 'Economic Factors,'" 1387. See also Clawson, "Multiple-Use Considerations," 28–32. Hays, "Public Values," 1811, 1823 (quotation).

See generally Worster, *Under Western Skies*; Hardt, "Federal Land Management"; Brubaker, *Rethinking the Federal Lands*.

4. Workman, Fairfax, and Burch, "Applying Socioeconomic Techniques," 1428. One economic tool for assessing passive-use or nonuse values (e.g., so-called option and bequest values) is called contingent valuation. The method involves the use of survey techniques to evaluate a population's willingness to pay to preserve a species or a landscape. For instance, the researcher might ask whether a person would vote for a property tax increase of $20 per year where the additional revenues would be used to reduce by 30 percent the likelihood that some endangered species would become extinct over the next fifty years. Contingent valuation allows researchers to estimate "option" and "bequest" values by asking questions like, "How much is it worth to you to protect Chaco Canyon, even if you might never visit it?" or, "How much would you pay to help preserve high sagebrush desert for future generations?" Contingent valuation has been approved for use by both the Department of the Interior's U.S. Fish and Wildlife Service and the Department of Commerce's National Oceanic and Atmospheric Administration. Each agency incorporates the methodology in its regulations for assessing natural resource damages due to oil or hazardous substance spills. See 50 C.F.R. part 11, 15 C.F.R. part 990. Contingent valuation measures were used to assess the damage to beaches, marine life, and other natural resources caused when the *Exxon Valdez* oil tanker ran aground and spilled 11 million gallons of crude oil into Alaska's Prince William Sound in 1989.

5. Workman, Fairfax, and Burch, "Applying Socioeconomic Techniques," 1430–31. Kneip, "In Supplying Areas for Recreation," 368.

6. Hays, "Public Values," 1826, citing the new disciplines of forest sociology and forest psychology, which have emerged to analyze these values. Ibid., 1812–14 (citing a 1976 Gallup poll), 1831–32.

7. NRC, *Land Use and Wildlife Resources*, 259. Ehrenfeld, "Why Put a Value on Biodiversity?" 215. For more traditional examinations of the economics of public land grazing, readers are directed to the National Research Council report *Developing Strategies for Rangeland Management* (1984), in particular the sections within it entitled "Manipulative Range Improvements" and "Applying Socioeconomic Techniques to Range Management Decision Making." See also generally Markandya and Richardson, eds., *Environmental Economics*.

8. Ehrenfeld, "Why Put a Value on Biodiversity?" 216.

9. Peffer, *Closing of the Public Domain*, 22. See Hays, *Conservation*, 50–52; Adams, *Renewable Resource Policy*, 90–91. Merrill, "Private Spaces," 30–32. See Hays, *Conservation*, 51–52; Pelzer, *Cattlemen's Frontier*; Clawson, *Western Range Livestock Industry*, 14. See also chapters 1 and 2.

10. 43 U.S.C. § 315. USDA, *The Western Range*.

11. Roberts, "Integrated Part of Western Agriculture," 379–82. Roberts included in this figure all crop production, irrigation expenditures, etc.

12. USDA, *The Western Range*, iii. Roberts, "Integrated Part of Western Agriculture," 378–79.

13. Roberts, "Integrated Part of Western Agriculture," 378–81.

14. Ibid., 417, 416.

15. Ibid. See also Rowley, *Forest Service Grazing*, 159–60.

16. Roberts, "Integrated Part of Western Agriculture," 417–18.

17. Forsling et al., "Range Conservation the Exception," 287–88. Show, "Probable Future Use," 454.

18. Show, "Probable Future Use," 454. Forsling et al., "Range Conservation the Exception," 286–88.

19. Clapp, "Major Range Problems," 37–38, 61. See generally ibid., 37–67. Forsling et al., "Administration of Public Range," 454.

20. Bailey and Connaughton, "In Watershed Protection," 337. Clapp, "Major Range Problems," 25. Gates, *History of Public Land Law*, 620.

21. Clapp, "Major Range Problems," 25–27. See also Kneip, "In Supplying Areas for Recreation," 372-73.

22. Clapp, "Major Range Problems," 45, 27–28.

23. Ibid., 44–45 (emphasis added), 57. See also Forsling et al., "Administration of Public Range," 454–55. See Clapp, "Major Range Problems," 39–40, 55, 58, 61.

24. Kneip, "In Supplying Areas for Recreation," 366–67. Show, "Probable Future Use," 455.

25. Kneip, "In Supplying Areas for Recreation," 367.

26. Clapp, "Major Range Problems," 41.

27. See, e.g., Heinz, "Continued Grazing," 708–9; Jamieson, "Sustainability and Beyond," 7.

28. Kneip, "In Supplying Areas for Recreation," 368, 364, 371.

29. Ibid., 369. See Adams, *Renewable Resource Policy*, 205, quoting National Conference on Outdoor Recreation, *Report Epitomizing Results*, 89.

30. Clawson, *Western Range Livestock Industry*, 109–10.

31. Ibid., 14, 84 (emphasis added), 378. Compare Graf, *Wilderness Preservation*, 163; Voigt, *Public Grazing Lands*, 244; Hagenstein, "Federal Lands Today," 86.

32. Clawson, *Western Range Livestock Industry*, 14–16, 104–6.

33. Ibid., 385. Peffer, *Closing of the Public Domain*, 311–12, quoting a 1958 article in *American Cattle Producer*. See Clawson, *Western Range Livestock Industry*, 112.

34. Muhn and Stuart, *Story of BLM*, 167, quoting Mike Harvey, former PLLRC staffer and chief of BLM's Division of Legislation and Regulation. For a discussion of the PLLRC and its recommendations, see generally Coggins, "Public Rangeland Management IV," 7–9.

35. *PLLRC Report*, 48, 115–16 (emphasis added).

36. Ibid., 38, 42, 45–56, 51, 115 (emphasis deleted).

37. Ibid., 33–34, 46. See Taylor Grazing Act § 1, 43 U.S.C. § 315.

38. *PLLRC Report*, 105, 36. See also University of Idaho, *The Forage Resource*, S-51.

39. *PLLRC Report*, 115–16.

40. Ibid., 47–48.

41. University of Idaho, *The Forage Resource*.

42. Ibid., S-19, facing page S-20 (tables S-2, S-3). See also *PLLRC Report*, 105. University of Idaho, *The Forage Resource*, S-27. By way of comparison, the GAO reports that more than 160 acres are "sometimes required to support one cow for 1

month in southern New Mexico, Arizona, southwestern Utah, southeastern California, and most of Nevada," although the "average rate" is 16 acres. GAO, *BLM's Hot Desert Grazing Program*, 18–19.

43. University of Idaho, *The Forage Resource*, S-20, S-23.

44. Ibid., S-61, S-35 to S-37.

45. Ibid., S-51. See also *United States v. Fuller*, 409 U.S. 488, 490, 495–98 (1973), concerning the capitalized value of grazing permits; Klyza, *Who Controls Public Lands?* 140. University of Idaho, *The Forage Resource*, S-55 to S-57, S-61. See also Libecap, *Locking Up the Range*, 50.

46. University of Idaho, *The Forage Resource*, S-62, S-57 to S-58. See 48 Stat. 1269 (1934) (Taylor Act preamble). See Rowley, *Forest Service Grazing*, 159–60.

47. *PLLRC Report*, 105, 3; see ibid., 11, 36. FLPMA, 43 U.S.C. § 1701(a)(9).

48. *PLLRC Report*, 161, 160 (emphasis in original; some emphasis deleted).

49. Ibid., 108, 168. Cf. Ferguson and Ferguson, *Sacred Cows*, 139.

50. *PLLRC Report*, 168, 87.

51. Ibid., 198, 202, 205 (emphasis in original). See ibid., 47.

52. Ibid., 282 (emphasis added).

53. Nelson, "Economic Analysis," 53, citing USDA, Forest Service, *National Range Resources*.

54. Nelson, "Economic Analysis," 53–54. Cf. Bock, Bock, and Smith, "Proposal for a System," 731.

55. Nelson, "Economic Analysis," 54.

56. Ibid., 55, quoting U.S. Department of Agriculture, *Opportunities to Increase Red Meat Production*, 51.

57. See Coggins, "Public Rangeland Management IV," 7. Pub. L. No. 94-579, 43 U.S.C. §§ 1701–84 (1994). See, e.g., *PLLRC Report*, 48–51. See, e.g., 43 U.S.C. § 1701. FLPMA § 401(a), 43 U.S.C. § 1751(a) (emphasis added).

58. *Study of Grazing Fees*, 1-7, citing FLPMA § 102(a)(9), 43 U.S.C. § 1701(a)(9).

59. *Study of Grazing Fees*, 3-3.

60. Graf, *Wilderness Preservation*, 198. Regarding Yellowstone visitation, see www.yellowstone.net. Clapp, "Major Range Problems," 27. Kneip, "In Supplying Areas for Recreation," 372–73. Voigt, *Public Grazing Lands*, 234. Adams, *Renewable Resource Policy*, 215.

61. Muhn and Stuart, *Story of BLM*, 132. Department of the Interior, *Rangeland Reform Summary*, 23.

62. Graf, *Wilderness Preservation*, 25, 200, 240–42, 259.

63. Nelson, "Ideology and Public Land Policy," 288. See, e.g., *Public Lands News; Casper [Wyoming] Star-Tribune*.

64. Nelson, "Ideology and Public Land Policy," 288. See also Nelson, "Economic Analysis," 62. Graf, *Wilderness Preservation*, 236.

65. Nelson, "Ideology and Public Land Policy," 292, 287 (emphasis added). Clawson, *Federal Lands Revisited*, 200–211 (quotation on 209). See Nelson, "Economic Analysis," 65.

66. Nelson, "Ideology and Public Land Policy," 292, 287–88, 296. See also Nelson, "Economic Analysis," 60.

67. Conner, "Social and Economic Influences," 197.

68. For readers not familiar with the economic terms "option" and "existence" values, Howard Zahniser's comparison of wildernesses to art galleries is apropos and enlightening. As he explained, both are "available to everyone, visited by relatively few, [and] highly valued by many who never visit them." To Zahniser personally, option and existence values of wilderness were paramount. Graf contrasted Zahniser, who suffered from "a sciatic condition in his legs and a poor heart condition," with the energetic outdoorsman and mountaineer Robert Marshall. For Zahniser, who "was hardly up to a wilderness experience in any case," "wilderness was more of an ideal than an experience." Graf, *Wilderness Preservation*, 234 (citation omitted).

69. Costanza et al., "Value of the World's Ecosystem Services." See also Workman, Fairfax, and Burch, "Applying Socioeconomic Techniques," 1430. See Gray, "Response to 'Economic Factors,'" 1393; Nielsen, "Economic Factors"; Krutilla, "Conservation Reconsidered"; NRC, *Rangeland Health*, 21. See generally Markandya and Richardson, eds., *Environmental Economics*.

70. Wilson, *The Diversity of Life*, 320 (emphasis in original). See also ibid., 319–20; Caro, Pelkey, and Grigione, "Effects of Conservation Biology Education"; Kellert, *Attitudes—I*, 36–37; Kellert, *Attitudes—II*, 71, 75–76. See Krutilla, "Conservation Reconsidered," 784–85.

71. Wilkinson, *Crossing the Next Meridian*, 81. USDI, BLM, *Public Lands Statistics*, 1, 23.

72. Rowley, *Forest Service Grazing*, 177, 208.

73. Webb, *The Great Plains*, 226. Pisani, *To Reclaim a Divided West*, 226–27. According to Pisani, the "end of the cattle boom came several years before the notorious 'white winter' of 1886–87. Thousands of animals died during the winter of 1884–85 and the unusually dry summer that followed." Ibid.

74. Rowley, *Forest Service Grazing*, 14, 17–18. Senate Committee, *Grazing on Public Lands and National Forests*, 7. Barth and McCullough, *Grazing Impacts on Riparian Areas*, 19. Collins, "Sheepwagons," B1. Worster, *Nature's Economy*, 264. University of Idaho, *The Forage Resource*, S-23.

75. Clawson, *Western Range Livestock Industry*, 112. See USDI, BLM, *Public Lands Statistics*, 23–24. U.S. Department of the Interior, *Rangeland Reform*, 1-6. Regarding the declining AUMs, see *Land Letter*, 10 October 1997, 10, citing BLM's assistant director of Renewable Resources and Planning. See also Baden, "Range Resources," 1683, reporting that "AUMs authorized on BLM lands declined from nearly 15 million in 1960 to approximately 10 million in 1975" and citing E. Bruce Godfrey, "Public Land Grazing: Going, Going, Gone?" (paper presented at annual meetings of SRM, 8 February 1978).

76. Department of the Interior, *Rangeland Reform*, 3-64. Godfrey and Pope, "Case for Removing Livestock," 10 (quotation). *Study of Grazing Fees*, 3-5. Wilkinson, *Crossing the Next Meridian*, 75–81, 101–3.

77. *Study of Grazing Fees*, 3–5. Harvey, "Uses and Limits of the Federal Lands Today," 115. *PLLRC Report*, 105.

78. Gillis, "Should Cows Chew Cheatgrass," 669. Department of the Interior, *Rangeland Reform*, 1-6. USDI, BLM, *Public Lands Statistics*, 24. Department of the

Interior, *Rangeland Reform Summary*, 24. Department of the Interior, *Rangeland Reform*, 3-68 (citation omitted; emphasis added).

79. Department of the Interior, *Rangeland Reform*, 3-64 to 3-66 (citation omitted). See Carlson, Horning, and Alberswerth, "Naming Names," 20; GAO, *Profile of the BLM's Grazing Allotments*, 13; USDI, BLM, *Public Lands Statistics,* 23–24. BLM's own "Home Page" data, retrieved April 1996, but dated May 1995, reported that 18,800 farmers or ranchers held permits to graze.

80. Department of the Interior, *Rangeland Reform*, 3-66 (quotation). Department of the Interior, *Rangeland Reform Summary*, 24. Godfrey and Pope, "Case for Removing Livestock," 19. St. Clair, "Talkin' about Cows," 7, quoting Montana congressman Pat Williams. Lacey and Johnson, "Livestock Grazing on Federal Lands," 23. Godfrey and Pope, "Case for Removing Livestock," 9 (quotation). Burgess, "You Say You Want," 16 (quotation).

81. Hearings on H.R. 106, at 107, 109 (statement of George N. Swallow), 258 (statement by spokesman for Public Lands Coordinating Committee and Nevada Central Committee of Grazing Boards), 252. Comptroller General of the United States, *Public Rangelands*, 1.

82. Department of the Interior, *Rangeland Reform Summary*, 41; see also Department of the Interior, *Rangeland Reform*, 4-118 to 4-121.

83. Department of the Interior, *Rangeland Reform Summary*, 41; see also Godfrey and Pope, "Case for Removing Livestock," 10. The substantial environmental consequences of eliminating grazing are addressed in chapter 5.

84. Department of the Interior, *Rangeland Reform*, 3-68. See Hagenstein, "Federal Lands Today," 86–87. See Godfrey and Pope, "Case for Removing Livestock," 13, 18. Driscoll, "Big Beef Supply," 15.

85. Lacey and Johnson, "Livestock Grazing on Federal Lands," 23, 26 (emphasis added). Nielsen, "Economic Factors," 1376. See also Hagenstein, "Federal Lands Today," 87.

86. Micheli, "Response to 'Role of Land Treatments,'" 1421–23. See "Micheli Says Agriculture Suffering," 7.

87. Young, "Historical and Evolutionary Perspectives," 7–9. See Box, "American Rangeland," 2.

88. Young, "Historical and Evolutionary Perspectives," 7–9.

89. S. 852, § 101(a)(8); accord S. 1459, § 101(a)(9) (emphasis added). Holechek and Hess, "Free Market Policy," 63.

90. Department of the Interior, *Rangeland Reform*, 3-65 (emphasis added). Department of the Interior, *Rangeland Reform Summary*, 24. Department of the Interior, *Rangeland Reform*, at 3-78. See also McConnell, *Private Power*, 211, asserting that the western livestock industry and public grazing lands "are of only minor importance to the nation's economy." Holechek and Hess asserted that "discontinuation of federal land grazing . . . would severely harm some local economies." Holechek and Hess, "Free Market Policy," 63. They gave no examples and cited no statistics, however.

91. Gardner, "Role of Economic Analysis," 1463.

92. Department of the Interior, *Rangeland Reform*, 3-77. See USDA, Forest Service, *Social and Economic Assessment*; Department of the Interior, *Rangeland Reform*,

4-118 to 4-119; Ferguson and Ferguson, *Sacred Cows*, 225. See also the discussion later in the chapter of the disparity between permit revenues and grazing program administration costs.

93. GAO, *BLM's Hot Desert Grazing Program*, 47–48, 4.

94. Smith and Martin, "Socioeconomic Behavior," 224 (emphasis added). Power, *Lost Landscapes*, 188.

95. See Hearings on H.R. 106, at 252, 253, statement by George W. Abbott. USDA, Forest Service, *Social and Economic Assessment*.

96. Power, *Lost Landscapes*, xiii, 1–5, 181–86, 191 (quotation), 253–54.

97. Ibid., 183, 5 (emphasis added), citing U.S. Census of Agriculture (1987).

98. Power, *Lost Landscapes*, 182.

99. Ibid., 182–83 and table 8-1, citing New Mexico State University College of Agriculture, *Importance of Public Lands*.

100. Power, *Lost Landscapes*, 182–85 and table 8-2, 189 (citation omitted).

101. Department of the Interior, *Rangeland Reform Summary*, 24; see ibid., 41. Department of the Interior, *Rangeland Reform*, 3-56 to 3-63 (emphasis added).

102. Krza, "While the New West Booms," 12. Bishop, "Who's Waging War," E4. Department of the Interior, *Rangeland Reform Summary*, 41. Martin, "Mitigating the Economic Impacts," 1673 (emphasis in original). See also generally Jacobs, *Waste of the West*; Ferguson and Ferguson, *Sacred Cows*.

103. Box, "American Rangeland," 2–3. Godfrey and Pope, "Case for Removing Livestock," 10, 9, citing Hahn et al., *Estimating Forage Values*.

104. Holechek, Hawkes, and Darden, "Macro Economics and Cattle Ranching," 122–23. See also Hagenstein, "Federal Lands Today," 87. Roten, "Prairie Rides," 21. Department of the Interior, *Rangeland Reform*, 3-74 to 3-75.

105. Limerick, *Desert Passages*, 170–71, quoting Powell, *Report on the Lands*, at 7, 8, 30. GAO, *BLM's Hot Desert Grazing Program*, 48–49. Similarly, Libecap reported studies in the Southwest, which "revealed a sharp drop in costs as ranch size expanded up to eight hundred cattle" and similar economies of scale for sheep operations. Libecap, *Locking Up the Range*, 50–51.

106. Smith and Martin, "Socioeconomic Behavior of Cattle Ranchers," 217, 223–24 (citations omitted; emphasis added). See GAO, *BLM's Hot Desert Grazing Program*, 3.

107. Fowler and Gray, "Rangeland Economics," 78, 82–83 (emphasis added; citation omitted). See GAO, *BLM's Hot Desert Grazing Program*, 48–49.

108. Fowler and Gray, "Rangeland Economics," 82–83. Holechek and Hess, "Free Market Policy," 63.

109. Stevens, *Wyoming Mountain Valley Cattle Ranching*, 1, 3. Rea, "Staying on the Land," B1, quoting rancher Bruce Weeter, owner of Double H Ranch south of Ten Sleep, Wyoming, who received the Wyoming Stock Growers Association Environmental Stewardship Award in 1996.

110. Fowler and Gray, "Rangeland Economics," 71–78. A Farm Credit Services banker, describing the influence of the cattle price cycle, recently reported that a typical ranch's profit was around 1 percent, based on an average price of 88 cents per pound. Rea, "Staying on the Land," B1.

111. Fowler and Gray, "Rangeland Economics," 83.

112. Budinsky et al., "Eating into the Deficit," 74 (emphasis in original). Power, *Lost Landscapes*, 186 (citing U.S. Bureau of the Census, *Census of Agriculture*), 187, and table 8-3.

113. See Brunson and Steel, "National Public Attitudes." Department of the Interior, *Rangeland Reform*, 3-78, 3-64.

114. Davis, "Catron County's Politics," 8. Smith and Martin, "Socioeconomic Behavior of Cattle Ranchers," 224, based on 89 personal interviews obtained in a random sample of Arizona ranch owners. Robbins, "Discouraging Words," 81–82. University of Idaho, *The Forage Resource*, S-35. Gardner, "Role of Economic Analysis," 1453 (emphasis deleted).

115. Department of the Interior, *Rangeland Reform*, 3-75 to 3-76, 3-78.

116. GAO, *BLM's Hot Desert Grazing Program*, 48–50. Peryam and Olson, *Impact of Potential Changes*, 15. Smith and Martin, "Socioeconomic Behavior of Cattle Ranchers," 217–19.

117. Smith and Martin, "Socioeconomic Behavior of Cattle Ranchers," 217–19.

118. Ibid.

119. S. 1459, § 134(a)(3). *PLLRC Report*, 214–15 (emphasis deleted in part).

120. Smith and Martin, "Socioeconomic Behavior of Cattle Ranchers," 219–20 (emphasis added).

121. Ibid., 220, 222.

122. Ibid., 222–23.

123. Olson and Jackson, *Impact of Change*, 17–19. The researchers pointed out that their results "correspond to the findings of the Economic Research Service administrative report to the B.L.M. and Forest Service." Ibid., 18. Unlike Peryam and Olson, Olson and Jackson found that increased fees and reduced AUMs affected net income similarly. Ibid., 19.

124. Peryam and Olson, *Impact of Potential Changes*, 12, 15–17.

125. Feuz and Kearl, *Economic Analysis*, 46.

126. Martin, "Mitigating the Economic Impacts," 1676, 1678, citing the Economic Emergency Loan Program, Farm Operating Loan Program, Feed Grains Set Aside Program, Emergency Livestock Feed Program, Emergency Disaster Loan Program, Farmers Home Administration loans, and ASCS cost-sharing programs, quoting p. 18 of a "report prepared for the House of Representatives and the Senate Committees on Appropriation in Compliance with Public Law 968-126 [*sic*]."

127. See University of Idaho, *The Forage Resource*, S-55; *PLLRC Report*, 105.

128. Smith and Martin, "Socioeconomic Behavior of Cattle Ranchers," 224; see also Power, *Lost Landscapes*, 188. Martin, "Mitigating the Economic Impacts," 1676.

129. Smith and Martin, "Socioeconomic Behavior of Cattle Ranchers," 224. See Clawson, *Western Range Livestock Industry*, 12–13, 381–82; Davis, "Catron County's Politics"; Stiles, "Utah County Sweeps Away Old Guard."

130. Godfrey and Pope, "Case for Removing Livestock," 10 (emphasis added, citations omitted). Nijhuis, "Oil Clashes with Elk," 8, 10. See also Jones, "Drought Cuts to the Bone," reporting the story of an Arizona businessman and absentee "hobby type" operator.

131. Culhane, *Public Lands Politics*, 173–74. Department of the Interior, *Rangeland Reform*, 3-80 to 3-81.

132. *Natural Resources Defense Council v. Hodel*, 624 F. Supp. 1045, 1056 (D. Nev. 1985), *affirmed*, 819 F. 2d 927 (9th Cir. 1987). See generally Department of the Interior, *Rangeland Reform Summary*.

133. Department of the Interior, *Rangeland Reform Summary*, 42; see also Department of the Interior, *Rangeland Reform*, 4-121 to 4-123.

134. Armstrong's comment was made to a meeting of the National Cattlemen's Association on 29 January 1995. Quigley and Bartlett, "Livestock on Public Lands," 2.

135. Nelson, "Economic Analysis," 55.

136. See, e.g., GAO, *BLM's Hot Desert Grazing Program*, 3, 49–50; Jacobs, *Waste of the West*, 500–501, 504–5; Godfrey and Pope, "Case for Removing Livestock," 10. McConnell, *Private Power and American Democracy*, 207.

137. Department of the Interior, *Rangeland Reform Summary*, 25. Godfrey and Pope, "Case for Removing Livestock," 18 (citations omitted).

138. Godfrey and Pope, "Case for Removing Livestock," 9. See, e.g., Reed, "County Supremacy Movement." Quigley and Bartlett, "Livestock on Public Lands," 2.

139. Hays, "Public Values," 1817. See generally Kellert, *Attitudes I*. See also Behan, "Multiple Use Management," 2003.

140. See Malone, "Reflections on the Jeffersonian Ideal." See Department of the Interior, *Rangeland Reform Summary*, 24–25. Nelson, "Economic Analysis," 58, citing a 1979 internal OMB document; Kellert, *Activities II*, 118, reporting that survey respondents who were members of the national stockmen's organizations "had extremely high incomes and education means," while livestock producers generally "had significantly lower education and income means" than respondents in other activity groups.

141. Carlson, Horning, and Albersworth, "Naming Names," 21–22, citing GAO, *Profile of the BLM's Grazing Allotments*, 15 (emphasis added). Carlson et al. were reporting the results of a review by the National Wildlife Federation of BLM data on its grazing permittees and of a GAO study. Chadd reported that "J. R. Simplot's company runs livestock on nearly 2 million acres of [mostly federal] public grazing land." Chadd, "Manifest Subsidy," 20. Egan, "Grazing Bill," A1, C18. Egan also asserted: "Without support from the government, which provides roads, water and forage to ranchers for little or, in some cases, no fees, many cattle operations would leave public land, some experts believe." Ibid., C18. Egan noted that Hewlett and Packard are both in their eighties. Ibid. Compare the discussion of the average age of public land ranchers earlier in this chapter. Contrary views have been expressed on the income issue. Gardner commented in the context of a rhetorical question about the fairness of increasing grazing fees that many public land ranchers "have incomes below the national average." Gardner, "Role of Economic Analysis," 1452–53. He cited no authority for the assertion. In the same volume, Baden referred to "ranchers with relatively low incomes," also citing no authority. Baden, "Range Resources," 1683. And a National Cattlemen's Association official, describing in 1991 the "vulnerability" of ranchers to grazing fee increases, reported that "87% of all BLM permittees own fewer

than 500 cows and many net only $28,000 to $30,000 a year." Gillis, "Should Cows Chew Cheatgrass," 675, citing Jim Connelly. But 500-cow operations would be considered medium or large in most categorizations of ranches by size, and Connelly didn't define "many" or mention what the average or upper incomes of ranchers are.

142. Carlson, Horning, and Alberswerth, "Naming Names," 22. Egan, "In Battle over Public Lands," A12. Egan, "Grazing Bill," C18.

143. Department of the Interior, *Rangeland Reform Summary*, 42.

144. The pertinent sections in Domenici's bills are § 101(a)(9) of S. 852, and § 101(a)(10) of S. 1459. Armstrong's comment was made to a meeting of the National Cattlemen's Association on 29 January 1995. Thomas's remarks were heard on a Wyoming Public Radio news broadcast. Cotton and Cotton, *Wyoming CRM*, 16.

145. Wuerthner, "Subdivisions versus Agriculture," 905, quoting a TNC official. Lenderman, "A Ranch Rescued," 7, quoting TNC spokesperson Libby Ellis. St. Clair, "Talkin' about Cows," 8, quoting a Wilderness Society spokesperson.

146. Wuerthner, "Subdivisions versus Agriculture," 905–6. Ferguson and Ferguson, *Sacred Cows*, 224.

147. Wuerthner, "Subdivisions versus Agriculture," 906. Quigley and Bartlett, "Livestock on Public Lands," 1; see ibid., 1–5. See also Obermiller, "Introduction to the Economics Session," ii. See Vanvig and Hewlett, *Wyoming Farm and Ranch*, 33–34, noting that "[s]cenic and recreational values and high carrying capacities were factors closely associated with higher prices" of grazing lands and that Forest Service grazing permits enhanced ranch price more than did BLM permits.

148. See Godfrey and Pope, "Case for Removing Livestock," 10. GAO, *BLM's Hot Desert Grazing Program*, 48–49. Department of the Interior, *Rangeland Reform*, 3-73 to 3-78. Smith and Martin, "Socioeconomic Behavior of Cattle Ranchers," 219, 223–24.

149. Wuerthner, "Subdivisions versus Agriculture," 906.

150. See, e.g., U.S. House, *Hearings on H.R. 106*, 107–12; Micheli, "Response to 'Role of Land Treatments,'" 142; Egan, "In Idaho," C18. Nelson, "Economic Analysis," 50.

151. See Vesilind, "Anything But Empty," 46. Lacey and Johnson, "Livestock Grazing on Federal Lands," 23, 26. Stevens, *Wyoming Mountain Valley Cattle*, 1.

152. Rowley, *Forest Service Grazing*, 223, 233–34. Hess and Holechek, "If Rain Doesn't Fall," 20. The plant (locoweed) to which Holechek refers is probably a species of *Astragalus* or *Oxytropis*.

153. Nelson, "Economic Analysis," 58. Holechek and Hess, "Free Market Policy," 63.

154. See Lacey and Johnson, "Livestock Grazing on Federal Lands," 23. Herbel, "Manipulative Range Improvements," 1172 (citation omitted). "[N]onuse of grazing animals" is a cost of range improvements, Herbel explains, because "[v]irtually any range improvement practice requires deferment of grazing." Ibid., 1170.

155. Gillis, "Should Cows Chew Cheatgrass," 669; Burgess, "You Say You Want," 16. Clawson, "Multiple-Use Considerations," 32. Schlebecker, *Cattle Raising on the Plains*, 177, 200. Jacobs, *Waste of the West*, 380. Holechek and Hess, "Free Market Policy," 63. Klyza, *Who Controls Public Lands?* 135. Nelson, "Ideology and Public Land Policy," 280. Nelson, "Economic Analysis," 66 (emphasis added).

156. Godfrey and Pope, "Case for Removing Livestock," 6, citing an unpublished paper by R. H. Nelson, Office of Policy Analysis, Department of the Interior. Rimbey, "Economic Factors," 408. Range improvement costs were $1.13 and $0.79 per AUM for the BLM and USFS, respectively. Ibid. GAO, *BLM's Hot Desert Grazing Program*, 4.

157. Ferguson and Ferguson, *Sacred Cows*, 225. Holechek and Hess. "Free Market Policy," 63. Nelson, "Economic Analysis," 65.

158. Burgess, "You Say You Want," 16.

159. See, e.g., Holechek and Hess, "Free Market Policy," 64; Holechek and Hess, "Emergency Feed Program," 135; Martin, "Mitigating the Economic Impacts," 1676.

160. Holechek and Hess, "Emergency Feed Program," 133–34.

161. Ibid. Public Law 127, § 171(b), 104th Cong., 2d sess., 4 April 1996.

162. Godfrey and Pope, "Case for Removing Livestock," 9 (citations omitted), noting that these studies all emphasized wildlife and livestock.

163. See generally USDA, *The Western Range*. GAO, *BLM's Hot Desert Grazing Program*, 50. Workman et al., "Applying Socioeconomic Techniques," 1434, 1439. Bishop, "Who's Waging War," E4.

164. Quigley and Bartlett, "Livestock on Public Lands," 2. Fowler and Gray, "Rangeland Economics," 86. Martin, "Mitigating the Economic Impacts," 1482. As to what those "marginal rates of substitution" might be, Martin says we "certainly have no idea." Ibid. See also chapter 5. See Westoby, Walker, and Noy-Meir, "Opportunistic Management," regarding use of livestock as a range management tool.

165. Cotton and Cotton, *Wyoming CRM*, 16. See, e.g., ibid., 7–8. See "Preliminary Summary of Findings," I-B-2; Wuerthner, "Subdivisions versus Agriculture," 905, citing EPA, *Livestock Grazing on Western Riparian Areas*.

166. Micheli, "Response to 'Role of Land Treatments,'" 1424. Nielsen, "Economic Factors," 1379.

167. Power, *Lost Landscapes*, 188–89.

168. Ibid., 189–90.

169. Ibid., 5 (emphasis added).

170. Krutilla, "Conservation Reconsidered," 784–85.

CONCLUSION

1. Martin, "Mitigating the Economic Impacts," 1677.

2. Brunson and Steel, "National Public Attitudes," 77–81. See Department of the Interior, *Rangeland Reform*, 3-80 to 3-81.

3. Brunson and Steel, "National Public Attitudes," 77–81.

4. Department of the Interior, *Rangeland Reform*, 3-80 to 3-81.

5. Brunson and Steel, "National Public Attitudes," 79–80.

6. Department of the Interior, *Rangeland Reform*, 3-80 to 3-81.

7. Magill, "Visual Perceptions," 339–42.

8. See chapter 4 for a discussion of the power of education to influence attitudes about animals and nature.

9. Quigley and Bartlett, "Livestock on Public Lands," 2.

10. Evans, "Nature Protection," 42, citing a 1977 survey by the American Forest Institute, which revealed that nearly two-thirds of Americans thought there should be no logging of national forests. *Public Lands Council v. Babbitt*, 154 F. 3d 1160, 1172 (10th Cir. 1998).

11. Coggins, "Law of Public Rangeland Management V," 546.

12. Noss and Cooperrider, *Saving Nature's Legacy*, 262 (emphasis added). Dwyer, Buckhouse, and Huey, "Impacts of Grazing Intensity," 875.

13. Tarpy, "New Zoos," 11, noting that the annual visitation "exceeds the combined attendance at all big-league baseball, football, and basketball games."

14. Sax, "Claim for Retention of the Public Lands," 129, referring to the "considerable" private benefits derived from uses of the federal lands such as grazing.

15. Wuerthner, "Subdivisions versus Agriculture," 907. Wuerthner included grazing within the category of "marginal uses."

16. Leopold, *Sand County Almanac*, quoted in Noss, "Issues of Scale," 247.

Bibliography

GOVERNMENT PUBLICATIONS

Allen, Edith B. "Restoration Ecology: Limits and Possibilities in Arid and Semiarid Lands." In *Proceedings—Wildland Shrub and Arid Land Restoration Symposium*, compiled by Bruce A. Roundy, E. Durant McArthur, Jennifer S. Haley, and David K. Mann. Las Vegas, Nev., 19–21 October 1993. General Technical Report INT-GTR-315. Ogden, Utah: U.S. Forest Service Intermountain Research Station, September 1994.

Barrow, Jerry R., and Kris M. Havstad. "Natural Methods of Establishing Native Plants on Arid Rangelands." In *Proceedings—Wildland Shrub and Arid Land Restoration Symposium*, compiled by Bruce A. Roundy, E. Durant McArthur, Jennifer S. Haley, and David K. Mann. Las Vegas, Nev., 19–21 October 1993. General Technical Report INT-GTR-315. Ogden, Utah: U.S. Forest Service Intermountain Research Station, September 1994.

Barth, Richard C., and Edgar J. McCullough. *Livestock Grazing Impacts on Riparian Areas within Capitol Reef National Park*. Final Report prepared for the National Park Service by Soil-Plant Systems, Golden, Colo., 1988.

Belnap, Jayne. "Potential Role of Cryptobiotic Soil Crusts in Semiarid Rangelands." In *Proceedings—Ecology and Management of Annual Rangelands*, edited by Stephen B. Monsen and Stanley G. Kitchen. General Technical Report INT-GTR-313. Ogden, Utah: U.S. Forest Service Intermountain Research Station, September 1994.

Briggs, Mark. "Evaluating Degraded Riparian Ecosystems to Determine the Potential Effectiveness of Revegetation." In *Proceedings—Wildland Shrub and Arid Land Restoration Symposium*, compiled by Bruce A. Roundy, E. Durant McArthur, Jennifer S. Haley, and David K. Mann. Las Vegas, Nev., 19–21 October 1993. General Technical Report INT-GTR-315. Ogden, Utah: U.S. Forest Service Intermountain Research Station, September 1994.

Brokaw, Howard P., ed. *Wildlife and America*. Washington, D.C.: Council on Environmental Quality (U.S. Government Printing Office), 1978.

Comptroller General of the United States. *Public Rangelands Continue to Deteriorate*. 5 July 1977. A report to Congress pursuant to *U.S. Code*, vol. 31, secs. 53, 67.

Council on Environmental Quality. *Incorporating Biodiversity Considerations into Environmental Impact Analysis under the National Environmental Policy Act*. January 1993.

Downs, Janelle L., William H. Rickard, and Larry L. Cadwell. "Restoration of Big Sagebrush Habitat in Southeastern Washington." In *Proceedings—Wildland Shrub and Arid Land Restoration Symposium*, compiled by Bruce A. Roundy, E. Durant McArthur, Jennifer S. Haley, and David K. Mann. Las Vegas, Nev., 19–21 October 1993. General Technical Report INT-GTR-315. Ogden, Utah: U.S. Forest Service Intermountain Research Station, September 1994.

Ensign, Edgar T. *Report on the Forest Conditions of the Rocky Mountains*. 2d ed. U.S. Department of Agriculture, Forestry Division, Report. Washington, D.C.: Government Printing Office, 1889.

Feuz, Dillon M., and W. Gordon Kearl. *An Economic Analysis of Enterprise Combinations on Mountain Valley Cattle Ranches*. Department of Agricultural Economics, Agricultural Experiment Station, University of Wyoming. Research Journal 207. April 1987.

Gates, Paul W. *History of Public Land Law Development*. Washington, D.C.: U.S. Government Printing Office, 1968.

General Accounting Office. *Management of Public Rangelands by the Bureau of Land Management*. Testimony of James Duffus III, Associate Director, before the Subcommittee on National Parks and Public Lands of the House Committee on Interior and Insular Affairs, Attachment I. 1988.

————. *Public Land Management: Issues Related to the Reauthorization of the Bureau of Land Management*. Testimony of James Duffus III, Division Director, before the Subcommittee on National Parks and Public Lands of the House Committee on Interior and Insular Affairs, 1991 (GAO/T-RCED-91-20).

————. *Public Rangelands: Some Riparian Areas Restored But Widespread Improvement Will Be Slow*. June 1988.

————. *Rangeland Management: Assessment of Nevada Consulting Firm's Critique of Three GAO Reports*. May 1992.

————. *Rangeland Management: BLM Efforts to Prevent Unauthorized Livestock Grazing Need Strengthening*. December 1990.

————. *Rangeland Management: BLM's Hot Desert Grazing Program Merits Reconsideration*. November 1991.

————. *Rangeland Management: BLM's Range Improvement Project Data Base Is Incomplete and Inaccurate*. April 1993.

————. *Rangeland Management: Comparison of Rangeland Condition Reports*. July 1991.

————. *Rangeland Management: Interior's Monitoring Has Fallen Short of Agency Requirements*. February 1992.

————. *Rangeland Management: More Emphasis Needed on Declining and Overstocked Allotments*. June 1988.

————. *Rangeland Management: Profile of the Bureau of Land Management's Grazing Allotments and Permits*. June 1992.

Godfrey, E. Bruce, and C. Arden Pope III. "The Case for Removing Livestock from Public Lands." In *Current Issues in Rangeland Resource Economics*, edited by Frederick W. Obermiller. Special Rep. 852. Corvallis: Oregon State University Extension Service, February 1990.

Great Plains Agricultural Council, Water Quality Task Force. *Agriculture and Water Quality in the Great Plains: Status and Recommendations*. College Station: Texas Agricultural Experiment Station, 1992.

Griffiths, D. *Forage Conditions on the Northern Border of the Great Basin*. Bureau of Plant Industry Bulletin No. 15. Washington, D.C.: U.S. Department of Agriculture, 1902.

Hahn, W. F., T. L. Crawford, K. E. Nelson, and R. A. Bowl. *Estimating Forage Values for Grazing National Forest Lands*. Staff Report No. 89-51. Washington, D.C.: U.S. Department of Agriculture, ERS, CED, 1989.

Hironaka, Min. "Medusahead: Natural Successor to the Cheatgrass Type in the Northern Great Basin." In *Proceedings—Ecology and Management of Annual Rangelands*, edited by Stephen B. Monsen and Stanley G. Kitchen. Intermountain Research Station General Technical Report INT-GTR-313. Ogden, Utah: U.S. Forest Service, September 1994.

Kellert, Stephen R. *Activities of the American Public Relating to Animals, Phase II*. Washington, D.C.: U.S. Department of the Interior, Fish and Wildlife Service, 1980.

———. *Knowledge, Affection and Basic Attitudes toward Animals in American Society, Phase III*. Washington, D.C.: U.S. Department of the Interior, Fish and Wildlife Service, 1980.

———. *Public Attitudes toward Critical Wildlife and Natural Habitat Issues, Phase I*. Washington, D.C.: U.S. Department of the Interior, Fish and Wildlife Service, 1979.

Legislative Administrative Committee. *Oregon 1997 Legislative Guide*. 1997.

Legislative Counsel Bureau. Research Division. *Biographies of Members of the Nevada Legislature: 1997 Legislative Session*. 1997.

Linhart, Yan B. "Restoration, Revegetation, and the Importance of Genetic and Evolutionary Perspectives." In *Proceedings—Wildland Shrub and Arid Land Restoration Symposium*, compiled by Bruce A. Roundy, E. Durant McArthur, Jennifer S. Haley, and David K. Mann. Las Vegas, Nev., 19–21 October 1993. General Technical Report INT-GTR-315. Ogden, Utah: U.S. Forest Service Intermountain Research Station, September 1994.

Magill, Arthur W. "Visual Perceptions of Management on Arid Lands." In *Proceedings—Wildland Shrub and Arid Land Restoration Symposium*, compiled by Bruce A. Roundy, E. Durant McArthur, Jennifer S. Haley, and David K. Mann. Las Vegas, Nev., 19–21 October 1993. General Technical Report INT-GTR-315. Ogden, Utah: U.S. Forest Service Intermountain Research Station, September 1994.

McClure, Beaumont C. "Meeting the Biodiversity Challenge Land Ownership." In U.S. Bureau of Land Management et al., *Meeting the Biodiversity Challenge: A Shortcourse for Decision-Makers*, sec. 6, 5. Phoenix and Silver Creek, Colo., 26–29 July 1993.

McVicker, Gary. "Ecosystem Management—A Process for Restoring Biodiversity." In U.S. Bureau of Land Management, U.S. Forest Service, and U.S. Fish and Wildlife Service, Applied Biodiversity Conservation, sec. 3, 1. Sacramento, 22–26 February 1993.

Monsen, Stephen B., and Stanley G. Kitchen. *Proceedings—Ecology and Management of Annual Rangelands*. General Technical Report INT-GTR-313. Ogden, Utah: U.S. Forest Service Intermountain Research Station, September 1994.

Muhn, James, and Hanson R. Stuart. *Opportunity and Challenge: The Story of BLM*. Washington, D.C.: U.S. Department of the Interior—Bureau of Land Management, September 1988.

Munda, Bruce D., and Steven E. Smith. "Genetic Variation and Revegetation Strategies for Desert Rangeland Ecosystems." In *Proceedings—Ecology and Management of Annual Rangelands*, edited by Stephen B. Monsen and Stanley G. Kitchen. General Technical Report INT-GTR-313. Ogden, Utah: U.S. Forest Service Intermountain Research Station, September 1994.

National Conference of State Legislatures. *State Legislators' Occupations, 1993 and 1995*. March 1996.

New Mexico State University College of Agriculture. *The Importance of Public Lands to Livestock Production in the United States*. Las Cruces: New Mexico State University College of Agriculture, June 1992.

Noss, Reed F. "Guidelines for Biodiversity Management." In U.S. Bureau of Land Management, U.S. Forest Service, and U.S. Fish and Wildlife Service, *Applied Biodiversity Conservation*, § 14. Sacramento, 22–26 February 1993.

Obermiller, Frederick W., ed. *Current Issues in Rangeland Resource Economics*. Special Rep. 852. Corvallis: Oregon State University Extension Service, February 1990.

———. "Introduction to the Economics Session." In *Current Issues in Rangeland Resource Economics*, edited by Frederick W. Obermiller. Oregon State University Extension Service. Special Rep. 852. February 1990.

Office of Legislative Research and General Counsel. *Utah Legislative Manual, 1997–1998*. 7 February 1997.

Olson, Carl E., and John W. Jackson. *The Impact of Change in Federal Grazing Policies on Southcentral Wyoming Mountain Valley Cattle Ranches*. Research Journal 96. Laramie: Agricultural Experiment Station, University of Wyoming, November 1975.

Peryam, J. Stephen, and Carl E. Olson. *Impact of Potential Changes in BLM Grazing Policies on West-Central Wyoming Cattle Ranches*. Research Journal 87. Laramie: Agricultural Experiment Station, University of Wyoming, April 1975.

Powell, John Wesley. *Report on the Lands of the Arid Regions of the United States*. Washington, D.C.: U.S. Geological Survey, 1878.

Public Land Law Review Commission. *One Third of the Nation's Lands*. Washington, D.C.: U.S. Government Printing Office, 1970.

Quigley, Thomas M., and E. T. Bartlett. "Livestock on Public Lands: Yes!" In *Current Issues in Rangeland Resource Economics*, edited by Frederick W. Obermiller. Special Rep. 852. Corvallis: Oregon State University Extension Service, February 1990.

Rimbey, Neil R. "Economic Factors for Consideration in Converting Annual Grasslands to Improved Rangelands." In *Proceedings—Ecology and Management of Annual Rangelands*, edited by Stephen B. Monsen and Stanley G. Kitchen. General Technical Report INT-GTR-313. Ogden, Utah: U.S. Forest Service Intermountain Research Station, September 1994.

Rosentreter, Roger. "Displacement of Rare Plants by Exotic Grasses." In *Proceedings—Ecology and Management of Annual Rangelands*, edited by Stephen B. Monsen and Stanley G. Kitchen. General Technical Report INT-GTR-313. Ogden, Utah: U.S. Forest Service Intermountain Research Station, September 1994.

Roundy, Bruce A., E. Durant McArthur, Jennifer S. Haley, and David K. Mann, compilers. *Proceedings—Wildland Shrub and Arid Land Restoration Symposium*, Las Vegas, Nev., 19–21 October 1993. General Technical Report INT-GTR-315. Ogden, Utah: U.S. Forest Service Intermountain Research Station, September 1994.

Ryan, Michael G., Linda A. Joyce, Tom Andrews, and Kate Jones. *Research Natural Areas in Colorado, Nebraska, North Dakota, South Dakota, and Parts of Wyoming*. General Technical Report RM-251. Fort Collins, Colo.: U.S. Department of Agriculture–Forest Service, September 1994.

Sanders, Kenneth D. "Can Annual Rangelands Be Converted and Maintained as Perennial Grasslands through Grazing Management?" In *Proceedings—Ecology and Management of Annual Rangelands*, edited by Stephen B. Monsen and Stanley G. Kitchen. General Technical Report INT-GTR-313. Ogden, Utah: U.S. Forest Service Intermountain Research Station, September 1994.

Shafer, Craig L. "Land Conservation Strategy Reserve Design." In U.S. Bureau of Land Management, U.S. Forest Service, and U.S. Fish and Wildlife Service, *Applied Biodiversity Conservation*, sec. 14, no pagination. Sacramento, 22–26 February 1993.

Sheridan, David. *Desertification of the United States*. Washington, D.C.: Council on Environmental Quality, 1981.

———. *Off-Road Vehicles on Public Lands*. Washington, D.C.: Council on Environmental Quality, 1979.

Smeins, Fred E. "Concepts for Solving Biodiversity Problems: Rangeland Ecosystems." In U.S. Bureau of Land Management, U.S. Forest Service, and U.S. Fish and Wildlife Service, *Meeting the Biodiversity Challenge: A Shortcourse for Decision-Makers*, sec. 5. Phoenix and Silver Creek, Colo., 26–29 July 1993.

Smith, R. J. "Conclusions." In *Proceedings of a Seminar on Improving Fish and Wildlife Benefits in Range Management*, edited by J. E. Townsend and R. J. Smith. FWS/OBS-77-1. U.S. Fish and Wildlife Service, 1977.

Sowell, R. F., et al. *Cattle Nutrition in Wyoming's Red Desert*. Science Monograph 45. Laramie: University of Wyoming Agricultural Experiment Station, March 1985.

State of California. *Assembly Weekly History*. 1997. Telefax copy.

———. *Senate Daily File*. 1997. Telefax copy.

State of Idaho. *54th Idaho Legislature: 1997 Directory*. 1997.

State of New Mexico. "Forty-third Legislature, First Session, 1997." 15 January 1997. Photocopy.

State of Washington. House and Senate. *Legislative Manual of State of Washington, 1997–1998*. 1997.

Stevens, Delwin M. *Wyoming Mountain Valley Cattle Ranching in 1973 and 1974: An Economic Analysis*. Research Journal 95. Laramie: Agricultural Experiment Station, University of Wyoming, October 1975.

Study of Grazing Fees for Grazing Livestock on Federal Lands—A Report from the Secretary of the Interior and the Secretary of Agriculture. 21 October 1977.

Stutz, Howard C. "Evolution of Weedy Annuals." In *Proceedings—Ecology and Management of Annual Rangelands,* edited by Stephen B. Monsen and Stanley G. Kitchen. General Technical Report INT-GTR-313. Ogden, Utah: U.S. Forest Service Intermountain Research Station, September 1994.

Tausch, Robin J., Jeanne C. Chambers, Robert R. Blank, and Robert S. Nowak. "Differential Establishment of Perennial Grass and Cheatgrass Following Fire on an Ungrazed Sagebrush-Juniper Site." In *Proceedings—Wildland Shrub and Arid Land Restoration Symposium,* compiled by Bruce A. Roundy, E. Durant McArthur, Jennifer S. Haley, and David K. Mann. Las Vegas, Nev., 19–21 October 1993. General Technical Report INT-GTR-315. Ogden, Utah: U.S. Forest Service Intermountain Research Station, September 1994.

U.S. Bureau of the Census. *Census of Agriculture.* Washington, D.C., 1987.

U.S. Bureau of Land Management, U.S. Forest Service, and U.S. Fish and Wildlife Service. *Applied Biodiversity Conservation.* Sacramento, 22–26 February 1993.

U.S. Comptroller General, *Public Rangelands Continue to Deteriorate.* Washington, D.C.: U.S. Comptroller General, 5 July 1977.

U.S. Department of Agriculture. *Opportunities to Increase Red Meat Production from Ranges of the USA (Nonresearch, Phase 1).* Washington, D.C.: USDA, 1974.

U.S. Department of Agriculture. Forest Service. *Biological Diversity Assessment.* Denver: U.S. Forest Service Rocky Mountain Region, May 1992.

———. *The National Range Resources—A Forest-Range Environmental Study.* Forest Resource Report No. 19, by Forest-Range Task Force. Washington, D.C.: U.S. Government Printing Office, 1972.

———. *Social and Economic Assessment.* Denver: U.S. Forest Service Rocky Mountain Region, May 1992.

U.S. Department of the Interior. Bureau of Land Management. *1992 Annual Report.*

———. "Ecosystem Management in the BLM: A Process to Promote Biological Diversity and Sustainable Development." In *Applied Biodiversity Conservation,* by U.S. Bureau of Land Management, U.S. Forest Service, and U.S. Fish and Wildlife Service, Sacramento, 22–26 February 1993.

———. *Effects of Livestock Grazing on Wildlife, Watershed, Recreation and Other Resource Values in Nevada.* April 1974.

———. *Fish and Wildlife 2000: A Plan for the Future.* n.d.

———. *Management Plan for Afton Canyon Natural Area and the Surrounding Area.* Barstow Resource Area, California Desert District. May 1989.

———. *Managing the Nation's Public Lands.* FY 1992 Annual Report.

———. *Public Lands Statistics: 1991.* 23 September 1992.

———. *Rangeland Reform '94: Draft Environmental Impact Statement.* May 1994.

———. *Rangeland Reform '94: Draft Environmental Impact Statement Executive Summary.* May 1994.

———. *Rangeland Reform '94: Final Environmental Impact Statement.* n.d.

———. *Riparian Area Management: Process for Assessing Proper Functioning Condition.* TR1737-9. 1993.

————. *Riparian-Wetland Initiative for the 1990's.* September 1990.

————. *State of Arizona Wilderness Status Map.* Scale 1:500,000. 1984.

————. *State of California Wilderness Status Map.* Scale 1:1,000,000. November 1991.

————. *State of Colorado Wilderness Status Map.* Scale 1:1,000,000. 1992.

————. *State of Nevada.* Scale 1:1,000,000. 1990.

————. *State of New Mexico Land Status Map.* Scale 1:531,915. 1990.

————. *State of Wyoming Land Status.* Scale 1:500,000. 1984.

————. *Surface Management Responsibility, State of Idaho.* Scale 1:500,000. 1991.

U.S. Department of the Interior and U.S. Department of Agriculture. *Meeting the Biodiversity Challenge: A Shortcourse for Decision-Makers.* Phoenix and Silver Creek, Colorado, 26–29 July 1993.

————. *Study of Fees for Grazing Livestock on Federal Lands.* 21 October 1977. Report to Congress.

U.S. Department of Labor. Bureau of Labor Statistics. *Geographic Profile of Employment and Unemployment, 1995.* Bulletin 2486. February 1997.

U.S. Environmental Protection Agency. *Livestock Grazing on Western Riparian Areas.* Washington, D.C., 1990.

————. *Water Quality Standards for Wetlands: National Guidance.* 1990.

University of Idaho, with Pacific Consultants. *The Forage Resource: A Study for the Public Land Law Review Commission.* Vol. 1, Summary. Moscow, Idaho, 1969.

University of Wyoming Agricultural Experiment Station. "A Ranch Land Price Model for Wyoming." Science Monograph 44. May 1983.

Vail, Delmar. "Symposium Introduction: Management of Semiarid Rangelands-Impacts of Annual Weeds of Resource Values." In *Proceedings—Ecology and Management of Annual Rangelands*, edited by Stephen B. Monsen and Stanley G. Kitchen. General Technical Report INT-GTR-313. Ogden, Utah: U.S. Forest Service Intermountain Research Station, September 1994.

Vanvig, Andrew, and John P. Hewlett. *Wyoming Farm and Ranch Land Market, 1988–90.* Research Journal 210. Laramie: University of Wyoming Agricultural Experiment Station, October 1990.

Vickerman, Sara. "Integrating Biodiversity Strategies at Different Scales." In U.S. Bureau of Land Management, U.S. Forest Service, and U.S. Fish and Wildlife Service, *Applied Biodiversity Conservation.* Sacramento, 22–26 February 1993.

Wagner, Frederic H. "Livestock Grazing and the Livestock Industry." In *Wildlife and America*, edited by Howard P. Brokaw. Washington, D.C.: Council on Environmental Quality/U.S. Government Printing Office, 1978.

Walker, Scott C., Richard Stevens, Stephen R. Monsen, and Kent R. Jorgensen. "Interaction between Native and Seeded Introduced Grasses for Twenty-three Years Following Chaining of Juniper-Pinyon Woodlands." In *Proceedings— Wildland Shrub and Arid Land Restoration Symposium*, compiled by Bruce A. Roundy, E. Durant McArthur, Jennifer S. Haley, and David K. Mann. Las Vegas, Nev., 19–21 October 1993. General Technical Report INT-GTR-315. Ogden, Utah: U.S. Forest Service Intermountain Research Station, September 1994.

Whitson, Tom D., ed. *Weeds and Poisonous Plants of Wyoming and Utah.* Laramie: University of Wyoming Cooperative Extension Service, 1987.

BOOKS AND ARTICLES

Abbey, Edward. "Even the Bad Guys Wear White Hats." *Harper's*, January 1986, 51.

Adams, David A. *Renewable Resource Policy: The Legal-Institutional Foundations*. Washington, D.C.: Island Press, 1993.

Aguirre, A. Alonso, and Edward E. Starkey. "Wildlife Disease in U.S. National Parks: Historical and Coevolutionary Perspectives." *Conservation Biology* 8 (1994): 654–61.

Anderson, J. R., R. W. Merritt, and E. C. Loomis. "The Insect-Free Cattle Dropping and Its Relationship to Increased Dung Fouling of Rangeland Pastures." *Journal of Economic Entomology* 77 (1984): 133–41.

Antognini, Joe et al. "Implementing Effective Noxious Weed Control on Rangelands." *Rangelands* 17 (1995): 158–63.

"Applying Socioeconomic Techniques to Range Management Decision Making," Part 5. In *Developing Strategies for Rangeland Management*, prepared by the Committee on Developing Strategies for Rangeland Management, National Research Council/National Academy of Sciences. Boulder, Colo.: Westview Press, 1984.

Archer, Steven. "Woody Plant Encroachment into Southwestern Grasslands and Savannas: Rates, Patterns, and Proximate Causes." In *Ecological Implications of Livestock Herbivory in the West*, edited by Martin Vavra, William A. Laycock, and Rex D. Pieper. Denver: Society for Range Management, 1994.

Archer, Steven, and Fred E. Smeins. "Ecosystem-Level Processes." In *Grazing Management: An Ecological Perspective*, edited by Rodney K. Heitschmidt and Jerry W. Stuth. Portland: Timber Press, 1991.

————. "Non-linear Dynamics in Grazed Ecosystems: Thresholds, Multiple Steady States and Positive Feedbacks." In *Is the Range Condition Concept Compatible with Ecosystem Dynamics?* Spokane, Wash.: Society for Range Management, 1992.

Arizona Retailers Association. *43rd Legislature, 1997–1998*. n.d.

Athearn, R. G. *The Mythic West in Twentieth Century America*. Lawrence: University of Kansas Press, 1986.

Atkins, A. P. "Report of the President, 1955." *Journal of Range Management* 9 (1956): 63–64.

Baden, John. "Range Resources and Institutional Change." In *Developing Strategies for Rangeland Management*. Boulder, Colo.: Westview Press, 1984.

Bahre, C. J. *A Legacy of Change: Historic Human Impact on Vegetation of the Arizona Borderlands*. Tucson: University of Arizona Press, 1991.

Baker, Beth. "A Reverent Approach to the Natural World." *Bioscience* 46 (1996): 475–78.

Barnes, Will C. "Sheepmen on the National Forests." *National Wool Grower* (February 1921): 23.

Barns, Cass G. *The Sod House*. Lincoln: University of Nebraska Press, 1930.

Bates, Sarah. *The Changing Management Philosophies of the Public Lands*, Western Lands Rep. Series No. 3. Boulder: University of Colorado Natural Resources Law Center, 1993.

Bazzaz, F. A. "Characteristics of Populations in Relation to Disturbance in Natural and Man-Modified Ecosystems." In *Disturbance and Ecosystems: Components of Response*, edited by H. A. Mooney and M. Godron. Berlin: Springer-Verlag, 1983.

Bear, Dinah. "The Promise of NEPA." In *Biodiversity and the Law*, edited by William Snape III. Covelo, Calif.: Island Press, 1996.

Beatley, Timothy. *Ethical Land Use: Principles of Policy and Planning*. Baltimore: Johns Hopkins University Press, 1994.

Beattie, Mollie. "Biodiversity Policy and Ecosystem Management." In *Biodiversity and the Law*, edited by William Snape III. Covelo, Calif.: Island Press, 1996.

Behan, Richard W. "Multiple Use Management." In *Developing Strategies for Rangeland Management*. Boulder, Colo.: Westview Press, 1984.

Belsky, A. Joy. "Does Herbivory Benefit Plants? A Review of the Evidence." *American Naturalist* 127 (1986): 870–92.

———. Letter. *Fremontia* 20 (1992): 30–31.

Bender, Gordon L. *Reference Handbook on the Deserts of North America*. Westport, Conn.: Greenwood Press, 1982.

Bennion, G. "A Pioneer Cattle Venture of the Bennion Family." *Utah Historical Quarterly* 34 (1966): 315–25.

Billings, W. D. "Bromus tectorum, A Biotic Cause of Ecosystem Impoverishment in the Great Basin." In *The Earth in Transition: Patterns and Processes of Biotic Impoverishment*, edited by George M. Woodwell. Cambridge: Cambridge University Press, 1990.

———. "Man's Influence on Ecosystem Structure, Operation, and Ecophysiological Processes." In *Physiological Plant Ecology IV: Encyclopedia of Plant Physiology*, edited by O. L. Lange et al. New Series, Vol. 12D. Berlin: Springer-Verlag, 1983.

"Bill to Conduct Grazing Study in Wyoming Park Becomes Law." *Land Letter*, 26 November 1997, 12.

"Bill Would Allow Civil Lawsuits over Defamation of Agricultural Industry." *Laramie [Wyoming] Daily Boomerang*, 31 January 1997, 8.

"Biologists Studying Reasons for Sage Grouse Decline." *Laramie [Wyoming] Daily Boomerang*, 23 July 1996, 7.

Bishop, Tom. "Who's Waging War on the West?" Casper [Wyoming] *Star Tribune*, 30 November 1995, E4.

Bjork, Gordon C. "Ownership and Outcome: An Economic Analysis of the Privatization of Land Tenure on Forest and Rangeland." In *Rethinking the Federal Lands*, edited by Sterling Brubaker. Washington, D.C.: Resources for the Future, 1984.

"BLM Whistleblower Restored to Job after Grazing Case Settled." *Laramie [Wyoming] Daily Boomerang*, 24 January 1995, 7.

Blumler, Mark A. "Some Myths about California Grasslands and Grazers." *Fremontia* 20 (1992): 22–27.

Bock, Carl E., Jane H. Bock, and Hobart M. Smith. "Proposal for a System of Federal Livestock Exclosures on Public Rangelands in the Western United States." *Conservation Biology* 7 (1993): 731–33.

Borman, Michael M., and David A. Pyke. "Successional Theory and the Desired Plant Community Approach." *Rangelands* 16 (1994): 82–84.

Bosselman, Fred P., and A. Dan Tarlock. "The Influence of Ecological Science on American Law: An Introduction." *Chicago-Kent Law Review* 69 (1994): 847, 854–56.

Boulding, Kenneth. *Ecodynamics*. Thousand Oaks, Calif.: Sage Publications, 1978.

Box, Thadis W. "The American Rangeland in a Time of Change." In *Achieving Efficient Use of Rangeland Resources*, edited by Richard S. White and Robert E. Short. Papers presented at the Fort Keogh Research Symposium, Miles City, Montana, September 1987. February 1988.

———. "Rangelands." In *Natural Resources for the 21st Century*. Washington, D.C.: American Forestry Association, 1990.

Box, T. W., and W. B. Sisson. "Public Ranges Are in Better Condition Than They Have Been for Seventy Years—But More Range Managers Could Make Them Even Better! *Rangelands* 2 (1975): 44–46.

Boylan, Karen Day, and Donald R. MacLean. "Linking Species Loss with Wetlands Loss." *National Wetlands Newsletter*, (November–December 1997): 1, 13–17.

Brady, W. W., et al. "Response of a Semidesert Grassland to Sixteen Years of Rest from Grazing." *Journal of Range Management* 42 (1989): 284–88.

Brandt, C. A., and W. H. Rickard. "Alien Taxa in the North American Shrub-Steppe Four Decades after Cessation of Livestock Grazing and Cultivation Agriculture." *Biological Conservation* 68 (1994): 95–105.

Braun, Clait (Colorado Division of Wildlife). Presentation at Wyoming Conservation Congress, Rock Springs, Wyoming, April 1996.

Braun, Richard H. "Emerging Limits on Federal Land Management Discretion: Livestock, Riparian Ecosystems, and Clean Water Law." *Environmental Law* 17 (1986): 43–79.

Brick, Phil. "Determined Opposition: The Wise Use Movement Challenges Environmentalism." *Environment* 37 (October 1995): 16–20, 36–42.

Brown, James H., and William McDonald. "Livestock Grazing and Conservation on Southwestern Rangelands." *Conservation Biology* 9 (1995): 1644–47.

Brubaker, Sterling, ed. *Rethinking the Federal Lands*. Washington, D.C.: Resources for the Future, 1984.

Brunson, Mark W., and Brent S. Steel. "National Public Attitudes toward Federal Rangeland Management." *Rangelands* 16 (1994): 77–81.

Bryant, F. C., B. E. Dahl. R. D. Pettit, and C. M. Britton. "Does Short-Duration Grazing Work in Arid and Semiarid Regions?" *Journal of Soil and Water Conservation* 44 (July–August 1989): 290–96.

Buchanan, Bruce A. *Rangelands*. Albuquerque: University of New Mexico Press, 1988.

Budinsky, Steven, David Hage, Robert F. Black, and Sara Collins, with Jennifer Smith. "Eating into the Deficit: Efforts to Slash Farm Subsidies Will Be a Bellwether for Budget Balancers." *U.S. News and World Report*, 6 March 1995, 73–78.

Burgess, Jeff. "You Say You Want to Cut Government Spending? Kick Off Cows." *High Country News* (Paonia, Colorado), 20 March 1995, 16.

Calef, Wesley. *Private Grazing and Public Lands*. Chicago: University of Chicago Press, 1960.

Campbell, Thomas M., III, and Tim W. Clark. "Colony Characteristics and Vertebrate Associates of White-Tailed and Black-Tailed Prairie Dogs in Wyoming." *American Midland Naturalist* 105 (1981): 269–76.

Carlson, Cathy, John Horning, and David Alberswerth. "Naming Names on the Public Range." *Forest Watch* (November–December 1992): 20–22.

Caro, T. M., N. Pelkey, and M. Grigione. "Effects of Conservation Biology Education on Attitudes toward Nature." *Conservation Biology* 8 (1994): 846–52.

Carpenter, Farrington R. "Range Stockmen Meet the Government." In *The 1967 Denver Westerners Brand Book*, edited by Richard A. Ronzio. Denver: Westerners, 1968.

Carpenter, F. R. "Establishing Management under the Taylor Grazing Act." *Rangelands* 3 (June 1981): 105–15.

Carrier, Jim. "Rebels on the Range: Nevadans Take on Federal Sovereignty." *Denver Post*, 21 January 1996, 1A, 16A.

Chadd, Edward A. "Manifest Subsidy: Government Subsidies on Private Companies." *Common Cause*, 1 September 1995, 18–21.

Chapin, F. Stuart, III. "Patterns of Nutrient Absorption and Use by Plants from Natural and Man-Modified Environments." In *Disturbance and Ecosystems: Components of Response*, edited by H. A. Mooney and M. Godron. Berlin: Springer-Verlag, 1983.

Cheever, Federico. "The Road to Recovery: A New Way of Thinking about the Endangered Species Act." *Ecology Law Quarterly* 23 (1996): 1–78.

Chilson, Peter. "Did Ranchers Fire a University President?" *High Country News*, 23 June 1997, 5.

———. "Peter Chilson Responds." *High Country News*, 4 August 1997, 9.

Clark, Tim W., et al. "Prairie Dog Colony Attributes and Associated Vertebrate Species." *Great Basin Naturalist* 42 (1982): 572–82.

Clawson, Marion. *The Federal Lands Revisited*. Washington, D.C.: Resources for the Future, 1983.

———. *From Sagebrush to Sage—The Making of a Natural Resource Economist*. Washington, D.C.: Ana Publications, 1987.

———. "Multiple-Use Considerations." In *Managing Public Lands in the Public Interest*, edited by Benjamin C. Dysart III and Marion Clawson. New York: Praeger, 1988.

———. *The Western Range Livestock Industry*. New York: McGraw-Hill Book Co., 1950.

Clements, Frederic E. *Dynamics of Vegetation: Selections from Writings of Frederic E. Clements*, edited by B. W. Allred and E. S. Clements. New York: H. W. Wilson, 1949.

———. "Ecology in the Public Service." In *Dynamics of Vegetation: Selections from Writings of Frederic E. Clements*, edited by B. W. Allred and E. S. Clements. New York: H. W. Wilson, 1949.

———. "Plant Succession: An Analysis of the Development of Vegetation." Publication 1-512. Carnegie Institute of Washington, 1916.

Coggins, George C. " 'Devolution' in Federal Land Law." *West-Northwest* 3 (1996): 211.

———. "The Law of Public Rangeland Management III: A Survey of Creeping Regulation at the Periphery." *Environmental Law* 13 (1983): 295–365.

———. "The Law of Public Rangeland Management IV: FLPMA, PRIA, and the Multiple Use Mandate." *Environmental Law* 14 (1983): 1–131.

————. "The Law of Public Rangeland Management V: Prescriptions for Reform." *Environmental Law* 14 (1984): 497–546.

————. "Of Succotash Syndromes and Vacuous Platitudes: The Meaning of 'Multiple Use, Sustained Yield' for Public Land Management (Part I)." *University of Colorado Law Review* 53 (1982): 229–87.

————. "Some Disjointed Observations on Federal Public Land and Resources Law." *Environmental Law* 11 (1981): 471–87.

Coggins, George C., and Robert L. Glicksman. *Public Natural Resources Law*. Secs. 19.02, 19.03. Webster, N.Y.: Clark Boardman Callaghan, 1996.

Coggins, George C., and Margaret Lindeberg-Johnson. "The Law of Public Rangeland Management II: The Commons and the Taylor Act." *Environmental Law* 13 (1982): 1–101.

Coggins, George C., Charles F. Wilkinson, and John D. Leshy. *Federal Public Land and Resources Law*. Westbury, N.Y.: Foundation Press, 1993.

Collins, Katharine. "Sheepwagons Relegated to Quaintness as Utilitarian Role Dwindles." *Casper [Wyoming] Star Tribune*, 27 October 1996, B1.

Committee on Agricultural Land Use and Wildlife Resources. National Research Council. *Land Use and Wildlife Resources*. Washington, D.C.: National Academy of Sciences, 1970.

Committee on Developing Strategies for Rangeland Management. National Research Council/National Academy of Sciences. *Developing Strategies for Rangeland Management*. Boulder, Colo.: Westview Press, 1984.

Committee on Rangeland Classification. National Research Council. *Rangeland Health: New Methods to Classify, Inventory and Monitor Rangelands*. Washington, D.C.: National Academy Press, 1994.

Conner, J. R. "Social and Economic Influences on Grazing Management." In *Grazing Management: An Ecological Perspective*, edited by Rodney K. Heitschmidt and Jerry W. Stuth. Portland: Timber Press, 1991.

Cook, C. W., and J. Stubbendieck. *Range Research: Basic Problems and Techniques*. Denver: Society for Range Management, 1986.

Cooperrider, Allen. "Conservation of Biodiversity on Western Rangelands." In *Landscape Linkages and Biodiversity*, edited by Wendy E. Hudson. Washington, D.C.: Island Press, 1991.

Coppelman, Peter D. "The Federal Government's Response to the County Supremacy Movement." *Natural Resources and Environment* (Summer 1997): 30–33, 79–80.

Costanza, R., R. d'Arge, and M. van den Belt. "The Value of the World's Ecosystem Services and Natural Capital." *Nature* 387 (1997): 253–60.

Cotton, Scott E., and Ann C. Cotton, *Wyoming CRM: Enhancing Our Environment*. N.p., n.d.

"County Officials Formally Protest Grass Creek Plan." *Casper [Wyoming] Star-Tribune*, 18 September 1996, B1.

Cox, J. R., H. L. Morton, T. N. Johnson, G. L. Jordan, S. C. Martin, and L. C. Fierro. "Vegetation Restoration in the Chihuahuan and Sonoran Deserts of North America." Agriculture Reviews and Manuals, No. 28. Tucson: USDA-Agricultural Research Service, 1982.

Crawley, M. J. "Benevolent Herbivores?" *Trends in Ecology and Evolution* 2 (1987): 167–68.

Cronon, William. *Nature's Metropolis: Chicago and the Great West*. New York: W. W. Norton & Co., 1991.

Cronon, William, George Miles, and Jay Gitlin, eds. "Becoming West: Toward a New Meaning for Western History." In *Under an Open Sky: Rethinking America's Western Past*, edited by William Cronon, George Miles, and Jay Gitlin. New York: W. W. Norton & Co., 1992

———. *Under an Open Sky: Rethinking America's Past*. New York: W. W. Norton & Co., 1992.

Crumpacker, David W., Stephen W. Hodge, Dale Friedley, and William P. Gregg, Jr. "A Preliminary Assessment of the Status of Major Terrestrial and Wetland Ecosystems on Federal and Indian Lands in the United States." *Conservation Biology* 2 (1988): 103–15.

Culhane, Paul J. *Public Lands Politics: Interest Group Influence on the Forest Service and the Bureau of Land Management*. Baltimore: Johns Hopkins University Press, 1981.

Dale, Richard E. *The Range Cattle Industry: Ranching on the Great Plains from 1865 to 1925*. Norman: University of Oklahoma Press, 1960.

Dana, Samuel Trask. *Forest and Range Policy: Its Development in the United States*. New York: McGraw-Hill Book Co., 1956.

Dasmann, Raymond F. "Wildlife and Ecosystems." In *Wildlife and America*, edited by Howard P. Brokaw. Washington, D.C.: Council on Environmental Quality, 1978.

Davidson, Diane W., et al. "Selecting Wilderness Areas to Conserve Utah's Biological Diversity." *Great Basin Naturalist* (April 1996): 95–118.

Davis, Tony. "Catron County's Politics Heat Up as Its Land Goes Bankrupt." *High Country News*, 24 June 1996, 1, 8–9.

Dobie, J. Frank. *I'll Tell You a Tale*. Austin: University of Texas Press, 1986.

"Dombeck Says Ranching Will Have Role in Land Management." *Laramie [Wyoming] Daily Boomerang*, 27 July 1996, 7.

Donahue, Debra L. "The Untapped Power of Clean Water Act Section 401." *Ecology Law Quarterly* 23 (1996): 201–302.

Donaldson, Thomas. *The Public Domain: Its History, with Statistics*. 1884. Reprint, New York: Johnson Reprint Corp., 1970.

Donart, Gary P. "The History and Evolution of Western Rangelands in Relation to Woody Plant Communities." In *Developing Strategies for Rangeland Management*. Boulder, Colo.: Westview Press, 1984.

Doyle, Jim. "Ranches Agree to Limit Grazing in Tortoise Country." *San Francisco Chronicle*, 23 March 1993, A13.

Dregne, Harold E. "Desertification of Arid Lands." *Economic Geography* 53 (1977): 322–31.

Driscoll, Paul A. "Big Beef Supply Sends Cattle Futures Tumbling." *Laramie [Wyoming] Boomerang*, 21 July 1998, 15.

Duerk, Adam. "BLM Manager in Wyoming Gets Trampled." *High Country News*, 22 February 1993, 3.

Dwyer, Donald D., John C. Buckhouse, and William S. Huey. "Impacts of Grazing Intensity and Specialized Grazing Systems on the Use and Value of Rangeland: Summary and Recommendations." In *Developing Strategies for Rangeland Management*. Boulder, Colo.: Westview Press, 1984.

Dyksterhuis, E. J. "Condition and Management of Range Land Based on Quantitative Ecology." *Journal of Range Management* 2 (1949): 104–15.

Dysart, Benjamin C., III, and Marion Clawson, eds. *Managing Public Lands in the Public Interest*. New York: Praeger, 1988.

Echeverria, John D., and Raymond Booth Eby, eds. *Let the People Judge: Wise Use and the Private Property Rights Movement*. Washington, D.C.: Island Press, 1995.

Eckert, R. E., and J. S. Spencer. "Vegetation Response on Allotments Grazed under Rest-Rotation Management." *Journal of Range Management* 39 (1986): 166–74.

Egan, Timothy. "Grazing Bill to Give Ranchers Vast Control of Public Lands." *New York Times*, 21 July 1995, A1, C18. Also published in a different edition of the 21 July 1995 *New York Times* under the title "In Battle over Public Lands, Ranchers Push Public Aside," A1, A12.

———. "In Idaho, Wily Opponent Who Takes on Ranchers." *New York Times*, 21 July 1995, C18. Also published in a different edition of the 21 July 1995 *New York Times* under the same title, A1, A12.

Ehrenfeld, David. "Why Put a Value on Biodiversity?" In *Biodiversity*, edited by E. O. Wilson. Washington, D.C.: National Academy Press, 1988.

Ellison, Lincoln. "The Ecological Basis for Judging Condition and Trend on Mountain Range Land." *Journal of Forestry* 47 (1949): 787–95.

Elmore, Wayne, and Boone Kauffman. "Riparian and Watershed Systems: Degradation and Restoration." In *Ecological Implications of Livestock Herbivory in the West*, edited by Martin Vavra, William A. Laycock, and Rex D. Pieper. Denver: Society for Range Management, 1994.

Evans, M. Brock. "Nature Protection and Appreciation: A New or Old Concept?" In *Managing Public Lands in the Public Interest*, edited by Benjamin C. Dysart III and Marion Clawson. New York: Praeger, 1988.

Fabian, Ann. "History for the Masses: Commercializing the Western Past." In *Under an Open Sky: Rethinking America's Past*, edited by William Cronon, George Miles, and Jay Gitlin. New York: W. W. Norton & Co., 1992.

Fairfax, Sally K. "Coming of Age in the Bureau of Land Management: Range Management in Search of a Gospel." In *Developing Strategies for Rangeland Management*. Boulder, Colo.: Westview Press, 1984.

———. "Legal and Political Aspects of Range Management: Summary and Recommendations." In *Developing Strategies for Rangeland Management*. Boulder, Colo.: Westview Press, 1984.

Ferguson, Denzel, and Nancy Ferguson, *Sacred Cows at the Public Trough*. Bend, Ore.: Maverick, 1984.

Fischman, Robert L. "Endangered Species Conservation: What Would We Expect of Federal Agencies?" *Public Land Law Review* 13 (1992): 1–23.

Flader, Susan L., and J. Baird Callicott, eds. *The River of the Mother of God and Other Essays by Aldo Leopold*. Madison: University of Wisconsin Press, 1991.

Fleischner, Thomas L. "Ecological Costs of Livestock Grazing in Western North America." *Conservation Biology* 8 (September 1994): 629–44.

Flinders, Jerran. "Essential Habitat for Wildlife." In *Rangelands*, edited by Bruce A. Buchanan. Albuquerque: University of New Mexico Press, 1988.

Forman, R. T. T., and M. Godron. "Patches and Structural Components for a Landscape Ecology." *Bioscience* 31 (1981): 733–40.

Forsling, C. L. "The Grazing Lands Must Be Restored: Ravelling Watersheds." *American Forests* 69 (February 1963): 12–13, 59–63.

Foss, Phillip. *Politics and Grass*. Seattle: University of Washington Press, 1960.

Fowler, Charles W., and James A. MacMahon. "Selective Extinction and Speciation: Their Influence on the Structure and Functioning of Communities and Ecosystems." *American Naturalist* 119 (1982): 480–98.

Fowler, John M., and James R. Gray, "Rangeland Economics in the Arid West." In *Rangelands*, edited by Bruce A. Buchanan. Albuquerque: University of New Mexico Press, 1988.

Francis, John G. "Realizing Public Purposes without Public Ownership: A Strategy for Reducing Intergovernmental Conflict in Public Land Regulation." In *Western Public Lands: The Management of Natural Resources in a Time of Declining Federalism*, edited by John G. Francis and Richard Ganzel. Totowa, N.J.: Rowman & Allanheld, Publishers, 1984.

Francis, John G., and Richard Ganzel, eds. *Western Public Lands: The Management of Natural Resources in a Time of Declining Federalism*. Totowa, N.J.: Rowman & Allanheld, Publishers, 1984.

Freyfogle, Eric T. "Owning and Belonging: The Private Landowner as Ecosystem Member." *Sustain* 1 (Spring 1996): 16–23.

Friedel, M. H. "Range Condition Assessment and the Concept of Thresholds: A Viewpoint." *Journal of Range Management* 44 (1991): 422–26.

Friedel, M. H., B. D. Foran, and D. M. Stafford-Smith. "Where the Creeks Run Dry or Ten Feet High: Pastoral Management in Arid Australia." *Proceedings of the Ecological Society of Australia* 16 (1990): 185–94.

Gardner, B. Delworth. "The Role of Economic Analysis in Public Range Management." In *Developing Strategies for Rangeland Management*. Boulder, Colo.: Westview Press, 1984.

George, Uwe. *In the Deserts of This Earth*. New York: Harcourt Brace Jovanovich, 1979.

Gillis, Anna M. "Should Cows Chew Cheatgrass on Commonlands?" *Bioscience* 41 (1991): 668–75.

Glicksman, Robert L. "Pollution on the Federal Lands II: Water Pollution Law." *UCLA Journal of Environmental Law and Policy* 12 (1993): 61–118.

———. "Severability and the Realignment of the Balance of Power over the Public Lands: The Federal Land Policy and Management Act of 1976 after the Legislative Veto Decisions." *Hastings Law Journal* 36 (1984): 1–92.

Godfrey, E. Bruce. "Measuring the Economic Impact of Agency Programs on Users and Local Communities." In *Developing Strategies for Rangeland Management*. Boulder, Colo.: Westview Press, 1984.

Godron, M., and R. T. T. Forman. "Landscape Modification and Changing Ecological Characteristics." In *Disturbance and Ecosystems: Components of Response*, edited by H. A. Mooney and M. Godron. Berlin: Springer-Verlag, 1983.

Graf, William L. *Wilderness Preservation and the Sagebrush Rebellions*. Savage, Md.: Rowman & Littlefield Publishers, 1990.

Gray, James R. "Response to 'Economic Factors to Be Considered in Sagebrush/Grassland Management.'" In *Developing Strategies for Rangeland Management*. Boulder, Colo.: Westview Press, 1984.

Greeley, W. B. "Stabilizing the Use of Public Ranges." In *Proceedings of the American National Live Stock Association*. N.p., 1923.

Hackett, David. "Wool Subsidy Cut a 'Death Knell,' Paseneaux Claims." *Casper [Wyoming] Star Tribune*, 25 September 1993, B1.

Hage, Wayne. *Storm over Rangelands: Private Rights in Public Lands*. Bellevue, Wash.: Free Enterprise Press, 1989.

Hagenstein, Perry R. "The Federal Lands Today—Uses and Limits." In *Rethinking the Federal Land*, edited by Sterling Brubaker. Washington, D.C.: Resources for the Future, 1984.

Haines, Aubrey L. *The Yellowstone Story*. Vol. 2. Yellowstone Library and Museum Association, in cooperation with Colorado Associated University Press, 1977.

"Hansen and Cannon Forget Their Manners." *Southern Utah Wilderness Alliance* (Fall 1997): 11.

Hardt, Scott. "Federal Land Management in the Twenty-first Century: From Wise Use to Wise Stewardship." *Harvard Environmental Law Review* 18 (1994): 345–403.

Harris, Larry D. *The Fragmented Forest: Island Biogeography Theory and the Preservation of Biotic Diversity*. Chicago: University of Chicago Press, 1984.

Harris, Larry D., Michael E. McGlothlen, and Michael N. Manlove. "Genetic Resources and Biotic Diversity." In *The Fragmented Forest: Island Biogeography Theory and the Preservation of Biotic Diversity*, by Larry D. Harris. Chicago: University of Chicago Press, 1984.

Harvey, Ann. "The Aliens among Us: Introduced Species in the Greater Yellowstone Ecosystem." *NRCC News* (Spring 1994): 4–5, 7.

Harvey, D. Michael. "Uses and Limits of the Federal Lands Today." In *Rethinking the Federal Lands*, edited by Sterling Brubaker. Washington, D.C.: Resources for the Future, 1984.

Hays, Samuel P. *Conservation and the Gospel of Efficiency: The Progressive Conservation Movement, 1890–1920*. Cambridge: Harvard University Press, 1959.

———. "Public Values and Management Response." In *Developing Strategies for Rangeland Management*. Boulder, Colo.: Westview Press, 1984.

Heady, Harold F. *Rangeland Management*. New York: McGraw-Hill Book Co., 1975.

———. "Summary: Ecological Implications of Livestock Herbivory in the West." In *Ecological Implications of Livestock Herbivory in the West*, edited by Martin Vavra, William A. Laycock, and Rex D. Pieper. Denver: Society for Range Management, 1994.

———. "Valley Grassland." In *The Terrestrial Vegetation of California*, edited by M. E. Barbour and J. Major. New York: John Wiley & Sons, 1977.

"Hearing on the Livestock Grazing Act Held in Washington." *Laramie [Wyoming] Daily Boomerang*, 23 June 1995, 7.

Heinz, Dan. "Continued Grazing: A Presupposition" (Letter to Editor). *Conservation Biology* 9 (1995): 708–9.

Heitschmidt, Rodney K., and Jerry W. Stuth, eds. *Grazing Management: An Ecological Perspective*. Portland: Timber Press, 1991.

Herbel, Carlton H. "Manipulative Range Improvements: Summary and Recommendations." In *Developing Strategies for Rangeland Management*. Boulder, Colo.: Westview Press, 1984.

Hess, Karl, Jr., and Jerry L. Holechek. "If Rain Doesn't Fall, the Money Will." *High Country News*, 1 May 1995, 20.

———. "Ranchers Forced into the Numbers Game." *High Country News*, 24 July 1995, 20.

Hewlett, John. "No Easy Answer to Complexities of Ag Living." *Wyoming Rural Electric News*, May 1996, 19–20.

Hobbs, Richard J., and Laura F. Huenneke, "Disturbance, Diversity, and Invasion: Implications for Conservation." *Conservation Biology* 6 (1992): 324–27.

Hodgson, Bryan. "Buffalo—Back Home on the Range." *National Geographic* (November 1994): 64.

Holechek, Jerry L., and Karl Hess, Jr. "The Emergency Feed Program." *Rangelands* 17 (1995): 133–36.

———. "Free Market Policy for Public Land Grazing." *Rangelands* 16 (1994): 63–67.

Holechek, Jerry L., Jerry Hawkes, and Tim D. Darden. "Macro Economics and Cattle Ranching." *Rangelands* 16 (1994): 118–23.

Holechek, Jerry L., Rex D. Pieper, and Carlton H. Herbel. *Range Management: Principles and Practices*. Englewood Cliffs, N.J.: Prentice Hall, 1989.

Holst, Jon D. "The Unforeseeability Factor: Federal Lands, Managing for Uncertainty, and the Preservation of Biological Diversity." *Public Land Law Review* 13 (1992): 113.

"Hook, Line, and Sunk?" *Environment* 38 (June 1996): 23–24.

Hoose, Phillip M. *Building an Ark: Tools for the Preservation of Natural Diversity through Land Protection*. Covelo, Calif.: Island Press, 1981.

Horning, John. *Grazing to Extinction: Endangered, Threatened and Candidate Species Imperiled by Livestock Grazing on Western Public Lands*. Washington, D.C.: National Wildlife Federation, June 1994.

"House Committee Approves Range Bill That Babbitt Opposes." *Public Lands News*, 2 October 1997, 4.

"House-Passed Range Bill May Receive Western Aid in Senate." *Public Lands News*, 13 November 1997, 3–4.

Hudson, Wendy E., ed. *Landscape Linkages and Biodiversity*. Washington, D.C.: Island Press, 1991.

Hungerford, Andrea. " 'Custom and Culture' Ordinances: Not a Wise Move for the Wise Use Movement." *Tulane Environmental Law Journal* 8 (1995): 457–503.

Hunter, Malcolm L., Jr. "Coping with Ignorance: The Coarse-Filter Strategy for Maintaining Biodiversity." In *Balancing on the Brink of Extinction: The Endangered*

Species Act and Lessons for the Future, edited by Kathryn A. Kohm. Washington, D.C.: Island Press, 1991.

"Impacts of Grazing Intensity and Specialized Grazing Systems on the Use and Value of Rangeland." In *Developing Strategies for Rangeland Management*, 867–1166 (part 3). Boulder, Colo.: Westview Press, 1984.

"Irony Piles on Irony in Wyoming." *High Country News*, 7 August 1995, 7.

Jacobs, Lynn. *Waste of the West: Public Lands Ranching*. Tucson, Ariz.: Lynn Jacobs, 1992.

Jamieson, Dale. "Sustainability and Beyond." *Resource Law Notes,* April 1996, 5–7.

Jenkins, Peter. "Harmful Exotics in the United States." In *Biodiversity and the Law*, edited by William Snape III. Washington, D.C.: Island Press, 1996.

Jones, Ann. "Roundup of Ranch Vacations." *National Geographic Traveler* 12 (July–August 1995): 46–53.

Jones, Lisa. "Drought Cuts to the Bone on Southwest Range." *High Country News*, 22 July 1996.

———. "An In-Your-Face Range Scientist." *High Country News*, 1 May 1995, 19.

———. "Straight Arrow." *High Country News*, 24 July 1995, 15.

Joyce, Linda A. "The Life Cycle of the Range Condition Concept." *Journal of Range Management* 46 (1993): 132–38.

Keiter, Robert B. "Conservation Biology and the Law: Assessing the Challenges Ahead." *Chicago-Kent Law Review* 69 (1994): 911–33.

Keiter, Robert B., and Peter H. Froelicher. "Bison, Brucellosis, and Law in the Greater Yellowstone Ecosystem." *Land and Water Law Review* 28 (1993): 1–75.

Kelso, M. M. "Current Issues in Federal Land Management in the Western United States." *Journal of Farm Economics* (November 1947): 1295–1313.

The Keystone Center. *Final Consensus Report of the Keystone Policy Dialogue on Biological Diversity on Federal Lands*. Keystone, Colo.: Keystone Center, April 1991.

Klyza, Christopher McGrory. *Who Controls Public Lands?: Mining, Forestry, and Grazing Policies, 1870–1990*. Charlotte: University of North Carolina Press, 1996.

Knight, Dennis H. *Mountains and Plains*. Cambridge: Yale University Press, 1994.

Knowles, C. "Some Relationships of Black-Tailed Prairie Dogs to Livestock Grazing." *Great Basin Naturalist* 46 (1986): 198–203.

Koppes, Clayton R. "Efficiency, Equity, Esthetics: Shifting Themes in American Conservation." In *Under Western Skies: Nature and History in the American West*, edited by Donald Worster. New York: Oxford University Press, 1992.

Krutilla, John V. "Conservation Reconsidered." *American Economic Review* 57 (1967): 777–86.

Krza, Paul. "Cow Coup: Wyoming Governor Usurps Federal Grazing Group." *High Country News*, 23 December 1996, 4.

———. "While the New West Booms, Wyoming Mines, Drills . . . and Languishes." *High Country News*, 7 July 1997, 1, 8–10, 12–13.

Lacey, John B., and James B. Johnson. "Livestock Grazing on Federal Lands: A Boon to Montana's Economy." *Western Wildlands* 16 (Summer 1990): 23–26.

Lamar, Howard R. "Westering in the Twenty-first Century: Speculation on the Future of the American Past." In *Under an Open Sky: Rethinking America's Past*, edited by William Cronon, George Miles, and Jay Gitlin. New York: W. W. Norton & Co., 1992.

Lamotte, M. "Research on the Characteristics of Energy Flows within Natural and Man-Altered Ecosystems." In *Disturbance and Ecosystems: Components of Response*, edited by H. A. Mooney and M. Godron. Berlin: Springer-Verlag, 1983.

Land Letter. Newsletter published by Environmental and Energy Study Institute, 122 C Street, NW, Washington, D.C. 20001.

Larsen, Erik. "The Revolt of the West." *Time*, 23 October 1995, 52–55.

Larson, T. A. *Wyoming: A History*. New York: W. W. Norton & Co., 1984.

Lauenroth, W. K., D. G. Michulnas, J. L. Dodd, R. H. Hart, R. K. Heitschmidt, and L. R. Rittenhouse. "Effects of Grazing on Ecosystems of the Great Plains." In *Ecological Implications of Livestock Herbivory in the West*, edited by Martin Vavra, William A. Laycock, and Rex D. Pieper. Denver: Society for Range Management, 1994.

Lavelle, Marianne. "'Wise Use' Movement Grows." *National Law Journal*, 5 June 1995, A1–A3.

Laycock, William A. "Implications of Grazing vs. No Grazing on Today's Rangelands." In *Ecological Implications of Livestock Herbivory in the West*, edited by Martin Vavra, William A. Laycock, and Rex D. Pieper. Denver: Society for Range Management, 1994.

———. "Stable States and Thresholds of Range Condition on North American Rangelands: A Viewpoint." *Journal of Range Management* 44 (1991): 427–33.

Lee, William P. "FLPMA's Legislative Veto Provisions after *INS v. Chadha*: Who Controls the Federal Lands?" *Environmental Affairs* 12 (1985): 791–821.

Lenderman, Jason. "A Ranch Rescued." *High Country News*, 24 November 1997, 7.

Leopold, Aldo. *Game Management*. New York: Charles Scribner's Sons, 1933.

———. *A Sand County Almanac, with Essays on Conservation from Round River*. New York: Sierra Club/Ballantine Books, 1974.

Leshy, John D. "Sharing Federal Multiple-Use Lands: Historic Lessons and Speculation for the Future." In *Rethinking the Federal Lands,* edited by Sterling Brubaker. Washington, D.C.: Resources for the Future, 1984.

Libecap, Gary D. *Locking Up the Range: Federal Land Controls and Grazing*. Cambridge, Mass.: Ballinger Publishing Co., 1981.

Ligorner, K. Lesli. "Congressman Miller's Natural Resource and Subsidy Report: Exposing Governmental Inefficiency and Environmental Disasters." *Eco-Notes Environmental Law and Policy* 1 (Fall 1995): 29–30.

Limerick, Patricia Nelson. *Desert Passages: Encounters with the American Deserts*. Albuquerque: University of New Mexico Press, 1985.

"Listing Actions Published for Wetland Species." *National Wetlands Newsletter* 19 (July–August 1997): 24.

Long, Michael E. "The Vanishing Prairie Dog." *National Geographic* (April 1998): 116–30.

Low, Bobbi S., and Jesse A. Berlin. "Natural Selection and the Management of Rangelands." In *Developing Strategies for Rangeland Management*. Boulder, Colo.: Westview Press, 1984.

Madson, Chris, "Dog Days." *Wyoming Wildlife*, May 1995, 6–13.

Malone, Linda A. "Reflections on the Jeffersonian Ideal of an Agrarian Democracy and the Emergence of an Agricultural and Environmental Ethic in the 1990 Farm Bill." *Stanford Environmental Law Journal* 12 (1993): 3–49.

Manning, Elizabeth. "The Mojave National Preserve: 1.4 million Acres of Contradictions." *High Country News,* 14 April 1997, 12–13.

Margolis, Jon. "Utah's Bumbling Obscures a Valid Complaint." *High Country News*, 1 September 1997, 5.

———. "Waaaaaaaaaaaaagh! The West Refuses to Be Weaned." *High Country News*, 20 February 1995, 16.

Markandya, Anil, and Julie Richardson, eds. *Environmental Economics: A Reader*. New York: St. Martin's Press, 1992. Reprint, 1993.

Marston, Ed. "Coming into a New Land." In *Reopening the Western Frontier*, edited by Ed Marston. Washington, D.C.: Island Press, 1989.

———. *Reopening the Western Frontier*. Washington, D.C.: Island Press, 1989.

Martin, William E. "The Distribution of Benefits and Costs Associated with Public Rangelands." In *Public Lands and the U.S. Economy: Balancing Conservation and Development*, edited by George M. Johnston and Peter M. Emerson. Proceedings of a conference sponsored by the Wilderness Society. Boulder, Colo.: Westview Press, 1984.

———. "Mitigating the Economic Impacts of Agency Programs for Public Rangelands." In *Developing Strategies for Rangeland Management*. Boulder, Colo.: Westview Press, 1984.

May, Robert M. "Thresholds and Breakpoints in Ecosystems with a Multiplicity of Stable States." *Nature* 269 (1977): 471–77.

McClaran, Michael P. "Livestock in Wilderness: A Review and a Forecast." *Environmental Law* 20 (1990): 857–89.

McClure, S. W. "Address by Dr. S. W. McClure before the National Convention." *National Wool Grower* (February 1932): 39–40, 57–58.

McConnell, Grant. *Private Power and American Democracy*. New York: Alfred A. Knopf, 1967.

McGerr, Michael E. "Is There a Twentieth-Century West?" In *Under an Open Sky: Rethinking America's Past*, edited by William Cronon, George Miles, and Jay Gitlin. New York: W. W. Norton & Co., 1992.

Meagher, Mary, and Margaret E. Meyer. "On the Origin of Brucellosis in Bison of Yellowstone National Park: A Review." *Conservation Biology* 8 (1994): 645–53.

Merrill, Karen R. "Private Spaces on Public Lands: Constructing State Sovereignty on the Western Range, 1900–1934." Ph.D. dissertation, University of Michigan, Lansing, 1994.

Micheli, Ronald A. "Response to 'Role of Land Treatments on Public and Private Lands.'" In *Developing Strategies for Rangeland Management*. Boulder, Colo.: Westview Press, 1984.

"Micheli Says Agriculture Suffering." *Laramie [Wyoming] Daily Boomerang*, 14 April 1995, 7.

Miller, Brian, Gerardo Ceballos, and Richard Reading. "The Prairie Dog and Biotic Diversity." *Conservation Biology* 8 (1994): 677–81.

Miller, Ken. "Economics of 'Old West' Fading, Professor Writes." *Denver Post*, 30 June 1986, 8A.

Miller, Richard F., Tony J. Svejcar, and Neil E. West. "Implications of Livestock Grazing in the Intermountain Sagebrush Region: Plant Composition." In *Ecological Implications of Livestock Herbivory in the West*, edited by Martin Vavra, William A. Laycock, and Rex D. Pieper. Denver: Society for Range Management, 1994.

Mitchell, John E., George N. Wallace, and Marcella D. Wells. "Visitor Perceptions about Cattle Grazing on National Forest Lands." *Journal of Range Management* 49 (1996): 81–86.

Mooney, H. A., and M. Godron, eds. *Disturbance and Ecosystems: Components of Response*. Vol. 44 in the series Ecological Studies: Analysis and Synthesis. Berlin: Springer-Verlag, 1983.

Morrissey, Katherine G. "Engendering the West." In *Under an Open Sky: Rethinking America's Past*, edited by William Cronon, George Miles, and Jay Gitlin. New York: W. W. Norton & Co., 1992.

Murie, Olaus J. *The Elk of North America*. Rpt. Jackson, Wyo.: Teton Bookshop, 1979. Originally published by Stackpole and the Wildlife Management Institute in 1951.

Nash, Roderick Frazier. *The Rights of Nature: A History of Environmental Ethics*. Madison: University of Wisconsin Press, 1989.

Nelson, Robert H. "Economic Analysis in Public Rangeland Management." In *Western Public Lands: The Management of Natural Resources in a Time of Declining Federalism*, edited by John G. Francis and Richard Ganzel. Totowa, N.J.: Rowman & Allanheld, Publishers, 1984.

————. "Ideology and Public Land Policy: The Current Crisis." In *Rethinking the Federal Lands*, edited by Sterling Brubaker. Washington, D.C.: Resources for the Future, 1984.

Ness, Erik. "You're Picking on Ranchers." *High Country News*, 4 August 1997, 9.

"A New Lease on Life." *Environment* 39 (March 1997): 21.

Nielsen, Darwin B. "Economic Factors to Be Considered in Sagebrush/Grassland Management." In *Developing Strategies for Rangeland Management*. Boulder, Colo.: Westview Press, 1984.

Nijhuis, Michelle. "Oil Clashes with Elk in the Book Cliffs." *High Country News*, 13 April 1998, 1, 8–10.

Nokkentved, N. S. "Idaho Ranchers Finally Get Their Man." *High Country News*, 14 June 1993.

Norton, B. E. "Impacts of Grazing Intensity and Specialized Grazing Systems on Vegetation Production and Composition." A paper presented at the workshop on grazing systems, National Research Council, 16–17 March 1981.

Norton, Bryan. "Commodity, Amenity, and Morality: The Limits of Quantification in Valuing Biodiversity." In *Biodiversity*, edited by E. O. Wilson. Washington, D.C.: National Academy Press, 1988.

Noss, Reed F. "Cows and Conservation Biology." *Conservation Biology*, 8 (1994): 613–16.

———. "From Endangered Species to Biodiversity." In *Balancing on the Brink of Extinction: The Endangered Species Act and Lessons for the Future*, edited by Kathryn A. Kohm. Washington, D.C.: Island Press, 1991.

———. "Issues of Scale in Conservation Biology." In U.S. Bureau of Land Management et al., *Meeting the Biodiversity Challenge: A Shortcourse for Decision-Makers*. Phoenix and Silver Creek, Colo., 26–29 July 1993. Reprint from *Conservation Biology: The Theory and Practice of Nature Conservation Preservation and Management*, edited by P. L. Fiedler and S. K. Jain. New York: Chapman and Hall, 1992.

———. "Landscape Connectivity: Different Functions at Different Scales." In *Landscape Linkages and Biodiversity*, edited by Wendy E. Hudson. Washington, D.C.: Island Press, 1991.

———. "A Regional Landscape Approach to Maintain Diversity." *Bioscience* 33 (1983): 700–706.

———. "Some Principles of Conservation Biology, as They Apply to Environmental Law." *Chicago-Kent Law Review* 69 (1994): 893–909.

Noss, Reed F., and Allen Y. Cooperrider. *Saving Nature's Legacy*. Washington, D.C.: Island Press, 1994.

Noy-Meir, Immanuel. "Compensating Growth of Grazed Plants and Its Relevance to the Use of Rangelands." *Ecological Applications* 3 (1993): 32–34.

Odum, Eugene P. *Fundamentals of Ecology*. 3d ed. Philadelphia: W. P. Saunders Co., 1971.

Patlis, Jason. "Biodiversity, Ecosystems, and Endangered Species." In *Biodiversity and the Law*, edited by William Snape, III. Covelo, Calif.: Island Press, 1996.

Pearson, G. A. "Multiple Use in Forestry." *Journal of Forestry* 42 (1944): 243–49.

Peck, Norm. "Ecosystem Management: High-Level Spin Control or the Real Thing?" *Forest Watch*, November–December 1992, 23.

Peffer, E. Louise. *The Closing of the Public Domain*. Stanford: Stanford University Press, 1951.

Pelzer, Louis. *The Cattlemen's Frontier*. Glendale, Calif.: Arthur H. Clark Co., 1936.

Pendergrass, John A. "Rediscovering Old Tools." In *Biodiversity and the Law*, edited by William Snape III. Covelo, Calif.: Island Press, 1996.

Perry, David A., and Jeffrey G. Borchers. "Climate Change and Ecosystem Responses." *Northwest Environmental Journal* 6 (1990): 293–313. Reprint in U.S. Bureau of Land Management, U.S. Forest Service, and U.S. Fish and Wildlife Service, *Meeting the Biodiversity Challenge: A Shortcourse for Decision-Makers*. Phoenix and Silver Creek, Colo., 26–29 July 1993.

Peterson, C. S. "Grazing in Utah: A Historical Perspective." Proceedings of the Society for Range Management Annual Meeting. Salt Lake City, February 1985.

Pieper, Rex D. "Ecological Implications of Livestock Grazing." In *Ecological Implications of Livestock Herbivory in the West*, edited by Martin Vavra, William A. Laycock, and Rex D. Pieper. Denver: Society for Range Management, 1994.

———. "Grazing Systems and Management." In *Rangelands,* edited by Bruce A. Buchanan. Albuquerque: University of New Mexico Press, 1988.

Pinchot, Gifford. *The Fight for Conservation*. New York: Doubleday, 1910.

Pisani, Donald J. *To Reclaim a Divided West: Water, Law, and Public Policy, 1848–1902*. Albuquerque: University of New Mexico Press, 1992.

Popper, Frank J. "A Nest-Egg Approach to the Public Lands." In *Managing Public Lands in the Public Interest*, edited by Benjamin C. Dysart III and Marion Clawson. New York: Praeger, 1988.

Power, Thomas M. *Lost Landscapes and Failed Economies*. Washington, D.C.: Island Press, 1996.

"Preliminary Summary of Findings: Western States Water Council's Nonpoint Source Pollution Survey." In *Nonpoint Source Pollution Control Workshop—Technical Issues*. Midvale, Utah: Western States Water Council, 25–28 July 1989.

Public Lands News. Biweekly newsletter published by Resources Publishing Co., 1010 Vermont Avenue, Suite 708, Washington, D.C. 20005.

Quillen, Ed. "The Mountain West: A Republican Fabrication." *High Country News*, 13 October 1997, 8–9.

Quinn, Bernard, Herman Anderson, Martin Bradley, Paul Goetting, and Peggy Shriver. *Churches and Church Membership in the United States, 1980*. Atlanta: Glenmary Research Center, 1982.

Quinn, D. Michael. "Religion in the American West." In *Under an Open Sky: Rethinking America's Past*, edited by William Cronon, George Miles, and Jay Gitlin. New York: W. W. Norton & Co., 1992.

Raup, David M. "Diversity Crises in the Geological Past." In *Biodiversity*, edited by E. O. Wilson. Washington, D.C.: National Academy Press, 1988.

Rea, Tom. "Predator 'Problem' Lamented, Doubted in Gillette." *Casper [Wyoming] Star Tribune*, 11 April 1996, B1.

———. "Staying on the Land: Prize-Winning Rancher Outlines Conservation Methods." *Casper [Wyoming] Star Tribune*, 3 July 1997, C1.

———. "Strange Bedfellows Work to Keep Space Open: Ranchers, Environmentalists Team Up to Fight Subdividers." *Casper [Wyoming] Star Tribune*, 3 July 1997, C1.

Reed, Scott W. "The County Supremacy Movement: Mendacious Myth Marketing." *Idaho Law Review* 30 (1993–94): 525–53.

Reid, Walter V., and Kenton R. Miller. *Keeping Options Alive: The Scientific Basis for Conserving Biodiversity*. Washington, D.C.: World Resources Institute, 1989.

Reisner, Marc. "The Next Water War: Cities versus Agriculture." *Issues in Science and Technology* 5 (Winter 1988–89): 98.

Richardson, Elmo. *BLM's Billion-Dollar Checkerboard: Managing the O&C Lands*. Santa Cruz, Calif.: Forest History Society, 1980.

Richardson, Valerie. "No-Nonsense Idaho Sheriff Tells Federal Law Officers to Steer Clear." *Washington Times*, 27 August 1995, A1.

Riebsame, William E. "Ending the Range Wars?" *Environment* 38 (May 1996): 4–9, 27–29.

Robbins, Jim. "Discouraging Words in Montana." In *Reopening the Western Frontier*, edited by Ed Marston. Washington, D.C.: Island Press, 1989.

Robbins, Roy M. *Our Landed Heritage: The Public Domain, 1776–1970*. 2d ed. Lincoln: University of Nebraska Press, 1976.

Rodgers, William H., Jr. "'The Relevance of Management Information Systems to Policy Choices': Comment and Discussion." In *Developing Strategies for Rangeland Management*. Boulder, Colo.: Westview Press, 1984.

Roosevelt, Theodore. *Hunting Trips of a Ranchman*. New York: G. P. Putnam's Sons, 1899.

———. *Ranch-Life and the Hunting Trail*. New York: Century Co., 1989.

Roten, Robert. "Prairie Rides a New Career Path for a Traditional Ranch Family." *Laramie [Wyoming] Daily Boomerang*. 21 July 1996, 21.

Rowley, William D. *U.S. Forest Service Grazing and Rangelands: A History*. College Station: Texas A&M University Press, 1985.

Ruhl, J. B. "Section 7 of the 'New' Endangered Species Act: Rediscovering and Redefining the Untapped Power of Federal Agencies' Duty to Conserve Species." *Environmental Law* 25 (1995): 1107–63.

Russell, Sharman Apt. *Kill the Cowboy: A Battle of Mythology in the New West*. Reading, Mass.: Addison-Wesley Publishing Co., 1993.

St. Clair, Jeffrey. "Talkin' about Cows." *Forest Watch*, June 1993, 7–8.

St. Clair, Larry, and Jeffrey R. Johansen. "Introduction to the Symposium on Soil Crust Communities." *Great Basin Naturalist*. 53 (31 March 1993): 1–4.

Salwasser, Hal, Christine Schonewald-Cox, and Richard Baker. "The Role of Interagency Cooperation in Managing for Viable Populations." In *Viable Populations for Conservation*, edited by Michael E. Soule. Cambridge: Cambridge University Press, 1987.

Sampson, Arthur W. *Range and Pasture Management*. New York: John Wiley & Sons, 1923.

Savory, Allan. *Holistic Resource Management*. Washington, D.C.: Island Press, 1988.

Sax, Joseph L. "The Claim for Retention of the Public Lands." In *Rethinking the Federal Lands*, edited by Sterling Brubaker. Washington, D.C.: Resources for the Future, 1984.

———. "Nature and Habitat Conservation and Protection in the United States." *Ecology Law Quarterly* 20 (1993): 47–56.

Schlebecker, John T. *Cattle Raising on the Plains, 1900–1961*. Lincoln: University of Nebraska Press, 1963.

Schwartz, Bernard. *Administrative Law*. 3d ed. Boston: Little, Brown & Co., 1991.

Scott, J. M., et al. "Gap Analysis of Species Richness and Vegetation Cover: An Integrated Biodiversity Conservation Strategy." In *Balancing on the Brink of Extinction: The Endangered Species Act and Lessons for the Future*, edited by Kathryn A. Kohm. Washington, D.C.: Island Press, 1991.

Scott, Valerie Weeks. "The Range Cattle Industry: Its Effect on Western Land Law." *Montana Law Review* 28 (1967): 155–83.

Seigel, Barry. "A Lone Ranger; U.S. Forest Service Ranger Guy Pence Is a Persistent and Passionate Defender of Public Lands. Is That Why Someone Bombed His Office and His Home?" *Los Angeles Times Magazine*, 26 November 1995, 20.

Severson, Keith E., and Philip J. Urness. "Livestock Grazing: A Tool to Improve Wildlife Habitat." In *Ecological Implications of Livestock Herbivory in the West*, edited by Martin Vavra, William A. Laycock, and Rex D. Pieper. Denver: Society for Range Management, 1994.

Sharp, L. A., K. Sanders, and N. Rimbey. "Forty Years of Change in a Shadscale Stand in Idaho." *Rangelands* 12 (1990): 313–28.

Siemans, James A. "A 'Hard Look' at Biodiversity and the National Forest Management Act." *Tulane Environmental Law Journal* 6 (1992): 157–77.

Sindelar, Brian W., Clifford Montagne, and Roland R. H. Kroos. "Holistic Resource Management: An Approach to Sustainable Agriculture on Montana's Great Plains." *Journal of Soil and Water Conservation* 50 (1995): 45–49.

Smith, Arthur F., and William E. Martin. "Socioeconomic Behavior of Cattle Ranchers, with Implications for Rural Community Development in the West." *American Journal of Agricultural Economics* 54 (1972): 217–25.

Smith, Helen H. *The War on Powder River: The History of an Insurrection*. Lincoln: University of Nebraska Press, 1966.

Smith, Jeffery. "Evangelical Christians Preach a Green Gospel." *High Country News*, 28 April 1997.

Snape, William J., III, ed. *Biodiversity and the Law*. Washington, D.C.: Island Press, 1996.

Society for Range Management. "Society for Range Management Guidelines for Rangeland Assessment." July 1992. Reprint in U.S. Bureau of Land Management, U.S. Forest Service, and U.S. Fish and Wildlife Service, *Applied Biodiversity Conservation*. Sacramento, 22–26 February 1993.

Soulé, Michael E., ed. *Viable Populations for Conservation*. New York: Cambridge University Press, 1987.

Southern Utah Wilderness Alliance. 1471 South 1100 East, Salt Lake City, UT 84105.

Stack, Peggy Fletcher. "Free-Market Grazing Unites Foes." *Salt Lake Tribune*, 8 October 1995, C1.

Standing Bear, Luther. *Land of the Spotted Eagle*. Boston: Houghton Mifflin Co., 1933.

Stebbins, G. Ledyard. Letter. *Fremontia* 20 (1992): 31–32.

Stiles, Jim. "Utah County Sweeps Away Old Guard." *High Country News*, 8 February 1993.

"Stockgrowers Association Criticizes Dumping Dead Bison." *Laramie [Wyoming] Daily Boomerang*, 22 July 1997, 7.

Stoddart, Lawrence A., and Arthur D. Smith. *Range Management*. New York: McGraw-Hill Book Co., 1943.

Stoddart, L. A., A. D. Smith, and T. W. Box. *Range Management*. 3d ed. New York: McGraw-Hill Book Co., 1975.

"Study of Pacific Northwest Concludes Economy Aided by Environmental Protection." *Environment Reporter (Current Developments)*, 12 January 1996, 1615.

Summers, Ken, et al. *World Desertification Bibliography*. Office of Arid Lands Studies, University of Arizona, and United Nations Environment Programme (UNEP). Nairobi: UNEP Desertification Control Programme Activity Centre, August 1991.

Symposium on Soil Crust Communities. *Great Basin Naturalist* 53 (1993): 1–95.

Tarpy, Cliff. "New Zoos: Taking Down the Bars." *National Geographic* 184 (July 1993): 2–37.

"These Guns for Hire: ADC and the Hidden War on Predators." *Forest Watch*, July 1992, 18.

Thurow, Thomas L. "Hydrology and Erosion." In *Grazing Management: An Ecological Perspective*, edited by Rodney K. Heitschmidt and Jerry W. Stuth. Portland: Timber Press, 1991.

Tueller, P. T. "Secondary Succession, Disclimax, and Range Condition Standards in Desert Shrub Vegetation." In *Arid Shrublands*, edited by D. N. Hyder. Denver: Society for Range Management, 1973.

Udall, Stewart L. *The Quiet Crisis*. New York: Avon Books, 1963.

United Nations Center for Economic and Social Information. *United Nations Conference on Desertification: Roundup, Plan of Action and Resolutions*. New York: United Nations, 1978.

U.S. West Communications. *Montana 1997 Directory, Fifty-fifth Session*. N.p.: U.S. West Communications, n.d.

"Utahans Don't Take Kindly to DoI Review of BLM Wilderness." *Public Lands News*, 5 September 1996, 6.

Van Vuren, Dirk. "Bison West of the Rocky Mountains: An Alternative Explanation." *Northwest Science* 61 (1987): 65–69.

Van Vuren, Dirk, and Frank C. Deitz. "Evidence of *Bison bison* in the Great Basin." *Great Basin Naturalist* 53 (1993): 318–19.

Vavra, Martin, William A. Laycock, and Rex D. Pieper, eds. *Ecological Implications of Livestock Herbivory in the West*. Denver: Society for Range Management, 1994.

Verkaar, H. J. "When Does Grazing Benefit Plants?" *Trends in Research in Ecology and Evolution* 1 (1986): 168–69.

Vesilind, Priit J. "Anything But Empty: The Sonoran Desert." *National Geographic* 186 (September 1994): 37–63.

Vileisis, Ann, and Ed Marston. "What Did the Land Look Like? What Should the Land Look Like?" *High Country News*, 23 March 1992, 14–15.

Voigt, William, Jr. *Public Grazing Lands: Use and Misuse by Industry and Government*. New Brunswick, N.J.: Rutgers University Press, 1976.

Wagner, Frederic H. "Changing Institutional Arrangements for Setting Natural-Resources Policy." In *Ecological Implications of Livestock Herbivory in the West*, edited by Martin Vavra, William A. Laycock, and Rex D. Pieper. Denver: Society for Range Management, 1994.

Waller, Donald M. "Introduction." In *Landscape Linkages and Biodiversity*, edited by Wendy E. Hudson. Washington, D.C.: Island Press, 1991.

Warner, V. G. "Elk and Game Wardens vs. Live Stock and Human Beings." *National Wool Grower* (May 1912): 31–33.

Webb, Walter Prescott. *The Great Plains*. Boston: Ginn & Co., 1931.

West, Neil E. "Biodiversity of Rangelands." *Journal of Range Management* 46 (1993): 2–13.

———. "Successional Patterns and Productivity Potentials of Pinyon-Juniper Ecosystems." In *Developing Strategies for Rangeland Management*. Boulder, Colo.: Westview Press, 1984.

West, Patrick C. "Power, Dependency, and Conflict Management: Implications for Adaptive Strategies in BLM Management." In *Developing Strategies for Rangeland Management*. Boulder, Colo.: Westview Press, 1984.

Westoby, Mark, Brian Walker, and Immanuel Noy-Meir. "Opportunistic Management for Rangelands Not at Equilibrium." *Journal of Range Management* 42 (1989): 266–74.

White, Lynn, Jr. "The Historical Roots of Our Ecologic Crisis." *Science* 155 (1967): 1203–7.

White, Richard S., and Robert E. Short, eds. *Achieving Efficient Use of Rangeland Resources*. Papers presented at the Fort Keogh Research Symposium, Miles City, Montana, September 1987. N.p., February 1988.

Whittaker, Robert H. *Communities and Ecosystems*. 2d ed. New York: Macmillan Publishing Co., 1975.

Wilcox, David, et al. *Rebuilding the Ark: Toward a More Effective Endangered Species Act for Private Land*. New York: Environmental Defense Fund, 1996.

Wilkinson, Charles F. *Crossing the Next Meridian: Land, Water, and the Future of the West*. Covelo, Calif.: Island Press, 1992.

Wilkinson, Todd. "Utah Ushers Its Frogs toward Oblivion." *High Country News*, 27 May 1996, 1, 10–13.

Williams, David C., and Faith Campbell, "How the Bureau of Land Management Designates and Protects Areas of Critical Environmental Concern: A Status Report, with a Critical Review by the Natural Resources Defense Council." *Natural Areas Journal* 8 (1988): 231.

Williams, Jack E., and John N. Rinne. "Biodiversity Management on Multiple-Use Federal Lands: An Opportunity Whose Time Has Come." *Fisheries*, May–June 1992, 4–5.

Williams, Terry Tempest, and Thomas J. Lyon. "An Open Letter to Utah Sens. Orrin Hatch and Robert Bennett." *High Country News*, 29 November 1993.

Wilson, Edward O., ed. *Biodiversity*. Washington, D.C.: National Academy Press, 1988.

———. *The Diversity of Life*. Cambridge, Mass.: Belknap Press of Harvard University Press, 1992.

———. "The Environmental Ethic." *West-Northwest* 3 (1996): 327–31.

Winner, Cherie. "The Sagebrush Steppe: Familiar Grassland-Shrub Landscape Contains Complex Life Systems." *Casper [Wyoming] Star-Tribune*, 8 August 1996, E1, E4.

Winter, Charles E. *Four Hundred Million Acres: The Public Land and Resources*. Casper, Wyo.: Overland Publishing Co., 1932. Reprint, New York: Arno Press, 1979.

Wolf, Tom. "'Wyoming' Is Dead—Long Live 'Wyoming.'" In *Reopening the Western Frontier*, edited by Ed Marston. Washington, D.C.: Island Press, 1989.

Woodwell, George M., ed. *The Earth in Transition: Patterns and Processes of Biotic Impoverishment*. Cambridge: Cambridge University Press, 1990.

Workman, John P., Sally K. Fairfax, and William Burch. "Applying Socioeconomic Techniques to Range Management Decision Making: Summary and Recommendations." In *Developing Strategies for Rangeland Management*. Boulder, Colo.: Westview Press, 1984.

Worster, Donald. "Appendix: Doing Environmental History." In *The Ends of the Earth: Perspectives on Modern Environmental History*, edited by Donald Worster. Cambridge: Cambridge University Press, 1988.

————, ed. *The Ends of the Earth: Perspectives on Modern Environmental History.* Cambridge: Cambridge University Press, 1988.

————. *Nature's Economy: A History of Ecological Ideas.* Cambridge: Cambridge University Press, 1977.

————. *Under Western Skies: Nature and History in the American West.* New York: Oxford University Press, 1992.

Wuerthner, George. "Grazing Myths: A Top Ten List." *Forest Watch*, July 1993, 17–19.

————. "Grazing the Western Range: What Costs, What Benefits?" *Western Wildlands*, Summer 1990, 27–29.

————. "Living behind the Bovine Curtain." *Forest Watch*, July 1992, 15–18.

————. "Montana State University to Local Environmentalist: Get Lost!" *High Country News*, 1 May 1995, 21.

————. "Subdivisions versus Agriculture." *Conservation Biology* 8 (1994): 905–8.

Wyant, William K. *Westward in Eden: The Public Lands and the Conservation Movement.* Berkeley: University of California Press, 1982.

Wyoming Trucking Association. *Lawmakers of Wyoming: Fifty-fourth Wyoming State Legislature, 1997–98.* N.p., n.d.

Yoakum, Jim, and William P. Dasmann. "Habitat Manipulation Practices." In *Wildlife Management Techniques*, 3d ed., edited by R. H. Giles, Jr. Washington, D.C.: Wildlife Society, 1971.

Young, James A. "Historical and Evolutionary Perspectives on Grazing of Western Rangelands." In *Ecological Implications of Livestock Herbivory in the West*, edited by Martin Vavra, William A. Laycock, and Rex D. Pieper. Denver: Society for Range Management, 1994.

Young, James A., and Raymond A. Evans. "The Grand Experiment—Ranching in the Great Basin." In *Symposium of Cultural, Physical, and Biological Characteristics of the Range Livestock Industry.* Denver: Society for Range Management, 1985.

————. "Plant Manipulation." In *Rangelands*, edited by Bruce A. Buchanan. Albuquerque: University of New Mexico Press, 1988.

Zukoski, Edward B. "Multiple Uses Must Be Considered before Setting Stocking Rates." *Wildlife Law News Quarterly* (Spring 1996): 14.

CASES, STATUTES, REGULATIONS, EXECUTIVE ORDERS, LEGISLATIVE MATERIALS

Administrative Procedure Act, U.S. Code. Vol. 5, secs. 551–706 (1994).

Amending the Taylor Grazing Act. S. Rep. No. 505, 76th Cong., 1st sess., 1939.

Amendment to the Taylor Grazing Act. 14 July 1939. *U.S. Statutes at Large* 53 (1939): 1002–3.

American Iron & Steel Institute v. EPA. 526 F. 2d 1027 (3d Cir. 1975).

Anthony Wilkinson Livestock Co. v. McIlquam. 83 Pac. 364 (Wyo. 1905).

Association of Pacific Fisheries v. EPA. 615 F. 2d 794 (9th Cir. 1980).

Babbitt v. Sweet Home Chapter of Communities for a Great Oregon. 115 S. Ct. 2407 (1995).

Bailey, Reed W., and Charles A. Connaughton. "In Watershed Protection." In U.S. Department of Agriculture, Forest Service, *The Western Range: A Report on the Western Range—A Great But Neglected Natural Resource*. 74th Cong., 2d sess., 1936. S. Doc. No. 199. Washington, D.C.: U.S. Government Printing Office, 1936. Reprint, Arno Press, 1979.

Barton v. United States. 609 F. 2d 977 (10th Cir. 1979).

Bleamaster v. Morton. 448 F. 2d 1289 (9th Cir. 1971).

Brooks v. Dewar. 313 U.S. 354 (1941).

Buford v. Houtz. 133 U.S. 320 (1890).

Camfield v. United States. 167 U.S. 518 (1897).

Carl v. Udall. 309 F. 2d 653 (D.C. Cir. 1962).

Chournos v. United States. 193 F. 2d 321 (10th Cir. 1951).

Chrysler Corp. v. Brown. 441 U.S. 281 (1979).

Clapp, Earl H. "The Major Range Problems and Their Solution: A Resume." In U.S. Department of Agriculture, Forest Service, *The Western Range: A Report on the Western Range—A Great But Neglected Natural Resource*. 74th Cong., 2d sess., 1936. S. Doc. No. 199. Washington, D.C.: U.S. Government Printing Office, 1936. Reprint, Arno Press, 1979.

Classification and Multiple Use Act of 1964. Public Law 606, 88th Cong., 2d sess., 19 September 1964 (expired 1970). *U.S. Statutes at Large* 78 (1964): 982–85.

Clean Water Act. U.S. Code. Vol. 33, secs. 1251–1387 (1994).

Code of Federal Regulations. Vol. 33, pt. 328 (1995).

Code of Federal Regulations. Vol. 40, pt. 230 (1995).

Code of Federal Regulations. Vol. 40, pt. 1500 (1995).

Code of Federal Regulations. Vol. 43, sec. 1610.7-2 (1995).

Code of Federal Regulations. Vol. 43, sec. 4110.3 (1994).

Code of Federal Regulations. Vol. 43, sec. 4110.4-2a2 (1994).

Congressional Record. 1934. Washington, D.C.

Diamond Ring Ranch, Inc. v. Morton. 531 F. 2d 1397 (10th Cir. 1976).

Endangered Species Act of 1973. U.S. Code. Vol. 16, secs. 1531–44 (1994).

Enlarged Homestead Act. U.S. Statutes at Large 35 (1909): 639–40, 43 U.S.C. §§ 218–21 (repealed 1976).

Federal Advisory Committee Act. U.S. Code. Vol. 5 app. 2, secs. 1–15 (1994).

Federal Agriculture Improvement and Reform Act. Public Law 127, sec. 171(b), 104th Cong. 2d sess., 4 April 1996. *U.S. Statutes at Large* 110 (1996): 937-38.

Federal Land Policy and Management Act of 1976. U.S. Code. Vol. 43, secs. 1701–84 (1994).

Federal Rules of Appellate Procedure, U.S. Code Annotated, Title 28, Federal Rules of Appellate Procedure, United States Court of Appeals for the Ninth Circuit. Rules 36-1 to 36-3. 1998.

Forsling, C. L., et al. "Range Conservation the Exception." In U.S. Department of Agriculture, Forest Service, *The Western Range: A Report on the Western Range—A Great But Neglected Natural Resource*. 74th Cong., 2d sess., 1936. S. Doc. No. 199. Washington, D.C.: U.S. Government Printing Office, 1936. Reprint, Arno Press, 1979.

Forsling, C. L., Fred P. Cronemiller, Percy E. Melis, Arnold R. Standing, Alva A. Simpson, and Rex King. "The Administration of Public Range Lands." In U.S. Department of Agriculture, Forest Service, *The Western Range: A Report on the Western Range—A Great But Neglected Natural Resource*. 74th Cong., 2d sess., 1936. S. Doc. No. 199. Washington, D.C.: U.S. Government Printing Office, 1936. Reprint, Arno Press, 1979.

Foundation for North American Wild Sheep v. U.S. Department of Agriculture. 681 F. 2d 1172 (9th Cir. 1982).

Grimaud v. United States. 220 U.S. 506 (1911).

Hall v. Hickel. 305 F. Supp. 723 (D. Nev. 1969).

Hinsdale Livestock Co. v. United States. 501 F. Supp. 773 (D. Mont. 1980).

Immigration and Naturalization Service v. Chadha. 462 U.S. 919 (1983).

Kleppe v. Sierra Club. 427 U.S. 390 (1976).

Kneip, Leon F. "In Supplying Areas for Recreation." In U.S. Department of Agriculture, Forest Service, *The Western Range: A Report on the Western Range—A Great But Neglected Natural Resource*. 74th Cong., 2d sess., 1936. S. Doc. No. 199. Washington, D.C.: U.S. Government Printing Office, 1936. Reprint, Arno Press, 1979.

LaRue v. Udall. 324 F. 2d 428 (D.C. Cir. 1963).

Leo Sheep Co. v. United States. 440 U.S. 668 (1979).

Mary A. Van Alen. Interior Board of Land Appeals, vol. 8, 77 (27 October 1972).

Motor Vehicle Manufacturers Association v. State Farm Mutual Auto Insurance Co. 462 U.S. 29 (1983).

Multiple-Use, Sustained-Yield Act of 1960. U.S. Code. Vol. 16, secs. 528–31 (1994).

National Conference on Outdoor Recreation. *A Report Epitomizing Results of Major Fact-Finding Surveys and Projects Which Have Been Undertaken under the Auspices of the National Conference on Outdoor Recreation*. 70th Congress, 1st sess. S. Doc. 158. Washington, D.C.: Government Printing Office, May 1928.

National Environmental Policy Act. U.S. Code. Vol. 42, secs. 4321–70d (1994).

National Forest Management Act. U.S. Code. Vol. 16, secs. 1600–14 (1994).

National Wildlife Federation v. Bureau of Land Management. UT-06-91-1 (U.S. Department of the Interior Office of Hearings and Appeals, 20 December 1993), *affirmed*, IBLA 94–264 (Interior Board of Land Appeals, 1 March 1994).

National Wildlife Federation v. Watt. 571 F. Supp. 1145 (D.D.C. 1983).

Natural Resources Defense Council v. Hodel. 618 F. Supp. 848 (E.D. Cal. 1985).

Natural Resources Defense Council v. Hodel. 624 F. Supp 1045 (D. Nev. 1985), *affirmed*, 819 F. 2d 927 (9th Cir. 1987).

Natural Resources Defense Council v. Morton. 388 F. Supp. 829 (D.D.C. 1974), *affirmed per curiam*, 527 F. 2d 1386 (D.C. Cir.), *certiorari denied*, 427 U.S. 913 (1976).

Northwest Indian Cemetery Protective Association v. Peterson. 764 F. 2d 581 (9th Cir. 1985), *reversed in part on other grounds sub nom. Lyng v. Northwest Indian Cemetery Protective Association*, 485 U.S. 439 (1988).

Oregon and California Act. U.S. Statutes at Large 50 (1937): 874–76.

Oregon Natural Desert Association v. Thomas. 940 F. Supp. 1534 (D. Ore. 1996), *reversed sub nom. Oregon Natural Desert Association v. Dombeck*, 46 ERC 1993 (9th Cir. 1998).

Pacific Legal Foundation v. Watt. 529 F. Supp. 982 (D. Mont. 1981).

Public Lands Council v. Secretary of the Interior. 929 F. Supp. 1436 (D. Wyo. 1996), *reversed in part and affirmed in part sub nom. Public Lands Council v. Babbitt*, 154 F. 3d 1160 (10th Cir. 1998).

Public Rangelands Improvement Act of 1978. U.S. Code. Vol. 43, secs. 1901–8 (1994).

PUD No. 1 v. Washington Department of Ecology. 511 U.S. 700 (1994).

Red Canyon Sheep Co. v. Ickes. 98 F. 2d 308 (D.C. Cir. 1938).

Richardson v. Udall. 253 F. Supp. 72 (D. Idaho 1966).

Roberts, Paul H. "As an Integrated Part of Western Agriculture." In U.S. Department of Agriculture, Forest Service, *The Western Range: A Report on the Western Range—A Great But Neglected Natural Resource.* 74th Cong., 2d sess., 1936. S. Doc. No. 199. Washington, D.C.: U.S. Government Printing Office, 1936. Reprint, Arno Press, 1979.

Robertson v. Methow Valley Citizens Council. 490 U.S. 332 (1989).

Roosevelt, Franklin D. Executive Order 6910. 26 November 1934.

Seidman v. Gunzel. No. CIV 94–2266 (D. Ariz., 16 January 1996).

Show, S. B. "The Probable Future Use and Ownership of Range Lands." In U.S. Department of Agriculture, Forest Service, *The Western Range: A Report on the Western Range—A Great But Neglected Natural Resource.* 74th Cong., 2d sess., 1936. S. Doc. No. 199. Washington, D.C.: U.S. Government Printing Office, 1936. Reprint, Arno Press, 1979.

Sierra Club v. Clark. 756 F. 2d 686 (9th Cir. 1985).

Stockraising Homestead Act of 1916. U.S. Statutes at Large 39 (1916): 862–65.

Taylor Grazing Act. U.S. Statutes at Large 48 (1934): 1269–75.

Tennessee Valley Authority v. Hill. 437 U.S. 153 (1978).

Three Year Homestead Act. U.S. Statutes at Large 38 (1912): 123–125 (repealed 1976).

U.S. Department of Agriculture. Forest Service. *The Western Range: A Report on the Western Range—A Great But Neglected Natural Resource.* 74th Cong., 2d sess., 1936. S. Doc. No. 199. Washington, D.C.: U.S. Government Printing Office, 1936. Reprint, Arno Press, 1979.

United States ex rel. Bergen v. Lawrence. 620 F. Supp. 1414 (D. Wyo. 1985), *affirmed*, 848 F. 2d 1502 (10th Cir. 1988).

U.S. House of Representatives. *Federal Land Policy and Management Act of 1976.* 94th Cong., 2d sess., 15 May 1976. H.R. Rep. No. 1163. Reprinted in *U.S. Code Congressional and Administrative News* (1976): 6175, 6179.

———. *To Provide for the Orderly Use, Improvement, and Development of the Public Range.* 73d Cong., 2d sess., 1934. H.R. Rep. No. 903.

———. Subcommittee on Public Lands of the House Committee on Interior and Insular Affairs. *Public Lands Review, Hearings before the Subcommittee on Public Lands of the Committee on Interior and Insular Affairs on H.R. 106, H.R. 255, H.R. 5498, and H.R. 5159.* 88th Cong., 1st sess., 1963. Serial No. 11, Part I, Public Land Law Review Commission.

———. *Public Lands Review, Hearings on H.R. 106, 255, 5498, and 5159.* 88th Cong., 1st sess., 1963. Serial No. 11, Part I, Use and Disposal of Public Lands.

———. *Public Lands Review, Hearings on H.R. 8070 to 8073 and H.J. Res. 52.* 88th Cong., 1st sess., 1962. Serial No. 11, Part II, Public Land Law Review Commission.

U.S. Senate. *Livestock Grazing Act*. 104th Cong., 1st sess., S. 852 (1995).

———. *Public Rangelands Management Act of 1996*. 104th Cong., 2d sess., S. 1459 (1996).

U.S. Senate Committee on Public Lands and Surveys. *Grazing on Public Lands and National Forests*. 69th Cong., 1st sess., 1926. S. Rept. 517.

———. *To Provide for the Orderly Use, Improvements, and Development of the Public Range*. 73d Cong., 2d sess., 1934. S. Rept. 1182.

United States v. Douglas-Willan Sartoris Co. 3 Wyo. 287, 22 Pac. 92 (1889).

United States v. Fuller. 409 U.S. 488 (1973).

United States v. Light. 220 U.S. 523 (1911).

United States v. New Mexico. 438 U.S. 696 (1978).

United States v. Riverside Bayview Homes, Inc. 474 U.S. 121 (1985).

Unlawful Inclosures Act of 1885. U.S. Statutes at Large 23 (1885): 321–22.

Watts, Lyle F. "Unsuitable Land Policy." In U.S. Department of Agriculture, Forest Service, *The Western Range: A Report on the Western Range—A Great But Neglected Natural Resource*. 74th Cong., 2d sess., 1936. S. Doc. No. 199. Washington, D.C.: U.S. Government Printing Office, 1936. Reprint, Arno Press, 1979.

Western Radio Services v. Espy. 79 F. 3d 896 (9th Cir. 1996).

Wild, Free-Ranging Horses and Burros Act. U.S. Statutes at Large 85 (1971): 649–50. *U.S. Code*. Vol. 16, secs. 1331–40.

Yellowstone Park Act. U.S. Statutes at Large 17 (1872): 32–33. *U.S. Code*. Vol. 30, secs. 21–22 (1994).

INTERNET RESOURCES

Bureau of Land Management home page: website www.blm.gov/.

Colorado legislative information: website www.aclin.org/other/government/gen_assembly/pb/. 1997 Directory, Sixty-first General Assembly, First Regular Session, State of Colorado.

High Country News: website www.hcn.org.

U.S. Geological Survey water use data: website www.cnr.colostate.edu/CWK/use_colo.htm.

Yellowstone National Park information: website www.yellowstone.net.

Index